Advanced International Trade

Advanced International Trade

THEORY AND EVIDENCE

Robert C. Feenstra

PRINCETON UNIVERSITY PRESS   PRINCETON AND OXFORD

Copyright © 2004 by Princeton University Press

Published by Princeton University Press, 41 William Street, Princeton,
New Jersey 08540

In the United Kingdom: Princeton University Press, 3 Market Place,
Woodstock, Oxfordshire OX20 1SY

Library of Congress Cataloging-in-Publication Data

Feenstra, Robert C.
    Advanced international trade : theory and evidence / Robert C. Feenstra.
      p. cm.
    Includes bibliographical references and index.
    ISBN 0-691-11410-2
    1. International trade—Mathematical models.   2. Commercial policy—Mathematical
models.   I. Title.
    HF1379.F44 2003
    382'.01—dc21   2003048604

British Library Cataloging-in-Publication Data is available

This book has been composed in Galliard

Printed on acid-free paper. ∞

www.pupress.princeton.edu

Printed in the United States of America

10 9 8 7 6 5 4 3 2

ISBN-13: 978-0-691-11410-1

ISBN-10: 0-691-11410-2

To Heather and Evan

Contents

Acknowledgments

A BOOK like this would not be possible without the assistance of many people, indeed, without a career full of teachers and colleagues who have shaped the field and my own views of it. I am fortunate to have had many of these who were all generous with their time and insights. As an undergraduate at the University of British Columbia, I first learned international trade from the original edition of Richard Caves and Ronald Jones, *World Trade and Payments* (Little, Brown, 1973), and then from the "dual" point of view with Alan Woodland. His continuing influence will be clear in this book. I also took several graduate courses in duality theory from Erwin Diewert, and while it took longer for these ideas to affect my research, their impact has been quite profound.

In 1977 I began my graduate work at MIT, where I learned international trade from Jagdish Bhagwati and T. N. Srinivasan, both leaders and collaborators in the field. These courses greatly expanded my knowledge of all aspects of international trade and stimulated me to become a trade economist. The book I have written probably does not do justice to the great breadth of research topics I learned there. These topics are well presented in the textbook by Jagdish Bhagwati, Arvind Panagariya and T. N. Srinivasan, *Lectures in International Trade* (MIT Press, 1998), to which the reader is referred. My own book does not aim to be a substitute for that important volume.

In 1981, I joined Jagdish Bhagwati as a colleague at Columbia University, and for the next five years enjoyed the company of Ronald Findlay, Guillermo Calvo, Robert Mundell, Maury Obstfeld, Stanislaw Wellisz, and other regular attendees at the Wednesday afternoon international seminar. Richard Brecher was also a visitor at Columbia during this period. I am much indebted to these colleagues for the stimulating seminars and conversations. My early work in trade did not stray too far from the familiar two-sector model, but in 1982 I was invited by Robert Baldwin to participate in a conference of the National Bureau of Economic Research (NBER) focusing on the empirical assessment of U.S. trade policies. For this conference I prepared a paper on the voluntary export restraint with Japan in automobiles, and thus my empirically oriented research in trade began.

Following this, I participated in more conferences of the NBER, and since 1992 have directed the International Trade and Investment group there. These conferences have been enormously influential to my research. During the 1980s, there was a large amount of research on trade and trade policy under imperfect competition. Some of this was done for NBER conferences, and I was able to witness all of it. In the 1990s the focus shifted very substantially to "endogenous" growth models, and this research was again supported by a working group at the NBER and by many other researchers. I was fortunate to spend a sabbatical leave in 1989 at the Institute for Advanced Study of the Hebrew University of Jerusalem, along with Wilfred Ethier, Gene Grossman, Paul Krugman, James Markusen, and organized by Elhanan Helpman and Assaf Razin, during which time these growth models were being developed. Furthermore, throughout the 1980s and 1990s there was an increased awareness of empirical issues in international trade, with fine work by many new colleagues. So in the span of just two decades since beginning my career, I have seen three great waves of research in international trade, and I attempt to summarize all three of these areas in this book. A fourth new area, having to do with the organization of the firm, is introduced in the final chapter, and it promises to be just as important.

Since moving to the University of California, Davis, in 1986, my research on empirical topics in trade has been greatly assisted by the Institute of Governmental Affairs (IGA). I wish to thank Alan Olmstead, Jean Stratford, and other staff at IGA for generously providing time and resources in securing datasets, computational resources, office space, and even directing research assistants. The datasets that I have accumulated and then distributed on CD-ROMs and over the web would not have been possible without their help, for which I am grateful.

Likewise, these datasets would not have been possible without generous funding from the National Science Foundation and Ford Foundation on several occasions, as well as the assistance of many graduate students over the years. Some of their research appears in this book, and many others have labored faithfully to construct datasets that have been widely distributed. Let me thank in particular Haiyan Deng, Hiau Looi Kee, Dorsati Madani, Maria Yang, and Shunli Yao for their past work on datasets, along with David Yue, Roger Butters, Seungjoon Lee, Songhua Lin, and especially Alyson Ma for their help with this textbook. Finally, I should especially like to thank a number of colleagues who contributed to this book: Lee Branstetter, my colleague at Davis and now at Columbia, provided a number of the empirical exercises, with the STATA programs written by Kaoru Nabeshima; Bin Xu read nearly all the chapters at an early stage and provided detailed comments; and Bruce Blonigen, Donald Davis, Earl Grinols, Doug Irwin, Jiandong Ju, Kala Krishna, James Levinsohn, Nina Pavcnik, James Rauch, Deborah Swenson, and Daniel Trefler provided comments or datasets for specific chapters. I am grateful to these individuals and many others whose input has improved this book.

Preface

THIS BOOK is intended for a graduate course in international trade. I assume that all readers have completed graduate courses in microeconomics and econometrics. My goal is to bring the reader from that common point up to the most recent research in international trade, in both theory and empirical work. This is not intended to be a difficult book, and the mathematics used should be accessible to any graduate student. The material covered will give the reader the skills needed to understand the latest articles and working papers in the field.

At the same time, I am aware that many readers will become teachers in the field, especially at the undergraduate level. I feel that it is suitable, then, to start most chapters by introducing simple graphical techniques that can be used in teaching. Following this, I move towards the equations for each model. A set of problems at the end of each chapter gives the reader some experience in manipulating these equations. An instructor's manual that accompanies this book provides solutions to the problems.[1] In addition, I have included empirical exercises that replicate the results in some chapters. Completing all of these could be the topic for a second course, but even in a first course there will be a payoff to trying some exercises. The data and programs for these can be found on my home page and also at the website www.internationaldata.org.[2]

A word on notation. I consistently use *subscripts* to refer to goods or factors, whereas *superscripts* refer to consumers or countries. In general, then, *subscripts refer to commodities and superscripts refer to agents.* The index used (h, i, j, k, ℓ, m, or n) will depend on the context. The symbol c is used for both costs and consumption, though in some chapters I instead use $d(p)$ for consumption to avoid confusion. The output of firms is consistently denoted by y and exports are denoted by x. Uppercase letters are used in some cases to denote vectors or matrixes, and in other cases to denote the number of goods (N), factors (M), households (H), or countries (C), and sporadically elsewhere. The symbols α and β are used generically for intercept and slope coefficients, including fixed and marginal labor costs.

The contents of several chapters included here have been previously published. Chapters 4 and 5 are revisions from articles appearing in

[1] Faculty wishing to obtain the instructor's manual should contact Princeton University Press.
[2] The programs for the empirical exercises are provided in STATA. Readers not familiar with STATA are encouraged to complete the web course developed by James Levinsohn and available at www.psc.isr.umich.edu/saproject.

E. Kwan Choi and James Harrigan, eds., *Handbook of International Trade* (Basil Blackwell, 2003) and the *Scottish Journal of Political Economy*, respectively. Some material from chapters 7–9 has appeared in articles published in the *Journal of International Economics* and the *Quarterly Journal of Economics*, and material from chapter 10 has appeared in the *Journal of Development Economics* and the *American Economic Review*.

Chapter 1

Preliminaries: Two-Sector Models

WE BEGIN our study of international trade with the classic Ricardian model, which has two goods and one factor (labor). The Ricardian model introduces us to the idea that technological differences across countries matter. In comparison, the Heckscher-Ohlin model dispenses with the notion of technological differences and instead shows how *factor endowments* form the basis for trade. While this may be fine in theory, the model performs very poorly in practice: as we show in the next chapter, the Heckscher-Ohlin model is hopelessly inadequate as an explanation for historical or modern trade patterns unless we allow for technological differences across countries. For this reason, the Ricardian model is as relevant today as it has always been. Our treatment of it in this chapter is a simple review of undergraduate material, but we will have the opportunity to refer to this model again at various places throughout the book.

After reviewing the Ricardian model, we turn to the two-good, two-factor model that occupies most of this chapter and forms the basis of the Heckscher-Ohlin model. We shall suppose that the two goods are traded on international markets, but we do not allow for any movements of factors across borders. This reflects the fact that the movement of labor and capital across countries is often subject to controls at the border and generally much less free than the movement of goods. Our goal in the next chapter will be to determine the pattern of international trade between countries. In this chapter, we simplify things by focusing primarily on *one* country, treating world prices as given, and examine the properties of this two-by-two model. The student who understands all the properties of this model has already come a long way in his or her study of international trade.

Ricardian Model

Indexing goods by the subscript i, let a_i denote the labor needed per unit of production of each good at home, while a_i^* is the labor need per unit of production in the foreign country, $i = 1, 2$. The total labor force at home is L and abroad is L^*. Labor is perfectly mobile between the industries in each

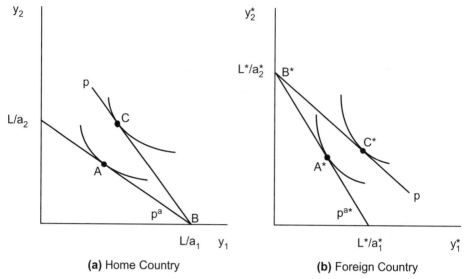

(a) Home Country   **(b)** Foreign Country

Figure 1.1

country, but immobile across countries. This means that both goods are produced in the home country only if the wages earned in the two industries are the same. Since the marginal product of labor in each industry is $1/a_i$, and workers are paid the value of their marginal products, wages are equalized across industries if and only if $p_1/a_1 = p_2/a_2$, where p_i is the price in each industry. Letting $p = p_1/p_2$ denote the *relative* price of good 1 (using good 2 as the numeraire), this condition is $p = a_1/a_2$.

These results are illustrated in Figure 1.1(a) and (b), where we graph the production possibility frontiers (PPFs) for the home and foreign countries. With all labor devoted to good i at home, it can produce L/a_i units, $i = 1, 2$, so this establishes the intercepts of the PPF, and similarly for the foreign country. The slope of the PPF in each country (ignoring the negative sign) is then a_1/a_2 and a_1^*/a_2^*. Under autarky (i.e., no international trade), the equilibrium relative prices p^a and p^{a*} must equal these slopes in order to have both goods produced in both countries, as argued above. Thus, the autarky equilibrium at home and abroad might occur at points A and A*. Suppose that the home country has a *comparative advantage* in producing good 1, meaning that $a_1/a_2 < a_1^*/a_2^*$. This implies that the home autarky relative price of good 1 is *lower* than that abroad.

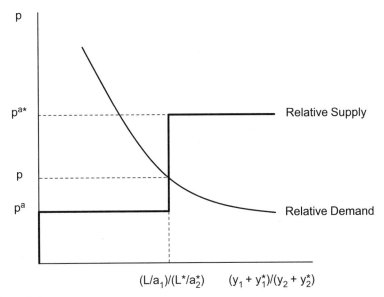

Figure 1.2

Now letting the two countries engage in international trade, what is the equilibrium price p at which world demand equals world supply? To answer this, it is helpful to graph the world relative supply and demand curves, as illustrated in Figure 1.2. For the relative price satisfying $p < p^a = a_1/a_2$ and $p < p^{a*} = a_1^*/a_2^*$ both countries are fully specialized in good 2 (since wages earned in that sector are higher), so the world relative supply of good 1 is zero. For $p^a < p < p^{a*}$, the home country is fully specialized in good 1, whereas the foreign country is still specialized in good 2, so that the world relative supply is $(L/a_1)/(L^*/a_2^*)$, as labeled in Figure 1.2. Finally, for $p > p^a$ and $p > p^{a*}$, both countries are specialized in good 1. So we see that the world relative supply curve has a "stair-step" shape, which reflects the linearity of the PPFs.

To obtain world relative demand, let us make the simplifying assumption that tastes are identical and homothetic across the countries. Then demand will be independent of the distribution of income *across* the countries. Demand being homothetic means that *relative* demand d_1/d_2 in either country is a downward-sloping function of the relative price p, as illustrated in Figure 1.2. In the case we have shown, relative demand intersects relative supply at the world price p that lies *between* p^a and p^{a*}, but this does not need to occur: instead, we can have relative demand intersect one of the flat segments of relative supply, so that the equilibrium price with trade *equals* the autarky price in one country.[1]

Focusing on the case where $p^a < p < p^{a*}$, we can go back to the PPF of each country and graph the production and consumption points with free trade. Since $p > p^a$, the home country is fully specialized in good 1 at point B, as illustrated in Figure 1.1(a), and then trades at the relative price p to obtain consumption at point C. Conversely, since $p < p^{a*}$, the foreign country is fully specialized in the production of good 2 at point B* in Figure 1.1(b), and then trades at the relative price p to obtain consumption at point C*. Clearly, *both* countries are better off under free trade than they were in autarky: trade has allowed them to obtain a consumption point that is above the PPF.

Notice that the home country exports good 1, which is in keeping with its comparative advantage in the production of that good, $a_1/a_2 < a_1^*/a_2^*$. Thus, *trade patterns are determined by comparative advantage*, which is a deep insight from the Ricardian model. This occurs even if one country has an *absolute disadvantage* in both goods, such as $a_1 > a_1^*$ and $a_2 > a_2^*$, so that more labor is needed per unit of production of *either* good at home than abroad. The reason that it is still possible for the home country to export is that its *wages* will adjust to reflect its productivities: under free trade, its wages are lower than those abroad.[2] Thus, while trade patterns in the Ricardian model are determined by *comparative advantage*, the level of wages across countries is determined by *absolute advantage*.

Two-Good, Two-Factor Model

While the Ricardian model focuses on technology, the Heckscher-Ohlin model, which we study in the next chapter, focuses on factors of production. So we now assume that there are two factor inputs—labor and capital. Restricting our attention to a single country, we will suppose that it produces two goods with the production functions $y_i = f_i(L_i, K_i)$, $i = 1, 2$, where y_i is the output produced using labor L_i and capital K_i. These production functions are assumed to be increasing, concave, and homogeneous

---

[1] This occurs if one country is very large. Use Figures 1.1 and 1.2 to show that if the home country is very large, then $p = p^a$ and the home country does not gain from trade.

[2] The home country exports good 1, so wages earned with free trade are $w = p/a_1$. Conversely, the foreign country exports good 2 (the numeraire), so wages earned there are $w^* = 1/a_2^* > p/a_1^*$, where the inequality follows since $p < a_1^*/a_2^*$ in the equilibrium being considered. Then using $a_1 > a_1^*$, we obtain $w = p/a_1 < p/a_1^* < w^*$.

of degree one in the inputs (L_i, K_i).[3] The last assumption means that there are *constant returns to scale* in the production of each good. This will be a maintained assumption for the next several chapters, but we should point out that it is rather restrictive. It has long been thought that *increasing returns to scale* might be an important reason to have trade between countries: if a firm with increasing returns is able to sell in a foreign market, this expansion of output will bring a reduction in its average costs of production, which is an indication of greater efficiency. Indeed, this was a principal reason that Canada entered into a free-trade agreement with the United States in 1989: to give its firms free access to the large American market. We will return to these interesting issues in chapter 5, but for now, ignore increasing returns to scale.

We will assume that labor and capital are *fully mobile* between the two industries, so we are taking a "long run" point of view. Of course, the amount of factors employed in each industry is constrained by the endowments found in the economy. These resource constraints are stated as

$$\begin{aligned} L_1 + L_2 &\leq L, \\ K_1 + K_2 &\leq K, \end{aligned} \tag{1.1}$$

where the endowments L and K are fixed. Maximizing the amount of good 2, $y_2 = f_2(L_2, K_2)$, subject to a given amount of good 1, $y_1 = f_1(L_1, K_1)$, and the resource constraints in (1.1) give us $y_2 = h(y_1, L, K)$. The graph of y_2 as a function of y_1 is shown as the PPF in Figure 1.3. As drawn, y_2 is a *concave* function of y_1, $\partial^2 h(y_1, L, K)/\partial y_1^2 < 0$. This familiar result follows from the fact that the production functions $f_i(L_i, K_i)$ are assumed to be concave. Another way to express this is to consider all points $S = (y_1, y_2)$ that are feasible to produce given the resource constraints in (1.1). This production possibilities set S is *convex*, meaning that if $y^a = (y_1^a, y_2^a)$ and $y^b = (y_1^b, y_2^b)$ are both elements of S, then any point between them $\lambda y^a + (1 - \lambda)y^b$ is also in S, for $0 \leq \lambda \leq 1$.[4]

The production possibility frontier summarizes the technology of the economy, but in order to determine where the economy produces on the PPF we need to add some assumptions about the market structure. We will assume perfect competition in the product markets and factor markets. Furthermore, we will suppose that product prices are given *exogenously*: we can think of these prices as established on world markets, and outside the control of the "small" country being considered.

[3] Students not familiar with these terms are referred to problems 1.1 and 1.2.
[4] See problems 1.1 and 1.3 to prove the convexity of the production possibilities set, and to establish its slope.

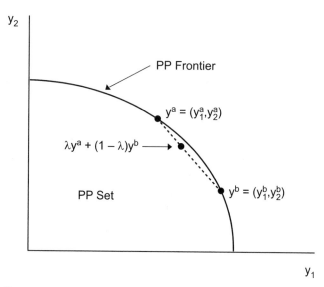

Figure 1.3

GDP Function

With the assumption of perfect competition, the amounts produced in each industry will maximize gross domestic product (GDP) for the economy: this is Adam Smith's "invisible hand" in action. That is, the industry outputs of the competitive economy will be chosen to maximize GDP:

$$G(p_1, p_2, L, K) = \max_{y_1, y_2} p_1 y_1 + p_2 y_2 \quad \text{s.t.} \quad y_2 = h(y_1, L, K). \quad (1.2)$$

To solve this problem, we can substitute the constraint into the objective function and write it as choosing y_1 to maximize $p_1 y_1 + p_2 h(y_1, L, K)$. The first-order condition for this problem is $p_1 + p_2(\partial h / \partial y_1) = 0$, or

$$p = \frac{p_1}{p_2} = -\frac{\partial h}{\partial y_1} = -\frac{\partial y_2}{\partial y_1}. \quad (1.3)$$

Thus, the economy will produce where the relative price of good 1, $p = p_1 / p_2$, is equal to the slope of the production possibility frontier.[5] This is illustrated by the point A in Figure 1.4, where the line tangent through point A has the slope of (negative) p. An increase in this price will *raise* the

---

[5] Notice that the slope of the price line tangent to the PPF (in absolute value) equals the relative price of the good on the *horizontal* axis, or good 1 in Figure 1.4.

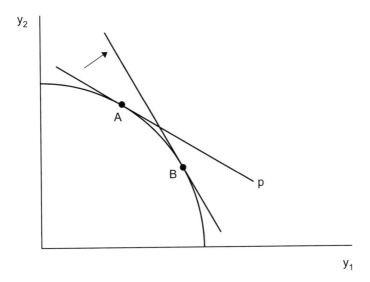

Figure 1.4

slope of this line, leading to a new tangency at point B. As illustrated, then, the economy will produce more of good 1 and less of good 2.

The GDP function introduced in (1.2) has many convenient properties, and we will make use of it throughout this book. To show just one property, suppose that we differentiate the GDP function with respect to the price of good i, obtaining

$$\frac{\partial G}{\partial p_i} = y_i + \left(p_1 \frac{\partial y_1}{\partial p_i} + p_2 \frac{\partial y_2}{\partial p_i} \right). \tag{1.4}$$

It turns out that the terms in parentheses on the right-hand side of (1.4) sum to zero, so that $\partial G/\partial p_i = y_i$. In other words, the derivative of the GDP function with respect to *prices* equals the *outputs* of the economy.

The fact that the terms in parentheses sum to zero is an application of the "envelope theorem," which states that when we differentiate a function that has been maximized (such as GDP) with respect to an exogenous variable (such as p_i), then we can *ignore* the changes in the endogenous variables (y_1 and y_2) in this derivative. To prove that these terms sum to zero, totally differentiate $y_2 = h(y_1, L, K)$ with respect to y_1 and y_2 and use (1.3) to obtain $p_1 dy_1 = -p_2 dy_2$, or $p_1 dy_1 + p_2 dy_2 = 0$. This equality must hold for any small movement in y_1 and y_2 around the PPF, and in particular, for the small movement in outputs *induced* by the change in p_i. In other words, $p_1(\partial y_1/\partial p_i) + p_2(\partial y_2/\partial p_i) = 0$, so the terms in parentheses on the right of (1.4) vanish and it follows that $\partial G/\partial p_i = y_i$.[6]

Equilibrium Conditions

We now want to state succinctly the equilibrium conditions to determine factor prices and outputs. It will be convenient to work with the *unit-cost functions* that are dual to the production functions $f_i(L_i, K_i)$. These are defined by

$$c_i(w, r) = \min_{L_i, K_i \geq 0} \{wL_i + rK_i \mid f_i(L_i, K_i) \geq 1\}. \tag{1.5}$$

In words, $c_i(w, r)$ is the minimum cost to produce one unit of output. Because of our assumption of constant returns to scale, these unit-costs are equal to both marginal costs and average costs. It is easily demonstrated that the unit-cost functions $c_i(w, r)$ are nondecreasing and concave in (w, r). We will write the *solution* to the minimization in (1.5) as $c_i(w, r) = wa_{iL} + ra_{iK}$, where a_{iL} is optimal choice for L_i, and a_{iK} is optimal choice for K_i. It should be stressed that these optimal choices for labor and capital *depend* on the factor prices, so that they should be written in full as $a_{iL}(w, r)$ and $a_{iK}(w, r)$. However, we will usually not make these arguments explicit.

Differentiating the unit-cost function with respect to the wage, we obtain

$$\frac{\partial c_i}{\partial w} = a_{iL} + \left(w\frac{\partial a_{iL}}{\partial w} + r\frac{\partial a_{iK}}{\partial w} \right). \tag{1.6}$$

As we found with differentiating the GDP function, it turns out that the terms in parentheses on the right of (1.6) sum to zero, which is again an application of the "envelope theorem." It follows that the derivative of the unit-costs with respect to the wage equals the labor needed for one unit of production, $\partial c_i/\partial w = a_{iL}$. Similarly, $\partial c_i/\partial r = a_{iK}$.

To prove this result, notice that the constraint in the cost-minimization problem can be written as the isoquant $f_i(a_{iL}, a_{iK}) = 1$. Totally differentiate this to obtain $f_{iL}\, da_{iL} + f_{iK}\, da_{iK} = 0$, where $f_{iL} \equiv \partial f_i/\partial L_i$ and $f_{iK} \equiv \partial f_i/\partial K_i$. This equality must hold for any small movement of labor da_{iL} and capital da_{iK} around the isoquant, and in particular, for the change in labor and capital *induced* by a change in wages. Therefore, $f_{iL}(\partial a_{iL}/\partial w) + f_{iK}(\partial a_{iK}/\partial w) = 0$. Now multiply this through by the product price p_i, noting that $p_i f_{iL} = w$ and $p_i f_{iK} = r$ from the profit-

---

[6] Other convenient properties of the GDP function are explored in problem 1.4.

maximization conditions for a competitive firm. Then we see that tl
terms in parentheses on the right of (1.6) sum to zero.

The first set of equilibrium conditions for the two-by-two economy is
that *profits equal zero*. This follows from free entry under perfect competition. The zero-profit conditions are stated as

$$p_1 = c_1(w, r),$$
$$p_2 = c_2(w, r). \tag{1.7}$$

The second set of equilibrium conditions is full employment of both
resources. These are the same as the resource constraints (1.1), except
that now we express them as equalities. In addition, we will rewrite the labor and capital used in each industry in terms of the derivatives of the
unit-cost function. Since $\partial c_i/\partial w = a_{iL}$ is the labor used for *one unit* of
production, it follows that the total labor used in $L_i = y_i a_{iL}$, and similarly
the total capital used is $K_i = y_i a_{iK}$. Substituting these into (1.1), the full-
employment conditions for the economy are written as

$$\underbrace{a_{1L} y_1}_{L_1} + \underbrace{a_{2L} y_2}_{L_2} = L,$$

$$\underbrace{a_{1K} y_1}_{K_1} + \underbrace{a_{2K} y_2}_{K_2} = K. \tag{1.8}$$

Notice that (1.7) and (1.8) together are *four* equations in *four* unknowns, namely, (w, r) and (y_1, y_2). The parameters of these equations, p_1,
p_2, L, and K, are given exogenously. Because the unit-cost functions are
nonlinear, however, it is not enough to just count equations and unknowns: we need to study these equations in detail to understand whether
the solutions are unique and strictly positive, or not. Our task for the rest
of this chapter will be to understand the properties of these equations and
their solutions.

To guide us in this investigation, there are three key questions that we
can ask: (1) what is the solution for factor prices? (2) if prices change, how
do factor prices change? (3) if endowments change, how do outputs
change? Each of these questions is taken up in the sections that follow.
The methods we shall use follow the "dual" approach of Woodland
(1977, 1982), Mussa (1979), and Dixit and Norman (1980).

Determination of Factor Prices

Notice that our four-equation system above can be decomposed into the
zero-profit conditions as *two* equations in *two* unknowns—the wage and

rental—and then the full-employment conditions, which involve both the factor prices (which affect a_{iL} and a_{iK}) and the outputs. It would be especially convenient if we could uniquely solve for the factor prices from the zero-profit conditions, and then just substitute these into the full-employment conditions. This will be possible when the hypotheses of the following lemma are satisfied.

Lemma (Factor Price Insensitivity)

So long as both goods are produced, and factor intensity reversals (FIRs) do not occur, then each price vector (p_1, p_2) corresponds to unique factor prices (w, r).

This is a remarkable result, because it says that the factor endowments (L, K) do not matter for the determination of (w, r). We can contrast this result with a one-sector economy, with production of $y = f(L, K)$, wages of $w = pf_L$, and diminishing marginal product $f_{LL} < 0$. In this case, any increase in the labor endowments would certainly reduce wages, so that countries with higher labor/capital endowments (L/K) would have lower wages. This is the result we normally expect. In contrast, the above lemma says that in a two-by-two economy, with a fixed product price p, it is possible for the labor force or capital stock to grow *without* affecting their factor prices! Thus, Leamer (1995) refers to this result as "factor price insensitivity." Our goal in this section is to prove the result and also develop the intuition for why it holds.

Two conditions must hold to obtain this result: first, that both goods are produced; and second, that factor intensity reversals (FIRs) do not occur. To understand FIRs, consider Figures 1.5 and 1.6. In the first case, presented in Figure 1.5, we have graphed the two zero-profit conditions, and the unit-cost lines intersect only *once*, at point A. This illustates the lemma: given (p_1, p_2), there is a *unique* solution for (w, r). But another case is illustrated in Figure 1.6, where the unit-cost lines interesect *twice*, at points A and B. Then there are two possible solutions for (w, r), and the result stated in the lemma no longer holds.

The case where the unit-cost lines intersect more than once corresponds to '*factor intensity reversals.*' To see where this name comes from, let us compute the labor and capital requirements in the two industries. We have already shown that a_{iL} and a_{iK} are the derivatives of the unit-cost function with respect to factor prices, so it follows that the vectors (a_{iL}, a_{iK}) are the *gradient vectors* to the iso-cost curves for the two industries in Figure 1.5. Recall from calculus that gradient vectors point in the direction of the maximum increase of the function in question. This means that they are *orthogonal* to their respective iso-cost curves, as shown by (a_{1L}, a_{1K}) and

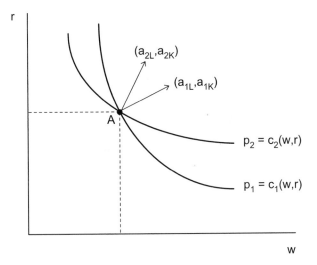

Figure 1.5

(a_{2L}, a_{2K}) at point A. Each of these vectors has slope (a_{iK}/a_{iL}), or the capital-labor ratio. It is clear from Figure 1.5 that (a_{1L}, a_{1K}) has a smaller slope than (a_{2L}, a_{2K}) which means that *industry 2 is capital intensive*, or equivalently, *industry 1 is labor intensive*.[7]

In Figure 1.6, however, the situation is more complicated. Now there are two sets of gradient vectors, which we label by (a_{1L}, a_{1K}) and (a_{2L}, a_{2K}) at point A and by (b_{1L}, b_{1K}) and (b_{2L}, b_{2K}) at point B. A close inspection of the figure will reveal that industry 1 is *labor intensive* $(a_{1K}/a_{1L}) < a_{2K}/a_{2L})$ at point A but is *capital intensive* $(b_{1K}/b_{1L}) < b_{2K}/b_{2L})$ at point B. This illustrates a *factor intensity reversal*, whereby the comparison of factor intensities changes at different factor prices.

While FIRs might seem like a theoretical curiosum, they are actually quite realistic. Consider the footwear industry, for example. While much of the footwear in the world is produced in developing nations, the United States retains a small number of plants. In sneakers, New Balance has a plant in Norridgewock, Maine, where employees earn some $14 per hour.[8] Some operate computerized equipment with up to 20 sewing

---

[7] Alternatively, we can totally differentiate the zero-profit conditions, holding prices fixed, to obtain $0 = a_{iL}dw + a_{iK}dr$. It follows that the slope of the iso-cost curve equals $dr/dw = -a_{iL}/a_{iK} = -L_i/K_i$. Thus, the slope of each iso-cost curve equals the relative demand for the factor on the horizontal axis, whereas the slope of the gradient vector (which is orthogonal to the iso-cost curve) equals the relative demand for the factor on the vertical axis.
[8] The material that follows is drawn from Aaron Bernstein, "Low-Skilled Jobs: Do They Have to Move?" *Business Week,* February 26, 2001, 94–95.

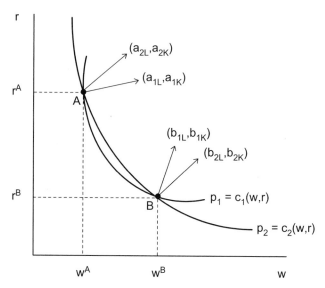

Figure 1.6

machine heads running at once, while others operate automated stitchers guided by cameras, which allow one person to do the work of six. This is a far cry from the plants in Asia that produce shoes for Nike, Reebok, and other U.S. producers, using century-old technology and paying less than $1 per hour. The technology used to make sneakers in Asia is like industry 1 at point A in Figure 1.5, using labor-intensive technology and paying low wages w^A, while industry 1 in the United States is at point B, paying higher wages w^B and using a capital-intensive technology.

As suggested by this discussion, when there are two possible solutions for the factor prices such as points A and B in Figure 1.6, then some countries can be at one equilibrium and others countries at the other. How do we know which country is where? This is a question that we will answer at the end of the chapter, where we will argue that a *labor abundant* country will likely be at equilibrium A of Figure 1.6, with a low wage and high rental on capital, whereas a *capital abundant* country will be at equilibrium B, with a high wage and low rental. Generally, to determine the factor prices in each country we will need to examine its full-employment conditions in addition to the zero-profit conditions.

Let us conclude this section by returning to the simple case of no FIR, in which the lemma stated above applies. What are the implications of this result for the determination of factor prices under free trade? To answer this question, let us sketch out some of the assumptions of the Heckscher-Ohlin model, which we will study in more detail in the next chapter. We assume that there are two countries, with identical technologies but different factor endowments. We continue to assume that labor and capital are the two factors of production, so that under free trade the equilibrium conditions (1.7) and (1.8) apply in *each* country with the *same* product prices (p_1, p_2) We can draw Figure 1.5 for each country, and in the absence of FIR, this *uniquely* determines the factor prices in each countries. In other words, the wage and rental determined by Figure 1.5 are *identical* across the two countries. We have therefore proved the factor price equalization (FPE) theorem, which is stated as follows.

Factor Price Equalization Theorem (Samuelson 1949)

Suppose that two countries are engaged in free trade, having identical technologies but different factor endowments. If both countries produce both goods and FIRs do not occur, then the factor prices (w, r) are equalized across the countries.

The FPE theorem is a remarkable result because it says that *trade in goods* has the ability to equalize factor prices: in this sense, trade in goods is a "perfect substitute" for trade in factors. We can again contrast this result with that obtained from a one-sector economy in both countries. In that case, equalization of the product price through trade would certainly not equalize factor prices: the labor-abundant country would be paying a lower wage. Why does this outcome *not occur* when there are two sectors? The answer is that the labor-abundant country can *produce more of, and export*, the labor-intensive good. In that way it can fully employ its labor while still paying the same wages as a capital-abundant country. In the two-by-two model, the opportunity to disproportionately produce more of one good than the other, while exporting the amounts not consumed at home, is what allows factor price equalization to occur. This intuition will become even clearer as we continue to study the Heckscher-Ohlin model in the next chapter.

Change in Product Prices

Let us move on now to the second of our key questions of the two-by-two model: if the product prices change, how will the factor prices change? To answer this, we perform comparative statics on the zero-profit conditions (1.7). Totally differentiating these conditions, we obtain

$$dp_i = a_{iL}dw + a_{iK}dr \Rightarrow \frac{dp_i}{p_i} = \frac{wa_{iL}}{c_i}\frac{dw}{w} + \frac{ra_{iK}}{c_i}\frac{dr}{r}, \quad i=1,2. \quad (1.9)$$

The second equation is obtained by multiplying and dividing like terms, and noting that $p_i = c_i(w, r)$. The advantage of this approach is that it allows us to express the variables in terms of *percentage changes*, such as $d \ln w = dw/w$, as well as *cost shares*. Specifically, let $\theta_{iL} = wa_{iL}/c_i$ denote the cost share of labor in industry i, while $\theta_{iK} = ra_{iK}/c_i$ denotes the cost share of capital. The fact that costs equal $c_i = wa_{iL} + ra_{iK}$ ensures that the shares sum to unity, $\theta_{iL} + \theta_{iK} = 1$. In addition, denote the percentage changes by $dw/w = \hat{w}$ and $dr/r = \hat{r}$. Then (1.9) can be rewritten as

$$\hat{p}_i = \theta_{iL}\hat{w} + \theta_{iK}\hat{r}, \quad i = 1, 2. \tag{1.9'}$$

Expressing the equation using these cost shares and percentage changes follows Jones (1965) and is referred to as the "Jones' algebra." This system of equation can be written in matrix form and solved as

$$\begin{pmatrix} \hat{p}_i \\ \hat{p}_2 \end{pmatrix} = \begin{pmatrix} \theta_{1L} & \theta_{1K} \\ \theta_{2L} & \theta_{2K} \end{pmatrix} \begin{pmatrix} \hat{w} \\ \hat{r} \end{pmatrix} \Rightarrow \begin{pmatrix} \hat{w} \\ \hat{r} \end{pmatrix} = \frac{1}{|\theta|} \begin{pmatrix} \theta_{2K} & -\theta_{1K} \\ -\theta_{2L} & \theta_{1L} \end{pmatrix} \begin{pmatrix} \hat{p}_1 \\ \hat{p}_2 \end{pmatrix}, \tag{1.10}$$

where $|\theta|$ denotes the determinant of the two-by-two matrix on the left. This determinant can be expressed as

$$\begin{aligned} |\theta| &= \theta_{1L}\theta_{2K} - \theta_{1K}\theta_{2L} \\ &= \theta_{1L}(1 - \theta_{2L}) - (1 - \theta_{1L})\theta_{2L} \\ &= \theta_{1L} - \theta_{2L} = \theta_{2K} - \theta_{1K}, \end{aligned} \tag{1.11}$$

where we have repeatedly made use of the fact that $\theta_{iL} + \theta_{iK} = 1$.

In order to fix ideas, let us assume henceforth that *industry 1 is labor intensive*. This implies that its cost share in industry 1 exceeds that in industry 2, $\theta_{1L} - \theta_{2L} > 0$, so that $|\theta| > 0$ in (1.11).[9] Furthermore, suppose that the relative price of good 1 *increases*, so that $\hat{p} = \hat{p}_1 - \hat{p}_2 > 0$. Then we can solve for the change in factor prices from (1.10) and (1.11) as

$$\hat{w} = \frac{\theta_{2K}\hat{p}_1 - \theta_{1K}\hat{p}_2}{|\theta|} = \frac{(\theta_{2K} - \theta_{1K})\hat{p}_1 + \theta_{1K}(\hat{p}_1 - \hat{p}_2)}{(\theta_{2K} - \theta_{1K})} > \hat{p}_1, \tag{1.12a}$$

since $\hat{p}_1 - \hat{p}_2 > 0$, and,

$$\hat{r} = \frac{\theta_{1L}\hat{p}_2 - \theta_{2L}\hat{p}_1}{|\theta|} = \frac{(\theta_{1L} - \theta_{2L})\hat{p}_2 - \theta_{2L}(\hat{p}_1 - \hat{p}_2)}{(\theta_{1L} - \theta_{2L})} < \hat{p}_2, \tag{1.12b}$$

since $\hat{p}_1 - \hat{p}_2 > 0$.

---

[9] As an exercise, show that $L_1/K_1 > L_2/K_2 \Leftrightarrow \theta_{1L} > \theta_{2L}$. This is done by multiplying the numerator and denominator on both sides of the first inequality by like terms, so as to convert it into cost shares.

From the result in (1.12a), we see that the wage increases *by more* than the price of good 1, $\hat{w} > \hat{p}_1 > \hat{p}_2$. This means that workers can afford to buy more of good 1 (w/p_1 has gone up), as well as more of good 2 (w/p_2 has gone up). When labor can buy more of *both goods* in this fashion, we say that the *real wage* has increased. Looking at the rental on capital in (1.12b), we see that the rental r changes by *less than* the price of good 2. It follows that the capital owner can afford less of good 2 (r/p_2 has gone down), and also less of good 1 (r/p_1 has gone down). Thus the *real return to capital* has fallen. We can summarize these results with the following theorem.

Stolper-Samuelson (1941) Theorem

An increase in the relative price of a good will increase the real return to the factor used intensively in that good, and reduce the real return to the other factor.

To develop the intuition for this result, let us go back to the differentiated zero-profit conditions in (1.9′). Since the cost shares add up to unity in each industry, we see from equation (1.9′) that $\hat{p}_i$ is a weighted average of the factor price changes $\hat{w}$ and $\hat{r}$. This implies that $\hat{p}_i$ necessarily lies in between $\hat{w}$ and $\hat{r}$. Putting these together with our assumption that $\hat{p}_1 - \hat{p}_2 > 0$, it is therefore clear that

$$\hat{w} > \hat{p}_1 > \hat{p}_2 > \hat{r}. \tag{1.13}$$

Jones (1965) has called this set of inequalities the "magnification effect": they show that any change in the product prices has a *magnified effect* on the factor prices. This is an extremely important result. Whether we think of the product price change as due to export opportunities for a country (the export price goes up), or due to lowering import tariffs (so the import price goes down), the magnification effect says that there will be both gainers and losers due to this change. Even though we will argue in chapter 6 that there are gains from trade in some overall sense, it is still the case that trade opportunities have strong *distributional* consequences, making some people worse off and some better off!

We conclude this section by illustrating the Stolper-Samuelson theorem in Figure 1.7. We begin with an initial factor price equilibrium given by point A, where industry 1 is labor intensive. An increase in the price of that industry will shift out the iso-cost curve, and as illustrated, move the equilibrium to point B. It is clear that the wage has gone up, from w_0 to w_1, and the rental has declined, from r_0 to r_1. Can we be sure that the wage has increased in percentage terms *by more* than the relative price of good 1? The answer is yes, as can be seen by drawing a ray from the origin

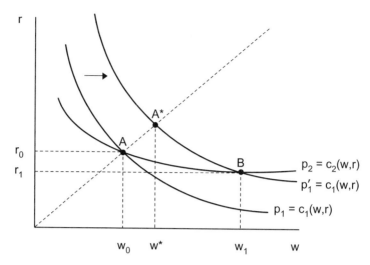

Figure 1.7

through the point A. Because the unit-cost functions are homogeneous of degree one in factor prices, moving along this ray increases p and (w, r) in the same proportion. Thus, at the point A*, the increase in the wage exactly matched the percentage change in the price p_1. But it is clear that the equilibrium wage increases by *more*, $w_1 > w^*$, so the percentage increase in the wage *exceeds* that of the product price, which is the Stolper-Samuelson result.

Changes in Endowments

We turn now to the third key question: if endowments change, how do the industry outputs change? To answer this, we hold the product prices *fixed* and totally differentiate the full-employment conditions (1.8) to obtain

$$a_{1L}dy_1 + a_{2L}dy_2 = dL,$$
$$a_{1K}dy_1 + a_{2K}dy_2 = dK. \tag{1.14}$$

Notice that the a_{ij} coefficients *do not* change, despite the fact that they are functions of the factor prices (w, r). These coefficients are fixed because p_1 and p_2 do not change, so from our earlier lemma, the factor prices are also fixed.

By rewriting the equations in (1.14) using the "Jones' algebra," we obtain

$$\frac{y_1 a_{1L}}{L}\frac{dy_1}{y_1} + \frac{y_2 a_{2L}}{L}\frac{dy_2}{y_2} = \frac{dL}{L} \qquad \lambda_{1L}\hat{y}_1 + \lambda_{2L}\hat{y}_2 = \hat{L}$$
$$\frac{y_1 a_{1K}}{K}\frac{dy_1}{y_1} + \frac{y_2 a_{2K}}{K}\frac{dy_2}{y_2} = \frac{dK}{K} \Rightarrow \quad \lambda_{1K}\hat{y}_1 + \lambda_{2K}\hat{y}_2 = \hat{K}. \qquad (1.14')$$

To move from the first set of equations to the second, we denote the percentage changes $dy_1/y_1 = \hat{y}_1$, and likewise for all the other variables. In addition, we define $\lambda_{iL} \equiv (y_i a_{iL}/L) = (L_i/L)$, which measures the *fraction of the labor force employed in industry i*, where $\lambda_{1L} + \lambda_{2L} = 1$. We define λ_{iK} analogously as the fraction of the capital stock employed in industry i.

This system of equations is written in matrix form and solved as

$$\begin{bmatrix} \lambda_{1L} & \lambda_{2L} \\ \lambda_{1K} & \lambda_{2K} \end{bmatrix}\begin{pmatrix} \hat{y}_1 \\ \hat{y}_2 \end{pmatrix} = \begin{pmatrix} \hat{L} \\ \hat{K} \end{pmatrix} \Rightarrow \begin{pmatrix} \hat{y}_1 \\ \hat{y}_2 \end{pmatrix} = \frac{1}{|\lambda|}\begin{bmatrix} \lambda_{2K} & -\lambda_{2L} \\ -\lambda_{1K} & \lambda_{1L} \end{bmatrix}\begin{pmatrix} \hat{L} \\ \hat{K} \end{pmatrix}, \quad (1.15)$$

where $|\lambda|$ denotes the determinant of the two-by-two matrix on the left, which is simplified as

$$\begin{aligned} |\lambda| &= \lambda_{1L}\lambda_{2K} - \lambda_{2L}\lambda_{1K} \\ &= \lambda_{1L}(1 - \lambda_{1K}) - (1 - \lambda_{1L})\lambda_{1K} \qquad (1.16) \\ &= \lambda_{1L} - \lambda_{1K} = \lambda_{2K} - \lambda_{2L}, \end{aligned}$$

where we have repeatedly made use of the fact that $\lambda_{1L} + \lambda_{2L} = 1$ and $\lambda_{1K} + \lambda_{2K} = 1$.

Recall that we assumed *industry 1 to be labor intensive*. This implies that the share of the labor force employed in industry 1 exceeds the share of the capital stock used there, $\lambda_{1L} - \lambda_{1K} > 0$, so that $|\lambda| > 0$ in (1.16).[10] Suppose further that the endowment of labor is increasing, while the endowment of capital remains fixed such that $\hat{L} > 0$, and $\hat{K} = 0$. Then we can solve for the change in outputs from (1.15)–(1.16) as

$$\hat{y}_1 = \frac{\lambda_{2K}}{(\lambda_{2K} - \lambda_{2L})}\hat{L} > \hat{L} > 0 \quad \text{and} \quad \hat{y}_2 = \frac{-\lambda_{1K}}{|\lambda|}\hat{L} < 0. \qquad (1.17)$$

From (1.17), we see that the output of the labor-intensive industry 1 expands, whereas the output of industry 2 contracts. We have therefore established the Rybczynski theorem.

---

[10] As an exercise, show that $L_1/K_1 > L/K > L_2/K_2 \Leftrightarrow \lambda_{1L} > \lambda_{1K}$ and $\lambda_{2K} > \lambda_{2L}$.

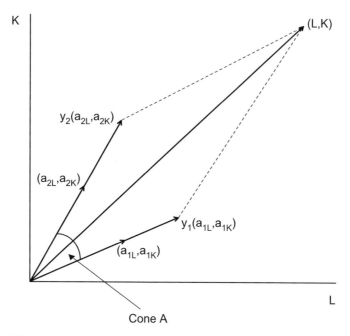

Figure 1.8

Rybczynski (1955) Theorem

An increase in a factor endowment will increase the output of the industry using it intensively, and decrease the output of the other industry.

To develop the intuition for this result, let us write the full-employment conditions in vector notation as

$$\begin{pmatrix} a_{1L} \\ a_{1K} \end{pmatrix} y_1 + \begin{pmatrix} a_{2L} \\ a_{2K} \end{pmatrix} y_2 = \begin{pmatrix} L \\ K \end{pmatrix}. \tag{1.8'}$$

We have already illustrated the gradient vectors (a_{iL}, a_{iK}) to the iso-cost curves in Figures 1.5 (with no FIR). Now let us take these vectors and re-graph them, in Figure 1.8. Multiplying each of these by the output of their respective industries, we obtain the total labor and capital demands $y_1(a_{1L}, a_{1K})$ and $y_2(a_{2L}, a_{2K})$ Summing these as in (1.8') we obtain the labor and capital endowments (L, K). But this exercise can also be performed in reverse: for any endowment vector (L, K), there will be a *unique* value for the outputs (y_1, y_2) such that when (a_{1L}, a_{1K}) and (a_{2L}, a_{2K}) are multiplied by these amounts, they will sum to the endowments.

How can we be sure that the outputs obtained from (1.8') are positive? It is clear from Figure 1.8 that the outputs in both industries will be positive

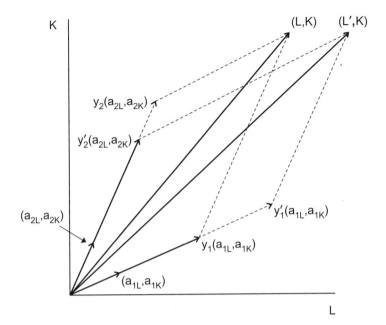

Figure 1.9

if and only if the endowment vector (L, K) lies *in between* the factor requirement vectors (a_{1L}, a_{1K}) and (a_{2L}, a_{2K}). For this reason, the space
spanned by these two vectors is called a '*cone of diversification*', which we
label by cone A in Figure 1.8. In contrast, if the endowment vector (L, K)
lies *outside* of this cone, then it is *impossible* to add together any positive
multiples of the vectors (a_{1L}, a_{1K}) and (a_{2L}, a_{2K}) and arrive at the endowment vector. So if (L, K) lies outside of the cone of diversification, then it
must be that only *one good* is produced. At the end of the chapter, we will
show how to determine which good it is.[11] For now, we should just recognize that when only one good is produced, then factor prices are determined by the marginal products of labor and capital as in the one-sector
model, and will certainly depend on the factor endowments.

Now suppose that the labor endowment increases to $L' > L$, with no
change in the capital endowment, as shown in Figure 1.9. Starting from the
endowments (L', K), the *only* way to add up multiples of (a_{1L}, a_{1K}) and
(a_{2L}, a_{2K}) and obtain the endowments is to *reduce* the output of industry
2 to y_2', and *increase* the output of industry 1 to y_1'. This means that not
only does industry 1 absorb the entire amount of the extra labor endowment, it also absorbs further labor and capital from industry 2 so that its

[11] See problem 1.5.

ultimate labor/capital ratio is unchanged from before. The labor/capital ratio in industry 2 is also unchanged, and this is what permits both industries to pay exactly the same factor prices as they did before the change in endowments.

There are many examples of the Rybczynski theorem in practice, but perhaps the most commonly cited is what is called the "Dutch Disease."[12] This refers to the discovery of oil off the coast of the Netherlands, which led to an increase in industries making use of this resource. (Shell Oil, one of the world's largest producers of petroleum products, is a Dutch company.) At the same time, however, other "traditional" export industries of the Netherlands contracted. This occurred because resources were attracted away from these industries and into those that were intensive in oil, as the Rybczynski theorem would predict.

We have now answered the three questions raised earlier in the chapter: how are factor prices determined; how do changes in product prices affect factor prices; and how do changes in endowments affect outputs? But in answering all of these, we have relied on the assumptions that *both goods are produced*, and also that factor intensity reversals do not occur, as was stated explicitly in the FPE theorem. In the remainder of the chapter we need to investigate both of these assumptions, to understand either when they will hold or the consequences of their not holding.

We begin by tracing through the changes in the outputs induced by changes in endowments, along the equilibrium of the production possibility frontier. As the labor endowment grows in Figure 1.9, the PPF will shift out. This is shown in Figure 1.10, where the outputs will shift from point A to point A' with an increase of good 1 and reduction of good 2, at the unchanged price *p*. As the endowment of labor rises, we can join up all points such as A and A' where the slopes of the PPFs are equal. These form a downward-sloping line, which we will call the *Rybczynski line* for changes in labor (ΔL). The Rybczynski line for ΔL indicates how outputs change as labor endowment expands.

Of course, there is also a Rybczynski line for ΔK, which indicates how the outputs change as the capital endowment grows: this would lead to an increase in the output of good 2, and reduction in the output of good 1. As drawn, we have illustrated both of the Rybczynski lines as *straight* lines: can we be sure that this is the case? The answer is yes: the fact that the product prices are fixed along a Rybczynski line, implying that factor prices are also fixed, ensures that these are straight lines. To see this, we can easily calculate their slopes by differentiating the full-employment conditions (1.8). To compute the slope of the Rybczynski line for ΔL, it is convenient

---

[12] See, for example, Corden and Neary 1982 and Jones, Neary, and Ruane 1987.

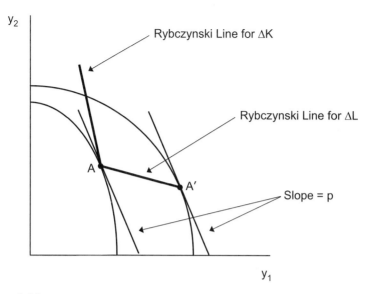

Figure 1.10

to work with the full-employment condition for *capital*, since that endowment does not change. Total differentiating (1.8) for capital gives

$$a_{1K}y_1 + a_{2K}y_2 = K \Rightarrow a_{1K}dy_1 + a_{2K}dy_2 = 0 \Rightarrow \frac{dy_2}{dy_1} = -\frac{a_{1K}}{a_{2K}}. \quad (1.18)$$

Thus, the slope of the Rybczynski line for ΔL is the negative of the ratio of capital/output in the two industries, which is constant for fixed prices. This proves that the Rybczynski lines are indeed straight.

If we continue to increase the labor endowment, outputs will move downwards on the Rybczynski line for ΔL in Figure 1.10, until this line hits the y_1 axis. At this point the economy is fully specialized in good 1. In terms of Figure 1.9, the vector of endowments (L, K) is coincident with the vector of factor requirements (a_{1L}, a_{1K}) in industry 1. For further increases in the labor endowment, the Rybczynski line for ΔL then *moves right along the* y_1 axis in Figure 1.10, indicating that the economy remains specialized in good 1. This corresponds to the vector of endowments (L, K) lying outside and below the cone of diversification in Figure 1.9. With the economy fully specialized in good 1, factor prices are determined by the marginal products of labor and capital in that good, and the earlier "factor price insensitivity" lemma no longer applies.

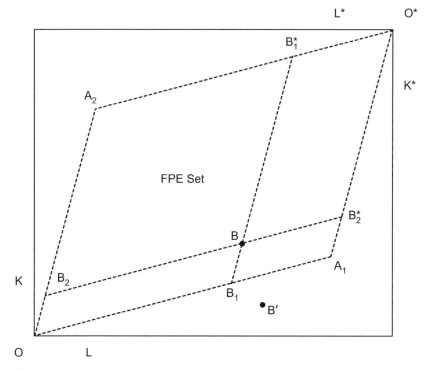

Figure 1.11

Factor Price Equalization Revisited

Our finding that the economy produces both goods whenever the factor
endowments remain *inside* the cone of diversification allows us to investigate the FPE theorem more carefully. Let us continue to assume that
there are no FIRs, but now rather than *assuming* that both goods are produced in both countries, we will instead derive this as an *outcome* from the
factor endowments in each country. To do so, we engage in a thought experiment posed by Samuelson (1949) and further developed by Dixit and
Norman (1980).

Initially, suppose that labor and capital are *free to move* between the two
countries until their factor prices are equalized. Then all that matters for
factor prices are the *world* endowments of labor and capital, and these are
shown as the length of the horizontal and vertical axis in Figure 1.11. The
amounts of labor and capital choosing to reside at home are measured relative to the origin 0, while the amounts choosing to reside in the foreign

country are measured relative to the origin 0^*—suppose that this allocation is at point B. Given the world endowments, we establish equilibrium
prices for goods and factors in this "integrated world equilibrium." The
factor prices determine the demand for labor and capital in each industry
(assuming no FIR), and using these, we can construct the diversification
cone (since factor prices are the same across countries, then the diversification cone is also the same). Let us plot the diversification cone relative
to the home origin 0, and again relative to the foreign origin 0^*. These
cones form the parallelogram $0A_1 0^* A_2$.

For later purposes, it is useful to identify precisely the points A_1 and A_2
on the vertices of this parallelogram. The vectors $0A_i$ and $0^* A_i$ are proportional to (a_{iL}, a_{iK}), the amount of labor and capital used to produce
one unit of good i in each country. Multiplying (a_{iL}, a_{iK}) by world demand for good i, D_i^w, we then obtain the *total* labor and capital used to
produce that good, so that $A_i = (a_{iL}, a_{iK}) D_i^w$. Summing these gives the
total labor and capital used in world demand, which equals the labor and
capital used in world production, or world endowments.

Now we ask whether we can achieve exactly the same world production
and equilibrium prices as in this "integrated world equilibrium," but *without* labor and capital mobility. Suppose there is some allocation of labor
and capital endowments across the countries, such as point B. Then can
we produce the same amount of each good as in the "integrated world
equilibrium"? The answer is clearly yes: with labor and capital in each
country at point B, we could devote $0B_1$ of resources to good 1 and $0B_2$
to good 2 at home, while devoting $0^* B_1^*$ to good 1 and $0^* B_2^*$ towards
good 2 abroad. This will ensure that the same amount of labor and capital
worldwide is devoted to each good as in the "integrated world equilibrium," so that production and equilibrium prices must be the same as before. Thus, we have achieved the same equilibrium but without factor
mobility. It will become clear in the next chapter that there is still *trade in
goods* going on to satisfy the demands in each country.

More generally, for *any allocation* of labor and capital within the parallelogram $0A_1 0^* A_2$ both countries remain diversified (producing both
goods), and we can achieve the same equilibrium prices as in the "integrated world economy." It follows that factor prices *remain equalized
across countries* for allocations of labor and capital within the parallelogram
$0A_1 0^* A_2$, which is referred to as the *factor price equalization (FPE) set*.
The FPE set illustrates the range of labor and capital endowments between countries over which both goods are produced in both countries,
so that factor price equalization is obtained. In contrast, for endowments
outside of the FPE set such as point B', then at least one country would
have to be fully specialized in one good and FPE no longer holds.

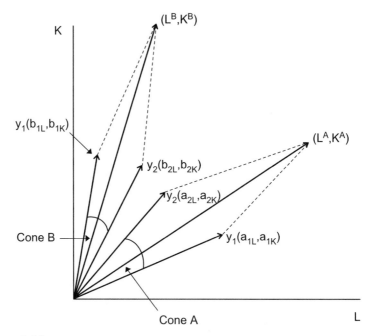

Figure 1.12

Factor Intensity Reversals

We conclude this chapter by returning to a question raised earlier: when there are "factor intensity reversals" giving multiple solutions to the zero-profit conditions, then how do we know which solution will prevail in each country? To answer this, it is necessary to combine the zero-profit with the full-employment conditions, as follows.

Consider the case in Figure 1.6, where the zero-profit conditions allow for two solutions to the factor prices. Each of these determine the labor and capital demands shown orthogonal to the iso-cost curves, labeled as (a_{1L}, a_{1K}) and (a_{2L}, a_{2K}) and (b_{1L}, b_{1K}) and (b_{2L}, b_{2K}). We have redrawn these in Figure 1.12, after multiplying each of them by the outputs of their respective industries. These vectors create *two* cones of diversification, labeled as cone A and cone B. Initially, suppose that the factor endowments for each country lie within one cone or the other (then we will consider the case where the endowments are outside both cones).

Now we can answer the question of which factor prices will apply in each country: a *labor abundant* economy, with a high ratio of labor/capital endowments such as (L^A, K^A) in cone A of Figure 1.12, will have factor prices given by (w^A, r^A) in Figure 1.6, with low wages; whereas a *capital abundant* economy, with a high ratio of capital/labor endowments, such as shown by (L^B, K^B) in cone B of Figure 1.12, will have factor prices given by (w^B, r^B) in Figure 1.6, with high wages. Thus, factor prices depend on the endowments of the economy. A labor-abundant country such as China will pay low wages and a high rental (as in cone A), while a capital-abundant country such as the United States will have high wages and a low rental (as in cone B). Notice that we have now reintroduced a link between factor endowments and factor prices, as we argued earlier in the one-sector model: when there are FIR in the two-by-two model, factor prices vary systematically with endowments *across* the cones of diversification, even though factor prices are independent of endowments *within* each cone.

What if the endowment vector of a country does not lie in either cone? Then the country will be fully specialized in one good or the other. Generally, we can determine which good it is by tracing through how the outputs change as we move through the cones of diversification, and it turns out that outputs depend *nonmonotonically* on the factor endowments.[13] For example, textiles in South Korea or Taiwan expanded during the 1960s and 1970s, but contracted later as capital continued to grow. Despite the complexity involved, many trade economists feel that countries do in fact produce in different cones of diversification, and taking this possibility into account is a topic of current research.[14]

Conclusions

In this chapter we have reviewed several two-sector models: the Ricardian model, with just one factor, and the two-by-two model, with two factors both of which are fully mobile between industries. There are other two-sector models, of course: if we add a third factor, treating capital as specific to each sector but labor as mobile, then we obtain the Ricardo-Viner or "specific factors" model, as will be discussed in chapter 3. We will have an opportunity to make use of the two-by-two model throughout this book, and a thorough understanding of its properties—both the equations and the diagrams—is essential for all the material that follows.

One special feature of this chapter is the dual determination of factor prices, using the unit-cost function in the two industries. This follows the

---

[13] See problem 1.5.

[14] Empirical evidence on whether developed countries fit into the same cone is presented by Debaere and Demiroglu (2003), and the presence of multiple cones is explored by Leamer (1987); Harrigan and Zakrajšek (2000); Schott (2003); and Xu (2002). The latter papers draw on empirical methods that we introduce in chapter 3.

dual approach of Woodland (1977, 1982), Mussa (1979), and Dixit and Norman (1980). Samuelson (1949) used a quite different diagramatic approach to prove the FPE theorem. Another method that is quite commonly used is the so-called Lerner (1952) diagram, which relies on the production rather than cost functions.[15] We will not use the Lerner diagram in this book, but it will be useful to understand some articles, for example, Findlay and Grubert (1959) and Deardorff (1979), so we include a discussion of it in the appendix to this chapter.

This is the only chapter where we do not present any accompanying empirical evidence. The reader should not infer from this that the two-by-two model is unrealistic: while it is usually necessary to add more goods or factors to this model before confronting it with data, the relationships between prices, outputs, and endowments that we have identified in this chapter will carry over in some form to more general settings. Evidence on the pattern of trade is presented in the next chapter, where we extend the two-by-two model by adding another country, and then many countries, trading with each other. We also allow for many goods and factors, but for the most part restrict attention to situations where factor price equalization holds. In chapter 3, we examine the case of many goods and factors in greater detail, to determine whether the Stolper-Samuelson and Rybczynski theorems generalize and also how to estimate these effects. In chapter 4, evidence on the relationship between product prices and wages is examined in detail, using a model that allows for trade in intermediate inputs. The reader is already well prepared for these chapters that follow, based on the tools and intuition we have developed from the two-by-two model. Before moving on, you are encouraged to complete the problems at the end of this chapter.

Appendix: The Lerner Diagram and Factor Prices

The Lerner (1952) diagram for the two-by-two model can be explained as follows. With perfect competition and constant returns to scale, we have that revenue = costs in both industries. So let us choose a special isoquant in each industry such that revenue = 1. In each industry, we therefore choose the isoquant $p_i y_i = 1$, or

$$y = f_i(L_i, K_i) = 1/p_i \Rightarrow wL_i + rK_i = 1.$$

[15] This diagram was used in a seminar presented by Abba Lerner at the London School of Economics in 1933, but not published until 1952. The history of this diagram is described at the "Origins of Terms in International Economics," maintained by Alan Deardorff at http://www.personal.umich.edu/~alandear/glossary/orig.html. See also Samuelson 1949, 181 n. 1.

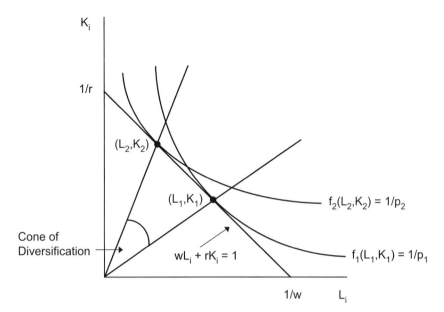

Figure 1.13

Therefore, from cost minimization, the $1/p_i$ isoquant in each industry will be *tangent* to the line $wL_i + rK_i = 1$. This is the same line for both industries, as shown in Figure 1.13.

Drawing the rays from the origin through the points of tangency, we obtain the cone of diversification, as labeled in Figure 1.13. Furthermore, we can determine the factor prices by computing where $wL_i + rK_i = 1$ intersects the two axes: $L_i = 0 \Rightarrow K_i = 1/r$, and $K_i = 0 \Rightarrow L_i = 1/w$. Therefore, given the prices p_i we determine the two isoquants in Figure 1.13, and drawing the (unique) line tangent to both of these, we determine the factor prices as the intercepts of this line. Notice that these equilibrium factor prices do not depend on the factor endowments, provided that the endowment vector lies within the cone of diversification (so that both goods are produced). We have thus obtained an alternative proof of the "factor price insensitivity" lemma, using a primal rather than dual approach. Furthermore, with two countries having the same prices (through free trade) and technologies, Figure 1.13 holds in both of them. Therefore, their factor prices will be equalized.

Lerner (1952) also showed how Figure 1.13 can be extended to the case of factor intensity reversals, in which case the isoquants intersect twice. In that case there will be *two* lines $wL_i + rK_i = 1$ that are tangent to both isoquants, and there are two cones of diversification. This is

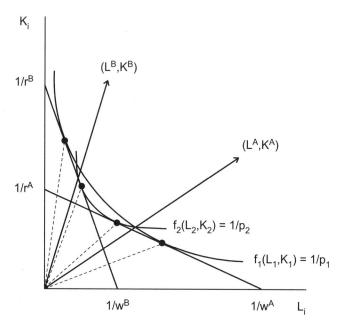

Figure 1.14

shown in Figure 1.14. To determine which factor prices apply in a particular country, we plot its endowments vector and note which cone of diversification it lies in: the factor prices in this country are those applying to
that cone. For example, the endowments (L^A, K^A) will have the factor
prices (w^A, r^A), and the endowments (L^B, K^B) will have the factor prices
(w^B, r^B). Notice that the labor-abundant country with endowments $(L^A,
K^A)$ has the low wage and high rental, whereas the capital-abundant
country with endowments (L^B, K^B) has the high wage and low rental.

How likely is it that the isoquants of industries 1 and 2 intersect twice, as
in Figure 1.14? Lerner (1952, 11) correctly suggested that it depends on
the elasticity of substitution between labor and capital in each industry. For
simplicity, suppose that each industry has a constant elasticity of substitution production function. If the elasticities are the same across industries,
then it is impossible for the isoquants to intersect twice. If the elasticities of
substitution differ across industries, however, and we choose prices p_i,
$i = 1, 2$, such that the $1/p_i$ isoquants intersect at least once, then it is
guaranteed that they intersect twice. Under exactly the same conditions,
the iso-cost lines in figure 1.6 intersect twice. Thus, the occurrence of FIR
is very likely once we allow elasticities of substitution to differ across industries. Minhas (1962) confirmed that this was the case empirically, and dis-

cussed the implications of FIR for factor prices and trade patterns. This line of empirical research was dropped thereafter, perhaps because FIR seemed too complex to deal with, and has been picked up again only recently (see note 14).

Problems

1.1 Rewrite the production function $y_1 = f_1(L_1, K_1)$ as $y_1 = f_1(v_1)$, and similarly, $y_2 = f_2(v_2)$. Concavity means that given two points $y_1^a = f_1(v_1^a)$ and $y_1^b = f_1(v_1^b)$, and $0 \le \lambda \le 1$, then $f_1(\lambda v_1^a + (1 - \lambda)v_1^b) \ge \lambda y_1^a + (1 - \lambda)y_1^b$. Similarly for the production function $y_2 = f_2(v_2)$. Consider two points $y^a = (y_1^a, y_2^a)$ and $y^b = (y_1^b, y_2^b)$, both of which can be produced while satisfying the full-employment conditions $v_1^a + v_2^a \le V$ and $v_1^b + v_2^b \le V$, where V are the endowments. Consider a production point midway between these, $\lambda y^a + (1 - \lambda)y^b$. Then use the concavity of the production functions to show that this point can *also* be produced while satisfying the full-employment conditions. This proves that the production possibilities set is *convex*. (Hint: Rather than showing that $\lambda y^a + (1 - \lambda)y^b$ can be produced while satisfying the full-employment conditions, consider instead allocating $\lambda v_1^a + (1 - \lambda)v_1^b$ of the resources to industry 1, and $\lambda v_2^a + (1 - \lambda)v_2^b$ of the resources to industry 2.)

1.2 Any function $y = f(v)$ is homogeneous of degree α if for all $\lambda > 0$, $f(\lambda v) = \lambda^\alpha f(v)$. Consider the production function $y = f(L, K)$, which we assume is homogeneous of degree one, so that $f(\lambda L, \lambda K) = \lambda f(L, K)$. Now differentiate this expression with respect to L, and answer the following: Is the marginal product $f_L(L, K)$ homogeneous, and of what degree? Use the expression you have obtained to show that $f_L(L/K, 1) = f_L(L, K)$.

1.3 Consider the problem of maximizing $y_1 = f_1(L_1, K_1)$, subject to the full-employment conditions $L_1 + L_2 \le L$ and $K_1 + K_2 \le K$, and the constraint $y_2 = f_2(L_2, K_2)$. Set this up as a Lagrangian, and obtain the first-order conditions. Then use the Lagrangian to solve for dy_1/dy_2, which is the slope of the production possibility frontier. How is this slope related to the marginal product of labor and capital?

1.4 Consider the problem of maximizing $p_1 f_1(L_1, K_1) + p_2 f_2(L_2, K_2)$, subject to the full-employment constraints $L_1 + L_2 \le L$ and $K_1 + K_2 \le K$. Call the result the GDP function $G(p, L, K)$, where $p = (p_1, p_2)$ is the price vector. Then answer the following:

(a) What is $\partial G/\partial p_i$? (Hint: we solved for this in the chapter,)
(b) Give an economic interpretation to $\partial G/\partial L$ and $\partial G/\partial K$.

(c) Give an economic interpretation to $\partial^2 G/\partial p_i \partial L = \partial^2 G/\partial L \partial p_i$, and $\partial^2 G/\partial p_i \partial K = \partial^2 G/\partial K \partial p_i$.

1.5   Trace through changes in outputs when there are factor intensity reversals. That is, construct a graph with the capital endowment on the horizontal axis, and the output of goods 1 and 2 on the vertical axis. Starting at a point of diversification (where both goods are produced) in cone A of Figure 1.12, draw the changes in output of goods 1 and 2 as the capital endowment grows outside of cone A, into cone B, and beyond this.

Chapter 2

The Heckscher-Ohlin Model

WE BEGIN this chapter by describing the Heckscher-Ohlin model with two countries, two goods, and two factors (or the two-by-two-by-two model). This formulation is often called the Heckscher-Ohlin-Samuelson (HOS) model, based on the work of Paul Samuelson, who developed a mathematical model from the original insights of Eli Heckscher and Bertil Ohlin.[1] The goal of that model is to predict the pattern of trade in goods between the two countries, based on their differences in factor endowments. Following this, we present the multigood, multifactor extension that is associated with the work of Vanek (1968), and is often called the Heckscher-Ohlin-Vanek (HOV) model. As we shall see, in this latter formulation we do not attempt to keep track of the trade pattern in individual goods, but instead compute the "factor content" of trade, that is, the amounts of labor, capital, land, and so on embodied in the exports and imports of a country.

The factor-content formulation of the HOV model has led to a great deal of empirical research, beginning with Leontief (1953) and continuing with Leamer (1980), Bowen, Leamer, and Sveikauskas (1987), Trefler (1993a, 1995), and Davis and Weinstein (2001), with many other writers in between. We will explain the twists and turns in this chain of empirical research. The bottom line is that the HOV model performs quite poorly empirically unless we are willing to dispense with the assumption of identical technologies across countries. This brings us back to the earlier tradition of the Ricardian model of allowing for technological differences, which also implies differences in factor prices across countries. We will show several ways that technological differences can be incorporated into an "extended" HOV model, with their empirical results, and this remains an area of ongoing research.

Heckscher-Ohlin-Samuelson (HOS) model

The basic assumptions of the HOS model were already introduced in the previous chapter: identical technologies across countries; identical and homothetic tastes across countries; differing factor endowments; and free

---

[1] The original 1919 article by Heckscher and the 1924 dissertation by Ohlin have been translated from Swedish and edited by Harry Flam and June Flanders and published as Heckscher and Ohlin 1991.

trade in goods (but not factors). For the most part, we will also assume away the possibility of factor intensity reversals. Provided that all countries have their endowments *within* their "cone of diversification," this means that factor prices are equalized across countries.

We begin by supposing that there are just two countries, two sectors and two factors, exactly like the two-by-two model we introduced in chapter 1. We shall assume that the home country is labor abundant, so that $L/K > L^*/K^*$. We will also assume that good 1 is labor intensive. The countries engage in free trade, and we also suppose that trade is balanced (value of exports = value of imports). Then the question is: what is the pattern of trade in goods between the countries? This is answered by the following theorem.

Heckscher-Ohlin Theorem

Each country will export the good that uses its abundant factor intensively.

Thus, under our assumptions the home country will export good 1 and the foreign country will export good 2. To prove this, let us take a particular case of the factor endowment differences $L/K > L^*/K^*$, and assume that the labor endowments are identical in the two countries, $L^* = L$, while the foreign capital endowment exceeds that at home, $K^* > K$.[2] In order to derive the pattern of trade between the countries, we proceed by first establishing what the relative product price is in each country *without* any trade, or *in autarky*. As we shall see, the pattern of autarky prices can then be used to predict the pattern of trade: a country will export the good whose free-trade price is higher than its autarky price, and import the other.

Let us begin by illustrating the *home autarky* equilibrium, at point A in Figure 2.1. We have assumed a representative consumer with homothetic tastes, so we can use indifference curves to reflect demand. The autarky equilibrium is established where an indifference curve is tangent to the home PPF, at point A. The price line drawn tangent to the PPF and indifference curve has a slope of (negative) the autarky relative price of good 1, $p^a \equiv p_1^a/p_2^a$. Let us now consider the foreign PPF, which is drawn outside the home PPF in Figure 2.1. In order to determine where the foreign autarky equilibrium lies, let us initially suppose that p^a is *also* the autarky equilibrium abroad, and see whether this assumption leads to a contradiction.

---

[2] Because of the assumptions of identical homothetic tastes and constant returns to scale, the result we are establishing remains valid if the labor endowments also differ across countries.

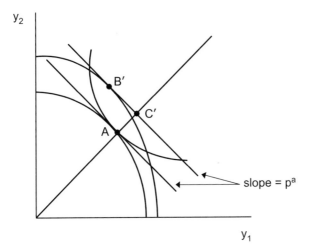

Figure 2.1

If p^a is also the autarky price in the foreign country, then production must occur at the tangency between the price line with slope p^a and the foreign PPF, or at point B'. Notice that from the Rybczynski theorem, point B' must lie *above and to the left* of point A: the higher capital endowment abroad leads to more of good 2 and less of good 1. The price line through point B' acts like a budget constraint for the representative consumer in the foreign country, so that the consumer chooses the highest indifference curve on this price line. Since tastes are homothetic, the foreign representative consumer will demand the two goods in exactly the same proportion as the home representative consumer. In other words, the foreign consumption point must lie on the budget constraint through point B', and also on a ray from the origin through point A. Thus, foreign consumption must occur at point C', which is *above and to the right* of point A. Since points B' and C' do not coincide, we have arrived at a contradiction: the relative price p^a at home *cannot* equal the autarky price abroad, and on the contrary, at this price there is an excess demand for good 1 in the foreign country. This excess demand will bid up the relative price of good 1, so that the foreign autarky price must be *higher* than at home, $p^{a*} > p^a$.

To establish the free trade equilibrium price, let $z(p)$ denote the excess demand for good 1 at any prevailing price p at home, while $z^*(p^*)$ denotes the excess demand for good 1 abroad. World excess demand at a common price is therefore $z(p) + z^*(p)$, and a free-trade equilibrium occurs when world excess demand is equal to zero. The home autarky equilibrium

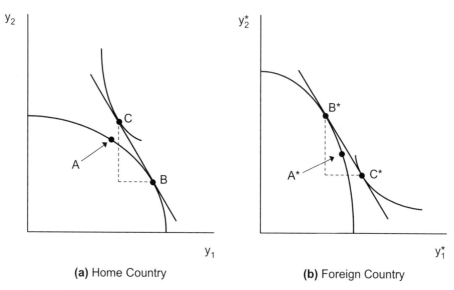

(a) Home Country

(b) Foreign Country

Figure 2.2

satisfies $z(p^a) = 0$, and we have shown above that $z*(p^a) > 0$. It follows that $z(p^a) + z*(p^a) > 0$. If instead we reversed the argument in Figure 2.1 and started with the foreign autarky price satisfying $z*(p^{a*}) = 0$, then we could readily prove that $z(p^{a*}) < 0$, so at the foreign autarky price there is excess supply of good 1 at home. It follows that world excess demand would satisfy $z(p^{a*}) + z*(p^{a*}) < 0$. Then by continuity of the excess demand functions, there must be a price p, with $p^{a*} > p > p^a$, such that $z(p) + z*(p) = 0$. This is the equilibrium price with free trade.

Let us illustrate the free trade equilibrium, in Figure 2.2. In panel (a) we show the equilibrium at home, and in panel (b) we show the equilibrium in the foreign country. Beginning at the home autarky point A, the relative price of good 1 *rises* at home, $p > p^a$. It follows that production will occur at a point like B, where the price line through point B has the slope p. Once again, this price line acts as a budget constraint for the representative consumer, and utility is maximized at point C. The difference between production at point B and consumption at point C is made up through exporting good 1 and importing good 2, as illustrated by the "trade triangle" drawn. This trade pattern at home establishes the HO theorem stated above. In the foreign country, the reverse pattern occurs: the relative price of good 1 *falls*, $p^{a*} > p$, and production moves from the autarky equilibrium point A* to production at point B* and consumption at point C*, where good 1 is imported and good 2 is exported. Notice that the trade triangles drawn at home and abroad are *identical* in size: the exports of one country must be imports of the other.[3]

In addition to establishing the trade pattern, the HO model has precise implications for who gains and who loses from trade: the *abundant* factor in each country gains from trade, and the *scarce* factor loses. This result follows from the pattern of price changes ($p^{a*} > p > p^a$) and the Stolper-Samuelson theorem. With the relative price of good 1 rising at home, the factor used intensively in that good (labor) will gain in real terms, and the other factor (capital) will lose. Notice that labor is the abundant factor at home. The fact that $L/K > L^*/K^*$, means that labor would have been earning less in the home autarky equilibrium than in the foreign autarky equilibrium: its marginal product at home would have been lower (in both goods) than abroad. However, with free trade the home country can shift production towards the labor-intensive good, and export it, thereby absorbing the abundant factor without lowering its wage. Indeed, factor prices are *equalized* in the two countries after trade, as we argued in the previous chapter. Thus, the abundant factor, whose factor price was bid down in autarky, will gain from the opening of trade, while the scarce factor in each country loses.

Our presentation of the HO model above is about as far as discussion of this model goes at the undergraduate level. After showing something like Figure 2.2, it would be common to provide some rough data or anecdotes to illustrate the HO theorem (e.g., the United States is abundant in scientists, so it exports high-tech goods; Canada is abundant in land, so it exports natural resources, etc.). As plausible as these illustrations are, it turns out that the HO model is a *rather poor* predictor of actual trade patterns, indicating that its assumptions are not realistic. It has taken many years, however, to understand why this is the case, and we begin this exploration by considering the earliest results of Leontief (1953).

Leontief's Paradox

Leontief (1953) was the first to confront the HO model with data. He had developed the set of input-output accounts for the U.S. economy, which allowed him to compute the amounts of labor and capital used in each industry for 1947. In addition, he utilized U.S. trade data for the same year to compute the amounts of labor and capital used in the production of $1 million of U.S. exports and imports. His results are shown in Table 2.1.

---

[3] Also notice that the slope of the hypotenuse of the trade triangle for the home country is $(\text{import}_2/\text{export}_1) = p$. It follows that $(p \cdot \text{export}_1) = \text{import}_2$, so that trade is balanced, and this also holds for the foreign country.

TABLE 2.1
Leontief's (1953) Test

	Exports	*Imports*
Capital ($ million)	$2.5	$3.1
Labor (person-years)	182	170
Capital/labor ($/person)	$13,700	$18,200

Note: Each column shows the amount of capital or labor needed per $1 million worth of exports or imports into the United States, for 1947.

Leontief first measured the amount of capital and labor required for $1 million worth of U.S. exports. This calculation requires that we measure the labor and capital used *directly*, that is, in each exporting industry, and also these factors used *indirectly*, that is, in the industries that produce intermediate inputs that are used in producing exports. From the first row of Table 2.1, we see that $2.5 million worth of capital was used in $1 million of exports. This amount of capital seems much too high, until we recognize that what is being measured is the *capital stock*, so that only the annual depreciation on this stock is actually used. For labor, 182 person-years were used to produce the exports. Taking the ratio of these, we find that each person employed in producing exports (directly or indirectly) is working with $13,700 worth of capital.

Turning to the import side of the calculation, we immediately run into a problem: it is not possible to measure the amount of labor and capital used in producing imports unless we have knowledge of the *foreign* technologies, which Leontief certainly did not know in 1953! Indeed, it is only very recently that researchers have begun to use data on foreign technologies to test the HO model, as we will describe later in the chapter. So Leontief did what many researchers have done since: he simply used the *U.S. technology* to calculate the amount of labor and capital used in imports. Does this invalidate the test of the HO model? Not really, because recall that an assumption of the HO model is that technologies are the same across countries. Thus, under the null hypothesis that the HO model is true, it would be valid to use the U.S. technology to measure the labor and capital used in imports. If we find that this null hypothesis is rejected, then one explanation would be that the assumption of identical technologies is false.

Using the U.S. technology to measure the labor and capital used in imports, both directly and indirectly, we arrive at the estimates in the last column of Table 2.1: $3.1 million of capital, 170 person-years, and so a capital/labor ratio in imports of $18,200. Remarkably, this is *higher* than the capital/labor ratio found for U.S. exports! Under the presumption that the United States was capital abundant in 1947, this appears to contradict the HO theorem. Thus, this finding came to be called "Leontief's paradox."

A wide range of explanations have been offered for this paradox:

- U.S. and foreign technologies are not the same.
- By focusing only on labor and capital, Leontief ignored land.
- Labor should have been disaggregated by skill (since it would not be surprising to find that U.S. exports are intensive in skilled labor).
- The data for 1947 may be unusual, since World War II had just ended.
- The U.S. was not engaged in free trade, as the HO model assumes.

These reasons are all quite valid criticisms of the test that Leontief performed, and research in the years following his test aimed to redo the analysis while taking into account land, skilled versus unskilled labor, other years, and so on. This research is well summarized by Deardorff (1984a), and the general conclusion is that the paradox continued to occur in some cases. It was not until two decades later, however, that Leamer (1980) provided the definitive critique of the Leontief paradox: it turned out that Leontief had performed the wrong test! That is, even if the HO model is true, it turns out the capital/labor ratios in export and imports, as reported in Table 2.1, should not be compared. Instead, an alternative test should be performed. The test that Leamer proposed relies on the "factor content" version of the Heckscher-Ohlin model, developed by Vanek (1968), which we turn to next.

Heckscher-Ohlin-Vanek (HOV) Model

Let us now consider many countries, indexed by $i = 1, \ldots, C$; many industries, indexed by $j = 1, \ldots, N$; and many factors, indexed by k or $\ell = 1, \ldots, M$. We will continue to assume that technologies are identical across countries, and that factor price equalization prevails under free trade. In addition, we assume that tastes are identical and homothetic across countries.

Let the $(M \times N)$ matrix $A = [a_{jk}]'$ denote the amounts of labor, capital, land, and other primary factors needed for one unit of production in each industry.[4] Notice that this matrix applies in any country. The *rows*

---

[4] This matrix should include both the *direct* primary factors used in the production of each good and the *indirect* primary factors used through the intermediate inputs. In practice, the indirect factors are measured using the input-output matrix for the economy. That is, denoting the $(M \times N)$ *direct* factor requirements by $\bar{A}$ and the $(N \times N)$ input-output matrix by B, we compute the *total* factor requirements as $A = \bar{A}(I - B)^{-1}$.

measure the different factors $k, \ell = 1, \ldots, M$, while the *columns* of this matrix measure the different industries $j = 1, \ldots, N$. For example, with just two industries using only labor and capital, this matrix would be

$$A = \begin{bmatrix} a_{1L} & a_{2L} \\ a_{1K} & a_{2K} \end{bmatrix}.$$

Next, let Y^i denote the $(N \times 1)$ vector of outputs in each industry for country i, and let D^i denote the $(N \times 1)$ vector of demands of each good, so that $T^i = Y^i - D^i$ equals the vector of *net exports* for country i. The *factor content of trade* is then defined as $F^i \equiv AT^i$, which is an $(M \times 1)$ vector. We will denote individual components of this vector as F_k^i, where a positive value indicates that the factor is exported, while a negative value indicates that the factor is imported. For example, with just labor and capital, the factor content of trade is

$$\begin{pmatrix} F_\ell^i \\ F_k^i \end{pmatrix} \equiv AT^i.$$

The goal of the HOV model is to relate the factor content of trade AT^i to the underlying endowments of country i. To do so, we can proceed by computing AY^i and AD^i. The term AY^i equals the demand for factors in country i. Analogous to the full-employment conditions studied in chapter 1, AY^i equals the endowments of country i, which we write as $AY^i = V^i$. Turning to AD^i, this term is simplified by using our assumption of identical and homothetic tastes. Since product prices are equalized across countries by free trade, it follows that the consumption vectors of all countries must be *proportional* to each other. We shall write this as $D^i = s^i D^w$, where D^w denotes the *world* consumption vector and s^i is the share of country i in world consumption.[5] It follows that $AD^i = s^i AD^w$. Note that if trade is balanced, then s^i also equals country i's share of world GDP.[6] Since world consumption must equal world production, we therefore obtain $AD^i = s^i AD^w = s^i AY^w = s^i V^w$, where the last equality is the full-employment condition at the world level.

Making use of these expressions for AY^i and AD^i, we have therefore proved

$$F^i \equiv AT^i = V^i - s^i V^w, \tag{2.1}$$

which is a statement of the Heckscher-Ohlin-Vanek (HOV) theorem. In terms of individual factors, this is written as $F_k^i = V_k^j - s^i V_k^w$. If country i's endowment of factor k relative to the world endowment *exceeds* country i's share of world GDP $(V_k^i / V_k^w > s^i)$, then we say that country i is *abun-*

---

[5] Letting p denote the vector of prices, then $p'D^i = s^i p'D^w$ so that $s^i = p'D^i / p'D^w$.
[6] Continuing from note 5, if trade is balanced so that expenditure = income in each country, then $p'D^i = p'Y^i$ and so $s^i = p'Y^i / p'Y^w = GDP^i / GDP^w$.

dant in that factor. In that case, (2.1) says that the factor content of trade in factor k should also be positive ($F_k^i > 0$), and conversely if country i is scarce in factor k ($V_k^i/V_k^w < s^i$).

What does the HOV theorem tell us about the Leontief test? To answer this, let us focus on just two elements of the factor content vector, for labor and capital. These are written as

$$F_k^i = K^i - s^i K^w, \tag{2.2a}$$

$$F_\ell^i = L^i - s^i L^w, \tag{2.2b}$$

where F_k^i and F_ℓ^i are the computed factor contents of trade, and K^i and L^i are the capital and labor endowments for country i. Following Leamer (1980), we define capital to be abundant relative to labor in country i if $K^i/K^w > L^i/L^w$. Then using (2.2), the implications of capital abundance are:

Theorem (Leamer 1980)

If capital is abundant relative to labor in country i, then the HOV theorem (2.1) implies that the capital/labor ratio embodied in *production* for country i exceeds the capital/labor ratio embodied in *consumption*:

$$K^i/L^i > (K^i - F_k^i)/(L^i - F_\ell^i). \tag{2.3}$$

Proof

From equation (2.2), we have $K^w = (K^i - F_k^i)/s^i$ and $L^w = (L^i - F_\ell^i)/s^i$. It follows that $K^i/K^w = s^i K^i/(K^i - F_k^i)$ and $L^i/L^w = s^i L^i/(L^i - F_\ell^i)$. Then $K^i/K^w > L^i/L^w$ implies that $K^i/(K^i - F_k^i) > L^i/(L^i - F_\ell^i)$, which is rewritten as (2.3).   QED

To interpret this result, note that K^i and L^i are simply the endowments of capital and labor, or alternatively, the capital and labor embodied in *production*. If we subtract the content of these factors embodied in trade, then what we end up with can be defined as the factor content of *consumption*, or $K^i - F_k^i$ and $L^i - F_\ell^i$. Then equation (2.3) states that the capital/labor ratio embodied in *production* (on the left) must exceed the capital/labor ratio embodied in *consumption* (on the right).

The results from making this comparison for the United States in 1947 are shown in Table 2.2. In the first column we list the capital and labor endowments for the United States, and in the second column we show the capital and labor embodied in consumption. Taking the ratio of these, it is indeed the case that the capital/labor ratio embodied in production

TABLE 2.2
Leamer's (1980) Reformulation of the Leontief Test

	Production	*Consumption*
Capital ($ billion)	$327	$305
Labor (million person-years)	47	45
Capital/labor ($/person)	$6,949	$6,737

Note: Each column shows the amount of capital or labor embodied in production or consumption in the United States, for 1947.

exceeds that in consumption. This is the precise application of the HOV theorem, and it turns out to be satisfied for the United States in 1947, contrary to what Leontief concluded. Thus, there was no paradox after all!

It is useful to see the HOV theorem and Leamer's result in a diagram. In Figure 2.3, the length of the horizontal axis is the world labor endowment $L^w = L^1 + L^2$, and the length of the vertical axis is the world capital endowment $K^w = K^1 + K^2$. The origin for country 1 is in the lower left corner, and for country 2 is in the upper right corner. Thus, any point in the world endowment box measures the endowments (L^i, K^i) of the two countries. Suppose that the endowments are at the point V^i where country 1 is capital abundant, $K^1/L^1 > K^w/L^w > K^2/L^2$.

Under the assumptions of the HOV model, the consumption of each country D^i is proportional to world consumption D^w, which means that the factor content of consumption AD^i is proportional to $AD^w = V^w$. In other words, the factor content of consumption must lie along the *diagonal* in the world endowment box, as illustrated by point AD^i. Therefore, a line from point V^i to point AD^i measures the factor content of trade. In Figure 2.3, country 1 exports F_k^1 of capital services and imports F_ℓ^1 of labor services. With balanced trade, the slope of the line between V^i and AD^i measures the ratio of factor prices.

The theorem of Leamer (1980) states that if country 1 is capital abundant, as illustrated, then the capital/labor ratio embodied in *production* must exceed the capital/labor ratio embodied in *consumption*. That is, since the consumption point AD^i must lie on the diagonal, it is necessarily to the right of and below the endowment point V^i. While this is graphically obvious, note that it does not depend in any way on whether trade is balanced or not. For example, if country 1 is running a trade surplus (with the value of production exceeding consumption), then we should move the consumption point AD^i *to the left* down the diagonal. This would have no effect whatsoever on the capital/labor *ratio* embodied in consumption as compared to the capital/labor *ratio* embodied in production. So Leamer's test of the HOV theorem in (2.3) is completely robust to having nonbalanced trade. Indeed, Leamer

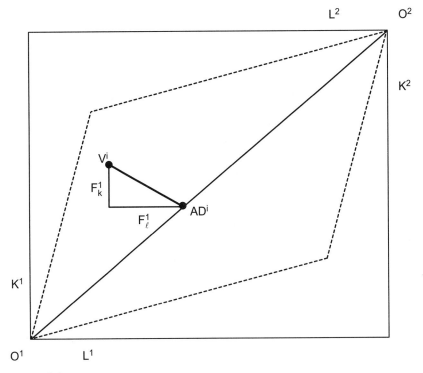

Figure 2.3

(1980) argues that this was the key problem with the way that Leontief did the original test: Leontief's method of testing the HOV theorem was not valid with nonbalanced trade, and in 1947, the United States had a trade surplus and was exporting both labor and capital as embodied in trade.[7]

Partial Tests of the HOV Theorem

The statement of the HOV theorem in (2.1) tells us immediately how a complete test of the theory should be performed: simply compute the left-hand side (using data on trade T^i and technology A), compute the

---

[7] This situation is shown in Figure 2.3 by moving the consumption point AD^i so far to the left and down the diagonal that both capital services F_k^i and labor services F_ℓ^i are exported. Brecher and Choudhri (1982a) point out that the United States being a net exporter of labor is itself a paradox: from (2.2b), $F_\ell^i > 0$ if and only if $L^i > s^i L^w$, which implies $p'D^i/L^i < p'D^w/L^w$ using the expression for s^i from note 5. In words, the United States will be exporting labor if and only if its per capita income is less than the world average, which is plainly false!

right-hand side (using data on endowments V^i and V^w), and compare them. Depending on how well they match up, we can judge whether the theorem is an empirical success or not. This complete test requires both trade and endowments data for many countries, and technology data for at least one country. While such data is readily available today,[8] this was not the case two or three decades ago. Accordingly, many researchers, including Leontief himself, performed what we can call "partial tests" of the HOV model, using only two rather than all three types of data. Before considering the complete test, we will review several other partial tests that were performed.

Let us assume that the number of goods equals the number of factors, so that A is a square matrix, which we assume is invertible. Then we can rewrite (2.1) as

$$T^i = A^{-1}(V^i - s^i V^w). \tag{2.4}$$

This equation could be tested in several ways. First, if we think about the matrix A^{-1} as data, then we could run a regression of T^i on A^{-1}, and coefficients obtained would serve as an estimate of the relative abundance $(V^i - s^i V^w)$ of each factor. Baldwin (1971) performed a test similar to this, but instead of regressing T^i on A^{-1}, he actually regressed T^i on A'. With two factors and three goods, for example, A' is the matrix

$\begin{bmatrix} a_{1L} & a_{1K} \\ a_{2L} & a_{2K} \\ a_{3L} & a_{3K} \end{bmatrix}$. Thus, Baldwin regressed the *adjusted net exports* of each

industry[9] on their *labor and capital requirements* needed for one unit of production.

Using data for 60 U.S. industries for years around 1960, and disaggregating workers by their types, Baldwin (1971) obtained the following result:

Adjusted net exports = -1.37^* (physical capital/worker)
$+ 7011^*$ (scientists/worker)
$- 1473$ (managers/worker)
$+ 71$ (clerical staff/worker)
$+ 1578^*$ (craftsmen and foremen/worker)
$+ 248$ (operatives/worker)
$+ 761$ (unskilled employees/worker)

---

[8] Input-output tables as well as bilateral trade data for many countries are available from the Organization for Economic Cooperation and Development (OECD) STAN and I-O datasets. Also see the trade and production data available at www.internationaldata.org.
[9] Adjusted net exports are defined as industry exports per million dollars of total exports minus industry imports per million dollars of total imports.

$+ 845^*$ (farmers/worker)
$+$ (other variables included for
    indutry scale and unionization),
$N = 60$, $R^2 = 0.44$,
$^* =$ significant at 95% level

Thus, looking across the U.S. industries, Baldwin finds that those industries using more scientists, craftsmen and foremen, or farmers relative to total workers will tend to have *higher* exports. The importance of scientists and farmers in predicting U.S. exports is not surprising at all, since the United States is abundant in skilled labor and land; and the importance of craftsmen and foremen is perhaps reasonable, too. What is surprising, however, is the *negative* coefficient found on the very first variable, physical capital/worker. Taken literally, this coefficient says that U.S. industries using *more* capital per worker will tend to export *less*. This is exactly the opposite of what we would expect if the United States were capital abundant. Thus, this result appears to be similar to the "paradox" found by Leontief.

Various writers after Baldwin have redone the type of regression shown above, with mixed results: sometimes the capital coefficient is positive, but other times it is again negative (see the survey in Deardorff 1984a). What are we to make of these results? Well, as we argued for Leontief's original paradox, it can be questioned whether Baldwin's approach is a *valid test* of the HOV model. From (2.4), a valid test would be to regress T^i on A^{-1}, but instead, Baldwin regressed T^i on A'. To see the consequences of this, use the ordinary least squares (OLS) formula for the coefficients β that would be obtained from this regression:

$$T^i = A'\beta \Rightarrow \hat{\beta} = (AA')^{-1}AT^i = (AA')^{-1}(V^i - s^iV^w), \qquad (2.5)$$

where the final equality follows from using the HOV theorem (2.1).

Thus, we see that $\hat{\beta}$ is a *contaminated estimate* of the vector of relative factor endowments ($V^i - s^iV^w$). Namely, rather than equaling the relative factor endowments vector, $\hat{\beta}$ equals the positive definite matrix $(AA')^{-1}$ times ($V^i - s^iV^w$). Because $(AA')^{-1}$ is certainly not the identity matrix, it is entirely possible that the *sign pattern* of the elements in $\hat{\beta}$ will differ from the sign pattern of ($V^i - s^iV^w$).[10] In other words, even if the United States was capital abundant and the HOV theorem held, it would still be possible for the Baldwin regression to find a negative coefficient on capital: this does not contradict the HOV theorem, because like the original Leontief approach, it is the wrong test.

---

[10] See Leamer and Bowen 1981 and Aw 1983.

The careful reader might point out, however, that possible differences in the sign pattern of $\hat{\beta}$ and $(V^i - s^i V^w)$ can presumably be *checked for* using the actual data on $(AA')^{-1}$. This is exactly the approach taken by Bowen and Sveikauskas (1992), who argue that such sign reversals are very unlikely to occur in practice. Thus, the Baldwin regression may be acceptable in practice, and in fact, it has been used in recent research by Romalis (2001).[11] As a descriptive tool to show how trade is related to industry factor requirements, this regression makes good sense, but as a definitive *test* of the HOV theorem it is inadequate for the reasons we have described.

A second "partial test" of the HOV theorem in equation (2.4) has been undertaken by Leamer (1984). In contrast to Baldwin, Leamer tested (2.4) by treating factor endowments $(V^i - s^i V^w)$ as data, while estimating the elements of A^{-1}. To follow this test, notice that (2.4) applies across all countries i. Focusing on a single industry j, and letting the elements of A^{-1} be written as β_{jk}, we can write (2.4) in scalar form as

$$T_j^i = \sum_{k=1}^{M} \beta_{jk}(V_k^i - s^i V_k^w), \quad i = 1, \dots, C. \tag{2.6}$$

Notice that the summation in (2.6) is across factors, while the observations are across countries. Thus, to estimate this regression we would combine the observation for a *single* industry j across multiple countries $i = 1, \dots, C$, where the coefficients β_{jk} are estimated. These coefficients should be interpreted as Rybczynski effects and, as shown in chapter 1, can be positive or negative.

To run this regression, we first need to choose some aggregation scheme for net exports and factors of production. Leamer (1984) works with the trade data for 60 countries in two years, 1958 and 1975. The trade data is organized according to the Standard Industrial Trade Classification (SITC). Because these are *traded* goods, they include only merchandise, that is, agriculture, mining, and manufacturing. Leamer organizes these goods into 10 aggregates, as shown in the first column of Table 2.3: two primary products (petroleum and raw materials); four crops (forest products, tropical agricultural products, animal products, and cereals); and four manufactured products (labor-intensive manufactures, capital-intensive manufactures, machinery, and chemicals).[12] Implicitly there is an eleventh

---

[11] Romalis's model relies on the monopolistic competition framework, which we do not cover until chapter 5. It is recommended for further reading after that.

[12] The method used to form these aggregates involves looking at the cross-country correlations of the disaggregate products in each group with the aggregate itself. That is, "cereals" is an aggregate because countries that export this product in total tend to have high exports of all the products within this group. It turns out that the ratios of capital to worker and professionals to all workers are also reasonably similar within the aggregates. Feenstra and Hanson (2000) consider how the aggregation scheme might lead to bias in calculations of the factor content of trade.

TABLE 2.3
Estimates of Rybczynski Effects from Leamer 1984

	Capital	Professional & Technical Workers	Non-professional Workers	Illiterate Workers	Land 1	Land 2	Land 3	Land 4	Coal	Minerals	Oil	R^2
GNP	453**	15,683**	-445*	-480**	30**	-49**	81*	-27*	9.0**	2.8*	2.1**	0.997
Primary products												
Petroleum	-18.4**	-248	-.8	31*	0.5	7.9**	-5.4	0.3	-1.0**	-0.4	0.6**	0.92
Raw materials	-8.9**	127	-31.2*	-2.3	0.89	0.47	1.1	3.3**	0.45**	0.86**	0.04*	0.86
Crops												
Forest products	-1.7	34	-18.8	8.4	-0.45	-2.7*	0.3	3.3*	-0.17	0.53*	0.08*	0.53
Tropical Agricultural products	-2.9**	-30.1	8.9	5.6	2.0**	-1.1	4.5*	-3.9**	-0.30**	0.44**	0.05*	0.72
Animal products	-0.5	-42	-29.3	14.0	0.09	-0.34	5.6*	-1.3	0.17	0.28	0.05	0.22
Cereals	-4.5**	70	-51.0*	-6.8	1.3*	-4.8**	16.1**	-3.6	0.39**	0.97**	0.24**	0.86
Manufacturing												
Labor intensive	1.9	-397	42*	7.4	-0.97	.00	-0.6	-1.6	-0.10	-0.09	-0.07*	0.13
Capital intensive	18**	-1,900**	116**	49**	-0.89	3.2*	-12**	-0.63	-0.12	-0.46*	-0.17**	0.86
Machinery	29**	-1,471*	38	33	-1.6	-1.5	-24**	-7.9*	1.0**	-1.1*	-0.27**	0.76
Chemicals	4.1**	-154	-16.0	3.0	-0.57	-0.30	-6.0*	-1.0	0.3**	-0.15	-0.04*	0.51

Source: Leamer 1984, 163.
Note: GNP is scaled in thousands of dollars; capital is in millions.
* $|t| > 1$. ** $|t| > 2$.

product in the economy, making up all the nontraded goods, so Leamer includes total GNP as an aggregate to reflect this. There are also 11 factors of production, listed along the top row of Table 2.3: capital, three types of workers (distinguished by skill), four types of land (distinguished by climate), and three natural resources. So the number of goods equals the number of factors by construction.

The estimates of β_{jk} from regressing the 1975 net exports of each of these aggregates on the country factor endowments are shown in Table 2.3. Leamer stresses that the point estimates should not be taken too seriously, but the sign pattern of the coefficients is of interest, especially when the estimates are significantly different from zero. In interpreting the coefficients as Rybczynski effects, it is noteworthy that an increase in the capital endowment is associated with a *rise* in the net exports of all the manufactured goods, and the same is true for an increase in the endowments of nonprofessional or illiterate workers. Conversely, increases in most types of land, or of professional and technical workers, are associated with *declines* in the net exports of the manufactured products. The interpretation of these results is that increases in land favor agriculture over manufacturing, and increases in professional and technical workers favor nontraded services over manufacturing.

Because the estimated coefficients can be positive or negative, they do not provide any basis to *test* the HOV theorem. Instead, we have to rely on the overall fit of the regression: a *linear* relationship between endowments and trade, as in (2.6), is implied by the theory and can be assessed by the R^2 of the regressions. In the final column of Table 2.3 we show the R^2 from each cross-country regression, and these vary from 0.13 to nearly unity. Admittedly, these fits are a *very weak* test of the theory, because we generally do not want to rely on only the R^2 of an equation to judge the validity of the theory underlying it. So while this early approach of Leamer (1984) provides valid results on the Rybczynski effects (which we shall refer to again in the next chapter), it is of limited usefulness in testing the HOV theorem.

We summarize our results so far in Table 2.4, which indicates the data used and the basic methods of the various authors. These "partial tests" have used only two sources of data, and we now turn to various complete tests of the HOV theorem, using all three sources of data (trade, technology, and factor endowments).

Complete Test of the HOV Theorem

The first complete test of the HOV theorem was by Bowen, Leamer, and Sveikauskas (1987). They proposed two tests of equation (2.1), a *sign test*

$$\text{sign}(F_k^i) = \text{sign}(V_k^i - s^i V_k^w), \qquad i = 1, \ldots, C; k = 1, \ldots, M$$

TABLE 2.4
Tests of the Heckscher-Ohlin Model

	Trade	*Technology*	*Factor Endowments*	*Method*
		Data Used		
Leontief (1953)	Yes	U.S.	No	Compared (K/L) ratio of exports and imports
Leamer (1980)	Yes	U.S.	No	Compared (K/L) ratio in production and consumption
Baldwin (1971)	Yes	U.S.	No	$\underset{\text{data}}{T^i} = \underset{\text{data}}{A'}(V^i - s^i V^w)$
Leamer (1984)	Yes	No	Yes	$\underset{\text{data}}{T^i} = A^{-1}\underbrace{(V^i - s^i V^w)}_{\text{data}}$
Bowen, Leamer and Sveikauskas (1987)	Yes	U.S.	Yes	Sign test and rank test
Trefler (1993a)	Yes	U.S.	Yes	Allowed for productivity parameters π_k^i
Trefler (1995)	Yes	U.S.	Yes	Allowed for productivity parameters δ^i (and more)
Davis and Weinstein (2001)	Yes	Many countries	Yes	Estimated A^i from data

and a *rank test*,

$$F_k^i > F_\ell^i \Leftrightarrow (V_k^i - s^i V_k^w) > (V_\ell^i - s^i V_\ell^w), \quad i = 1, \ldots, C; k, l = 1, \ldots, M$$

The first of these tests simply compares the sign pattern on the left and right sides of (2.1). With M factors and C countries, there are MC observations in total, and we are interested in what *percentage* of these have the same sign on the two sides of the equation. Notice that a completely random pattern of signs such as obtained by flipping a coin would still generate correct signs 50% of the time in a large sample. Therefore, the sign test must do considerably better than this in order to conclude that the HOV theorem is successful.

The rank test involves a pairwise comparison of all factors for each country, so there are $M(M-1)/2$ pairs for each of C countries. If the computed factor contents of one factor exceed that of a second factor, then we check whether the relative abundance of that first factor also exceeds the relative abundance of the second factor. Again, a completely random assignment of factor abundance and relative endowments would imply that in 50% of the comparisons in a large sample, the rank test would be satisfied, so we would hope that the actual data perform considerably better than this.

In fact, the sign and rank test both fail miserably when confronted with actual data. Using data for 27 countries and 12 factors, Bowen, Leamer, and Sveikauskas found that the sign test was satisfied in about 61% of the cases, and the rank test was satisfied in about 49% of the cases: about what we would expect from flipping a coin. These negative results were confirmed in later calculations by Trefler (1995), with a sample of 33 countries and 9 factors, and his results for each country are shown in Table 2.5. Overall, the sign test was successful in only 50% of the cases when using U.S. technology to measure matrix A (column (2) in Table 2.5).[13] The rank test was successful in only 60% of cases (column (4)). This lack of success indicates that some assumption of the HOV model is drastically wrong![14]

Bowen, Leamer, and Sveikauskas along with Trefler (1995) perform several diagnostic tests on the data to determine which assumptions of the HOV model are most likely to be responsible for its failure, and conclude that the assumption of *equal technologies across countries* is especially bad. Accordingly, they develop an extended version of the HOV model that allows for different technologies across countries—a proposal originally made by Leontief (1953) as one explanation for the "paradox."

Modeling Different Technologies across Countries

There are two ways that technological differences can be introduced into the HOV model. One approach is to model the *productivity of factors* in different countries; another approach is to model *differences in the factor*

[13] Table 2.5 corrects the expenditure shares s^i for trade imbalance. From note 6, $s^i = p'D^i/p'D^w$. Noting that $GDP^i = p'Y^i = p'D^i + p'T^i$, it follows that when $p'T^i \neq 0$ due to trade imbalances, we should measure the shares by $s^i = (GDP^i - p'T^i)/GDP^w$.

[14] Rather than conduct this test over the entire sample of countries, we might instead restrict attention to the factor content of trade for northern versus southern countries, whose factor endowments are quite different. Taking this approach, Debaere (2003) obtains much greater success with the sign test, which is reformulated to compare the difference in endowments of two factors with the difference in their factor content of trade. Then comparing northern and southern countries using Trefler's (1995) data, Debaere finds that the reformulated sign test is successful in 84% of cases for capital relative to labor, whereas for northern countries it is successful in 60% of cases and for southern countries in only 49% of cases.

TABLE 2.5
Results from the HOV Model

Country	GDP per Capita (1)	Sign HOV F (2)	Sign HOV F^δ (3)	Rank HOV F (4)	Rank HOV F^δ (5)	Estimates δ^i (6)	Estimates t-statistic (7)
Bangladesh	0.04	0.33	0.78	0.75	0.78	0.03	47.71
Pakistan	0.08	0.33	0.67	0.72	0.78	0.09	32.10
Indonesia	0.11	0.22	0.67	0.67	0.67	0.10	39.51
Sri Lanka	0.12	0.22	0.56	0.42	0.67	0.09	14.85
Thailand	0.16	0.22	0.67	0.69	0.72	0.17	23.80
Colombia	0.21	0.33	0.89	0.81	0.86	0.16	18.41
Panama	0.23	0.33	0.78	0.56	0.78	0.28	3.24
Yugoslavia	0.30	0.56	0.67	0.44	0.61	0.29	11.35
Portugal	0.30	0.22	0.78	0.53	0.58	0.14	9.63
Uruguay	0.31	1.00	0.11	0.72	0.53	0.11	19.46
Greece	0.35	0.11	0.56	0.47	0.75	0.45	4.63
Ireland	0.39	0.67	0.44	0.53	0.39	0.55	2.91
Spain	0.41	0.22	0.78	0.39	0.69	0.42	9.40
Israel	0.60	0.67	0.89	0.39	0.69	0.49	2.91
Hong Kong	0.61	0.67	0.89	0.83	0.72	0.40	4.12
New Zealand	0.62	0.44	0.22	0.53	0.61	0.38	7.89
Austria	0.65	0.56	0.67	0.53	0.47	0.60	3.03
Singapore	0.66	0.56	1.00	0.61	0.61	0.48	2.11
Italy	0.66	0.67	0.33	0.78	0.67	0.60	7.16
U.K.	0.66	0.67	0.78	0.58	0.64	0.58	8.04
Japan	0.66	0.78	0.67	0.78	0.78	0.70	7.15
Belgium	0.67	0.67	0.78	0.61	0.53	0.65	2.73
Trinidad	0.69	0.67	1.00	0.50	0.53	0.47	1.25
Netherlands	0.69	0.44	0.44	0.53	0.47	0.72	2.66
Finland	0.70	0.33	0.44	0.47	0.50	0.65	2.17
Denmark	0.72	0.44	0.44	0.53	0.42	0.73	1.92
West Germany	0.73	0.56	0.67	0.81	0.78	0.78	3.80
France	0.73	0.33	0.33	0.08	0.22	0.74	4.84
Sweden	0.75	0.44	0.44	0.67	0.36	0.57	4.09
Norway	0.82	0.44	0.44	0.61	0.78	0.69	1.80
Switzerland	0.91	0.89	0.89	0.56	0.47	0.79	1.41
Canada	0.95	0.56	0.22	0.89	0.56	0.55	9.82
U.S.A.	1.00	0.89	0.56	0.92	0.72	1.00	
All countries		0.50	0.62	0.60	0.62		

Source: Trefler 1995 and empirical exercises 2.1 and 2.2.

Note: Column (1) is capita GDP relative to U.S. per capita GDP. Columns (2) and (4) report the results of the sign and rank tests, assuming that all countries have the U.S. technology. Columns (3) and (5) report the results of the sign and rank tests, allowing for uniform technological differences δ^i across countries. Column (6) reports the estimates of δ^i and column (7) their asymptotic t-statistic for the null hypothesis $\delta^i = 1$.

requirements matrix A. These approaches are closely related, of course: saying that a factor is 10% less productive in one country is the same as saying that 10% more of that factor is needed per unit of production. But thinking about them as distinct will be convenient for our discussion.

Trefler (1993a) takes the first approach and allows *all factors in every country to differ in their productivities.* The only exception to this is for the United States, which he uses as the benchmark country, with factor productivities normalized at unity. So let π_k^i denote the productivity of factor k in country i relative to its productivity in the United States. In terms of efficiency units, the *effective endowment* of factor k in country i becomes $\pi_k^i V_k^i$. Let A now denote the amount of effective factors needed per unit of output in each industry. We continue to assume that factor price equalization holds in terms of effective factor prices, so with identical technologies, the matrix A is the same across countries. Thus, we continue to measure the factor content of trade as $F^i \equiv AT^i$. Then the HOV equation (2.1) is rewritten in terms of effective factor endowments as

$$F_k^i = \pi_k^i V_k^i - s^i \sum_{j=1}^{C} \pi_k^j V_k^j, \quad i=1,\ldots,C; k=1,\ldots,M. \qquad (2.7)$$

There are MC equations in (2.7), and $M(C-1)$ productivity parameters. These equations are not independent, however. For any factor k, if we sum (2.7) across countries $i=1,\ldots,C$, then we must obtain zero on both sides: exports equal imports for the world, even when measured in terms of factor contents. So we can drop the equations for one country, and we do so for the U.S. This leaves $M(C-1)$ equations in $M(C-1)$ parameters. These equations will be independent "almost everywhere," that is, for almost all sets of data on endowments and factor contents of trade. Furthermore, the productivity parameters enter (2.7) *linearly,* so the $M(C-1)$ equations in (2.7) can be inverted to solve for these uniquely. Thus, we have established the following theorem.

Theorem (Trefler 1993a)

Allowing for all factors in all but one country to differ in their productivities π_k^i, for almost all datasets there will be a solution for productivities π_k^i such that the HOV equation (2.7) holds *with equality* for $i=1,\ldots,C$, $k=1,\ldots,M$.

The unusual feature of this result is that the HOV equation no longer becomes testable: it holds as an identity by the choice of productivity parameters! How, then, are we to judge whether the HOV model is a reasonable description of reality? Trefler recommends two methods: first, we need to check whether the productivity parameters are *positive* (there is

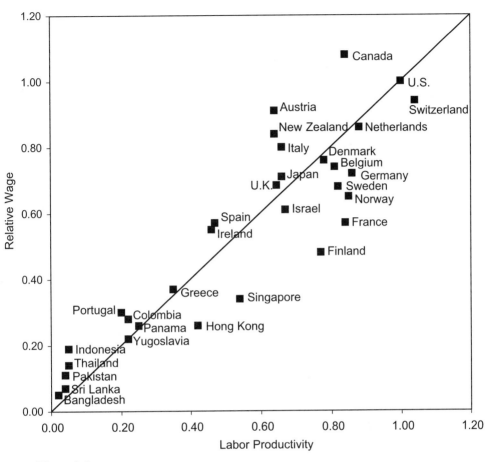

Figure 2.4

nothing in the inversion of (2.7) that guarantees this); second, we might compare these parameters to other economic data to evaluate how "reasonable" the productivity parameters are. For example, it makes sense to compare the labor productivity parameters to wages across countries. If factor price equalization holds in terms of *effective* endowments, then it should be the case that the productivity parameters π_k^i match the factor prices of country i quite closely.

In Figure 2.4, we show the results that Trefler (1993a) obtains for *labor*.[15] On the horizontal axis we measure the estimated productivities

---

[15] In empirical exercise 2.3 you are provided with Trefler's data and are asked to compute the productivities π_k^i.

π_ℓ^i, and on the vertical axis are data on wages across countries (both of these are relative to the United States). It is clear that the observations on these two variables across countries follow each other quite closely: the correlation between estimated π_ℓ^i and actual wages is 0.9. Since we think that cross-country differences in wages should indeed reflect workers' productivities, this close correspondence between the two in Figure 2.4 lends support to Trefler's extension of the HOV model.[16]

Turning to the second method of introducing productivity differences, Trefler (1995) allows the factor requirements matrix A^i to differ across countries, while assuming that the factor endowments do not differ in efficiency units. In this analysis, he chooses to *restrict* the range of differences in matrices A^i so that the HOV equations give *less than a perfect fit*. This means that we are back in the traditional econometric approach: choosing the parameters of A^i so as to minimize the sum of squared residuals of the HOV equations. To implement this, we need to model A^i in terms of some productivity differences across countries. The initial case that Trefler considers is where the matrices A^i differ by a *uniform amount* across countries:

$$\delta^i A^i = A^{US}, \qquad (2.8)$$

which implies $A^i = A^{US}/\delta^i$. With $\delta^i < 1$, this means that $A^i > A^{US}$, so that country i is *less productive* and requires more labor, capital, and other resources for a unit of production relative to the United States.

With the assumption (2.8), we need to rederive the HOV equation. From the assumption of full employment, we still have $A^i Y^i = V^i$. We continue to make the assumption of identical and homothetic tastes across countries, so the factor content of trade is computed as

$$A^i T^i = A^i Y^i - A^i D^i = V^i - A^i(s^i D^w) = V^i - A^i \left(s^i \sum_{j=1}^{C} Y^j \right). \quad (2.9)$$

To make further progress with (2.9), let us multiply both sides by δ^i. On the left, we would obtain $\delta^i A^i T^i = A^{US} T^i \equiv F^{i\,US}$ That is, we define $F^{i\,US}$ as the factor content of trade for country i, computed by using the U.S. factor requirements matrix. (Recall that this is what Leontief used, as well as all other researchers discussed above.) By also multiplying the right-hand side of (2.9) by δ^i, the matrix A^i appearing in the last term becomes instead $\delta^i A^i = A^{US}$. Since this term now does not depend on the

---

[16] Gabaix (1999) disagrees, and argues that even when the labor content of trade is *zero*, the solution for the productivities of labor π_ℓ^i from equation (2.7) is simply GDP per capita, as you are asked to show in problem 2.1. Because the labor content of trade is small, it is therefore not surprising that the solution for π_ℓ^i is highly correlated with wages, which are highly correlated with GDP per capita.

country i, it can be brought *inside* the summation on the far right of (2.9), to obtain $\sum_{j=1}^{C} A^{US} Y^{j} = \sum_{j=1}^{C} \delta^{j} A^{j} Y^{j} = \sum_{j=1}^{C} \delta^{j} V^{j}$, where the final equality makes use of the full-employment conditions in country $j = 1, \ldots, C$. Substituting these results back into (2.9), we have therefore derived

$$F^{iUS} \equiv A^{US} T^{i} = \delta^{i} V^{i} - \left(s^{i} \sum_{j=1}^{C} \delta^{j} V^{j} \right). \qquad (2.10)$$

This becomes the statement of the HOV theorem when we allow for uniform technological differences across countries: the factor content of trade, measured with the U.S. technology on the left, should equal the relative factor endowments on the right, where these are each adjusted by the technological parameter of each country. Unlike equation (2.7), however, (2.10) will certainly not hold exactly. We therefore introduce an additive error and choose the parameters δ^{i} to minimize the sum of squared residuals of this equation.

The estimates for δ^{i} obtained by Trefler (1995) from equation (2.10) are shown in column (6) of table 2.5, and column (7) reports their asymptotic t-statistic to test the null hypothesis $\delta^{i} = 1$. Clearly, most countries have a technological development that is significantly less advanced than that in the United States. Furthermore, these is a close relationship between δ^{i} in column (6) and each country's GDP per capita relative to the United States reported in column (1): the correlation between them is 0.89. If we presume that the differences in GDP per capita across countries are principally explained by technology, then this strong correlation lends support to the model.

How should we compare the models estimated by Trefler 1993a and Trefler 1995? The complete set of cross-country factor productivity differences π_{k}^{i} allows for a perfect fit in the HOV equations, but this is because there are so many "free" parameters. Allowing only scalar productivity differences δ^{i} is much more parsimonious, with $(C - 1)$ free parameters rather than $M(C - 1)$. One approach is to ask how much the fit of the HOV equations improves by this more limited choice of parameters. That is, we can compare the variance of the left side and estimated right side of the HOV equation in (2.1), (2.7), or (2.10) and use this as a measure of the R^{2} of the model. In conjunction with the "reasonableness" of the estimates themselves, this method can be used to evaluate the model.

Consider the original HOV equation (2.1), without any productivity parameters at all. For Trefler's data, the variance of the factor contents F_{k}^{i} relative to the variance of the country endowments $V_{k}^{i} - s^{i} V_{k}^{w}$ turns out to be only 0.032! Trefler (1995) refers to this as the mystery of "missing trade": measured factor contents of trade are very small in comparison with relative endowments $V_k^i - s^i V_k^w$. At the other extreme, when we allow for the complete set of cross-country factor productivity differences π_k^i, we obtain a perfect fit in the HOV equations (2.7), so that the ratio of the left side and right side is unity. In between these, we can consider the uniform productivity differences δ^i, chosen to minimize the sum of squared residuals in (2.10). Then the R^2 from this equation turns out to be 0.486. In other words, nearly *one-half* of the "missing trade" is explained by allowing for uniform productivity differences across countries. This is an encouraging result! Recomputing the sign test—which compares the signs of the left- and right-hand sides of (2.10)—it turns out that the correct sign is obtained in 62% of cases (column 3 in table 2.6), rather than the 50% obtained without the scalar productivity differences δ^i.[17]

Trefler (1995) goes on to consider other modifications to the HOV framework, including a *limited* set of factor productivity differences (allowed to differ between rich and poor countries), distinguishing consumption versus investment goods, and a "home country" bias in consumption. He concludes that the contribution of these to further explaining "missing trade" is more limited, and prefers the initial model that allows for uniform productivity differences.[18]

Using Data on Different Technologies across Countries

The reader will notice in Table 2.4 that most complete tests of the HOV theorem, using all three types of data, have still relied on the U.S. technology matrix. This is again due to data limitations: factor requirements for other countries, concorded to the same set of factors and industries, have only recently become available.[19] With the availability of this data, the next logical step is to make use of it to construct A^i across countries, rather than only using the U.S. technology matrix. This is the approach taken by Davis and Weinstein (2001). We will defer a discussion of their approach until the next chapter, since it relies on material that we have not yet covered. We note at this point, however, that Davis and Weinstein are careful to *estimate* the differences in the technology matrices A^i across countries, rather than using the *actual data* for A^i, since

---

[17] If instead we compute the sign test while *weighting* each observation in (2.10) by the factor content of trade, then the same signs are obtained in 71% of cases without allowing for any technological differences between countries, and 93% of cases when allowing for the scalar differences δ^i.

[18] Another extension not considered by Trefler is nonhomothetic tastes. Hunter and Markusen (1988) argue that differences in per capita income are indeed an important determinant of trade, and show how the HOV equations can be extended to allow for a non homothetic linear expenditure system. You are asked to work through this case in problem 2.2.

[19] See note 8.

the latter approach would run the risk of having the constructed factor content of trade equal to the countries' relative endowments by construction. This is the same issue that Trefler (1993a) had, where he allowed for enough productivity parameters for the HOV equations to fit perfectly. If the actual technology matrices are used to construct the factor content of trade, the HOV equation can again hold as an identity, as we now show.

In addition to using the actual data on A^i across countries, let us assume that the output of every good is exported to each country in proportion to the purchasing country's GDP.[20] We now keep track of the *bilateral* trades between countries, so let X^{ij} denote the *gross exports of goods from country i to country j*. (Note that this is related to the net exports of country i by $T^i = \sum_{j \neq i} X^{ij} - \sum_{j \neq i} X^{ji}$). Using our assumption regarding bilateral exports, these may be written as

$$X^{ij} = s^j Y^i, \qquad (2.11)$$

where $s^j = \mathrm{GDP}^j/\mathrm{GDP}^w$ is the ratio of country j's GDP to world GDP.[21] In order to measure the factor content of these bilateral exports, we use the primary factor requirements of the exporting country i, and define $F^{ij} \equiv A^i X^{ij}$ as the factor contents of exports from country i to country j. It follows from (2.11) that

$$F^{ij} \equiv A^i X^{ij} = s^j A^i Y^i = s^j V^i, \qquad (2.11')$$

where the final equality follows from full employment.

Using simple algebra, we can rewrite the relative endowments of country i as

$$
\begin{aligned}
V^i - s^i \left(\sum_j V^j \right) &= (1 - s^i) V^i - s^i \left(\sum_{j \neq i} V^j \right) \\
&= \left(\sum_{j \neq i} s^j \right) V^i - s^i \left(\sum_{j \neq i} V^j \right).
\end{aligned}
\qquad (2.12)
$$

Now make use of the factor content of exports in $(2.11')$, $F^{ij} = s^j V^i$. This term is summed over all destination countries $j \neq i$, and appears as the first term on the right side of (2.12), which is interpreted as the *factors used in country i to produce exports for all countries $j \neq i$*. Similarly, the second term on the right side of (2.12) is the *factors used in every country $j \neq i$ to produce exports to country i*. Thus, using $(2.11')$ to replace the terms on the right of (2.12), we have shown the following theorem.

[20] This assumption is somewhat stronger than identical and homothetic tastes, and is modeled by the "gravity equation." We will discuss this equation in detail in chapter 5.
[21] We are ignoring trade imbalances, as discussed in footnote 13.

Theorem (Trefler 1998)

If the output of every good is exported to each country in proportion to the purchasing country's GDP, and the factor content of bilateral trade is measured with the exporting countries' technologies, then

$$V^i - s^i \left(\sum_j V^j \right) = \left(\sum_{j \neq i} F^{ij} \right) - \left(\sum_{j \neq i} F^{ji} \right). \qquad (2.13)$$

The first term on the right side of (2.13) is the factor content of exports from country i to all countries $j \neq i$, and the second term is the factor content of imports from all countries $j \neq i$ to country i. The factor content of country i's multilateral net exports is measured by the difference between these, and (2.13) therefore shows that the factor content of country i's multilateral net exports (on the right) equals its relative factor endowments (on the left). We stress that this HOV equation is *automatically satisfied* if the hypotheses of the theorem holds true.

This result, due to Trefler (1998), serves as a warning about using actual technology data to construct the factor content of trade. As in Trefler 1993a, which allowed for unlimited differences in factor productivities across countries, using the actual technologies can quickly lead us to an *identity* between the factor content of trade and a country's relative endowments, as in (2.13). This would not then be a test of the theory. Trefler (1998) further shows how this result can be extended to accommodate trade in intermediate inputs, and rightfully suggests that future work needs to take this identity into account.

Other Tests of Trade

We conclude this chapter by briefly considering some other approaches to testing models of trade. We begin with the most general test of the "law of comparative advantage," as proposed by Deardorff (1984b), which does not depend on the Heckscher-Ohlin model. While this test is completely general, it unfortunately relies on information on *autarky* prices, which is seldom available. Accordingly, we move towards alternative tests of the HO model that do not rely on factor price equalization, and also do not require information on autarky prices. Such a test has been proposed by Helpman (1984a), building on the earlier work of Brecher and Choudhri (1982b). We shall review this test and the recent empirical application by Choi and Krishna (2001).

Deardorff's test of comparative advantage can be motivated with the simple two-by-two-by-two model with which we began this chapter. In

Figure 2.2(a), the home country has its production shifted from point A to point B, and its consumption shifted from point A to point C, when moving from autarky to free trade. But both the shift in production and the shift in consumption can be linked by some inequalities that follow from profit maximization and revealed preference. To develop these, let us denote the autarky production of country i by the vector Y^{ia}, the autarky price vector by p^{ia}, and the free-trade production by Y^i. Then profit maximization ensures that $p^{ia\prime}Y^{ia} \geq p^{ia\prime}Y^i$. In other words, the value of production in autarky must exceed the value obtained if producers choose the feasible (but not optimal) point Y^i instead. In autarky, production equals consumption, so that $p^{ia\prime}Y^{ia} = p^{ia\prime}D^{ia}$. Now consider the consumption vector chosen under free trade, D^i. As is evident from Figure 2.2 and will be proven carefully in chapter 6, the representative consumer is *better off* with this free-trade consumption than in autarky: there are gains from trade. It follows from revealed preference that the representative consumer in country i *could not* afford the free-trade consumption vector at the autarky prices, that is, $p^{ia\prime}D^i \geq p^{ia\prime}D^{ia}$. Pulling together these various inequalities, we therefore have

$$p^{ia\prime}D^i \geq p^{ia\prime}D^{ia} = p^{ia\prime}Y^{ia} \geq p^{ia\prime}Y^i. \tag{2.14}$$

Comparing the first and last of these expressions, we see that $p^{ia\prime}(D^i - Y^i) \geq 0$. But since the net exports of country i are denoted by $T^i = Y^i - D^i$, it follows that $p^{ia\prime}T^i \leq 0$. In addition, we have implicitly assumed above that trade is balanced for all countries, meaning that $p'T^i = 0$, where p is the vector of free-trade prices. Therefore, we have derived the key result of Deardorff (1984b):

$$(p^{ia} - p)'T^i \leq 0. \tag{2.15}$$

In words, countries will tend to export those goods $(T^i_j > 0)$ whose autarky prices are below their trade prices, and import those goods $(T^i_j < 0)$ whose autarky prices are above their trade prices. This certainly held in our two-by-two-by-two model at their beginning of the chapter, where the home country exported good 1 (with $p > p^a$) and imported good 2. The inequality in (2.15) shows that this type of result holds in general, with any number of goods and factors.

While we have derived this result for a comparison of autarky and free trade, Deardorff (1984b) shows that it also holds for a comparison of autarky with any form of trade that may be *restricted* by the use of tariffs. So we can measure the trade prices and quantities using actual data, but as we have already mentioned, it is difficult to measure the autarky equilibrium. One unique case where this equilibrium was observed in historical data was Japan in the mid-1850s, which then rapidly moved to more open trade with the Meiji restoration in the late 1860s. Bernhofen and Brown (2001) use data on Japan's pattern of trade from 1868 to 1872, together with various sources of autarky price information from around the 1850s, to directly test the prediction in (2.15). They find that this prediction is strongly confirmed, thereby supporting this general statement of comparative advantage.

To develop a test that does not rely on autarky information, let us return to the assumptions of the HO model: identical technologies across countries, with constant returns to scale. In contrast to our initial formulation of the HOV model, however, we no longer assume that FPE holds. We are then allowing the countries to be in different cones of diversification. When countries trade freely in goods at the price vector p, we denote the GDP of country i by $G(p, V^i)$, where V^i are the endowments of country i. Note that under our assumption of identical technologies, we do not need to index the GDP function itself by the country i. We again keep track of the *bilateral* trades between countries, and let X^{ij} denote the *gross exports* of goods *from country i to country j*. In order to measure the factor content of these exports, we use the primary factor requirements of the *exporting* country i, and define $F^{ij} \equiv A^i X^{ij}$ as the factor content of exports from country i to country j, measured with the exporting country's technology.

Suppose, however, that rather than having country j import X^{ij} of goods, we directly allow it to import the amount F^{ij} *in factors*. Under our maintained assumption that technologies are the same in both countries, it would be *feasible* for country j to directly produce the amount X^{ij} in goods, using the same methods as employed in country i. In general, however, country j could do better than that: because factor prices differ between the countries, the importing country might not want to use the same methods as the exporter, and will end up producing more by choosing methods attuned to its own factor prices. Thus, if we evaluate GDP in country j using the hypothetical factor imports F^{ij}, it must *exceed* the value obtained with the import of goods:

$$
\begin{aligned}
p'(Y^j + X^{ij}) &\leq G(p, V^j + F^{ij}) \\
&\leq G(p, V^j) + [\partial G(p, V^j)/\partial V^j]'F^{ij} \quad (2.16) \\
&= p'Y^j + w^{j\prime}F^{ij}.
\end{aligned}
$$

The second line of (2.16) follows because the GDP function is concave in the factor endowments, and the last line follows because the derivative of the GDP function with respect to endowments equals the vector of factor prices w^j.

Taking the difference between the first and last lines of (2.16), we therefore have $p'X^{ij} \leq w^{j\prime}F^{ij}$, so that the value of bilateral exports in goods is less than the value of embodied factors, using the *importing* country's factor prices. If instead we had used the *exporting* country's factor prices, however, then with constant returns to scale the value of output would just equal the value of factors used, so that $p'X^{ij} = w^{i'}F^{ij}$. Combining this with the previous inequality we therefore have

$$(w^j - w^i)'F^{ij} \geq 0. \tag{2.17}$$

Furthermore, by repeating this exercise but focusing on net exports from country j to country i, measured using country j's technology, we can derive that

$$(w^j - w^i)'F^{ji} \leq 0. \tag{2.18}$$

Putting together these two inequalities, we therefore obtain the key result of Helpman (1984a):

$$(w^j - w^i)'(F^{ij} - F^{ji}) \geq 0. \tag{2.19}$$

These inequalities can be interpreted as saying that factors embodied in trade should flow towards the country with the higher factor price; that is, if factor k has a higher price in country j, $(w_k^j - w_k^i) > 0$ then we should have $F_k^{ij} > 0$ in (2.17) or $F_k^{ji} < 0$ in (2.18) for at least some factors k, so that (2.17)–(2.19) hold when we add up across factors.

To summarize, (2.17)–(2.19) give us testable hypotheses on bilateral factor content of trade between countries that *do not* depend on FPE, though they do presume identical technologies. Choi and Krishna (2001) implement this test for bilateral trade flows between eight countries (Canada, Demark, France, Germany, Korea, Netherlands, the United Kingdom and the United States) using data for 1980. They consider two different ways of measuring the rental price of capital, and two different levels of disaggregating labor. Considering first the one-way trade flows in (2.17) and (2.18), they find that these equations have the correct sign in about 52% to 55% of cases, depending on the methods used for measuring factors. Even when a one-way flow has the incorrect sign, but is small in magnitude, it is still possible that the two-way factor flow in equation (2.19) will have the correct sign. This is confirmed by Choi and Krishna, who find that the *combined* equation (2.19) is satisfied for 72% to 75% of cases, which is a quite respectable success rate.

Choi and Krishna (2004) also show how (2.17) and (2.18) can be generalized to allow for scalar technological differences across countries, much as in (2.8). In that case, they find that the one-way trade flows in (2.17) and (2.18) have the correct sign in 55% to 59% of cases, while the two-way trade flows in (2.19) have the correct sign in 79% of cases. It is somewhat surprising that correcting for scalar technology differences between countries did not lead to a greater improvement in the test results, but then again, this correction improved the "sign test" for Trefler (1995) from 50% to only 62%. Trefler's acceptance of the scalar productivity differences as an *improvement* over the conventional HOV model was based on other criteria, and in particular, their ability to help explain the "missing trade." For the bilateral flows analyzed by Choi and Krishna, the fact that the combined equation (2.19)—emphasized by Helpman (1984a)—is satisfied in about three-quarters of cases indicates support for the theory and suggests that dropping FPE is an important direction for further research.

Conclusions

We started this chapter with the Leontief paradox and, after explaining this away using the results of Leamer (1980), went on to argue that the complete tests of the HOV model fail sadly under the conventional assumptions of this model: identical homothetic tastes and identical technologies with FPE across countries. As we begin to loosen these assumptions, the model performs better, and when we allow for unlimited differences in productivities of factors across countries, as in Trefler (1993a), then the resulting HOV equations will hold as an identity. Between these two extremes, Trefler (1995) shows that a parsimonious specification of technological differences between countries—allowing for a uniform difference from the United States—is still able to greatly improve the fit of the HOV equation. Recent research such as Davis and Weinstein 2001, which we review in the next chapter, generalizes these technological differences and further explains how we account for the differences between the factor content of trade and relative endowments.

So what is left for further research? While it is dangerous to predict the course of future research, we can suggest two areas that deserve further attention. First, it is worth making a distinction between *accounting* for global trade volumes and *testing hypotheses* related to trade. When we attempt to match the right- and left-hand sides of the HOV equation, such as by introducing productivity parameters, we are engaged in an accounting exercise. With enough free parameters this is bound to lead to equality of the HOV equation, as we found in (2.13), which uses the actual technologies of each country but relies on an assumption about exports. On the other hand, when we test hypotheses such as (2.17)–(2.19), we are making use of economic behavior: the GDP function is concave in the factor endowments, leading to (2.17)–(2.19), if and only if producers economize on factor inputs when their prices rise. There seems to be a difference between these two approaches, and ordinarily in economics, we are more interested in testing economic behavior.

Second, even if we accept that the HOV equation can fit perfectly by allowing for sufficient differences between technologies across countries, this begs the question: *where do these differences in technology come from?* In the original work of Heckscher and Ohlin, they rejected the technology differences assumed by Ricardo in favor of a world where knowledge flowed across borders. We have since learned that this assumption of technological similarity across countries was empirically false at the time they wrote (see Estevadeordal and Taylor 2002a, 2002b), as well as in recent years (Trefler 1993a, 1995; Davis and Weinstein 2001). So we are back in the world of Ricardo, where technological differences are a major determinant of trade patterns. Such differences can hardly be accepted as exogenous, however, and surely must be explicable based on underlying causes. Increasing returns to scale might be one explanation, and this has been incorporated into the HOV framework by Antweiler and Trefler (2002), as will be discussed in chapter 5. Economy-wide increasing returns are also suggested by the literature on "endogenous growth," which we will discuss in chapter 10. Beyond this, some recent authors have argued that geography and climate (Sachs 2001), or colonial institutions (Acemoglu, Johnson and Robinson 2001), or social capital (Jones and Hall 1999), or the efficiency with which labor is utilized (Clark and Feenstra 2003) must play an important role. Whatever the answer, this issue will no doubt occupy researchers for some years to come.

Problems

2.1 Suppose that the factor content of trade is zero on the left side of equation (2.7). Then solve for the implied values of the productivities π_k^i in one country relative to another.

2.2 An assumption of the Heckscher-Ohlin-Vanek model, as outlined in this chapter, is that tastes are identical across countries and also homothetic. The latter is an unrealistic assumption because of Engel's law: expenditures on food are a declining share of total income. Following Hunter and Markusen (1988), we can introduce nonhomothetic tastes using a linear expenditure system. Denoting per capita consumption of good i in any country j by d_i^j, we suppose that the utility function is given by

$$U^j = \prod_{i=1}^{N} (d_i^j - \bar{d}_i)^{\phi_i},$$

$$\text{with } \sum_{i=1}^{N} \phi_i = 1.$$

The parameters $\bar{d}_i \geq 0$ in the utility function are interpreted as the "minimum consumption" of each commodity $i = 1, \ldots, N$. They are assumed to be the same across countries, as are the parameters $\phi_i > 0$.

(a) Assuming that *per-capita* income I^j is large enough to afford the "minimum consumption," show that per capita demand for each commodity in country j is given by

$$d_i^j = \bar{d}_i + \phi_i \left(I^j - \sum_{j=1}^{N} p_j \bar{d}_j \right) / p_i,$$

where p_j, $j = 1, \ldots, N$, are the commodity prices.

(b) Assuming that prices are the same across countries due to free trade, we can normalize them at unity, and rewrite demand in the more compact form

$$d_i^j = \delta_i + \phi_i I^j,$$

where $\delta_i \equiv (\bar{d}_i - \phi_i \sum_{j=1}^{N} \bar{d}_j)$ are the values of "minimum consumption" measured relative to their mean. Interpret the coefficients δ_i.

(c) Multiply the per capita demand by country population L^j to obtain total demand, $D_i^j = L^j d_i^j = \delta_i L^j + \phi_i E^j$, where $E^j \equiv L^j I^j$ denotes *total expenditure* in country j. We can write this in vector notation as $D^j = \delta L^j + \phi E^j$. Using this demand function, rederive the HOV equation (2.1) and interpret the new equation.

Empirical Exercises

In these exercises, you will reproduce some of the empirical results from Trefler (1993a, 1995). To complete the exercise, the Excel file "hov_pub. csv" should be stored in the directory c:\Empirical_Exercise\Chapter_2\ hov_pub.csv. After this, run the STATA program "hov_pub.do", which will create a new STATA data file "trefler.dta". Then do the following exercises:

2.1   Given identical technologies across countries, run the program "sign_rank_1.do" to conduct the sign test, rank test, and test for missing trade. Use the results in "sign_rank_1.log" to replicate columns (2) and (4) in Table 2.5.

2.2   Given uniform technological differences across countries, run the program "sign_rank_2.do" to redo the sign test, rank test, and missing trade. Use the results in "sign_rank_2.log" to replicate column (3) and (5), given column (6), in Table 2.5.

2.3   Allowing all factors in each country to have different productivities, now run the program "compute_pi.do" to compute factor productivities π_k^i as in Trefler 1993a. Note that there are nine factors in the original data set, but these are now aggregated to just four factors, which are labor (endowment 1), capital (endowment 2), cropland (endowment 3), and pasture (endowment 4). Using the results in "pi.log" or alternatively in the data files "pi_1.dta", "pi_2.dta", "pi_3.dta", "pi_4.data" to answer the following:

(a) Which factor has the most *negative* productivities estimated?

(b) What is the correlation between the estimated labor productivity and the productivities of other factors? What is the correlation between each factor productivity and GDP per capita (which you can find in the file "trefler.dta")?

Chapter 3

Many Goods and Factors

THE HECKSCHER-OHLIN-VANEK (HOV) model we studied in the previous chapter allowed for many goods and factors, but for much of that discussion we maintained the assumption of factor price equalization. This theorem was proved in chapter 1 only for the case of two goods and two factors (and no factor intensity reversals). A natural question to ask, with many goods and factors, is whether factor price equalization will continue to hold. More generally, what happens to the other theorems we discussed in chapter 1—the Stolper-Samuelson and Rybczynski theorems? Are there some generalizations of these that apply to the many-good and many-factor case? These are the topics we shall address in this chapter.

We begin with the case where the number of goods and factors is the same, the so-called "even" case. We will see that the factor price equalization theorem naturally generalizes from the case of two goods and two factors to N goods and N factors. Versions of the Stolper-Samuelson and Rybczynski theorems also continue to hold, though not quite as strong as we obtained in the two-by-two case.

Then we turn to "uneven" cases, beginning with two goods and three factors. We can think of the factors as labor, which is mobile between both industries, and a specific factor in each industry, such as capital or land, which does not move between them. This is the so-called "specific factors" or Ricardo-Viner model. It will become immediately clear that factor price equalization *does not* hold, but rather, that factor prices prevailing in a country depend on its factor endowments. The results of the Stolper-Samuelson and Rybczynski theorems are also modified, depending on whether we are considering a change in the mobile factor (labor) or the specific factors. The results we obtain for this case illustrate those that apply whenever there are more factors than goods.

Empirically, the case of an equal number of goods and factors or more factors than goods can be neatly analyzed using a country's GDP function. We discuss how these functions can be estimated using data on a set of industries over time. These techniques have been pioneered by Diewert (1974) and applied in an international context by Kohli (1978, 1991), Woodland (1982), and others.[1] Harrigan (1997) provides an application to

---

[1] Burgess (1974a, 1974b, 1976) provides estimates of an aggregate cost rather than GDP function for the United States, as we shall discuss.

the OECD (Organization for Economic Cooperation and Development) countries that we shall review, whereby the output shares of various industries are related to country prices, productivity, and factor endowments. By estimating these share equations, we can then compute the effect of endowment changes on output shares, namely, the Rybczynski effects. This methodology allows us to explain the specialization of countries across various industries. In addition, the GDP function allows us to estimate the dual Stolper-Samuelson effects, as we shall discuss in this chapter and the next.

Finally, we consider the case of more goods than factors, starting with three goods and two factors. Using the results of Dixit and Norman (1980), we argue that there is a wide range of possible factor endowments across countries such that factor price equalization continues to hold, provided that technologies are the same across countries. However, the amount of production occurring in each country is indeterminate when factor prices are equalized. A test for production indeterminacy has been implemented by Bernstein and Weinstein (2002), as we review.[2] An elegant generalization of the case with more goods than factors is when there is a *continuum* of goods, as in Dornbusch, Fischer, and Samuelson 1980. This model allows us to complete our presentation of empirical results from Davis and Weinstein (2001) that we introduced in the last chapter.

Equilibrium Conditions

We will suppose that there are $i = 1, \ldots, N$ goods, and $j = 1, \ldots, M$ factors. The production functions are written $y_i = f_i(v_i)$, where $v_i = (v_{i1}, \ldots, v_{iM})$ is the vector of factor inputs. As usual we assume that the production functions are positive, increasing, concave, and homogeneous of degree one for all $v_i \geq 0$. Denoting the vector of factor prices by w, the unit-cost functions are $c_i(w) \equiv \min_{v_i \geq 0} \{w'v_i \mid f_i(v_i) \geq 1\}$, which are also positive, nondecreasing, concave, and homogeneous of degree one for all $w > 0$. The zero-profit conditions are then stated as

$$p_i = c_i(w), \qquad i = 1, \ldots, N. \tag{3.1}$$

The second set of equilibrium conditions is full employment of resources. As in chapter 1, we write $\partial c_i / \partial w = a_i(w)$ as the amount of factors used for *one unit* of production, and it follows that the total inputs used in industry i are $v_i = y_i a_i(w)$. We denote the elements of the vector $a_i(w)$ by $a_{ij}(w), j = 1, \ldots, M$. Then the full-employment conditions are stated as

$$\sum_{i=1}^{N} a_{ij}(w)y_i = V_j, \qquad j = 1, \ldots, M, \tag{3.2}$$

---

[2] The empirical methods discussed in this chapter draw upon the survey by Harrigan (2003).

where V_j is the endowment of resource j. In matrix notation, let $A = [a_1(w)', \ldots, a_N(w)']$ denote the $M \times N$ matrix of primary factors needed for one unit of production in each industry, where the *columns* of this matrix measure the different industries $i = 1, \ldots, N$. The full-employment conditions (3.2) are then written compactly as

$$AY = V, \qquad (3.2')$$

where Y is the $(N \times 1)$ vector of output and V is the $(M \times 1)$ vector of factor endowments.

The equilibrium conditions (3.1) and (3.2) are $(N + M)$ equations in $N + M$ unknowns, namely, the factor prices w_j, $j = 1, \ldots, M$ and outputs y_i, $i = 1, \ldots, N$. To analyze these, it will be helpful to use the GDP function for the economy, which is defined as

$$G(p, V) \equiv \max_{v_i \geq 0} \sum_{i=1}^{N} p_i f_i(v_i) \quad \text{subject to} \quad \sum_{i=1}^{N} v_i \leq V, \qquad (3.3)$$

where $p = (p_1, \ldots, p_N)$ and $V = (V_1, \ldots, V_M)$ are the price and endowment vectors. To solve this maximization problem, we substitute the constraint (written with equality) into the objective function, and write the output of good 1 as $f_1(V - \sum_{i=2}^{N} v_i)$, so that the maximized value of GDP becomes $G(p, V) = p_1 f_1(V - \sum_{i=2}^{N} V_i) + \sum_{i=2}^{N} p_i f_i(v_i)$. From the envelope theorem, we can differentiate this with respect to p and V while holding the optimal inputs choices v_i fixed, $i = 2, \ldots, N$. Then we obtain

(a) $\partial G / \partial p_i = f_i(v_i) = y_i$,

which is the output of industry i;

(b) $\partial G / \partial V_j = p_1 \partial f_1 / \partial v_{1j} = w_j$,

which is the factor price w_j.

Furthermore, by Young's theorem we know that $\partial^2 G / \partial p_i \, \partial V_j = \partial^2 G / \partial V_j \, \partial p_i$, so it follows that

(c) $$\frac{\partial^2 G}{\partial p_i \partial V_j} = \frac{dw_j}{dp_i} = \frac{\partial^2 G}{\partial V_j \partial p_i} = \frac{dy_i}{dV_j}. \qquad (3.4)$$

Samuelson (1953–54) called conditions (3.4) the "reciprocity relations," and they show that the Stolper-Samuelson derivatives are identical to the Rybczynski derivatives! Results (a)–(c) hold regardless of the number of

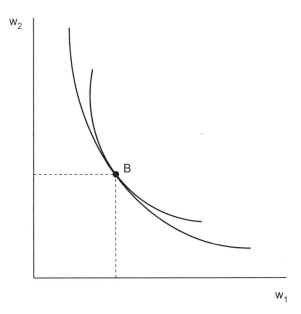

Figure 3.1

goods and factors, but require differentiability of the GDP function. We shall comment on the validity of this assumption below.

We now consider some special cases.

Same Number of Goods and Factors

With $N = M$, the zero-profit conditions (3.1) become N equations in N unknowns. The question, then, is whether we can obtain a solution for the wages w and if this solution is unique. In chapter 1, we discussed the case of "factor intensity reversals," whereby the iso-cost lines of the unit-cost curves for two industries intersect twice (see Figure 1.6). This means that there are some prices for the two industries such that the iso-cost lines are tangent, as shown in Figure 3.1 at point B. At these factor prices, the factor requirements vectors $a_i(w)$ in the two industries are proportional.

A factor intensity reversal (FIR) means that there are factor prices w at which two columns of the matrix A are proportional, so that A is singular. Actually, a factor intensity reversal occurs even if the components of $a_i(w)$ and $a_j(w)$ *for just two factors* are proportional, that is, point B in Figure 3.1 holds for factors 1 and 2, even though the demand for the other factors in these industries is not proportional. To rule out this case, we therefore require a stricter assumption than the nonsingularity of A.

Samuelson (1953–54) first proposed the condition that the leading principal minors of A are all nonnegative, that is,

$$a_{11} \neq 0, \begin{vmatrix} a_{11} & a_{21} \\ a_{12} & a_{22} \end{vmatrix} \neq 0, \ldots, \begin{vmatrix} a_{11} & \cdots & a_{N1} \\ \vdots & \ddots & \vdots \\ a_{1N} & \cdots & a_{NN} \end{vmatrix} \neq 0 \qquad (3.5)$$

By a natural reordering of the goods and factors, the signs of all these determinants can be taken as positive. However, Nikaido (1972) showed that this condition was not enough to ensure that the system of equations (3.1) has a unique solution for w given any $p > 0$. Instead, it had to be strengthened in the following way: there exist bounds $b > 0$ and $B > 0$ such that

$$0 < b \leq a_{11}, \begin{vmatrix} a_{11} & a_{21} \\ a_{12} & a_{22} \end{vmatrix}, \ldots, \begin{vmatrix} a_{11} & \cdots & a_{N1} \\ \vdots & \ddots & \vdots \\ a_{1N} & \cdots & a_{NN} \end{vmatrix} \leq B. \qquad (3.6)$$

Then we have the following "factor price insensitivity" result, as named by Leamer (1995).

Lemma (Samuelson 1953–54; Nikaido 1972)

Assume $N = M$ and that condition (3.6) holds for all $w > 0$. Then for all $p > 0$, the set of equations (3.1) has a unique solution for factor prices $w > 0$.

This lemma implies that the factor prices can be written as a function of product prices, or $w(p)$, independent of endowments. Note that this implies a special form for the GDP function (3.3). With constant returns to scale in all industries, GDP can be written in general as $G(p, V) = \sum_{j=1}^{M} w_j(p, V)V_j$, which is just the sum of payment to primary factors. Under the conditions of the above lemma, this formula is simplified to

$$G(p, V) = \sum_{j=1}^{M} w_j(p)V_j. \qquad (3.7)$$

In particular, this implies that $\partial^2 G/\partial V_j \partial V_i = 0$, so there are no diminishing returns to the accumulation of a factor in the economy overall.

Now suppose that two countries share the same technologies, and therefore the same unit-cost functions, and through free trade they face the same prices p. Provided that both countries are producing all $i = 1, \ldots, N$ goods, then this lemma establishes that they will have the same factor prices, so factor price equalization (FPE) is obtained. The set of endowments that allow both countries to be producing $y_i > 0$ for $i = 1, \ldots, N$, can be computed from the full-employment conditions (3.2). This will be an FPE set, analogous to Figure 1.9. In the case of equal goods and factors, the FPE set is a higher-dimension analogue to Figure 1.9: rather than a parallelogram in two dimensions, we would have a hyperparallelogram in N dimensions. So for factor price equalization, the extension from two goods and two factors to N goods and N factors is obtained quite easily.

What about the Stolper-Samuelson and Rybczynski theorems? To see what sort of generalization can be obtained for these, let us totally differentiate the zero-profit conditions (3.1), and apply the Jones' (1965) algebra, to obtain

$$\hat{p}_i = \sum_{j=1}^{M} \theta_{ij} \hat{w}_j, \qquad i = 1, \ldots, N, \tag{3.8}$$

where $\theta_{ij} = w_j a_{ij}/c_i$ denotes the cost share of factor j in industry i. As we saw in chapter 1, the changes in commodity prices are *weighted averages* of the changes in factor prices. For a change in the price of each commodity i, holding other goods prices fixed, there must then exist factors j and k such that $\hat{w}_j \geq \hat{p}_i$ and $\hat{w}_k \leq 0$. Under additional conditions we can establish that these inequalities are strict,[3] and therefore, factor j has gained in real terms and factor k has lost in real terms. The Stolper-Samuelson theorem generalizes in this sense: *for a change in the price of each good, there will exist some factor that gains in real terms and another that loses.*

A similar generalization holds for the Rybczynski theorem. To see this, differentiate the full-employment conditions (3.2) with respect to endowment V_k, holding prices (and therefore factor prices) fixed, obtaining

$$\sum_{i=1}^{N} \frac{dy_i}{dV_k} a_{ij}(w) = 0, \qquad j = 1, \ldots, M, j \neq k, \tag{3.9a}$$

$$\sum_{i=1}^{N} \frac{dy_i}{dV_k} a_{ik}(w) = 1. \tag{3.9b}$$

Provided that the matrix A is nonsingular at the prevailing factor prices, we can use the conditions (3.9) to uniquely determine the Rybczynski derivatives dy_i/dV_k. From condition (3.9b), it must be the case that $dy_i/dV_k > 0$ for some good i. Using this in (3.9a), there must exist some

---

[3] Ethier (1974, 1984) assumed that $a_{ij} > 0$ for all factors and industries. Jones and Scheinkman (1977, 929) use the weaker assumption that every industry employs at least two inputs, and each input is employed in at least two industries. However, they both assume that with a small change in prices every good is still produced. This means that the factor intensities a_{ij} cannot be proportional in two industries.

other good j for which $dy_j/dV_k < 0$. Thus, we have shown that *for an increase in the endowment of each factor, there must be a good whose output rises and another good whose output falls.*

This generalization of the Rybczynski theorem is fine, but our results for the Stolper-Samuelson theorem are not fully satisfactory. Recall that in the two-by-two model, labor and capital *each* suffers from an increase in the price of *some* good. Does this apply in the $N \times N$ case? Jones and Scheinkman (1977) answer this in the affirmative.

Theorem (Jones and Scheinkman 1977)

Assume that $N = M$, and that the matrix A is nonsingular at the prevailing factor prices. Then for each factor, there must be a good such that an *increase* in the price of that good will *lower* the real return to the factor.

The proof of this theorem follows from (3.9) and the reciprocity relations (3.4): starting with any factor k, we know that $dy_j/dV_k < 0$ for some good j, and so it follows that $dw_k/dp_j < 0$ for some good j. Since all other prices are fixed, it follows that w_k/p_i has fallen, along with w_k/p_j, so that the real return to factor k has been reduced. Jones and Scheinkman interpret this theorem as saying that "each factor has a good that is a natural enemy," in the sense that raising the price of that good will *lower* the real return to the factor. However, in the general case of $N = M > 2$ goods and factors, we *cannot* prove in general that "each factor has a good that is a natural friend"; that is, for each factor, there need not exist a good such that increasing the price of that good will *raise the real return* to the factor.[4] We have already argued that raising a price will increase the real return to *some* factor, but we cannot establish that *each* factor will benefit in real terms due to an increase in the price of some good. So factors have "natural enemies" but not necessarily "natural friends."

Empirical estimates of the Rybczynski effects in the "even" case have already been shown in the previous chapter, from Leamer (1984). Harrigan (1995) reexamines a similar set of regressions but using industry outputs as the dependent variable rather than net trade. The explanatory variables are country factor endowments, and the linear relationship between outputs and factor endowments follows directly from inverting (3.2′), obtaining $Y = A^{-1}V$, or

$$y_j^i = \sum_{k=1}^{M} \beta_{jk} V_k^i, \qquad i = 1, \ldots, C; \, j = 1, \ldots, N, \qquad (3.10)$$

---

[4] Ethier (1984, proposition 20) argues that there will be a "qualified" friend, in the sense that raising some commodity price will raise that factor price enough to *lower* the aggregate income of all other factors.

where i now indexes countries, j indexes goods, k indexes factors, and β_{jk} denotes the elements of A^{-1}. Harrigan uses data for the OECD countries over 1970–85 for 10 manufacturing sectors and four factor supplies: capital, skilled and unskilled labor, and land. Notice that the number of goods exceeds the number of factors in this formulation, even though inverting (3.2′) assumes that $N = M$. We can think of Harrigan's approach as assuming $N = M$ in terms of the "true" number of goods and factors, but then aggregating factors in the data so that there are only four. More generally, this discussion points out that whether or not there is an equal number of goods and factors cannot be judged by simply "counting" them: instead, we would need to test some hypotheses to make a judgment, as we shall discuss in the sections that follow.

The results obtained by regressing industry outputs on factor endowments, over the panel of OECD countries and years, are similar to those obtained by Leamer (1984): for each manufacturing industry there is at least one factor with a negative Rybczynski effect, indicating that an increase in that endowment would reduce the manufacturing output. These factors were usually skilled or unskilled labor, and sometimes land. Conversely, capital has a positive coefficient β_{jk} in all 10 regressions, indicating that an increase in this endowment will raise manufacturing output. Beyond these results, Harrigan (1995) is able to explore properties of the panel dataset that Leamer (1984) could not since he only had data for two years. Harrigan finds that *fixed effects* for countries are very important, indicating that there are systematic differences across countries not captured by the theory underlying (3.10). The most significant assumption in applying (3.10) to panel data is that *technologies are the same* across countries and time. We will be eliminating this assumption later in this chapter.

More Factors Than Goods

We turn now to the case of more factors than goods, $M > N$. We can again differentiate the zero-profit conditions to obtain (3.8), so our generalization of the Stolper-Samuelson theorem continues to hold: an increase in the price of each good will lead to a rise in the real return to *some* factor, and a fall in the real return to another. However, our generalization of the Rybczynski theorem *does not* hold: when we differentiate the full-employment conditions, we do not obtain (3.9), because now a change in factor endowments leads to a change in their prices, so the factor intensities a_{ij} will change. Furthermore, the fact that (3.9) does not hold means that the theorem due to Jones and Scheinkman (1977) will not hold either: it is no longer that case that each factor has a good that is a "natural enemy."

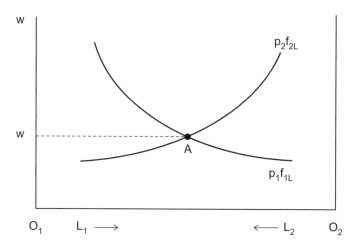

Figure 3.2

To illustrate these results, we focus on the special case of two goods and three factors, in what is called the "specific factors," or the Ricardo-Viner, model. This model has been analyzed by Jones (1971), Mayer (1974), Mussa (1974), and Neary (1978), among others. Let us return to the notation that the two sectors use labor and capital, with production functions $y_i = f_i(L_i, K_i)$. We now assume that the capital stocks K_i are *fixed* in each industry, so that labor is the only factor that moves between them. This framework is sometimes viewed as a "short run" version of the Heckscher-Ohlin model, for a time span short enough such that capital is fixed.

The full-employment condition for labor is $L_1 + L_2 \leq L$, and so the GDP function for the economy is

$$G(p, L, K_1, K_2) \equiv \max_{L_i \geq 0} \sum_{i=1}^{2} p_i f_i(L_i, K_i) \text{ subject to} \qquad (3.11)$$

$$L_1 + L_2 \leq L.$$

To maximize GDP, labor will flow between the two industries until its marginal value product is the same in each. This first-order condition is stated as

$$w = p_1 f_{1L}(L_1, K_1) = p_2 f_{2L}(L_2, K_2). \qquad (3.12)$$

With the capital stocks fixed, (3.12) is easily solved for the labor allocation, as is illustrated in Figure 3.2. The horizontal axis measures the total labor endowment L, which is allocated between industry 1 (measured

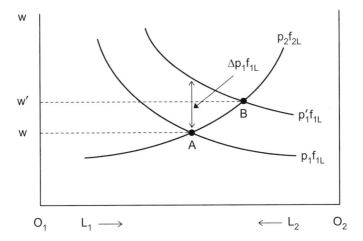

Figure 3.3

from its origin 0_1) and industry 2 (measured from its origin 0_2). Concavity of the production functions implies a diminishing marginal product of labor, so both curves $p_i f_{iL}$ are drawn as downward sloping relative to their origins. The equilibrium wage is determined at the intersection of these two curves, point A.

Note that the position of the marginal product curves depends on the amount of capital in each industry, and, therefore, so does the equilibrium wage at point A. Thus, with two countries having the same technology and facing the same prices due to free trade, but with differing endowments, there will *not be* factor price equalization: rather, the price of each factor will be inversely related to the countries' endowments.[5]

Now suppose that there is an exogenous increase in the price of good 1. What is the effect on factor prices? In Figure 3.3, the marginal value product curve of industry 1 will shift up by $\Delta p_1 f_{1L}$, as illustrated. It is immediately clear that the wage increases along with the allocation of labor to industry 1. From (3.12), we can compute the increase in the wage as

$$\frac{dw}{dp_1} = f_{1L} + p_1 f_{1LL} \frac{dL_1}{dp_1} < f_{1L} = \frac{w}{p_1}, \qquad (3.13)$$

where the inequality follows from $f_{1LL} < 0$ and $dL_1/dp_1 > 0$. With $dp_1 > 0$, it follows immediately from (3.13) that $dw/w = \hat{w} < dp_1/p_1 = \hat{p}_1$. The fact that $\hat{w} > 0$ means that workers can buy more of good 2, whose price is fixed, but the fact that $\hat{w} < \hat{p}_1$ means that (w/p_1) has fallen, so that

[5] See problem 3.1.

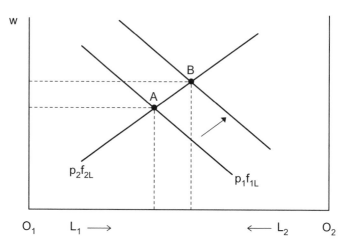

Figure 3.4

workers can afford of less of good 1.[6] Thus, the change in the real wage is *ambiguous*: whether a worker is better off or worse off depends on his or her relative consumption of the two goods. This illustrates that the theorem due to Jones and Scheinkman (1977) no longer holds with more factors than goods.

What about the rental to capital in each industry? From the zero-profit conditions (3.8) the change in the prices of the goods is a weighted average of the change in the wage and rentals. Denoting the latter by r_i, the fact that $0 < \hat{w} < \hat{p}_1$ implies

$$\hat{r}_2 < 0 < \hat{w} < \hat{p}_1 < \hat{r}_1. \qquad (3.14)$$

If we allow for a change in the price of good 2, with $\hat{p}_2 < \hat{p}_1$, then these inequalities become

$$\hat{r}_2 < \hat{p}_2 < \hat{w} < \hat{p}_1 < \hat{r}_1. \qquad (3.14')$$

This shows how the "magnification effect" present in the two-by-two model is modified when capital is specific to each sector. In that case, the wage of labor is "caught in the middle," whereas the returns to the *specific factors* are still a *magnified* version of the price changes.

The effects of changes in the endowments of factors are also straightforward to derive. Suppose first that the capital stock in industry 1 rises.

---

[6] This result can also be seen from Figure 3.3, since the vertical shift of the marginal value product curve *exceeds* the increase in the relative wage, $\Delta w < \Delta p_1 f_{1L}$, with f_{1L} evaluated at the initial labor allocation at point A. Dividing both sides of this equation by $w = p_1 f_{1L}$, we obtain $\Delta w / w < \Delta p_1 / p_1$.

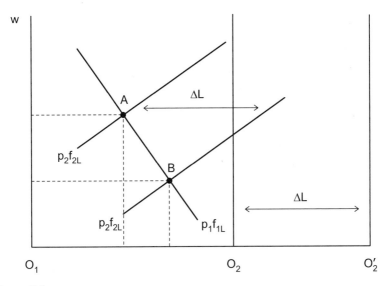

Figure 3.5

This increases the marginal product of labor in that industry, which leads to a higher wage, as shown in Figure 3.4.[7] Thus, labor benefits from an increase in the capital stock in either industry. Furthermore, we can apply (3.8) while setting $\hat{p}_1 = 0$ since we are assuming that product prices are fixed. The increase in the wage must be offset by a *fall* in the rental on capital *in both industries*.[8] So all specific factors suffer from an increase in their stock in any industry. Figure 3.4 also shows that the labor allocated to industry 1 increases, while the labor allocated to industry 2 decreases. It follows that y_1 rises but y_2 falls. So an increase in either specific factor will raise the output of that industry but lower the output of the other industry.

Next, consider an increase in the labor endowment. This expands the labor axis in Figure 3.5, and as the origin 0_2 shifts to the right, it carries along with it the $p_2 f_{2L}$ curve. The equilibrium shifts from point A to point B, and it is clear that the wage falls while the increase in labor in industry 1 is less than the total increase in the labor endowment. These two results imply that the specific factors in *both* industries experience a rise in their rentals, and the output of both industries increases. So for an increase in labor, which is the mobile factor, there is no longer a Rybczynski-like effect.

[7] With only two factors, and a production function $f(L, K)$ that is concave and homogeneous of degree one, it must be the case that $f_{LK} > 0$.
[8] Exercise: use (3.8) with $\hat{p}_i = 0$ to show which specific factor has the greatest fall in its rental.

Estimating the GDP Function

The number of goods and factors, as well as whether factors are mobile or not, influences the form of the GDP function. To capture these effects empirically we can hypothesize a very general functional form for GDP and then use data on industry output and prices, as well as factor endowments and prices, to estimate the GDP function. By taking the derivatives of the estimated GDP function with respect to prices and factor endowments, we can then obtain the Rybczynski and Stolper-Samuelson derivatives that apply to an actual economy.

The first step is to choose a functional form for GDP. A convenient choice is the translog function, which was introduced by Diewert (1974, 139) and initially used in the international trade literature by Kohli (1978). This function is written as

$$\ln G = \alpha_0 + \sum_{i=1}^{N} \alpha_i \ln p_i + \sum_{k=1}^{M} \beta_k \ln V_k + \frac{1}{2}\sum_{i=1}^{N}\sum_{j=1}^{N} \gamma_{ij} \ln p_i \ln p_j$$

$$+ \frac{1}{2}\sum_{k=1}^{M}\sum_{\ell=1}^{M} \delta_{k\ell} \ln V_k \ln V_\ell + \sum_{i=1}^{N}\sum_{k=1}^{M} \phi_{ik} \ln p_i \ln V_k, \tag{3.15}$$

where p_i denotes the prices of products $i = 1, \ldots, N$, and V_k denotes the endowments of factors $k = 1, \ldots, M$. In order to ensure that the translog GDP function is homogeneous of degree one in prices, we impose the requirements,[9]

$$\sum_{i=1}^{N} \alpha_i = 1 \quad \text{and} \quad \sum_{i=1}^{N} \gamma_{ij} = \sum_{i=1}^{N} \phi_{ik} = 0. \tag{3.16}$$

In addition, to ensure that the GDP function is homogeneous of degree one in endowments, we impose the requirements

$$\sum_{k=1}^{M} \beta_k = 1 \quad \text{and} \quad \sum_{k=1}^{M} \delta_{k\ell} = \sum_{k=1}^{M} \phi_{ik} = 0. \tag{3.17}$$

The usefulness of the translog function comes from computing its first derivatives, $\partial \ln G/\partial \ln p_i = (\partial G/\partial p_i)(p_i/G)$. Because $\partial G/\partial p_i$ equals the output of sector i, it follows that $(\partial G/\partial p_i)(p_i/G)$ equals the *share of sector i in*

---

[9] Without loss of generality, we also impose the symmetry restrictions $\gamma_{ij} = \gamma_{ji}$ and $\delta_{k\ell} = \delta_{\ell k}$. See problem 3.2 to show that (3.16) and symmetry ensures that the translog cost function is homogeneous of degree one in prices.

GDP, which we denote by the output shares $s_i = p_i y_i / G$. Thus, differentiating (3.15) with respect to ln p_i, we obtain

$$s_i = \alpha_i + \sum_{j=1}^{N} \gamma_{ij} \ln p_j + \sum_{k=1}^{M} \phi_{ik} \ln V_k, \quad i = 1, \ldots, N. \quad (3.18)$$

In addition, we can compute the first derivatives with respect to factor endowments, obtaining $\partial \ln G / \partial \ln V_k = (\partial G / \partial V_k)(V_k / G)$. Because $\partial G / \partial V_k$ equals the factor price of endowment k, it follows that $(\partial G / \partial V_k)(V_k / G)$ equals the *share of GDP devoted to factor k*, which we denote by the factor shares $s_k = w_k V_k / G$. Thus, differentiating (3.15) with respect to ln V_k, we obtain

$$s_k = \beta_k + \sum_{\ell=1}^{M} \delta_{k\ell} \ln V_\ell + \sum_{i=1}^{N} \phi_{ik} \ln p_i, \quad k = 1, \ldots, M. \quad (3.19)$$

Equations (3.18) and (3.19) are $N + M$ linear equations that can be estimated using annual data on output and factor shares, product prices, and endowments. The dependent variables in each of (3.18) and (3.19) sum to unity, which means that one of the equations can be derived from the others. Under these conditions, one of the equations is dropped from each of (3.18) and (3.19) before the system is estimated, leaving $(N + M - 2)$ equations. With annual observations over T years, this means that there are $(N + M - 2)T$ observations used to estimate the coefficients γ_{ij}, ϕ_{ik}, and δ_{kl}.[10] The great advantage of estimating this system of share equations, rather than just the GDP function in (3.15), is that there are more observations and degrees of freedom. Even with just a modest number of annual observations, such as 20, the researcher can expect to obtain reasonably precise estimates of the coefficients.

The coefficients ϕ_{ik} in (3.18) measure the response of each output share to changes in the endowments, and are referred to as *output elasticities*. These are similar to the Rybczynski effects, which are normally defined as the impact of a change in endowments on the *level* of output rather than its *share*. To make this conversion, write the quantity of each output as ln $y_i = \ln(s_i G / p_i)$. Differentiating this with respect to an endowment ln V_k using (3.15) and (3.18), we obtain the Rybczynski elasticity:

$$\frac{\partial \ln y_i}{\partial \ln V_k} = \frac{\phi_{ik}}{s_i} + s_k. \quad (3.20)$$

[10] The hypotheses of symmetry and homogeneity, in (3.16) and (3.17), can be tested by first estimating the translog system without these restrictions and comparing the system estimated with the restrictions.

Thus, the coefficients ϕ_{ik} together with the input and output shares can be used to calculate the Rybczynski elasticity.

Similarly, write the price of each factor as $\ln w_k = \ln(s_k G/V_k)$. Differentiating this with respect to $\ln p_i$ using (3.15) and (3.19), it follows that the Stolper-Samuelson elasticities are

$$\frac{\partial \ln w_k}{\partial \ln p_i} = \frac{\phi_{ik}}{s_k} + s_i. \tag{3.21}$$

In addition, we can differentiate $\ln w_k = \ln(s_k G/V_k)$ with respect to the factor endowments to obtain

$$\frac{\partial \ln w_k}{\partial \ln V_\ell} = \begin{cases} \dfrac{\delta_{kk}}{s_k} + s_k - 1, & \text{if } k = \ell, \\[2ex] \dfrac{\delta_{k\ell}}{s_k} + s_\ell, & \text{if } k \neq \ell. \end{cases} \tag{3.22}$$

These elasticities allow us to test the hypothesis of "factor price insensitivity," meaning that the GDP function takes the special form in (3.7). While this functional form cannot be imposed globally for the translog GDP function, it can be evaluated locally by testing whether (3.22) is zero. This means that we test $\delta_{kk} = s_k(1 - s_k)$ and $\delta_{kl} = - s_k s_l$, which can be performed at one year (e.g., the midpoint) of the sample. In summary, given the estimated coefficients from the translog share equations, we can readily compute the Rybczynski and Stolper-Samuelson elasticities and also test for "factor price insensitivity."

Turning to empirical applications, Kohli (1978) estimates a translog GDP function for Canada, while Kohli (1990a) estimates it for U.S. data. Focusing on the U.S. application, Kohli uses the five major GDP components as goods: consumption (C), investment (I), government services (G), exports (X), and imports (M). Notice that he treats exports and imports as an output and input, respectively, in the production process. This is quite different from our treatment in the previous chapter, where net exports were the difference between consumption and production: now we are defining exports and imports independently from consumption. This makes sense if exports are differentiated from domestic goods and if imports are mainly intermediate inputs. Both of these are plausible hypotheses, and we will explore the role of imports as intermediate inputs more in the next chapter.

For primary inputs Kohli (1990a) identifies labor and capital, so he obtains five output share equations (3.18) (where imports have a negative share) and two factor share equations (3.19). Dropping one equation from each system, we then have five equations in total, and with data over

40 years (1948–87) this gives 200 observations to estimate a total of 25 parameters of the translog system.[11] In his results, Kohli finds that the Rybczynski elasticities (3.20) are *positive* for the impact of labor on the supply of exports, investment goods, and the demand for imports, and also for the impact of the capital stock on the production of consumption goods. In other words, exports and investment goods appear to be *labor* intensive, while consumption goods appear to be *capital* intensive, as measured by these Rybczynski elasticities. The signs of the Stolper-Samuelson elasticities in (3.21) are the same, of course, so that an increase in the import price hurts labor, while an increase in the export price benefits labor.

This sign pattern of elasticities found by Kohli is somewhat puzzling, since we normally think of investment goods as capital intensive in their production, and the same is true for U.S. exports, whereas consumption goods (including many nontraded services) would seem to be labor intensive. Kohli (1990a) finds the opposite of these expected results, confirmed in Kohli 1993a using a different functional form. Perhaps the difficulty is that the macroeconomic variables C, I, and G are not the best way to form output aggregates, despite the fact that these categories are readily available from the national accounts. Indeed, the finding that U.S. exports appear to be labor intensive already appeared in the early results of Leontief (1953), discussed in chapter 2, and one explanation for this "paradox" (besides the critique of Leamer 1980) was that goods or factors should be disaggregated further.

An alternative aggregation scheme is used by Burgess (1974a, 1974b, 1976), who estimates an aggregate cost rather than GDP function for the United States. He also includes imports as an input into the cost function, along with labor and capital, and for outputs uses traded goods (durables and nondurables) and nontraded goods (nongovernment services and structures). Burgess notes that the relative price movements within each of these aggregates are similar, which is one justification for the formation of an aggregate. Using data for the United States over 32 years (1948–69), Burgess finds that traded goods are *capital* intensive, whereas nontraded goods are *labor* intensive. This matches our prior beliefs about U.S. exports versus nontraded services. In addition, he finds that nontraded goods have a lower cost-share of imports than do traded goods. This

---

[11] In addition to five constant terms α_i and β_k in the share equations (3.18) and (3.19) (after dropping one from each system), Kohli (1990a) includes five time trends reflecting technological change. In addition, the five-by-five matrix $[\gamma_{ij}]$ has 10 free parameters after taking into account symmetry $\gamma_{ij} = \gamma_{ji}$ and the homogeneity restrictions (3.16); the two-by-two matrix $[\delta_{k\ell}]$ has one free parameter after taking into account symmetry and the homogeneity restrictions (3.17); and the five-by-two matrix $[\phi_{ik}]$ has four free parameters after taking into account (3.16) and (3.17).

means that an increase in the price of imports has a greater impact on traded goods and, because this sector is capital intensive, leads to a fall in the return to capital and a rise in the relative wage.[12] In this sense, tariffs benefit labor in the United States (which is the opposite of the result found by Kohli).

Burgess (1976) also tests the hypothesis that the aggregate cost function $C(Y, w)$ can be written in the linear form

$$C(Y, w) = \sum_{i=1}^{N} y_i c_i(w), \tag{3.23}$$

where the functions $c_i(w)$ are interpreted as *unit-cost* functions within the industries $i = 1, \ldots, N$. When (3.23) *does not* hold, it means that we cannot identify distinct industries producing each of the outputs; rather, these outputs are produced *jointly* from the economy's factor endowments. So (3.23) is referred to as a test of "nonjoint production." We have not yet emphasized that nearly all of our results on the Stolper-Samuelson and Rybczynski theorems so far in this book rely on *nonjoint* production. In contrast, if outputs are produced jointly from one or more inputs, there is no presumption that "magnification effects" of the type we have discussed hold. Notice the similarity between the linear form for the aggregate cost function in (3.23) and the linear form for the GDP function in (3.7). We argued that (3.7) is a test of "factor price insensitivity," whereas (3.23) is a test of nonjoint production, but sometimes these concepts are used nearly interchangeably.[13]

Burgess (1976) finds that (3.23) is rejected at exactly the 1% level of significance. Thus, there is some evidence for the United States that the production of traded and nontraded goods occurs under *joint* production. Likewise, Kohli (1981) also rejects the hypothesis of a nonjoint aggregate cost function using U.S. data. Considering the hypothesis of 'factor price insensitivity,' which means that the GDP function can be written in the linear form (3.7), this can be evaluated from the elasticities (3.22) reported by Kohli (1990a, 1993a). He finds that factor returns do depend on endowments—with higher endowments leading to lower returns on that factor—but only weakly so (standard errors are not reported).

Notice that these tests of (3.7) and (3.23) are actually combining two distinct hypotheses: perfect mobility of capital between sectors and nonjointness in production. So when we reject (3.7) and (3.23), we are not sure which of these hypotheses is really responsible. Kohli (1993b) addresses this by developing a model where capital is *sector specific*, though the researcher does not observe the amount of capital in each sector. Only

---

[12] This result is developed in problem 3.3.

[13] For example, Kohli (1983; 1991, 44) refers to (3.23) as "nonjointness in input quantities" and (3.7) as "nonjointness in output quantities."

observing the *aggregate* capital stock, one way to proceed is to assume that the capital devoted to each sector is always in *fixed proportion* to the aggregate stock. In that case, the GDP function is written as a function of aggregate labor (mobile between the two sectors) and aggregate capital (in fixed proportion in each sector).

Using this sector-specific structure, Kohli (1993b) develops a test for nonjointness in production that he refers to as "almost nonjointness." This test can be applied to either the GDP or cost function, and is weaker than the tests in (3.7) and (3.23) because the return to capital in each sector need not be the same. He implements this test on a two-by-two aggregation structure of the U.S. economy, where labor and capital produce consumption and investment goods. In the results, he finds that "almost nonjointness" is rejected for the aggregate cost function but is *not rejected* for the GDP function. Even on the cost side, the parameter estimates of the cost function do not differ that much when "almost nonjointness" is imposed. So Kohli concludes that a *sector-specific structure* of the U.S. economy is broadly consistent with the annual data, and is much preferable to perfect mobility of capital combined with nonjointness as in (3.7) and (3.23). The implied Stolper-Samuelson and Rybczynski elasticities for the sector-specific structure are as we discussed in the previous section.

A final application of the translog GDP function that we shall discuss is due to Harrigan (1997). Building on the prior work of Leamer (1984) and Harrigan (1995), he is interested in estimating Rybczynski elasticities on cross-country and time-series data. A limitation of early work was the assumption that technologies were the same across countries. Harrigan (1997) argues that this can be generalized by instead assuming that the GDP function is the same across countries while *allowing* for Hicks-neutral differences in the industry production functions. Thus, if industry production functions are denoted by $y_i = A_i f_i(v_i)$, where the coefficients A_i can differ across countries, then the GDP function becomes

$$G(A_1 p_1, \ldots, A_N p_N, V) \equiv \max_{v_i \geq 0} \sum_{i=1}^{N} p_i A_i f_i(v_i) \text{ subject to}$$

$$\sum_{i=1}^{N} v_i \leq V. \tag{3.24}$$

Notice that we have multiplied the prices p_i appearing in the GDP function by the Hicks-neutral productivity parameters A_i, because that is how they appear on the right side of (3.24). If we adopt a translog form for the GDP function, then the output share equations in (3.18) would be written as

$$s_i = \alpha_i + \sum_{j=1}^{N} \gamma_{ij} \ln(A_j p_j) + \sum_{k=1}^{M} \phi_{ik} \ln V_k, \quad i = 1, \ldots, N. \tag{3.25}$$

That is, the output shares of each industry depend on their prices *and* productivities (with the same coefficient applying to each), as well as the factor endowments.

We will be discussing the measurement of industry productivity further in chapters 4 and 10, as well as properties of the GDP function in (3.24). For present purposes, we note that Harrigan (1997) assumes that countries are engaged in free trade, so that industry prices are the same and no longer appear in (3.25):[14] it follows that the determinants of the output shares are productivities and endowments. It is the inclusion of the productivity variables in (3.25) that distinguishes this approach from Leamer (1984) and Harrigan (1995), and this is an important generalization from earlier research.[15]

Harrigan estimates (3.25) over a panel dataset consisting of 10 OECD countries over about 20 years (from 1970 to 1988–90). He distinguishes seven major manufacturing sectors (food, apparel, papers, chemicals, glass, metals, and machinery), which consist of aggregates from the International Standard Industrial Classification (ISIC). For endowments he uses six factors: two types of capital (producer durables and nonresidential construction), three types of labor (high-educated with some postsecondary schooling, medium-educated with some high school, and low-educated without high school), and arable land. Because he only has data on factor quantities but not prices, he does not estimate the corresponding system of factor share equations. The output shares are measured relative to GDP, so these sum to less than unity over the seven manufacturing sectors, and there is no need to drop one of the equations. He therefore has seven equations with about 200 observations for each, or some 1,400 observations to estimate a total of 77 parameters.[16]

The calculation of the Rybczynski elasticities in (3.20) requires both the output shares and the factor shares. Since the latter are not available, we simply report the estimated coefficients ϕ_{ik} from the share equations (3.25), in Table 3.1. These "Rybczynski effects" have signs that match our expectations. Thus, producer durable investment has a positive impact on the share of each of the seven manufacturing sectors, but nonresidential construction has a negative coefficient in most cases. This is consistent with nontraded services being intensive in nonresidential construction

---

[14] The prices can be normalized at unity in the first year, and then Harrigan assumes that their values in ensuing years can be captured by a simple time trend in each share equation.

[15] The model proposed by Harrigan (1997) has also been used in recent work by Redding (2002), which is recommended for further reading.

[16] Along with seven constant terms α_i in the share equations (3.18), Harrigan also includes seven time trends. In addition, the seven-by-seven matrix $[\gamma_{ij}]$ has 28 free parameters after taking into account symmetry $\gamma_{ij} = \gamma_{ji}$, and the seven-by-six matrix $[\phi_{ik}]$ has 35 free parameters after taking into account (3.16).

TABLE 3.1
Estimates of Rybczynski Effects from Harrigan (1997)

	Producer Durables	Non-residential Construction	High-Education Workers	Medium-Education Workers	Low-Education Workers	Arable Land
Food	1.31	−0.20	−0.17	0.68	−0.02	−1.60
	(0.19)	(0.29)	(0.13)	(0.20)	(0.14)	(0.30)
Apparel	0.94	−0.35	−0.66	0.69	0.10	−0.71
	(0.14)	(0.20)	(0.09)	(0.14)	(0.10)	(0.23)
Paper	−0.02	0.16	−0.22	−0.04	−0.15	−0.26
	(0.11)	(0.17)	(0.07)	(0.11)	(0.08)	(0.70)
Chemicals	1.19	−1.53	−0.002	−0.89	−0.40	1.63
	(0.21)	(0.29)	(0.10)	(0.20)	(0.15)	(0.32)
Glass	0.36	−0.24	−0.19	0.38	−0.10	−0.20
	(0.09)	(0.14)	(0.06)	(0.09)	(0.07)	(0.15)
Metals	0.19	−0.07	−0.50	−0.21	−0.22	0.81
	(0.20)	(0.28)	(0.13)	(0.19)	(0.14)	(0.31)
Machinery	0.91	−1.75	−2.11	1.01	1.82	0.12
	(0.48)	(0.72)	(0.32)	(0.48)	(0.35)	(0.88)

Source: Harrigan 1997, 488.
Note: Standard errors are in parentheses.

and drawing resources away from manufacturing. Only two of the sectors have a positive and significant Rybczynski effect with arable land, and these are chemicals and metals, which depend on natural resources. With the exception of these two, most other sectors have a positive Rybczynski effect with either medium-educated or low-educated labor, but a negative effect with highly educated labor, which is consistent with highly educated workers being used intensively in nontraded services. These results are broadly consistent with, and build upon, the findings of Leamer (1984) and Harrigan (1995).

More Goods Than Factors

We now consider a model with more goods than factors, and for convenience, suppose that there are three goods and two factors (labor and capital). We assume that there is perfect factor mobility between the industries. The zero-profit conditions (3.1) then become three equations in two

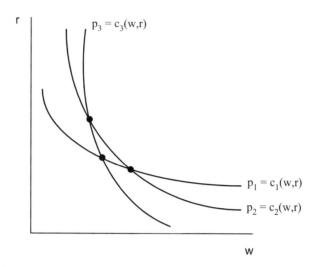

Figure 3.6

unknowns, so we cannot find a solution except at special values of the
prices (p_1, p_2, p_3). This situation is illustrated in Figure 3.6. If we consider
one of these special prices (p_1, p_2, p_3) at which all three goods are produced, then the full-employment conditions (3.2) give two equations in
three unknowns, so these are underdetermined: there are *many solutions*
for (y_1, y_2, y_3). What is the explanation for these unusual results?

Using the result that there are multiple solutions for (y_1, y_2, y_3), we can
graph these as a *line* of outputs on the PPF in Figure 3.7. Therefore, the PPF
has "ruled segments" on it, as illustrated. Any price vector $p = (p_1, p_2, p_3)$
that allows for zero profits in all three industries will correspond to a *line of
outputs* along the PPF. At the same time, a slight movement in prices away
from this point will very likely lead to a *corner solution*, where only two of the
goods are produced. Thus, for most price vectors there will be specialization
in a subset of goods, equal to the number of factors. Conversely, if the price
vector just happens to allow for zero profits in all goods, then there will be
multiple solutions for the outputs.[17]

With these initial observations, what can we say about factor price equalization? At first glance, the problem seems intractable: the set of goods
produced in a country will be extremely sensitive to the product prices. But
let us recall that the prices being considered must be the *equilibrium prices*
with free trade. Let us make the strong assumption that the countries have
identical technologies. Since all goods must be produced in equilibrium, it
follows that for a wide range of factor endowments the equilibrium prices

---

[17] This means that the GDP function is not differentiable in the product prices.

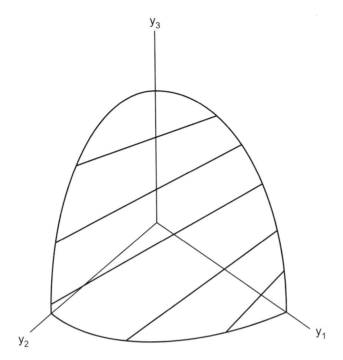

Figure 3.7

will indeed be one of the special vectors (p_1, p_2, p_3) that is consistent with all goods being produced in each country. In other words, it will not be unusual to find that the plane with normal vector (p_1, p_2, p_3) is tangent to one of the ruled segments on the PPF for each country, with indeterminate outputs in each country, but adding up to world demand in total.

To demonstrate these claims, we will construct the factor price equalization (FPE) set for two countries, similar to that constructed in chapter 1 but now using multiple goods. Recall from chapter 1 that we construct the FPE set by first considering an "integrated world equilibrium" where labor and capital are *free to move* between countries, ensuring that their factor prices are equalized. In this equilibrium we establish product prices that are consistent with all goods being produced. These can be used to construct factor prices (the same in both countries) and the factor intensities a_{ij}. Then the question is whether we can reproduce the same equilibrium but having fixed endowments in each country, without factor mobility. The range of endowment over which we can obtain the same equilibrium is the FPE set.

To determine this range, let us rank the goods in terms of decreasing labor/capital ratio, so that $a_{1L}/a_{1K} \geq a_{2L}/a_{2K} \geq \cdots \geq a_{NL}/a_{NK}$. Then using the world demands D_1^w for each good in the integrated equilibrium, compute the labor and capital demands in each industry, $(a_{iL}, a_{iK})D_1^w$. Summing these, we must obtain the world endowments of labor and capital,

$$\sum_{i=1}^{N}(a_{iL}, a_{iK})D_1^w = (L^w, K^w). \qquad (3.26)$$

This full-employment condition is illustrated in Figure 3.8, where the axes measure the world endowments of labor and capital. Starting at the origin 0 for the home country, we sum the usage of labor and capital in each industry as in (3.26), obtaining the consecutive points shown in Figure 3.8 that reach the opposite origin 0*. Conversely, starting at the foreign origin 0*, we can sum the usage of labor and capital in each industry to arrive at the home origin 0.

Now consider any point B inside this region in Figure 3.8. We leave it to the reader to confirm that there is a positive linear combination of the vectors (a_{iL}, a_{iK}) that sum to point B from either origin. Indeed, there are most likely *many positive combinations* of the vectors (a_{iL}, a_{iK}) that sum to point B, which illustrates the indeterminacy of production in each country. But this indeterminacy does not really matter, because the world equilibrium is maintained at the same product and factor prices as in our initial hypothetical equilibrium. Thus, all points inside the region labeled the FPE set in Figure 3.8 lead to factor price equalization, with equilibrium product prices that are consistent with zero profits for all goods in both countries.[18]

An empirical test for the indeterminacy of production is proposed by Bernstein and Weinstein (2002). They note that the full-employment condition (3.2′) holds regardless of the number of goods and factors, where the $M \times N$ matrix A is the same across countries. If $N = M$ and A is nonsingular, then we could invert (3.2′) to obtain the regression (3.10), which is estimated by Harrigan (1995). Denoting the coefficients of that regression by the matrix $A^{-1} = B = [\beta_{jk}]$, it follows that

$$AB = I_M, \qquad (3.27)$$

where I_M is an identity matrix of dimension M. Thus, a test for the indeterminacy of production proceeds by estimating the regression (3.10) as in Harrigan, and using the coefficients to test the linear restriction in (3.27). If these fail, we conclude that production is indeterminate.

Bernstein and Weinstein use data across 47 Japanese prefectures around 1985, with 29 sectors and three factors (college-educated workers, other

---

[18] This construction of the FPE set is due to Dixit and Norman (1980, 114–21), and we will have an opportunity to use it again in chapter 11, in our discussion of multinationals.

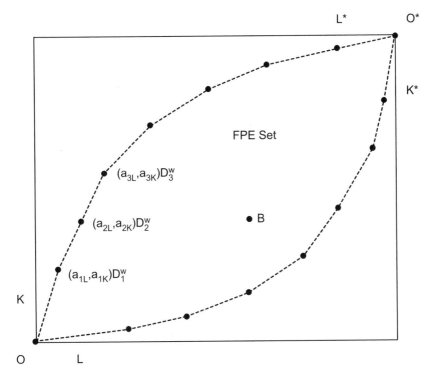

Figure 3.8

workers, and capital). They first check whether the full-employment condition $AY^i = V^i$ holds for *each* prefecture $i = 1, \ldots, 47$. In this test, the matrix A is held fixed at its national value for Japan. This means that the national full-employment condition $A\sum_{i=1}^{47} Y^i = \sum_{i=1}^{47} V^i$ holds by construction, and the first test is to see whether this condition also holds for each prefecture. This first test is passed easily. However, Bernstein and Weinstein strongly reject the second test, which consists of estimating regression (3.10) using the cross-prefecture data and testing restriction (3.27). The implication is that the location of production across the prefectures in Japan is not simply explained by the endowments in each region: some other features must be at work.[19]

---

[19] Other features are suggested by Davis and Weinstein (2002b), which is recommend for further reading. Bernstein and Weinstein (2002) go on to compare their results for Japan to those obtained with international data. They find that even the full-employment condition $AY^i = V^i$ fails when using the Japanese national data for A, but this is not the case for (3.27) when using other countries data for Y^i and V^i. This is the familiar finding that production techniques differ across countries.

Is there any way to resolve production indeterminacy when there are more goods than factors? Bhagwati (1972), responding to Jones (1956–57), suggested that a determinate production structure would occur when factor prices were unequal across countries: in that case, *every commodity* exported by a country with high labor/capital endowment would need to have a higher labor/capital ratio than the exports of the other country. A proof of this so-called "chain proposition" was provided by Deardorff (1979). Bhagwati also suggested that the existence of transportation costs would be enough to make factor prices unequal, and therefore resolve the production indeterminacy. Deardorff argued that this is true when there is trade only in final goods (and no subsidies to trade), but it breaks down when there is also trade in intermediate inputs. Setting aside this concern, are there any other cases where production indeterminacy can be resolved? Instead of relying on transportation costs to generate factor price differences, it would seem that we could instead rely on *endowment differences* between the countries, large enough to move them *outside* of the factor price equalization set. This turns out to be a fruitful line of inquiry, and to model it most elegantly, it will be useful to introduce a continuum of products into the Heckscher-Ohlin model. This is done by Dornbusch, Fischer, and Samuelson 1980, which we discuss next.

Continuum of Goods

Let $z \in [0, 1]$ denote the range of goods, and let $y(z)$ denote the *quantity* produced of each of these goods:

$$y(z) = f[L(z), K(z), Z], \qquad (3.28)$$

where these production functions are increasing, concave, and linearly homogeneous in $[L(z), K(z)]$. It will be convenient to work with the dual unit-cost functions, which are

$$c(w, r, z) \equiv \min_{L(z), K(z) \geq 0} \{wL(z) + rK(z) \mid f[L(z), K(z), z] \geq 1\}. \qquad (3.29)$$

We let $a_L(w, r, z) \equiv \partial c(w, r, z)/\partial w$ and $a_K(w, r, z) \equiv \partial c(w, r, z)/\partial r$ denote the amount of labor and capital, respectively, needed to produce one unit of $y(z)$. These will depend on the factor prices, but we assume that there are no factor intensity reversals, which means that we can order the activities z such that $a_K(w, r, z)/a_L(w, r, z)$ is nondecreasing in z. That is, we rank the activities by *increasing order of capital intensity*.

Consider first the home country under autarky. Demand is assumed to come from a Cobb-Douglas utility function:

$$\ln U = \int_0^1 \alpha(z) \ln y(z) dz, \quad \text{with} \quad \int_0^1 \alpha(z) dz = 1. \qquad (3.30)$$

Thus, a constant share of income $\alpha(z)$ is spent on each final good $y(z)$. Under autarky, then, the expenditure on each final good at home would be $\alpha(z)(wL + rK)$, where L and K are the factor endowments, with equilibrium prices w and r. Dividing this by the prices $p(z) = c(w, r, z)$, we obtain demand for each output, which must equal supply under autarky:

$$y(z) = \alpha(z)(wL + rK)/c(w, r, z). \qquad (3.31)$$

To complete the equilibrium conditions, we use the equality of factor demand and factor supply, which is written in relative terms as

$$\frac{L}{K} = \frac{\int_0^1 a_L(w, r, z)y(z)dz}{\int_0^1 a_K(w, r, z)y(z)dz}. \qquad (3.32)$$

The numerator on the right of (3.32) is the total demand for labor, and the denominator is the total demand for capital, which must equal their relative endowments. Substituting (3.31) into (3.32), we obtain one equation to determine the factor price ratio (w/r) in autarky.[20]

Let us now introduce the foreign country, denoted with an asterisk, and having the identical technology and tastes as at home. The key issue for trade is to determine *which goods* are produced in each country. Under factor price equalization this will be impossible to determine. In that case, the equilibrium prices are still $p(z) = c(w, r, z)$ and condition (3.31) is modified as

$$y(z) + y^*(z) = \alpha(z)[(wL + rK) + (wL^* + rK^*)]/c(w, r, z), \qquad (3.31')$$

where $y(z)$ is the home outputs and $y^*(z)$ is foreign output. The only condition that ties down these outputs is (3.32) in each country: the relative demand for labor must equal its relative endowments. But there are many combinations of outputs $y(z)$ and $y^*(z)$ that will simultaneously satisfy (3.31') and condition (3.32) in each country. Neither outputs nor the set of goods produced in each country is uniquely determined, just as we found in the previous section under factor price equalization.

If factor endowments are sufficiently different, however, factor price (w^*, r^*) will differ from (w, r). Notice that the FPE set can be constructed just as we did in the previous section, and it is illustrated in Figure 3.9. Instead of the piece-wise linear segments obtained from the full-employment condition (3.26), we instead have smooth curves in Figure 3.9 obtained by

---

[20] Notice that demand on the right of (3.31) depends only on the factor price ratio, since $c(w, r, z)$ is homogeneous of degree one in (w, r). Similarly, $a_L(w, r, z) \equiv c_w(w, r, z)$ and $a_K(w, r, z) \equiv c_r(w, r, z)$ in (3.32) depend on the factor price ratio, since these factor demands are homogeneous of degree zero in (w, r).

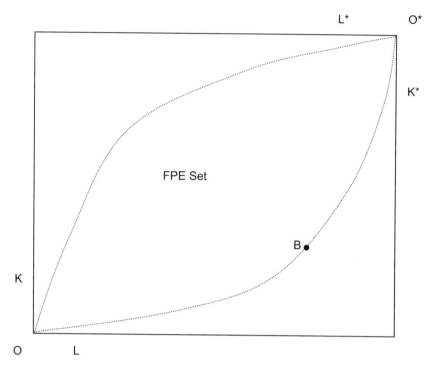

Figure 3.9

integrating over the factor demands $[a_L(w, r, z), a_K(w, r, z)]D^w(z)$, where world demand $D^w(z)$ in the integrated equilibrium equals (3.31'). A point like B right on the boundary of the FPE set would allow for factor price equalization, but for endowments just slightly to the right of point B we would be outside the set, and factor prices would differ.

Outside the FPE set the indeterminacy of outputs no longer applies. To see this, note that the equilibrium prices will be determined by

$$p(z) = \min \{c(w, r, z), c(w^\star, r^\star, z)\}, \qquad (3.33)$$

since goods will only be produced in the country where unit-costs are lowest. In general, each country will produce and export those goods with lower unit-costs than abroad. Thus, to determine the trade patterns, we need to compare unit-cost across countries.

To fix ideas, we will suppose that the home country is relatively abundant in labor, and has a lower wage/rental ratio than that abroad, $(w/r) < (w^\star/r^\star)$. With this assumption, we can graphically illustrate the problem of choosing the minimum cost location for each good. Let us begin by graphing the locus of unit-costs for the foreign country, given fixed

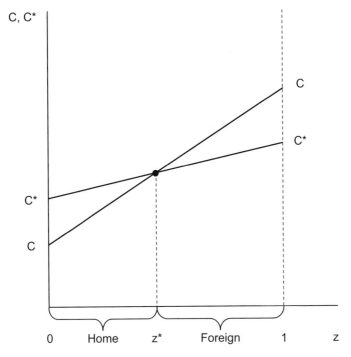

Figure 3.10

factor prices. The unit-costs $c(w^*, r^*, z)$ as a function of z can have any shape whatsoever, and need not even be a continuous function. For convenience, however, we will assume that this function is continuous, and illustrate it as the upward-sloping curve C*C* in Figure 3.10. Then the question is: how does the locus of unit-costs $c(w, r, z)$ at home, denoted by CC, compare to that abroad?

If the unit-costs of all activities were *lower* at home, for example, then all goods would be produced there, and vice-versa if all unit-costs were lower abroad. This would violate the full-employment condition in one country, so it follows that the curves C*C* and CC intersect *at least once*, and we denote this good by z^*, with $c(w, r, z^*) = c(w^*, r^*, z^*)$. Then consider an activity $z' > z^*$ with slightly higher capital/labor demand. Because of our assumption that $(w/r) < (w^*/r^*)$, the higher capital/labor requirements should have a greater impact on *home* costs than on *foreign* costs. We therefore expect that $c(w, r, z') > c(w^*, r^*, z')$, for $z' > z^*$. Similarly, we expect that the converse is also true, $c(w, r, z') < c(w^*, r^*, z')$, for $z' < z^*$. Thus, the loci C*C* and CC can intersect *at most once*, as shown in Figure 3.10.[21]

---

[21] This is confirmed by Feenstra and Hanson (1996), in a model where the production functions (3.28) have a special functional form. This model is discussed in the next chapter.

Given this unique intersection, we see that home unit-costs are less than those abroad for all $z' < z^*$, so that the home country will specialize in the products $[0, z^*)$, whereas the foreign country will specialize in $(z^*, 1]$. Thus, the outputs in each country are determined by

$$y(z) = \alpha(z)[(wL + rK) + (w^* L^* + r^* K^*)]/c(w, r, z),$$
$$\text{for } z \in [0, z^*) \qquad (3.34a)$$

and,

$$y^*(z) = \alpha(z)[(wL + rK) + (w^* L^* + r^* K^*)]/c(w^*, r^*, \quad (3.34b)$$
$$\text{for } z \in (z^*, 1],$$

Using this information, we can then calculate the demand for labor in each country. At home, for example, the relative demand for labor/capital is

$$\frac{L}{K} = \frac{\int_0^{z^*} a_L(w, r, z)y(z)dz}{\int_0^{z^*} a_K(w, r, z)y(z)dz}, \qquad (3.35a)$$

and in the foreign country, the relative demand is

$$\frac{L^*}{K^*} = \frac{\int_{z^*}^1 a_L(w^*, r^*, z)y^*(z)dz}{\int_{z^*}^1 a_K(w^*, r^*, z)y^*(z)dz}. \qquad (3.35b)$$

The equality of relative labor demand and supply for the home country is illustrated in Figure 3.11, where we show the relative labor demand on the right side of (3.35a) as $D(z^*)$, depending on the relative wage and z^*. This must equal the relative endowment L/K.

The two-country equilibrium is determined by conditions (3.34) and (3.35), combined with $c(w, r, z^*) = c(w^*, r^*, z^*)$, and also trade balance between the countries:

$$\int_{z^*}^1 \alpha(z)(wL + rK)dz = \int_0^{z^*} \alpha(z)(w^* L^* + r^* K^*)dz. \qquad (3.36)$$

The left side of (3.36) is the value of home imports of the goods $(z^*, 1]$, while the right side is home exports of those products $[0, z^*)$. Substituting (3.34) into (3.35), we have four equations (i.e., (3.35a), (3.35b), $c(w, r, z^*) = c(w^*, r^*, z^*)$, and (3.36)) to determine z^* and the four factor prices (w, r), and (w^*, r^*), where one factor price can be normalized at unity.

Summing up, we have shown that when factor prices are *not* equalized across the countries, each country is specialized in a different range of final goods. Not only have we resolved the indeterminacy of outputs, we

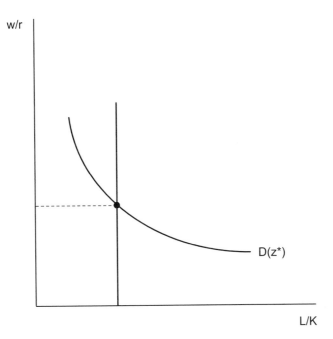

Figure 3.11

have gone much further: there is an extremely strong connection between the labor/capital ratios in production and the labor/capital endowments, with *all the goods* $[0, z^*)$ produced by the labor-abundant country having a higher labor/capital ratio in production than *all the goods* $(z^*, 1]$ produced by the capital-abundant country. This holds even for slight differences in the factor prices across countries, that is, for factor endowments just slightly to the right of point B in Figure 3.9.

Estimating the HOV Model Once Again

We return now to the estimation of the Heckscher-Ohlin-Vanek (HOV) model, and the recent results of Davis and Weinstein (2001). Recall that the key issue in estimating the HOV model is to allow for some technological differences across countries, while avoiding the introduction of so many free parameters that the HOV equation holds as an equality (as in Trefler 1993a, 1998). In other words, we want to model the technological differences in a parsimonious manner.

Our discussion of the Dornbusch, Fischer, and Samuelson (1980) model immediately suggests a simple empirical technique. If factor prices are not equal, then the capital/labor ratios of traded goods must be systematically related to each country's endowments: a country with a capital/labor endowment higher than its neighbor's must have higher capital/labor intensities in *all of its* traded goods. Let us model this relation by

$$\ln a^i_{jk} = \alpha^i + \beta_{jk} + \gamma_k \left(\frac{K^i}{L^i} \right) + \varepsilon^i_{jk}, \tag{3.37}$$

where $i = 1, \ldots, C$ denotes countries, $j = 1, \ldots, N$ denotes traded goods, $k = 1, \ldots, M$ denotes factors, (K^i/L^i) is the relative capital/labor endowment, and ε^i_{jk} is a random error.

Davis and Weinstein use a sample of 20 OECD countries (plus the rest of the world), 34 sectors, and two factors (labor and capital) around 1985. The regression in (3.37) is run over countries, goods, and factors, where the estimated right-hand side is a measure of "predicted" factor requirements. We can think of the parameters β_{jk} as providing *average* estimates of the factor requirements across countries. The predicted factor requirements in *each* country differ from this average depending on the parameters α^i, which measure uniform technology difference across countries, as in chapter 2,[22] and depending on $\gamma_k(K^i/L^i)$, which measures the impact of factor endowments. Thus, this simple regression permits a parsimonious description of technology differences across countries.

As noted by Harrigan (2003), there is considerable prior evidence that a specification like (3.37) will fit the data quite well: Dollar, Wolff, and Baumol (1988, table 2.3), for example, find that capital per worker in individual industries is highly correlated with capital per worker in overall manufacturing. Davis and Weinstein (2001) likewise find that the simple linear relationship (3.37) fits well, and that the parameters γ_k linking factor requirements to country endowments are highly significant. Using several variants of this regression, they construct the estimated technology matrix $\hat{A}^i$ for each country using the predictions from (3.37). This estimated matrix is then used to construct the factor content of trade and to evaluate how well the constructed factor contents match the relative endowments of countries. In other words, we can proceed much as in the earlier testing of the HOV model, but now using technology matrices $\hat{A}^i$, which differ across countries.

As discussed near the end of the last chapter, when the technology matrices differ across countries, we should use the technology of the *exporting* country to construct the factor content of trade. Davis and Weinstein

---

[22] In chapter 2 we used the parameter δ^i, which was unity for the most efficient country (the United States) and less than unity otherwise. This can be related to α^i by $\delta^i = \exp(-\alpha^i)$, where now δ^i will be unity for the *average* country.

follow this approach, so the factor content of exports from country i to country j is

$$\hat{F}^{ij} \equiv \hat{A}^i X^{ij}, \tag{3.38}$$

where X^{ij} is the vector of gross exports of goods from country i to j. Davis and Weinstein sometimes use an additional assumption, whereby these exports are themselves estimated *in proportion to the purchasing country's GDP*. In that case, the factor content of export is

$$\hat{F}^{ij} \equiv \hat{A}^i \hat{X}^{ij}. \tag{3.39}$$

In either case, the prediction of the HOV model is that the factor content of trade reflects a country's relative endowments, or that

$$V^i - s^i \left(\sum_j V^j \right) = \left(\sum_{j \neq i} \hat{F}^{ij} \right) - \left(\sum_{j \neq i} \hat{F}^{ji} \right). \tag{3.40}$$

In the sign test, for example, if we assume that all OECD countries use the same *average* technology matrix, then we include only the parameters β_{jk} in regression (3.37) and construct the predicted technology matrix $\hat{A}$, which is the same across countries. In that case, Davis and Weinstein initially find that the right and left sides of (3.40) have the same sign in only 46% of the cases.[23] This is no better than a coin toss, much as we found in chapter 2. If instead we allow for uniform productivity differences between countries, so the regression (3.37) is estimated with α^i in addition to β_{jk}, then we find that the sign test is satisfied in 50% of the cases. If we also include $\gamma_k(K^i/L^i)$ in regression (3.37), so that the estimated technologies differ systematically with countries' factor endowments, then the sign test is satisfied in fully 86% of the cases. Finally, if we model exports as proportional to the purchasing countries GDP, so factor contents are measured with (3.39) rather than (3.38), the sign test is satisfied in 92% of the cases!

Clearly, we are getting closer to a 100% match between relative endowments and constructed factor contents, on the left and right side of (3.40). The theorem of Trefler (1998) reviewed in the previous chapter tells us that this is no coincidence: if regression (3.37) fit perfectly, and assuming that every good is exported in proportion to the purchasing country's GDP, then (3.40) would automatically hold. What is remarkable is that even the simple specification in (3.37) is enough to greatly improve the fit of the HOV model. The contribution of Davis and Weinstein is to

---

[23] We average the results reported for labor and capital in Davis and Weinstein (2001, Table 4).

systematically show the importance of each modeling assumption to "closing the gap" between factor contents and endowments.

Conclusions

We have covered a lot of ground in this chapter. As we leave the "even" structure of the two-by-two or the $N \times N$ model, many of the results we found in chapter 1 are lost. With more factors than goods, the "factor price insensitivity" lemma no longer applies. This can be tested by estimating a GDP function for a country (or a group of countries), and determining whether it is linear in the factor endowments, that is, whether the functional form in (3.7) holds globally or the elasticities in (3.22) are locally insignificantly different from zero. The results of Kohli (1990a, 1993a) for the United States indicate that the elasticities in (3.22) are nonzero, but only weakly so. This can be interpreted as evidence in favor of "more factors than goods." One reason for this is that capital might be slow to move between sectors, so with N sectors there are N fixed factors (capital in each sector) plus the additional mobile factors (types of labor). Kohli (1993b) develops a test for this production structure and finds some evidence to support it using annual data for the United States.

With more factors than goods, the GDP function is generally well behaved: it will be differentiable in prices and endowments provided that industries do not have the same factor intensities. With more goods than factors, however, the GDP function is poorly behaved: the fact that the production possibility frontier has "ruled segments," as illustrated in Figure 3.7, indicates that the GDP function is not differentiable in prices. A test for "more goods than factors" is developed by Bernstein and Weinstein (2002), and they find evidence to support it using data from prefectures in Japan. This may seem inconsistent with the results of Kohli (1993b) for the United States, but note that Kohli used time-series data, whereas Bernstein and Weinstein used cross-sectional data. We should not be surprised to find differing conclusions when comparing the time series of national data versus the cross-section of provincial data. In any case, the results of both Kohli and Bernstein and Weinstein support the idea that we are *not* in an "even" model, with equal numbers of goods and factors. This structure had been assumed by Leamer (1984) and Harrigan (1995), for example. The more general approach of Harrigan (1997), using a GDP function estimated across OECD countries, could also be used to test "factor price insensitivity" by evaluating the elasticities in (3.22), though this was not done due to data limitations.

We have also reviewed the Heckscher-Ohlin model with a continuum of goods, due to Dornbusch, Fischer, and Samuelson (1980). This was used to motivate the empirical work of Davis and Weinstein (2001). Using the idea that industry factor intensities should depend systematically on economy-wide factor endowments, Davis and Weinstein estimate technology matrices across the OECD countries and use these to test the HOV equation. We already know from the theorem of Trefler (1998), discussed at the end of the last chapter, that using *actual* technology matrices (and an assumption on exports) can lead to a perfect fit for this equation. What is surprising is that Davis and Weinstein are able to obtain a very close fit even with a parsimonious specification of the technology matrices across countries. In case the reader thinks that this is the last word on the HOV model, however, we note that there are still important issues left unresolved by Davis and Weinstein (2001).

First, their sample consists of the OECD countries, and in any evaluation of the Heckscher-Ohlin model we ideally want to introduce data on a wider range of countries. Xu (2002) has recently estimated a regression like (3.37) over a sample of 14 developing countries. By systematically examining the sign of the regression coefficient γ_k (which indicates the impact of the countries' capital/labor endowments on their industry capital/labor ratios), he is able to arrange countries into three distinct groups, ranked by their capital/labor abundance. His evidence supports the idea that these countries are in different cones of diversification.

Second, Trefler and Zhu (2000) have criticized Davis and Weinstein's approach for not adequately distinguishing between trade in final goods and trade in intermediate inputs. All of the theory we have developed for the HOV equation assumes trade in final goods, and yet a great deal of actual trade is in steel, chemicals, textiles, and other intermediate inputs. Indeed, component parts can cross borders multiple times before being incorporated into a finished good. This makes the construction of the factor content of trade very difficult: if Germany imports steel from Korea, and Korea relied on coal from Australia to produce the steel, and Australia used imported mining equipment from Germany, then whose factor requirements should we use to construct the factor content of steel trade? These types of flows tend to cancel out when we consider only *net* exports of each country, as in the original formulation of the HOV model. However, once the technology matrices differ across countries, then totaling up the *gross* exports, as on the right side of (3.40), can lead to considerably larger values for trade, much of which is due to intermediate inputs. It is hard to see, then, how achieving near equality of (3.40) amounts to a validation of the HOV model, when that model has so little to say about trade in intermediate inputs. Trefler (1998) and Davis and Weinstein (2003) concur that this is an important area for further research, and one that we begin to investigate in the next chapter.

Problems

3.1   In the sector-specific model, suppose that the home and foreign countries have identical labor endowments, and identical capital in sector 2, but the *home* country has more capital in sector 1. Technologies and tastes are the same across countries.

(a) Can we predict the trade pattern between the countries? What factor(s) at home benefits from the opening of trade, and which factor(s) loses?

(b) Repeat part (a), but now assume that the endowments of capital are identical across the countries, but the *home* country has more *labor*. Can we predict the trade pattern between the countries? Try to use assumptions on the factor cost shares to help determine this.

3.2   Consider the translog GDP function $\ln G(p, V)$ in (3.15).

(a) Show that $G(p, V)$ is homogeneous of degree one in prices when (3.16) and $\gamma_{ij} = \gamma_{ji}$ hold.

(b) Show that $G(p, V)$ is homogeneous of degree one in endowments when (3.17) and $\delta_{k\ell} = \delta_{\ell k}$ hold.

3.3   Suppose that there are two outputs—nontraded good 1 and traded good 2—and three inputs—labor, capital, and imported inputs. Assume that the cost share of labor is higher in good 1 and the cost share of capital is higher in good 2. The prices of both outputs are treated as fixed initially, but the price of the imported input increases.

(a) Write down the zero-profit conditions and totally differentiate these.

(b) Determine the impact of the increase in the imported input price on the wage and rental, assuming that the traded good has a higher cost share of imports.

(c) If the price of the nontraded good changes endogenously due to the increase in the price of imported inputs, how will this affect your conclusions in (b)?

Chapter 4

Trade in Intermediate Inputs and Wages

SINCE THE EARLY 1980s there has been a marked change in the pattern of wage payments in the United States: the wage of skilled workers relative to unskilled workers has experienced a sustained increase that continued through the 1990s. A similar pattern has been observed in other countries. This led to a great deal of research on the possible causes of the change in relative wages.[1] From the material we have already covered, we can identify three methods to determine whether the change in relative wages is due to international trade.

First, we could estimate a GDP or cost function for the U.S. economy, or for specific industries, and compute the Stolper-Samuelson effect of a change in traded goods prices. We will discuss this approach at several points throughout the chapter. Second, we could proceed as in the Heckscher-Ohlin-Vanek (HOV) model and compute the change in the factor content of trade and associated changes in factor prices. Theoretically, this second approach is justified by Deardorff and Staiger (1988), who show that

$$(w^2 - w^1)(F^2 - F^1) \geq 0, \qquad (4.1)$$

where w^t is equilibrium wages in a country in two years $t = 1, 2$, and F^t is the factor content of exports for that country. The equilibria $t = 1, 2$ are computed with changing international prices but fixed endowments within the country. Equation (4.1) is interpreted as saying that a *higher* content of imports for some factor k, $F_k^2 < F_k^1 < 0$ so $(F_k^2 - F_k^1) < 0$, will tend to be associated with a *falling* wage for that factor, $(w_k^2 - w_k^1) < 0$. The same would be true for the *direct* imports of a factor, as with immigration. Among the most careful assessments of these effects for the United States, Borjas, Freeman, and Katz (1997, 62) find that immigration into the United States during 1980–95 accounts for about

---

[1] See the surveys by Feenstra (1998), Freeman (1995), Johnson and Stafford (1999), Katz and Autor (1999), Richardson (1995), and Wood (1995), and the volumes by Bhagwati and Kosters (1994), Cheng and Kierzkowski (2001), Collins (1998), and Feenstra (2000). This chapter draws upon Feenstra and Hanson 2003.

one-quarter to one-half of the decline in the relative wages of high school dropouts. The increasing factor content of imports from less-developed countries also reduces the wages of high school dropouts, but by less than immigration. Both channels have only a small impact on the wages of more highly educated workers.

Note the similarity between (4.1), which refers to a comparison over time, and equation (2.19) (from Helpman 1984a), which refers to a comparison across countries. This suggests that all the observations we have made about testing the HOV model apply equally well to implementing formula (4.1): the results of a factor content approach when applied over time will depend on the assumptions about technology (which year or country's technology matrix is used); assumptions on tastes; and also whether or not there are traded intermediate inputs.[2] For these reasons, there is considerable controversy about the suitability of using a factor content approach to infer the effects of trade on wages.[3]

These concerns suggest a third approach: rather than relying on an HOV equation, let us directly model the presence of traded intermediate inputs, caused by firms splitting apart their production process across several countries. This is sometimes called *production sharing* by the companies involved, or simply *outsourcing*.[4] The idea that trade in intermediate inputs can have an effect on production and factor prices that is different from trade in final goods is gaining widespread acceptance among trade economists,[5] and no graduate trade course today is complete without a discussion of this topic (I think the same is true at the undergraduate level). Fortunately, the tools we have developed in the previous chapters can be readily extended to deal with trade in intermediate inputs.

After reviewing the initial evidence concerning the change in wages for the United States in the next section, we present a simple three-good, three-factor model that can be used to analyze the link between input prices and wages. Two of the goods are traded intermediate inputs, and

---

[2] Note that Staiger (1986) argues that traded intermediate inputs *should not* be included in the calculation of factor contents in the bilateral test of Helpman (1984a), so their treatment in applying the factor content approach over time is open to question.

[3] See Deardorff 2000; Krugman 2000; Leamer 2000; and Panagariya 2000.

[4] Alternatively referred to as outsourcing (Katz and Murphy 1992; Feenstra and Hanson 1996), delocalization (Leamer 1996), fragmentation (Jones 2000; Arndt and Kierzkowski 2001; Marjit and Acharyya 2003), intraproduct specialization (Arndt 1998a, 1998b), intramediate trade (Antweiler and Trefler 2002), vertical specialization (Hummels, Ishii, and Yi 2001), and slicing the value chain (Krugman 1995), this phenomenon refers to the geographic separation of activities involved in producing a good (or service) across two or more countries. The term *production sharing* was coined by management consultant Peter Drucker ("The Rise of Production Sharing," *Wall Street Journal*, March 15, 1977).

[5] In addition to the references in the previous footnote, see the Ohlin lectures of Jones (2000) and the recent article by Paul Samuelson (2001).

the third is a final product. It is readily shown that a fall in the price of imported intermediate inputs *decreases* the relative wage of the factor used intensively in those imports, which would be unskilled labor for the United States. Next, we generalize this model and present a version with a continuum of inputs, analogous to the Dornbusch, Fischer, and Samuelson (1980) model. With the United States being more abundant in skilled labor than abroad, the model predicts that a growth in capital or technology abroad will lead to increased outsourcing from the United States, and an *increase in the relative wage of skilled labor in both countries*. Following this we discuss various methods of estimating the model, and summarize evidence for the United States and other countries.

Changes in Wages and Employment

The basic facts concerning wage movements in the United States are well understood.[6] For full-time U.S. workers, between 1979 and 1995 the real wages of those with 12 years of education fell by 13.4% and the real wages of those with less than 12 years of education fell by 20.2%. During the same period, the real wages of workers with 16 or more years of education rose by 3.4%, so that the *wage gap* between less-skilled and more-skilled workers increased dramatically.[7] To illustrate these trends, we can use data from the U.S. manufacturing sector for "nonproduction" and "production" workers. The former are often used as a proxy for more-skilled workers, and the latter as a proxy for less-skilled workers. The breakdown is far from perfect, of course, but has been used because the data are readily available.[8] These trends are shown in Figure 4.1, which graphs the relative annual earnings of nonproduction/production workers in U.S. manufacturing, and Figure 4.2, which illustrates their relative annual employment.

In Figure 4.1, we see that earnings of nonproduction relative to production workers in the United States moved erratically during the 1960s and 1970s, but then increased substantially during the 1980s and 1990s. Turning to Figure 4.2, we see that there has been a steady increase in the

---

[6] For a detailed discussion, see Katz and Autor 1999, whose wage figures we report next.

[7] Only the highly skilled have had large real-wage gains. For the 1979–95 period, real wages for those with 18 or more years of education rose by 14.0% and for those with 16 to 17 years of education rose by only 1.0%.

[8] The breakdown of workers according to whether or not they are engaged in production activity is made in the U.S. *Annual Survey of Manufactures* and is used as a proxy for the occupational class or skill-level of workers. In practice, this classification shows similar trends as using education or other skill categories (Berman, Bound, and Griliches 1994; Sachs and Shatz 1994). The increase in the nonproduction/production relative wage is only a small part of the total increase in wage inequality, however (Katz and Autor 1999).

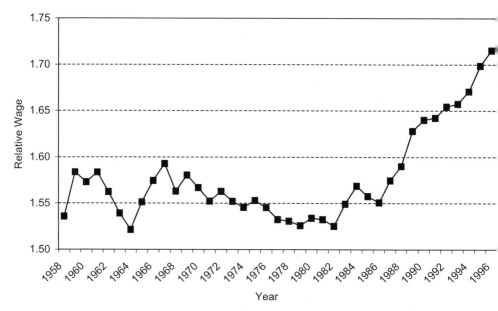

Figure 4.1   Relative Wage of Nonproduction/Production Workers, U.S. Manufacturing. *Source:* NBER productivity database (Bartelsman and Gray, 1996); see
empirical exercise 4.1.

ratio of nonproduction to production workers used in U.S. manufacturing, with some leveling off recently. This increase in the supply of workers
can account for the *reduction* in the relative wage of nonproduction workers from 1970 to the early 1980s, as shown in Figure 4.1, but is at odds
with the *increase* in the relative nonproduction wage after that. The rising
relative wage should have led to a shift in employment *away* from skilled
workers, along a demand curve, but it has not. Thus, the only explanation
consistent with these facts is that there has been an *outward shift* in the demand for more-skilled workers since the mid-1980s, leading to an increase in their relative employment and wages.[9]

What factors could lead to an outward shift in the relative demand for
skilled labor in the economy? One explanation suggested by the two-
sector model is that the output of skill-intensive sectors have risen relative
to those of unskilled-labor-intensive sectors: this would certainly increase
the relative demand for skilled labor. However, the evidence for the

[9] The same decline in the relative wages of blue-collar workers during the 1980s and into the
1990s can be found for Australia, Canada, Japan, Sweden, and the United Kingdom (Freeman
and Katz 1994; Katz and Autor 1999), and also for Hong Kong and Mexico (Cragg and
Epelbaum 1996; Hanson and Harrison 1999; Hsieh and Woo 1999; Robertson 2000).

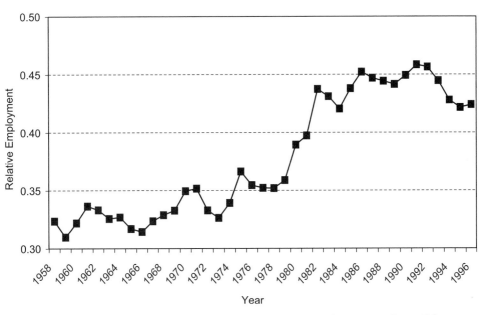

Figure 4.2   Relative Employment of Nonproduction/Production Workers, U.S. Manufacturing. *Source:* NBER productivity database (Bartelsman and Gray, 1996); see empirical exercise 4.1.

United States is that this sort of sectoral change in outputs *did not* occur. Rather, the bulk of the increase in the relative demand for skilled labor occurred *within* the manufacturing industries, and not by shifts in labor between industries. Some evidence on this *within versus between* industry distinction is contained in Table 4.1, which is revised from Berman, Bound, and Griliches 1994.

Table 4.1 decomposes the change in the relative employment and relative wages of nonproduction workers into those that occurred within and between industries. We can see that in the period 1979–87, the relative employment of nonproduction workers increased by slightly more than one-half of one percent per year (0.55%), with about two-thirds of that (0.36%) explained by *within* industry movements. On the wage side, the relative annual earnings of nonproduction workers increased by about seven-tenths of a percentage point per year (0.72%), with more than half of that change (0.41%) explained by *within*-industry movements. The conclusion suggested by Berman, Bound, and Griliches (1994) is that trade cannot be a dominant explanation for the wage and employment shifts, because the movements *between* industries are smaller than the movements *within* industries.

TABLE 4.1

Industry-Level Decomposition of the Change in the Share of Employment and Wages of Nonproduction Workers, 1973–79 and 1979–87

	Employment		*Wages*	
	Between	*Within*	*Between*	*Within*
1973–79	0.12	0.20	0.12	0.21
Total	0.32		0.33	
1979–87	0.18	0.36	0.31	0.41
Total	0.55		0.72	

Source: Bernard and Jensen, 1997, Table 1.

Notes: Numbers are percentage changes between years. *Between* numbers represent shifts across four-digit SIC industries, and *within* numbers represent changes within industries. All calculations have been annualized.

This conclusion was reinforced by consideration of the price movements. If the Stolper-Samuelson theorem holds, then the relative price of skilled labor in the United States would increase if the relative price of skill-intensive goods also increased, for example, if the price of computers rose relative to the price of apparel. In fact, this *did not* occur during the 1980s.[10] This can be seen from Table 4.2, which is taken from the work of Lawrence and Slaughter (1993) and Lawrence (1994). For each country, the first row is a weighted average of the change in manufacturing prices over the 1980s, where the weights are the industry's share of total manufacturing employment of *nonproduction* workers. The second row is again the weighted average of the change in prices over the 1980s, but now using the industry's share of employment of *production* workers. For U.S. import prices, for example, we can see that when industries are weighted by their production workers, the average price increase is *higher* than when they are weighted by nonproduction workers. The same pattern can be seen by comparing the rows for other industrial countries. This means that some of the industries that use the *most* production—or less-skilled—workers are those with the *highest* price increases. This finding led Lawrence and Slaughter (1993) to conclude that price movements due to international competition could not explain the wage movements.

The price movements shown in Table 4.2, combined with the shift in relative demand towards skilled labor *within* industries, as shown in Table 4.1, led many economists to conclude that international trade could not be

[10] But it did occur during the 1970s, in what Leamer (1998) has called the "Stolper-Samuelson decade."

TABLE 4.2
Average Percentage Changes in Domestic and Import Prices, Weighted by Employment

	Domestic Price	*Import Price*
United States (1980–89)		
All manufacturing industries		
Nonproduction labor weights	33.1	26.0
Production labor weights	32.3	28.1
Japan (1980–90)		
All manufacturing industries		
Nonproduction labor weights	−5.6	−18.2
Production labor weights	−3.9	−17.3
Without office machines		
Nonproduction labor weights	−7.1	−18.7
Production labor weights	−4.7	−17.5
Also without petroleum products		
Nonproduction labor weights	−7.0	−18.5
Production labor weights	−4.7	−17.4
Germany (1980–90)		
All manufacturing industries		
Nonmanual labor weights	24.0	15.2
Manual labor weights	26.0	17.1
Without office machines		
Nonmanual labor weights	24.8	15.4
Manual labor weights	26.2	17.1
Also without petroleum products		
Nonmanual labor weights	25.0	15.7
Manual labor weights	26.3	17.2

Source: Lawrence and Slaughter 1993, Tables 3 and 4 and Lawrence 1994, Table 4.
Note: The averages shown weight each industry's price change by that industry's share of total manufacturing employment of nonproduction or nonmanual workers, and production or manual workers. Industries are defined at the three-digit SIC level for the United States, and generally correspond to the two-digit level for Japan and Germany.

a substantial explanation for the rise in relative wages. Instead, they have looked to the introduction of skill-biased technological changes, such the introduction of computers, to provide the explanation. But should we really rule out trade? It may be true that the Heckscher-Ohlin model does not provide the explanation for the change in wages during the 1980s and 1990s. But surely trade can have an important impact on the structure of

TABLE 4.3

Plant-Level Decomposition of the Change in the Share of Employment and Wages of Nonproduction Workers, 1973–79 and 1979–87

	Employment		*Wages*	
	Between	*Within*	*Between*	*Within*
1973–79	0.10	0.17	0.14	0.13
Total		0.27		0.27
1979–87	0.18	0.22	0.32	0.22
Total		0.39		0.54

Source: Bernard and Jensen 1997, Table 1.

Note: Numbers are percentage changes between years. *Between* numbers represent shifts across four-digit SIC plants, and *within* numbers represent changes within plants. All calculations have been annualized.

production, and demand for labor *within* industries as well. This is certainly the case when we introduce trade in intermediate inputs: as we shall see, trade can then affect labor demand *within* an industry.

Some preliminary evidence that suggests that trade shifts the composition of activity *within* an industry is provided by Bernard and Jensen (1997), who do the same decomposition as Berman, Bound, and Griliches but with *plant-level* data rather than *industry-level* data. This is shown in Table 4.3. Looking again at the period 1979–87, we can see that nearly one-half of the relative increase in the employment of nonproduction workers (0.39%) occurred as a result of the shifts *between* plants (0.18%), and more than one-half of the increase in the relative wage of nonproduction workers (0.54%) is also explained by movements *between* manufacturing plants (0.32%). Furthermore, Bernard and Jensen found that the plants experiencing the greatest increase in relative nonproduction employment and earnings are precisely those that were engaged in exporting.

The results of Bernard and Jensen provide prima facie evidence that trade has had an impact on factor demand and wages, through shifting the demand for labor *within* industries. In order to understand how these shifts due to trade can occur, we present in the next section a simple model of outsourcing.

Trade in Intermediate Inputs: A Simple Model

Of the many activities that take place within any industry, let us identify just three: the production of an unskilled-labor-intensive input, denoted by y_1; the production of a skilled-labor-intensive input, denoted by y_2, and the "bundling together" of these two goods into a finished product. The two intermediate inputs are produced at home and also traded internationally. We shall simplify the analysis, however, by assuming that the production of these two inputs and the "bundling" activity are *always* performed at home. Thus, we are ruling out "corner solutions" where one of these activities is done entirely abroad. In reality, corner solutions such as this are very common: for example, many U.S. firms export intermediate inputs to the *maquiladora* plants in Mexico, where assembly of the inputs and other production activities take place rather than in the United States. A model that emphasizes the movement of entire activities across countries is presented in the next section.

We will suppose that the two inputs y_i, $i = 1, 2$, are each produced using unskilled labor (L_i), skilled labor (H_i), and capital (K_i), with concave and linearly homogeneous production functions

$$y_i = f_i(L_i, H_i, K_i), \qquad i = 1, 2. \tag{4.2}$$

For example, the unskilled-labor-intensive input y_1 might represent the activities done within a factory, while the skilled-labor-intensive input y_2 might represent the research and development activities within the industry, as well as marketing and after-sales service. These are both needed to produce the final manufacturing product. But some of the activities done within the factory can instead be outsourced, that is, imported from abroad; and conversely, the services associated with research, development, and marketing can be exported to support production activities abroad. We therefore let $x_1 < 0$ denote the imports of input 1, and $x_2 > 0$ denote the exports of input 2. Also let p_i denote the price of each input, $i = 1, 2$, and let $p = (p_1, p_2)$ denote the price vector of the traded intermediate inputs.

The production of the final good is given by $y_n = f_n(y_1 - x_1, y_2 - x_2)$, where this production function "bundles together" the amounts of goods 1 and 2 available, and is also concave and linearly homogeneous. We ignore any additional labor and capital inputs used in this bundling activity, so that the total factor usage in the manufacturing industry is

$$L_1 + L_2 = L_n, \quad H_1 + H_2 = H_n, \quad K_1 + K_2 = K_n. \tag{4.3}$$

We can now solve for the optimal output in the industry, which includes the three activities. With perfect competition, the value of output from the final good, plus net trade, will be maximized subject to the resource constraints

$$G_n(L_n, H_n, K_n, p_n, p) \equiv \max_{x_i, L_i, H_i, K_i} p_n f_n(y_1 - x_1, y_2 - x_2) + p_1 x_1$$
$$+ p_2 x_2, \text{ subject to } (4.2), (4.3), \tag{4.4}$$

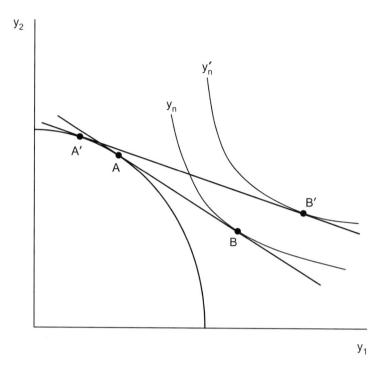

Figure 4.3

where p_n is the price of the final good, and p is the price vector of the traded intermediate inputs. The value of (4.4) can be thought of as value-added for the industry, that is, output including exports $p_2 x_2$ less the value of intermediate inputs $p_1 x_1$. Note that this function is very similar to the GDP function introduced in chapter 1, but now we apply it to *each* of the $n = 1, \ldots, N$ manufacturing industries. When applied to specific industries, it is common to call (4.4) a *revenue function*.

Note that the optimization problem in (4.4) does *not* require that trade be balanced on an industry-by-industry basis; that is, we do *not* require that $p_1 x_1 + p_2 x_2 = 0$. Of course, there will be some balance-of-trade constraint for the economy overall, but we ignore that here. Problem (4.4) can be easily illustrated, as in Figure 4.3, where we show the production possibility frontier between inputs 1 and 2, and several isoquants of the final good y_n. For the purpose of illustration we now add the condition that trade in inputs is balanced, $p_1 x_1 + p_2 x_2 = 0$, so that the output of the final good is maximized on the isoquant that is tangent to the balanced trade line. At initial prices, for example, the industry produces inputs at point A, and then trades to point B. With a *drop* in the relative price of the imported input, the industry shifts production towards the skilled-labor-intensive activity at point A′, and then trades to point B′, obtaining a higher output y_n'. All this will look very familiar to readers from the similar discussion for an economy in chapter 1: the special feature of Figure 4.3 is that we now think of these activities as taking place *within* a single manufacturing industry.

How will the drop in the relative price of imported inputs affect factor prices? To answer this, we can use the zero-profit conditions for producing inputs 1 and 2, which are

$$p_i = c_i(w, q, r). \tag{4.5}$$

These conditions must hold in order for the locally produced inputs y_i, $i = 1, 2$, to be competitive with those available from abroad, at the international prices p_i. Totally differentiating (4.5) and using the Jones' algebra (as in chapter 1), we can express the percentage change in factor prices $\hat{w}$, $\hat{q}$, and $\hat{r}$ as functions of the percentage change in prices $\hat{p}_i$:

$$\hat{p}_i = \theta_{iL}\hat{w} + \theta_{iH}\hat{q} + \theta_{iK}\hat{r}, \tag{4.6}$$

where θ_{ij} is the cost share of factor j in activity i, with $\Sigma_j \theta_{ij} = 1$.

Treating the change in the traded price $\hat{p}_i$ as exogenous, (4.6) gives *two* equations with which to determine *three* unknown factor prices changes— $\hat{w}$, $\hat{q}$, and $\hat{r}$. In general, these factor price changes will be difficult to pin down with only two equations. In terms of Figure 4.3, when production shifts towards the skilled-labor-intensive activity, from point A to point A′, we do not know in general how factor prices are affected. But there are some simplifying assumptions we can make that allow us to determine these prices.

Let us assume that *capital has equal cost shares in the two activities*, so that $\theta_{1K} = \theta_{2K}$. Using this, we take the difference between the two equations in (4.6) to obtain

$$\hat{p}_1 - \hat{p}_2 = (\theta_{1L} - \theta_{2L})\,\hat{w} + (\theta_{1H} - \theta_{2H})\,\hat{q} = (\theta_{1L} - \theta_{2L})(\hat{w} - \hat{q}), \quad (4.7)$$

where the second equality follows since with equal cost shares of capital, the total cost shares of labor are also equal, so that $(\theta_{1L} + \theta_{1H}) = (\theta_{2L} + \theta_{2H})$ $\Rightarrow (\theta_{1L} - \theta_{2L}) = -(\theta_{1H} - \theta_{2H})$. With activity 1 assumed to be unskilled labor intensive, we have that $(\theta_{1L} - \theta_{2L}) > 0$. Thus, (4.7) says that a *decrease* in the relative price of imported intermediate input, $\hat{p}_1 - \hat{p}_2 < 0$, leads to a *decrease* in the relative wage of unskilled labor, $(\hat{w} - \hat{q}) = (\hat{p}_1 - \hat{p}_2)/(\theta_{1L} - \theta_{2L}) < 0$.

These results are illustrated in Figure 4.4, where we graph the iso-curves of $c_i(w, q, r)$. With the wages of unskilled and skilled labor labeled on the axis, we are implicitly holding fixed the rental on capital, r. Now

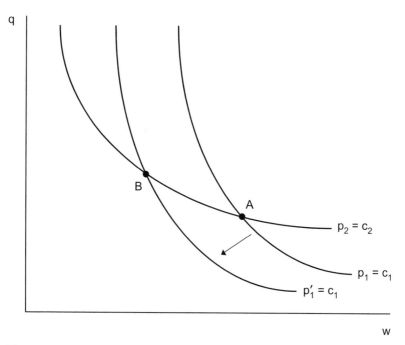

Figure 4.4

suppose that there is a fall in the price p_1 of activity 1, which is unskilled labor intensive. In Figure 4.4, this will shift inwards the iso-cost line of that activity, and as shown, will lead to a *fall* in the relative wage of unskilled labor (from point A to point B). There will be some additional change in the rental on capital, but under our assumption of equal cost share of capital in the two industries, this will lead to an *equiproportional* shift in the two iso-cost curves and therefore have no further effect on the relative wage. Thus, the drop in the price of the imported inputs leads to a fall in the relative wage (w/q) of unskilled labor.

We can also ask what happens to the price of the final good p_n. Let $c_n(p_1, p_2)$ denote the unit-cost function that is dual to $f_n(y_1, y_2)$, whereby the final good is assembled from the two intermediate inputs. Then the price of the final good satisfies $p_n = c_n(p_1, p_2)$, so that $\hat{p}_n = \theta_{n1}\hat{p}_1 + \theta_{n2}\hat{p}_2$, where θ_{ni} is the cost share of input i in the final product. Thus, the change in the price of the final good is a *weighted average* of the change in the input prices. In particular, with a fall in the relative price of imported inputs, $\hat{p}_1 - \hat{p}_2 < 0$, the price of the final good satisfies $\hat{p}_1 < \hat{p}_n < \hat{p}_2$. Stated differently, the price of the final good *relative to imported inputs rises*, $\hat{p}_n - \hat{p}_1 > 0$.

Thus, our model of outsourcing suggests a different way of looking at the link between product prices and factor prices. Rather that comparing prices *across* different industries, depending on their skill intensity, it now makes sense to compare import and domestic prices *within* each industry. The types of goods being imported within each industry (e.g., auto parts) are not the same as those being sold domestically (e.g., finished autos). Indeed, as U.S. firms find imported inputs at increasingly lower prices—through outsourcing activities that they used to do at home—we would expect to see that U.S. prices within each industry *rising* relative to import prices. In terms of Table 4.2, we should be comparing the price changes across *columns* rather than across *rows*. Looking at the United States, we see that during the 1980s it is indeed the case that domestic prices rose faster than import prices, and the same is true for Japan and Germany. These price movements are entirely consistent with the model of foreign outsourcing, whereby the United States and other industrial countries are continually seeking lower-cost sources of supply. Based on this logic, there is no "contradiction" at all between the movement of prices and relative wages!

Continuum of Inputs

The model we have presented above can be readily extended to incorporate a continuum of inputs, as in Feenstra and Hanson 1996, 1997. Let the index $z \in [0, 1]$ denote the many activities undertaken in the creation, production, and delivery of a product to the consumer. Rather than listing these activities in their *temporal* order, we will instead list them in *increasing order* of skilled/unskilled labor, where for example, the least skill-intensive activity is assembly and the most skill-intensive activity is R&D. Letting $x(z)$ denote the quantity produced of each one of these inputs, we let $a_H(z)$ and $a_L(z)$ denote the skilled and unskilled labor, respectively, needed to produce one unit of $x(z)$. As stated, we will order the activities z so that $a_H(z)/a_L(z)$ is nondecreasing in z.

We will suppose that there are two countries, with the foreign country denoted by an asterisk. The production functions for producing the two inputs are assumed to be the same up to a Hicks-neutral productivity parameter in each country:

$$x(z) = A\left[\min\left\{\frac{L(z)}{a_L(z)}, \frac{H(z)}{a_H(z)}\right\}\right]^{\theta} K^{1-\theta}, \quad z \in [0, 1]. \tag{4.8}$$

Thus, the amount of skilled and unskilled labor $H(z)$ and $L(z)$ are used in the home country to produce input z, using a Leontief technology between these two types of labor, and then a Cobb-Douglas technology between labor overall and capital K. The parameter θ denotes the share of labor in the costs of producing each input. The foreign production function is the same, except with a different productivity parameter A^*.

Rather than working with the production functions for the inputs in (4.8), it will be convenient to work with the dual unit-cost function:

$$c(w, q, r, z) = B[wa_L(z) + qa_H(z)]^\theta \, r^{1-\theta}, \qquad (4.9)$$

where $c(w, q, r, z)$ denotes the costs of producing one unit of $x(z)$ in the home country, given the wage of unskilled labor w, the wage of skilled labor q, and the rental on capital r. The inputs can be produced in *either country*, and are then combined into the production of a final product. The production function for the final good is assumed to be a Cobb-Douglas function over all the inputs:

$$\ln Y = \int_0^1 \alpha(z) \ln x(z) dz, \quad \text{with} \quad \int_0^1 \alpha(z) dz = 1. \qquad (4.10)$$

Notice that in (4.10) we have not included labor as an input, so the final good is assembled "costlessly" from all the individual inputs $z \in [0, 1]$. This means that we do not need to keep track of which country the assembly takes place, because there is zero value added (and zero demand for labor) in this activity.

In general, firms doing the assembly will wish to source the inputs from the minimum-cost location. To determine this, we will make the following assumption on factor prices:

$$\frac{q}{w} < \frac{q^*}{w^*}, \quad \text{and} \quad r < r^*. \qquad (4.11)$$

The first assumption in (4.11) states that the relative wage of skilled labor is *lower* at home than abroad, which is realistic if the home country is skilled-labor abundant, like the United States: despite the increase in the relative wage of skilled labor in the United States during the past two decades, it is still much lower than in Mexico. The second assumption states that the rental on capital is lower at home, so that if capital is able to move, it will want to relocate abroad. This is also realistic if the home country is capital abundant, and will provide the basis for some comparative statics we shall consider.

With assumption (4.11), we can graphically illustrate the problem of choosing the minimum-cost location for each input. Let us begin by graphing the unit-costs (4.9) for the home country, given fixed factor prices. The unit-costs $c(w, q, r, z)$ as a function of z can have any shape whatsoever, and need not even be a continuous function. For convenience, however, we will assume that it is a continuous function, and illustrate it as

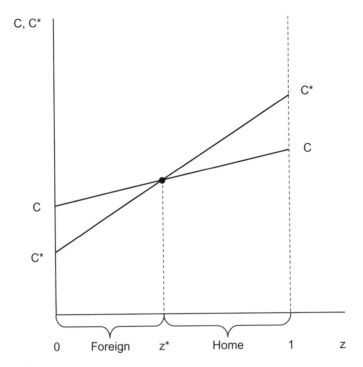

Figure 4.5

the upward-sloping curve CC in Figure 4.5. Then the question is, how does the locus of unit-costs $c^*(w^*, q^*, r^*, z)$ abroad, which we denote by C^*C^*, relate to that at home?

If the unit-costs of all activities were *lower* at home, for example, then all inputs would be produced there, and vice versa if all unit-costs are lower abroad. We are interested in the case where there is some "production sharing" across the countries, so assume that the curves C^*C^* and CC intersect *at least once*, and denote this input by z^*, with $c(w, q, r, z^*) = c(w^*, q^*, r^*, z^*)$. Then consider an activity $z' > z^*$ with slightly higher skilled/unskilled labor requirements. Because of our assumptions that $(q/w) < (q^*/w^*)$, the higher skilled/unskilled requirements should have a greater impact on *foreign* costs than on *home* costs. We therefore expect that $c(w, r, q, z') < c(w^*, q^*, r^*, z')$ for $z' < z^*$. Similarly, we expect that the converse is also true, $c(w, q, r, z') > c(w^*, q^*, r^*, z')$ for $z' < z^*$. Thus, the loci C^*C^* and CC can intersect *at most once*, as shown in Figure 4.5.[11] The similarity of this analysis with the model of Dornbusch, Fischer, and

---

[11] This is proved by Feenstra and Hanson (1996).

Samuelson (1980) in the previous chapter, where we used nearly the same diagrams, will be clear to the reader.

Given this unique intersection, we see that foreign unit-costs are less than those at home for all $z' < z^*$, so that the foreign country will specialize in the products $[0, z^*)$, whereas home unit-costs are less than those abroad for all $z' > z^*$, so the home country will specialize in $(z^*, 1]$. Using this information, we can then calculate the demand for labor in each country. At home, for example, the relative demand for skilled/unskilled labor is

$$D(z^*) = \frac{\int_{z^*}^1 \frac{\partial c}{\partial q} x(z) dz}{\int_{z^*}^1 \frac{\partial c}{\partial w} x(z) dz}. \qquad (4.12)$$

Because the final good is "costlessly" assembled from the intermediate inputs, without the use of any additional labor, we do not need to keep track of where this assembly occurs. An expression similar to (4.12) holds for the relative demand $D^*(z^*)$ in the foreign country, except that the integration is done over the range of goods $[0, z^*)$ rather than $(z^*, 1]$. Notice that the demands certainly depend on factor prices (since these enter the cost functions),[12] and it can be confirmed that $D(z^*)$ and $D^*(z^*)$ are *decreasing* in the relative wage of skilled/unskilled labor in each country, as shown in Figure 4.6.

The equilibrium conditions for the world economy are that supply equal demand in the market for skilled and unskilled labor in each country, as well as for capital, when each country is producing the range of products for which they have minimum cost. In terms of our diagrams, we will have z^* determined by Figure 4.5, which is then used to draw the relative demand for labor in each country. Supposing the *endowments* of labor and capital are fixed, the relative wage is determined by the intersection of supply and demand in Figure 4.6 for each country, which feeds back into the cost loci CC and C^*C^* in Figure 4.5, to determine z^*. When all these curves intersect simultaneously, we can do a final calculation to determine the rental on capital in each country. The wage bill at home is $wL + qH$. Because wages make up the fraction θ of total costs, it follows that GDP in each country is $(wL + qH)/\theta$. Multiplying this by $(1 - \theta)$, the cost share of capital, we therefore obtain

$$\frac{(wL + qH)}{\theta}(1 - \theta) = rK. \qquad (4.13)$$

[12] In addition, factor prices affect the prices of the intermediate inputs, which influence the equilibrium demand for $x(z)$.

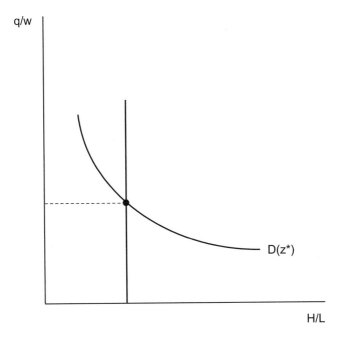

Figure 4.6

With the capital endowment K fixed on the right side of (4.13), this equation determines the rental r at home, with the analogous equation holding abroad.

Now suppose that we allow capital to move between the countries. In particular, with our earlier assumption that $r < r^*$, suppose that some capital moves from the home to the foreign country, so that K falls while K^* rises. From (4.13) and the analogous equation abroad, the *initial impact* of that capital movement will be to raise r and lower r^*. Of course, we expect a further effect on the wages appearing on the left side of (4.13). To work out how these will change, consider Figures 4.7 and 4.8. The increase in r *raises* the CC locus in Figure 4.7, while the reduction in r^* *lowers* the C^*C^* locus. At unchanged wages, this has the effect of *increasing* the equilibrium value of z, from z^* to z'. Therefore, the foreign country now specializes in the expanded range of activities $[0, z')$, while the home country specializes in the contracted range of activities $(z', 1]$. This will have an effect on the relative demand for labor in each country, as follows.

For the home country, the range of inputs being produced has contracted from $(z^*, 1]$ to $(z', 1]$. Notice that those activities that have been transferred abroad, in the interval (z^*, z'), are *less* skill intensive than the

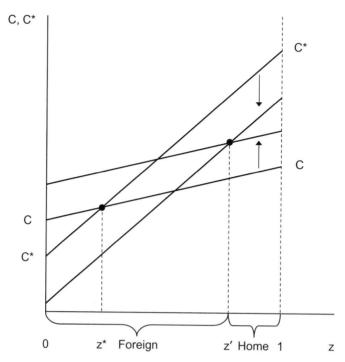

Figure 4.7

activities still performed at home. This makes sense, since we expect the least skill-intensive activities to be outsourced from the home country, such as the United States. This has the effect of *lowering* the relative demand for unskilled labor at home, or *increasing* the relative demand for skilled labor, so the curve $D(z^*)$ shifts rightward to $D(z')$ in Figure 4.8. What about the foreign country? Notice that in that country, the activities (z^*, z') being added are *more skill intensive* than any activities previously done there. For example, as TV manufacturing shifted into Mexico, first the chassis of the televisions were constructed there, then the electronic circuits, and later still the picture tubes (Kenney and Florida 1994). This shift in production has the effect of *increasing* the relative demand for skilled labor in the foreign country as well.

The rightward shift of the relative demand for skilled labor in both countries means that the *relative wage of skilled labor rises in both countries.* Of course, this change in wages has a feedback effect on the cost loci in Figure 4.7, which further changes the equilibrium value of z. In the final equilibrium, however, the changes are exactly as we have described: as more activities are outsourced, the relative demand for skilled labor rises in *both* countries. This is a realistic description of what has occurred in the

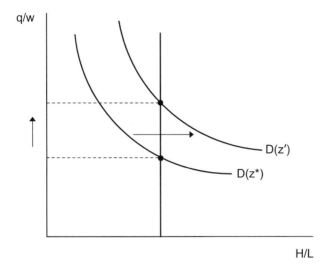

Figure 4.8

United States as well as in Mexico (Cragg and Epelbaum 1996; Hanson and Harrison 1999; Robertson 2000). In contrast, it is difficult to generate the *same direction of movements* in relative wages across countries from opening trade in the Heckscher-Ohlin model.

Can we say anything about absolute rather than relative wages? Feenstra and Hanson (1996) explore this question, and conclude that while the *relative* wage of unskilled workers falls in both countries, their *real wages* need not fall. Unskilled workers in the home country are the most disadvantaged by the outsourcing, but nevertheless, it is possible that they gain due to lower prices of the final good. These results hold regardless of whether the increased outsourcing is due to a capital flow, as we have described, or due to a variety of other causes: growth in the capital endowments abroad, at a rate exceeding that at home; or simply technological progress abroad exceeding that at home. In each of these cases, the comparative static effects are the same as we have just described.

Another question, not explored by Feenstra and Hanson, is the extent to which factor accumulation or a reduction in trade barriers increases trade between countries. With trade due to outsourcing, it would appear that modest shifts in the relative cost loci in Figure 4.7 could potentially lead to large changes in the borderline activity z^* and in the amount of outsourcing. Yi (2003) argues that this is indeed the case in a Ricardian model with a continuum of goods, and that "vertical specialization" accounts for more than 50% of the growth in U.S. trade since 1962. Yi's paper is recommended for further reading.

Estimating the Relative Demand for Skilled Labor

Summarizing our argument so far, the decision of companies to purchase intermediate inputs from overseas will most certainly affect their employment at home, and can be expected to differentially affect skilled versus unskilled workers. With firms in industrial countries facing a higher relative wage for unskilled labor than that found abroad, the activities that are outsourced would be those that use a large amount of unskilled labor, such as assembly of components and other repetitive tasks. Moving these activities overseas will reduce the relative demand for unskilled labor in the industrial country, in much the same way as replacing these workers with automated production. *This means that outsourcing has a qualitatively similar effect on reducing the relative demand for unskilled labor within an industry as does skilled-biased technological change, such as the increased use of computers.* Thus, determining which of these is most important is an empirical question.

We will examine two methods that have been used to estimate the effects of trade versus technological change on wages and employment. The first method estimates the demand for skilled and unskilled labor. Let us return to the simple three-good, three-factor model introduced above, where we derived the revenue function $G_n(L_n, H_n, K_n, p_n, p)$ in (4.4) for each industry $n = 1, \ldots, N$, where $p = (p_1, p_2)$ is the vector of imported input prices. It will be convenient to work with a "short run" cost function that is dual to (4.4). Note that the function $G_n(L_n, H_n, K_n, p_n, p)$ is linearly homogeneous in prices, so we can alternatively write it as $p_n G_n(L_n, H_n, K_n, 1, p/p_n)$. Thus, a natural measure of *real value-added* is

$$Y_n = G_n(L_n, H_n, K_n, 1, p/p_n). \tag{4.14}$$

This measure of output is nearly the same as y_n, except it now includes real net exports. Provided that the underlying production functions f_i, $i = 1, 2, n$, are increasing and concave, then the function G_n will also be increasing and concave in (L_n, H_n, K_n).

Then the *short-run cost function*, obtained when the levels of capital and output are fixed, is defined as

$$C_n(w, q, K_n, Y_n, p/p_n) \equiv \min_{L_n, H_n} wL_n + qH_n, \tag{4.15}$$

subject to (4.14).

Notice that we have included the relative price of traded inputs p/p_n in this cost function since they also appear in the revenue function (4.14). More generally, *any structural variables that shift the production function and therefore affect costs* should be included as arguments. In the model discussed above with a continuum of input, the *range of inputs* imported into each country should appear as an argument in (4.15). That is, it is not enough to just keep track of import prices—we also need to keep track of newly imported intermediate inputs. In practice, we will measure this by the *expenditure* on imported inputs for each industry, though this does not fully capture the idea of newly imported inputs.[13] We will denote all such structural variables that affect costs in industry n by the vector z_n; in addition to imported inputs, this can include expenditures on computers and other new types of capital equipment. We therefore rewrite the cost function in (4.15) as $C_n(w, q, K_n, Y_n, z_n)$.

The next step is to choose a functional form for costs. As in our discussion of the GDP function in chapter 3, a convenient choice is the translog cost function, which is written in a general notation (dropping the industry subscript n) as

$$\ln C = \alpha_0 + \sum_{i=1}^{M} \alpha_i \ln w_i + \sum_{k=1}^{K} \beta_k \ln x_k + \frac{1}{2} \sum_{i=1}^{M} \sum_{j=1}^{M} \gamma_{ij} \ln w_i \ln w_j$$

$$+ \frac{1}{2} \sum_{k=1}^{K} \sum_{\ell=1}^{K} \delta_{k\ell} \ln x_k \ln x_\ell + \sum_{i=1}^{M} \sum_{k=1}^{K} \phi_{ik} \ln w_i \ln x_k, \qquad (4.16)$$

where w_i denotes the wages of the optimally chosen inputs $i = 1, \ldots, M$, and x_k denotes either the quantities of the *fixed* inputs or outputs $k = 1, \ldots, K$, or any other shift parameters.[14] In terms of the cost function in (4.15), there are just two optimally chosen factors—skilled and unskilled labor—while capital and output are treated as fixed in the short run.

The usefulness of the translog function comes from computing its first derivatives, $\partial \ln C / \partial \ln w_i = (\partial C / \partial w_i)(w_i / C)$. Because $\partial C / \partial w_i$ equals the demand for the chosen input i, it follows that $(\partial C / \partial w_i)(w_i / C)$ equals the *payments to factor i relative to total costs*, which we denote by the cost shares s_i. Thus, differentiating (4.16) with respect to $\ln w_i$, we obtain

$$s_i = \alpha_i + \sum_{j=1}^{M} \gamma_{ij} \ln w_j + \sum_{k=1}^{K} \phi_{ik} \ln x_k, \quad i = 1, \ldots, M. \qquad (4.17)$$

Given annual data on factor cost shares, wages, and fixed inputs and outputs, this set of linear equations can be estimated over time for a given

---

[13] In chapter 10 we discuss methods to directly measure the product variety of imports. Dinopoulos and Segerstrom (1999b), Zhu (2001a), and Zhu and Trefler (2001) develop models that emphasize the link between new varieties of traded goods and wages, with corresponding empirical work by Zhu (2001b). These papers are recommended for further reading.

[14] Without loss of generality we impose the symmetry requirement that $\gamma_{ij} = \gamma_{ji}$. In addition, to ensure that the translog cost function is homogeneous of degree one in wages, we impose $\sum_{i=1}^{M} \alpha_i = 1$ and $\sum_{i=1}^{M} \gamma_{ij} = \sum_{i=1}^{M} \phi_{ik} = 0$.

industry to obtain the coefficients γ_{ij} and ϕ_{ik}.[15] Alternatively, the equations can be estimated for a single year, or the change between two years, by pooling data across industries. In the latter case, we are assuming that the *same* cost function applies across the industries. Despite this strong assumption, the cross-industry approach is popular, and we will follow it here.

Returning now to the notation $C_n(w, q, K_n, Y_n, z_n)$ as in (4.15), we have two chosen inputs—skilled and unskilled labor. Focusing on the share equation for skilled labor, it will depend on wages for both types of labor, as well as capital, output, and all other structural variables, z_n. When (4.17) is estimated by pooling data across industries, as in Berman, Bound, and Griliches (1994), for example, it is felt the cross-industry variation in wages has little information: wages differ across industries principally due to quality variation of workers, so we do not expect high-wage industries to economize on those (high-quality) workers. Accordingly, the wage terms are typically dropped from the right of (4.17) when pooling data across industries. This leaves just fixed capital, output, and other structural variables. Taking the difference between two years, the estimating equation for the wage share of skilled labor (s_{nH}) in industries $n = 1, \ldots, N$ becomes

$$\Delta s_{nH} = \phi_0 + \phi_K \Delta \ln K_n + \phi_Y \Delta \ln Y_n + \phi_z' \Delta z_n, \quad n = 1, \ldots, N, \quad (4.18)$$

where z_n denotes the vector of structural variables that shifts costs, and ϕ_z is the corresponding vector of coefficients. In particular, when the wage share of skilled labor is increasing, we are interested in determining how much of that increase is due to changes in capital, output, and the structural variables.

Estimates of (4.18) for 447 industries within the U.S. manufacturing sector, over 1979–90, are shown in Table 4.4. The data are from the NBER Productivity Database at the 4-digit Standard Industrial Classification (SIC) level (Bartelsman and Gray 1996, which is available at http: //www.nber.org/nberces/).[16] In these regressions we use nonproduction labor as a proxy for skilled labor, so the dependent variable is the change in the share of nonproduction labor in total wages within each industry. Over all manufacturing industries, the nonproduction wage share increased from 35.4% to 42.4% between 1979 and 1990, for an annual growth of 0.4% (four-tenths of one percent) per year. It is common to weight regressions like those in Table 4.4 by the industry share of the total manufacturing wage bill, as we shall do. In this way, large industries

---

[15] Generally, the dependent variables in the system (4.17) sum to unity, which means that one of the equations can be derived from the others. Under these conditions, one of the equations is dropped before the system is estimated.

[16] In empirical exercise 4.1, you are asked to download this dataset and reproduce Figures 4.1–4.2, and in exercise 4.2 you are asked to reproduce Table 4.4.

TABLE 4.4
Change in Nonproduction Wage Share, 1979–90, as Dependent Variable

	Mean (1)	Regression (2)	Regression (3)	Regression (4)	Contribution (5)
$\Delta\ln(K/Y)$	0.71	0.05 (0.01)	0.04 (0.01)	0.04 (0.009)	7–9%
$\Delta\ln(Y)$	1.54	0.02 (0.006)	0.02 (0.006)	0.01 (0.006)	4–8%
Outsourcing	0.42	0.20 (0.096)	0.22 (0.10)	0.14 (0.09)	15–24%
Computer and other high-tech capital measured with ex post rental prices					
Computer share	0.25	0.20 (0.091)			13%
Other high-tech share	0.14	−0.07 (0.14)			—
Computer and other high-tech capital measured with ex ante rental prices					
Computer share	0.07		0.43 (0.17)		8%
Other high-tech share	0.17		0.005 (0.07)		0.2%
Computers measured as share of investment					
Computer share	6.56			0.02 (0.01)	31%
High-tech share (*ex post* rental prices)	0.40			0.03 (0.05)	3%
Constant		0.20 (0.04)	0.21 (0.04)	0.16 (0.05)	40–53%
R^2		0.16	0.16	0.19	
N		447	447	447	

Source: Feenstra and Hanson 2003, Table 3, as simplified from Feenstra and Hanson 1999, Table III), and empirical exercise 4.2.

Note: The mean of the dependent variable equals 0.389. Standard errors (in parentheses) are robust to heteroskedasticity and correlation in the errors within two-digit industries. The first column shows mean values of the dependent and independent variables for 1979–90. All regressions and means are computed over 447 four-digit SIC industries and are weighted by the average industry share of the manufacturing wage bill. $\Delta\ln(K/Y)$ is the average annual change in the log capital-shipments ratio, and $\Delta\ln(Y)$ is the average annual change in log real shipments. The outsourcing variables and the computer and high-technology shares are in annual changes.

receive more weight in the regressions. The regressors included are the shipments of each industry (as a proxy for real value-added Y_n); the capital/shipments ratio (reflecting the capital input K_n relative to Y_n); outsourcing, measured by imported intermediate inputs as a share of total intermediate purchases (one of the z_n variables); and the share of computers and other high-tech capital in the capital stock (other z_n variables). Several of these variables deserve further explanation.

The *imported intermediate inputs* have been estimated by Feenstra and Hanson (1999) using the input-output matrix of the U.S. economy, combined with trade data. For example, if the automobile industry purchases 10% of its inputs from the steel industry, and 30% of steel consumed in the United States is imported, then we conclude that 3% of the inputs in autos is due to *imported* steel. This is summed over all intermediate inputs to arrive at the overall share of imported inputs for each industry. The share of computers and other high-tech capital in the capital stock is constructed in three different ways: first, using *ex post* rental prices to measure capital services; second, using *ex ante* rental prices to measure capital services;[17] and third, by measuring computer expenditures as a share of *investment* rather than of the capital stock.[18] We think that it is preferable to measure the contribution of computers to the capital stock, rather than to new investment, but experiment with all three approaches.

In column (1) of Table 4.4, we report the mean values of the dependent and independent variables for 1979–90, and, following this, the regression coefficients in columns (2)–(4). Each regression uses alternative

[17] To explain the construction of rental prices, suppose that there is only one type of capital and labor, so that value-added in an industry is $pY_n = wL_n + rK_n$. Given data on sales and on compensation to labor, the *ex post* payments to capital are constructed as a residual, $rK_n = pY_n - wL_n$. Next, we need some measure of the physical capital stock K_n, which is typically constructed from investment data I_n using the perpetual inventory method: $K_{nt} = (1 - \delta)K_{nt-1} + I_{nt}$, where δ is a depreciation rate for capital. Then using the constructed physical capital in year t, and the total payments to capital in year t, these are divided to obtain the *ex post* rental on capital in year t: $r_t = (pY_{nt} - wL_{nt})/K_{nt}$. Then using the *purchase price* of capital p_{kt}, the implied *ex post rate of return* to capital would be constructed as $\rho_t = (r_t/p_{kt}) - \delta + [(p_{kt+1} - p_{kt})/p_{kt}]$. Thus, the *ex post rate of return* includes the rental relative to the purchase price, minus depreciation, plus any capital gains or losses on the capital equipment. In contrast, an *ex ante rate of return* would *ignore* the capital gains or losses. Thus, if we chose ρ^* as a "safe" rate of return such as on a bond, then the corresponding *ex ante* rental price would be obtained by ignoring capital gains and computing r_t from the equation, $r_t = (\rho^* + \delta)p_{kt}$. The formulas used for the rental prices become more complicated when we take into account business taxes, and when there are multiple types of capital. For further details see Harper, Berndt, and Wood 1989.

[18] The share of computer spending in *investment* is obtained from the *Census of Manufactures*, which simply asked firms to report what percentage of new investment was devoted to computers. This variable has been used previously by Berman, Bound, and Griliches (1994) and Autor, Katz, and Krueger (1998).

measures of the computer and other high-technology shares. In all the regressions, we see that outsourcing has a positive impact on the nonproduction share of the wage bill, as does the computer share. By multiplying the regression coefficients by the mean values for the change in each variable, we obtain the contributions of each to the total change in the nonproduction wage share, shown in column (5). We see that outsourcing accounts for 15–24% of the shift towards nonproduction labor.

The results for computers depend on the specification. Measuring computer services and other high-tech capital as a share of the *capital stock* using *ex post* rental prices, we see they account for 13% of the shift towards nonproduction labor. Measuring these shares using *ex ante* rental prices, we see that computers and other high-tech capital explain only 8% of this shift. In both cases, the contribution of computers and other high-tech capital is *less than* the contribution of outsourcing. In contrast, when computers are measured by their share of *investment* (and the high-technology capital share is also included), we see that these variables account for 31% of the shift toward nonproduction labor, which *exceeds* the contribution of outsourcing. Thus, whether outsourcing is more or less important than computers depends on whether the latter are measured as a share of the capital stock, or as a share of investment. Regardless of the specification, however, it is fair to conclude that *both* outsourcing and expenditure on computers and other high-technology capital are important explanations of the shift towards nonproduction labor in the United States, with their exact magnitudes depending on how they are measured.

A specification like (4.18) has also been used to investigate the demand shift towards nonproduction labor in various other countries. Following its liberalization of foreign investment and trade in the 1980s, Mexico experienced an increase in the relative wage of skilled labor (Hanson and Harrison 1999). In the period following reform, foreign direct investment (FDI) in Mexico was concentrated in foreign assembly plants, known as *maquiladoras*, most of which are located in Mexican states along the U.S. border. These assembly plants are created, in most cases, by U.S. firms outsourcing unskilled-labor-intensive production activities to Mexico. Feenstra and Hanson (1997) find that the shift in Mexican manufacturing towards foreign assembly plants over 1975–88 can account for 45% of the increase in the country's nonproduction wage share. Evidence supporting the link between outsourcing or import penetration and wages shares or relative employment is also available for Austria (Dell'mour et al. 2000), Germany (Geishecker 2002), Hong Kong (Hsieh and Woo 1999), Japan (Head and Ries 2002) and the United Kingdom (Anderton and Brenton 1999; Görg, Hijzen, and Cline 2001).

In the specification (4.18), outsourcing changes the relative wage by shifting out the relative demand for skilled labor. An alternative view is that international trade changes factor prices by flattening the labor demand curves, making them more elastic. Leamer (1998) presents an extreme version of this story, in which the transition of an economy from autarky to trade transforms an economy's labor demand curve from being downward sloping to being horizontal, at least over segments that correspond to diversified production.[19] Extending this logic, Rodrik (1997) identifies several mechanism through which greater economic integration between countries may make labor demand curves flatter. In one of the few attempts to test this hypothesis, Slaughter (2001) estimates the own-price elasticity of labor demand for production and nonproduction workers in two-digit U.S. manufacturing industries over the period 1960–91. Over the entire sample, demand became more elastic for production labor, but not for nonproduction labor. The sectors with the largest increase in elasticities were food and tobacco, apparel and textiles, wood and paper, and primary and fabricated metals, which include some of the least skill-intensive manufacturing industries. The demand for production labor became more elastic in industries with more outsourcing, more investment in computers, and more investment in high-tech capital overall. These results are robust to controls for industry-fixed effects but not time-fixed effects, suggesting that changes in labor demand elasticities are dominated by a time trend.

Estimating the Zero-Profit Conditions

The second empirical technique we will discuss assumes that both types of labor, as well as capital, are being optimally chosen. So we abandon the "short run" cost function in (4.15), and instead use the more familiar long-run cost function for the industry:

$$C_n(w_n, q_n, r_n, Y_n, p/p_n) \equiv \min_{L_n, H_n, K_n} w_n L_n + q_n H_n + r_n K_n,$$

$$\text{subject to (4.14).} \tag{4.19}$$

Notice that in (4.19) we have allowed the factor prices w_n, q_n, and r_n to *differ* across the industries $n = 1, \ldots, N$. This reflects the empirical fact that factor prices, and wages in particular, do differ across industries (Krueger and Summers 1988), and will turn out to be important. As before, the relative price of traded inputs p/p_n enters this cost function because it also appears in the revenue function (4.14); we will replace this by the vector z_n, which includes other structural variables.

---

[19] See problem 4.1.

Since the revenue function (4.14) is linearly homogeneous in inputs, then we can rewrite the cost function in (4.19) as

$$C_n(w_n, q_n, r_n, Y_n, z_n) = Y_n c_n(w_n, q_n, r_n, z_n), \qquad (4.20)$$

where $c_n(w_n, q_n, r_n, z_n)$ denotes the *unit-cost* function. The zero-profit conditions in the industries are therefore expressed as

$$p_n = c_n(w_n, q_n, r_n, z_n), \qquad n = 1, \ldots, N. \qquad (4.21)$$

Throughout this book, we have examined how changes in product prices affect factor prices. Now, however, the presence of the structural variables z_n means that the changes in prices reflect more than just changes in factor prices. Indeed, taking the difference between the log change in factor and product prices, we can define *total factor productivity* as

$$\text{TFP}_n \equiv (\theta_{nL}\Delta\ln w_n + \theta_{nH}\Delta\ln q_n + \theta_{nK}\Delta\ln r_n) - \Delta\ln p_n, \quad (4.22)$$

where the cost-shares of the three factors sum to unity, $\theta_{nL} + \theta_{nH} + \theta_{nK} = 1$, and Δ denotes the first difference. Productivity improvements mean that factor prices rise more than product prices, so that (4.22) is positive. Note that this is the "dual" definition of productivity, and empirically it is very close to the "primal" definition, which is the growth in output minus the weighted average of the growth in inputs.[20]

Shuffling the terms in (4.22) slightly, we obtain the equation

$$\Delta\ln p_n = -\text{TFP}_n + \theta_{nL}\Delta\ln w_n + \theta_{nH}\Delta\ln q_n + \theta_{nK}\Delta\ln r_n, \quad (4.23)$$
$$n = 1, \ldots, N.$$

We consider estimating (4.23) as a linear regression across industries, where the *data* are the change in log prices, total factor productivity, and the factor cost-shares θ_{nj}, while the change in factor prices are *estimated* as regression coefficients. That is, we estimate the *implied* change in factor prices β_L, β_H, and β_K from the regression

$$\Delta\ln p_n = -\text{TFP}_n + \theta_{nL}\beta_L + \theta_{nH}\beta_H + \theta_{nK}\beta_K + \varepsilon_n, \quad (4.24)$$
$$n = 1, \ldots, N,$$

where ε_n is an error term, specified more fully below. We interpret the co-efficients β_L, β_H, and β_K as the change in factor prices that are "mandated by" the change in product prices, which is the dependent variable in (4.24). We hope to find that the estimate factor prices changes β_L, β_H, and

---

[20] That is, the primal definition of productivity is $\text{TFP}_n \equiv \Delta\ln Y_n - (\theta_{nL}\Delta\ln L_n + \theta_{nH}\Delta\ln H_n + \theta_{nK}\Delta\ln K_n)$. With the log change in quantities or prices measured between two years, we should construct the factor cost shares as the *average* of the cost shares in the two years. This formulation is called the Törnqvist index of productivity and will be discussed further in chapter 10 and in Appendix A.

β_K from this regression are quite close to their actual changes, and if so, we can conclude that a Stolper-Samuelson linkage between product and factor prices works empirically. Baldwin and Hilton (1984) were among the first to estimate this price regression, and there are many recent applications of it (Baldwin and Cain 2000; Slaughter 2000), as discussed below.

Estimates of (4.24) for 447 U.S. manufacturing industries, over 1979–90, are provided in Table 4.5. The dependent variable is the log change in the industry output price over the period, and we use the primal measure of TFP. The other independent variables are the average cost-shares for production labor, nonproduction labor, and capital; the materials cost share times the log change in materials prices; and the energy cost share times the log change in energy prices. Note that we do not attempt to estimate the change in materials prices and energy prices, but simply include these cost shares times their prices as controls.

In columns (1) and (2), we constrain the coefficients on the materials share times the materials price, and the energy share times the energy price, to be unity. This approximates the specification in Leamer 1998. In column (1), the coefficients on the labor shares imply a *decrease* in the nonproduction/production relative wage of 2.3% – 3.1% = −0.8% per year, which is consistent with the results in Leamer 1998. But in reality, the nonproduction-production wage gap in the United States *rose* by 0.7% per year, or about seven-tenths of one percent.[21] So the regression in column (1) does *not reproduce at all* the actual factor prices changes in the United States! In column (2), we follow Sachs and Shatz (1994) and drop the computer industry (SIC 3573), which *reverses* the predicted change in wage inequality. Now nonproduction wages are mandated to rise by 1.5% per year *more* than production wages. In column (3), we approximate Krueger's (1997) specification by dropping TFP as a regressor, while estimating coefficients on materials and energy. There is again a mandated *rise* in the nonproduction-production wage gap, but one that is *much larger* than the actual increase in relative wages.

The estimates in Table 4.5 are troubling because they show that slight changes in the data, such as dropping the computer industry, have dramatic effects on the results. While it is true that the computer industry is an outlier, the sensitivity of the results to the specification suggests that something more basic is going on. To address this, let us ask, why do the estimates of β_L, β_H, and β_K from regression (4.24) differ at all from the *actual average* change in manufacturing wages, which we denote by

---

[21] After being weighted by each industry's share of manufacturing shipments, the average nominal wages of nonproduction workers rose by 5.4% per year over 1979–90, and the nominal wages of production workers rose by 4.7% per year. The difference between these, 0.7%, is the increasing "wage gap" that needs to be explained.

TABLE 4.5
Log Change in Industry Price, 1979–90, as Dependent Variable

	(1)	(2)	(3)	(4)	(5)
Effective TFP				−1.0	−1.0
				(0.01)	(0.001)
TFP	−1.0	−0.8			
	(0.1)	(0.1)			
Production labor	3.1	2.4	3.6	4.7	4.7
cost share	(1.2)	(1.2)	(1.9)	(0.02)	(0.01)
Nonproduction labor	2.3	4.1	6.2	5.5	5.4
cost share	(1.4)	(1.7)	(4.0)	(0.02)	(0.03)
Capital cost share	7.9	8.1	9.5	4.0	4.0
	(0.8)	(0.9)	(2.2)	(0.01)	(0.02)
Materials cost share	1.0[a]	1.0[a]	1.2	1.0[a]	1.0
times change in			(0.3)		(0.002)
materials price					
Energy cost share	1.0[a]	1.0[a]	−0.9	1.0[a]	1.0
times change in			(0.9)		(0.01)
energy price					
Constant	−0.7	−0.83	−1.9		0.01
	(0.3)	(0.29)	(0.9)		(0.005)
R^2	0.90	0.81	0.93	0.99	0.99
N	447	446	446	447	447

Source: Feenstra and Hanson 1999, and empirical exercise 4.3.
Note: Standard errors are in parentheses. All regressions omit three industries with missing data on materials purchases or prices (SIC 2067, 2794, 3483) and are weighted by the
industry share of total manufacturing shipments, averaged over the first and last periods. In
columns (1)–(3) and (5), the dependent variable is the log change in the gross industry
price, and the factor cost shares sum to one across all factors. The materials cost share is multiplied by the log change in the materials price; the energy cost share is treated similarly. In
column (4), the dependent variable is the log change in the industry value-added price, and
factor cost shares sum to one across primary factors. Column (1) uses primal TFP as a regressor; column (2) drops the computer industry (SIC 3573) from the sample; column (3)
also drops TFP as a regressor; and column (5) uses effective TFP as a regressor, where effective TFP equals primal TFP minus the change in wage differentials.
[a] Constrained at unity.

$\overline{\Delta \ln w}$, $\overline{\Delta \ln q}$, and $\overline{\Delta \ln r}$? The overbar indicates that we are averaging the
change in factor prices over all manufacturing industries. By just comparing
(4.23) and (4.24), it seems that there should be some close connection
between the estimates β_L, β_H, and β_K and these average actual factor price
changes, but we need to uncover what this connection is.

To find this connection, let us make the transition from (4.23) to an estimating equation more carefully. First, notice that we can rewrite (4.23) as

$$\Delta \ln p_n = -\text{TFP}_n + \theta_{nL} \overline{\Delta \ln w} + \theta_{nH} \overline{\Delta \ln q} + \theta_{nK} \overline{\Delta \ln r} + \varepsilon_n, \quad (4.25)$$

where

$$\varepsilon_n \equiv \theta_{nL}(\Delta \ln w_n - \overline{\Delta \ln w}) + \theta_{nH}(\Delta \ln q_n - \overline{\Delta \ln q}) \quad (4.26)$$
$$+ \theta_{nK}(\Delta \ln r_n - \overline{\Delta \ln r}).$$

That is, we replace the *industry* wage changes on the right of (4.23) by the *average* wage changes, and incorporate the difference between these two into an error term. In economic terms, ε_n reflects interindustry wage differentials: that is, the difference between wages paid in each industry and the manufacturing average. It is well known that these wage differentials vary systematically across industries, with capital-intensive industries paying higher wages.

Now that we have derived the regression equation more carefully, it is clear that it has an error term ε_n. Recognizing this, we can answer the question of whether the estimates from the equation will match the *actual* factor price changes or not: the estimates of β_L, β_H, and β_K obtained from (4.24) will be unbiased estimates of the *average actual* factor price changes in (4.25) if and only if the error term ε_n shown in (4.26) is *uncorrelated* with the cost shares θ_{nL}, θ_{nH}, and θ_{nK}. This result follows directly from the properties of ordinary least squares, whereby the independent variables need to be *uncorrelated* with the error term to obtain unbiased estimates. But this property is unlikely to be true in our data. Industries such as computers have both a high share of nonproduction labor (e.g., engineers), and probably the fastest-growing industry wage differential, as these workers have had very rapid wage gains. This suggests that the error term ε_n is correlated with the nonproduction labor cost share. Indeed, this correlation likely explains why the *estimated* change in nonproduction wages is *lower* in column (1) of Table 4.5, which includes the computer industry, than in column (2) or (3), which exclude this industry.

To correct this problem, we can simply include the error term ε_n as an additional regressor in the equation, reflecting the change in interindustry wage differentials. It is convenient to combine ε_n with TFP_n, obtaining a measure of "effective" TFP:

$$\text{ETFP}_n \equiv \text{TFP}_n - \varepsilon_n \quad (4.27)$$
$$= (\theta_{nL} \overline{\Delta \ln w} + \theta_{nH} \overline{\Delta \ln q} + \theta_{nK} \overline{\Delta \ln r}) - \Delta \ln p_n.$$

Thus, this measure of effective productivity shows how the *average manufacturing factor price changes*, weighted using the cost share in each industry, differ from the change in product price of that industry. Making use of (4.27), the regression in (4.24) is written once again as

$$\Delta \ln p_n = -\text{ETFP}_n + \theta_{nL}\beta_L + \theta_{nH}\beta_H + \theta_{nK}\beta_K, \qquad (4.28)$$
$$n = 1, \dots, N.$$

Now there is no error term in this regression, so it ought to provide a perfect fit when estimated. This will not be exactly true in our data, since we are using the primal rather than the dual measure of TFP to construct effective TFP in (4.28). These priors are confirmed in columns (4) and (5) of table 4.5. In column (4), we constrain the coefficients on the materials and energy shares to equal unity, while in column (5), we allow these coefficients to differ from unity. In either specification, the coefficients on the labor and capital shares are extremely close to the actual average annual percentage changes in factor prices, which are 4.7% for production labor, 5.4% for nonproduction labor, and 4.0% for capital. Thus, when we properly estimate (4.28), we end up with an identity!

Summarizing our results so far, we started with the goal of estimating the zero-profit conditions to obtain "mandated" changes in factor prices that are consistent with the change in product prices. A number of researchers have estimated an equation like (4.23), without much attention to the error term in this regression. When we carefully derive the error term, as in (4.26), we then realize that it is likely correlated with the factor cost shares that are the independent variables. To correct for this we can include the error term as data, by incorporating it into "effective" total factor productivity. But now we encounter another problem: this gives essentially a perfect fit, just reproducing the *actual* change in factor prices. That means the regression does not provide us with any new information! This discouraging finding suggests that a new approach is needed.

To make further progress, Feenstra and Hanson (1999) propose a two-step estimation procedure. In the first step, we combine the variables $\Delta \ln p_n + \text{ETFP}_n$, which appear in (4.28), and regress these on the structural variables z_n. Supposing that there are only two structural variables, z_{1n} and z_{2n}, we therefore run the regression

$$\Delta \ln p_n + \text{ETFP}_n = \alpha_0 + \alpha_1 \Delta z_{1n} + \alpha_2 \Delta z_{2n}, \quad n = 1, \dots, N. \qquad (4.29)$$

In the second step, we then use the estimated coefficients $\hat{\alpha}_1$ and $\hat{\alpha}_2$ to construct the dependent variables for the regressions

$$\hat{\alpha}_1 \Delta z_{1n} = \theta_{nL}\beta_{1L} + \theta_{nH}\beta_{1H} + \theta_{nK}\beta_{1K} \qquad (4.30a)$$

and

$$\hat{\alpha}_2 \Delta z_{2n} = \theta_{nL}\beta_{2L} + \theta_{nH}\beta_{2H} + \theta_{nK}\beta_{2K}, \quad n = 1, \dots, N. \qquad (4.30b)$$

That is, we use the estimated coefficients $\hat{\alpha}_1$ and $\hat{\alpha}_2$ times each structural variable as the dependent variables in (4.30), and regress these on the factor cost shares. The coefficients obtained from the second-stage regression, $\beta_{1L}, \beta_{1H}, \beta_{1K}$ and $\beta_{2L}, \beta_{2H}, \beta_{2K}$, are interpreted as *the portion of the total change in factor prices that is explained by each structural variable*. In this way, we are taking the total change in factor prices, and decomposing it into parts that are explained by each structural variable.

In their estimation of (4.29) for U.S. manufacturing industries over the period 1979–90, Feenstra and Hanson (1999) find positive and statistically significant correlations between dependent variable $\Delta \ln p_m + \text{ETFP}_m$ in the first-step regressions, and these structural variables: outsourcing, the computer share of the capital stock, and the computer share of investment. In the second step, these structural variables (times their estimated coefficients) are regressed on the factor cost shares to obtain "mandated changes" in factor prices. The results indicate that *both* outsourcing and capital upgrading contributed to rising wage inequality in the 1980s.

For example, when the share of the capital stock devoted to computers is measured using *ex post* rental prices, outsourcing accounts for 15% of the increase in the relative wage of nonproduction workers, while computers account for 35% of this increase; thus, computers are twice as important as outsourcing. When the computer share of the capital stock is measured using *ex ante* rental prices, outsourcing explains about 25% while computers explain about 20% of the increase in the relative wage. However, when the computer share of *investment* is used, then the contribution of outsourcing falls to about 10%, while the contribution of computers rises so much that it explains the *entire* increase in the relative wage. So as with our results when examining the change in the nonproduction labor *share*, when we now consider the factors influencing the *relative wage*, we find that both outsourcing and computer expenditure are important, with their exact magnitudes depending on how these variables are measured.

Haskel and Slaughter (2001) have also applied the two-stage estimation procedure to data on U.K. manufacturing industries over the period 1960–90. As structural variables they use union density (the share of union workers in industry employment), industry concentration (share of sales by the five largest firms), innovations per industry, import prices, and computerization (share of firms in the industry using computers). They find that TFP growth is higher in industries with more innovations, lower initial union density, lower initial sales concentration, and larger reductions in import prices (but is unrelated with computerization). Product price changes are lower in industries with smaller changes in import prices. During the 1980s, when U.K. wage inequality rose, the structural variable that appears to have contributed most to the increase in the skilled-unskilled wage gap is industry innovation. The contribution of import prices is comparatively small. This contrasts with research (Anderton and Brenton 1999) showing that rising imports over 1970–83 is a significant determinant of the non-production labor *share* in the United Kingdom.

The Role of Nontraded Goods

Our approach above has been to use disaggregate data for U.S. manufacturing, most of which is traded goods. As appealing as this approach may be, it misses the important fact that most of the U.S. economy—as with other industrial countries—is devoted to *nontraded* goods and services. It is highly desirable, therefore, to incorporate the nontraded sector into the estimation. One way to do this is to estimate aggregate GDP or cost functions, distinguishing nontraded and traded goods, as well as different types of labor. This approach has been taken by several authors, as follows.

Tombazos (1999) distinguishes types of labor by identifying industries that are intensive in skilled or unskilled labor, and then forming aggregate wage and employment indexes over each group of industries; these indexes are then used as a proxy for the price and quantity of skilled and unskilled labor. He incorporates skilled labor, unskilled labor, capital, and imports into the estimation of an aggregate cost function for the United States, over 1967–94, with a single aggregate output (including exports). His major conclusion is that a drop in the import price reduces the demand for unskilled labor, but raises the demand for skilled labor in the United States. This is highly consistent with our theoretical model in this chapter. Missing from his analysis, though, is a discussion of how much import prices have fallen, and therefore, how much of the shift towards skilled labor can be explained by this channel of influence.

Further results are obtained by Harrigan and Balaban (1999), Harrigan (2000), and Kumar (2000). Harrigan and Balaban estimate a translog GDP function for the United States over the period 1963–91 using data on four factors (high school dropouts, high school graduates, college graduates, and capital), and four sectors (skill-intensive traded goods, unskilled-intensive traded goods, skill-intensive nontraded goods, and unskilled-intensive nontraded goods). Thus, imports are not explicitly identified. In contrast, Harrigan (2000) has two categories of outputs (skill-intensive and unskilled-intensive final output), and seven factors including imports (oil imports, two other groups of imports, and the three types of labor and capital). It turns out that changes in the import prices have been *quite small* in comparison with other price changes, especially in nontraded goods, so that changes in import prices *are not* an important explanation for changes in wages. We therefore focus below on the results of Harrigan and Balaban, which except for imports are similar to those of Harrigan.

With the estimated coefficients from the translog share equations, Harrigan and Balaban calculate wage elasticities with respect to factor quantities and product prices. They find that the elasticity of each factor price with respect to its own endowment is negative (so the hypothesis of "factor price insensitivity" is rejected). Increasing the supply of capital raises wages for all workers, but these elasticities are rising in education levels, such that a 10% increase in the capital stock increases the college/high school graduate relative wage by about 3.5%, and the college/high school dropout relative wage by about 8%. The wage elasticities of *traded* goods prices are imprecisely estimated, while those for *nontraded* goods are somewhat surprising. Increases in prices of skill-intensive nontraded goods *raises* wages for college graduates and high school dropouts, but *lowers* wages for high school graduates, whereas increases in prices of unskilled-intensive nontraded goods have a large positive effect on high school graduate wages, a moderate positive effect on college wages, and a negative effect on high school dropout wages.

Putting the estimated wage elasticities together with observed changes in factor supplies and product prices, we can decompose the contribution of different variables to the observed change in factor prices. While capital accumulation contributed to an increase in the relative wage of college graduates, this effect was largely offset by increases in the supply of college graduates. The big changes during the latter part of the sample period were an *increase in the relative price of skill-intensive nontraded goods*, such as finance, insurance, and real estate. This had the largest impact on *raising* the college/high school graduate relative wage. Similarly, there was a *decrease in the relative price of unskilled-intensive nontraded goods*, such as wholesale and retail trade, which had the largest impact on *reducing* the relative wage of high school graduates relative to college graduates. In short, the increase in the relative wage of skilled labor, in the 1980s and beyond, is highly correlated with the rise in the price of nontraded goods that use skilled labor, but does not appear to depend on aggregate import prices.

This is a surprising finding, since it seems to suggest that the wage changes have little to do with trade. But Harrigan and Balaban's findings beg the question of whether the change in nontraded prices is caused by the change in wages, or conversely. Using the model of Sachs and Schatz (1998), it is not difficult to construct an example where capital leaves the country, increasing the relative wage of skilled labor, and therefore *raising* the price of skill-intensive nontradables and *lowering* the price of unskilled-intensive nontradables.[22] This story would be consistent with the estimates of Harrigan and Balaban, and supposes that the driving force behind the wage and price changes is international capital flows. We

---

[22] See problem 4.2.

cannot rule out, however, the idea that the nontradables prices are changing due to some other reason (e.g., rising incomes and demand leading to an increase in the price of skill-intensive nontradables), which is therefore the proximate cause of the change in wages.[23] As Harrigan (2000, 186) puts it: "To my knowledge, there are no scholarly studies of relative price determination in the United States that might shed light on the causes of the changes shown . . . and until we understand the cause of these price changes we cannot rule out an important role for import competition."

Conclusions

The model of intermediates inputs we have investigated has some similarities to the conventional Heckscher-Ohlin framework, but rather than focusing on *industries* of various skill intensities, we instead suppose that there are *activities within each industry* that vary in their factor intensities. These activities are modeled as intermediate inputs that are traded between countries and combined into some final product. With this modification from the conventional Heckscher-Ohlin framework, we have found that we can easily generate shifts in relative demand for skilled labor *within* an industry. We have further argued that a drop in the price of imported intermediates has effects that are *observationally equivalent* to the effect of skilled-biased technological change. The relative importance of trade versus technological change must be assessed on empirical grounds.

While models of production sharing are starting to take hold within international trade, this concept is already used in economic sociology (Gereffi and Korzeniewicz 1994; Kenney and Florida 1994), geography (Dicken et al. 2001; Yeung 2001) and other social sciences, where production sharing is referred to by the more general name *commodity chains*. A commodity chain consists of the sequence of activities involved in the manufacture of a product, from initial development through to production, marketing, and sales, especially as these activities cross international boundaries. In these disciplines, commodity chains are seen as an integral part of the development process for countries that are still industrializing. We have taken a less grand view, and have simply argued that production sharing has a substantial impact on wages.

Using these theoretical insights, we described the labor demand regression arising from a model where capital is fixed in the short run, while skilled and unskilled labor are chosen optimally. Additional terms are included in the demand regressions reflecting trade in intermediate inputs (outsourcing) as well as computer use. We find that both of these variables

---

[23] Blum (2003), for example, argues that capital accumulation in nontradables was a principal source of rising wage inequality during the 1980s and early 1990s.

can explain a portion of the shift towards skilled labor in the United States during the 1980s, with the exact contribution of each being sensitive to how computer use is measured (i.e., as a share of the capital stock, or as a share of new investment).

We also revisited the link between changes in product prices and factor prices. Contrary to the suggestion of Lawrence and Slaughter (1993), we argued that the movements in product prices (combined with growth in productivity) are *fully consistent* with the increase in the relative wage of skilled labor in the United States. Indeed, the zero-profit conditions ensure that, as an identity, the change in relative wages must be explained by product prices and productivity. The challenge for researchers is to uncover what structural factors explain the underlying movement in prices and productivity: are these changes due to skill-biased technological upgrades, or due to trade in intermediate inputs? We discussed a "two stage" estimation procedure due to Feenstra and Hanson (1999) that allows this to be determined. As with the labor demand regressions, we find that both outsourcing and computer use can account for a portion of the increase in the relative wage of skilled workers, with the exact contribution of each being quite sensitive to how computer use is measured.

Finally, we concluded this chapter with a discussion of nontraded goods. Harrigan and Balaban (1999), Harrigan (2000), and Kumar (2000) have argued that the variables *most highly* correlated with the movement in wages over the 1980s and 1990s are neither trade prices nor outsourcing nor high-technology capital, but rather, a sharp increase in the price of skill-intensive nontraded goods in the United States as well as a decrease in the price of unskilled-intensive nontradables. This finding poses a challenge to those who believe that either trade or technology is responsible for the change in wages and will no doubt be an important area for further research (see Blum 2003, for example).

Problems

4.1 In this question we will examine the aggregate demand curve for labor that arises in autarky, and under free trade. Make all the usual assumptions of the two-by-two economy.

(a) First consider the autarky economy, where there is a single representative consumer in the country, and the prices for the goods are determined by supply = demand. Suppose that the endowment of labor increases. Then verbally trace through the effects on the outputs of the goods, relative prices of the goods, and then factor prices. Graph the relationship between the labor endowment and the real wage.

(b) Now consider the same economy but with free trade and *fixed* world prices. If there is an increase in the labor endowment, what is the effect on the real wage? Graph this relationship.

(c) Reconsider your answer to part (b), supposing that the labor endowment grows so large that the country moves outside its cone of diversification. How will further increases in the labor endowment affect the real wage? Add this to your graph.

4.2 Consider an economy with two industries and three factors: unskilled labor (L), skilled labor (H), and capital (K).

(a) Suppose that industry 1 has a higher cost share of unskilled labor and also of capital (think of factory production). Suppose further than the product prices are *constant*, but that the rental on capital *goes up* (perhaps because capital is leaving the country). In this case, can we definitely predict what happens to the *relative wage* of unskilled labor?

(b) Now add a nontraded good, which uses only skilled and unskilled labor. What is the impact of the increase in the rental on capital, and the change in wages, on the price of the nontraded good? Contrast a high-skill-intensive versus low-skill-intensive nontraded good.

Empirical Exercises

4.1 Download the NBER productivity dataset at http://www.nber.org/nberces/nbprod96.htm, compute the relative wage and relative employment for 1958–96, and reconstruct Figures 4.1 and 4.2. Note: Given this data, you need to first compute the wage rates in production and nonproduction sectors using the following formula:

Production worker wage rate

$$= \frac{\sum_i \text{production worker wage bill}_i}{\sum_i \text{production workers}_i},$$

Nonproduction worker wage rate

$$= \frac{\sum_i \text{Nonproduction worker wage bill}}{\sum_i \text{Nonproduction workers}_i}$$

$$= \frac{\sum_i (\text{total pay roll}_i - \text{production worker wage bill}_i)}{\sum_i (\text{total employment}_i - \text{production workers}_i)},$$

where i = industry.

4.2   Store the files for this chapter in the directory c:\Empirical_Exercise\ Chapter_4\. Run the program "Problem_4_2.do" to reproduce the regressions in Table 4.4 (which is simplified from Table III in Feenstra and Hanson 1999). Then answer the following: what weights are used in these regressions, and how are the results affected if these weights are not used?

4.3   Run the STATA program "Problem_4_3a.do" to reproduce the regressions in Table 4.5 (i.e., Table I in Feenstra and Hanson 1999). Then run "Problem_4_3b.do" to perform the two-step regression, Table IV and Table V in Feenstra and Hanson 1999. Note that Table V is obtained using the coefficients in the first column of Table IV.

Chapter 5

Increasing Returns and the Gravity Equation

IN THIS CHAPTER, we make a significant departure from earlier trade models by allowing for increasing returns to scale. The idea that increasing returns might be a reason for trade between countries was well recognized by Bertil Ohlin (1933) and also Frank Graham (1923), and has been the motivation for policy actions.[1] In Canada, for example, arguments were made the 1960s to the effect that Canadian firms would benefit from unrestricted access to the U.S. market. It was believed that the Canadian market was too small to allow manufacturing industries to operate at a minimum efficient scale, and that with access to the U.S. market, firms could move down their average costs curves, which is a gain in efficiency.[2] Indeed, this was a principal reason that Canada entered into a free-trade agreement with the United States in 1989: to give its firms free access to the large American market. As promising as this line of argument is, however, it contains a puzzle: as firms in Canada and the United States move down their average cost curves due to access to the other market, surely not *all firms* can expand output that much, since who would buy it? Thus, an expansion by some firms seems to suggest that others will need to exit the market entirely. So we need a model to sort out these various effects.

The model that is most suited to this purpose is one of *monopolistic competition*: a market with a large number of firms, each producing a unique variety of a differentiated product, with freedom of entry and exit. This model dates back to Edward Chamberlin (1936) and Joan Robinson (1933), who presented graphical analyses. The widespread use of this model had to wait for a mathematical formulation, however, which was achieved by Lancaster (1975, 1979), Spence (1976), and Dixit and Stiglitz (1977). Lancaster presented a model in which consumers differed in their "ideal variety" of a differentiated good. In constrast, Spence and Dixit and Stiglitz had a single representative consumer demanding many varieties of the differentiated

[1] Graham (1923) argued that trade due to increasing returns to scale might be an argument for protection; that is, one country could lose from trade. Ethier (1982a) analyzed a model of this sort, relying on increasing returns that are *external* to the firm. In this chapter we will focus exclusively on increasing returns that are internal to the firm.

[2] See, for example, Eastman and Stykolt 1967.

good, in what is called the "love of variety" approach. Lancaster (1980) and Helpman (1981) applied the "ideal variety" approach to international trade, while Krugman (1979, 1980, 1981) applied the "love of variety" approach due to Dixit and Stiglitz. The comprehensive treatment by Helpman and Krugman (1985) shows that these two approaches lead to very similar results, so we will use the simpler "love of variety" approach. We begin by describing the model of Krugman (1979).

Monopolistic Competition Model

We will suppose that there are $i = 1, \ldots, N$ product varieties, where the number N will be endogenously determined. There is a fixed number L of consumers, each of whom receives the following utility from consuming c_i of each variety:

$$U = \sum_{i=1}^{N} v(c_i), \quad v' > 0, \ v'' < 0. \tag{5.1}$$

Notice that this utility function is *symmetric* over the product varieties; that is, the same function $v(c_i)$ applies to the consumption of each. Each consumer receives labor income of w, so the consumer's budget constraint is $w = \sum_{i=1}^{N} p_i c_i$. They choose consumption c_i of each variety to maximize utility in (5.1), subject to this budget constraint. The first-order conditions for this problem are

$$v'(c_i) = \lambda p_i, \quad i = 1, \ldots, N, \tag{5.2}$$

where λ is the Lagrange multiplier (i.e., the marginal utility of income).

The effect of a change in price on consumption can be derived by totally differentiating the system of equations in (5.2), together with the budget constraint. Normally, such a change in price would affect λ. However, it can be argued that if the number of varieties is sufficiently large, so that the budget share of each of them is small, then we can ignore the impact of a change in one price on λ. In that case, the effect of a change in price is simply

$$v'' dc_i = dp_i \lambda \Rightarrow \frac{dc_i}{dp_i} = \frac{\lambda}{v''} < 0. \tag{5.3}$$

Using (5.2) and (5.3), we define the elasticity of demand for variety i as

$$\eta_i = -\frac{dc_i}{dp_i} \frac{p_i}{c_i} = -\left(\frac{v'}{c_i v''}\right) > 0. \tag{5.4}$$

While the assumptions we have made on v (increasing and concave) ensure that the elasticity is positive, we do not in general know whether it is

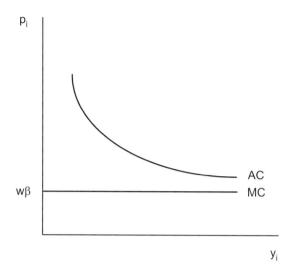

Figure 5.1

increasing or decreasing in c_i. This will turn out to be quite important, and we shall *assume* that $d\eta_i/dc_i < 0$, so that as we move up a demand curve (consumption falling), the elasticity rises. The reader should verify that this assumption holds for a linear demand curve, and more generally, for any demand curve that is "less convex" than a constant-elasticity curve.

On the production side, labor is the only resource, and each firm requires the following labor to produce output of y_i:

$$L_i = \alpha + \beta y_i,$$
(5.5)

where α is the fixed labor input needed for production and β is the marginal labor input. Given the equilibrium wage w, it follows that average costs for the firms are $AC_i = wL_i/y_i = w\alpha/y_i + w\beta$, while marginal costs are simply $w\beta$. These are both graphed in Figure 5.1.

Monopolistic competition has two key equilibrium conditions for firms. First, each firm maximizes its own profits, requiring that marginal revenue equal marginal cost ($MR = MC$). Second, there is free entry whenever economic profits are positive, so in the long-run equilibrium we must have zero profits, or price equal to average cost ($P = AC$). In addition to these, we will add the requirement that the equilibrium is "symmetric," meaning that prices and quantities are identical across varieties. Dropping the subscript i, we therefore have the equilibrium conditions

$$MR = MC: \quad p\left(1 - \frac{1}{\eta}\right) = w\beta, \quad \text{or} \quad \frac{p}{w} = \beta\left(\frac{\eta}{\eta - 1}\right);$$
(5.6)

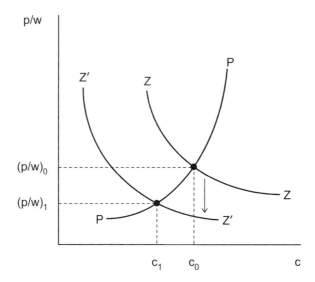

Figure 5.2

$$P = AC: \qquad p = \left(\frac{w\alpha}{y}\right) + w\beta \ \text{ or } \ \frac{p}{w} = \left(\frac{\alpha}{Lc}\right) + \beta. \qquad (5.7)$$

Notice that in (5.7), we have replaced supply of each good, y, by the demand for each good, Lc. Equations (5.6) and (5.7) form two equations to solve for the two unknowns, (p/w) and c. The first of these equations is graphed as the line PP in Figure 5.2. Our assumption that $d\eta_i/dc_i < 0$ ensures that the PP curve is *upward sloping*. Turning to equation (5.7), this is graphed as the *downward sloping* line ZZ in Figure 5.2, which is simply the firm's average cost curve. The intersection of these two curves determines the equilibrium values of (p/w) and c. Then to determine the equilibrium number of product N, we make use of full employment in the economy, which is stated as

$$L = \sum_{i=1}^{N} L_i = \sum_{i=1}^{N} (\alpha + \beta y_i) = N(\alpha + \beta y) = N(\alpha + \beta Lc), \qquad (5.8)$$

from which it follows that

$$N = \frac{1}{[(\alpha/L) + \beta c]}. \qquad (5.9)$$

The equilibrium value of c therefore determines the number of products N.

So far, we have represented the equilibrium for a single economy. But the effects of trade are easily introduced. For example, suppose that two countries of identical size move from autarky to free trade. Notice that because the economies are identical, in the Heckscher-Ohlin model there would be absolutely no reason for trade between them. But in the monopolistic competition model, there will be a rationale for trade: because firms produce differentiated products, they will begin to export to the other country, and at the same time, face competition from firms abroad. This increase in the number of competitors can be expected to lower the equilibrium price. This is exactly what happens, as can be confirmed from the equilibrium conditions, as follows.

Having the two identical countries trading is just like doubling the population L. This has no impact on the PP curve (since L does not appear in (5.6)), but it does shift the ZZ curve *down* (as can be seen from (5.7)). Therefore, the equilibrium consumption of each variety *falls*, from c_0 to c_1, while the real wage *rises*, from $(w/p)_0$ to $(w/p)_1$. Consumption falls because individuals are spreading their expenditures over more product varieties, and this raises the elasticity of demand, reducing the equilibrium prices and therefore raising real wages. This is a source of gain for consumers. But there is also a second source of gain from trade, because with the rise in L and fall in c, it can be verified from (5.9) that total product variety *increases*. That is, the sum of varieties from both countries under free trade exceeds the number in any single country before trade.

But notice that the *number of varieties produced in each country* necessarily *falls* with the opening of trade. This can be seen by noting that the fall in (p/w), as firms move down their average cost curve, necessarily implies that output y increases. This means that any firm that produces both in autarky and under free trade will be selling more with trade. But the full-employment condition for *each* economy is $L = N(\alpha + \beta y)$, where now L is fixed. So the increase in y, as firms exploit economies of scale, necessarily implies a *reduction in the number of firms in each country*. This resolves the puzzle raised at the beginning of the chapter: opening trade between countries indeed implies that firms must exit in each, while the remaining firms expand their output and take advantage of scale economies.

Evidence from the Canada-U.S. Free Trade Agreement

To summarize, Krugman's model contains two predictions concerning the impact of trade on the productivity of firms: the *scale* effect, as surviving firms expand their outputs, and the *selection* effect, as some firms are forced to exit. Which one of these effects is most important in practice? This is a question of some importance since the dislocation of workers caused by the bankruptcy of firms is bound to cause unemployment. This was certainly true in Canada after it entered into the free-trade agreement with the United States on January 1, 1989, because at the same time, Canada also had a tight monetary policy that led to further job loss. The early computable general equilibrium model of Harris (1984) and Cox and Harris (1985, 1986), done *before* the 1989 agreement, presumed substantial scale economies based on engineering estimates for various industries, and predicted very high efficiency gains for Canada. These estimates were influential in Canadian policy circles as the merits of the agreement with the United States were being debated. With more than a decade since the Canada-U.S. FTA began there are now several studies we can look to that quantify the scale versus selection effect empirically.

The scale effect—that surviving firms will expand their scale of production following trade liberalization—has unfortunately not been borne out empirically. Head and Ries (1999) use plant-level data for a sample of 230 Canadian industries over 1988–94 to examine the impact on plant scale in the six years following the free-trade agreement with the United States. They find that the tariff reductions in the United States increased plant scale in Canada by some 10% on average, but this was largely offset by a 8.5% *reduction* in plant scale due to the reductions in Canadian tariffs. On net, therefore, the free-trade agreement had only a small impact on scale. This type of evidence is also found from tariff reductions in a wide range of developing countries, where the average scale of firms in import-competing industries either shrank following liberalization, or expanded only slightly.[3] The only silver lining to this result is that it appears the extent of economies of scale is not very great in the first place, so that any reduction in scale does not really cause higher costs. In addition, evidence from developing countries shows that the markup of price over marginal costs is indeed reduced following tariff reductions, so consumers gain in that respect.[4]

Turning to the selection effect, this is another avenue through which productivity in an industry can change following liberalization. In particular, if the *least efficient* firms are the ones to exit, then *average industry productivity* will rise. Note that this is outside the framework of the original Krugman model, which makes the "symmetry" assumption that all firms are of the same size and efficiency (it follows that the exit of some would not automatically change average productivity). This assumption was made for analytical convenience, but contradicts the empirical fact

---

[3] Tybout and Westbrook (1995) obtain this result for liberalization in Mexico during 1984–90, whereas Tybout, de Melo, and Corbo (1991) find evidence of small increases in scale following liberalization in Chile.

[4] We will discuss the empirical link between tariffs and markups in chapter 10.

that every industry has a very wide range of firms operating within it. Indeed, it is only recently that trade theory has caught up with this empirical fact, and there are now several models that allow for a range of firms with differing productivities, due to Yeaple (2003) and Melitz (2003), that can predict the effects of tariff reductions. In these models, the gains from the Canada-U.S. free-trade area would come not from scale effects, but rather from selection effects, whereby the least efficient firms exit after liberalization.

The empirical evidence on this comes from Trefler (2001), which is the first attempt to comprehensively assess the impact of this agreement on productivity within Canada. Trefler (2001, abstract) concludes that

> For industries subject to large tariff cuts (these are typically "low-end" manufacturing industries), the short-run costs included a 15% decline in employment and about a 10% decline in both output and the number of plants. Balanced against these large short-run adjustment costs were long-run labour productivity gains of 17% or a spectacular 2.0% per year. Although good capital stock and plant-level data are lacking, an attempt is made to identify the sources of FTA-induced labour productivity growth. Surprisingly, this growth is not due to rising output per plant, increased investment, or market share shifts to high-productivity plants. Instead, half of the 17% labour productivity growth appears due to favourable plant turnover (entry and exit) and rising technical efficiency.

Thus, productivity in Canada was increased due to free trade with the United States from the selection effect, not the scale effect.

The finding that the scale of Canadian firms did not change much (on net) following the FTA can be explained from several models, as discussed by Head and Ries (1999, 2001). We note here one particularly simple theoretical result: if the elasticity of demand for product varieties is *constant*, then firm scale will not change at all due to tariffs or trade liberalization. A utility function that leads to this case is the constant elasticity of substitution (CES) function:

$$U = \sum_{i=1}^{N} c_i^{(\sigma-1)/\sigma}, \tag{5.10}$$

The elasticity of substitution between products is equal to $\sigma > 1$, which also equals the elasticity of demand η when N is large.[5] This implies that the markup of prices over marginal costs is fixed, $p/(\beta w) = [\sigma/(\sigma - 1)]$.

---

[5] In problem 5.2 you are asked to derive the elasticity of demand and investigate other properties of the utility function (5.10).

Substituting this optimal price into the expression for profits of the firm, we obtain

$$\pi = py - w(\alpha + \beta y) = w\left[\left(\frac{\beta y}{\sigma - 1}\right) - \alpha\right]. \tag{5.11}$$

In order to have zero profits in equilibrium, the output of firms is therefore *fixed* at

$$\bar{y} = (\sigma - 1)\alpha/\beta. \tag{5.12}$$

So there is no scale effect in a model using (5.10), though trade will still affect the product variety available to consumers. The product variety produced in *each country* is readily solved from (5.12) and the full-employment condition (5.8), obtaining $N = L/(\alpha + \beta\bar{y})$. Thus, the number of varieties *produced* does not change due to trade in this CES model, so there is no selection effect either, but the number of varieties *consumed* will increase due to those available from imports.[6]

The key advantage of using the CES functional form is that it is *homothetic*, whereas this will not hold for any other choice of $v(c_i)$ in (5.1). For this reason the CES functional form is commonly used in the monopolistic competition literature despite its special properties, and we shall also make use of it later in the chapter.[7]

The Gravity Equation

In the monopolistic competition model, each country will be exporting varieties of the differentiated product to another. While firms in different countries may produce the same product varieties in autarky, we assume they can costlessly leave one variety and produce another, so that with trade it is profit maximizing to produce *different* varieties. In other words, the countries are completely specialized in different product varieties. Trade in these product varieties is referred to as *intraindustry trade*. Notice that complete specialization and intraindustry trade does not occur in the two-sector Heckscher-Ohlin model: countries may be producing in the same industries, but they either export or import in each industry—not both. In the Heckscher-Ohlin model with a *continuum* of goods, however, we do have complete specialization in different products when factor prices are unequal, as described in chapter 3. The common feature of the monopolistic competition model and the HO model with a continuum of

---

[6] If firms are heterogeneous, as in the model of Melitz (2002) and Yeaple (2002), then a selection effect will reappear even using CES preferences.

[7] In problem 5.4, we provide an example of an *indirect* utility function that is still homothetic, but does not require constant price elasticities of demand.

goods is that they both have *many more goods than factors*: that is what allows for complete specialization in different product varieties across countries. In this case, it turns out that trade patterns can be described by a remarkably simple equation called the "gravity equation."

In its simplest form, the gravity equation states that the bilateral trade between two countries is directly proportional to the product of the countries' GDPs. Thus, larger countries will tend to trade more with each other, and countries that are more *similar* in their relative sizes will also trade more. This equation performs extremely well empirically, as has been known since the original work of Tinbergen (1962). Our goal in this section is to derive this simple version of the gravity equation, under the assumption of free trade, so that *all countries have identical prices*. In later sections, we will loosen this assumption and allow for differing prices due to trade barriers between countries, which turns out to be quite important.

To the assumption that countries are specialized in different varieties of a final product, let us add that demand is identical and homothetic across countries, and that trade is free (no tariffs or transport costs). Then it follows that a good produced in any country is sent to all other countries in proportion to the purchasing country's GDP. To formalize this, consider a multicountry framework where $i, j = 1, \ldots, C$ denotes countries, and $k = 1, \ldots, N$ denotes products (any variety of a good counts as a distinct product). Let y_k^i denote country i's production of good k. Since prices are the same across all countries, we normalize them to unity, so y_k^i actually measures the *value* of production. The total GDP in each country is measured by $Y^i = \Sigma_{k=1}^N y_k^i$, and world GDP is $Y^w = \Sigma_{i=1}^C y^i$.

Let s^j denote country j's share of world expenditure. Assuming that trade is balanced in each country, then s^j also denotes country j's share of world GDP, so that $s^j = Y^j/Y^w$. Then under the assumptions that all countries are producing different products, and demand is identical and homothetic, the exports *from country i to county j of product k* are given by

$$X_k^{ij} = s^j y_k^i. \qquad (5.13)$$

Summing over all products k, we obtain

$$X^{ij} = \sum_k X_k^{ij} = s^j \sum_k y_k^i = s^j Y^i = \frac{Y^j Y^i}{Y^w} = s^j s^i Y^w = X^{ji}. \qquad (5.14)$$

Summing the first and last of these terms, we therefore find that bilateral trade between two countries equals

$$X^{ij} + X^{ji} = \left(\frac{2}{Y^w}\right) Y^i Y^j. \qquad (5.15)$$

This gives our simplest derivation of the gravity equation, where the bilateral exports from country i to country j are proportional to the product of their GDPs. This simple model has many empirical applications, and we shall discuss two.

Empirical Applications of the Gravity Equation

Trade within and outside the OECD

As a first application of the gravity equation, we consider the work of Helpman (1987). The goal of his work is to give an alternative characterization of the gravity equation, emphasizing the role of *differential country size*. Thus, consider an economic region consisting of two countries. Then holding fixed the economic size of this region, two countries of unequal size will not trade as much as would two countries of similar size. To demonstrate this, let us sum the first and last of terms in (5.14) to obtain

$$X^{ij} + X^{ji} = 2s^i s^j Y^w. \tag{5.16}$$

It will be convenient to reexpress this equation as depending on each country's share of GDP *relative to each other*. So let us say that these two countries belong to "region A" of the world, and denote the sum of the GDPs of these two countries by $Y^A = Y^i + Y^j$. Then their relative shares of regional GDP are expressed as $s^{iA} = Y^j/Y^A$, and the GDP of region A relative to the world is $s^A = Y^A/Y^w$. Then (5.16) can be rewritten as $(X^{ij} + X^{ji})/Y^A = 2s^{iA} s^{jA} s^A$. The shares of regional GDP sum to unity, $s^{iA} + s^{jA} = 1$, and squaring this we obtain $2s^{iA} s^{jA} = 1 - (s^{iA})^2 - (s^{jA})^2$. Substituting this back into the previous equation, we have therefore shown the following theorem.

Theorem (Helpman 1987)

If countries are completely specialized in their outputs, tastes are identical and homothetic, and there is free trade worldwide, then the volume of trade among countries in region A relative to their GDP is

$$\frac{\text{Volume of trade in A}}{\text{GDP}^A} = s^A \left(1 - \sum_{i \in A} (s^{iA})^2\right). \tag{5.17}$$

We have derived this result above for the case of two countries in a region, but Helpman shows that it holds for a region of many countries. The term $(1 - \Sigma_{i \in A}(s^{iA})^2)$ appearing on the right side of (5.17) is a "size dispersion index." It shows how the volume of trade will be related to the *relative size of countries*. To understand the properties of this index, suppose that there are N countries in region A. Then the index is maximized for countries of the same relative size $1/N$, in which case it equals $[1 - (1/N)]$. Conversely, as any country has a share approaching unity, then the dispersion index also approaches zero. The theorem says that the volume of trade relative to GDP will be proportional to the dispersion index.

Helpman (1987) tests (5.17) for a group of OECD countries. In the simplest test, he graphs the dispersion index against the volume of trade relative to GDP for these countries. Both of these variables are indeed increasing over time; that is, countries are becoming more similar in size and trade is growing. Hummels and Levinsohn (1995) extended this comparison to non-OECD countries as well. We will discuss the results of Debaere (2002), who provides the most complete treatment. Let us specify the region A as *any pair of countries, $A = \{i, j\}$*. Then (5.17) is written in natural logs as

$$\ln\left(\frac{X^{ij} + X^{ji}}{Y^i + Y^j}\right) = \ln(s^i + s^j) + \ln\left[1 - \left(\frac{Y^i}{Y^i + Y^j}\right)^2 - \left(\frac{Y^j}{Y^i + Y^j}\right)^2\right].$$

(5.18)

Debaere tests these relations using a dataset covering 1970–89, over a sample of OECD and non-OECD countries. Recognizing that the variables also depend on time, let us rewrite the estimating equation in (5.18) as

$$\ln\left(\frac{X^{ij}_t + X^{ji}_t}{Y^i_t + Y^j_t}\right) = \alpha_{ij} + \gamma\ln(s^i_t + s^j_t) + \beta\ln(\text{Dispersion}^{ij}_t), \quad (5.19)$$

where α_{ij} is a fixed effect for each country pair, γ is a coefficient on the log sum of country shares, and β is a coefficient on the size dispersion index, which equals the final bracketed term on the right side of (5.18). Notice that if the country shares are roughly constant over time, then the fixed effect α_{ij} in (5.19) would absorb this term. This was implicitly assumed by Hummels and Levinsohn (1995), so Debaere runs two versions of (5.19): first excluding the term $\ln(s^i_t + s^j_t)$, which treats the country shares as constant over time; and then including this term, which allows the country share to vary over time. These two versions are shown in panels (a) and (b) of Table 5.1.

Debaere also uses several different methods to measure the country GDP shares and dispersion index. Since GDP should be measured in a common currency—the U.S. dollar—it can be converted from national currencies using either nominal exchange rates or purchasing power parity (PPP) exchange rates. The former—nominal GDP in U.S. dollars—is available from

TABLE 5.1

Tests of the Gravity Equation with Value of (Trade/GDP) for Country Pairs as Dependent Variable

	OECD Countries				Non-OECD Countries			
	(1)	*(2)*	*(3)*	*(4)*	*(5)*	*(6)*	*(7)*	*(8)*
Measure								
of GDP	PWT	IFS	PWT	IFS	PWT	IFS	PWT	IFS
Estimator	OLS	OLS	IV[a]	IV[a]	OLS	OLS	IV[a]	IV[a]
	(a) With constant GDP shares							
ln (Dispersion)	1.01	0.55	1.97	2.10	−2.05	−0.14	−2.30	1.54
	(0.10)	(0.04)	(0.21)	(0.34)	(0.85)	(0.20)	(1.69)	(0.71)
R^2	0.59	0.43	0.58	0.39	0.02	0.12	0.02	0.13
N	1820	1820	1820	1820	1320	1320	1320	1320
	(b) With time-varying GDP shares							
ln (Dispersion)	1.57	0.89	3.28	3.52	−0.96	0.40	−1.43	2.10
	(0.11)	(0.06)	(0.25)	(0.24)	(0.99)	(0.24)	(1.77)	(0.73)
$\ln(s_t^i + s_t^j)$	1.30	0.47	2.54	2.76	1.98	0.99	7.51	4.39
	(0.13)	(0.06)	(0.28)	(0.26)	(0.95)	(0.10)	(2.83)	(1.18)
R^2	0.61	0.45	0.60	0.43	0.02	0.14	0.02	0.14
N	1820	1820	1820	1820	1320	1320	1320	1320

Source: Debaere 2002.

Note: Standard errors are in parentheses.

[a] Column uses country populations as an instrumental variable for GDP, and then calculates the country shares and dispersion index using predicted GDPs.

the International Financial Statistics (IFS) of the International Monetary Fund, which is a standard source for macroeconomic data across countries. The latter—real GDP converted to dollars using PPP exchange rates—is available from the Penn World Tables (PWT). We would expect that the latter is more reliable to construct the country GDP shares and dispersion index, but report results from both PWT and IFS. In addition, Debaere reports results obtained when country populations are used as an instrumental variable for GDP, so the country shares and dispersion index are calculated using predicted GDPs from this first-stage regression.

We are especially interested in testing whether β is close to unity, as Helpman's equation implies. The estimates of (5.19) over 14 OECD countries are shown in columns (1)–(4) of Table 5.1. Looking first at part (a), which ignores the term $\ln(s_t^i + s_t^j)$, in regression (1) using country GDPs from the PWT, we find that β is insignificantly different from unity. In regression (2), using the GDPs in nominal dollars from the IFS, β is estimated at 0.55, which is obviously less than unity but is still positive and highly significant. The instrumental variable regressions in columns (3) and (4) both have higher estimates of β on the dispersion index, but again they are positive and highly significant. When the log sum of country shares is introduced in part (b), the estimates of β are generally increased further.

For the group of non-OECD countries, the results are quite different. Using real GDPs from the PWT, in columns (5) and (7), the dispersion index has a *negative* coefficient. This contradicts Helpman's results in (5.17), and more generally, contradicts the gravity equation. We should not be surprised by this, however, because the gravity equation was based on the assumption that countries are *specialized in different goods*. This may be a reasonable description of trade between industrialized countries (e.g., Italian shoes are different from American shoes), but it is a poor description of trade between developing countries that export basic agricultural goods or low-skilled commodities. In that case, there is no reason at all for the gravity equation to hold, and this is what we are finding in the non-OECD results where β is negative.

It turns out that when nominal GDPs from the IFS are used instead for the non-OECD countries, as in columns (6) and (8), then β is instead positive in some cases but is just barely significant. In addition, the regressions for the non-OECD countries have much lower R^2 than for the OECD countries. In summary, the results in Table 5.1 show that Helpman's formulation of the gravity equation in (5.17) is strongly supported for the OECD countries, but receives little or no support for the non-OECD countries. This accords with our expectation that specialization in different goods is much more prevalent for the industrialized countries.

Trade within and between Canada and the United States

A second application of the gravity model, and one that has stimulated a large amount of research, came from comparing *intranational* trade between Canadian provinces to *international* trade between Canadian provinces and U.S. states. This was the question posed by McCallum (1995) in a study using 1988 data, just before the Canada-U.S. FTA was signed. He estimated a gravity model like (5.15), where the dependent variable is exports from each Canadian province to other provinces or to U.S. states. Exports depend on the province or state GDPs, so the regression estimated by McCallum is

$$\ln X^{ji} = \alpha + \beta_1 \ln Y^i + \beta_2 \ln Y^j + \gamma \delta^{ij} + \rho \ln d^{ij} + \varepsilon_{ij}, \quad (5.20)$$

where δ^{ij} is an indicator variable that equals unity for trade between two Canadian provinces and zero otherwise, and d^{ij} is the distance between any two provinces or states. The results from estimating (5.20) using 1988 data are shown in column (1) of Table 5.2. The same regression using 1993 data

TABLE 5.2

Comparison of Gravity Equations with Value of Exports for Province/State Pairs
as Dependent Variable

	McCallum (1995) and Other Samples			Anderson and van Wincoop 2001	With Fixed Effects[a]
	(1)	*(2)*	*(3)*	*(4)*	*(5)*
Year of data	*1988*	*1993*	*1993*	*1993*	*1993*
Regions included			US-US	US-US	US-US
	CA-CA	CA-CA	CA-CA	CA-CA	CA-CA
	CA-US	CA-US	CA-US	CA-US	CA-US
Independent variables					
ln Y^i	1.21	1.22	1.13	1	1
	(0.03)	(0.04)	(0.02)		
ln Y^j	1.06	0.98	0.97	1	1
	(0.03)	(0.03)	(0.02)		
lnd^{ij}	−1.42	−1.35	−1.11	−0.79	−1.25
	(0.06)	(0.07)	(0.03)	(0.03)	(0.04)
Indicator Canada	3.09	2.80	2.75		
	(0.13)	(0.14)	(0.11)		
Indicator U.S.			0.40		
			(0.05)		
Indicator border				−1.65	−1.55
				(0.08)	(0.06)
Border effect Canada[b]	22.0	16.4	15.7	10.5	
	(2.9)	(2.0)	(1.9)	(1.2)	
Border effect U.S.[b]			1.5	2.6	
			(0.1)	(0.1)	
Border effect-average[c]			4.8	5.2	4.7
			(0.3)	(0.4)	(0.3)
R^2	0.81	0.76	0.85	n.a.	0.66
Observations	683	679	1511	1511	1511

Source: McCallum 1995; Anderson and van Wincop 2003, Table 2; Feenstra 2002; and
empirical exercises 5.1 and 5.2.

Note: Standard errors are in parentheses.

[a] Includes fixed effects for source and destination provinces or states.

[b] Computed as the exponent of the Canada or U.S. indicator variable, except for the calculation in column (4), which is explained in the text.

[c] Computed as the geometric mean of the Canada and U.S. border effects in columns
(3)–(4), and as the exponent of the (absolute value of the) coefficient on the border indicator in columns (4)–(5).

is shown in column (2). Note that McCallum's dataset included trade between Canadian provinces, and provinces and states, but not trade between the U.S. states. This is added in column (3) using 1993 data, in which case we also include an indicator variable that equals 1 when trade is between two U.S. states and zero otherwise.

The results in columns (1)–(3) show coefficients on provincial or state GDP close to unity, and strong negative relationship between distance and trade. This is no surprise. What is unexpected is the very large coefficient on cross-provincial trade: ranging from 3.09 in column (1) to 2.75 in column (3). Taking the exponents of these, we obtain the estimates on "Canada trade" shown at the bottom of the table, indicating the cross-provincial trade is some 22 times larger than cross-border trade in 1988, and 15.7 times larger in 1993. These numbers are extraordinarily high! They are meant to capture any and all factors that might impede trade between the United States and Canada, or what we might call "border effects." It seems nearly unbelievable, however, that these factors would lead to 16 or 22 times more internal trade in Canada than external trade.

How is it that the Canada-U.S. border can apparently have an impact this large? The answer from recent work of Anderson and van Wincoop (2003) is that border effects have an *asymmetric effect* on countries of different size, and in particular, have a larger effect on small countries. To understand their argument, we can run through a numerical example using Canada-U.S. trade. Let us make the realistic assumption that the United States is 10 times bigger economically. It follows that

- With frictionless trade, Canada exports 90% of GDP to the United States, so it sells 10% internally
- Suppose the border effect reduces cross-border trade by a factor of one-half
- Then, Canada exports 45% of its GDP to the United States, so it must trade 55% internally
- So internal trade went up by 5.5 times (from 10% to 55%), cross-border down by one-half (from 90% to 45%), and so internal trade has increased by 11 times more than cross-border trade
- If we ask what has happened in the United States, it used to export 10% of its output to Canada, and now it exports only 5%. So internal trade has risen from 90% to 95% of output—a modest change—while external trade has fallen in half. We conclude that cross-state trade has increased by slightly more than 2 times cross-border trade.

We can see from this example that comparing cross-state trade to cross-border trade for the United States (a large country) gives a reasonable estimate of the true border effect (which was a factor of one-half), but that comparing cross-provincial trade with cross-border trade for Canada (a small country) gives a really exaggerated estimate of the border effect. To avoid this bias, we need to rederive the gravity equation while introducing trade barriers (such as transport costs or tariffs) right from the start. This means that prices differ across countries. Anderson (1979) was the first to derive the gravity equation while taking into account these "price effects." Estimating the resulting equation still presents a challenge, however, and we shall discuss three approaches: the use of *prices indexes* to measure the price effects in the gravity equation, as in Bergstrand 1985, 1989 and Baier and Bergstrand 2001; the use of *estimated border effects* to measure the price effects, as in Anderson and van Wincoop 2003; and the use of *fixed effects* to account for the price effects, as in Redding and Venables 2000 and Rose and van Wincoop 2001. Our derivation of the gravity equation follows Redding and Venables.

Border Effects in the Gravity Model

When there are border effects, such as transport costs or tariffs, then it is no longer the case that prices are equalized across countries, so the pattern of trade is more complex than in the gravity equation (5.15). The only way to sort this out is to assume a specific utility function, and we shall adopt the CES specification. We let c_k^{ij} denote the exports *from country i to country j of good k*. Because each country produces unique product varieties, the *exports* of good k from country i to j are identical to the *consumption* of good k in country j. In contrast to Krugman's model, we now let c_k^{ij} denote *total* consumption of good k in country j, rather than *per capita* consumption. We will suppose that country $i = 1, \ldots, C$ produces N^i products. Then utility for country j is

$$U^j = \sum_{i=1}^{C} \sum_{k=1}^{N^i} (c_k^{ij})^{(\sigma-1)/\sigma}.$$

$$(5.21)$$

The triple index on consumption is a bit unwieldy, but this can be simplified by assuming that all products exported by country i sell for the same price p^{ij} in country j. These prices are inclusive of transport costs from country i to j, on a c.i.f. (cost, insurance, freight) basis. In contrast, the local prices p^i for goods produced in country i are net of any transport costs, on a f.o.b. (free on board) basis. Let us model the relationship between these as $p^{ij} = T^{ij} p^i$, where $T^{ii} = 1$ and $T^{ij} \geq 1$, indicating that T^{ij} units of the product must be shipped to country j in order for one unit to arrive; the amount $(T^{ij} - 1)$ "melts" along the way. This formulation is called "iceberg" transport costs and was introduced by Samuelson (1952).

With equal prices p^{ij} across varieties, then consumption in country j is also equal over all the products $k = 1, \ldots, N^i$ sold by country i, so that $c_k^{ij} = c^{ij}$.

Then the utility function is simplified as

$$U^j = \sum_{i=1}^{C} N^i (c^{ij})^{(\sigma-1)/\sigma}, \qquad (5.22)$$

where c^{ij} now denotes the consumption of any product sent *from country i to country j.*

The representative consumer in country maximizes (5.22) subject to the budget constraint

$$Y^j = \sum_{i=1}^{C} N^i p^{ij} c^{ij}, \qquad (5.23)$$

where Y^j is aggregate expenditure and income in country j (we will assume balanced trade).

Maximizing (5.22) subject to (5.23), we can derive the following expression for the demand for each product c^{ij}:[8]

$$c^{ij} = (p^{ij}/P^j)^{-\sigma} (Y^j/P^j), \qquad (5.24)$$

where P^j refers to country j's overall price index, defined as

$$P^j = \left(\sum_{i=1}^{C} N^i (p^{ij})^{(1-\sigma)} \right)^{1/(1-\sigma)}. \qquad (5.25)$$

To compare this with our earlier derivation of gravity equation in (5.15), let us express the total value of exports from country i to j. This will be $X^{ij} \equiv N^i p^{ij} c^{ij}$, or from (5.24) and (5.25),

$$X^{ij} = N^i Y^j \left(\frac{p^{ij}}{P^j} \right)^{1-\sigma}. \qquad (5.26)$$

Estimating the Gravity Equation

Using Price Index Data

In order to estimate (5.26), we should recognize that the "true" number of products N^i in each country is unobservable. One approach, then, is to solve for this using the zero-profit conditions. Assuming that labor is the only factor of production and using the same production functions as in Krugman (1979), it follows that firm output is fixed as in (5.12). Then GDP in

---

[8] See problem 5.2 to derive (5.24) and (5.25) when there are two goods.

country i is $Y^j = N^i p^i \bar{y}$, and substituting this into (5.26), we obtain

$$X^{ij} = \frac{Y^i Y^j}{p^i \bar{y}} \left(\frac{p^{ij}}{P^j} \right)^{1-\sigma} = \frac{Y^i Y^j}{p^{i\sigma} \bar{y}} \left(\frac{T^{ij}}{P^j} \right)^{1-\sigma}, \tag{5.26'}$$

where we use $p^{ij} = T^{ij} p^i$ to obtain the last expression. The approach of Bergstrand (1985, 1989) and Baier and Bergstrand (2001) is to estimate (5.26′) directly, where the variables on the right side are country GDPs, T^{ij} is broken into tariffs and transport costs (measured with IFS data), and country prices p^i or P^j are measured with GDP deflators.

Specifically, taking the logs and first differences of the variables in (5.26′), we obtain the estimating equation

$$\Delta \ln X^{ij} = \Delta \ln(Y^i Y^j) + (1-\sigma)\Delta \ln T^{ij} - \sigma \Delta \ln p^i + (\sigma-1)\Delta \ln P^j. \tag{5.27}$$

The term $(Y^i Y^j)$ appearing in (5.27) can be further decomposed as $(Y^i + Y^j)^2 (s^i s^j)$, where s^i and s^j here denote the shares of each country's GDP relative to their sum, that is, $s^i = Y^i/(Y^i + Y^j)$, and similarly for s^j. Therefore, we can rewrite (5.27) as

$$\Delta \ln X^{ij} = 2\Delta \ln(Y^i + Y^j) + \Delta \ln(s^i s^j) + (1-\sigma)\Delta \ln T^{ij}$$
$$- \sigma \Delta \ln p^i + (\sigma-1)\Delta \ln P^j. \tag{5.27'}$$

In this formulation, we see that the growth of trade depends on changes in transport costs, changes in the sum of GDP, changes in relative country size measured by $(s^i s^j)$, and changes in the prices of each country, measured with GDP deflators. Because $s^i + s^j = 1$, then squaring both sides we obtain $s^i s^j = [1 - (s^i)^2 - (s^j)^2]/2$, so the variable $(s^i s^j)$ in (5.27′) is the same as Helpman's size dispersion index in (5.17).

Using data for 16 OECD countries, and taking differences between the averages in 1958–60 and 1986–88, Baier and Bergstrand (2001, 19) estimate the following regression (with standard errors in parentheses):

$$\Delta \ln X^{ij} = 0.05 + 2.37\,\Delta \ln(Y^i + Y^j) + 0.60\,\Delta \ln(s^i s^j)$$
$$\phantom{\Delta \ln X^{ij} =} (0.56)\ (0.38) (0.34)$$
$$- 4.49\,\Delta \ln(1 + \tau^{ij}) - 3.19\,\Delta \ln(1 + a^{ij})$$
$$ (1.00) \phantom{\Delta \ln(1 + \tau^{ij}) -} (0.37) \tag{5.28}$$
$$- 0.68\,\Delta \ln Y^j - 0.25\,\Delta \ln(p^i/P^j) - 0.08\,\ln X_0^{ij},$$
$$ (0.24) (0.09) (0.03)$$
$$R^2 = 0.40,\ N = 240.$$

The first variables appearing on the right side of (5.28) follow directly from the specification in (5.27′), where the term T^{ij} has been broken up into tariffs (τ^{ij}) and transport costs (a^{ij}). Both of these enter with negative and highly significant coefficients. The log sum of country GDPs has a co-efficient that is close to 2, as expected from (5.27′), while the product of shares ($s^i s^j$) has a coefficient that is insignificantly different from unity, as expected from the gravity equation and Helpman's (1987) formulation.

The final terms appearing on the right side of (5.28) are slightly differ-ent from those in (5.27′). First, Baier and Bergstrand's modeling of sup-ply is somewhat more general than ours, which leads to the extra term $\ln Y^j$ in (5.28), which has a negative coefficient. Second, the prices that appear separately in (5.27′) are combined as a ratio in (5.28), and meas-ured with GDP price deflators.[9] Third, they include the *initial* amount of trade in 1958–60, $\ln X_0^{ij}$, as a regressor in (5.28) to allow for the lagged adjustment of trade flows.

Overall, with an R^2 of 0.40, this gravity equation explains nearly one-half of the changes in bilateral trade flows for the OECD countries. Further-more, we can use the first variables that appear on the right side of (5.28) to explain the growth in trade between 1958–60 and 1986–88. Over these three decades, bilateral trade between the 16 OECD countries used in the sample grew by 150%. Of this, 100% or *two-thirds of the total*, was explained by the growth in GDP (i.e., the first variable on the right of (5.28) after the constant, times its coefficient). Next, the actual reductions in tariffs, times its coefficient in (5.28), explains another 38% increase in trade, or roughly *one-quarter of the total*. Third, the actual reduction in transport costs, times its coefficient in (5.28), explains a further 12% increase in trade, or *one-twelfth of the total*. So we conclude that the reduction in tariffs is about three times as important as the reduction in transport costs in explaining increased OECD trade.

Notice that these three variables (sum of GDPs, tariffs, and transport costs) explain the *entire increase* in trade, leaving no role at all for the convergence in relative country size, which is the term $\Delta\ln(s^i s^j)$ in (5.28). While this term is positive on average across all OECD countries for 1958–60 to 1986–88, it is actually negative but very small (-3%) for the 16 countries used in the sample. In other words, there is a slight *diver-gence* in size of real GDP among the 16 OECD countries used, which ex-plains a *slight reduction* in trade (of 2%) rather than an increase in trade. Note that this occurs despite the fact that the coefficient on the GDP shares $\Delta\ln(s^i s^j)$ is insignificantly different from unity in (5.28), as pre-dicted by the gravity equation and Helpman's (1987) formulation. So while this variable passed the statistical test of having a coefficient of the correct sign and magnitude (as we also found for the OECD countries in Table 5.1), it fails to be economically important in explaining the growth in trade among the OECD countries.

---

[9] Actually, all of the variables in (5.27′) are measured by Baier and Bergstrand (2001) in real rather than the nominal terms as we have used. When that modification is made, the prices p^i and P^i should indeed appear as a ratio.

Using Estimated Border Effects

An objection to using published price indexes to measure p^i and P^j is that these indexes may not accurately reflect the "true" border effects. That is, the myriad of costs (in money, time, and currency risk) involved in making transactions across the border are probably not reflected in aggregate price indexes.[10] So instead of using data to measure prices, we might want to model the c.i.f. prices p^{ij} as differing from the f.o.b. prices p^i due to distance and other factors, as with

$$\ln T^{ij} = \tau^{ij} + \rho \ln d^{ij} + \varepsilon_{ij}, \qquad (5.29)$$

where d^{ij} is the distance between countries i and j, τ^{ij} is any other "border effect" associated with selling from country i to country j, and ε_{ij} is a random error. We should think of ρ and τ^{ij} as being estimated, though we will have to explain how this is done. Generally, T^{ij} is meant to include *all effects* limiting trade between countries i and j, so referring to it as "iceberg" transportation costs is something of a misuse of language.

Substituting (5.29) back into the gravity equation (5.26) to eliminate the terms $p^{ij} = T^{ij} p^i$, we obtain a set of equations where the exports between country i and country j depend on the parameters τ^{ij} and ρ. This set of equations is highly nonlinear, however, so it is difficult to estimate these parameters directly. Instead, the approach of Anderson and van Wincoop (2003) is to further simplify the gravity equation making use of the market-clearing conditions, as follows.

Notice that with the iceberg transportation costs, the output of the firm exceeds the net amount received by consumer, since these are related by

$$y^i = \sum_{j=1}^{C} c^{ij} T^{ij}. \qquad (5.30)$$

Multiplying this by the price p^i, we obtain $p^i y^i = \Sigma_{j=1}^{C} p^{ij} c^{ij}$, which is an equality between the value of output of the firm (using the f.o.b. prices but before the output has "melted") and the expenditure of consumers (using the c.i.f. prices but after the quantity delivered has "melted"). In principle, we can use the market-clearing conditions (5.30) to solve for the unknown prices p^i. Rather than obtain an *explicit* solution for prices, Anderson and van Wincoop (2003) make use of a convenient *implicit*

---

[10] Another problem with using price indexes is that they are nearly always measured relative to an arbitrary base period. This makes it impossible to compare the "level" of prices in a Canadian province and U.S. state, when the base period for each index differs. Engel and Rogers (1996) neatly avoid this problem by measuring the correlation of prices across locations, rather than their levels.

solution. To develop their result, we again denote country i's GDP by $Y^i = N^i p^i y^i$, world GDP by $Y^w = \Sigma_{j=1}^{C} Y^j$, and country i's share by $s^i = Y^i/Y^w$).

Theorem (Anderson and van Wincoop 2003)

Suppose that the transportation costs are symmetric, $T^{ij} = T^{ji}$. Then an implicit solution to the market-clearing conditions (5.30) is

$$\tilde{p}^i = (s^i/N^i)^{1/(1-\sigma)}/\tilde{P}^i, \tag{5.31}$$

in which case the price indexes are solved as

$$(\tilde{P}^j)^{1-\sigma} = \sum_{i=1}^{C} s^i(T^{ij}/\tilde{P}^i)^{1-\sigma}. \tag{5.32}$$

Proof

We will show that substituting (5.31) into the price index (5.25), and substituting (5.31) into the market-clearing conditions (5.30), both lead to equation (5.32). First, substituting $\tilde{p}^{ij} = \tilde{p}^i T^{ij} = (s^i/N^i)^{1/(1-\sigma)} T^{ij}/\tilde{P}^i$ into (5.25), we immediately obtain (5.32). Second, rewrite the market-clearing conditions (5.30) as

$$Y^i = N^i p^i y^i = N^i p^i \sum_{j=1}^{C} c^{ij} T^{ij} = N^i \sum_{j=1}^{C} c^{ij} p^{ij}$$
$$= N^i \sum_{j=1}^{C} (p^i T^{ij}/P^j)^{1-\sigma} Y^j, \tag{5.33}$$

where the final equality makes use of (5.24) and $p^{ij} = T^{ij} p^i$. Then substituting (5.31) into the final expression of (5.33), we obtain

$$Y^i = s^i \sum_{j=1}^{C} (T^{ij}/\tilde{P}^i \tilde{P}^j)^{1-\sigma} Y^j. \tag{5.34}$$

Summing this over $i = 1, \ldots, C$, we have, $Y^w = \Sigma_{j=1}^{C} (T^{ij}/\tilde{P}^i \tilde{P}^j)^{1-\sigma} Y^j$, which is identical to (5.32) provided that $T^{ij} = T^{ji}$.   QED

To see the usefulness of this result, substitute (5.31) into the gravity equation (5.26) to obtain

$$X^{ij} = s^i Y^j \left(\frac{T^{ij}}{\tilde{P}^i \tilde{P}^j}\right)^{1-\sigma} = \left(\frac{Y^i Y^j}{Y^w}\right)\left(\frac{T^{ij}}{\tilde{P}^i \tilde{P}^j}\right)^{1-\sigma}. \tag{5.35}$$

This is a remarkably simple equation, whereby bilateral trade between countries depends on their GDPs and also their implicit price indexes. Anderson and van Wincoop call $\tilde{P}^i$ "indexes of multilateral resistance," because they depend on the transport costs T^{ij} in (5.32). These indexes are unobserved, but Anderson and van Wincoop argue that we can solve for them by using equation (5.32) in combination with a formula for the transportation costs such as (5.29′).[11]

Specifically, the estimation strategy of Anderson and van Wincoop is to move the GDP terms from the right to the left side of (5.35), take logs, and substitute (5.29) for the transportation costs, obtaining (without the constant term Y^w)

$$\ln(X^{ij}/Y^iY^j) = \rho(1-\sigma)\ln d^{ij} + (1-\sigma)\tau^{ij} + \ln(\tilde{P}^i)^{\sigma-1}$$
$$+ \ln(\tilde{P}^j)^{\sigma-1} + (1-\sigma)\varepsilon_{ij}. \qquad (5.36)$$

The dependent variable on the left side is bilateral trade relative to the product of GDPs. On the right side we have distance between regions i and j, followed by all other border effects $(1-\sigma)\tau^{ij}$, and then the multilateral resistance terms $(\tilde{P}^i)^{\sigma-1}$. These multilateral resistance terms can be solved from (5.32) once we know the transportation costs $T^{ij} = T^{ji}$. The transport costs, in turn, are obtained from (5.29) using the estimated value of $\rho(1-\sigma)\ln d^{ij} + (1-\sigma)\tau^{ij}$, which comes from (5.36). The estimation of this system must be custom programmed to minimize the sum of squared residuals in (5.36), while simultaneously using (5.29) to obtain the values of $T^{ij} = T^{ji}$ at each iteration, and with these, solving for the multilateral resistance terms $(\tilde{P}^i)^{\sigma-1}$ from (5.32).

To perform this estimation, we need to be more specific about the form of the border effects $(1-\sigma)\tau^{ij}$, in (5.36). Recall that in McCallum's (1995) gravity equation in (5.20), we introduced an indicator variable δ^{ij} that equaled unity for trade between two Canadian provinces, and zero otherwise. Anderson and van Wincoop instead work with an indicator variable that is $(1-\delta^{ij})$, or *unity for trade between the United States and Canada, and zero otherwise.* Introducing the coefficient γ on this variable, we replace $(1-\sigma)\tau^{ij}$ with $\gamma(1-\delta^{ij})$ in (5.36) and also use the coefficient

---

[11] Notice that (5.32) determines $\tilde{P}^i$ as a function of the transport costs T^{ij}. We can write (5.32) alternatively as $1 = \Sigma_{i=1}^C s^i(T^{ij}/\tilde{P}^i\tilde{P}^j)^{1-\sigma}$, which shows that a weighted average of the terms $(T^{ij}/\tilde{P}^i\tilde{P}^j)^{1-\sigma}$ sums to unity, implying that these terms themselves are centered around unity. When $T^{ij} = 1$ for all i, j, for example, then the solution to (5.32) is $\tilde{P}^i = 1$ for all i. Note that in general the solution to (5.32) involves a normalization on the absolute level of prices, and therefore, on the absolute level of the implicit price indexes.

$\alpha = \rho(1-\sigma)$ on distance, to obtain

$$\ln(X^{ij}/Y^iY^j) = \alpha \ln d^{ij} + \gamma(1-\delta^{ij}) + \ln(\tilde{P}^i)^{\sigma-1}$$
$$+ \ln(\tilde{P}^j)^{\sigma-1} + (1-\sigma)\varepsilon_{ij}. \tag{5.37}$$

Their estimates of (5.37) are shown in column (4) of Table 5.2. Notice that the provincial and states GDP terms have their coefficients constrained at unity, since they have been brought to the left side of (5.37). The coefficient on the indicator variable on cross-border trade in column (4) is estimated at $\hat{\gamma} = -1.65$. This can be compared to the estimates on the indicator variables for intra-Canada trade and intra-U.S. trade, in column (3), of 2.75 and 0.40, respectively. We certainly expect the indicator variables in columns (3) and (4) to have coefficients that are opposite in sign, since in the one case we are measuring *intranational* trade and in the other case measuring *international* trade. It is noteworthy, however, that Anderson and van Wincoop's estimate in column (4) is roughly midway between the conventional gravity estimates in column (3), in absolute value. This appears to occur because Anderson and van Wincoop only allow a single indicator variable to measure cross-border trade, rather than distinguishing two indicator variables (i.e., one for Canadian exports to the United States, and another for American exports to Canada). The use of a single indicator variable is related to their assumption that transport costs are symmetric, $T^{ij} = T^{ji}$.

How should we interpret the estimate $\hat{\gamma} = -1.65$? One approach is to recall that $(1 - \sigma)\tau^{ij}$ was replaced by $\gamma(1 - \delta^{ij})$ in (5.37), so setting these equal and taking the exponent, we solve for $\exp(\tau^{ij}) = \exp[\gamma(1 - \delta^{ij})/(1 - \sigma)]$. For cross-border trade we have $\delta^{ij} = 0$, so $\exp(\tau^{ij}) = \exp[\gamma/(1 - \sigma)]$. Taking values for the elasticity of substitution of $\sigma = 5, 10,$ and 20, we would therefore obtain estimates of $\exp(\tau^{ij})$ of 1.5, 1.2, and 1.09, indicating border barriers of between 9% and 50% in terms of their implied effect on price. The upper end of these estimates is certainly high, but the lower end is not unreasonable.

We would like to turn the coefficient $\hat{\gamma} = -1.65$ into an estimate of how much more trade there is *within* Canada as compared to *across* the border. For regressions (1)–(3) in Table 5.2, we simply took the exponent of the indicator coefficient, as reported near the bottom of the table. That approach is no longer appropriate, however, because if the border did not exist, then the multilateral resistance terms in (5.37) would also be affected. Let us denote by $(\overline{P}^i)^{\sigma-1}$ the multilateral resistance terms in the *absence* of the border effect, that is, what we obtain from formula (5.32), but now using *only* distance (times its estimated coefficient) to compute T^{ij} in (5.29). Taking exponents of (5.37), and comparing this equation *with* and *without* border effects, the ratio of trade in these two cases is, therefore,[12]

$$\frac{X^{ij}}{\overline{X}^{ij}} = \left[e^{\dot{\gamma}(1-\delta^{ij})} \right] \frac{(\tilde{P}^i)^{\sigma-1}(\tilde{P}^j)^{\sigma-1}}{(\overline{P}^i)^{\sigma-1}(\overline{P}^j)^{\sigma-1}}. \qquad (5.38)$$

For example, consider intra-Canadian trade, where $\delta^{ij} = 1$, so the first term on the right side of (5.38) vanishes. Anderson and van Wincoop find that (5.38) equals 4.3, meaning that intra-Canadian trade is *4.3 times larger with the border effects than without.*[13] In addition, for the United States, Anderson and van Wincoop find that intra-U.S. trade is *1.05 times larger with the border effects than without.* Finally, they find that cross-border trade is *0.41 times smaller with the border effects than without.* All these numbers are computed from the ratio on the right side of (5.38), averaged across the provinces or states in Canada or the United States, as appropriate. With intra-Canadian trade being 4.3 times higher due to the border effect, and cross-border trade being 0.41 times smaller, it is immediately clear that *intra-Canadian trade is 4.3/0.41 = 10.5 times higher than cross-border trade.* This estimate is shown near the bottom of column (4) in Table 5.2, along with its standard error. The analogous calculation for the United States shows that *intra-American trade is 1.05/0.41 = 2.6 times higher than cross-border trade,* which is again shown at the bottom of column (4).

These estimates show that small economies, such as Canada, experience a much larger impact of the border effects. This is consistent with our numerical example earlier in the chapter, and indeed, the estimates of border effects obtained by Anderson and van Wincoop (10.5 and 2.6) are nearly the same as in our simple numerical example. Furthermore, these estimates have the following special property. The geometric mean of the border effects is $(10.5 \cdot 2.6)^{1/2} = 5.2$. Notice that this is the same as what we obtain by taking the exponent of the coefficient on the cross-border indicator variable (in absolute value), $e^{1.65} = 5.2$. So the geometric mean of the Canada and U.S. border effects, computing using formula (5.38), turns out to be identical to what we obtain by just using the cross-border indicator variable! This is no coincidence, and we provide a proof of this simple relation in the appendix to this chapter (as in Feenstra 2002). This result means that using a cross-border indicator variable is a completely valid way to infer the *average* impact of the border on intranational relative to international trade.

---

[12] We treat the province or state GDPs Y^i as unaffected by border effects, so that (5.38) follows by taking the exponent of (5.37) and its ratio *with* and *without* border effects.

[13] This calculation requires the use of σ in (5.38). Anderson and van Wincoop use $\sigma = 5$, but find that the implied borders effects are not sensitive to this choice.

Using Fixed Effects

A drawback to the estimation strategy of Anderson and van Wincoop is that it requires custom programming to perform the constrained minimization (and obtain standard errors). A third and final approach to estimating the gravity equation, while using ordinary least squares, is to use fixed effects to take account of the unobserved price indexes. Fixed effects have been introduced into the gravity equation by a number of authors, including Harrigan (1996), Hummels (1999), Redding and Venables (2000), and Rose and van Wincoop (2001). We will summarize the results of the latter authors, as well as use fixed effects in estimating the Canada-U.S. gravity equation in Table 5.2.[14]

Since the multilateral indexes in (5.37) are unobserved, rather than calculating them according to (5.32), we could instead measure them as the coefficients of source and destination region fixed effects. That is, let δ_1^i denote an indicator variable that is unity if region i is the exporter, and zero otherwise; and let δ_2^j denote an indicator variable that is unity if region j is the importer, and zero otherwise. Then the gravity equation in (5.37) can be rewritten as

$$\ln(X^{ij}/Y^i Y^j) = \alpha \ln d^{ij} + \gamma(1-\delta^{ij}) + \beta_1^i \delta_1^i + \beta_2^j \delta_2^j + (1-\sigma)\varepsilon_{ij}, \quad (5.39)$$

where the coefficients $\beta_1^i = \ln(\tilde{P}^i)^{\sigma-1}$ and $\beta_2^j = \ln(\tilde{P}^j)^{\sigma-1}$ on the source and destination indicator variables estimate the multilateral indexes.

An estimate of (5.39) for Canada-U.S. intranational and international trade is shown in column (5) of Table 5.2. Rather than the border estimate $\hat{\gamma} = -1.65$ as in Anderson and van Wincoop (2003), we now obtain $\hat{\gamma} = -1.55$. Taking its exponential, we obtain $e^{1.55} = 4.7$, as reported near the bottom of column 5. The value 4.7 is a consistent estimate of the *average* impact of the border barrier on Canada and U.S. trade relative to cross-border trade (as shown in the appendix to this chapter). Notice that this estimate is nearly the same as the average border effect of 5.2 obtained by Anderson and van Wincoop (2003), who explicitly introduced the multilateral resistance term computed from (5.32) into the estimation. In contrast, the fixed-effect approach estimates this terms as part of the regression without relying on formula (5.32). *Both* approaches give consistent estimates of the average border effect. While using the explicit multilateral resistance terms should result in more efficient estimates, this benefit seems to be relatively small compared to the computational simplicity of the fixed-effect approach. Since the fixed-effects method pro-

---

[14] The use of fixed effects in the Canada–United States dataset draws on Feenstra 2002. Helliwell (1998, 2002) and Helliwell and Verdier (2001) provide a detailed examination of international versus intranational border effects for Canada, as does Wolf (1997, 2000) for the United States.

duces consistent estimates of the *average* border effect across countries, and is easy to implement, it might be considered to be the preferred empirical method.

It is also interesting that the average border effect of 4.7 is nearly the same as the *average* effect obtained by a conventional gravity equation (like McCallum 1995): in column (3) of Table 5.2, we compute the geometric mean of the border effect for Canada and the United States as 4.8. In contrast to columns (4) and (5), the estimates in columns (1)–(3) are *not consistent*, because these regressions do not incorporate the price indexes. This appears to have the effect of *overstating* the border effect for Canada (15.7 in column (3) as compared to 10.5 in column (4)), and *understating* the effect for the United States (1.5 in column (3) as compared to 2.6 in column (4)). Still, for this dataset, the geometric mean of these inconsistent estimates gives an average border effect that is very close to the consistent estimates in columns (4) and (5).

The fixed-effect approach has been used by Rose and van Wincoop (2001) to estimate the impact of monetary unions on international trade. They include an indicator variable that is unity if the two countries belong to a monetary union, and interpret its coefficient of $\hat{\gamma} = 0.86$ as a consistent estimate of the average impact of monetary unions on trade. Surprisingly, they find that monetary unions increase trade by $e^{\hat{\gamma}} = 2.36$, or more than doubling trade on average between union members relative to non–union members. The actual mechanism by which monetary unions lead to such a large increase in trade remains quite unclear. Results like this have led Obstfeld and Rogoff (2000) to identify large border effects from the gravity equations as the cause of the "six major puzzles in international macroeconomics."

The fixed-effect method has also been used by Redding and Venables (2000) to determine *wages* across countries. They do not rely on symmetric transportation costs, or the above theorem of Anderson and van Wincoop, but instead work directly from the gravity equation in (5.26). In their approach, the differentiated product is used as both consumer goods and as intermediate inputs to production. Thus, proximity to trading partners affects a country's ability to export the differentiated good and import the differentiated inputs: both of these activities will impact wages. Redding and Venables show that the fixed effects of the gravity equation are directly related to equilibrium wages. In other words, the economic geography of a country—measured by its distance from and access to trading partners—determines its wages and hence its standard of living.

In the next section, we turn to another question of economic geography that has to do with the *location* of firms. Specifically, as we consider regions or countries of differing size, will the higher demand in large areas serve to attract more firms? Since each product is produced by only one firm in our model, asking about the location of firms is the same as asking about how many products N^i each country produces. We address this in the next section, using a simplified framework where wages are constant and equal across countries.

The Home Market Effect

We will make the same assumptions on the differentiated good as in Krugman's original model: labor is the only input, and output y^i of the typical firm in country i requires the labor input $L^i = \alpha + \beta y^i$. In addition, we will suppose that there is a homogeneous good, and one unit of that good requires one unit of labor. There are no transport costs in this good, so its price is equalized across countries.[15] Choosing the homogeneous good as the numeraire, and provided that each country produces that good under trade, wages are therefore *unity* in all countries. Having wages fixed will simplify our determination of N^i.

On the demand side, we assume that a fixed share of income ϕ is spent on the differentiated product, which provides utility given by the CES function in (5.21) or (5.22).[16] Therefore, demand for each differentiated product is still given by (5.25), but replacing income Y^j by the amount ϕL^j actually spent on the differentiated product, we obtain

$$c^{ij} = (p^{ij}/P^j)^{-\sigma}\,\phi L^j/P^j. \tag{5.40}$$

The output of firms is still given by (5.30), $y^i = \Sigma_{j=1}^{C} c^{ij}T^{ij}$. Because of the CES utility function, this output will be fixed in a zero-profit equilibrium, $\bar{y} = (\sigma-1)\alpha/\beta$, as obtained in (5.12). So in principle, the number of products in each country can be derived from the market-clearing conditions

$$\bar{y} = \sum_{j=1}^{C} c^{ij}T^{ij}, \quad i = 1,\dots,C, \tag{5.41}$$

where consumption depends on the price indexes P^j given by (5.25), which depend on the number of products.

Rather than solving for the number of products in each country, we will instead solve for the *change* in these as country size L^j varies. The fact that

---

[15] The assumption of zero transport costs on the numeraire good is important. Davis (1998) argues that we need higher transport costs on the differentiated good than in the homogeneous product to obtain the home market effect, as derived below. See also Fujita, Krugman, and Venables 1999, chap. 7.

[16] Denoting consumption of the homogeneous good by c_0, the utility function is $U = c_0^{1-\phi}(\Sigma_{i=1}^{N}c_i^{(\sigma-1)/\sigma})^{\phi\sigma/(\sigma-1)}$.

the firm outputs are fixed on the left-hand side of (5.41) implies that on the right-hand side some combination of the consumptions in each country must also be fixed. As a guess, let us suppose that *consumption of every variety in each country is fixed*. Under our framework where wages are equalized across countries, the prices p^i and p^{ij} are also fixed. Then we can totally differentiate (5.40), holding c^{ij} fixed, to obtain

$$0 = (\sigma-1)\hat{P}^j + \hat{L}^j \Rightarrow \hat{P}^j = -\hat{L}^j/(\sigma-1), \qquad (5.42)$$

where $\hat{z} = dz/z$ for any variable. This equation states that the price indexes in each country j will fall in direct proportion to the rise in country GDP. Recall from (5.25) that the price indexes depend on the number of products in each country. Thus, provided that there is a change in the number of products consistent with $\hat{P}^j$ in (5.42), then our initial assumption that consumption c^{ij} is fixed is indeed correct.

To determine the change in the number of products, let us differentiate (5.25) to obtain

$$\hat{P}^j = \left(\frac{1}{1-\sigma}\right)\left(\sum_{i=1}^{C} \hat{N}^i \phi^{ij}\right), \qquad (5.43)$$

where $\phi^{ij} = N^{ij}(p^{ij}/P^j)^{1-\sigma}$ denotes the share of products from country i in the differentiated goods purchased by country j, with $\Sigma_{i=1}^{C}\phi^{ij} = 1$. Combining (5.42) and (5.43), we obtain an extremely simple relationship between the change in GDP of each country and the change in the number of products,

$$\hat{L}^j = \sum_{i=1}^{C} \hat{N}^i \phi^{ij}. \qquad (5.44)$$

We can use (5.44) to solve for the change in number of product $\hat{N}^i$ provided that the matrix of expenditure shares $\Phi = [\phi^{ij}]$ is invertible. This will be true, for example, if each country i devotes a larger share of its budget to purchasing its own differentiated products than the budget share that country j uses to buy products from i, so that $\phi^{ii} > \phi^{ij}$ for $i \neq j$, as we shall assume.

When there are just two countries, we can express (5.44) in matrix notation as

$$(\hat{N}^1, \hat{N}^2)\begin{pmatrix} \phi^{11} & \phi^{12} \\ \phi^{21} & \phi^{22} \end{pmatrix} = (\hat{L}_1, \hat{L}_2) \Rightarrow$$

$$(\hat{N}^1, \hat{N}^2) = \frac{(\hat{L}_1, \hat{L}_2)}{|\Phi|}\begin{pmatrix} \phi^{22} & -\phi^{12} \\ -\phi^{21} & \phi^{11} \end{pmatrix}, \qquad (5.45)$$

where $|\Phi|$ denotes the determinant of the two-by-two matrix above. This determinant can be alternatively expressed as

$$|\Phi| = \phi^{11}\phi^{22} - \phi^{12}\phi^{21}$$
$$= \phi^{11}(1-\phi^{12}) - \phi^{12}(1-\phi^{11}) \qquad (5.46)$$
$$= \phi^{11} - \phi^{12} = \phi^{22} - \phi^{21},$$

where we have repeatedly made use of the fact that $\phi^{1j} + \phi^{2j} = 1$, that is, the consumption shares of products from both sources to country j sum to unity. This determinant is positive under our assumption that $\phi^{ii} > \phi^{ij}$ for $i \neq j$.

To fix ideas, suppose that country 1 and 2 start off as identical, with equal transport costs between them. Similar to Krugman's model at the beginning of this chapter, trade between the identical countries will lead them to export equal numbers of the differentiated product to each other: $N^1 = N^2$, and trade is balanced in the differentiated good. Now suppose that the labor endowment of country 1 grows, with no change in country 2, so that $\hat{L}^1 > 0$, and $\hat{L}^2 = 0$. Then we can solve for the changing number of products from (5.45) and (5.46) as

$$\hat{N}^1 = \frac{\phi^{22}}{(\phi^{22} - \phi^{21})}\hat{L}^1 > \hat{L}^1 > 0 \ \text{ and } \ \hat{N}^2 = \frac{-\phi^{12}}{|\Phi|}\hat{L}^1 < 0. \qquad (5.47)$$

Thus, the number of products in the larger country will grow by *more than* the increase in country size, while those in the smaller country will *shrink*. Because consumption c^{ij} and prices p^{ij} are both fixed, exports $X^{ij} = N^i p^{ij} c^{ij}$ from each country to the other will change in proportion to the number of products. Thus, with N^1 growing and N^2 falling, country 1 will become a *net exporter* of the differentiated good to country 2, $X^{21} > X^{12}$ (where trade is balanced overall through flows of the homogeneous good). Summarizing these results, we have the following theorem.

Theorem (Krugman 1980)

With two countries trading, the larger market will produce a greater number of products and be a net exporter of the differentiated good.

This result is known as the '*home market effect*,' because it shows that a larger home market will attract disproportionately more firms, and therefore become a net exporter. This is quite different from what we expect in a model where the number of products N^i is constant: in that case, a larger market would have larger demand, and would therefore become a *net importer* of the good in question.[17]

---

[17] The assumption that products are differentiated by their country of origin, but the number of varieties supplied by each country is *fixed*, is known as the "Armington assumption," from

Davis and Weinstein (1996, 1999) provide the most direct test of the 'home market' effect, using industry level data for the OECD. They first measure "idiosyncratic" demand differences across countries, and then argue that having higher home demand should lead a country to be an exporter of a good if the 'home market effect' operates.[18] They test this by regressing production of industries on the estimated demand differences across countries. In their pooled sample, they obtain an estimated coefficient of 1.6 on the demand differences, indicating that having 10% greater demand for a product will lead to 16% additional production in that country, meaning that net exports will rise. This provides confirmation of the home market effect. When disaggregating across industries, they find that the impact of local demand on production exceeds unity in a majority of industries, though there are a few exceptions. When using data for Japanese industries locating in various prefectures, they find significant evidence of home market effects in about one-half of the industries, and these effects are economically large.

Head and Ries (2002) test for the home market effect between Canada and the United States. With only two countries, they need to rely on cross-industry or time-series variation in the data, rather than the cross-country demand differences used by Davis and Weinstein. For the cross-industry regression they find a weak home market effect, but for the time-series regression the home market effect is reversed (i.e., higher demand leads to imports rather than exports).

A similar reversal is found by Feenstra, Markusen, and Rose (2001), when comparing cross-country trade in *differentiated* versus *homogeneous* products.[19] In the gravity equation for differentiated products, they find that the coefficient on exporter GDP exceeds unity, whereas the coefficient of the importer GDP is less than unity. Having the coefficient on exporter GDP exceed unity is like the comparative static effect reported in (5.47): the change in exports from country 1 to country 2 is $\hat{X}^{12} = \hat{N}^1 > \hat{L}^1$, so having higher country 1 income (L^1) leads to a *magnified* increase in exports. For the homogeneous products, however, this result is reversed and the

---

Armington (1969). This was used as a convenient assumption before the introduction of monopolistic competition models. The fact that the number of varieties per country is fixed in the Armington assumption gives it quite different properties than monopolistic competition, where the number of varieties produced in each country varies due to free entry.

[18] Note that we could have let ϕ differ between the countries, and then the home market effect still operates.

[19] The classification of goods according to whether they are differentiated or homogeneous is due to Rauch (1999). He has classified products at the five-digit SITC level according to whether they are (*a*) traded in an organized exchange, and therefore treated as homogeneous; (*b*) not traded in an organized exchange, but having some quoted "reference price," such as in industry publications; (*c*) not having any quoted prices, and therefore treated as differentiated.

exporter GDP has a coefficient smaller than importer GDP. The latter result is what we would expect from a model where the number of products in each country is fixed, so that higher demand leads to net imports rather than net exports.

Conclusions

This chapter has covered material in two topics—trade under monopolistic competition and the gravity equation—that are often linked, though they need not be. As we have mentioned, the gravity equation arises quite naturally whenever countries are specialized in different goods. Such specialization is sometimes called '*national product differentiation*,' and cross-border trade in different varieties of a good is referred to as '*intra-industry trade*.' This occurs under the monopolistic competition model, but also occurs in other contexts, for example, Dornbusch, Fischer, and Samuelson's (1977) Ricardian model with a continuum of goods, or their (1980) Heckscher-Ohlin (HO) model where factor price are not equalized, as studied in chapter 3. Davis (1995) has combined Ricardian and HO elements to generate intraindustry trade in a model where product varieties have identical capital/labor ratios, but differ across countries by a Hicks-neutral productivity term.[20]

So while complete specialization in goods can arise in a number of contexts, the CES monopolistic competition model proves to be a convenient way to derive the gravity equation, especially when we allow for transport costs and other trade barriers. Unlike early work on the gravity equation that assumed identical prices across countries, once we introduce transportation costs or any other border barriers, prices must differ internationally, so we need to take account of the overall price indexes in each country. We have reviewed three methods to do so: using published data on price indexes; using the computational method of Anderson and van Wincoop (2003); or using country fixed effects to measure the price indexes. The latter two methods were compared on a dataset dealing with trade between and within Canada and the United States. The fixed-effects method produces consistent estimates of the *average* border effect across countries, and is simple to implement, so it might be considered to be the preferred empirical method.

---

[20] An elegant extension of Ricardian differences is provided by Eaton and Kortum (2002), who consider *stochastic* differences in the technologies across countries, with the lowest-cost country becoming the exporter of each product variety. They obtain a gravity-like equation, which should include country fixed effects that are related to the probability distribution of technologies within each country.

The fact that the gravity equation works well empirically cannot be taken as evidence in support of the monopolistic competition model, however: it simply suggests that countries are specialized in different products, for whatever reason.[21] To really test whether trade patterns are due to monopolistic competition, we must look for hypotheses arising from this model that would not occur otherwise. One such hypothesis is the '*home market effect*,' whereby firms tend to locate in the larger market due to higher profits available there. Under alternative explanations for national product differentiation, the home market effect need not occur: if the number of products N^i produced in each country is constant, then a larger market would have larger demand, and would therefore become a *net importer* of the good in question. So evidence of the home market effect, as found by Davis and Weinstein (1996, 1999) and more weakly by Feenstra, Markusen, and Rose (2001) as well as Head and Ries (2001), lends support to the idea that monopolistic competition explains national product specialization.

An important area for further research is to test other hypotheses arising from that model. One direction to look is in the area of economic geography. An expanded discussion of that topic is beyond the scope of this book, but the reader is referred to Fujita, Krugman, and Venables (1999), who describe many results building on increasing returns to scale and the monopolistic competition model. For example, this literature suggests that proximity to markets will raise wages, and Redding and Venables (2000) apply this idea to estimate wages across countries based on the gravity equation. A similar approach can be used to determine wages across cities or regions *within* a country, as in Hanson 1997, 1998.[22] In other empirical work, Davis and Weinstein (2002a) have used the location of economic activity in Japan, going from prehistoric times to wartime dislocations to the present day, to evaluate the importance of increasing returns versus alternative explanations for industry location.

Another direction to look for hypotheses is to loosen some of the assumptions of the monopolistic competition model. Two key assumptions are that firms are *symmetric* (their costs are all the same) and that they each produce a *single product*. Both of these assumptions are patently false: every industry has a wide range of firms of various efficiencies, and many of them produce multiple products. The theoretical difficulty with

---

[21] Actually, Evenett and Keller (2002) argue that even with incomplete specialization, a modified version of the gravity equation occurs in the HO model. It appears that this result depends on having just two countries, however, since otherwise the HO model makes no prediction at all about *bilateral* trade flows. Evenett and Keller test the increasing returns versus HO version of the gravity equation, and reject both in favor of a combined framework.

[22] See also the survey by Overman, Redding, and Venables (2003). A theoretical model linking outsourcing and wages in an economic geography framework is provided by Gao (2002).

allowing for firms with differing efficiency is that the zero-profit condition of monopolistic competition will no longer apply: if the less efficient firms earn zero profits, then the more efficient firms will not. This difficulty has been resolved in different ways by Melitz (2003) and Yeaple (2003). In Melitz's model, firms have random productivities and earn zero *expected* profits, while in Yeaple's model, the *workers* in more efficient firms receive higher wages, so profits are still zero. Both of these models suggest empirical applications.

The assumption that firms in the monopolistic competition model each produce a single product has be weakened by Feenstra, Huang, and Hamilton (2003). They motivate the idea of multiproduct companies by the "business groups" that are found in many countries, such as the *keiretsu* in Japan and the *chaebol* in South Korea. In their model, a business group chooses its range of upstream and downstream products to maximize profits, while free entry of groups ensures that profits are zero in equilibrium. They show that having multiproduct groups has a sharp implication for trade patterns: economies dominated by business groups will produce *less product variety* than with single-product firms. This hypothesis can be tested by comparing two economies of similar size but with differing structure of business groups. For that purpose, Feenstra, Yang, and Hamilton (1999) compare South Korea and Taiwan, where Korea has the large and strongly integrated *chaebol*, whereas Taiwan has much smaller business groups that are mainly located upstream. By comparing their sales of disaggregate products to the United States, it is strongly confirmed that Taiwan sells a *greater product variety* to the United States in nearly all industries than does Korea. Differences in the export patterns from South Korea and Taiwan are also observed by Martins (1992) and Rodrik (1993), who attribute this to the group structure in the two countries. Thus, the influence of business groups on the structure of trade, as predicted by monopolistic competition with multiproduct companies, is supported by this empirical evidence.

Appendix: Using the Gravity Model to Measure Border Effects

The estimates of 10.5 for Canada and 2.6 for the United States, shown in column (4) of Table 5.2, are Anderson and van Wincoop's (2003) "best" estimates of the impact of the Canada-U.S. border on intra-Canadian and intra-American trade relative to cross-border trade. These are unbiased estimates of the Canada-U.S. border effect, as opposed to the other estimates reported near the bottom of columns (1)–(3), which are biased because the price terms are omitted from the gravity equation. While the estimates of 10.5 and 2.6 require a complex calculation from (5.38), the *geometric mean* of these two values can be obtained very simply from the gravity equation, as indicated by the following result.

Lemma

Let $\hat{\gamma}$ denote the estimated coefficient of the border indicator in the gravity equation, and use (5.38) to compute the impact of the border on intranational trade *relative to* international trade, for each country. Then the geometric mean of the impact on each country equals $e^{-\hat{\gamma}}$.

Proof

The multilateral resistance terms in (5.38) are obtained from (5.32) using the transportation costs $T^{ij} = (d^{ij})^{\hat{\alpha}} e^{\hat{\gamma}(1-\delta^{ij})}$ (i.e., including border effects) to compute $(\tilde{P}^i)^{\sigma-1}$, while using $T^{ij} = (d^{ij})^{\hat{\alpha}}$ (i.e., just distance) to compute $(\overline{P}^i)^{\sigma-1}$. Taking the geometric mean of trade X^{ij} between Canadian provinces with border effects, and the predicted value $\overline{X}^{ij}$ without border effects, we obtain from (5.38):

$$\prod_{i,j\in CA} \left(\frac{X^{ij}}{\overline{X}^{ij}}\right)^{1/N} = \prod_{i,j\in CA} \left(\frac{(\tilde{P}^i)^{\sigma-1}(\tilde{P}^j)^{\sigma-1}}{(\overline{P}^i)^{\sigma-1}(\overline{P}^j)^{\sigma-1}}\right)^{1/N}. \tag{5.48}$$

With $CA = \{1,\ldots,10\}$ Canadian provinces, they can each sell to 9 others, making $N = 90$ bilateral flows in (5.48). (Notice that we exclude $i = j$ from the calculations in (5.48), since we are not considering sales by a province to itself.) In each of the bilateral flows, *two* indexes appear on the right-hand side, so there are a total of 180 multilateral indexes in the numerator and in the denominator of (5.48). Since each of the 10 provinces appears on the right-hand side of (5.48) an equal number of times, that is, $180/10 = 18$ times, this expression can be simplified as

$$\prod_{i,j\in CA} \left(\frac{X^{ij}}{\overline{X}^{ij}}\right)^{1/N} = \prod_{i\in CA} \left(\frac{(\tilde{P}^i)^{\sigma-1}}{(\overline{P}^i)^{\sigma-1}}\right)^{1/5}, \tag{5.48'}$$

where the exponent on the right is obtained as $18/90 = 1/5$.

Using the same approach for the $US = \{1,\ldots,30\}$ American states in the sample, we can compute that average trade between them with and without border effects as

$$\prod_{i,j\in US} \left(\frac{X^{ij}}{\overline{X}^{ij}}\right)^{1/N} = \prod_{i,j\in US} \left(\frac{(\tilde{P}^i)^{\sigma-1}(\tilde{P}^j)^{\sigma-1}}{(\overline{P}^i)^{\sigma-1}(\overline{P}^j)^{\sigma-1}}\right)^{1/N}, \tag{5.49}$$

where now $N = 30 \cdot 29 = 870$. Again, for each bilateral flow there are *two* multilateral indexes in the numerator and denominator on the right, so each of these indexes appears $870 \cdot 2 = 1{,}740$ times. Since each of the 30 states appears on the right of (5.49) an equal number of times, that is, $1740/30 = 58$ times, this expression can be simplified as

$$\prod_{i,j\in US}\left(\frac{X^{ij}}{\overline{X}^{ij}}\right)^{1/N} = \prod_{i\in US}\left(\frac{(\tilde{P}^i)^{\sigma-1}}{(\overline{P}^i)^{\sigma-1}}\right)^{1/15}, \qquad (5.49')$$

where the exponent on the right is obtained as $58/870 = 1/15$.

Finally, consider the effects on cross-border trade. In this case $\delta^{ij} = 0$, so the term $(d^{ij})^{\hat{\alpha}} e^{\hat{\gamma}(1-\delta^{ij})} = (d^{ij})^{\hat{\alpha}} e^{\hat{\gamma}}$ appears in (5.38). The ratio of United States–to-Canada exports with the border effects and without is given by

$$\prod_{i\in US, j\in CA}\left(\frac{X^{ij}}{\overline{X}^{ij}}\right)^{1/N} = \left[e^{\hat{\gamma}(1-\delta^{ij})}\right]\prod_{i\in US, j\in CA}\left(\frac{(\tilde{P}^i)^{\sigma-1}(\tilde{P}^j)^{\sigma-1}}{(\overline{P}^i)^{\sigma-1}(\overline{P}^j)^{\sigma-1}}\right)^{1/N}. \qquad (5.50)$$

On the left side, we average the flow from the United States to Canada, so $N = 30 \cdot 10 = 300$. On the right side, each pair of state-provinces appears an equal number of times, which means that each province appears 30 times and each state appears 10 times. It follows that we can rewrite this expression as

$$\prod_{i\in US, j\in CA}\left(\frac{X^{ij}}{\overline{X}^{ij}}\right)^{1/N} = (e^{\hat{\gamma}})\prod_{i\in US}\left(\frac{(\tilde{P}^i)^{\sigma-1}}{(\overline{P}^i)^{\sigma-1}}\right)^{1/30}\prod_{j\in CA}\left(\frac{(\tilde{P}^j)^{\sigma-1}}{(\overline{P}^j)^{\sigma-1}}\right)^{1/10}, \qquad (5.50')$$

where the exponent on the U.S. multilateral indexes is obtained as $10/300 = 1/30$, and the exponent on the Canadian provinces is obtained as $30/300 = 1/10$.

We also need to compute the ratio of Canada-to–United States exports with the border effects and without, but this turns out to be identical to $(5.50')$. Then taking the geometric mean of $(5.48')$ and $(5.49')$, and dividing by the square of $(5.50')$, we obtain $e^{-\hat{\gamma}}$. QED

Problems

5.1 For the utility function in (5.1), with $v(0) = 0$, $v' > 0$, and $v'' < 0$, show that when the number of goods rises holding income fixed, the consumer is better off.

5.2 In Krugman's monopolistic competition model, suppose that the utility function takes on the CES form shown in (5.10), rewritten for simplicity with two goods as

$$U(c_1, c_2) = c_1^\theta + c_2^\theta, \quad 0 < \theta = (\sigma - 1)/\sigma < 1.$$

Maximize this subject to the budget constraint, $p_1 c_1 + p_2 c_2 \leq I$.

(a) Obtain an expression for the *relative* demand c_1/c_2 as a function of prices.
(b) The *elasticity of substitution* is defined as $d \ln(c_1/c_2)/d \ln(p_2/p_1)$. What is the value of the elasticity of substitution for this utility function?
(c) Obtain an expression for the demands c_1 and c_2 as a function of prices.
(d) What do these expressions imply about the elasticity of demand?

5.3 Suppose that industry 1 is monopolistically competitive, with a CES subutility function as described in problem 5.2. We let the marginal costs be denoted by $c_1(w, r)$, and the fixed costs in the industry by $\alpha c_1(w, r)$. That is, the fixed costs use labor and capital in the same proportions as the marginal costs. Industry 2 is a competitive industry, and each industry uses labor and capital.

(a) Write down the relationship between the prices of goods and factor prices. Does the Stolper-Samuelson theorem still apply?
(b) Write down the full-employment conditions for the two factors. Does the Rybczynski theorem still apply in some form?

How are your answers to parts (a) and (b) affected if the fixed costs in industry 1 use different proportions of labor and capital than the marginal costs?

5.4 Consider the translog expenditure function:

$$\ln E(p, U) = \ln U + a_0 + \sum_{i=1}^{N} a_i \ln p_i + \frac{1}{2} \sum_{i=1}^{N} \sum_{j=1}^{N} b_{ij} \ln p_i \ln p_j, \quad (5.51)$$

where

$$a_i = 1/N, \; b_{ii} = -\gamma(N-1)/N, \text{ and } b_{ij} = \gamma/N \text{ for} \atop i \neq j, \text{ with } i, j = 1, \dots, N, \qquad (5.52)$$

where $\gamma > 0$. Use this expenditure function to answer the following:

(a) Show that restrictions in (5.52) ensure that the expenditure function in (5.51) is homogeneous of degree one in prices;
(b) Derive the share of expenditure on good i by differentiating (5.51) with respect to $\ln p_i$;

(c) Differentiate the share of each good with respect to ln p_i to derive an expression for the elasticity of demand;
(d) Use the elasticity of demand to obtain an expression for the ratio of price to marginal cost for the firm. How will each firm's price depend on its competitor's prices?

Note that this expenditure function has been used by Bergin and Feenstra (2000, 2001), and is justified by Feenstra (2003).

Empirical Exercises

In these exercises, you are asked to reproduce the empirical results shown in Table 5.2. There are four datasets available: "dist.csv", which is distances; "gdp_ce_93.csv", which is GDP in exporting location in 1993; "gdp_ci_ 93.csv", which is GDP in importing location in 1993; and "trade_93.csv", which is trade in 1993. To complete the exercises, these files should be stored in the directory c:\Empirical_Exercise\Chapter_5\. When the files are located there, run the STATA program "data_trans.do," which will convert these datasets to STATA files with the same name. The trade data is already converted into U.S. dollars, but GDP data is in Canadian dollars, so this is converted with the exchange rate 1 Canadian dollar = 0.775 U.S. dollars. Then do the following:

5.1 Run the program "gravity_1.do" to replicate the gravity equations in columns (1)–(3) of Table 5.2.

5.2 Run the program "gravity_2.do" to replicate gravity equation using fixed effects, that is, column (5) in Table 5.2. Then answer the following:

(a) How are these results affected if we allow the provincial and state GDPs to have coefficients different from unity?
(b) What coefficients are obtained if we introduce separate indicator variables for intra-Canadian and intra-U.S. trade, rather than the border dummy?

Chapter 6

Gains from Trade and Regional Agreements

IN EARLIER CHAPTERS we suggested that trade brings gains to a country, but at the same time, there are both winners and losers. The Stolper-Samuelson theorem made that especially clear. In the Heckscher-Ohlin model the *abundant factor* gains from trade (through the rise in the relative export price, increasing the real return to that factor, used intensively in exports), while the *scarce factor* loses from trade (through the fall in the relative import price, lowering the real return to that factor). Can we be sure that the gains always exceed the losses? That is the topic of this chapter.

We begin with a discussion of "lump sum transfers," whereby the government has the ability to tax the gainers and transfer income to the losers, without changing their behavior in the process. That is, the lump sum transfers are assumed to be nondistorting. We show that it is indeed possible to achieve Pareto gains from trade, that is, a situation where everyone gains. This result is unrealistic, however, because any attempt by the government to achieve such a redistribution of income would lead people to change their behavior (so as to receive more transfers), and these effects are not taken into account.

As a second approach, we investigate a set of commodity and factor taxes/subsidies that has been proposed by Dixit and Norman (1980). By construction, this policy requires much less information than the lump sum transfers, and any changes in individuals' behavior due to the tax or subsidies are fully taken into account. We show that this policy can *also* lead to a situation where everyone gains. There are still some assumptions needed to achieve this result, as we will discuss, but the policy is generally thought to be much more feasible than lump sum transfers. Indeed, we provide an example from Akerlof et al. (1991) where factor subsidies were proposed as a means to obtain Pareto gains from trade after the unification of Germany.

The use of lump sum subsidies to achieve Pareto gains from trade can be readily extended to compare any two trading situations, and identify conditions under which the country in question is better off or not, as in Grinols and Wong 1991 and Ju and Krishna 2000a, 2000b. Furthermore, the analysis can be extended to cover tariff reform by multiple countries. This is the goal of the World Trade Organization (WTO): to reduce barriers to trade among its member countries, which include more than 140 countries. Among the newest members are the People's Republic of China, accepted into the WTO on November 10, 2001, with Taiwan joining the next day. The WTO was known before 1994 as the General Agreement on Tariffs and Trade (GATT), and was set up after World War II along with other international institution such as the International Monetary Fund and the World Bank. The GATT has made great progress in reducing trade barriers worldwide through "rounds" of discussion, which included the Uruguay Round lasting from 1986 to 1994, and the agreement in Doha, Qatar, on November 14, 2001, to launch a new round of negotiations.

Some of the founding principles of GATT, known as articles, are displayed in Table 6.1. The most fundamental of these is the "most favored nation" (MFN) principle (see Article I), which states that all countries belonging to the GATT should be treated equally; that is, if the United States reduces its tariffs on goods coming from Europe, it must do the same for those goods coming from any other member country. Such tariff reductions are called *multilateral*, and all the GATT rounds have been aimed at multilateral reductions in trade barriers.

There are instances, however, where a group of countries will decide to completely eliminate all tariffs between them, *without* eliminating tariffs on goods imported from the rest of the world. This is called a *regional agreement* or *preferential agreement* between the countries involved. In the case where this group of countries also *unify* their tariffs against the rest of the world, with zero tariffs internally, this is called a *customs union*. The European Economic Community (EEC) is one example of a customs union, and another is MERCOSUR, established in 1995, which includes Argentina, Brazil, Paraguay and Uruguay. In contrast, if the group of countries maintains *their own* tariffs against the rest of the world, with zero tariffs internally, then this is called a *free-trade area*. Examples of free-trade areas are the Canada-U.S. Free Trade Agreement (CUSFTA) of 1989, which later led to the North American Free Trade Agreement (NAFTA) of 1994, which consists of Canada, the United States, and Mexico. Both customs unions and free-trade areas violate the MFN principle, since the countries within the union or area are treated differently from those outside. But such agreements are permitted under Article XXIV of the GATT, provided that "the duties [with outside parties] shall not on the whole be higher or more restrictive than the general incidence of the duties . . . prior to the formation."

Because customs unions and free-trade areas involve only partial elimination of tariffs, they can lead to unexpected results: as pointed out by

TABLE 6.1
Key Provisions of the GATT Agreement Preamble

Recognizing that their relations in the field of trade and economic endeavour
should be conducted with a view to raising standards of living, ensuring full
employment and a large and steadily growing volume of real income and
effective demand, developing the full use of the resources of the world and
expanding the production and exchange of goods.

Being desirous of contributing to these objectives by entering into reciprocal and
mutually advantageous arrangements directed to the substantial reduction of
tariffs and other barriers to trade and to the elimination of discriminatory
treatment in international commerce.

Have through their Representatives agreed as follows:

ARTICLE I

General Most-Favoured-Nation Treatment

1. With respect to customs duties . . . and with respect to all rules and formalities
   in connection with importation and exportation . . . any advantage, favour,
   privilege or immunity granted by any contracting party to any product
   originating in or destined for any other country shall be accorded immediately
   and unconditionally to the like product originating in or destined for the
   territories of all other contracting parties . . .

ARTICLE III

National Treatment on Internal Taxation and Regulation

1. The contracting parties recognize that internal taxes and other internal
   charges, and laws, regulations and requirements affecting the internal
   sale . . . should not be applied to imported or domestic products so as to
   afford protection to domestic production . . .

ARTICLE VI

Anti-dumping and Countervailing Duties

1. The contracting parties recognize that dumping, by which products of one
   country are introduced into the commerce of another country at less than
   the normal value of the products, is to be condemned if it causes or
   threatens material injury to an established industry. . . . [A] product is to be
   considered . . . less than its normal value, if the price of the product exported
   from one country to another
   a. is less than the comparable price . . . for the like product when destined for
      consumption in the exporting country, or,
   b. in the absence of such domestic price, is less than either
1) the highest comparable price for the like product for export to any third
   country in the ordinary course of trade, or

TABLE 6.1 (*cont.*)

---

2) the cost of production of the product in the country of origin plus a reasonable addition for selling cost and profit . . .

ARTICLE X

Publication and Administration of Trade Regulations

1. Laws, regulations, judicial decisions and administrative rulings of general application, made effective by any contracting party, pertaining to the classification or the valuation of products for customs purposes, or to rates of duty, taxes or other charges, or to requirements, restrictions or prohibitions on imports or exports or on the transfer of payments therefore . . . shall be published promptly in such a manner as to enable governments and traders to become acquainted with them. . . . The provisions of this paragraph shall not require any contracting party to disclose confidential information which would impede law enforcement or otherwise be contrary to the public interest or would prejudice the legitimate commercial interests of particular enterprises, public or private.

ARTICLE XI

General Elimination of Quantitative Restrictions

1. No prohibitions or restrictions other than duties, taxes or other charges, whether made effective through quotes, import or export licenses or other measures, shall be instituted or maintained by any contracting party on the importation of any product of the territory of any other contracting party or on the exportation or sale for export of any product destined for the territory of any other contracting party . . .

ARTICLE XVI

Subsidies

1. If any contracting party grants or maintains any subsidy, including any form of income or price support, which operates directly or indirectly to increase exports of any product from, or to reduce imports of any product into, its territory, it shall notify the contracting parties in writing of the extent and nature of the subsidization, of the estimated effect of the subsidization on the quantity of the affected product or products imported into or exported from its territory and of the circumstances making subsidization necessary. In any case in which it is determined that serious prejudice to the interests of any other contracting party is caused or threatened by any such subsidization, the contracting party granting the subsidy shall, upon request, discuss with the other contracting party . . . the possibility of limiting the subsidization.

TABLE 6.1 (*cont.*)

ARTICLE XVII

Restrictions to Safeguard the Balance of Payments

1. Notwithstanding the provisions of paragraph 1 of Article XI, any contracting party, in order to safeguard its external financial position and its balance of payments, may restrict the quantity or value of merchandise permitted to be imported.

ARTICLE XIX

Emergency Action on Imports of Particular Products

1. (a) If, as a result of unforeseen developments and of the effect of the obligations incurred by a contracting party under this Agreement, including tariff concessions, any product is being imported into the territory of that contracting party in such increased quantities and under such conditions as to cause or threaten serious injury to domestic producers in that territory of like or directly competitive products, the contracting party shall be free, in respect of such product, and to the extent and for such time as may be necessary to prevent or remedy such injury, to suspend the obligation in whole or in part or to withdraw or modify the concession . . .

ARTICLE XXIV

Territorial Application—Frontier Traffic—Customs Unions and Free-Trade Areas

4. The contracting parties recognize the desirability of increasing freedom of trade by the development, through voluntary agreements, of closer integration between the economies of the countries party to such agreements. They also recognize that the purpose of a customs union or of a free-trade area should be to facilitate trade between the constituent territories and not to raise barriers to the trade of other contracting parties with such territories.
5. Accordingly, the provisions of this Agreement shall not prevent [the formation of customs unions and free-trade areas, provided that]
(a) . . . the duties [with outside parties] shall not on the whole be higher or more restrictive than the general incidence of the duties . . . prior to the formation . . .

Source: Yoffie and Gomes-Casseres 1994, pp. 420–22.

Viner (1950), the countries left out of the union and even the countries *inside* the union can become worse off. We discuss this possibility at the end of the chapter, and identify conditions under which this outcome can be avoided, as in Kemp and Wan 1976. This also provides us with an important area for empirical research, that is, measuring the gains and losses from preferential agreements, of which there have been an increasing number in recent years. We discuss several empirical studies: Grinols 1984 on Britain's membership in the EEC; Clausing 2001 and Romalis 2002 on trade creation and diversion due to CUSFTA and NAFTA; and Chang and Winters 2002 on the terms of trade effects of MERCOSUR. We conclude the chapter by extending the results to include imperfect competition and increasing returns to scale, and also briefly discussing the welfare effects of regional agreements under monopolistic competition.

Lump Sum Transfers

Our discussion of lump sum transfers follows Dixit and Norman (1980, 76–78). We want to distinguish the various consumers in the economy, so we index them by $h = 1, \ldots, H$. We will suppose that individual h has the increasing and quasi-concave utility function $u^h(c^h, v^h)$, where c^h is the N-dimensional vector of consumption, and v^h is the M-dimensional vector of factor supplies. Under autarky, each consumer maximizes utility subject to the budget constraint

$$p^{a\prime} c^{ha} \leq w^{a\prime} v^{ha}, \tag{6.1}$$

where p^a is the autarky vector of commodity prices, and w^a is the autarky vector of factor prices. The resulting utility for each consumer is $u^h(c^{ha}, v^{ha})$.

Summing over all consumption and factor supplies, the total output in the economy is therefore $\Sigma_{h=1}^{H} c^{ha} = y^a$, and the total factor inputs are $\Sigma_{h=1}^{H} v^{ha} = v^a$. Of course, the point (y^a, v^a) must be feasible for producers, and also optimal at the prices (p^a, w^a). We will assume that the technology for the economy is subject to constant returns to scale. This means that the payments to factors are exactly equal to the revenue collected, so that profits in the economy are

$$p^{a\prime} y^a - w^{a\prime} v^a = 0.$$

We now consider the free-trade equilibrium, which includes a system of lump sum taxes or transfers from the government to each individual. We will let R^h denote the transfer to each individual h, so that $R^h < 0$ is a lump sum tax. Then the total revenue collected by the government is $-\Sigma_{b=1}^{H} R^{b}$, and we will need to establish that this is nonnegative in order for this system of lump sum transfers to be feasible.

Denote the equilibrium commodity and factor prices under free trade by (p, w). With each individual receiving the transfer R^{b}, the budget constraint is

$$p'c^{b} \le w'v^{b} + R^{b}. \tag{6.2}$$

We want to choose a pattern of transfers that allows all individuals to be as well off as they were in autarky. To this end, consider the following system:

$$R^{b} = (p - p^{a})'c^{ba} - (w - w^{a})'v^{ba}. \tag{6.3}$$

To interpret this, if a price for a commodity rises going from autarky to free trade, the government will subsidize each individual by the price rise times the individual's autarky consumption. Conversely, if the earnings of a factor rise going from autarky to free trade, the government will tax each individual by the wage increase times the individual's autarky factor supply. The goal of this transfer system is to ensure that all individuals can still afford their autarky choices (c^{ba}, v^{ba}). To see that this is indeed the case, substitute these autarky choices into the budget constraint (6.2), and make use of (6.3), to obtain

$$p'c^{ba} \le w'v^{ba} + (p - p^{a})'c^{ba} - (w - w^{a})'v^{ba} \iff p^{a}{}'c^{ba} \le w^{a}{}'v^{ba}.$$

Since the second equation above is just the individual's autarky budget constraint in (6.1), we know that it is satisfied. This proves that the autarky choices (c^{ba}, v^{ba}) are feasible for the budget constraint in (6.2) and transfers in (6.3).

This result can also be seen from Figure 6.1. We illustrate there the indifference curves for an individual choosing between a single consumption good c^{b} and a single factor supply v^{b}. Under autarky the budget constraint is $p^{a}c^{b} \le w^{a}v^{b}$, or $c^{b} \le (w^{a}/p^{a})v^{b}$, as shown by the line through the origin with slope (w^{a}/p^{a}), and the individual chooses point A. Suppose that the free-trade prices lead to a decline in the real wage, $(w/p) < (w^{a}/p^{a})$. Then in order to ensure that the consumer can still afford point A, the government would transfer the amount R/p in terms of the consumption good, leading to the budget constraint starting at that point and rising with slope (w/p). On this budget constraint the individual can still afford point A, but would prefer to consume at point B. This illustrates the consumer gains available using the lump sum transfers described in (6.3).

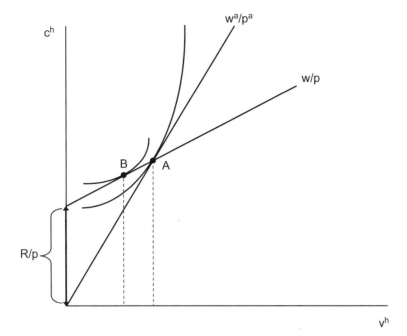

Figure 6.1

Let us now sum up the transfers, and reverse its sign, to obtain total government revenue:

$$
\begin{aligned}
-\sum_{b=1}^{H} R^{b} &= (p^{a} - p)' \sum_{b=1}^{H} c^{ba} - (w^{a} - w)' \sum_{b=1}^{H} v^{ba} \\
&= (p^{a} - p)' y^{a} - (w^{a} - w)' v^{a} \\
&= (p^{a\prime} y^{a} - w^{a\prime} v^{a}) - (p' y^{a} - w' v^{a}) \\
&= -(p' y^{a} - w' v^{a}) \\
&\geq -(p' y - w' v) = 0,
\end{aligned}
\tag{6.4}
$$

where the second line follows by using $\sum_{b=1}^{H} c^{ba} = y^{a}$ and $\sum_{b=1}^{H} v^{ba} = v^{a}$, the third line follows by rearranging terms, and the fourth line follows because autarky profits are zero as in (6.2). The expression $(p' y^{a} - w' v^{a})$ in the fourth line shows the value of profits under free trade if producers chose the feasible but nonoptimal point (y^{a}, v^{a}), which will be *less than* profits at the optimal point (y, v), and these profits are zero from constant returns to scale. This establishes the final line.

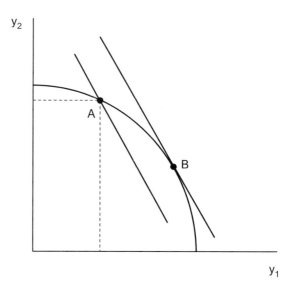

Figure 6.2

Therefore, we see that $-\sum_{h=1}^{H} R^{h} \geq 0$, so this system does not cost the government anything: the lump sum taxes collected from those gaining from trade are more than enough to cover the subsidies to those harmed by trade. No one is harmed by the move to free trade, and there will generally be gains of two sorts: the *consumption gains* shown in Figure 6.1 from consuming at a point different from autarky; and the *efficiency gains* that arise when the value of output $(p'y - w'v)$ is strictly greater than $(p'y^{a} - w'v^{a})$, so that the inequality on the last line of (6.4) is strict. To understand this source of gains, consider a special case where the factor supplies chosen by consumers do not change, so that the total factor inputs $\bar{v}$ are fixed. Then we have that $w'v^{a} = w'\bar{v} = p'y$, so that the revenue collected by the government in (6.4) is

$$-\sum_{h=1}^{H} R^{h} = -(p'y^{a} - w'v^{a}) = p'y - p'y^{a}. \qquad (6.4')$$

In Figure 6.2, for example, suppose that the autarky equilibrium is at point A and the free-trade production point at B. Then the revenue collected by the government is exactly the difference between the value of production at these points (with free-trade prices p), or the difference between the two budget lines that are drawn. Figure 6.2 thus illustrates the *production or efficiency gains* due to opening trade, and with this revenue given back to consumers via the lump sum transfers, they enjoy a rise in welfare for that reason in addition to the *consumption gains* illustrated in Figure 6.1.

How large are these gains from trade? There are a few historical examples where countries have moved from autarky to free trade, or vice versa, rapidly enough that we can use time-series data to estimate the gains from trade. One such episode in the United States occurred during December 1807 to March 1809, when Congress imposed a nearly complete embargo on international trade at the request of President Jefferson. Irwin (2001) calculates that the welfare cost to the United States was some 8% of GDP, which compares to pre-embargo exports of about 13% of GDP. Another case was Japan's rapid opening to the world economy in 1859 after some two hundred years of self-imposed autarky. Bernhofen and Brown (2002) calculate an upper bound to the gains from trade for Japan of 4 to 5% of GDP.

As appealing as these results on the gains from trade are, the idea of using lump sum transfers is not realistic because this policy requires too much information to implement. This can be seen from (6.3), where the transfers require knowledge of *each individual's autarky consumption and factor supplies*. Suppose that the government announced a plan to collect this information using a survey, and then implement the transfers in (6.3). Given knowledge of the formula used in (6.3), people would then have an incentive to change their consumptions and factor supplies so as to have more beneficial values of (c^{ha}, v^{ha}) recorded in the survey, and therefore get more transfers, thereby leading to a government budget deficit. This is an example of an *incentive compatibility* problem: the attempt to implement a policy would lead individuals to not truthfully report the information needed.

There are two possible solutions to such a problem. The first, which we describe next, is to use policy instruments that do not require individual information. A second solution is to *build into the policy itself* an incentive for people to tell the truth. The transfers in (6.3) certainly will not do this: everyone would claim that they had consumed more of goods whose prices increased from autarky to trade, and supplied more of factors whose wages fell. But perhaps there is some other system of transfers that would lead to truthful reporting of individual information, and is therefore incentive compatible, while at the same time leading to Pareto gains. This topic is explored in Feenstra, McMillan, and Lewis 1990; Feenstra and Lewis 1991a; and Facchini and Willmann 1999, but is beyond the scope of the present chapter.

Commodity Taxes and Subsidies

Dixit and Norman (1980, 79–80) and Dixit (1986) have proposed a system of commodity taxes and subsidies that is designed to achieve Pareto gains from trade, without requiring individual information (or at least, requiring much less information). Specifically, their idea is to allow good and factor prices *for producers* to move to their free-trade levels, but hold good and factor prices *for consumers* fixed at their autarky levels. Let us denote the autarky prices by (p^a, w^a) and the equilibrium prices with free trade (and the commodity tax/subsidies in place) by (p, w). We let firms face these free-trade prices, and set the vector of consumer taxes on goods at $(p^a - p)$ and the vector of consumer subsidies on factors at $(w^a - w)$. It follows that consumers face the price vector (p^a, w^a), which is the same as in autarky. Therefore, they would make exactly the same decisions as in autarky, and achieve their autarky utility $u^h(c^{ha}, v^{ha})$.

Next, we check the government budget. The revenue collected from this system of commodity taxes and subsidies equals

$$(p^a - p)'\sum_{h=1}^{H} c^{ha} - (w^a - w)'\sum_{h=1}^{H} v^{ha} = (p^a - p)'y^a - (w^a - w)'v^a. \quad (6.5)$$

Notice that this is *identical* to the expression in (6.4), and is therefore nonnegative for exactly the same reasons. As we discussed in (6.4') and Figure 6.2, this expression is strictly positive whenever there are efficiency gains from having producers face free-trade rather than autarky prices. If this is the case, then the government redistributes this revenue back to consumers as a "poll subsidy" (i.e., an equal amount to each person). In that way, all consumers receive *more than* their autarky utility level, and Pareto gains from trade are achieved!

This system of commodity taxes and subsidies just requires information on the goods and factor prices (p^a, w^a) and (p, w), which is obviously much less than required to compute the lump sum transfers in (6.3). On the other hand, it should not be thought that the factor price information is always available. If we can think of the quantity of a factor supplied as measuring *effort* rather than just hours worked, then the factor prices need to be measured *per unit of effort*. If effort is not observed, then neither are the true prices or factor supplies. To state this problem differently, a worker who was *guaranteed* his autarky wage even when trade is opened would no longer have an incentive to work hard. Thus, there is again an incentive compatibility problem related to the collection of factor prices whenever individuals' effort cannot be observed. A similar problem occurs for workers paid annual salaries rather than wages, so that we observe their income wv^h rather than wages w. In this case, we would have to infer their factor supply (or effort level) v^h before knowing their wage w.[1]

---

[1] This difficulty occurs especially for specific factors in an industry, where at most we would observe their total income but not their wage. This is an important example because of our earlier assumption that the technology of the economy has constant returns to scale. Suppose instead that the technology has decreasing returns, in which case the revenue earned

A second potential difficulty with this system of commodity taxes and subsidies occurs when individuals have *moving costs*. To model this, suppose that the vector of factor supplies v^h appearing in the utility function is indexed by the *location where the individual works*. That is, if the economy has M primary factors and L locations, the vector v^h is of dimension LM rather than M. An individual who is indifferent between working in one location versus the other would have indifference curves that are linear between these two factor supplies: when offered a wage slightly higher in one location, the individual would shift entirely there. But if instead the utility function $u^h(c^h,\ v^h)$ is *strictly* quasi-concave, then this individual would *not* be willing to shift between locations when wages are unchanged. This formulation is a simple way to capture the idea that individuals have preferences over where to work and psychic costs to relocating. Notice that it is still consistent with the Arrow-Debreu general equilibrium model; which allows goods or factor to be indexed by location.

What are the implications of this for the system of commodity tax and subsidies proposed by Dixit and Norman (1980)? Suppose that we use the factor subsidies to bring all individuals back to their autarky factor prices. Since v^h is indexed by location, and $u^h(c^h,\ v^h)$ is *strictly* quasi-concave, this means that individuals have a unique choice of where to work and are unwilling to shift between locations at the autarky wages. Assume that the various goods in the economy are produced at different locations. Then opening the economy up to trade, but holding wages fixed at w^a, means that it is *impossible* for the economy to shift from a point like A to point B in Figure 6.2: if workers are unwilling to move between industry/locations at constant wages, the economy will be stuck at point A despite the change in producer prices. It is appropriate to think of the preferences over locations, combined with wages fixed at their autarky level, as introducing a "kink" into the production possibility frontier at point A, as illustrated by the dashed lines in Figure 6.2. Because production no longer changes in response to the free-trade prices, there are no efficiency gains, and government revenue in (6.5) is zero. In this case, the scheme of commodity tax/subsidies proposed by Dixit and Norman fails to achieve any gains.

Feenstra and Lewis (1994) have investigated this case, and argue that *moving subsidies* can restore Pareto gains through subsidizing workers to move between industries or locations. An example of such subsidies in the

---

exceeds the sum of factor payments, so (6.2) does not hold. Then define the difference between revenue earned and factor payments as the income of a hypothetical fixed factor of production, so that including payments to this fixed factor, we have constant returns and (6.2) holds again. Then we would only observe income of this fixed factor, and *not* the separate wage and factor supply.

United States is Trade Adjustment Assistance (TAA). As described in
Richardson 1982, this program was established in the United States under
the Trade Act of 1974 to compensate workers in industries that experienced unemployment due to import competition. It was used heavily by
autoworkers during the U.S. recession of the early 1980s, for example.
However, it has often been the case that workers using this program have
not shifted into new jobs, but instead used TAA as an income supplement
during their period of unemployment (see the evidence in Aho and
Bayard 1984). This was especially true for the automobile workers laid off
in Detroit in 1979 and 1980: many of them simply collected the TAA
benefits, and when the automobile industry recovered, they returned to
their former jobs. Findings such as this eventually led Congress to realize
that the program was not encouraging relocation of workers, and its funding was cut drastically. A much smaller TAA program was later implemented along with NAFTA in 1994, and this program requires job
retraining (see Irwin 2002, 106–10).

There is some theoretical validity to the idea that a TAA program is
worthwhile only if it leads to the relocation of workers between industries.
In terms of Figure 6.2, the economy achieves production gains of going
from point A to point B only if workers are willing to move between
industry/locations: simply giving income supplements to workers but
having production remain at point A cannot be a self-financing policy.
Furthermore, it is essential that workers move in the "right" direction,
that is, towards those industries whose international prices have increased,
or from point A to point B in Figure 6.2. Feenstra and Lewis (1994) show
that a program of moving subsidies can be designed to achieve this goal,
so that in conjunction with the commodity taxes proposed by Dixit and
Norman, the program achieves Pareto gains and is self-financing.[2]

As a final example of how the commodity tax/subsidies proposed by
Dixit and Norman relate to actual policies, consider the case of the unification of East and West Germany. As described by Akerlof et al. (1991, 1):
"At midnight on June 30, 1990, German economic, monetary, and social
union occurred: the mark of the German Democratic Republic [East
Germany] was replaced by the deutsche mark; trade barriers were lifted;
legal, tax, and social insurance system were harmonized; and all existing
barriers to capital and labor movement were removed." The replacement
of the mark with the deutsche mark at par, and the pressure from labor

---

[2] A richer comparison of trade adjustment assistance with wage and employment subsidies is
provided by Davidson and Matusz (2002), in a model where workers search for new jobs
and therefore have temporary spells of unemployment. They argue that *temporary* wage subsidies (in industries to which workers should be moving) and *temporary* employment subsidies (in industries that workers have difficulty leaving) are preferable to adjustment assistance
and can be used to achieve Pareto gains.

unions to achieve wage parity between the east and west, meant that companies in former East Germany were faced with wages that were far above their market levels. Indeed, Akerlof et al. (1991) estimate that only 8% of former East German conglomerates would have been profitable at those high wages. In the absence of government intervention, it could be expected that wages in the industries located in eastern Germany would fall dramatically, or severe bankruptcy and unemployment would result.

The government attempted to increase wages in the east to levels closer to those in the west in order to avoid migration out of the east. Thus, not only did government policies explicitly allow workers in former East Germany to maintain their standard of living following unification, these policies attempted to achieve an increase in living standards in order to avoid migration. At the same time, it was expected that workers in former West Germany should not be harmed by unification. This historical episode is therefore a perfect example of an attempt to achieve Pareto gains from trade in practice.

How could such gains be achieved in the face of non-market-clearing wages in East Germany, combined with unemployment? The answer proposed by Akerlof et al. (1991, 4) is that "flexible employment bonuses" or *wage subsidies* be used in the east:

> So far . . . the package of policies that has been enacted fails to deal realistically with the questions of how to preserve existing jobs, how to speed new job creation, and how to make existing companies viable enough to be privatized. The major problem is that wages in the East are too high for most former state-owned enterprises to cover their costs. High wages also deter new investment. This creates an obvious need for governmental measures to close the gap between the high private cost of labor, caused by high Eastern wages, and the low marginal product of labor, caused by outmoded capital and technology. We propose a program of self-eliminating flexible employment bonuses . . . to eliminate this gap. Our analysis shows that such a program would give many workers a chance to keep their jobs and would also raise the level of new job creation through faster private investment. According to our estimates, even deep wage subsidies (for example, an employment bonus equal to 75 percent of current wages) would have very low budgetary costs. They might even *reduce* the budget deficits—largely for the same reason that infrastructure investment is not costly: the government is already committed to a high level of income support even if workers are unemployed.

Thus, by subsidizing workers in East Germany the government could save enough income from unemployment benefits that the policy could be self-financing. This is very similar to the commodity tax/subsidies proposed by

Dixit and Norman (1980), and shows that wage subsidies have an potentially important role to play in an actual attempt to achieve Pareto gains
from trade. Unfortunately, the wage subsidy proposal of Akerlof et al.
(1991) was not followed in Germany, and migration from east to west
continues to be a policy issue.[3]

Partial Reform of Tariffs

We now consider a country that undertakes a partial reform of its tariff
structure, moving from one situation of restricted trade (possible autarky)
to another. This is a very realistic example, since countries undertake partial reform of their tariffs frequently (though it is often done *in conjunction* with tariff reforms abroad). The question is: are individuals better off in
this country or not? To answer this, we make use of the lump sum transfers as a means to compensate individuals for this move, so we will need to
check whether the government budget constraint allows this compensation or not. While the use of lump sum transfers is not realistic, the reader
should think of this as simply a method to evaluate the desirability of the
tariff reform; that is, if tariff reform combined with lump sum transfers
could make everyone better off, then we accept the tariff reform itself as a
worthwhile policy, even when the transfers are not made. This criterion
for evaluating a reform is called the "compensation principle" (see Chipman
1987). Our analysis will follow that in Grinols and Wong 1991 and Ju and
Krishna 2000a, though the latter authors also show how the results can be
extended to non–lump sum transfers, using commodity tax and subsidies
as in Dixit and Norman 1980 and Dixit 1986.[4]

   To set up our notation, let the domestic price vector for consumers and
producers be denoted by $p = p^* + t$, where p^* is the vector of world
prices, and t is the vector of trade taxes and subsidies. Notice that $t_i > 0$
for an imported good indicates a tariff (raising the domestic price above
the world price), whereas $t_i < 0$ for an imported good indicates a subsidy.
Conversely, $t_i > 0$ for an exported good indicates a subsidy (since firms
receive $p_i^* + t_i$ from exporting, so the domestic price would also have to
rise by the same amount), while $t_i < 0$ for an exported good indicates a tax.
It follows that the total revenue collected by the government from the trade

---

[3] Interestingly, Phelps (1997) also proposes a system of wage subsidies to offset the drop in
wages for unskilled workers in the United States, whose wages fell during the 1980s and
1990s, as discussed in chapter 4.

[4] See problems 6.2 and 6.3, provided by Jiandong Ju. An alternative approach to the piecemeal reform of tariffs, relying on small reforms and using calculus, is provided in Diewert,
Turunen-Red, and Woodland 1989; Ju and Krishna 2000b; and Turunen-Red and Woodland
1991, 2000.

tax/subsidies is $t'(c - y)$, where $c = \Sigma_{h=1}^{H} c^h$ is total consumption and y is the output of the economy at the prices p. For convenience, let us denote the *import* vector as $m = c - y$, so that revenue collected is simply $t'm$.

We compare two different trade tax/subsidies t^0 and t^1, with the equilibrium domestic price vectors $p^0 = p^{*0} + t^0$ and $p^1 = p^{*1} + t^1$. We stress that the world price p^* *changes* in these two situations, and in general, the world prices are endogenously determined by the tariffs chosen at home. More generally, our setup allows for a change in tariffs abroad simultaneously with those at home, as part of a bilateral or multilateral tariff reform.

Our argument will follow the earlier discussion of lump sum compensation quite closely. In the initial situation, we suppose that consumers maximize utility subject to their budget constraints

$$p^{0\prime}c^{h0} \leq w^{0\prime}v^{h0} + (t^{0\prime}m^0)/H, \qquad (6.6)$$

where p^0 is the autarky vector of commodity prices, w^0 is the autarky vector of factor prices, and we include the redistributed tariff revenue $t^{0\prime}m^0/H$, where H is the number of consumers. The resulting utility for each consumer is $u^h(c^{h0}, v^{h0})$.

Summing over all consumption and factor supplies, the total consumption in the economy is therefore $\Sigma_{h=1}^{H} c^{h0} = c^0$, and the total factor inputs are $\Sigma_{h=1}^{H} v^{h0} = v^0$. Firms will be maximizing profits at the equilibrium prices (p^0, w^0), resulting in the outputs y^0 and factor demands v^0. Again, we assume constant returns to scale, so that the resulting profits are zero, $p^{0\prime}y^0 - w^{0\prime}v^0 = 0$. Imports in this equilibrium are $m^0 = c^0 - y^0$, so the revenue collected is $t^{0\prime}m^0$, which has been transferred back to consumers in (6.6).

After the tariff reform, domestic prices change to $p^1 = p^{*1} + t^1$, and the revenue collected from the trade tax/subsidies becomes $t^{1\prime}m^1$. We denote the transfer to consumers by R^h, which may differ from just the revenue $t^{1\prime}m^1$. The budget constraint for consumers is

$$p^{1\prime}c^h \leq w^{1\prime}v^h + R^h. \qquad (6.7)$$

Our goal is to identify conditions under which the government can compensate individuals for the change in prices, and at the same time, balance the government budget. Using a similar system of lump sum transfers that we considered earlier, this can be achieved by the following theorem.

Theorem (Grinols and Wong 1991; Ju and Krishna 2000a)

When the prices change from $p^0 = p^{*0} + t^0$ to $p^1 = p^{*1} + t^1$, suppose that the government transfers the following amount to each individual:

$$R^h = (p^1 - p^0)'c^{h0} - (w^1 - w^0)'v^{h0} + (t^{0\prime}m^0)/H. \qquad (6.8)$$

Provided that $(p^{\star 0} - p^{\star 1})'m^0 + t^{1\prime}(m^1 - m^0) \geq 0$, then no individual is worse off and the government budget is balanced.

Proof

Substituting the transfers in (6.8) into the individual's budget constraint (6.7), we can confirm that the initial choices (c^{b0}, v^{b0}) are still feasible:

$$
\begin{aligned}
p^{1\prime}c^{b0} &\leq w^{1\prime}v^{b0} + (p^1 - p^0)'c^{b0} - (w^1 - w^0)'v^{b0} + (t^{0\prime}m^0)/H \\
&\Leftrightarrow p^0c^{b0} \leq w^{0\prime}v^{b0} + (t^{0\prime}m^0)/H.
\end{aligned}
\tag{6.9}
$$

Since the second equation shown is just the initial budget constraint in (6.6), the initial choices (c^{b0}, v^{b0}) are feasible and utility is at least $u^b(c^{b0}, v^{b0})$.

To check the government budget, we subtract the transfers from the tariff revenue, obtaining

$$
\begin{aligned}
t^{1\prime}m^1 - \sum_{b=1}^{H} R^b &= t^{1\prime}m^1 - (p^1 - p^0)'\sum_{b=1}^{H} c^{b0} + (w^1 - w^0)'\sum_{b=1}^{H} v^{b0} - t^{0\prime}m^0 \\
&= (p^0 - p^1)'c^0 - (w^0 - w^1)'v^0 + t^{1\prime}m^1 - t^{0\prime}m^0 \\
&= (p^0 - p^1)'y^0 - (w^0 - w^1)'v^0 \\
&\quad + (p^0 - p^1)'m^0 + t^{1\prime}m^1 - t^{0\prime}m^0 \\
&= (p^{0\prime}y^0 - w^{0\prime}v^0) - (p^{1\prime}y^0 - w^{1\prime}v^0) \\
&\quad + (p^{\star 0} - p^{\star 1})'m^0 + t^{1\prime}(m^1 - m^0) \\
&\geq (p^{\star 0} - p^{\star 1})'m^0 + t^{1\prime}(m^1 - m^0).
\end{aligned}
\tag{6.10}
$$

The second, third, and fourth equalities follow from simple algebra, and the inequality on the final line follows because initial profits $(p^{0\prime}y^0 - w^{0\prime}v^0)$ are zero, while $(p^{1\prime}y^0 - w^{1\prime}v^0)$ is less than $(p^{1\prime}y^1 - w^{1\prime}v^1)$ which is also zero. Provided that the final line of (6.10) is nonnegative, then so is the government budget.   QED

This theorem provides us with two expressions that summarize the welfare impact of tariff reforms. The first of these is $(p^{\star 0} - p^{\star 1})'m^0$, which indicates the impact of the reform on the *terms of trade*, or international prices: if the price of imports goes up or the price of exports goes down, this expression will be negative and gains cannot be assured. The second term is $t^{1\prime}(m^1 - m^0)$, which is interpreted as the *change in imports* evaluated at the *final tariff vector*. The tariff vector reflects the difference between domestic and international prices: a positive value indicates that marginal costs at home exceed international prices, so it would be more efficient for the country to import the good; and if the value is negative, the country should be exporting the good. Therefore the term $t^{1\prime}(m^1 - m^0)$ gives a measure of the efficiency gain (if positive) due to attracting imports towards protected sectors. Thus, policies to raise welfare must avoid adverse terms of trade or efficiency effects to ensure Pareto gains.

Notice that the term $t^{1\prime}(m^1 - m^0)$ can also be interpreted as the *change in tariff revenue* evaluated at the *final tariff vector*. In some cases, this will equal the overall change in tariff revenue. For example, suppose that a small country starts with prohibitive tariffs on some goods, and then moves to free trade in those goods. Since they have zero tariff revenue before and after the change, the term $t^{1\prime}(m^1 - m^0)$ shows what happens to revenue collected on the *other* goods, whose tariffs are unchanged. If tariff revenue falls, then we cannot be sure that the country gained from the partial movement towards free trade. Working with a one-consumer small economy, Ohyama (1972) was the first to identify the sufficient condition that tariff revenue (evaluated at the final tariff vector) must rise to ensure gains.

Two special cases of the above theorem can be noted.

Corollary

Applying the transfers to individuals as in (6.8):

    (a) Starting in autarky and moving to trade with tariffs and subsidies makes no one worse off provided that $t^{1\prime} m^1 \geq 0$.

    (b) For a small country with constant world prices, $p^{*0} = p^{*1}$, a change in tariffs and subsidies makes no one worse off provided that $t^{1\prime}(m^1 - m^0) \geq 0$.

In the first case, we set $m^0 = 0$ in the above theorem, and see that the criterion to achieve Pareto gains is just $t^{1\prime} m^1 \geq 0$, that is, the tariffs and subsidies must raise nonnegative revenue. Ohyama (1972) described this condition as "self-financing" tariffs. The result in corollary (a) is interpreted as saying that "some trade is better than no trade." If we suppose that the second situation has free trade, $t^1 = 0$, then the condition in corollary (a) is clearly satisfied, and this result is interpreted as "free trade is better than autarky" (Samuelson 1962; Kemp 1962). Corollary (b) considers a "small country," facing fixed world prices, and shows that a tariff reform will raise welfare provided that the efficiency effects are non-negative. Again, if we suppose that the second situation has free trade, $t^1 = 0$, then the condition in corollary (b) is clearly satisfied, and this result can be interpreted as "free trade is better than restricted trade for a small country." We will provide another demonstration of this result in the next chapter.

Regional Trade Agreements

We now extend our results to the case where a group of countries decides to pursue free trade internally, while maintaining tariffs against the rest of the world. Under a customs union, the countries involved choose a *common* external tariff with the rest of the world, whereas under a free-trade area the countries maintain different tariffs on imports from the rest of the world. Let us consider the customs union case first, since it is easier.

The analysis of customs unions dates back to Viner (1950), who introduced the terms '*trade creation*' versus '*trade diversion*.' Trade creation refers to a situation where two countries within the customs union begin to trade with each other, whereas formerly they produced the good in question for themselves. In terms of corollary (a) above, the countries go from autarky (in this good) to trading with zero tariffs, and they both gain. Trade diversion, on the other hand, occurs when two countries begin to trade within the union, but one of these countries had formerly imported the good from *outside* the union. We may presume that the importing country formerly had the same tariffs on all other countries, but purchased from *outside* the union because that price was lowest. After the union, the country *switches* its purchases from the lowest-price to a higher-price country, so in terms of corollary (b) there is a negative efficiency effect, and the country could lose from joining the union.

To verify these results more formally, we need to expand our notation to incorporate the customs union. In our analysis above we implicitly assumed that each country i had a single tariff vector t^i applied against *all other* countries. This is no longer the case: countries in the union will face zero tariffs among themselves, and still maintain the same external tariff with respect to outside countries. An easy way to capture this is to *index goods by their region of origin and their region of destination.* That is, let the first N goods denote those produced in the union and sent to the union; the next N goods are produced outside the union and sent outside the union; the next N are produced in the union and sent outside the union; and the last N are produced outside the union and sent into the union. In total we therefore have $4N$ goods, but only the last $2N$ of these involve trade between the union and outside countries. This treatment of goods still is consistent with the Arrow-Debreu model, where goods can be indexed by location.[5]

With this notation, the above theorem and corollary continue to hold. For a union country i, the first N tariffs are zero, the second N tariffs are irrelevant (since these goods are traded between nonunion countries), and

---

[5] Note that if consumers are indifferent between a good coming from two locations, the indifference curves between these locations are linear.

the last $2N$ tariffs are equalized for all countries of the union. We will denote this postunion tariff vector by t^1. Notice that with zero tariffs on countries within the union, the term $t^{1\prime}(m^{i1} - m^{i0})$ measures the *change in tariff revenue for country i's imports from outside the union*. Trade diversion means that country i switches from the lowest-price supplier from outside the union (where tariff revenue is collected) to another supplier within the union (with no tariff revenue), so that $t^{1\prime}(m^{i1} - m^{i0}) < 0$ and tariff revenue has fallen. Therefore, country i can be worse off. This result illustrates what is called a "second best" problem: by eliminating its tariffs with all other countries, a small country would necessarily be better off, but if it goes only part way towards this goal (eliminating tariffs with the union countries only), there is no guarantee of gains.

This outcome makes it seem as if no general result on the desirability of customs unions is possible. Remarkably, Kemp and Wan (1976) were still able to obtain such a result. Their goal was to ensure that the customs union benefit its members, and also do no harm to the rest of the world. To achieve this end, Kemp and Wan used the following rule: *the customs union should keep the world price p* fixed, or equivalently, keep the purchases from the rest of the world x* fixed*. This rule can be contrasted with the criterion used in the WTO on customs unions. In Article XXIV in Table 6.1, we see that customs unions are "not prevented" provided that "the duties [with outside parties] shall not on the whole be higher or more restrictive than the general incidence of the duties . . . prior to the formation." Thus, the criterion used in WTO is that the *tariffs with respect to countries outside the union* should not be higher than before, whereas the rule used by Kemp and Wan is that *trade with respect to outside countries* is not affected by the formation of the customs union. The Kemp-Wan rule is the correct one to avoid losses, not the existing WTO criterion.

To develop the result of Kemp and Wan, let us denote the countries in the customs union by $i = 1, \ldots, C$. Prior to the union they have tariffs t^{i0}. We let p^{*0} denote the world prices in this equilibrium, and m^{i0} denote the import vector of country i. Let the net export vector of the rest of the world be denoted by $x^*(p^{*0})$. Notice that this vector is zero for the first $2N$ goods (which refer to trade strictly inside or outside the union), and potentially nonzero otherwise. Summing imports over all countries in the union, the equilibrium condition is

$$\sum_{i=1}^{C} m^{i0} = x^*(p^{*0}). \tag{6.11}$$

After the customs union the countries involved have a unified tariff t^1, the elements of which are zero for purchases from within-union countries. Let m^{i1} denote the vector of imports of country i in this situation. Kemp and Wan (1976) prove that there exists a unified tariff t^1 that ensures that

$$\sum_{i=1}^{C} m^{i1} = x^*(p^{*0}).$$ (6.12)

The fact that the prices p^{*0} and exports from the rest of the world $x^*(p^{*0})$ are *unchanged* due to the customs union guarantees that the *rest of the world is not affected by it*. The question now is whether the members of the customs union also gain, and whether this requires some transfers between the countries. This is answered by the following theorem.

Theorem (Kemp and Wan 1976; Grinols 1981)

Let the countries $i = 1, \ldots, C$ form a customs union, with the common external tariff such that prices and purchases from the rest of the world are unchanged. Suppose that each country within the customs union receives the transfers $- t^{1\prime}(m^{i1} - m^{i0})$ from the rest of the union. Then there is a pattern of lump sum transfers within each country such that no individual is worse off, and the government budget in each country is nonnegative.

Proof

Consider the transfers described in (6.8), but applied within each country. It follows that all consumers in every country of the union can still afford their previous consumption bundles. Furthermore, noting that prices p^* from the rest of the world are fixed, then from (6.10) the government budget in each country is no less than $t^{1\prime}(m^{i1} - m^{i0})$. Therefore, each country can afford to give up this amount (or receive it if negative), and have a nonnegative budget. It remains to be shown that these transfers within the union are self-financing, that is, $\sum_{i=1}^{C} t^{1\prime}(m^{i1} - m^{i0}) = 0$. But this follows immediately from the fact that total union imports are equal in (6.11) and (6.12), $\sum_{i=1}^{C} m^{i1} = \sum_{i=1}^{C} m^{i0}$.   QED

It is apparent that the way losses are avoided for the union is by keeping total imports fixed: in that way, the total tariff revenue (evaluated at post-union external tariffs) is also fixed. But keeping total imports fixed also means that world prices are fixed, which eliminates any terms of trade impacts for the union and the rest of the world. Thus, keeping total union imports fixed immediately satisfies the criterion identified in the earlier theorem: when summed over the countries of the union, the term $(p^{*0} - p^{*1})' m^{i0} + t^{1\prime}(m^{i1} - m^{i0})$ is zero, so the union as a whole is no worse off. An individual country may experience a loss in its own tariff revenue of $t^{1\prime}(m^{i1} - m^{i0})$, but this loss could be compensated by transfers from other countries within the union.

It has been more than 25 years since Kemp and Wan demonstrated this result, and in the meantime, regional agreements under GATT Article XXIV have proliferated. Many of them have not been customs unions, but free-trade areas (FTAs). Is it possible to extend the Kemp-Wan theorem to cover these FTAs? As explained above, FTAs differ from customs unions in that the countries involved have their own tariff vector with respect to the rest of the world. At the same time, tariffs are zero within the union, so goods can be sent between these countries freely. This means that *producer prices* must be equalized within the union, but by virtue of their differing tariffs on outside countries, *consumer prices* can differ within the union. It follows that the method of proof used by Kemp and Wan (1976) cannot be used for free-trade areas. Recently, however, Krishna and Panagariya (2002) have developed a new proof, which shows that Kemp-Wan theorem can indeed be extended to cover FTAs. Their approach can be described quite easily using our notation above.

Let $x^*(p^{*0})$ denote the initial net exports from the rest of the world to the countries planning to form a FTA. Recall that this vector is zero for the first $2N$ goods (which refer to trade strictly inside or outside the union), and potentially nonzero otherwise. The approach of Krishna and Panagariya is to ensure that *every country in the FTA* has exactly the same trade with the rest of the world as it did initially. Letting m^{i0} and m^{i1} denote the imports of country $i = 1, \ldots, C$, which is a member of the FTA, we require that

$$m_j^{i0} = m_j^{i1}, \quad \text{for goods } j = 2N+1, \ldots, 4N. \tag{6.13}$$

Thus, we require every FTA member import and export the same quantity with the rest of world as it did before the free-trade area. While Krishna and Panagariya do not provide a general existence result, we can certainly construct examples where there are country-specific tariffs ensuring that (6.13) holds, and denote these by t^{i1}, $i = 1, \ldots, C$. Notice that (6.13) implies that (6.12) still holds; that is, *total* net exports from the FTA to the rest of the world equal $x^*(p^{*0})$, the value initially. So we conclude that the equilibrium world prices are still given by p^{*0}.

Since trade with the outside world is not affected by the FTA, and neither are prices, we have obtained the result in the following theorem.

Theorem (Krishna and Panagariya 2002)

Let the countries $i = 1, \ldots, C$ form a free-trade area, with external tariffs t^{i1} for *each country* such that prices and purchases from the rest of the world are unchanged. Then there is a pattern of lump sum transfers within each country such that no individual is worse off, and the government budget in each country is nonnegative.

Proof

Again we use the transfers described in (6.8) applied within each country. It follows that all consumers in every country of the FTA can still afford their previous consumption bundle, and from (6.11), the government budget in each country is no less than $t^{i1\prime}(m^{i1} - m^{i0})$. The first N elements of t^{i1} are zero due to free trade within the FTA, and the next N elements of m^{i0} and m^{i1} are zero because those goods are produced and delivered outside the FTA. Then (6.13) ensures that $t^{i1\prime}(m^{i1} - m^{i0}) = 0$, so the budget is nonnegative in every country $i = 1, \ldots, C$.   QED

One feature of FTAs and the above theorem should be emphasized. Because tariffs with respect to the rest of world differ between the member countries, outside countries would have an incentive to export their goods into the *lowest-tariff* country of the FTA, and then transship it to other member countries. This type of activity needs to be ruled out to obtain the above theorem. That is, transshipment through the lowest-tariff country would *violate* condition (6.13), which specifies that each country must import the same quantity from outside countries as before the FTA. More generally, transshipment through the lowest-tariff country would lead to a drop in tariff revenue for other countries of the FTA, violating the condition to obtain Pareto gains. To ensure welfare gains, therefore, we need to rule out transshipment of goods not produced in the FTA.

In practice, restrictions on such transshipment within FTAs are known as *rules of origin* (ROO). Within NAFTA, for example, each and every good must be certified as "North American made" before it can be shipped freely between Mexico, the United States, and Canada. This certification is typically made based on the percentage of value added coming from North American production, or the use of some key input produced in North America. This prevents a foreign country from exporting into Canada, for example, and then sending the good to the United States or Mexico, unless it had enough further processing to certify it as "North American made." Such rules are enormously complex, since they require a specification of the production process for each and every good. Due to their complexity and the fact that the ROO are an artificial restriction on the movement of goods, they can have unexpected consequences (see Krishna and Krueger 1995; Krishna, 2002). But the theorem of Krishna and Panagariya sheds new light on these practices, since the welfare-improving FTA depends on their use.[6]

[6] Let us be more careful in this statement. Starting at any FTA, the theorem of Kemp and Wan ensures that there is a customs union that is Pareto superior. But that customs union is not achieved by simply dropping the ROO from the FTA; rather, it would require dropping the ROO, changing the external tariffs for all countries to a common level that ensures the

Evidence on Regional Agreements

The above theorems allow us to conclude that welfare-improving customs unions and FTAs exist, but from this result we should not infer that regional trade agreements in practice are necessarily a good thing. The possibility of trade diversion identified by Viner (1950) and any changes in the terms of trade need to be evaluated empirically before judging actual agreements. More generally, we should be concerned with whether regional trade agreements *help* or *hinder* the movement towards global free trade through multilateral negotiations under the WTO. This issue of political economy will be discussed in chapter 9.

Grinols (1984) was among the first to measure the gains or losses from membership in a customs union. He examined Britain's joining the European Economic Community in 1973. This meant that Britain had to adopt the common external tariff of the EEC. Not only would this tariff affect domestic prices p^i in Britain, it could also be expected to have an impact on the foreign prices p^{*i} facing Britain, that is, on its terms of trade. We are recognizing here that the prices charged by foreign exporting firms are often responsive to a change in tariffs by just one importing country. This occurs when foreign firms segment their export markets, charging different prices in each. This behavior is related to imperfect competition, as will be discussed in the next chapter.

Grinols measured the prices for British exports and imports during the years after its membership in the EEC. Multiplying these prices by initial quantities gives $(p^{*i0} - p^{*i1})' m^{i0}$, or the value of changes in the terms of trade. In every year from 1973 to 1980, it turned out that the British terms of trade had fallen from 1972, and the amount of this decline averaged about 2.3% of British GDP. (This amount includes the lost tariff revenue on imports, which automatically become property of the customs union, but the average drop in the terms of trade without including tariff revenue was still 1.7% of GDP.)

In order to compensate for this loss, Britain would have needed to obtain some transfer from the EEC, that is, the amount $t^{1'}(m^{i1} - m^{i0})$ in our discussion above. There was a wide range of transfers between countries as part of EEC membership, including the regional development funds (allocated to projects in lower-income regions), special funds in agriculture, coal, and steel, value-added taxes, and so on. The net transfers were slightly in Britain's favor, but not enough to offset the terms of trade

---

same total imports from the rest of the world, and also implementing income transfers across countries within the union. If these actions are politically infeasible, then the ROO are needed in order for the FTA to ensure Pareto gains, as in the theorem of Krishna and Panagariya.

loss, so that summing $(p^{\star i0} - p^{\star i1})' m^{i0} + t^{1\prime}(m^{i1} - m^{i0})$ still gives an average loss for Britain of 2.26% of GDP annually.

We conclude that the sufficient condition to ensure Britain's gain from joining the EEC, that is, $(p^{\star i0} - p^{\star i1})' m^{i0} + t^{1\prime}(m^{i1} - m^{i0}) > 0$, did not hold. This does not necessarily imply that Britain was worse off, however, since it still enjoys free trade within the EEC, and so had efficiency gains on both the consumption and production side for that reason. In Figure 6.1, for example, these gains are illustrated by the movement from point A to point B. Grinols attempts to evaluate these gains for Britain and finds that they are quite small. The conclusion is that its membership in the EEC in 1973 led to a welfare loss that averaged about 2% of GDP annually through 1980.

One criticism that can be made of Grinols's methodology is that he simply accepts the trade prices as data, and presumes that any change from 1972 represents the effect of Britain's membership in the EEC. Thus, the terms of trade decline is *attributed to* Britain's changing its external tariff to the common EEC level. This does not allow for any exogenous changes in the terms of trade due to factors affecting supply and demand on world markets. To control for such factors, we need to specify prices as functions of the tariffs, as well as other relevant factors. Using a log-linear regression to estimate prices as a function of tariffs and other factors allows us to *infer* the specific impact of the tariff change. This is the approach taken by Chang and Winters (2002) for MERCOSUR.

Specifically, Chang and Winters (2002) consider prices from various countries (United States, Japan, German, etc.) to Brazil, which is the largest market in MERCOSUR. This customs union had the effect of eliminating tariffs between Brazil and Argentina, Paraguay, and Uruguay, as well as equalizing their external tariffs. Of interest, then, is the *direct* effect of the change in the external tariff of Brazil on the prices charged by foreign firms; as well as the *indirect* effect of the elimination of the tariffs between Brazil and Argentina on the prices charged by foreign firms to Brazil. Both direct and indirect effects will lead to a terms of trade change for Brazil, as well as to the countries selling in that market. The regression framework used to measure these effects draws on Feenstra 1989, as discussed in detail in the next chapter, and specifies prices as a log-linear function of tariffs and other factors. By pooling data across disaggregate products and years, Chang and Winters can use annual fixed effects to control for any changes in prices that are common across commodities.

For the case of MERCOSUR, Chang and Winters find that many of the prices charged by external countries, including the United States, Japan, Germany, Korea, and Chile, indeed fell as a result of the change in Brazilian tariffs. The *direct* impact of the change in the Brazilian external tariff is smaller than the *indirect* effect of the elimination of its tariff with Argentina. On average, foreign prices charged to Brazil fall by one-third as much as the drop in the tariff with Argentina (and by even more if yearly fixed effects are used). This implies a significant terms of trade gain for Brazil and loss for the exporting countries. For example, Chang and Winters evaluate this loss in 1996 as $624 million for the United States (which exceeds 10% of its export sales to Brazil of $5.4 billion in 1991), $59 million for Japan, $236 million for Germany, $14 million for Korea, and $17 million for Chile. These figures illustrate the potential losses that a customs union can impose on the countries left out.[7]

For the North American Free Trade Agreement (NAFTA) of 1994 and the earlier Canada-U.S. Free Trade Agreement (CUSFTA) of 1989, Clausing (2001) and Romalis (2002) estimate the impact on trade quantities rather than prices, using highly disaggregate data for the United States. Clausing estimates the impact of CUSFTA on U.S. imports from Canada over 1989–94, and on U.S. imports from the rest of the world. These trade quantities are modeled as log-linear function of tariffs and other factors, and pooling across commodities and years allows annual fixed effects to be used. Romalis examines where the United States sources its imports of some 5,000 commodities, and compares this where the European Union sources the same commodities, using a "differences in differences" technique to identify the impact of both CUSFTA and NAFTA.

Clausing finds that U.S. imports from Canada responded predictably to CUSFTA, with a 10% drop in the U.S. tariff leading to a 1% expansion of its imports from Canada. This is an example of trade creation between the countries. At the same time, the drop in U.S. tariffs had a negative but statistically *insignificant* impact on its imports from the rest of the world, so there is little evidence to support trade diversion. This conclusion suggests that the Canada-U.S. Free Trade Agreement was relatively benign for other countries, but should be interpreted with caution: to make welfare conclusions, it is better to estimate the effect of tariff changes on *prices*, as done by Chang and Winters (2002), rather than quantities. Romalis also finds a significant impact of CUSFTA on U.S. imports from Canada, along with a large impact of NAFTA on U.S. imports from Mexico. However, he suggests that NAFTA may have led to substantial trade diversion, because the largest tariff reductions were often in commodities where the United States relied on imports from outside of North America.

---

[7] Schiff and Chang (2003) extend the work of Chang and Winters to examine whether the *possibility* of Argentine exports to Brazil (as indicated by its exports to another country in the same product category) served to lower the foreign prices charged in Brazil. They find evidence in support of this "contestability" effect.

Imperfect Competition and Increasing Returns to Scale

An omitted topic in the chapter thus far is the role of imperfect competition. This raises two distinct issues. First, in industries with monopolistic pricing there is a gap between price and marginal costs. Because prices reflect consumer valuations of a product, this gap indicates that consumers would be better off by *increasing* the output of that industry. If this occurs due to the opening of trade, we might expect that the economy is better off; but if trade reduces the outputs of industries with imperfect competition, this seems to indicate potential losses.

Second, models of imperfect competition often have increasing returns to scale, such as in the monopolistic competition model we studied in chapter 5. The presence of increasing returns creates a reason to be concerned about losses from trade. Many years ago, Graham (1923) argued that with increasing returns an industry facing strong import competition might be forced to contract, leading to higher average costs, and that this would be a reason for protection. Ethier (1982a) has confirmed this result in a model relying on increasing returns that are *external* to the firm, finding that the *small country* may experience losses from trade due to the contraction of its increasing-returns industry. Interestingly, Markusen (1981) found that the monopolistic firm in the *large* country might be forced to contact due to trade, so the large country potentially faced losses. So once again, a sufficient condition for gains from trade under increasing returns appears to be that the increasing-returns industries do not contract. We will derive a condition that is weaker than this using the analysis of Grinols (1991), and then summarize other results that apply under monopolistic competition, due to Helpman and Krugman (1985, chap. 9).

In contrast to the perfectly competitive case used earlier in the chapter, we will now need to be more specific about the structure of industry production and costs. With industry i output denoted by y_i, we will suppose that total minimum costs are $C_i(y_i, w)$. This formulation rules out having several goods produced jointly within an industry, and also rules out having firms in an industry produce with differing costs. But we allow for constant or increasing returns to scale and also allow for zero or positive profits in each industry.[8] Define $AC_i(y_i, w) \equiv C_i(y_i, w)/y_i$ as average costs, so that under increasing returns to scale $AC_i(y_i, w)$ *falls* as output rises.

Total profits earned by firms in the autarky equilibrium are $p^{a\prime} y^a - w^{a\prime} v^a$, and each consumer is entitled to some fixed fraction λ^h of these.

---

[8] The case of decreasing returns to scale can be handled by defining an artificial factor of production that transforms the technology into constant returns to scale, as in note 1.

Then the autarky budget constraint of consumer h is rewritten from (6.1) as

$$p^{a'}c^{ha} \leq w^{a'}v^{ha} + \lambda^h(p^{a'}y^a - w^{a'}v^a).$$
(6.14)

Let us now open the economy to trade at the prices p, and introduce a system of lump sum transfers, so the post-trade budget constraint of each consumer is

$$p'c^h \leq w'v^h + R^h + \lambda^h(p'y - w'v),$$
(6.15)

and the lump sum transfers to each individual are

$$R^h = (p - p^a)'c^{ha} - (w - w^a)'v^{ha}$$
$$+ \lambda^h(p^{a'}y^a - w^{a'}v^a) - \lambda^h(p'y - w'v).$$
(6.16)

It is straightforward to show that these transfers will allow each individual to obtain at least their autarky consumption bundle, so that they are no worse off. The question, then, is whether the government can afford this policy.

Summing the transfers in (6.16), and reversing the sign, we obtain

$$
\begin{aligned}
-\sum_{h=1}^{H} R^h &= (p^a - p)' \sum_{h=1}^{H} c^{ha} - (w^a - w)' \sum_{h=1}^{H} v^{ha} \\
&\quad - \sum_{h=1}^{H} \lambda^h [(p^{a'}y^a - w^{a'}v^a) - (p'y - w'v)] \\
&= (p^a - p)'y^a - (w^a - w)'v^a \\
&\quad - (p^{a'}y^a - w^{a'}v^a) + (p'y - w'v) \\
&= (p'y - p'y^a) + \left[w'v^a - \sum_{i=1}^{N} C_i(y_i, w) \right] \\
&= (p'y - p'y^a) - \sum_{i=1}^{N} [C_i(y_i, w) - C_i(y_i^a, w)] \\
&\quad + \left[w'v^a - \sum_{i=1}^{N} C_i(y_i^a, w) \right],
\end{aligned}
$$
(6.17)

where the second equality follows by using $\Sigma_{h=1}^{H} c^{ha} = y^a$ and $\Sigma_{h=1}^{H} \lambda^h = 1$, the third equality follows by canceling terms and using total economy costs $w'v = \Sigma_{i=1}^{N} C_i(y_i, w)$, and the fourth equality follows by adding and subtracting the term $\Sigma_{i=1}^{N} C_i(y_i^a, w)$.

If condition (6.17) is positive, then this is sufficient to ensure that Pareto gains can be achieved. The final term in brackets is guaranteed to be nonnegative, because it is *feasible* to produce the autarky output y^a using the autarky factor supplies v^a, but not necessarily optimal with the wages w, so that economy-wide costs are $\Sigma_{i=1}^{N} C_i(y^a, w) \leq w'v^a$. Thus, by combining the first two terms, the condition to ensure Pareto gains from trade becomes

$$\sum_{i=1}^{N} p_i \omega_i (y_i - y_i^a) > 0,\tag{6.18}$$

where[9]

$$\omega_i \equiv 1 - \left[\frac{C_i(y_i, w) - C_i(y_i^a, w)}{p_i(y_i - y_i^a)}\right], \quad \text{for } y_i \neq y_i^a.\tag{6.19}$$

The terms ω_i act as weights in the summation of (6.18). To interpret these weights, consider the case of constant returns to scale, so that $C_i(y_i, w) = p_i y_i = y_i AC_i(w)$ and $C_i(y_i^a, w) = y_i^a AC_i(w)$, where average costs AC_i are independent of output. Then (6.19) readily becomes $\omega_i = (p_i - AC_i)/p_i$, which is the markup of prices over average costs. Industries with perfect competition then have $\omega_i = 0$, and more generally these weights satisfy $0 \leq \omega_i \leq 1$. We argue in the next result that these bounds hold under increasing returns to scale, too.

Theorem (Grinols 1991)

A sufficient condition to obtain Pareto gains from trade is that a weighted average of the outputs in industries subject to increasing returns to scale or imperfect competition expands, or (6.18) holds, where the weights ω_i defined in (6.19) satisfy $0 \leq \omega_i \leq 1$.

Proof

From (6.17) and (6.18) the government budget is positive, so everyone can be made better off with a poll subsidy. Then the only thing left to show is that $0 \leq \omega_i \leq 1$. Since costs are nondecreasing in output, the numerator and denominator of the bracketed term in (6.19) have the same sign, and it follows that the bracketed term is nonnegative, so that $\omega_i \leq 1$.

---

[9] If $y_i = y_i^a$ then (6.20) is not defined, and we simply exclude that industry i from the summation in (6.18).

The numerator of the bracketed term can be written as $C_i(y_i, w) - C_i(y_i^a, w)$ $= AC_i(y_i, w)y_i - AC_i(y_i^a, w)y_i^a$. Consider the case where output is increasing, $y_i > y_i^a$. Since average costs are constant or falling in output, it follows that $AC_i(y_i, w) \leq AC_i(y_i^a, w)$, and so the numerator satisfies $C_i(y_i, w) - C_i(y_i^a, w) \leq AC_i(y_i, w)(y_i - y_i^a)$. Using this in (6.19), it follows that $\omega_i \geq [p_i - AC_i(y_i, w)]/p_i \geq 0$, where the final inequality is obtained since profits are nonnegative, so that $p_i \geq AC_i(y_i, w)$. A similar proof that $\omega_i \geq 0$ applies when $y_i < y_i^a$.   QED

Corollary

A sufficient condition for Pareto gains from trade is that the output of every industry subject to increasing returns to scale or imperfect competition does not fall when going from autarky to free trade, and at least one such industry expands.

Versions of this corollary have been obtained by Kemp and Negishi (1970), Markusen (1981), and Helpman (1984b). The theorem of Grinols is more general in its assumptions than any of these authors, and also shows how output increases in some industries and decreases in others can be summed together using the weights ω_i.

One concern with the above results is that it may be hard to achieve increases in industry output across several countries: if output increases in one country, is it not more likely to fall in another? This was the case analyzed by Markusen (1981) with a single industry subject to imperfect competition. For two countries that are identical except for size, he found that the smaller country would experience an increase in the imperfect competitive industry, but not the larger country. This means that gains from trade are assured only for the smaller country.

Sufficient conditions to have *all* countries gain from trade have been derived using a monopolistic competition model, by Helpman and Krugman (1985, chap. 9). In this case, each firm is producing a differentiated product, and there is free entry and exit from the industry. As a first step in their argument, they find that Pareto gains from trade for a single country are assured if (*a*) the output of *each firm still producing* does not fall going from autarky to free trade; (*b*) total *industry output* (equal to the number of firms times the output of each) in that country does not fall going from autarky to free trade; (*c*) the set of goods available to consumers is *not reduced* due to the opening of trade. Notice that condition (a) allows some firms to exit due to the opening of trade, as discussed in chapter 5. Indeed, their departure gives room for other firms to increase their outputs and take advantage of economies of scale.

Then extending the argument to deal with multiple countries opening to free trade, Helpman and Krugman (1985, 187–90) have identified quite weak assumptions to ensure that conditions (a)–(c) hold across all countries.[10] Specifically, they assume that each industry in the economy is organized like the Krugman model considered at the beginning of chapter 5, with consumption in each industry coming from an additively separable subutility function. Assume that (*a*) the elasticity of demand in nondecreasing in output; (*b*) there is a constant share of expenditure spent on each differentiated goods industry; (*c*) the production function for each differentiated good is homothetic; (*d*) equilibria in each differentiated goods industry are symmetric, with identical costs, prices, and output. Then Helpman and Krugman demonstrate that the opening of trade will lead to at least as many goods, and at least as much output of each, provided only that the *world output of each differentiated goods industry does not contract*. This becomes a very weak condition to ensure Pareto gains from trade across all countries.

Conclusions

The idea that countries gain from trade is as old as the idea of comparative advantage itself—Ricardo wrote his model of trade between England and Portugal to demonstrate both claims. But gains "for a country" does not have a well-defined meaning unless we specify what this condition implies for the many different individuals located there. In this chapter we have taken the heterogeneity of individuals seriously, and identified conditions under which *all agents* can gain from trade, that is, Pareto gains are achieved. The lump sum transfers that we have discussed require too much information to be implemented in practice, but are still valuable because they allow us to show that Pareto gains are *in principle* possible. The commodity tax/subsidies introduced by Dixit and Norman (1980) are an alternative means of achieving Pareto gains. In the presence of mobility costs, however, they may need to be supplemented with some form of trade adjustment assistance.

Our results for Pareto gains within a country can be extended to cover the comparison of any two trading situations, and also to cover multiple countries, as with customs unions and free-trade areas. In addition, we showed how imperfect competition and increasing returns to scale can be incorporated. Missing from our analysis, however, is an important topic

---

[10] Examples can be constructed, however, where one or more of these conditions is violated so that losses from trade are possible. See Lawrence and Spiller 1983 and Francois and van Ypersele 2002.

related to imperfect competition and the gains from regional trade agreements. Suppose that trade in differentiated products occurs under monopolistic competition, subject to "iceberg" transportation costs as discussed in chapter 5. Furthermore, suppose that the countries forming a regional agreement do not aim to keep welfare in the rest of world unchanged; on the contrary, these countries adjust the tariffs applied to the rest of the world to their own optimal advantage. In the next chapter, we will call this the "optimal" tariff, and it is applied to shift a country's terms of trade in its favor. Finally, suppose that the world splits up into a number of such regional areas, each of them equally sized. Then how does the formation of these areas impact world welfare?

This question has been addressed by Krugman (1991a, 1991b), with two quite distinct answers. First, ignoring transportation costs, Krugman (1991a) argues that with the world divided into a number of equally sized regional trading areas, the *worst* number of such areas is *three*. The logic of this proposition is that with just one area, encompassing all countries, we have the highest level of world welfare (i.e., global free trade). Conversely, with many equal-sized areas, each group of countries will have little influence in changing their terms of trade, so tariffs are low and we are again close to free trade. But at some intermediate number of areas, tariffs will be higher and world welfare lower. Stylized calculations suggests that world welfare is *minimized* with three areas, which is a depressing result in view of the possible formation of three trading regions in reality: the Americas, Europe, and Asia.

But this view of the world ignores the fact that actual trading regions are often between geographically close countries (e.g., the EEC and NAFTA), so the "natural" trading advantages of these countries are just enhanced by the regional agreement. To see how this affects the argument, suppose now that there are three continents (America, Europe, and Asia) with multiple countries in each. As in Krugman (1991b), take an extreme case where transportation costs are infinite for trade between the continents, but zero within each continent. In the absence of any regional agreements, the countries in each continent will be applying optimal tariffs against each other. But with a regional free-trade agreement on each continent, tariffs are eliminated, and world welfare is maximized: the fact that outside countries are excluded from each regional agreement is irrelevant, since transportation costs between the continents are so high. So in this case, three regional trading areas *maximize* world welfare!

These two starkly different results suggest that the pattern and level of transportation costs between countries is crucial to determining the welfare effects of regional agreements. Obviously, we need to go beyond the two extreme cases of Krugman (1991a, 1991b), and this is done by Frankel (1997). Continuing with Krugman's example of a world divided

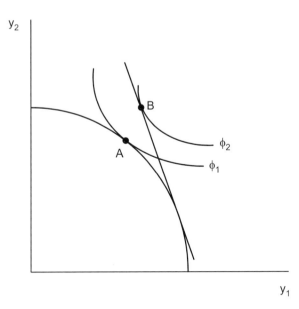

Figure 6.3

into continents, each of which is divided into multiple countries, Frankel explores the welfare impact of regional agreements within or across continents. An agreement within a continent (where transportation costs are low) is called "natural," while an agreement across continents (where transportation costs are high) is called "unnatural." Frankel confirms that "natural" trading areas are more likely to lead to world welfare gains than "unnatural" areas.[11] However, it turns out that having regional agreements *within* continents is not always welfare improving, and the case where these "natural" areas fail to lead to world gains is called "supernatural." This brief summary is meant to suggest that the impact of regional trade agreements—in theory or in practice—is still a wide open area for research, and we shall return to this topic in chapter 9.

Problems

In earlier chapters, our only demonstration of the gains from trade has been a diagram like Figure 6.3, where we show the indifference curves ϕ being lifted off the PPF due to free trade. The question is this: should we think of these indifference curves as applying to a single "representative"

---

[11] In a test of this proposition, Krishna (2003) provides empirical evidence that raises doubts on the link between "natural" trading areas (between close countries) and welfare gains.

consumer, or is there some other interpretation that allows for consumers who differ in their utility functions? The following results are due to Samuelson (1956) and give a precise interpretation to the indifference curves shown.

Suppose that we have H consumers with utility functions $u^h(c^h)$, $h = 1, \ldots, H$, where we ignore individual supplies of factors for simplicity. We assume that these are increasing and quasi-concave. Further, suppose that we have a social welfare function $W(u^1, \ldots, u^H)$, which is nondecreasing and quasi-concave. Then Samuelson defined the social utility function as

$$\phi(c) = \max_{c^h \geq 0} W[u^1(c^1), \ldots, u^H(c^H)] \quad \text{st.} \quad \sum_{h=1}^{H} c^h \leq c. \quad (6.20)$$

Thus, this social utility function takes the total amount of consumption goods available, c, and allocates it across individuals so as to maximize social welfare. This allocation is a form of "lump sum" transfers where we are physically allocating the goods (though the outcome would be similar if we instead used lump sum transfers of income).

Samuelson argued that we could think of the indifference curves in Figure 6.3 as being iso-curves of the function ϕ, so moving to a higher indifference curve due to trade (as illustrated) means that social welfare has indeed increased.

To further understand Samuelson's approach, answer the following:

6.1 The fact that we are moving from a welfare level of ϕ_1 in Figure 6.3 to ϕ_2 due to the opening of trade proves that *some person's utility must have increased*, but it does not prove that *everyone's* utility has increased. Can you think of a special form for the welfare function W that will ensure that when ϕ goes up, *everyone's* utility must go up? (This social welfare function is used by Chipman [1987, 528], for example.)

6.2 In this problem we extend the analysis of partial tariff reform to use the commodity taxes and subsidies suggested by Dixit and Norman (1980), rather than lump sum transfers. Suppose that the government imposes taxes of $(p^0 - p^1)$ on goods and subsidies of $(w^0 - w^1)$ on factors. In addition, we will suppose that the poll subsidy of $R \equiv (t^{0\prime} m^0)/H - (t^{1\prime} m^1)/H$ is given to each person (which is a tax if negative), in addition to the tariff revenue.

(a) Show that consumers can still afford their initial consumption bundles (c^{h0}, v^{h0}).
(b) Show that the government budget is nonnegative if $(p^{*0} - p^{*1})^\prime m^0 + t^{1\prime}(m^1 - m^0) \geq 0$.

6.3   Using the assumption of trade balance at international prices, show that the condition $(p^{*0} - p^{*1})'m^0 + t^{1'}(m^1 - m^0) \geq 0$ can be alternatively expressed as $p^{1'}(m^1 - m^0) \geq 0$, and interpret the latter condition. (This formulation of the condition to ensure Pareto gains under partial reform is used by Ju and Krishna 2000a.)

Chapter 7

Import Tariffs and Dumping

THERE ARE VARIOUS reasons why countries use import tariffs and other types of trade policies. Nearly all countries have used these instruments in early stages of their development to foster the growth of domestic industries, in what is called *import substitution*. Such policies have been heavily criticized for protecting inefficient domestic industries from international competition. Many countries have later switched to an *export promotion* regime, under which industries are expected to meet international competition through exports, albeit with subsidies (hopefully temporary) given to exporters. The more than 140 members of the WTO have all committed to abandon such heavily regulated trade regimes and move towards substantially freer trade. One question, then, is whether the use of import tariffs and other trade policies at early stages of the development process has any rationale, especially when other markets (such as for capital) might not be functioning well. While this is too big a question to deal with adequately in this chapter, we will briefly discuss the rationale for temporary tariffs in what is called "infant industry" protection.

A second question concerns the welfare cost of tariffs and quotas in situations where other markets are working well. Even under the GATT/WTO, countries are permitted to apply tariffs in a number of cases, including: (*a*) "escape clause" tariffs, under which countries temporarily escape from their promise to keep tariffs low, due to injury in an import-competing industry; (*b*) antidumping duties, under which tariffs are applied to offset import prices that are "too low." For theoretical purposes, we can think of escape clause tariffs as *exogenously imposed* on exporting firms, and this will be our assumption in the first part of the chapter. We will examine the response of the exporters, as well as the response of import-competing firms, to such tariffs. In particular, we are interested in whether there is any "strategic" role for trade policy, whereby it gives an advantage to importing firms that leads to a welfare gain for the importing country. This possibility is associated with the work of Brander and Spencer (1984a, 1984b). The response of firms to the tariff depends on the market structure, and we shall investigate a series of cases, concluding with an empirical investigation of these tariffs as applied to U.S. imports of compact trucks and heavyweight motorcycles (Feenstra 1989).

Following this, we turn to a discussion of dumping. We suggest that this phenomenon can be viewed as a natural attempt of imperfectly competitive firms to enter each other's markets, as in the "reciprocal dumping" model of Brander (1981) and Brander and Krugman (1983). As such, it is likely to bring gains to consumers through lower prices. These gains will be offset by the use of antidumping duties, especially since these duties must be treated as *endogenous*: their application will depend on the prices charged by the exporting firms. Exporting firms will have an incentive to raise their prices even if there is only a threat of antidumping duties being imposed, and to raise them even further if the duties are actually imposed. For these reasons, consumer and social losses due to antidumping actions are particularly high. We review empirical work by Prusa (1991, 1992), Staiger and Wolak (1994), and Blonigen and Haynes (2002), who estimate the price and quantity effects of antidumping actions.

Tariffs under the GATT/WTO

For member countries of the WTO the use of tariffs or quotas is allowed under some circumstances. For example, Article XIX of the GATT (see Table 6.1), called the "escape clause," allows for the temporary use of protection when domestic industries are experiencing unusual import competition. In order for the articles of GATT to have legal standing in its member countries, they must be reflected in a set of trade laws within each country. In the United States, Article XIX was incorporated into Title II, Section 201 of the Trade Act of 1974:

> Title II. Relief from Injury Caused by Import Competition
> Section 201. Investigation by International Trade Commission
> (a) (1) A petition for eligibility for import relief for the purpose of facilitating orderly adjustment to import competition may be filed with the International Trade Commission . . . by an entity, including a trade association, firm, certified or recognized union, or a group of workers, which is representative of the industry . . .
> (b) (1) . . . upon the filing of a petition under subsection (a) (1), the Commission shall promptly make an investigation to determine whether an article is being imported into the United States in such increased quantities as to be a substantial cause of serious injury, or threat thereof, to the domestic industry producing an article like or directly competitive with the imported article . . .
> (4) For the purposes of this section, the term "substantial cause" means a cause which is important and not less than any other cause.
> Source: U.S. Public Law 93-618, January 3, 1975

It can be seen that in order to qualify for tariffs protection under Section 201, several criteria need to be met, the most important of which is that imports must be a "substantial cause of serious injury, or threat thereof, to the domestic industry," where a "substantial cause" must be "not less than any other cause." This legal language is very important in practice: it means that a tariff will be granted only if rising imports are the *most important* cause of injury to the domestic industry. This criterion is difficult enough to establish that escape clause protection is used infrequently. This is shown in Table 7.1, taken from Hansen and Prusa 1995. Over the years 1980–88, there were only 19 escape clause case files in the United States, of which 12 obtained a *negative* recommendation from the U.S. International Trade Commission (ITC). The remaining 7 affirmative cases went to the president for a final ruling, and he gave a positive recommendation for import protection in only 5 cases, or less than 1 per year. We will investigate two of these U.S. cases in this chapter, one of which (heavyweight motorcycles) received import protection under Section 201, and the other of which (compact trucks) was denied under Section 201 but was able to get tariff protection by other means.

As an alternative to the escape clause, firms can file for import protection under the antidumping provision of the WTO, which is Article VI (see Table 6.1). This provision has been incorporated into Title VII of U.S. trade laws, where Section 303 deals with "countervailing duties" and Section 731 deals with "antidumping duties." Countervailing duties are applied to offset foreign subsidies that lower the price of the foreign export good in the home market. Antidumping deals with cases where it is believed that a foreign firm is selling goods in the home (i.e., importing) market at either a *lower price* than in its own market, or if there is no foreign price to observe, then at less than its *average costs* of production. The cases filed in the United States under each of these provisions are also shown in Table 7.1, and it can be seen that the number of these vastly exceeds escape clause cases.

Over 1980–88, there were more than 400 antidumping cases files in the United States, and of these, about 150 were rejected and another 150 had duties levied. In order to have duties applies, a case must first go to the Department of Commerce (DOC), which rules on whether imports have occurred as "less than fair value," that is, below the price or average costs in their own market. These rulings were positive in 94% of cases during this period (Hansen and Prusa 1995, 300). The case is then brought before the ITC, which must rule on whether imports have caused "material injury" to the domestic industry (defined as "harm that is not inconsequential, immaterial, or unimportant"). This criterion is much easier to meet than the "substantial cause of serious injury" provision of Section 201, and as a result, the ITC more frequently rules in favor of antidumping

TABLE 7.1
Administered Protection Cases in the United States

	Escape Clause Outcome				Antidumping Outcome				Countervailing Duty Outcome			
	Negative ITC	Affirmative ITC	Affirmative President	Total	Duty Levied	Case Rejected	Withdrawn	Total	Duty Levied	Case Rejected	Withdrawn	Total
1980	1	1	1	2	4	15	10	29	3	15	5	23
1981	1	0	0	1	5	6	4	15	2	0	5	7
1982	1	2	2	3	13	29	23	65	40	54	42	136
1983	0	0	0	0	19	24	3	46	12	5	5	22
1984	4	3	1	7	8	21	44	73	19	10	15	44
1985	3	1	1	4	27	21	15	63	16	14	18	48
1986	1	0	0	1	44	20	7	71	17	6	4	27
1987	0	0	0	0	8	5	2	15	3	2	1	6
1988	1	0	0	1	19	15	0	34	3	7	2	12
All	12	7	5	19	147	156	108	411	115	113	97	325

Source: Hansen and Prusa 1995.

duties. Furthermore, the application of duties does not require the additional approval of the president. These legal factors explain the much greater use of antidumping than the escape clause in the United States, and it is also becoming more commonly used in other countries, as described by Prusa (2001).

There is a surprising third category of antidumping cases shown in Table 7.1: of the roughly 400 cases in the United States over this period, about 100, or one-quarter, of these were *withdrawn* prior to a ruling by the ITC. What are we to make of these cases? U.S. antidumping law actually permits the U.S. firm to withdraw its case and then, acting through an intermediary at the DOC, agree with the foreign firm on the level of prices and market shares! (Prusa 1991, 1992). This type of communication between two American firms would be illegal under U.S. antitrust law, of course, but is exempted from prosecution in antidumping cases under the so-called Noerr-Pennington doctrine. As we would expect, these withdrawn and settled cases result in a significant increase in market prices, with losses for consumers, as will be discussed at the end of the chapter.

Social Welfare

In the previous chapter we were careful to allow for heterogeneous consumers, and considered systems of lump sum transfers or commodity taxes and subsidies such that everyone could be better off (Pareto gains from trade). It will now be convenient to adopt a simpler measure of overall social welfare, without worrying about whether every individual is better off or not. To construct this we need to have a method to "add up" the utilities of consumers. This will be achieved by assuming that every individual has a quasi-linear utility function, given by $c_0^h + U^h(c^h)$, where c_0^h is the consumption of a numeraire good, and c^h is the consumption vector of all other goods for consumer $h = 1, \ldots, H$, with U^h increasing and strictly concave. Each consumer maximizes utility subject to the budget constraint $c_0^h + p'c^h \le I^h$.

Let $c^h = d^h(p)$ denote the optimal vector of consumption for each individual, with remaining income spent on the numeraire good, $c_0^h = I^h - p'c^h(p)$.[1] Then we can define social welfare as the sum of individual utilities,

$$W(p, I) \equiv \sum_{h=1}^{H} I^h - p'd^h(p) + U^h[d^h(p)], \qquad (7.1)$$

[1] Notice that demand for the nonnumeraire goods does not depend on income; see problem 7.1.

where total income is $I = \sum_{h=1}^{H} I^h$. Notice that the sum over individuals of the last two terms on the right-hand side of (7.1) gives consumer surplus. By the envelope theorem, the derivative of (7.1) is the negative of total consumption, $\partial W/\partial p = \sum_{h=1}^{H} -d^h(p) \equiv -d(p)$. Thus, we can use the social welfare function just like an indirect utility function for the economy as a whole.

Let us further simplify the analysis by supposing that there is only a *single import good* subject to a tariff. Holding the prices of all other goods fixed, we will therefore treat p as a *scalar*, denoting the price of that good in the importing country. Its world price is denoted by the scalar p^*, and the difference between these is the *specific* import tariff t, so $p = p^* + t$. We suppose that the numeraire good is also traded, at a fixed world price of unity. Labor is assumed to be the only factor of production, and each unit of the numeraire good requires one unit of labor. It follows that wages in the economy are also unity, so that total income equals the fixed labor supply of L. These assumptions allow the economy to mimic a partial-equilibrium setting, where wages are fixed and trade is balanced through flows of the numeraire good.

Output of the good in question is denoted by the scalar y, which may be produced by competitive or imperfectly competitive firms. We suppose that the industry costs of producing the good are denoted by $C(y)$, with marginal costs $C'(y)$.[2] Imports are denoted by the scalar $m = d(p) - y$, where $d'(p) < 0$ from the assumption that U^h is strictly concave for all h. We assume that revenue raised from the tariff, tm, is redistributed back to consumers, who are also each entitled to profits from the import-competing industry, which are $py - C(y)$. It follows that social welfare is written as

$$W[p, L + tm + py - C(y)] \equiv W(t). \tag{7.2}$$

This general expression for social welfare holds under perfect or imperfect competition. In the former case, it is common to refer to profits $[py - C(y)]$ as producer surplus, that is, the return to fixed factors of production in the industry. In the latter case, we denote profits of the domestic industry by $\pi = py - C(y)$, and will need to specify how these depend on actions of foreign firms. We will be considering three cases: (*a*) perfect competition in the home and foreign industries; (*b*) foreign monopoly, with no domestic import-competing firms; (*c*) duopoly, with one home firm and one foreign firm engaged in either Cournot or Bertrand competition. A fourth case of

---

[2] Under perfect competition $C(y)$ denotes industry costs, and under monopoly it denotes the firm's costs. Under oligopoly with a homogeneous product, we should replace $C(y)$ with $NC(y)$, where N is the number of firms and $C(y)$ is the costs of each. Similarly, we replace sales py in (7.2) by Npy.

monopolistic competition is discussed by Helpman (1990) and is not covered here. We begin with perfect competition, where we distinguish a *small importing country*, meaning that the world price p^* is fixed even as the tariff varies, and a *large country*, whose tariff affects the foreign price p^*.

In each case, we are interested in how social welfare in (7.2) varies with the tariff. To determine this, let us first derive a general expression for the change in welfare. Treating the price p and output y as depending on the tariff, we can totally differentiate (7.2) to obtain

$$
\begin{aligned}
\frac{dW}{dt} &= -d(p)\frac{dp}{dt} + m + \left(t\frac{dm}{dp} + y\right)\frac{dp}{dt} + [p - C'(y)]\frac{dy}{dt} \\
&= m\left(1 - \frac{dp}{dt}\right) + t\frac{dm}{dp}\frac{dp}{dt} + [p - C'(y)]\frac{dy}{dt} \\
&= t\frac{dm}{dp}\frac{dp}{dt} - m\frac{dp^*}{dt} + [p - C'(y)]\frac{dy}{dt}.
\end{aligned}
\tag{7.3}
$$

The second line of (7.3) follows by noting that $d(p) - y = m$ and combining terms, while the third line follows because $p = p^* + t$, so that $[1 - (dp/dt)] = -dp^*/dt$.

We will be discussing each of the terms on the last line of (7.3) throughout this chapter, but note here the similarity between these terms and those derived in the previous chapter. The first term on the last line of (7.3) can be interpreted as the efficiency cost of the tariff, much like the term $t^{1\prime}(m^1 - m^0)$ in chapter 6; the second term is the effect of the tariff on the foreign price p^*, or the terms of trade effect, like $(p^{*0} - p^{*1})'m^0$ in chapter 6; and the third term reflects the change in industry output times the price-cost margin, like (6.18). This third term reflects the fact that with imperfect competition there is a gap between the price or consumer valuation of a product, and the marginal costs to firms. This distortion due to monopolistic pricing creates an efficiency loss, and any increase in domestic output will therefore offset that loss and serve to raise welfare.

Perfect Competition, Small Country

Holding p^* fixed, we already argued in the previous chapter that "free trade is better than restricted trade for a small country." In other words, the optimal tariff is zero. We now provide a more direct demonstration of this result, and also show how the welfare loss due to a tariff can be measured. Under perfect competition profits are maximized when $p = C'(y)$, so the final term in (7.3) is zero. When world prices are fixed and domestic prices given by $p = p^* + t$, then $dp^*/dt = 0$ and $dp/dt = 1$. Using these various relations in (7.3), we readily obtain

$$\frac{dW}{dt} = t\frac{dm}{dp}. \qquad (7.4)$$

Evaluating this expression at a zero tariff, we have

$$\left.\frac{dW}{dt}\right|_{t=0} = 0. \qquad (7.4')$$

This proves that social welfare has a critical point at a zero tariff, but we still need to determine whether this is a maximum or not. Differentiating (7.4) and evaluating at $t = 0$,

$$\left.\frac{d^2W}{dt^2}\right|_{t=0} = \frac{dm}{dp} < 0, \qquad (7.5)$$

where this sign is obtained because $dm/dp = d'(p) - (1/C'')$, with $d'(p) < 0$ from concavity of the utility functions and $C'' > 0$ from the second-order condition for profit maximization. This proves that the critical point at $t = 0$ is a local *maximum*, and in fact, it is also a global maximum since with $dm/dp < 0$ then $t = 0$ is the *only* tariff at which (7.4) equals zero. Therefore, the *optimal tariff for a small country is zero*.

It is relatively easy to obtain an expression for the loss in welfare from applying a tariff. To do so, let us take a second-order Taylor series approximation of welfare, around the free-trade point,

$$W(t) \approx W(0) + t\left.\frac{dW}{dt}\right|_{t=0} + \frac{1}{2}t^2\left.\frac{d^2W}{dt^2}\right|_{t=0}. \qquad (7.6)$$

Evaluating this using (7.4') and (7.5), we see that

$$W(t) - W(0) \approx \frac{1}{2}t^2\left.\frac{d^2W}{dt^2}\right|_{t=0} = \frac{1}{2}t^2\frac{dm}{dp} = \frac{1}{2}\Delta p\Delta m < 0. \qquad (7.7)$$

The final expression in (7.7) is negative since the tariff reduces imports, so the welfare loss equals one-half times the increase in price times the change in imports. This loss is illustrated in Figure 7.1. In panel (a) we show the domestic demand curve D and supply curve S, together with the constant world price p^*. Under free trade, domestic demand is at c_0 and supply at y_0, so imports are $m_0 = c_0 - y_0$. This is shown in panel (b), which graphs the import demand curve $M = D - S$. We can think of the fixed world price p^* as establishing a horizontal export supply curve X, which intersects M at the equilibrium imports m_0.

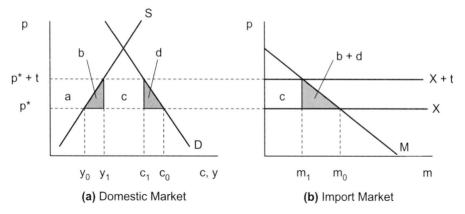

Figure 7.1 Small Country

With the import tariff of t, the export supply curve shifts up to $X + t$ in panel (b), leading to the equilibrium domestic price of $p = p^* + t$. Thus, the domestic price increases by the full amount of the tariff. In panel (a), this leads to reduced demand of c_1 and increased supply of y_1. The change in welfare in Figure 7.1(a) can be decomposed as $-(a + b + c + d)$ consumer surplus loss $+(a)$ producer surplus gain $+(c)$ tariff revenue $= -(b + d)$, which is always negative. Area $(b + d)$ is the deadweight loss of the tariff, and also shown as the triangle under the import demand curve in panel (b). The area d is interpreted as the consumer surplus loss for those units no longer purchased (i.e., $c_0 - c_1$), while area b is interpreted as the increase in marginal costs (along the supply curve) for the extra units produced (i.e., $y_1 - y_0$).

So we see that the deadweight loss of the tariff can be measured by a triangle under the import demand curve. Since both the height and the base of the triangle depend on the tariff, the area of the triangle itself is of the second order of smalls for a small tariff; that is, the deadweight loss in (7.7) depends on the *square* of the tariff. Notice that we can rewrite (7.7) to measure the deadweight loss as a fraction of import expenditure:

$$\frac{W(t) - W(0)}{pm} \approx \frac{1}{2}\left(\frac{t}{p}\right)^2\left(\frac{dm}{dp}\frac{p}{m}\right). \tag{7.7'}$$

For example, with a 10% tariff and an import demand elasticity of 2, the deadweight loss relative to import expenditure will be 1%. As is typical for triangle calculations, we see that the deadweight loss is quite small for moderate tariffs. This has led many researchers to conclude that a formula like (7.7') does not capture the inefficiencies present in import substitution regimes. We will be investigating some reasons why the deadweight loss of trade restrictions may well be greater than (7.7′). This can occur if foreign firms anticipate the tariffs, as with antidumping duties (discussed later in this chapter), or if quotas are used instead of tariffs (discussed in the next chapter), or if tariffs have the effect of decreasing the *variety* of import products available. This latter effect has been emphasized by Feenstra (1992) and Romer (1994). Both authors provide simple formulas to compute welfare losses due to a reduction in import varieties, and these are much greater than (7.7′). In addition, Feenstra (1988b) and Klenow and Rodríguez-Clare (1997) provide estimates of the welfare *gain* due to new import varieties, which can be substantial.

Perfect Competition, Large Country

For a large country, we suppose that the world price of imports depends on the tariff chosen, which is written as $p^*(t)$. Generally, we define the *terms of trade* as the price of a country's exports divided by the price of its imports, so that a fall in the import price p^* is an *improvement* in the terms of trade. We will argue that a tariff leads to such an improvement in the terms of trade under perfect competition, as we assume in this section. In the next section we will examine the sign of this derivative under foreign monopoly.

The domestic price of the import good is $p = p^* + t$, so now $dp^*/dt \neq 0$ and $dp/dt \neq 1$. We still have $p = C'(y)$ under perfect competition, so (7.3) becomes

$$\frac{dW}{dt} = t \frac{dm}{dp} \frac{dp}{dt} - m \frac{dp^*}{dt}. \tag{7.8}$$

The first term is interpreted as the marginal deadweight loss from the tariff; and the second term is the terms of trade effect of the tariff, that is, the reduction in the price of p^* times the amount of imports. The sign of dp^*/dt can be determined from Figure 7.2. In panel (a), we show the domestic demand curve D and supply curve S, which lead to the import demand curve $M = D - S$ in panel (b). Also shown is the foreign supply curve X, which we assume is upward sloping. The initial equilibrium foreign and domestic price is $p_0^* = p_0$. The tariff shifts up the export supply curve to $X + t$, which intersects import demand at the new domestic price $p = p^* + t$. It is clear from the diagram that the increase in the domestic price from p_0 to $p^* + t$ is *less than* the amount of the tariff t, which implies that the new foreign price p^* is less than its initial value p_0^*. This is a terms of trade gain for the importing country.

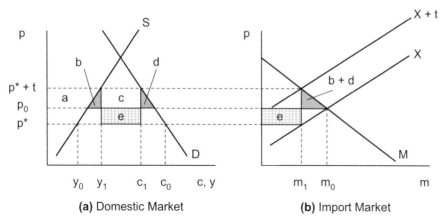

Figure 7.2 Large Country

Using the result that $dp^*/dt < 0$, we obtain from (7.8),

$$\left.\frac{dW}{dt}\right|_{t=0} = -m\frac{dp^*}{dt} > 0, \tag{7.9}$$

so that a small tariff will necessarily raise welfare. The change in welfare in Figure 7.2 is $-(a + b + c + d)$ consumer surplus loss $+ (a)$ producer surplus gain $+ (c + e)$ tariff revenue $= e - (b + d)$. The area e equals the drop in the price p^* times the import quantity $m_1 = c_1 - y_1$, which is a precise measure of the terms of trade gain. The deadweight loss triangle $(b + d)$ is still measured by (7.7), and depends on the square of the tariff, so it is of the second order of smalls. This does not apply to the terms of trade gain e, however, which depends on t rather than t^2. For these reasons, the net welfare gain $e - (b + d)$ is positive for tariffs sufficiently small, while it is negative for large tariffs.

The *optimal tariff t^** is computed where (7.8) equals zero:

$$\frac{dW}{dt} = 0 \implies \frac{t^*}{p^*} = \left(\frac{dp^*}{dt}\frac{m}{p^*}\right)\bigg/\left(\frac{dm}{dp}\frac{dp}{dt}\right). \tag{7.10}$$

To interpret this expression, we simplify it in two different ways:

(1) Since domestic imports equal foreign exports, then

$$m = x \implies \frac{dm}{dp}\frac{dp}{dt} = \frac{dx}{dt}.$$

Substituting this into (7.10) we obtain,

$$\frac{t^*}{p^*} = \left(\frac{dp^*}{dt}\frac{x}{p^*}\right)\bigg/\left(\frac{dx}{dt}\right) = 1\bigg/\left(\frac{dx}{dp^*}\frac{p^*}{x}\right), \qquad (7.11)$$

where the second term is obtained because $\left(\dfrac{dx}{dt}\bigg/\dfrac{dp^*}{dt}\right) = \dfrac{dx}{dp^*}$, which is the slope of the foreign export supply curve. Thus, (7.11) states that the *optimal percentage tariff*, t^*/p^*, equals the *inverse of the elasticity of foreign export supply*.

This is a good formula for comparing the case of a small country, where the elasticity of foreign export supply is infinite and so the optimal tariff is zero, to the large country, where the elasticity of foreign export supply is finite and positive, and so is the optimal tariff. Beyond this, however, the formula is not very helpful because there is little that we know empirically about the elasticity of foreign export supply: how "large" does an importing country have to be before it is reasonable to treat the elasticity of foreign export supply as less than infinite? There is no good answer to this question. We therefore turn to a second interpretation of the optimal tariff.

(2) An alternative way of writing (7.10) is to just rearrange terms, obtaining

$$\frac{t^*}{p} = \left(\frac{dm}{dp}\frac{p}{m}\right)^{-1}\left(\frac{dp^*}{dt}\bigg/\frac{dp}{dt}\right). \qquad (7.12)$$

Now the optimal tariff equals the *inverse of the elasticity of import demand supply*, times the ratio of the change in the relative *foreign* and *domestic* price of imports. Since the import demand elasticity is negative, and presuming that $dp/dt > 0$ (which we will confirm below), then the optimal tariff is positive provided that $dp^*/dt < 0$.

Think about the foreign price p^* as being chosen strategically by exporting firms. When these firms are faced with a tariff, how will they adjust the *net of tariff* price p^* that they receive? Will they absorb part of the tariff, meaning that $dp^*/dt < 0$ and $dp/dt < 1$, in an attempt to moderate the increase in the import price $p = p^* + t$? This may well be a profit-maximizing strategy. Generally, we will refer to the magnitude of the derivative dp/dt as the "pass-through" of the tariff: if domestic prices rise by less than the tariff, so that $dp/dt < 1$, this means that foreign exporters have absorbed part of the tariff, $dp^*/dt < 0$, which is a terms of trade gain. The smaller the pass-through of the tariff, the larger the optimal tariff from (7.12). The nice feature of this formula is that it puts the emphasis on the pricing decisions made by foreign exporters, which is entirely appropriate. We analyze this decision of foreign firms next.

Foreign Monopoly

We turn now to the case of a single foreign exporter, selling into the home market. The idea that this firm does not have any competitors in the home market is not very realistic: tariffs are designed to protect domestic firms, and if there are none, we would not expect a tariff! So the assumption of a foreign monopolist should be thought of as a simplification. Our analysis of this case follows Brander and Spencer (1984a, 1984b).

Let x denote the sales of the exporting firm into the home market, which equals home consumption, so $x = d(p)$. We will invert this expression and work with the inverse demand curve, $p = p(x)$, with $p' < 0$. The price received by the foreign exporter is $p^* = p(x) - t$, so that foreign profits are

$$\pi^*(x) = x[p(x) - t] - C^*(x), \tag{7.13}$$

where $C^*(x)$ is foreign costs. Maximizing this over the choice of x, the first-order condition is

$$\pi^{*'}(x) = p(x) + xp'(x) - [C^{*'}(x) + t] = 0. \tag{7.14}$$

The term $p(x) + xp'(x)$ is just marginal revenue, while $C^{*'}(x) + t$ is marginal costs inclusive of the tariff, and these are equalized to maximize profits.

Totally differentiating (7.14) we obtain $\pi^{*''}(x)dx - dt = 0$, so that

$$\frac{dx}{dt} = \frac{1}{\pi^{*''}(x)} < 0, \tag{7.15}$$

where the sign is obtained from the second-order condition for profit maximization. It follows that the change in the import price is

$$\frac{dp}{dt} = p'(x)\frac{dx}{dt} = \frac{p'(x)}{\pi^{*''}(x)} > 0. \tag{7.16}$$

Not surprisingly, the tariff inclusive price $p = p^* + t$ rises. We are interested in whether it rises *less than* the amount of the tariff, that is, whether the pass-through of the tariff is less than complete. Notice that with $p = p^* + t$, then $dp/dt < 1$ if and only if $dp^*/dt < 0$. Thus, "partial pass-through" of the tariff to domestic prices is equivalent to having the foreign firm absorb part of the tariff, which is a terms of trade gain.

Noting that the numerator and denominator of (7.16) are both negative, then $dp/dt < 1$ if and only if

$$p'(x) > \pi^{*''}(x) = 2p'(x) + xp''(x) - C^{*''}(x). \tag{7.17}$$

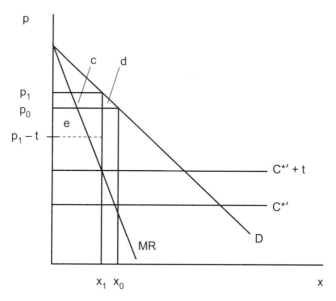

Figure 7.3

The left side of (7.17) is the slope of the inverse demand curve, while the right side is interpreted as the slope of the marginal revenue curve, $[2p'(x) + xp''(x)]$, less the slope of marginal costs. Suppose that marginal costs are constant, $C^{*''} = 0$. Then (7.17) will hold if and only if

$$p'(x) + xp''(x) < 0, \tag{7.17'}$$

which guarantees that marginal revenue is steeper than demand. This condition will hold for linear or concave demand curves, or for any demand curve that is not "too convex."

To illustrate these results, in Figure 7.3 we show the initial equilibrium with the domestic and foreign price of p_0. With the increase in the marginal costs due to the tariff t, the import price rises to p_1. Provided that the marginal revenue is *steeper* than demand, we see this increase in price is less than t, so that the *foreign* price received by the exporters falls, $p_1 - t < p_0$. In that case, $dp^*/dt < 0$ and then the optimal tariff from (7.8) is positive. The change in welfare is shown in Figure 7.3 by $- (c + d)$ consumer surplus loss $+ (c + e)$ revenue gain $= (e - d)$, which is positive if the tariff is sufficiently small.

If marginal revenue is *flatter* than demand, however, then $dp^*/dt > 0$ and the optimal policy is an *import subsidy*. We regard this as a relatively unusual case, but it is certainly possible. For example, if the elasticity of demand is constant, then since marginal revenue is $mr(x) = p(x)[1 - (1/\eta)]$, we have that $-mr'(x) = -p'(x)[1 - (1/\eta)] < -p'(x)$, and it follows that marginal revenue is flatter than demand.

We next check whether an ad valorem tariff τ leads to similar results. The net of tariff price received by the foreign exporters is now $p^* = p(x)/(1 + \tau)$, so that profits are

$$\pi^*(x) = \frac{xp(x)}{(1 + \tau)} - C^*(x). \tag{7.18}$$

Maximizing this over the choice of x, the first-order condition is $p + xp' = (1 + \tau)C^{*'}$, which can be written as

$$p(x)\left(1 - \frac{1}{\eta}\right) = (1 + \tau)C^{*'}(x), \tag{7.19}$$

using the elasticity $\eta(x) = (dx/dp)(p/x) = p/xp'(x)$.

It is straightforward to show that $dx/d\tau < 0$ and $dp/d\tau > 0$, as with the specific tariff. To determine the change in the foreign price p^*, rewrite (7.19) as

$$p^* = \frac{p(x)}{(1 + \tau)} = \left(\frac{\eta}{\eta - 1}\right)C^{*'}(x). \tag{7.19'}$$

Consider the case where the exporter's marginal costs $C^{*'}(x)$ are constant. Then differentiating (7.19'), we obtain

$$\frac{dp^*}{d\tau} = \left[\frac{\eta'}{\eta - 1} - \frac{\eta\eta'}{(\eta - 1)^2}\right]\frac{dx}{d\tau}C^{*'} = -\frac{\eta'(x)}{(\eta - 1)^2}\frac{dx}{d\tau}C^{*'}. \tag{7.20}$$

Using the fact that $dx/d\tau < 0$, we see that $dp^*/d\tau < 0$ when $\eta'(x) < 0$, meaning that the elasticity of demand *increases* as consumption of the importable *falls*. In that case the tariff leads to a fall in the price-cost margin set by the foreign exporter, so that p^* falls, which is a terms of trade gain for the importer. Thus, we summarize our results with the following theorem.

Theorem (Brander and Spencer 1984a, 1984b)

When the home country imports from a foreign monopolist with constant marginal costs,

(a) a small specific tariff improves the terms of trade and raises home welfare if marginal revenue is steeper than demand;

(b) a small ad valorem tariff improves the terms of trade and raises home welfare if the elasticity of demand increases as consumption of the importable falls.

Notice that the condition the $\eta'(x) < 0$ in part (b) is identical to the assumption on the elasticity of demand used by Krugman (1979), as discussed at the beginning of chapter 5. This case applies for linear or concave demand curves, and more generally, any curve that is "less convex" than a constant-elasticity demand curve.

Cournot Duopoly

Let us now introduce a domestic firm that is competing with the foreign firm in the domestic market. We will have to specify the strategic variables chosen by the firms and will assume Cournot competition in quantities in this section, and Bertrand competition in prices in the next. To avoid covering too many cases, we will focus on a *specific* tariff with Cournot competition, and the *ad valorem* tariff with Bertrand competition. To preview our results in this section, we confirm the finding of Helpman and Krugman (1989, sec. 6.1) that a positive tariff is very likely to be the optimal policy under Cournot duopoly.

We let x denote the sales of the foreign exporter in the domestic market, and y denote the sales of the home firm, so total consumption is $z = x + y$. As before, we invert the demand curve $z = d(p)$ to obtain inverse demand $p = p(z)$, with $p' < 0$. Profits of the foreign and home firms are then

$$\pi^* = x[p(z) - t] - C^*(x), \tag{7.21a}$$

$$\pi = yp(z) - C(y). \tag{7.21b}$$

Maximizing these over the choice of x and y, respectively, the first-order conditions are

$$\pi_x^* = p(z) + xp'(z) - [C^{*\prime}(x) + t] = 0. \tag{7.22a}$$

$$\pi_y = p(z) + yp'(z) - C'(y) = 0. \tag{7.22b}$$

The second-order conditions are $\pi_{xx}^* = 2p' + xp'' - C^{*\prime\prime} < 0$ and $\pi_{yy} = 2p' + yp'' - C'' < 0$. In addition, we assume that the stability condition $\pi_{xx}^*\pi_{yy} - \pi_{xy}^*\pi_{yx} > 0$ holds.

Using (7.22a), we can solve for foreign exports x as a function of domestic sales y, written as the reaction curve $x = r^*(y, t)$. From (7.22b), we can also solve for domestic output y as a function of foreign sales x, written as a reaction curve $y = r(x)$. These reaction curves are graphed as R*R* and RR in Figure 7.4, and their intersection determines the Cournot equilibrium denoted by point C. The typical property of these reaction curves is that they are both downward sloping. For stability, the

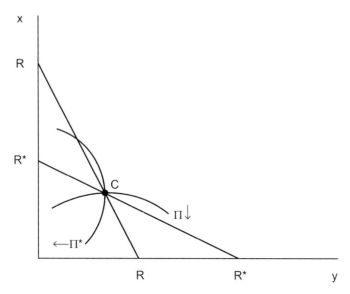

Figure 7.4

home reaction curve RR needs to cut the foreign reaction curve R*R* from above, as illustrated.[3] Notice that the iso-profit curves of π have higher profits in the downwards direction (i.e., for reduced x), and similarly the iso-profit curve π^* has higher foreign profits in the leftward direction (for reduced y), as illustrated.

With the tariff, the foreign firm will reduce the amount it wishes to export (from (7.22b), $dx/dt = 1/\pi^*_{xx} < 0$), and its reaction curve shifts down to R'R', as shown in Figure 7.5. The equilibrium therefore shifts from point C to point D, involving reduced sales of export sales x but increased domestic sales y, together with increased home profits. To determine the effect on the domestic prices we need to calculate the impact on *total sales* $z = x + y$, and then on $p(z)$. To determine this, it is convenient to sum the first-order conditions, obtaining

$$2p(z) + zp'(z) = C'(y) + [C*'(x) + t].$$ (7.23)

Suppose that domestic and foreign marginal costs are *both constant*. Then we can totally differentiate (7.23) to obtain

$$\frac{dz}{dt} = \frac{1}{[3p'(z) + zp''(z)]},$$ (7.24a)

[3] In problem 7.3, you are asked to derive these properties of the reaction curves.

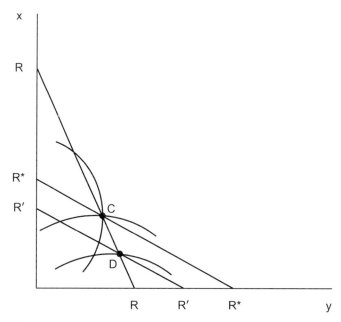

Figure 7.5

and

$$\frac{dp}{dt} = \frac{p'(z)}{[3p'(z) + zp''(z)]}.$$ (7.24b)

From (7.24a) we see that total consumption falls due to the tariff if $3p'(z) + zp''(z) < 0$. In that case the numerator and denominator of (7.24b) are both negative, so that $dp/dt < 1$ if

$$p'(z) > 3p'(z) + zp''(z) \Leftrightarrow 2p'(z) + zp''(z) < 0.$$ (7.25)

The condition on the right-hand side of (7.25) states that marginal revenue for the market as a whole, which is $p(z) + zp'(z)$, *slopes down*. This is a significantly weaker condition than (7.17′), which involved a comparison of the slopes of marginal revenue and demand; now, we only need to check the slope of marginal revenue, and most demand curves will satisfy (7.25). This includes the constant-elasticity curve, for which $mr'(z) = p'(z)[1 - (1/\eta)] < 0$. When (7.25) is satisfied, then $dz/dt < 0$ in (7.24a) and $dp/dt < 1$ in (7.24b), so there is a beneficial terms of trade impact ($dp^*/dt < 0$) for the importing country.

Checking social welfare, we again use the general change in social welfare in (7.3), rewritten here using foreign exports (x) rather than home imports (m):

$$\frac{dW}{dt} = t\frac{dx}{dt} - x\frac{dp^*}{dt} + [p - C'(y)]\frac{dy}{dt}, \qquad (7.3')$$

where the final term reflects the change in domestic output from equilibrium point C to point D. The first term on the right-hand side of (7.3) vanishes for small tariffs, and the second term is positive when (7.25) holds, so that a positive tariff improves the terms of trade. For the third term, in the typical case where both reaction curves are downward sloping, with the home curve cutting the foreign curve from above as shown in Figure 7.5, then we will have $dy/dt > 0$: the tariff will lead to an increase in domestic output, which brings an additional terms of trade gain. In this case, the optimal tariff is unambiguously positive.

However, the typical pattern of the reaction curves shown in Figure 7.5 need not hold, and it is possible that the home curve slope upwards instead, in which case $dy/dt < 0$, so the tariff *reduces* home output. This will tend to offset the terms of trade gains due to the tariff. With constant marginal costs, it can be shown that this case is avoided, so that $dy/dt > 0$, provided that $p'(z) + yp''(z) < 0.$[4] This condition states that "perceived" marginal revenue for the foreign firm, $p(z) + yp'(z)$, is steeper than the demand curve $p(z)$ and is somewhat weaker than (7.17'). Combining this condition with our finding that $dp/dt < 1$ when (7.25) holds, so that $dp^*/dt < 0$, we have two distinct reasons why a tariff will raise social welfare: the terms of trade effect; and the efficiency effect, whereby the tariff moves the home firm to a higher level of output at point D and offsets the distortion between price and marginal cost.

The idea that imperfect competition might justify the "strategic" use of trade policy was an area of very active research during the 1980s. In the tariff case we are discussing, it is tempting to refer to the last term in (7.3') as a "profit shifting" motive for the use of tariffs, suggesting that a "strategic" use of tariffs is to shift profits towards the home firm. But this terminology must be interpreted with caution. There is no direct relation between the sign of the last term in (7.3') and the change in profits for the domestic firm. In the case we are considering, profits of the home firm *always* rise from point C to point D in Figure 7.5 due to the tariff, but nevertheless, the last term in (7.3') can be positive or negative.[5]

In addition, Horstmann and Markusen (1986) argue the "profit shifting" motive for the tariff disappears if there is *free entry* into the domestic industry with Cournot competition. That is, suppose we allow free entry

[4] You are asked to prove this in problem 7.4.
[5] See problem 7.4.

of home firms. Then the tariff, which would cause an incipient rise in profits, leads to the entry of domestic firms until profits are returned to zero. Domestic welfare is written in this case as $W[p, L + tm + N(py - C(y))]$, where N is the number of domestic firms, but with profits equal to zero this becomes $W(p, L + tm)$. Differentiating this with respect to the tariff t, we obtain the total change in utility:

$$\frac{dW}{dt} = -d(p)\frac{dp}{dt} + m + t\frac{dm}{dp}\frac{dp}{dt}. \tag{7.26}$$

This very simple expression is the alternative to (7.3) when profits are identically zero. For small tariffs, the final term vanishes, so the change in welfare depends on a comparison of the first two terms. It is immediately clear that welfare of the importing country increases for a small tariff if and only if $dp/dt < m/d(p)$. The interpretation of this condition is that the pass-through of the tariff to domestic prices must be *less than* the import share $m/d(p)$. Thus, having a terms of trade gain due to the tariff (meaning that $dp/dt < 1$) is no longer sufficient to obtain a welfare improvement; instead, we must have $dp/dt < m/d(p)$. We will be reviewing estimates of the pass-through later in the chapter, and it is not unusual to find that 50–75% of a tariff is reflected in the import price. Under Cournot competition and free entry, this would be welfare improving (due to tariff revenue raised) only in an industry where the import share *exceeds* this magnitude.

Bertrand Duopoly

We turn next to the case of Bertrand competition between the home and foreign firms, where they are choosing prices as strategic variables. If the domestic and imported goods are perfect substitutes, as we assumed in the previous section, then Bertrand competition leads to marginal cost pricing. To avoid this case, we will suppose that the domestic and import goods are *imperfect substitutes*, with the price of the import good denoted by p and the domestic good by q. Let us momentarily depart from our assumption at the beginning of this chapter that there is an additively separable numeraire good that absorbs all income effects, and instead model demand for the domestic good as $y = d(p, q, I)$, and demand for the imported good as $x = d^*(p, q, I)$, where I is the expenditure on both of these goods. We will treat this expenditure as constant, though this is a strong assumption and will be weakened below. Both these demand functions should be homogeneous of degree zero in prices and expenditure I.

With an ad valorem tariff of τ on imports, their domestic price is $p = p^*(1 + \tau)$. So profits of the foreign and home firms are

$$\pi^* = \frac{pd^*(p, q, I)}{(1 + \tau)} - C^*[d^*(p, q, I)], \tag{7.27a}$$

$$\pi = qd(p, q, I) - C[d(p, q, I)]. \tag{7.27b}$$

Maximizing these over the choice of p and q, respectively, treating total expenditure I as fixed, the first-order conditions $\pi_p^* = \pi_q = 0$ can be simplified as

$$p\left(1 - \frac{1}{\eta^*}\right) = (1 + \tau)C^{*\prime}[d^*(p, q, I)], \tag{7.28a}$$

$$q\left(1 - \frac{1}{\eta}\right) = C'[d(p, q, I)], \tag{7.28b}$$

where $\eta^* \equiv -(\partial d^*(p, q, I)/\partial p)(p/d^*)$ and $\eta \equiv -(\partial d(p, q, I)/\partial q)(q/d)$ are the (positive) elasticities of import and domestic demand, respectively. The second-order conditions are $\pi_{pp}^* < 0$ and $\pi_{qq} < 0$, and for stability we require that $\pi_{qq}\pi_{pp}^* - \pi_{qp}\pi_{pp}^* > 0$.

Given the domestic price q, income I, and the tariff, we can use (7.28a) to solve for the tariff-inclusive import price p, obtaining the reaction curve $p = r^*(q, \tau)$. In addition, given the tariff-inclusive import price p and income I, we can use (7.28b) to solve for the domestic price q, obtaining the reaction curve $q = r(p)$. Their intersection determines the Bertrand equilibrium, at point B in Figure 7.6. The iso-profit curves of π have higher profits in the rightward direction (i.e., for higher p), and similarly the iso-profit curve π^* has higher foreign profits in the upward direction (for higher q), as illustrated. To derive the properties of the reaction curves, it is helpful to simplify the elasticities of demand. If the demand functions d and d^* have income elasticities of unity, it turns out that a change in income I does not affect the price elasticities nor the reaction curves. It follows that the price elasticities can be written as functions of the *price ratio* of p and q, or $\eta^*(p/q)$ and $\eta(q/p)$.[6]

The assumption that we used earlier to ensure that the ad valorem tariff led to a fall in the import price p^*, or a terms of trade gain, was that the elasticity of demand was decreasing in *quantity*. Since we are now thinking of the elasticities as functions of relative prices, the analogous assumption would be $\eta^{*\prime}(p/q) > 0$ and $\eta'(q/p) > 0$; that is, elasticities increase as the *relative price* of that good rises. Treating foreign and domestic marginal costs as constant in (7.29), this assumption will ensure that both

---

[6] See problem 7.5 to prove these properties of the elasticities.

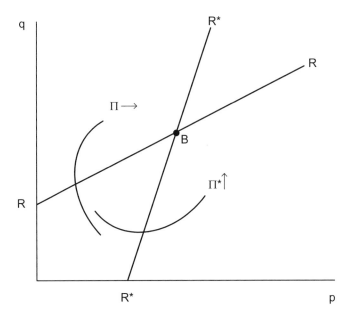

Figure 7.6

reaction curves $p = r^*(q, \tau)$ and $q = r(p)$ slope upwards, as shown in Figure 7.6. As the relative price of the competing good rises, the elasticity falls, and each firm will charge a higher price for its own good. Furthermore, there is a *dampened* response of each price to that of the competing good, so that $\dfrac{dp}{dq}\dfrac{q}{p} = r_q^*(q, \tau)\dfrac{q}{p} < 1$, and $\dfrac{dq}{dp}\dfrac{p}{q} = r_p(p)\dfrac{p}{q} < 1$.[7]

Suppose that the ad valorem tariff τ increases. From the second-order conditions for profit maximization, we will have an increase in the tariff-inclusive import price p. In Figure 7.7, the foreign reaction curve shifts rightward to $R'R'$. This leads to an induced increase in the domestic price q, and a further increase in the import price p, until the new equilibrium is reached at point D. We are interested in whether the percentage increase in p is *less than* the amount of the tariff, that is, $(dp/d\tau)(1 + \tau)/p < 1$, which will ensure that $dp^*/d\tau < 0$, so that there is a terms of trade gain.[8] It turns out that the assumptions we have already made, that $\eta^{*\prime}(p/q) > 0$ and $\eta'(q/p) > 0$, are enough to guarantee this outcome. These conditions are analogous to what we used above to ensure that the ad valorem tariff on a foreign monopolist led to a fall in the import price p^*, or a

---

[7] In problem 7.6 you are asked to demonstrate these properties of the reaction curves.
[8] Note that with $p = p^*(1 + \tau)$, then $dp/d\tau = p^* + (1 + \tau)dp^*/d\tau$, so $(dp/d\tau)(1 + \tau)/p = 1 + (dp^*/d\tau)(1 + \tau)/p^*$. Therefore, if $(dp/d\tau)(1 + \tau)/p < 1$ then $dp^*/d\tau < 0$.

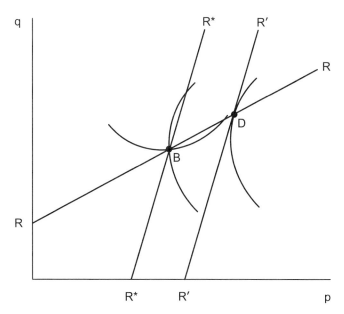

Figure 7.7

terms of trade gain. Thus, whether there is a single foreign firm or a duopoly in the import market, the key condition to ensure a terms of trade gain is that the elasticity of demand is increasing in price or decreasing in quantity. This condition holds for any demand curve that is "less convex" than a constant-elasticity demand curve.

To demonstrate the effect of the tariff on p^*, write the import price *net* of the tariff as $p^* = p/(1 + \tau)$. From (7.28a) this equals

$$p^*\left(1 - \frac{1}{\eta^*}\right) = C^{*\prime}. \qquad (7.29)$$

Totally differentiate this, holding marginal cost constant, to obtain

$$\frac{dp^*}{d\tau}\left(1 - \frac{1}{\eta^*}\right) + p^*\left(\frac{\eta^{*\prime}}{\eta^{*2}}\right)\frac{d(p/q)}{d\tau} = 0 \Rightarrow$$

$$\frac{dp^*}{d\tau} = -\left[\frac{p^*\eta^{*\prime}}{\eta^*(\eta^* - 1)}\right]\frac{d(p/q)}{d\tau}. \qquad (7.30)$$

Since we have assumed that $\eta^{*\prime} > 0$, we see that $dp^*/d\tau < 0$, provided that $d(p/q)/d\tau > 0$, that is, provided that the tariff leads to a higher increase in the price of the importable than the domestic good. But this condition is easily confirmed from Figure 7.7. With a rightward shift of the foreign reaction curve, and a dampened response of the domestic price q, the new equilibrium given by point D will lie *below* a ray from the origin going through the initial equilibrium given by point B. In other words, the relative price of the importable (p/q) must rise, and it follows from (7.30) that the net-of-tariff foreign price falls, which is a terms of trade gain for the importer.

To calculate the change in social welfare under Bertrand duopoly, we rewrite the social welfare function as $W[p, q, L + \tau p^*x + qy - C(y)]$, including both the import price $p = p^*(1 + \tau)$ and domestic price q. Totally differentiating this, and using steps similar to those in (7.3), we find that the welfare change due to the change in the ad valorem tariff is

$$\frac{dW}{d\tau} = \tau p^* \frac{dx}{d\tau} - x\frac{dp^*}{d\tau} + [q - C'(y)]\frac{dy}{d\tau}. \qquad (7.31)$$

The first term on the right-hand side of (7.31) vanishes for small tariffs, and the second term is positive when $\eta^{*\prime}(p/q) > 0$ and $\eta'(q/p) > 0$, so there is a terms of trade gain. The third term in (7.31) depends on the change in equilibrium output from point B to point D, and is of ambiguous sign in general: the increase in prices from point B to point D reduces demand, while the fall in (p/q) shifts demand towards the domestic good, so the effect on domestic output depends on the relative strength of these effects. It turns out that if the increase in domestic price is not too large, then an increase is domestic output occurs. The condition to ensure this is that the elasticity of the home reaction curve does not exceed

$$\frac{dq}{dp}\frac{p}{q} = r_p(p)\frac{p}{q} < \left(\frac{\eta - 1}{\eta}\right).^9 \text{ In that case, domestic output increases due to}$$
the tariff, which generates a welfare gain additional to the terms of trade gain.

The finding that domestic output may rise due to the tariff depends on our maintained assumption that total expenditure I on the imported and domestic products is *constant*. This would apply, for example, with a Cobb-Douglas utility function between an aggregate of the products (d, d^*) and all other goods in the economy, but would not be true otherwise. Generally, total expenditure on the imported and domestic products can *rise or fall* due to the tariff, and the latter case could lead to a fall in domestic output and a welfare loss.[10] So the "profit shifting" motive for

---

[9] See problem 7.7.

[10] The change in domestic output due to tariffs is investigated in a monopolistic competition model by Helpman (1990), using a utility function that allows expenditure on the differentiated good to change. He confirms that output of the domestic good can rise or fall due to the tariff. The latter possibility was first suggested by Markusen (1990), who referred to the

import protection is not very robust, as we also found under Cournot competition. Instead, the terms of trade motive for tariffs becomes the best indicator of gain or loss for the importing country. Under our assumptions that the elasticity of demand is *increasing* in price, there is a terms of trade gain for the importer, and the optimal tariff is positive for that reason. Conversely, with constant elasticities of demand, the optimal tariff is zero. Finally, in the somewhat unusual case where the elasticity of demand is *decreasing* in price, an import subsidy is optimal.

Tariffs on Japanese Trucks and Motorcycles

We have found that with imperfect competition, a terms of trade argument for a tariff is likely but not guaranteed. The "strategic" response of foreign firms in adjusting their price p^* then becomes an interesting empirical question. Feenstra (1989) provides some empirical evidence on this for two U.S. tariffs initially applied during the early 1980s: a 25% tariff on imports of compact trucks, coming from Japan; and a temporary, declining tariff beginning at 45% on imports of heavyweight motorcycles from Japan. The history of how these tariffs came to be applied is itself an important lesson in trade policy.

In 1979, Paul Volcker was appointed as chairman of the Board of Governors of the Federal Reserve Bank in the United States. Inflation exceeded 10% and showed signs of getting worse, so Volcker was committed to bring this rate down. A period of tight monetary policy followed, which led to very high interest rates, a strong dollar, and a deep recession beginning in January 1980. There may well have been long-term gains resulting from this policy, since following the recovery in late 1982, from the recession the United States began nearly two decades of expansion, interrupted only by a mild recession in 1990–91. But at the same time, one short-term cost was higher unemployment, and one of the sectors hardest hit was automobiles.

Accordingly, in June 1980 the United Automobile Workers applied to the ITC for protection under Section 201 of U.S. trade laws. A similar petition was received in August 1980 from Ford Motor Company. As described at the beginning of the chapter, Section 201 protection can be given when increased imports are a "substantial cause of serious injury to the domestic industry," where "substantial cause" must be "not less than any other

---

phenomena as a "de-rationalizing tariff." This might hold, for example, if the imported goods are intermediate inputs, and the tariff leads to reduced sales of the industry using the inputs. This was found to hold in a simulation model of the Mexican automobile industry by Lopez de Silanes, Markusen, and Rutherford (1994).

cause." In fact, the ITC determined that the U.S. recession was a more important cause of injury in autos than were increased imports. Accordingly, it *did not* recommend that the auto industry receive protection.

With this negative determination, several congressmen from midwestern states pursued import limits by other means. For cars imported for Japan, this protection took the form of a "voluntary" restraint on the quantity of imports, as described in the next chapter. For trucks imported from Japan, however, another form of protection was available. During the 1970s, Japan had exported an increasing number of compact trucks to the United States, most as cab/chassis with some final assembly needed. These were classified as "parts of trucks," which carried a tariff rate of 4%, whereas "complete or unfinished trucks" carried a tariff rate of 25%. That unusually high tariff was a result of the "Chicken War" between the United States and West Germany in 1962. At that time, Germany joined the European Economic Community (EEC), and was required to adjust its external tariffs to match those of the other EEC countries. This resulted in an increase in its tariff on poultry, which was imported from the United States. In retaliation, the United States increased its tariffs on "complete or unfinished trucks" and other products, so the 25% tariff on trucks became a permanent item of the U.S. tariff code. With prodding from the Congress, in 1980 the U.S. Customs Service announced that effective August 21 imported lightweight cab/chassis would be reclassified as complete trucks. This raised the tariff rates on nearly all Japanese trucks from 4% to 25%, a rate that remains in effect today.[11]

A second increase in tariffs occurred during the 1980s on heavyweight motorcycles (i.e., over 700 cc displacement), produced by Harley-Davidson. That company also applied to the ITC for Section 201 protection in 1983. Harley-Davidson was affected not so much by the U.S. recession, as by a long period of lagging productivity combined with intense competition from Japanese producers. Two of these (Honda and Kawasaki) had plants in the United States and also imported, whereas two others (Suzuki and Yamaha) produced and exported from Japan. In the early 1980s, these firms were engaged in global price war that spilled over into the U.S. market. As a result, inventories of imported heavyweight cycles rose dramatically in the United States: the ITC estimated that inventories as of September 1982 exceeded actual U.S. consumption during January–September of that year (USITC 1983, 13).

From our description of Section 201 at the beginning of the chapter, recall that protection can be recommended if increased imports are a "substantial cause of serious injury, *or threat thereof*, to the domestic industry."

---

[11] Japanese producers sued in U.S. court to have the reclassification reversed, but lost that case.

The very high level of inventories held by Japanese producers was judged by the ITC to be a threat to the domestic industry, and protection was indeed granted. This protection took the form of a five-year declining tariff schedule: 45% effective April 16, 1983, and then declining annually to 35%, 20%, 15% and 10%, and scheduled to end in April 1988.[12] In fact, Harley-Davidson petitioned the ITC to end the tariff early, after the 15% rate expired in 1987, by which time it had cut costs and introduced new and very popular products, so profitability had been restored.

U.S. imports of compact trucks and heavyweight cycles from Japan provide ideal industry cases to study the pass-though of the tariffs to U.S. prices. We are especially interested in whether Japanese producers absorbed part of the tariff, which would be a terms of trade gain for the United States, or whether they fully passed it through to U.S. prices. There are few studies of the pass-through of tariffs, but many studies of the pass-through of exchange rates, that is, the response of import prices to change in the value of the exporter's currency. Most studies at either the aggregate or disaggregate level suggest that the pass-through of exchange rates is *less than* complete, and averages about 0.6 (Goldberg and Knetter 1997, 1250), though this depends on the industry being studied.[13] We will argue that the pass-through of tariffs and exchange rates ought to be "symmetric" in a given industry, and will test this hypothesis for trucks and motorcycles. In addition, we will include U.S. imports of Japanese cars before the "voluntary" export restraint, though for that product we will only estimate the pass-through of the exchange rate.

Estimating the Terms of Trade Effect

To obtained an estimating equation, let us begin with the first-order condition of a typical foreign exporter, in (7.28a), where we treat foreign marginal costs $C^{*\prime}$ as constant, and rewrite this as c^*, in the foreign currency.

---

[12] Actually, the protection took the form of a "tariff-rate quota," which means that the declining tariffs rates were applied to imports of heavyweight motorcycles from each source country when imports *exceeded* a quota limit for the exporting country. The United States was also importing heavyweight cycles from BMW in Germany, but that country was granted a quota large enough that none of the imports were subject to the tariff. In contrast, Japan was allocated a quota (ranging from 6,000 to 10,000 units per year) that was less than its imports, so that declining tariffs applied to all imports in excess of this amount.

[13] The disaggregate results of Knetter (1989, 1993) show that exchange rate pass-through varies quite substantially across products and source countries, with U.S. exporters absorbing the *least* of any exchange rate change. In recent work, Campa and Goldberg (2002) investigate the pass-through of exchange rates in broad import sectors of the OECD countries, and find average long-run elasticities ranging from 0.61 to 0.89 across sectors.

We need to convert this to the domestic currency using an expected exchange rate e, so we rewrite (7.28a) as

$$p\left(1 - \frac{1}{\eta^*}\right) = (1 + \tau)ec^*. \tag{7.32}$$

Using the assumption that the income elasticity of demand is unity, we express the elasticity of import demand, $\eta^*(p/q)$, as a function of the import/domestic price ratio. More generally, $\eta^*(p, q, I)$ will depend on consumer income, too, but is homogeneous of degree zero in (p, q, I).[14] So treating the domestic price, income, tariff rate, exchange rate, and foreign marginal cost as parameters, (7.32) is one equation in one unknown—the import price p. We can therefore solve for the import prices as a function of the parameters:

$$p = \phi[(1 + \tau)ec^*, q, I]. \tag{7.33}$$

With $\eta^*(p, q, I)$ homogeneous of degree zero in (p, q, I), it is readily verified that $\phi[(1 + \tau)ec^*, q, I]$ is homogeneous of degree one in its arguments. This is our first testable hypothesis, which checks the overall specification of the pricing equation. Second, notice that we have written the tariff, exchange rate, and marginal costs as multiplied together in the arguments of $\phi[(1 + \tau)ec^*, q, I]$, because that is how they appear in the first-order condition (7.32). This is another testable hypothesis. To implement both these tests, let us specify (7.33) as a log-linear function of its arguments, which are indexed by time t:

$$\ln p_t = \alpha_t + \sum_{i=0}^{L} \beta_i \ln(c_t^* s_{t-i}) + \beta \ln(1 + \tau_t)$$

$$+ \sum_{j=1}^{M} \gamma_j \ln q_{jt} + \delta \ln I_t + \varepsilon_t. \tag{7.34}$$

The first term on the right-hand side of (7.34), α_t, is a simple quadratic function of time, which will allow the import price to change in a smooth fashion for reasons not specified elsewhere in the equation. To obtain the second term, we specify that the expected exchange rate e_t is a weighted average of lagged spot rates, $s_{t-i}, i = 0, 1, \ldots, L$ (in dollars/yen). This allows us to write $\ln(c_t^* s_{t-i})$ as having the coefficients $\beta_i, i = 0, 1, \ldots, L$, the *sum* of which will indicate the *total* pass-through of the exchange rate to import prices. Next, we write the ad valorem tariff $\ln(1 + \tau_t)$ as having the coefficient β, which is the pass-through of the tariff. The hypothesis of

---

[14] See problem 7.5.

symmetric pass-through of the tariff and exchange rate is therefore tested as

$$\sum_{i=0}^{L} \beta_i = \beta. \tag{7.35a}$$

The next terms appearing on the right-hand side of (7.34) are the price of domestic or rival imported products, $j = 1, \ldots, M$. For Japanese imports, this would include the average price of U.S. products, as well as German imported cars or motorcycles. Finally, total consumer expenditure on the broad category of transportation equipment is included as a measure of "income." Notice that if the income elasticity of demand is unity, then the foreign elasticity $n^*(p/q)$ does not depend on I, and neither will the optimal price p_t in (7.34), so $\delta = 0$. In any case, the hypothesis that the whole equation is homogeneous of degree one can be tested by

$$\sum_{i=0}^{L} \beta_i + \sum_{j=1}^{M} \gamma_j + \delta = 1. \tag{7.35b}$$

The results of estimating (7.34) using quarterly data for U.S. imports are shown in Table 7.2. The first row indicates the sample period of quarterly data used for each product. There are two distinct samples used for heavyweight motorcycles. The first sample consists of *interview* data reported by the ITC (USITC 1983, Table 8; 1983–84). The advantage of this data is that it gives the unit-value of imports for *consumption*, inclusive of duty, for the major Japanese importers (Honda, Suzuki, and Yamaha). However, the disadvantage is that the data end in 1984:4 and include a small number of German heavyweight motorcycles within the reported unit-value. A second source was collected at the border by the U.S. Dept of Commerce giving the unit-value of imports *shipments*, distinguishing Japanese and German heavyweight cycles up to 1987:1.[15] We experiment with both data sources and also the pooled sample.

In the first regression of Table 7.2 for Japanese imported cars, the coefficients on the exchange rate terms sum to 0.71, which is the estimate of the pass-through elasticity. For Japanese imported trucks, the sum of coefficients on the exchange rates is 0.63, while the coefficient on the tariff is 0.57. The hypothesis (7.35a) that these are equal is easily accepted, as is hypothesis (7.35b) that the pricing equation is homogeneous of degree one. When both of these restrictions are imposed, the pass-through elasticity (for the exchange rate or the tariff) becomes 0.58. Thus, there is

---

[15] Import shipments include motorcycles going into inventory. These data were adjusted to include the tariff.

TABLE 7.2
Regressions for Japanese Imported Products with Import Price as Dependent Variable

	Cars	Trucks	Cycles (consumption)	Cycles (shipments)	Cycles (pooled)
Period	74.1–81.1	77.1–87.1	78.1–84.4	78.1–87.1	78.1–87.1
$c_t^* s_t$	0.44*	0.28*	0.29	0.80	0.45*
	(0.11)	(0.06)	(0.26)	(0.72)	(0.21)
$c_t^* s_{t-1}$	0.32*	0.14*	0.17*	−0.042	0.10
	(0.04)	(0.03)	(0.10)	(0.28)	(0.09)
$c_t^* s_{t-2}$	0.17*	0.06	0.12	−0.34	−0.031
	(0.08)	(0.050)	(0.15)	(0.57)	(0.16)
$c_t^* s_{t-3}$	−0.01	0.05	0.12	−0.083	0.042
	(0.05)	(0.03)	(0.08)	(0.23)	(0.087)
$c_t^* s_{t-4}$	−0.21*	0.10	0.19	0.72	0.32
	(0.10)	(0.08)	(0.23)	(0.82)	(0.22)
Exchange rate[a]	0.71*	0.63*	0.89*	1.05*	0.89*
	(0.10)	(0.08)	(0.36)	(0.56)	(0.22)
Tariff	–	0.57*	0.95*	1.39*	1.13*
	–	(0.14)	(0.22)	(0.30)	(0.16)
U.S. price	1.00	0.03	0.68	1.14	0.57
	(0.93)	(0.40)	(0.60)	(2.17)	(0.59)
German price	0.08	–	0.06	0.12	0.06
	(0.09)	–	(0.11)	(0.23)	(0.11)
Income	−0.03	−0.03	−0.23	−0.23	0.02
	(0.12)	(0.06)	(1.69)	(0.65)	(0.01)
N, K[b]	29, 9	41, 9	28, 13	37, 13	65, 13
Adjusted R^2	0.988	0.989	0.907	0.769	0.833
Durbin-Watson	2.43	1.75	2.73	1.69	–

Note: Standard errors are in parentheses.
* Significant at the 95% level with conventional *t*-test.
[a] Sum of coefficients for $\ln(c_t^* s_{t-i})$, $i = 0, 1, \ldots 4$, where c_t^* is an aggregate of foreign factor prices, and s_{t-i} is the spot exchange rate (\$/yen).
[b] N is the number of observation, and K the number of independent variables. Coefficients for time trends and quarterly dummies are not reported.

strong evidence that the increase in the truck tariff was only partially reflected in U.S. prices: of the 21% increase, about $0.58 \cdot 21 = 12\%$ was passed through to U.S. prices, whereas the other 9% was absorbed by Japanese producers, leading to a terms of trade gain for the United States.

For Japanese imports of heavyweight motorcycles, however, the story is quite different. Regardless of which sample is used (consumption, shipments, or pooled), we find that the pass-throughs of the exchange rate and the tariff are both insignificantly different from *unity*! So while the hypothesis (7.35a) of "symmetric" pass-through is still confirmed, as is (7.35b), it is no longer the case that the United States experienced a terms of trade gain in this product. Rather, the *full amount* of the tariff in each year was passed through to U.S. prices.

What explains the differing results for compact trucks and heavyweight motorcycles? In the case of trucks, we note that prior to the increase of the tariff in August 1980, nearly all compact trucks sold in the United States were produced by Japanese firms, some of which were marketed through American auto companies. But after the tariff was imposed, U.S. producers introduced their own compact truck models, with characteristics very similar to the Japanese imports (see Feenstra 1988b). The Japanese producers (Isuzu and Mitsubishi) that had formerly been selling to American firms began to market compact trucks independently. In this environment of relatively intense competition, we can expect that Japanese firms would be reluctant to pass through the full amount of the tariff and risk losing more market share in the United States.

In heavyweight motorcycles, by contrast, recall that there was already a global price war, so that prices were likely close to marginal cost. This leaves little room for Japanese producers to absorb part of the tariff. This explanation is reinforced by the fact that the tariff was temporary, and that U.S. inventories were high: there would be little reason to sell to the United States at a reduced price in one year, if instead sales could be made out of inventory and some exports delayed to a later year when the tariff was lower.[16] By this logic, it is not surprising that the pass-through of the tariff in motorcycles was complete.

How should we assess the efficacy of the tariff in these two products? The tariff on trucks led to a terms of trade gain, and if this exceeded the deadweight loss, then it generated a welfare gain for the United States. This is not the case for the tariff on motorcycles, however, where there is a deadweight loss but no offsetting terms of trade gain. By our conventional welfare criterion, then, the tariff on trucks looks better than the tariff on heavyweight cycles. But this criterion ignores the fact that the tariff on motorcycles was *temporary*, whereas that on trucks is still in place today. Furthermore, it is well documented (see Reid 1990) that Harley-Davidson

---

[16] It was still the case that exports from Japan of heavyweight motorcycles (over 700 cc) were positive in every year of the tariff. In addition, Japanese firms began to sell a 699 cc motorcycle in the United States, which was a way to evade the tariff. See the discussion in Irwin 2002a, 135–37.

was on the brink of bankruptcy in 1982–83 and was able to secure a bank loan only after receiving protection, so the tariff may well have contributed to its continued survival. Its near-bankrupt status was due to problems of poor management and lagging productivity, while its revival after 1983 was due to the introduction of improved products and production techniques. It cannot be argued that this broad change in company practices was *caused* by the tariff, but it appears that the temporary tariff bought it some breathing room.[17] In view of the improved products later offered by Harley-Davidson (which were emulated by its Japanese rivals), the temporary tariff may well have contributed to long-run welfare gains for consumers. In contrast, the compact trucks introduced by American firms after the tariff were quite similar to the existing Japanese models, and brought little additional welfare gain (Feenstra 1988b).

Infant Industry Protection

Our discussion of the motorcycle tariff in the United States suggests a case where protection may have allowed the domestic industry to avoid bankruptcy. Without arguing that this was definitely the case, let us use this as a possible example of "infant industry" protection. Theoretically, infant industry protection occurs when a tariff in one period leads to a increase in output, and therefore a reduction in future costs, sufficient to allow the firm to survive, whereas otherwise it would not. Such protection is a very old idea, dating back to Hamilton (1791), List (1856), and Mill (1909).[18] An essential assumption of the argument is that the firm needs to earn positive profits each period to avoid bankruptcy. That is, there must be some reason that the capital market does not allow the industry to cover current losses by borrowing against future profits. A model of infant industry protection is developed by Dasgupta and Stiglitz (1988), and more recent treatment is in Melitz 2004. A historical example from the U.S. steel rail industry is provided by Head (1994).

An infant industry is an example of *declining marginal costs*, that is, when the future marginal costs are a decreasing function of current output. We have pretty much ignored this case throughout the chapter and have treated the marginal costs as either constant or increasing in output. When marginal costs are declining, however, then there may be additional

---

[17] This is the view expressed by the chief economist at the ITC at the time: "if the case of heavyweight motorcycles is to be considered the only successful escape-clause, it is because it caused little harm and it helped Harley-Davidson get a bank loan so it could diversify" (Suomela 1993, 135, as cited by Irwin 2002a, 136–37).

[18] Cited by Baldwin (1969), who provides a number of reasons why the "infant industry" argument is *not* valid. See also the survey of Corden (1984, 91–92).

scope for "strategic" trade policies. Krugman (1984) uses a model of declining marginal costs to argue that import promotion might act as export promotion: that protecting an import industry today might turn it into an export industry tomorrow. This intriguing idea is investigated for the production of random access memory chips by Baldwin and Krugman (1988a), and further empirical work would be desirable.

Dumping

If there is a case to be made for infant industry protection, whereby an increase in the import price allows a firm to survive, then the reverse should also be true: a decrease in the import prices might lead a firm to shut down. This would be an example of "predatory dumping," in which a foreign exporter lowers its prices in anticipation of driving rivals in the domestic country out of business. A model of predatory dumping is developed by Hartigan (1996), and like the infant industry argument, it relies on a capital market imperfection that prevents the home firm from surviving a period of negative profits.

Predatory dumping is presumably rare. In contrast, allegations of dumping are a widespread phenomenon and growing ever more common. Furthermore, charges of dumping are often made against trading partners in the same industry; for example, the United States will charge European countries and Japan with dumping steel in the United States, and likewise those other countries will charge the United States with dumping steel there! This does not sound like "predatory dumping," but must have some other rationale.

In his classic list of reasons for dumping, Jacob Viner referred to "long-run" or "continuous" dumping, to "maintain full production from existing facilities without cutting prices" (1966, 23, as cited by Staiger and Wolak 1992, 266). This can occur in markets with oligopolistic competition and excess capacity. Ethier (1982b) presents a model emphasizing demand uncertainty and excess capacity, leading to dumping. But subsequent literature has focused on a simpler framework without uncertainty, where dumping is a natural occurrence under imperfect competition as oligopolists enter each other's markets. This is demonstrated in the next section, using the "reciprocal dumping" model of Brander (1981) and Brander and Krugman (1983).

Reciprocal Dumping

To model the oligopolistic competition between foreign and domestic firms, we return again to the Cournot model used earlier in the chapter, but now allow for a number of firms N in the home country and N^* abroad. The home firms sell y_i in the home market and export y_i^*, $i = 1, \ldots, N$, while the foreign firms sell x_j in the home country and x_j^* in their own local market, $j = 1, \ldots, N^*$. The equilibrium price in the home market will be denoted by $p(z)$, where $z = \sum_{i=1}^{N} y_i + \sum_{j=1}^{N^*} x_j$, and the foreign price is $p^*(z^*)$, where $z^* = \sum_{i=1}^{N} y_i^* + \sum_{j=1}^{N} x_j^*$.

Let us also assume that there are "iceberg" transportation costs involved in delivering the product from one country to the other, as in chapter 5: the amount $T > 1$ of the product must be shipped in order for one unit to arrive, so that $(T - 1)$ "melts" along the way. The home price $p(z)$ denotes the c.i.f. (cost, insurance, freight) price, while the f.o.b. (free on board) price received by the foreign exporter per unit shipped is p/T. This can be compared to p^*, which is the price received by the foreign firms in its own market. Notice that when computing prices to assess allegations of dumping, the U.S. DOC works with these f.o.b. prices; that is, it *deducts* transportation costs from import prices before assessing whether dumping has occurred. So it would conclude that dumping has occurred at home if $p/T < p^*$. Similarly, the f.o.b. price received by the home firm per unit exported is p^*/T, and it could be charged with dumping in the foreign market if $p^*/T < p$.

From this setup, it is apparent that if we had an equilibrium where the c.i.f. prices *were equal* across the countries, $p = p^*$, then "reciprocal dumping" must be occurring, that is, $p/T < p^*$ and $p^*/T < p$. This was the outcome obtained by Brander and Krugman (1983) in a symmetric model, where the home and foreign markets were equal in size and had identical marginal costs. More generally, we are interested in whether reciprocal dumping will occur even in markets that are not necessarily the same size. Let us suppose that the home and foreign firms have identical marginal costs, but that the demand curves $p(z)$ and $p^*(z^*)$ are not the same. Will we observe reciprocal dumping?

To answer this question, denote the marginal cost of producing in either country by c. The fixed costs of production are α. A firm located in country i and selling to country j will face "iceberg" transport costs, so the marginal cost of delivering one unit abroad is cT. The home firms solve the profit maximization problem

$$\max_{y_i, y_i^*} \pi = [p(z) - c]y_i + [p^*(z^*) - cT]y_i^* - \alpha \tag{7.36}$$

with the first-order conditions

$$\pi_{y_i} = p(z) + y_i p'(z) - c = 0, \tag{7.37a}$$

$$\pi_{y_i^*} = p^*(z^*) + y_i^* p^{*\prime}(z^*) - cT = 0. \tag{7.37b}$$

Impose the symmetry condition that every home firm is selling the same amount in each of the home and foreign markets, so $y_i = y$ and $y_i^* = y*$. Then the first-order conditions are written as

$$p\left(1 - \frac{(y/z)}{\eta}\right) = c, \quad p*\left(1 - \frac{(y*/z*)}{\eta*}\right) = cT, \tag{7.38}$$

where $\eta = z/p'(z)p$ and $\eta* = z*/p*'(z*)p*$ are the home and foreign demand elasticities.

In a similar manner, we can derive the first-order conditions for the foreign firms,

$$p*\left(1 - \frac{(x*/z*)}{\eta*}\right) = c, \quad p\left(1 - \frac{(x/z)}{\eta}\right) = cT, \tag{7.39}$$

where each of these firms is selling $x*$ in its own market and x in the home market.

By adding up the market shares of all firms selling in each country, we must obtain

$$N(y/z) + N*(x/z) = 1,$$
$$N(y*/z*) + N*(x*/z*) = 1. \tag{7.40}$$

Notice that we can write this simple system in matrix notation as

$$(N, N*)\begin{bmatrix} (y/z) & (y*/z*) \\ (x/z) & (x*/z*) \end{bmatrix} = (1, 1), \tag{7.40'}$$

which can be inverted to solve for the number of firms in each country:

$$(N, N*) = \frac{(1,1)}{D}\begin{bmatrix} (x*/z*) & -(y*/z*) \\ -(x/z) & (y/z) \end{bmatrix} \Rightarrow \begin{aligned} N &= \frac{1}{D}\left(\frac{x*}{z*} - \frac{x}{z}\right), \\ N* &= \frac{1}{D}\left(\frac{y}{z} - \frac{y*}{z*}\right), \end{aligned} \tag{7.41}$$

where D is the determinant of the two-by-two matrix of market shares shown in (7.40'). From the first-order conditions (7.38) and (7.39) it is clear that $(y/z) > (x/z)$ and $(x*/z*) > (y*/z*)$, so that local sales in each county exceed imports (due to the assumption of equal marginal costs but positive transport costs). This ensures that $D > 0$.

Notice that the solutions for N and $N*$ from (7.41) are not guaranteed to be positive, though this occurs if each firm sells more in its local market than in its export market, $(y/z) > (y*/z*)$ and $(x*/z*) > (x/z)$. To determine when this will be the case, let us make the simplifying assumption that the elasticity of demand is equal in the two markets, $\eta = \eta^*$. Then we can substitute the market shares from the first-order conditions (7.38) and (7.39) into (7.41) and use $\eta = \eta^*$ to obtain

$$N = \frac{\eta}{D}\left(\frac{cT}{p} - \frac{c}{p^*}\right) > 0 \text{ if and only if } p/T < p^*, \quad (7.42\text{a})$$

$$N^* = \frac{\eta}{D}\left(\frac{cT}{p^*} - \frac{c}{p}\right) > 0 \text{ if and only if } p^*/T < p. \quad (7.42\text{b})$$

Thus, we have obtained the following result.

Theorem (Weinstein 1992; Feenstra, Markusen, and Rose 1998)

When the elasticities of demand and marginal costs of production are equal across countries, and firms in both countries are selling in both markets, then reciprocal dumping necessarily occurs: $p/T < p^*$ and $p^*/T < p$.

Remarkably, reciprocal dumping is guaranteed whenever the firms are selling in both markets! Our hypothesis that the elasticities of demand are equal across countries is a simplifying assumption: Weinstein (1992) establishes the theorem without this assumption (but using the weak condition (7.17'), that the market's marginal revenue curve is steeper than the demand curve). Weinstein also discusses what happens as the number of firms in one country grows. As N^* grows, the equilibrium price p^* in the foreign market falls. For a sufficiently high number of foreign firms, the inequality $p/T < p^*$ becomes an equality, and at this point the number of domestic firms from (7.42a) is zero: import competition has eliminated the domestic industry. However, note from (7.42b) that we still have $p^*/T < p$, so that the foreign firms are dumping into the domestic market. Thus, even when the number of firm in one country has grown large enough to eliminate competition in the other, unilateral dumping still occurs.

Welfare Effect of Trade

This model of reciprocal dumping is an alternative explanation for "intraindustry" trade, which we studied in chapter 5 under a monopolistic competition model. In that case, we argued that trade would bring extra gains, due to the increased variety of products and also economies of scale. But in the Cournot model we are studying, the firms are selling a homogeneous product so that there are no gains due to product variety, but instead losses due to wasted transportation costs in "cross hauling." On the

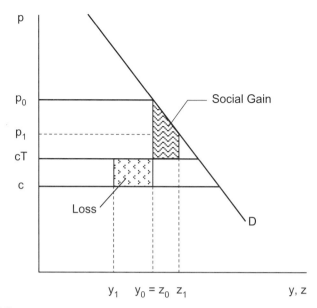

Figure 7.8

other hand, trade brings a reduction in the exercise of monopoly power, due to the competition introduced from foreign firms. So this raises the question of which effect dominates: the social loss due to wasted transportation, or the social gain due to reduced monopoly power?

Brander and Krugman (1983) argue that with a *fixed* number of firms, moving from autarky to free trade has an *ambiguous* effect on global welfare. This is illustrated in Figure 7.8. for a single home and foreign firm. Autarky occurs at the monopoly price p_0. Provided that this price is above the marginal costs for the foreign firm of exporting, cT, then with free trade the foreign firm will indeed sell to the home market.[19] Suppose that imports are $(z_1 - y_1)$, and these reduce the home price to p_1. This brings a rise in global welfare of the area shown (the top triangle of this area is consumer surplus in the importing country, and the remainder is profits of the foreign exporter), but a loss in global welfare due to added transport costs shown by the rectangle. A similar diagram would apply in the foreign country. The relative sizes of these areas are ambiguous, so we do not know whether trade raises or lowers global welfare.

---

[19] As noted by Brander and Krugman (1983), the condition to observe trade with a single firm in each country is that the monopoly price, $p_0 = c\eta/(\eta - 1)$, exceeds marginal cost of cT. This is written as $\eta/(\eta - 1) > T$, or alternatively, $\eta < T/(T - 1)$. So transport costs cannot be too high relative to the elasticity.

However, with free entry of firms in both countries, Brander and Krugman argue that global welfare necessarily improves due to free trade. The welfare function with multiple firms is $W(p, L + tm + N\pi)$, where π is the profits of each home firm, but with profits equal to zero this becomes $W(p, L + tm)$. Furthermore, comparing autarky and free trade, we have zero tariff revenue in each case, so welfare is just $W(p, L)$. Thus, welfare will rise going from autarky to free trade if and only if the import price falls. Brander and Krugman argue that this is indeed the case: with import competition, prices unambiguously fall, so welfare in both countries improves. The fall in prices is also reflected in a fall in average costs (since price equals average costs from zero profits), which implies the output of each firm increases going from autarky to free trade. So similar to the monopolistic competition model of chapter 5, we have the result that trade brings gains due to the exercise of economies of scale. But unlike the monopolistic competition model, these gains come despite the fact that trade is intrinsically wasteful due to the homogeneous product and transportation costs.

Impact of Antidumping Duties

Suppose that instead of comparing welfare under free trade and autarky, we instead consider the effect of an antidumping duty imposed by one country. When the number of firms is fixed at, say, one in each country, this corresponds to the case of Cournot duopoly analyzed earlier in the chapter. We found there that a small duty was likely to improve the terms of trade for the importing country, and may also contribute to an efficiency gain through increasing the output of the home firm. For both reasons, a small tariff was welfare improving for the importer. Should we think of antidumping duties in the same way?

The answer is no. Rather than leading to an improvement in the terms of trade, the application of antidumping law can often lead to a *worsening* of the terms of trade and a welfare loss for the importing country. To understand this, we need to review the administration of these laws in the United States. Antidumping actions go through several distinct phases (Staiger and Wolak 1994): an initial investigation by the DOC, which determines whether or not the imported product is being sold at "less than fair value"; followed by an initial investigation by the ITC to determine whether or not the domestic industry is "materially injured"; followed by a final determination of both agencies; followed by the application of duties if both findings are affirmative and the case is not withdrawn; and then also an annual administrative review in cases where duties are imposed (Blonigen and Haynes 2002). Let us consider how each of these stages affects prices.

Initial Investigation

In the first stage of an investigation, which we call period 1, the DOC compares the prices of imported products with their prices (or costs) abroad. This calculation involves comparing the f.o.b. price received by the foreign exporter, which we denote by p_1/T, with their own home price of p^*. If $p_1/T < p^*$, then there is pricing at "less than fair value." In nearly 95% of cases brought before the DOC, it concludes that this pricing occurs and recommends duties in period 2 of $(1 + \tau_2) = p^*/(p_1/T) > 1$.

Notice that the duty applied in period 2 *depends* on the price charged by the exporter in period 1. In this sense, we must treat the antidumping duty as *endogenous*, and the exporter will have an incentive to raise its period 1 price so as to lower the period 2 duty.[20] Furthermore, this increase in price occurs even *before* the duty has been imposed, so that the importing country does not collect any tariff revenues. This increase in the import price amounts to a pure terms of trade loss for the importer. Because there is no tariff revenue collected, and still allowing for free entry of home firms, the welfare criterion is modified from $W(p, L + tm)$ to $W(p, L)$. Thus, any increase in the import price leads to a welfare loss.

There is evidence that this investigation stage of dumping actions does indeed lead to an impact on imports, though this is often measured by the effect on quantities rather than prices. Using a sample of all antidumping cases in the United States from 1980 to 1985, Staiger and Wolak (1992) find that the initiation of an investigation has a substantial impact on imports, reducing them by about one-half as much as would have occurred under duties. The implication is that import prices must increase, leading to a loss for the importer.

Withdrawal of Cases

While the DOC finds evidence of "pricing at less than fair value" in most cases, the ITC rules in favor of "material injury" in only about one-half of the cases it considers. Thus, of some 400 cases in the United States during 1980–88, about 150 were rejected by the ITC and another 150 had duties levied. As shown in Table 7.1, the remaining 100 cases, or one-quarter of the total, were *withdrawn* prior to a ruling by the ITC. In these cases the U.S. firms can negotiate with the foreign firm on the level of prices and market shares (Prusa 1991, 1992). Prusa finds that the withdrawal and settlement of cases has about the same impact on reducing import quantity as do actual duties, which is also found by Staiger and Wolak

---

[20] See problems 7.8 and 7.9 to demonstrate this in a model with Bertrand competition.

(1992).[21] Again, the implication is that import prices rise, with a direct welfare loss for the importing country.

Continuing Investigations

Consider now the case where an antidumping duty has been imposed, and denote the period 2 import price (inclusive of duty) by p_2. Suppose that there is an administrative review to recalculate the amount of duty imposed in period 3. In calculating dumping margins during the administrative review, the DOC *removes* the tariff from the import price p_2, and also removes any transport costs, obtaining $p_2/[T(1 + \tau_2)]$ as the f.o.b. price for the foreign exporter. This is compared to the exporter's home price of p^* to determine whether the foreign firm is continuing in its practice of "pricing at less than fair value." Whenever $p_2/[T(1 + \tau_2)] < p^*$, duties of $(1 + \tau_3) = p^*/[p_2/T(1 + \tau_2)] > 1$ are imposed in period 3.

Notice that these duties can be rewritten as $(1 + \tau_3) = (1 + \tau_2)[p^*/(p_2/T)]$, so there is a built-in "continuation" of the antidumping duties: even if the foreign firm chooses $p^* = p_2/T$, so there would have been no initial evidence of dumping, it will *still* be faced with a tariff of $(1 + \tau_3) = (1 + \tau_2)$ in period 3. In other words, to avoid a charge of continued dumping during the administrative review, the foreign firm would not only need to increase its period 2 price above what was charged in period 1, it would need to further increase the period 2 price by the *full amount* of the period 2 duty. In the above notation, a charge of dumping is avoided in period 2 if and only if

$$p_2/[T(1+\tau_2)] \ge p^* \iff p_2 \ge p^* T(1+\tau_2) > p_1(1+\tau_2), \quad (7.43)$$

where the last inequality is obtained because dumping occurred in period 1, $p_1/T < p^*$.

Using the last inequalities in (7.43), we see that to avoid continuing antidumping duties the import price must rise between periods by the amount $p_2/p_1 > (1 + \tau_2)$, so there is *more than complete pass-through* of the period 2 duty. This hypothesis receives strong support from Blonigen and Haynes (2002). They estimate that the pass-through of the initial antidumping duties can be as high as 160% for the cases that are subject to an administrative review. This occurs because, as explained above, the DOC removes existing tariffs from import prices when computing the dumping margin. So in order to avoid duties after an administrative review, the tariff-inclusive price must rise by *more than* the amount of duties.

---

[21] There are some cases that are withdrawn for procedural reasons and are *not* settled between the home and foreign firms. Taylor (2003) argues that these have little or no impact on import quantity or price.

From a welfare point of view, this result very likely violates the criterion for welfare improvement. With the pass-through of duties exceeding unity, then $dp^*/dt > 0$, so there is a terms of trade loss. Then the only way that welfare can rise is if there is a large increase in domestic output with the associated efficiency gain (i.e., if the final term in (7.3) is positive). However, this source of gain vanishes if there is free entry into the domestic industry, so that profits are zero. In that case, the criterion for welfare gain is (7.26) rather than (7.3), and welfare can rise only if $dp/dt < m/d(p)$, meaning that the pass-through of the duty is less than the import share. This is clearly violated when the pass-through is greater than unity. Thus, in all three stages we have considered—initial investigation, withdrawal and settlement of cases, and continuing investigations—the presumption is that antidumping duties will lead to a welfare loss for the importer. This occurs because the duties being imposed are treated by the exporter as endogenous, and create an incentive to raise prices so as to avoid the duties.

Conclusions

Since this chapter has covered a large number of different models, a summary is appropriate. Consider tariffs that are *exogenously* imposed, such as under the escape clause provision of the GATT/WTO. In general, this will have three welfare effects on the importing country: (*a*) a deadweight loss; (*b*) a terms of trade effect; (*c*) a reduction in the monopoly distortion if the output of home firms increases (without leading to inefficient entry). The deadweight loss always harms the importer, but is of the second order of smalls for a small tariff. The change in the output of home firms, sometimes referred to as a "profit shifting" effect, is of ambiguous sign and cannot be relied upon to generate gains for the importer. Accordingly, the best indicator of the welfare impact of small tariffs is the terms of trade effect.

It is sometimes argued that countries must be very large in their sales or purchases of a product on world markets for their tariff to have an impact on the terms of trade. Even the United States, it is argued, should be treated as "small" in nearly all markets.[22] I disagree with this assessment. Under imperfect competition, it is quite plausible that a foreign exporter will absorb part of the tariff so the import price does not rise by its full amount; our detailed analysis of the Cournot and Bertrand cases has identified the exact conditions under which this outcome occurs. This depends on exporters treating their foreign markets as segmented (i.e., charging different prices to each), and holds regardless of the size of the importing country. The abundant

[22] See Irwin 2002a, 63.

evidence on partial pass-through of exchange rates (surveyed in Goldberg and Knetter 1997) suggests that the same is true for tariffs, though the exact magnitude of pass-through will depend on the industry being considered. For the comparison of the U.S. tariffs on truck and motorcycles we found quite different pass-through behavior, with the tariff on trucks generating a terms of trade gain but not the tariff on motorcycles.

Even if we accept that in many industries there will be a terms of trade and welfare gain due to a small tariff, this hardly justifies their use: the terms of trade gain comes *entirely* at the expense of foreign exporters, so this is a "beggar thy neighbor" policy. The use of tariffs can therefore invite retaliation from trading partners. A recent example occurred in the steel industry in the United States, which received Section 201 protection in March 2002.[23] Declining tariffs ranging from 8% to 30% were applied for three years to a range of steel products and various importers.[24] Shortly after these tariffs were imposed, the European Union, Japan, and Korea announced plans to file protests with the WTO and retaliate with tariffs of their own applied against U.S. products. Such retaliation means that the use of tariffs becomes a negative-sum game; that is, they can end up harming both trading partners.

What can prevent a country from attempting to move the terms of trade in its favor? One view of the GATT is that it was designed with exactly this goal in mind. Bagwell and Staiger (1999, 2002) argue that the provisions of GATT such as "reciprocity" (i.e., tariff reductions should be reciprocal across countries) are effective in preventing countries from using tariffs to improve their terms of trade. We will discuss this further in chapter 9. By a similar logic, I think that the escape clause provision of the GATT should be viewed as a way to promote free trade while allowing for exceptions in specific circumstances. The linkage was made explicit in the recent Section 201 protection to the steel industry in the United States, with which the Bush administration hoped to secure additional votes for "fast track" authority.[25] So Article XIX of the GATT and Section 201 of

[23] This was the first instance of a Section 201 action that was initiated by the president (and followed from a campaign promise made by George W. Bush while campaigning in steel-producing states).

[24] Some of the tariffs took the form of "tariff-rate quotas," which means that the tariffs are applied only for imports from each source country *in excess* of some amount. These quotas can be varied preferentially across source countries without violated the MFN principle of the GATT. Canada, Mexico, Israel, and Jordan are entirely exempt from the tariffs because of their free-trade agreements with the United States.

[25] "Fast track" authority refers to the ability of the executive branch to present to the U.S. Congress a proposal for an expansion of free trade, for an "up or down" vote without allowing amendments. This authority is used, for example, when negotiating free-trade areas, which the Bush administration intends to pursue in the Americas. Fast-track authority was renewed by the U.S. House of Representatives in July 2002 by a narrow vote.

U.S. trade law need to be assessed in a broader political-economy context of securing industry support for free trade. Given that these provisions are used rarely, and only temporarily, they can be viewed as rather effective.

The same is not true of the antidumping provisions of GATT. As we have argued, the GATT definition of dumping will apply in many markets subject to imperfect competition, and there has been an increasingly widespread use of the dumping provisions. The antidumping duties that are imposed must be treated as *endogenous*: they depend on the prices chosen by the exporter prior to, and during, the dumping action. This creates an incentive for exporters to raise their prices before dumping duties are imposed, and to raise them even further before an administrative review of the dumping case. These actions correspond to a terms of trade loss for the importer, as indicated by the empirical evidence of Blonigen and Haynes (2002). This can also be reflected in an increase in the price of import-competing products, of course, so the antidumping duties promote more collusive behavior. Gallaway, Blonigen, and Flynn (1999) estimate the combined welfare cost of antidumping and countervailing duty legislation in the United States to be some \$4 billion in 1993. In the next chapter, we will also find that import quotas can lead to more collusive behavior among firms, so that along with antidumping legislation, these policies must be judged as very costly.

Problems

7.1   Derive the optimal demands for the consumer with the quasi-linear utility function given by $c_0^h + U^h(c^h)$, where c_0^h is the consumption of a numeraire good and c^h is the consumption vector of all other goods, with U^h increasing and strictly concave. The consumer maximizes utility subject to the budget constraint $c_0^h + p'c^h \le I^h$.

7.2   Derive the optimal specific tariff from (7.12) in the case where there is a single foreign firm, the demand curve $d(p)$ is linear, and marginal costs are constant, $C''(y) = 0$.

7.3   Derive conditions under which the Cournot reaction curves in Figure 7.4 are both downward sloping.

7.4   By totally differentiating the equilibrium condition (7.22), show that

(a) $dy/dt > 0$ provided that $p'(x + y) + yp''(x + y) < 0$;
(b) The total change in home profits π due to the tariff is positive.

7.5   In this problem we derive the properties of the elasticities used with Bertrand competition.

(a) First review problem 1.2 of chapter 1 and show that if a function $y = f(v)$ is homogeneous of degree α, meaning that for all $\lambda > 0$, $f(\lambda v) = \lambda^\alpha f(v)$, then its first derivative is homogeneous of degree $\alpha - 1$.

(b) Thus, if demand $d(p, q, I)$ is homogeneous of degree zero in (p, q, I), then $d_q(p, q, I)$ is homogeneous of degree minus one. Use this to show that $\eta(p, q, I) \equiv - qd_q(p, q, I) / d(p, q, I)$ is homogeneous of degree zero in (p, q, I).

(c) Now assume that the income elasticity is unity, so that demand is written as $d(p, q, I) = \phi(p, q)I$. Show that the elasticity η does not depend on I. Therefore, show that the elasticity η can be written as a function of q/p.

7.6   Using the results from problem 7.5, assume that $\eta^{*\prime}(p/q) > 0$ and $\eta'(q/p) > 0$.

(a) Then by differentiating the first-order conditions (7.28), show that the reaction curves $p = r^*(q, \tau)$ and $q = r(p)$ both slope upwards, as shown in Figure 7.6, with elasticities less than unity.

(b) Also compute the elasticity of the foreign reaction curve $p = r^*(q, \tau)$ with respect to τ.

(c) Use the results in parts (a) and (b) to solve for the total change in q and p due to the tariff.

7.7   Output of the home firm is $y = d(q, p, I)$.

(a) Use the fact that $d(q, p, I)$ is homogeneous of degree zero in (q, p, I) to show that $d_q q + d_p p + d_I I = 0$. Then use the assumption that the income elasticity of demand is unity to show that $d_p p / d = (\eta - 1)$, where $\eta \equiv -d_q q / d$.

(b) Using part (a), compute the total change in home output $y = d(q, p, I)$ as p increases along the home reaction curve. Show that output increases if $0 < q\eta'/p\eta < (\eta - 1)^2$.

7.8   Under Bertrand competition, show that foreign profits fall due to the tariff when $\eta^{*\prime}(p/q) > 0$ and $\eta'(q/p) > 0$.

7.9   Consider the problem of an exporting firm facing the threat of an antidumping duty. Given the period 1 import price chosen by the exporting firm, the duty imposed in period 2 equals $(1 + \tau_2) = p^*/p_1$ whenever $p_1 < p^*$. This tariff is imposed with probability θ, and conversely, with probability $(1 - \theta)$ there will be no duty. Denote the value of period 2 profits when the duty is imposed by $\pi_2^*(\tau_2)$, where from problem 7.8 we have that $\pi_2^{*\prime}(\tau_2) < 0$. Let $\pi_2^*(0)$ denote the maximized value of period 2 profits for the foreign firm in the case of zero duty. Then the period 1 problem can be stated as

$$\max_{p_1} \pi^*(p_1, q_1) + \delta[\theta\pi_2^*(\tau_2) + (1-\theta)\pi_2^*(0)]$$

$$\text{s.t. } (1+\tau_2) = p^*/p_1.$$

(7.44)

We suppose that the home firm chooses q_1, under Bertrand competition. Derive the first-order conditions for the home and foreign firms, and show that the threatened duty leads to an *increase* in the foreign price p_1.

Empirical Exercises

In these exercises, you are asked to reproduce some of the empirical results from Feenstra 1989. To complete the exercises, the files "cars.csv, trucks.csv, cycon.csv, cyship.csv, cypool.csv" should be stored in the directory c:\Empirical_Exercise\Chapter_7\. Each of these can be used in STATA programs "cars.do, trucks.do, cycon.do, cyship.do, cypool.do" to create a dataset with the variables described in "Documentation_Chp7.doc." Use these "do" programs to complete the following exercises:

7.1   Replicate Table 7.2, that is, run the specifications of (7.34) without imposing the tests of symmetry or homogeneity. Duplicate all of the coefficients that are reported in this table, except the Durbin-Watson statistics.

7.2   Then replicate Feenstra's Table 7.2 by imposing the tests of homogeneity and symmetry, shown in (7.35a) and (7.35b). Instead of conducting the Wald test, as done in Feenstra 1989, instead conduct the analogous *F*-test. Do you accept or reject the hypotheses of symmetry and homogeneity?

Chapter 8

Import Quotas and Export Subsidies

IN ADDITION TO import tariffs, quotas and subsidies are widely used forms of trade policy. Quotas and subsidies can in principle be applied to either imports or exports, but we will focus here on *import* quotas and *export* subsidies. How do these policy instruments differ from tariffs, and does this difference depend on the type of competition in the market? These are the questions we shall investigate in this chapter.

We begin with the result of Bhagwati (1965) on the "equivalence" of tariffs and quotas. This means that under *perfect* competition, applying a quota that limits the number of units imported will have essentially the same effects as applying a certain level of tariff: for each quota, there is an "equivalent" tariff. This equivalence result no longer holds under *imperfect* competition, however. Bhagwati (1965) considered a monopolistic home importer subject to a quota, and that analysis was later extended to duopoly with a home firm and foreign firm subject to an import quota (Harris 1985; Krishna 1989). As we shall see, a quota and tariff that have comparable effects on the level of imports can then have quite different effects on the import price, and therefore on welfare in the importing country.

Another reason for tariffs and quotas to differ occurs when foreign firms can choose the *quality* of the good that they export. In that case, a limitation on the number of units exported (as under a quota) will have quite a different impact from a tariff on the value of exports (as with an ad valorem tariff). The importance of this case became apparent with the quota applied to Japanese auto exports to the United States during the 1980s. The evidence strongly supports the hypothesis that Japanese firms changed the characteristics of the cars they sold, shifting towards higher-quality and higher-priced models. We shall describe a theoretical model of quality choice and the empirical evidence for autos (Feenstra 1988a).

The finding that trade policies have differing effects depending on the market structure carries over to the case of export subsidies. In the conventional two-sector model, there is no reason to use export subsidies: they will lead to a deadweight loss (analogous to a tariff) for a small country, and have an additional terms of trade loss (the opposite of a tariff) for a large country. This seems to contradict the fact that many countries have used export subsidies to support their industries at some time. To explain this, we need to go beyond the two-sector model with perfect competition. Adding more goods turns out to make a difference, and there is a potential role for targeted export subsidies in models with many goods (Feenstra 1986; Itoh and Kiyono 1987).

Dropping perfect competition and instead allowing for duopoly between a home and foreign firm exporting to a third market also makes a difference. The question then is whether the home government can give its own firm a "strategic" advantage by subsidizing it. We shall require that the subsidy also be in the *national* interest, which means that profits for the exporter need to rise by more than the amount of the subsidy itself. Initial analysis of this problem (Brander and Spencer 1985) suggested that such an advantage would indeed occur, at least under Cournot-Nash competition. Later work (Eaton and Grossman 1986), however, showed that this advantage would be *reversed* under Bertrand competition. The conclusion is that export subsidies are in the national interest only under some forms of market competition, but not generally. We conclude the chapter by investigating the effects of subsidies to the production of commercial aircraft, produced by Boeing in America and Airbus in Europe. Irwin and Pavcnik (2001) have recently investigated the effects of subsidies on prices and profits in this industry, as we shall discuss.

Equivalence of Tariffs and Quotas

The analysis of quotas under perfect competition proceeds much like our graphical treatment of tariffs, in the previous chapter. In panel (a) of Figure 8.1 we show the domestic demand D and supply curve S, together with the constant world price p^*. Under free trade, domestic demand is at c_0 and supply at y_0, so imports are $m_0 = c_0 - y_0$. The import demand curve $M = D - S$ is shown in panel (b), together with the horizontal export supply curve X at the world price p^*. These intersect at the equilibrium imports m_0.

Now suppose that an import quota of $\overline{X}$ is imposed, meaning that the quantity imported cannot exceed this amount. This effectively established a *vertical* export supply curve denoted by $\overline{X}$ in panel (b), which now intersects import demand at m_1 with the price of p_1. In panel (a), the price of p_1 leads to increased supply of y_1 and reduced demand of d_1. Notice that there would be an equivalent effect on price, consumption, and production if instead the government had imposed a tariff of $t \equiv p_1 - p_0$. In this sense, for every quota there is an *equivalent* tariff.

The welfare change from having the quota in Figure 8.1 is $-(a + b + c + d)$ consumer surplus loss $+(a)$ producer surplus gain. However, the area c, which would be collected as revenue under a tariff, now needs to

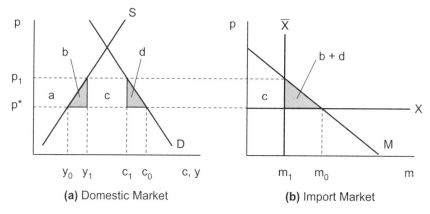

Figure 8.1   Small Country

be considered more carefully. This area is the difference between the domestic price p_1 and the world price p^*. Therefore, whoever is actually importing the good stands to collect the pure profits or "rents" equal to $(p_1 - p^*)m_1$, which is area c. There are four possible ways that these quota rents can be allocated.

First, the quota licenses can be given to home firms, who are then able to import at the world price p^* and sell domestically at p_1, earning the difference between these as rents. An example of this is the dairy industry in the United States, where U.S. producers of cheese also receive licenses to import from abroad.[1] With home firms earning the rents c, the net loss in domestic welfare due to the quota is $-(a + b + c + d)$ consumer surplus loss $+(a + c)$ producer surplus gain $= -(b + d)$, which is the same loss as we found for a tariff.

However, a second possibility is that while the quota licenses are given to home firms, these firms engage in some kind of inefficient activities in order to obtain the licenses. For example, if licenses for some imported input are allocated in proportion to the previous year's production of a final good, then firms will produce more final goods than they can sell (and probably of lower quality) just to obtain the import licenses. Krueger (1974) called this kind of activity "rent seeking," and it can include lobbying and other resource-using activities. It has been suggested that the waste of resources devoted to rent-seeking activities could be as large as the value of rents themselves, so that the area c would be wasted rather than accrue to domestic firms. In that case, the welfare loss due to the

---

[1] As described in Hornig et al. 1990, there is actually some sharing of the quotas rents between importers, exporters, and the U.S. government.

quota would be $-(a + b + c + d)$ consumer surplus loss $+(a)$ producer surplus gain $= -(b + d + c)$, which is greater than for the tariff.[2]

Third, the quota licenses can be auctioned by the government of the importing country. This has occurred in New Zealand, for example.[3] In a well-organized auction, we might expect that the revenue collected would equal the value of the rents, so that area c accrues to the home government. In that case, the net loss in domestic welfare due to the quota is $-(a + b + c + d)$ consumer surplus loss $+(a)$ producer surplus gain $+(c)$ auction revenue $= -(b + d)$, which is again the same loss as we found for a tariff.

Finally, the government of the importing country can give authority for implementing the quota to the government of the *exporting country*. Because the exporting country allocates the quota among its own producers, this is sometimes called a "voluntary" export restraint (VER), or "voluntary" restraint agreements (VRA). This arrangement has occurred for quotas that the United States has used in automobiles, steel, textiles, and other industries. In automobile imports for Japan after 1981, for example, the Ministry of International Trade and Industry (MITI) told each auto manufacturer in Japan how much it could export to the United States. We have discussed the background to this case in the previous chapter and will analyze it in detail later in this chapter. At this point, we note that the quota rents are then earned by *foreign producers*, so the loss in domestic welfare equals $-(a + b + c + d)$ consumer surplus loss $+(a)$ producer surplus gain $= -(b + d + c)$, which is larger than for a tariff.[4]

In Figure 8.2 we extend the analysis of the quota to a large country. In that case the quota rents might be measured as area c or $c + e$, and these accrue to the *foreign producers* under a VER. The deadweight loss for the importing country is still measured by area $b + d$, and it can be argued that the area f represents an analogous deadweight loss for the *foreign* country. In Table 8.1 we present some estimates of the home and foreign deadweight loss, along with the rents, for major U.S. quotas around 1985. In all cases except dairy, these rents were earned by foreign exporters. We will be discussing the case of automobiles later in the chapter, and estimates of the quota rents earned by foreigners range from $2 to 8 billion. Textiles and apparel also have very large quota rents and U.S. deadweight losses

---

[2] Bhagwati and Srinivasan (1980) have suggested, however, that there might also be "profit seeking" activities for tariff revenue, in which case we ought to take this into account for a tariff, too.

[3] See Bergsten et al. 1987.

[4] This raises the question of why a country would use a VER, since it gives the rents to foreigners. One answer is that this helps to prevent retaliation by the foreign countries. In addition, Feenstra and Lewis (1991b) argue that transferring the rents to foreigners serves as an "incentive compatibility" device, so that the importing country will only use the VER if the domestic industry is genuinely harmed.

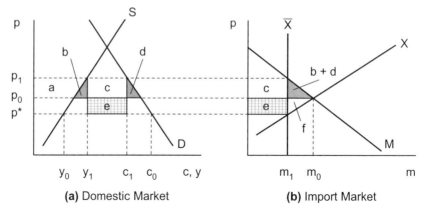

Figure 8.2   Large Country

(about \$5 billion each), under the global system of quotas known as the Multi-Fiber Arrangement (MFA). The *foreign* deadweight losses due to the MFA are even larger, with estimates ranging from \$4 to \$16 billion. The upper end of these estimates is obtained from models that include very costly rent-seeking activities by foreign producers in developing countries.

Summing the costs shown in Table 8.1, the total deadweight loss due to these quotas was in the range of \$8 to \$12 billion annually in the mid-1980s, while the quota rents transferred to foreigners are another \$7 to \$17 billion annually. Some of these costs for the United States are no longer relevant

TABLE 8.1
Annual Cost of U.S. Import Protection (\$billion, years around 1985)

	U.S. Deadweight Loss (area $b + d$)	Quota Rents (c or $c + e$)	Foreign Deadweight Loss (area f)
Automobiles	0.2–1.2	2.2–7.9	0–3
Dairy	1.4	0.25	0.02
Steel	0.1–0.3	0.7–2.0	0.1
Sugar	0.1	0.4–1.3	0.2
Textiles and Apparel	4.9–5.9	4.0–6.1	4–15.5
Average Tariffs	1.2–3.4	0	—
Total[a]	7.9–12.3	7.3–17.3	4.3–18.8

Source: Feenstra 1992, with detailed sources cited there.

[a] In dairy the quota rents are shared by U.S. importers, foreign exporters, and the U.S. government, and so are not included in the total.

today: the quota in automobiles ceased to be binding after 1987, as discussed later in the chapter, and under the Uruguay Round of the WTO it was agreed that the MFA would be dismantled. But that action is being delayed until 2005, and even for automobiles, there is always the possibility of new trade actions.[5] The quotas in the steel industry, whose costs are summarized in Table 8.1, have been recently replaced by tariffs (as described at the end of chapter 7). In addition, the "average tariffs" included in the last row of Table 8.1 reflect only conventional tariffs and do not include the additional cost due to U.S. antidumping duties (estimated as some $4 billion annually, also discussed at the end of chapter 7). In summary, the quotas and tariffs/duties used by the United States continue to impose a significant cost on the United States itself and on foreign trading partners.

Nonequivalence Due to Imperfect Competition

We have shown the equivalence of tariffs and quotas, in the sense that when each instrument is chosen to result in the same level of imports, it also has the same impact on prices. With imperfect competition in the domestic market, however, this result quickly breaks down. The reason is that the quota creates a "sheltered" market for the domestic firm, which will lead to higher prices and lower sales than under a tariff with the same level of imports. The case of a domestic monopoly, as analyzed by Bhagwati (1965), is demonstrated in Figure 8.3.

With the fixed world price of p^*, the demand curve facing the domestic monopolist is essentially horizontal at that price, so marginal revenue is also horizontal and the profit-maximizing quantity is y_0, where marginal revenue equals marginal cost. Note that this is the *same quantity* that a competitive firm or industry would produce if it had the same marginal costs as the monopolist. In this sense, free trade in a small country eliminates the market power of the monopolist, that is, eliminates its ability to restrict supply and raise price. This is a potential extra source of gains from trade.

Suppose initially that a *tariff* of t is applied to imports. In that case, the domestic monopolist can charge as much as $p^* + t$, but no more, so the demand curve is now horizontal at that price. This means that the marginal revenue curve is also horizontal at $p^* + t$, so the profit-maximizing quantity is where that price equals marginal cost, which is y_1 in Figure 8.3. Consumption at that price is c_1, so imports are $m_1 = c_1 - y_1$.

Now suppose that instead of the tariff, a quota of m_1 is applied. This means that for any price above p^*, the fixed amount m_1 will be imported,

---

[5] See Levinsohn 1997, who discusses a 1995 trade dispute in autos between the United States and Japan.

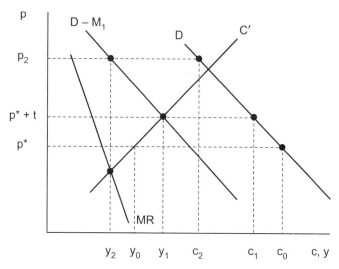

Figure 8.3   Domestic Monopoly

so the demand curve facing the monopolist is the initial demand curve D *less* the amount m_1, which we illustrate by $D - M_1$. Unlike the situation under the tariff, the monopolist retains the ability to influence the domestic price: it can choose the optimal price and quantity along $D - M_1$. So we graph the marginal revenue curve below $D - M_1$, which is denoted by MR, and find the profit-maximizing price and quantity where this intersects marginal cost, at p_2 and y_2. It will definitely be the case that $p_2 > p^* + t$, so that the quota *with the same level of imports as the tariff* has led to a higher domestic price. Therefore, the tariff and quota are no longer equivalent: the quota enables the monopolist to exercise market power, and has a higher welfare cost for this reason.

It is also the case that the quota might even lead to a *fall* in domestic output as compared to free trade. This is illustrated in Figure 8.3 by $y_2 < y_0$. This is not a necessary result, and we could instead have drawn the MR curve so that $y_2 > y_0$. It is rather surprising that $y_2 < y_0$ is even possible, because it suggests that workers in the industry would *fail to be protected* by the quota: that is, employment could fall due to the reduction in output under the quota. We see, then, that this policy instrument has quite undesirable results as compared to a tariff.

These results of Bhagwati (1965) give us good insight into the effect of a tariff versus a quota under imperfect competition, but the assumption that the domestic monopoly does not interact at all with foreign firms is not satisfactory. Presumably, the domestic firm competes with foreign firms,

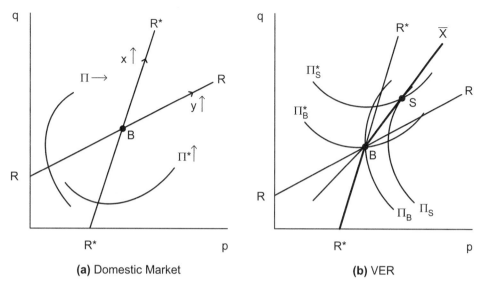

(a) Domestic Market   (b) VER

Figure 8.4   Bertrand Duopoly

under Cournot or Bertrand competition. In the first case, Cournot-Nash competition, the import quota has rather predictable effects: restricting the foreign firm to sell less than its free trade amount will shift sales towards the domestic firm, under the normal shape of reaction curves.[6] In order to obtain more dramatic results, we instead consider an import quota (restricting quantity) in a game where the two firms are initially engaged in Bertrand competition (taking each other's prices as given). This case has been analyzed by Harris (1985) and Krishna (1989), and we follow the exposition of Harris.

As in the previous chapter, we assume that the imported and domestic products are imperfect substitutes, and denote their prices by p and q, respectively. The amount exported by the foreign firm is x, and sold by the domestic firm is y. Under the assumption that the elasticity of demand for each product is increasing in the relative price of that product, the reaction curves $p = r^*(q)$ and $q = r(p)$ both slope upwards, with profits increasing in the directions shown in Figure 8.4(a). As the relative price of the competing good rises, the elasticity falls, and each firm will charge a higher price for its own good. Furthermore, there is a *dampened* response of each price to that of the competing good, so that

$$\frac{dp}{dq}\frac{q}{p} = r_q^*(q)\frac{q}{p} < 1, \text{ and } \frac{dq}{dp}\frac{p}{q} = r_p(p)\frac{p}{q} < 1.^7$$

[6] See problem 8.1.
[7] See problem 7.6.

In addition, under weak additional conditions the demand for each good will increase along its own reaction curve, as also illustrated in Figure 8.4(a).[8]

The Bertrand equilibrium under free trade occurs at point B. Suppose then that the foreign firm faces a "voluntary" export restraint (VER) on sales to the domestic market, of the amount $x(p, q) \le \bar{x}$. To make the argument as clear as possible, suppose further that the quota limit $\bar{x}$ is set at the free-trade level of exports, obtained at point B. Then what will be the response of the domestic and foreign firms to this export restraint? To answer this question, let us graph the prices at which the constraint $x(p, q) \le \bar{x}$ holds, as done in Figure 8.4(b). This constraint holds by choice of $\bar{x}$ at the Bertrand equilibrium. If we moved up the foreign reaction curve R^*R^*, then export sales x increase, so the constraint is violated. Accordingly, the constraint will hold at *higher* values of p, as illustrated by the line $B\overline{X}$ in Figure 8.4(b).

The fact that the foreign firm is restricted to sell $x(p, q) \le \bar{x}$ is common knowledge among all firms. In this situation, it is no longer appropriate to suppose that the firms engage in Bertrand competition, treating the prices of the other firm as fixed. In particular, the domestic firm will realize that if it *raises* its price and shifts export sales towards the foreign firm, thereby leading to $x(p, q) > \bar{x}$, the foreign firm will have no choice but to increase its own price to restore $x(p, q) = \bar{x}$. The reaction curve of the foreign firm is therefore $R^*B\overline{X}$. We can expect the domestic firm to take advantage of the export restraint and increase its prices, knowing that the foreign firm will have to respond. Essentially, the VER gives the domestic firm a "first mover advantage" in selecting its price, so it can act like a Stackelberg leader relative to the reaction curve of the foreign firm.

By this reasoning, the optimal action by the domestic firm will be to increase its price until an iso-profit curve is tangent to the constraint $B\overline{X}$, as shown at point S in Figure 8.4(b). This movement clearly increases the profits of the home firm, from π_B to π_S. Furthermore, the discrete increase in prices from point B to point S is much different from what we would expect from a tariff: since imports are equal at points B and S, a *zero* tariff would have the same impact on imports as the export restraint, but obviously no impact at all on prices. So as in the analysis of Bhagwati (1965), the quota has a much greater impact on import and domestic prices than would a tariff at the same level of imports.

What is new in the duopoly model is to realize that the *foreign* firm also benefits from the export restraint. This is clear from Figure 8.4(b) when exports are limited to the free-trade level: profits of the foreign firm increase from π_B^* to π_S^*. Harris (1985) refers to this as a reason why export

---

[8] See problem 7.7.

restraints are 'voluntary', and Krishna (1989) refers to the export restraint as a "facilitating practice"; that is, it facilitates a more collusive outcome between the firms. Notice that if we consider a quota at *less than* the free-trade level of exports, however, the profits of the foreign firm do not necessarily go up.[9] In any case, the losers from the export restraint are home consumers who are paying a higher price for the domestic good and imports, without the benefits of tariff revenue. This begs the question of why a government would ever use a VER rather than a tariff. One answer is that the VER may prevent retaliation from the foreign government, since its own firms may be gaining from the trade restriction.

Nonequivalence Due to Quality Choice

We turn now to a second reason for tariffs and quotas to differ, and that is due to the choice of product quality for the exporting firms. We think of quality as a characteristic of a product, which brings higher utility for consumers but also has higher costs for the firm. If an exporting firm is constrained in the *quantity* that it exports, how will this affect its choice of quality or product characteristics? Our argument in this section is that, under certain conditions, it will be optimal for the firm to increase product quality in response to the quota, whereas it would not do so with an ad valorem tariff.

To develop this argument, we will suppose that there are $i = 1, \ldots, N$ varieties of a differentiated product, each of which has characteristics given by the vector z_i. As in our treatment of monopolistic competition in chapter 5, we will suppose that the demand for these product varieties arises from an aggregate utility function, now given by

$$U[f(z_1)c_1, \ldots, f(z_N)c_N], \tag{8.1}$$

where c_i denotes the consumption of each variety, $i = 1, \ldots, N$, and the function $f(z_i)$ converts the vector of characteristics into a scalar "quality," which then multiplies consumption. Several features of the aggregate utility function in (8.1) deserve comment.

First, if we recognize that the product varieties are actually bought by *different* individuals, is it still legitimate to use an aggregate utility function like (8.1)? This question has been answered in the affirmative by McFadden (1978, 1981) and Anderson, de Palma, and Thisse (1992). McFadden (1981) provides a very general aggregation theorem that applies to the behavior of individuals making choices over a discrete number of products, where they each purchase one unit of their optimal variety. It

---

[9] See problem 8.2.

turns out that by summing over their quantity purchased of each product, their aggregate decisions are *equivalent* to those made by a representative consumer. We discuss McFadden's aggregation theorem and extensions in Appendix B, which allow us to use an aggregate utility function like (8.1).

Specific functional forms can also be obtained. One case that we shall consider is the CES aggregate utility function:

$$U = \sum_{i=1}^{N} [f(z_i)c_i]^{(\sigma-1)/\sigma}, \qquad (8.2)$$

again defined over the consumption c_i of each good times its quality $f(z_i)$. The fact that the CES utility function can arise from a discrete choice problem by individuals is demonstrated by Anderson, de Palma, and Thisse (1989; 1992, 85–90), provided that individuals consume continuous amounts of the differentiated good. A more conventional assumption is that they must consume zero or one unit, and in that case, the aggregate demands obtained are the "logit" formulation. We shall use those alternative demand functions at the end of the chapter.

Given that an aggregate utility function exists, however, it is still rather special to suppose that the product characteristics and consumption enter in the *separable* form shown in (8.1), that is, in the form $f(z_i)c_i$, which we can interpret as "quality times quantity." This functional form implies that every unit consumed of good i is evaluated as having the same quality. This form of the utility function was used by Swan (1970), but criticized as being too special by Spence (1975). Spence uses a more general formulation like $\phi(z_i, c_i)$, under which the marginal utility of characteristics per unit consumed, $\phi_z(z_i, c_i)/c_i$, can vary with the level of consumption c_i. If we interpret demand as coming from different individuals, then $\phi_z(z_i, c_i)/c_i$ depending on c_i means that consumers have differing valuations of characteristics. We will use the special form $f(z_i)c_i$ for convenience, but as we shall repeatedly emphasize, the results that we obtain on quality upgrading will not necessarily carry over to more general functional forms.

Free-Trade Equilibrium

We begin by analyzing the problem for consumers and firms in the absence of any quota restriction. Consumers are presented with a set of $i = 1, \ldots, N$ varieties, with fixed characteristics z_i and prices p_i, and then choose the optimal quantity of each variety. It will be convenient to work with the "quality adjusted" prices, which are defined by $q_i \equiv p_i/f(z_i)$. That is, the higher is overall product quality $f(z_i)$, the lower are the quality-adjusted prices q_i. The aggregate consumer maximizes utility in (8.1), subject to the budget constraint $\sum_{i=1}^{N} p_i c_i \leq I$. The Lagrangian for this problem is

$$
\begin{aligned}
L &= U[f(z_1)c_1, \ldots, f(z_N)c_N] + \lambda \left(I - \sum_{i=1}^{N} p_i c_i \right) \\
&= U(d_1, \ldots, d_N) + \lambda \left(I - \sum_{i=1}^{N} q_i d_i \right),
\end{aligned}
\tag{8.3}
$$

where the second line of (8.3) follows by defining $d_i \equiv f(z_i)c_i$ as the effective "quality-adjusted" demand, and also using the quality-adjusted prices $q_i \equiv p_i / f(z_i)$. This rewriting of the Lagrangian makes it clear that instead of choosing c_i given prices p_i and characteristics z_i, we can instead think of the aggregate consumer as choosing d_i given quality-adjusted prices q_i, $i = 1, \ldots, N$. Let us denote the solution to problem (8.3) by $d_i(q, I)$, where q is the vector of quality-adjusted prices.

Varieties of the differentiated product can be sold by domestic and foreign firms, which we do not distinguish in the notation. Producing one unit of product i with characteristics z_i requires unit-costs of $g_i(z_i)$, where we are treating factor prices as constant and suppress them in this cost function.[10] For simplicity, we are assuming constant returns to scale, so that the costs $g_i(z_i)$ do not depend on the level of output. Firms simultaneously choose prices p_i and characteristics z_i, for the $i = 1, \ldots, N$ varieties. Suppose that a given firm produces the first $i = 1, \ldots, M$ product varieties. Consumption of each of these is $c_i = d_i(q, I)/f(z_i)$. The profit-maximization problem for this firm is then

$$
\max_{p_i, z_i} \sum_{i=1}^{M} [p_i - g_i(z_i)]c_i = \max_{q_i, z_i} \sum_{i=1}^{M} \left[q_i - \frac{g_i(z_i)}{f(z_i)} \right] d_i(q, I).
\tag{8.4}
$$

Again, we have changed the variables from nominal prices p_i to quality-adjusted prices q_i when moving from the left side to the right side of (8.4). This transformation relies on our assumption that *prices and characteristics are chosen simultaneously*, as well as our special functional forms.

It is immediately clear that to maximize profits in (8.4), the firms must minimize $g_i(z_i)/f(z_i)$, which is interpreted as the costs per unit of quality for good i. Taking logs and minimizing this over the choice of characteristics z_i leads to the first-order conditions

$$
\frac{1}{f(z_i)} \frac{\partial f}{\partial z_i} = \frac{1}{g_i(z_i)} \frac{\partial g_i}{\partial z_i}, \quad i = 1, \ldots, M.
\tag{8.5}
$$

[10] We index the function $g_i(z_i)$ by i to reflect that firms might have access to different technologies. Then they will produce varieties with different characteristics in equilibrium.

Thus, we obtain equality between the relative marginal utility from each characteristic, on the left of (8.5), and its relative marginal cost, on the right. Notice that this condition holds despite the fact that the firm will be choosing its prices in a monopolistically competitive fashion, provided the prices and characteristics are chosen simultaneously.[11]

Maximizing (8.4) over the choice of prices q_i, we obtain the first-order conditions

$$d_i(q, I) + \sum_{j=1}^{M} \left[q_j - \frac{g_j(z_j)}{f(z_j)} \right] \frac{\partial d_j}{\partial q_i} = 0, \qquad i = 1, \ldots, M. \qquad (8.6)$$

This expression is slightly more complicated than usual because the firm is selling multiple products $j = 1, \ldots, M$, and therefore must take into account the effect of a change in price q_i on all these products. To simplify this expression, let us consider the case of a CES utility function in (8.2). Then it can be confirmed that the demand derivatives are symmetric, $\partial d_i / \partial q_j = \partial d_j / \partial q_i$.[12] Using this in (8.6) and dividing by effective demand d_i, we can reexpress it as

$$1 + \sum_{j=1}^{M} \left[1 - \frac{g_j(z_j)}{p_j} \right] \frac{\partial \ln d_i}{\partial \ln q_j} = 0, \qquad i = 1, \ldots, M. \qquad (8.7)$$

Let us denote the ratio of price to marginal cost for each product by $\mu_j = p_j / g_j(z_j) \geq 1$. We can see that the expression in brackets in (8.7) equals $(\mu_i - 1)/\mu_i = [p_i - g_i(z_i)]/p_i \geq 0$, which is the difference between price and marginal cost measured relative to price. This is the Lerner index of monopoly power for a single-product firm, and with price chosen optimally will equal the inverse of its elasticity of demand. To see how this Lerner pricing rule is modified with multiproduct firms, let us conjecture a solution where the price-cost ratios are *constant* across all products sold by the firm in question, $\mu_j = \mu$. Then it is immediately clear that the solution to (8.7) is

$$\left(\frac{\mu - 1}{\mu} \right) = - \left(\sum_{j=1}^{M} \frac{\partial \ln d_i}{\partial \ln q_j} \right)^{-1}. \qquad (8.8)$$

[11] It is well known that a condition like (8.5) holds in a competitive market, as described in the classic article by Rosen (1974), and Swan (1970) first showed that it holds under monopoly as well, using the special functional forms we have assumed. When prices and characteristics are not chosen simultaneously, then we do not obtain the equality shown in (8.5); see Feenstra 1995, for example.

[12] See problem 8.3 to derive this and also expression (8.9) below.

Expression (8.8) says that the Lerner index for the firm equals the inverse of the sum of demand elasticities. In order for this solution to be valid, we need to have the sum of elasticities on the right of (8.8) be *independent of good i*. That is, an equiproportional increase in all prices charged by a firm needs to lead to the same percentage drop in demand for *any* product sold by that firm. It turns out that this condition is satisfied for CES demands, in which case the sum of elasticities is

$$-\left(\sum_{j=1}^{M} \frac{\partial \ln d_i}{\partial \ln q_j}\right) = \sigma + (1 - \sigma)\left(\sum_{j=1}^{M} \frac{p_j c_j}{I}\right), \tag{8.9}$$

where $\sigma > 1$ is the elasticity of substitution between products. The expression on the right-hand side of (8.9) is the sum of sales over all products sold by the firm, measured relative to total expenditure I on the differentiated product. In other words, the expression on the right side is the *total market share* of the firm. As the market share grows, the sum of elasticities falls, and the markup of the firm will rise in (8.8).

Using the solution for μ from (8.8) and (8.9), the optimal prices of the firm are

$$p_i = \mu g_i(z_i), \qquad i = 1, \ldots, M. \tag{8.10}$$

Thus, in this CES case the firm charges the same markups over all products that it sells. This is certainly special and would not carry over to other functional forms. Bresnahan (1981) was the first to estimate a discrete choice model for autos that allowed for differing markups over products sold, and found that higher-priced models tended to have higher percentage markups. Similarly, Berry, Levinsohn, and Pakes (1995, 1999), Feenstra and Levinsohn (1995), and Goldberg (1995) use functional forms more general than CES that allow markups to differ across products. These discussions go beyond the scope of this chapter, though the theory behind them is discussed in Appendix B, and we shall comment on their empirical findings below.

Voluntary Export Restraint

Suppose now that the exports of a foreign firm are restricted to the amount $\sum_{i=1}^{M} c_i = \sum_{i=1}^{M} d_i/f(z_i) \le \overline{X}$, where $\overline{X}$ is the quota amount. Under the VER on Japanese autos, for example, the amounts $\overline{X}$ were allocated to each Japanese firm by the Ministry of International Trade and Industry (MITI). We do not introduce a subscript to denote the foreign

firms, but analyze the profit maximization problem for any such firm. The
Lagrangian is

$$
\begin{aligned}
L &= \max_{q_i,\, z_i} \sum_{i=1}^{M} \left[q_i - \frac{g_i(z_i)}{f(z_i)} \right] d_i(q_i, I) + \lambda \left(\overline{X} - \sum_{i=1}^{M} \frac{d_i(q, I)}{f_i(z_i)} \right) \\
&= \max_{q_i,\, z_i} \sum_{i=1}^{M} \left[q_i - \frac{g_i(z_i) + \lambda}{f(z_i)} \right] d_i(q_i, I) + \lambda \overline{X},
\end{aligned}
\tag{8.11}
$$

where the second line follows by simply combining terms. Thus, to maximize profits, it is now the case that the foreign firms will choose characteristics z_i to minimize $[g_i(z_i) + \lambda]/f(z_i)$. Taking logs, the first-order
condition for this minimization problem is

$$
\frac{1}{f(z_i)} \frac{\partial f}{\partial z_i} = \frac{1}{[g_i(z_i) + \lambda]} \frac{\partial g_i}{\partial z_i}, \qquad i = 1, \dots, M.
\tag{8.12}
$$

Thus, in contrast to the first-order condition in (8.5), we no longer obtain an equality between relative marginal utility and marginal cost of
characteristics. This equality is broken by the binding quota constraint,
and higher value of λ will be associated with higher levels of characteristics
chosen by the firm. To see this, totally differentiate (8.12) with respect to
z_i and λ to obtain

$$
\frac{dz_i}{d\lambda} = \frac{1}{[g_i(z_i) + \lambda]^2} \left[\frac{\partial^2 \ln(g_i + \lambda)}{\partial z_i^2} - \frac{\partial^2 \ln f}{\partial z_i^2} \right]^{-1} \frac{\partial g_i}{\partial z_i}.
\tag{8.13}
$$

The matrix of second derivatives shown in brackets on the right side of
(8.13) is positive definite from the second-order conditions for minimizing $[g_i(z_i) + \lambda]/f(z_i)$. While this does not establish the sign of the vector
$dz_i/d\lambda$, notice that we can premultiply (8.13) by the row vector $(\partial f/\partial z_i)'$,
which from (8.12) is proportional to the vector $(\partial g_i/\partial z_i)'$. Then we will
obtain a positive definite matrix that is pre- and postmultiplied by vectors
that are proportional and is therefore positive:

$$
\frac{df(z_i)}{d\lambda} = \frac{\partial f'}{\partial z_i} \frac{dz_i}{d\lambda} > 0, \qquad i = 1, \dots, M.
\tag{8.14}
$$

Thus, overall product quality is increased for every product sold by foreign firms due to the export restraint. This is our first demonstration of
the idea that quotas lead to an increase in product quality.[13] Notice that

---

[13] We stress again that this result depends on the special functional forms we have used.
Krishna (1987) uses a more general utility function like $\phi(z_i, c_i)$ as in Spence (1975), and finds

this would *not occur* under an ad valorem tariff, however. In that case the profit-maximization problem (8.4) would be rewritten as

$$\max_{p_i,\, z_i} \sum_{i=1}^{M} \left[\frac{p_i}{(1+\tau)} - g_i(z_i) \right] c_i = \max_{q_i,\, z_i} \sum_{i=1}^{M} \left[\frac{q_i}{(1+\tau)} - \frac{g_i(z_i)}{f(z_i)} \right] d_i(q, I), \quad (8.4')$$

where τ is the ad valorem tariff. Changes in the tariff would have no effect at all on the optimal choice of characteristics in (8.5), which continues to hold.

There is also a second sense in which product quality is increased, and that comes from looking at demand *across* product varieties sold by a firm, rather than at the characteristics *within* each variety. To motivate this, let us solve for the optimal prices that come from the Lagrangian in (8.11). Assuming again that the utility and demand functions are CES, the optimal prices are increased according to the Lagrange multiplier on the export restraint:[14]

$$p_i = \mu[g_i(z_i) + \lambda], \qquad i = 1, \ldots, M, \qquad (8.15)$$

where μ is once again the markup charged on all products sold by the firm, as solved from (8.8) and (8.9). With λ and μ both common across all products sold by a firm, we see that the effect of the VER is to introduce a *dollar* price increase of $\mu\lambda$ to the price of every product sold. In other words, the VER acts in the same way as a *specific* price increase, and not like a proportional price increase across products.[15]

Now consider two products sold by the firm, $i = 1, 2$, with marginal costs higher for product 1, $g_1(z_1) > g_2(z_2)$. In the absence of the VER, prices will be $p_1 = \mu g_1(z_1) > p_2 = \mu g_2(z_2)$, and it is natural to refer to the more expensive product 1 as having higher quality. Suppose that the quota is applied, and so that prices rise by the same dollar amount as in (8.15). Holding characteristics fixed, the new prices will be $p_1' = \mu'[g_1(z_1) + \lambda]$, and $p_2' = \mu'[g_2(z_2) + \lambda]$, where we allow for the fact that due to the VER the markup μ can change to μ'. Notice that the *ratio* of prices becomes $(p_1'/p_2') = [g_1(z_1) + \lambda]/[g_2(z_2) + \lambda] < g_1(z_1)/g_2(z_2) = p_1/p_2$, where the inequality is obtained because $g_1(z_1) > g_2(z_2)$. In other words, the

---

that the change in product quality is ambiguous. Similarly, Feenstra (1988a) uses marginal costs for the firm that depend on quantity, in which case the change in product quality is again ambiguous. An alternative formulation of the quality-choice problem, using an "address" specification, is in Das and Donnenfeld 1987, 1989. They also find that the impact of the quota on quality is ambiguous in general (1989), but leads to quality upgrading under specific functional forms (1987).

[14] In problem 8.4 you are asked to derive (8.15).
[15] This result is also obtained by Krishna (1990), for a monopolist selling a continuum of products.

same *dollar* increase in both prices will lead to a smaller *percentage* increase in the higher-priced product.

Assuming that there are just two goods and the utility function is homothetic, then the ratios of demands d_1/d_2 depends only on the price ratio q_1/q_2, and is decreasing in this relative price. With characteristics constant, the fall in p_1/p_2 will reduce q_1/q_2, which will *shift demand towards* the higher-priced product so that d_1/d_2 increases. This shift towards the higher-quality product corresponds to an increase in "average quality." Furthermore, notice that the change in average quality would *not* occur with an ad valorem tariff, since that would have no impact on the relative price or relative quantity demanded.

The above description of quality upgrading due to shifts in demand is called the "Washington apples" effect, after the example given by Alchian and Allen (1964, 74–75). They noted that while the state of Washington grows apples of many varieties, it appeared that the *best apples* were shipped the furthest distance, to east coast markets. This is explained by treating the transport costs as the same for each apple. Transport therefore acts like a specific price increase, which lowers the *relative price* of the higher-quality apples in more distance markets. Accordingly, we expect to see the best apples shipped to the east coast, which raises the average quality in those markets.[16]

In summary, there are two reasons to expect import quality to rise with a quota on the number of units sold: due to the increase in characteristics chosen by the exporting firms; and due to the shift in demand towards the higher-quality products. These two effects can certainly work together. In the model above, the demands $d_i(q_i, I)$ for quality-adjusted consumption $f(z_i)c_i$, are determined by the quality-adjusted prices $q_i \equiv p_i/f(z_i)$. So let us see how these prices are affected by the quota, even as characteristics change.

Using (8.15), the quality-adjusted prices are written as $q_i = \mu[g_i(z_i) + \lambda]/f_i(z_i)$. From our discussion following (8.8), we know that $[g_i(z_i) + \lambda]/f_i(z_i)$ is minimized over the choice of characteristics z_i. Then by the envelope theorem, when differentiating this expression we can treat the characteristics as fixed. Accordingly, we can compute the change in quality-adjusted prices due to the quota as

$$\frac{d \ln q_i}{d\lambda} = \frac{d \ln \mu}{d\lambda} + \frac{1}{[g_i(z_i) + \lambda]} = \frac{d \ln \mu}{d\lambda} + \frac{\mu}{p_i}. \tag{8.16}$$

The first term on the right of (8.16) is the change in markup due to the VER, which is common across products, while the second term is smallest

---

[16] Hummels and Skiba (2002) argue that this effect can be observed in trade data across countries.

for the highest-priced products. Therefore, we will observe the *smallest* relative increase in quality-adjusted price for those products with the *highest* prices. This can be expected to shift demand towards the highest-priced products, just as in the "Washington apples" effect.

Measuring Quality Upgrading Due to Quotas

We turn now to an application of the above theory to the "voluntary" export restraint (VER) imposed on Japanese autos by the United States. Recall that with unemployment in the automobile industry growing in 1979–80 and profits falling, Ford Motor Company and the UAW applied to the ITC for Section 201 protection. This application was denied on the grounds that the U.S. recession appeared to be a greater cause of unemployment than were rising imports from Japan.

Faced with this negative outcome, several congressmen from midwestern states pursued protection for automobiles via other means. Senators Danforth and Bentsen introduced a bill to restrict imports, which would have restricted Japanese automobiles imports into the United States to 1.6 million units during 1981, 1982, and 1983. Indeed, this bill was scheduled for revision in the Senate Finance Committee on May 12, 1981. Clearly aware of this pending legislation, the Japanese government announced on May 1 that it would "voluntarily" limit the sales of automobiles in the U.S. market. For the period April 1981–March 1982, this limit was set at 1.83 million autos, including 1.68 million cars exported to the United States, 82,500 utility vehicles, and 70,000 vehicles exported to Puerto Rico. This limit was in place until March 1984, after which it was raised to 2.02 and then 2.51 million vehicles annually until March 1992, as shown in Table 8.2, where we compare the actual imports with the VER limits. It is evident that the VER was nearly exactly satisfied in early years, and remained binding until 1987. After that, however, actual imports were below the VER, so that by March 1994 it was discontinued. The reason that imports fell below the VER after 1987 was because Japanese companies had begun assembling cars in the United States, so imports naturally fell.

Our interest, then, is in the effects of the VER during the early years. To estimate the change in product quality, initially consider the case where there is no VER. Assuming that marginal costs take the form $\ln g_i(z_{it}) = \beta' z_{it} + \xi_{it}$, where ξ_{it} is a random error that reflects unmeasured characteristics, and we add the subscript t to denote years. Then the first-order condition (8.10) is written in logs as

$$\ln p_{it} = \alpha_t + \beta' z_{it} + \xi_{it}, \qquad i = 1, \ldots, M, \qquad (8.17)$$

TABLE 8.2
Japanese Car Imports and VER limit, 1979–94

Time Period	U.S. Imports from Japan	VER Limit	Difference (Imports − VER)
April 1979–March 1980	1,779,497	None	
April 1980–March 1981	2,011,822	None	
April 1981–March 1982	1,833,313	1,832,500[a]	813
April 1981–March 1983	1,831,198	1,832,500	−1,302
April 1983–March 1984	1,851,694	1,832,500	19,194
April 1994–March 1985	2,031,250	2,016,000[b]	15,250
April 1985–March 1986	2,605,407	2,506,000[c]	99,407
April 1986–March 1987	2,518,707	2,506,000	12,707
April 1987–March 1988	2,377,383	2,506,000	−128,617
April 1988–March 1989	2,115,304	2,506,000	−390,696
April 1989–March 1990	2,015,920	2,506,000	−490,080
April 1990–March 1991	1,911,828	2,506,000	−594,172
April 1991–March 1992	1,728,446	2,506,000	−777,554
April 1992–March 1993	1,637,519	1,650,000	−12,481
April 1993–March 1994	1,549,587	1,650,000	−100,413

Source: Table 2 from "The U.S. Automobile Industry: Monthly Report on Selected Economic Indicators," U.S. International Trade Commission, May issue of each year, cited in Berry, Levinsohn, and Pakes 1999, 402.

Note: This table reports U.S. imports of cars and sport-utility vehicles from Japan, including imports to Puerto Rico.

[a] Computed as 1.68 million cars to the United States, 82,500 utility vehicles to the United States, and 70,000 vehicles to Puerto Rico.

[b] Of the 2.106 million total, 1.85 million were cars sold to the United States.

[c] Of the 2.506 million total, 2.30 million were cars sold to the United States.

where $\alpha_t = \ln \mu_t$ reflects the markups. We should also be indexing α_t by firms (since the markups differ across firms), but will omit this notation. Equation (8.17) is a log-linear regression of prices on characteristics and is called a "hedonic regression." Our derivation shows that this is a valid representation of the equilibrium under imperfect competition provided that markups are the same across products (as in the CES case). Furthermore, using the equality between relative marginal utility from each characteristic, on the left side of (8.5), and relative marginal cost on the right, we can interpret the coefficients β in (8.17) in either way.

Under the VER, the first-order condition becomes (8.15). For the same specification of marginal costs, $\ln g_i(z_{it}) = \beta' z_{it} + \xi_{it}$, this is rewritten as

$$p_{it} = \exp(\alpha_t + \beta' z_{it} + \xi_{it}) + s_t, \qquad i = 1, \ldots, M, \qquad (8.18)$$

where $\alpha_t = \ln \mu_t$ are the markups and $s_t = \mu_t \lambda_t$ are the specific price increases due to the VER. To convert the random error to an additive form, define

$$\varepsilon_{it} = \exp(\alpha_t + \beta' z_{it} + \xi_{it}) - \exp(\alpha_t + \beta' z_{it})$$
$$= [\exp(\xi_{it}) - 1]\exp(\alpha_t + \beta' z_{it}). \tag{8.19}$$

Then (8.18) is rewritten as

$$p_{it} = \exp(\alpha_t + \beta' z_{it}) + s_t + \varepsilon_{it}, \qquad i = 1, \ldots, M. \tag{8.20}$$

Thus, under the VER we need to allow for *specific* price increases s_t from year to year, as well as the *proportional* price changes captured by α_t.

Feenstra (1988a) estimates these hedonic regressions using a sample of U.S. imports of Japanese cars and trucks. Only cars and utility vehicles were subject to the VER, whereas trucks had a higher tariff imposed in August 1980, as discussed in the previous chapter. Summary statistics for the sample over 1979–85 are shown in Table 8.3. Notice that the unit-value (i.e., average price) of Japanese cars increased by 20% from 1980 to 1981, which was unusually high, and a further 10% from 1981 to 1982. We should not attribute this entire amount to the VER, however. The nominal increase in prices can also reflect general inflation, and in addition, increases in the quality of each product. Using the estimates for a hedonic regression, we can define quality as $(\alpha_0 + \beta' z_{it})$, which will increase whenever the characteristics z_{it} rise. Observing whether this occurred for Japanese autos under the VER, as predicted by the theory, is the goal of the empirical work, as well as to estimate the impact of the VER on prices as measured by the specific price terms s_t.

An initial estimate of (8.20) for 1979–85, using the base version of each Japanese car model sold in the United States, is shown in column (1) of Table 8.4.[17] The coefficients at the top of the table are estimates of β_k for each characteristic k. For example, an increase in width of one foot is estimated to raise the price of a car by $\exp(0.36) = 1.43$, while an increase in horsepower of 100 will increase price by $\exp(0.69) = 2$, or double the price. In the lower part of the table we report the estimates of α_t, referred to as the *proportional* price increases (measured relative to 1979), and then the estimates of s_t, referred to as the *specific* price increases (measured relative to 1980). Except for 1985, we see that the specific prices increase are positive but have high standard errors. This is due to the multicollinearity between the terms α_t and s_t, both of which are measuring annual price increases.

---

[17] Assuming that the random errors ξ_{it} have equal variance, then from (8.19) we see that the variance of ω_{it} is proportional to $\exp(\alpha_t + \beta' z_{it})^2$. Accordingly, we obtain preliminary estimates of α_t and β and then use of inverse of $\exp(\alpha_t + \beta' z_{it})^2$ as weights when estimating (8.20). See the empirical exercises to reproduce the results in Tables 8.3 and 8.4.

TABLE 8.3
Japanese Cars and Trucks, and U.S. Small Cars, 1979–85

	1979	*1980*	*1981*	*1982*	*1983*	*1984*	*1985*
Japanese cars							
Number of models	21	24	24	24	26	29	31
Unit-value ($)	4,946	5,175	6,211	6,834	7,069	7,518	8,153
(percent change)		(4.6)	(20.0)	(10.0)	(3.4)	(6.4)	(8.4)
Price index	96.6	100	119.8	128.9	131.3	138.9	147.8
(percent change)		(3.5)	(19.8)	(7.6)	(1.9)	(5.8)	(6.4)
Unit-quality ($)	4,361	4,473	4,867	5,253	5,637	5,862	6,130
(percent change)		(2.6)	(8.8)	(7.9)	(7.3)	(4.0)	(4.6)
Quality index	98.7	100	108.6	115.2	121.3	126.6	130.6
(percent change)		(1.3)	(8.6)	(8.6)	(5.3)	(4.4)	(3.2)
Japanese trucks[a]							
Number of models	10	10	11	11	10	11	12
Unit-value ($)	4,794	4,937	6,134	6,426	6,134	6,247	6,250
(percent change)		(3.0)	(24.2)	(4.8)	(−4.5)	(1.8)	(0.05)
Price index	97.02	100	127.8	130.9	121	123.1	125.2
(percent change)		(3.1)	(27.8)	(2.4)	(−7.6)	(1.7)	(1.7)
Unit-quality ($)	4,627	4,638	4,791	4,930	4,997	5,010	5,433
(percent change)		(0.2)	(3.3)	(2.9)	(1.4)	(0.3)	(8.4)
Quality index	99.6	100	103.5	105.9	105.7	105.3	116.0
(percent change)		(0.4)	(3.5)	(2.3)	(−0.2)	(−0.4)	(10.2)
U.S. small cars							
Number of models	24	22	23	27	33	34	
Unit-value ($)	4186	5067	5915	6446	6581	6781	
(percent change)		(21.0)	(16.7)	(9.0)	(2.1)	(3.0)	
Price index	81.9	100.0	116.8	125.6	125.4	127.5	
(percent change)		(22.1)	(16.8)	(7.5)	(−0.2)	(1.7)	
Unit-quality ($)	4195	4132	4183	4351	4497	4563	
(percent change)		(−1.5)	(1.2)	(4.0)	(3.4)	(1.5)	
Quality index	100.5	100.0	102.2	104.4	105.7	106.1	
(percent change)		(−0.5)	(2.2)	(2.1)	(1.3)	(0.4)	

Source: Revised from Feenstra 1985, 1988a; empirical exercises 8.1 and 8.4.
[a] Includes utility vehicles.

TABLE 8.4
Hedonic Regression for Japanese Cars and Trucks, 1979–85, with Price as
Dependent Variable

	Cars (1)	Trucks (2)	Cars (3)	Trucks (4)
Constant	6.33*	7.71*	5.83*	6.63*
	(0.58)	(0.50)	(0.86)	(0.77)
Weight (tons)	0.03	0.41*	0.05	0.48*
	(0.12)	(0.08)	(0.11)	(0.12)
Width (feet)	0.36*	0.01	0.39*	0.21
	(0.11)	(0.10)	(0.14)	(0.14)
Height (feet)	−0.06	0.01	−0.06*	−0.03
	(0.06)	(0.05)	(0.06)	(0.07)
Horsepower (100)	0.69*	0.20	0.81*	0.24
	(0.09)	(0.10)	(0.10)	(0.15)
Transmission (5-speed or auto)	0.14*	0.03	0.18*	0.05
	(0.02)	(0.03)	(0.04)	(0.04)
Power steering	0.06*	0.09	0.07*	0.06
	(0.03)	(0.04)	(0.03)	(0.06)
Air conditioning	0.15*		0.16*	
	(0.03)		(0.04)	
Four-wheel drive		0.22*		0.30*
		(0.03)		(0.06)
Proportional				
Year 1980	0.01	0.004	0.01	0.01
	(0.03)	(0.033)	(0.03)	(0.03)
Year 1981	0.05	0.21*	0.07	0.23*
	(0.11)	(0.03)	(0.04)	(0.04)
Year 1982	0.09	0.23*	0.07	0.23*
	(0.11)	(0.03)	(0.04)	(0.04)
Year 1983	0.02	0.17*	−0.001	0.16*
	(0.11)	(0.04)	(0.05)	(0.05)
Year 1984	0.09	0.19*	0.02	0.18*
	(0.10)	(0.04)	(0.05)	(0.05)
Year 1985	0.22*	0.18*	0.10	0.11
	(0.10)	(0.04)	(0.06)	(0.06)
Specific				
Year 1981	410		367	
	(619)		(239)	
Year 1982	378		600*	
	(650)		(254)	
Year 1983	770		887*	
	(601)		(243)	
Year 1984	624		1,104*	
	(618)		(251)	
Year 1985	−123		856*	
	(719)		(366)	
Observations	179	75		254
R^2	0.990	0.996		0.992

Source: Revised from Feenstra 1988a; empirical exercises 8.2 and 8.3.

Note: Standard errors are in parentheses.

* Significant at 95 percent level.

To address this multicollinearity, we consider pooling data for U.S. imports of Japanese cars and trucks. Denoting trucks with an asterisk, we rewrite the hedonic regression (8.17) as,

$$\ln p_{it}^* = \alpha_t^* + \beta^{*\prime} z_{it}^* + \xi_{it}^*, \quad i = 1, \ldots, M. \tag{8.21}$$

Thus, we are allowing trucks to have different coefficient on its characteristics than cars, and also differing proportional price increases α_t^*. Because trucks were not subject to the VER, we do not include any specific price increases in this regression. Estimates of (8.21) using the data on trucks are shown in regression (2) of Table 8.4.[18]

We now consider testing the hypothesis that the year-to-year price changes in Japanese car and truck exports to the United States would be the same, *after correcting for the trade policies in each product.* Cars were subject to the VER after April 1981, whereas trucks imported from Japan were subject to an increase in the tariff from 4% to 25% after August 1980, as discussed in the previous chapter. Feenstra (1988a) argues that the 21% increase in the wholesale price of trucks as they cross the border would be reflected by at most a 16% increase in the retail price.[19] Accordingly, we consider testing the hypothesis that the proportional year increase for trucks, α_t^*, is 0.16 greater than the proportional year increase for cars, α_t, for 1981 and later years:

$$\alpha_t^* = \alpha_t + 0.16 \quad \text{for} \quad t = 1981, 82, \ldots, 85. \tag{8.22}$$

Feenstra (1988a) finds that this hypothesis is accepted in all years except 1985, and so it is imposed on the subsequent estimation except for that year.

In columns (3) and (4) of Table 8.4, we reestimate the regressions for cars and trucks, while imposing the cross-equation restraint (8.22) for $t = 1981, \ldots, 84$. Notice that this reduces the standard errors on the specific price increases for cars substantially. By 1984–85, the impact of the VER is to increase the price of cars by about $1,000 on average. This is an estimate of the pure price increase due to the quota, after correcting for changes in the characteristics of Japanese cars. Multiplying this by the average 1984–85 imports of some 2.2 million, we obtain an estimate of the quota rents of $2.2 billion annually in 1984–85.

This estimate equals lower end of the quota rents for autos shown in Table 8.1. Where do the higher estimates come from? It turns out that

---

[18] Utility vehicles are given the same hedonic coefficients β^* as trucks, but use the year coefficients s_t and α_t of cars, since utility vehicles were subject to the VER.

[19] This can be thought of as a pass-through of 0.75 from the 21% increase in tariff to a 16% increase in retail price. This is somewhat higher than the pass-through of 0.58 for the truck tariff estimated in Feenstra 1989 and discussed in the previous chapter.

along with the increase in Japanese car prices, European producers selling in the U.S. also raised their prices substantially—by nearly one-third, as estimated by Dinopoulos and Kreinin (1988). They calculate a U.S. welfare loss due to this increase in European prices of some $3.4 billion in 1984, which exceeds the loss due to quota rents transferred to Japan. This nicely illustrates the result argued by Harris (1985) and Krishna (1989), that a VER will act as a "facilitating practice" and leads to more collusive behavior in the market where it is imposed. For American small cars we also show a substantial increase in prices at the bottom of Table 8.3: by 21% from 1979–80 and 17% from 1980–81. Some of this increase occurred before the VER, but it appears that this quota allowed American producers to maintain and continue large prices increases.

What about the change in product quality for Japanese imports? In fact, there was a considerable upgrading of model characteristics at just the time that the VER was imposed. In Table 8.3, we show the "unit-quality," which is computed as $(\alpha_0 + \beta' z_{it})$ and then averaged across all models. This increases by 8.8% from 1980 to 1981, and another 7.9% over 1981–82 and 7.3% over 1982–83. The dollar increase in quality over 1980–85 is $1,650, which reflects higher values of the characteristics applied to each model. This vastly exceeds the quality change for trucks or U.S. small cars as shown in Table 8.3. These observations strongly support the theoretical prediction that Japanese producers raised characteristics to increase the quality of cars due to the VER, but this did not occur under the ad valorem tariff in trucks.

Aside from characteristics, recall that there is a second way that average quality can increase following the VER, and that is from shifting *demand* towards the highest-quality products because their effective prices have the lowest percentage increase in prices. Evidence supporting this "Washington apples" effect can also be seen from Table 8.3. In addition to the unit-value and unit-quality, we show there a price and quality index. The difference between the unit-value and price index is that the former uses the quantity sold of each car *in that year* as a weight in forming the average, whereas the price index uses *fixed weights from year to year* when forming the index.[20] In other words, a shift in demand towards more expensive models will increase the unit-value, but will have no effect on the price index. It follows that the *ratio of the unit-value to the price index* can be used as a measure of "product mix," that is, an increase in the unit-value exceeding the price index indicates that demand has shifted towards more expensive models.

---

[20] The price and quality indexes shown in Table 8.3 are constructed as the Fisher Ideal index. The formula for this index is discussed in Appendix A, and you are asked to calculate this index in empirical exercises 8.1 and 8.4.

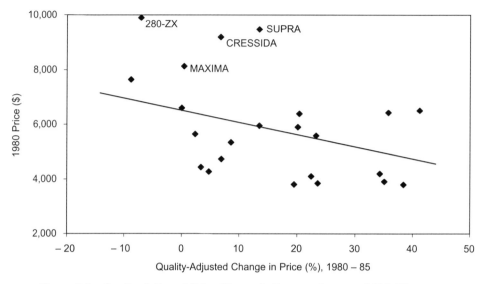

Figure 8.5   Quality-Adjusted Price Change in Japanese imports, 1980-85.

Returning to Table 8.3, we see that the unit-value indeed increased by more than the price index: the cumulative rise in the unit-value is $(8,153 - 5,175)/5,175 = 57.5\%$ over 1980–85, whereas the price index increased by 47.8%. Similarly, the cumulative rise in the unit-quality is $(6,130 - 4,473)/4,473 = 37\%$ over 1980–85, whereas the quality index increased by 30.6%. By either measure, there is a noticeable shift in demand towards the higher-priced and higher-quality cars, as predicted by the "Washington apples" effect. In addition, the change in the quality-adjusted prices (measured by $\Delta \ln p_{it} - \Delta \beta' z_{it}$) is graphed in Figure 8.5, for 1980–85. It can be seen that many of the highest-priced models had below-average increases in their quality-adjusted price, as predicted by (8.16).

We note that the nonuniform change in prices illustrated in Figure 8.5 can be expected to have a deadweight loss (as compared to a uniform percentage change in prices). A formula for measuring the deadweight loss is developed in Boorstein and Feenstra (1991), who studied quality upgrading due to the "Washington applies" effect for the quota on U.S. steel imports during 1969–74.[21] That formula was extended to incorporate rising characteristics due to the autos VER by Feenstra (1993), who finds that the deadweight loss is high: between one-quarter and one-third of the

---

[21] Goolsbee (2003) applies this formula to measure the deadweight loss due to nonuniform capital taxation.

value of quality upgrading in each year, or about $500 by 1985. This loss is *in addition* to the foregone rents of about $1,000 per imported Japanese car in 1984–85, which indicates that the deadweight loss of quality change adds a substantial component to the welfare cost of the VER.[22]

Our estimate of the quota rents over 1980–85 can be compared to other studies. Ries (1993) studies the change in stock prices of Japanese auto producers and parts suppliers during the weeks in 1981 when this policy was being formulated. He finds strong evidence of positive returns to the stocks of Japanese auto producers during this period, though only after it became clear that MITI would administer the quotas to each producer (so that they would capture the rents). In contrast, only the largest parts suppliers obtain abnormal stock during this period. Further supportive evidence is obtained by Goldberg (1995), who finds that the VER was binding in 1983–84 and 1986–87, with the highest rents in the earlier years.

The only study to question this conclusion is Berry, Levinsohn, and Pakes (1999) (hereafter BLP), who argue that the VER was *not binding* in the early years and became binding in 1986. They obtain the highest estimates for the price effect of the quota (like s_t in our notation) in the years 1987–90. This is a puzzling finding, since from Table 8.2 we know that Japanese imports fell short of the VER limit during March 1987–April 1988 and in later years. For the remainder of this section, we discuss possible explanations for the differing findings of Feenstra (1988a) and BLP.

We begin by extending our sample from 1979 to 1985, used in the regressions of Table 8.4, to 1979–90. The new estimates of the car and truck regressions (8.20) and (8.21) are shown in Table 8.5. In columns (1) and (2) we report the car and truck regressions without any cross-equation constraints, while in columns (3) and (4) we make use of the constraint in (8.22) for $t = 1981, \ldots, 84$.[23] As before, making use of this cross-equation constraint is effective in reducing the standard errors of the specific price increases.

Including the additional five years of data turns out to have a substantial impact on some of the hedonic coefficients: for example, the coefficient on width in the car regression is much higher than in Table 8.4, while the coefficient on horsepower is smaller. With this change in the hedonic coefficients, the specific price effect of the VER in the *early years is reduced* somewhat: in 1984, we estimate a price increase due to the VER of $812 in column (3) of Table 8.5, as compared with $1,104 in column (3) of

---

[22] The deadweight loss due to quality change under quotas in U.S. dairy imports is estimated by Anderson (1985, 1988). Anderson and Neary (1996) develop general methods for measuring the deadweight loss of nonuniform tariff or quota structures.

[23] As in note 18, utility vehicles are given the same hedonic coefficients $\beta^\star$ as trucks, but using the year coefficients s_t and α_t of cars, since utility vehicles were subject to the VER.

TABLE 8.5

Hedonic Regression for Japanese Cars and Trucks, 1979–90, with Price as Dependent Variable

	Cars (1)	Trucks (2)	Cars (3)	Trucks (4)
Constant	4.05*	6.96*	4.61*	6.58*
	(1.25)	(1.25)	(0.77)	(0.42)
Weight (tons)	0.48*	0.49*	0.37*	0.48*
	(0.20)	(0.09)	(0.14)	(0.09)
Width (feet)	0.82*	0.07	0.73*	0.16*
	(0.21)	(0.06)	(0.13)	(0.08)
Height (feet)	−0.27*	−0.03	−0.22*	−10.07
	(0.10)	(0.05)	(0.07)	(0.06)
Horsepower (100)	0.42*	0.36*	0.42*	0.35*
	(0.09)	(0.08)	(0.07)	(0.09)
Transmission	0.16*	0.09	0.14*	0.09*
(5-speed or auto)	(0.05)	(0.02)	(0.04)	(0.02)
Power steering	0.16*	0.01	0.15	−0.002
	(0.05)	(0.06)	(0.03)	(0.05)
Air conditioning	0.15*		0.15*	
	(0.05)		(0.04)	
Four-wheel drive		0.09		0.30*
		(0.10)		(0.06)

Year dummy	Cars Proportional	Cars Specific	Trucks Proportional	Cars Proportional	Cars Specific	Trucks Proportional
Year 1980	−0.04		−0.01	−0.03		−0.03
	(0.07)		(0.02)	(0.03)		(0.03)
Year 1981	0.06	256	0.31*	0.16*	−137	0.32*
	(0.13)	(472)	(0.06)	(0.05)	(283)	(0.05)
Year 1982	0.09	360	0.31*	0.17	43	0.33*
	(0.13)	(512)	(0.06)	(0.05)	(305)	(0.05)
Year 1983	0.05	510	0.19*	0.06	523*	0.22*
	(0.13)	(482)	(0.04)	(0.05)	(252)	(0.05)
Year 1984	0.09	695	0.20*	0.07	812*	0.23*
	(0.12)	(477)	(0.05)	(0.05)	(254)	(0.05)
Year 1985	0.23*	60	0.05*	0.22*	59	0.06*
	(0.07)	(93)	(0.02)	(0.05)	(67)	(0.02)
Year 1986	0.28*	672	0.21*	0.26*	726	0.24*
	(0.13)	(602)	(0.05)	(0.09)	(515)	(0.06)
Year 1987	0.36*	1317*	0.19*	0.34*	1164*	0.22*
	(0.13)	(583)	(0.05)	(0.09)	(502)	(0.06)
Year 1988	0.41*	859	0.05	0.43*	502	0.10
	(0.14)	(1067)	(0.15)	(0.10)	(886)	(0.12)
Year 1989	0.40*	852	0.11	0.47*	−253	0.29*
	(0.15)	(1134)	(0.16)	(0.10)	(1021)	(0.12)
Year 1990	0.32*	850	0.21	0.42*	−550	0.43*
	(0.14)	(1123)	(0.17)	(0.10)	(1012)	(0.13)
Observations	404			404		
R^2	0.995			0.993		

Source: Updated from Feenstra 1988a, as in empirical exercise 8.5.

Note: Standard errors are in parentheses.

* Significant at 95 percent level.

Table 8.4. This price impact is small in 1985 in both tables, but the effect of the VER grows after that and peaks in 1987, where we estimate quota rents of $1,164 per vehicle in column (3) of Table 8.5. So by extending the sample, we find that the VER is still binding in 1987. After that year, however, our estimates give highly imprecise estimates of the price impact of the VER, ranging from positive in column (1) to negative in column (3), but in all cases *insignificantly different from zero*. Consistent with the fact that Japanese exports to the United States fell short of the VER limit, we do not identify any significant impact of this trade restriction on prices after 1987.

In contrast, BLP continue to find a significant price impact of the VER through 1990, but no significant effect before 1986. I believe that the reason for this has to do with the way that BLP model the supply side of the market. They model marginal costs for Japanese producers as determined by time trends and wages, with the exchange rate entering insignificantly. This formulation predicts that a steady increase in prices would have occurred over 1980–85 *even without* the VER, so the VER does not appear to be binding in their estimates. But this predicted increase in prices is contradicted by the *actual* movement in truck prices, which rose due to the tariff in 1980–81 but were quite stable or fell in some years after this (see Table 8.3). The free-trade change in car prices that we have used is the same as for trucks, correcting for the tariff as in (8.22). Therefore, we are using a *lower* increase in free-trade car prices than BLP, which accounts for difference in our findings through 1985.

We find that, like BLP, the VER is binding in 1986 and 1987, but after this time we begin to estimate a rather large *proportional* increase in car prices, so the *specific* price effect of the VER becomes smaller and insignificant. In contrast, the free-trade increase in prices allowed by BLP is still dominated by the time trends and wages entering marginal costs, and it turns out that these are not enough to explain the actual increase in Japanese prices: hence, they estimate that the VER is binding after 1987, even though actual exports fell short of the VER limit.

Export Subsidies

We turn now to our second major topic for the chapter, which is the application of export subsidies. These are used by developing and industrial countries alike to support their industries. There is little doubt that these subsidies are welcomed by the firms receiving them, and this might explain their use in a political economy model, as we examine in the next chapter. But in this chapter we are concerned with social welfare, which means that the *revenue cost* of the subsidies must be counted against any increase in profits of the receiving industries: only if the revenue cost is *less*

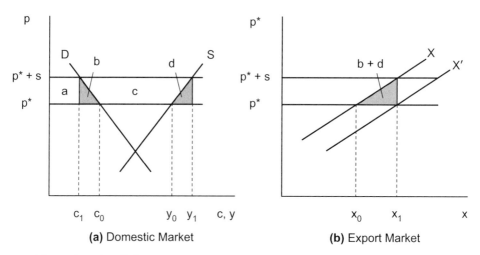

Figure 8.6   Small Country.

than the net change in producer plus consumer surplus are the subsidies in the national interest. As we shall see, this cannot occur in a two-good model with perfect competition, and after presenting these results we will consider other frameworks.

Perfect Competition

We consider first the case of a small country, in Figure 8.6. In panel (a) we show the domestic demand D and supply S curves, together with the constant world price p^*. Under free trade, domestic demand is at c_0 and supply at y_0, so exports are $x_0 = y_0 - c_0$. This is shown in panel (b), which graphs the domestic export supply curve $X = S - D$. We can think of the fixed world price p^* as establishing a horizontal import demand curve from the rest of the world, which intersects X at the equilibrium exports x_0.

Now suppose that firms in the home industry are given a subsidy of s dollars per unit exported. With this subsidy, the home industry would be able to earn $p^* + s$ on all quantities that are exported. Accordingly, firms in this industry would be unwilling to sell at home for anything less than that amount, and the domestic price must also rise to $p^* + s$. At this price, domestic demand falls to c_1 and supply rises to y_1, so exports rise to the amount $x_1 = y_1 - c_1$. This corresponds to a *rightward shift* of the domestic export supply curve in panel (b), because at the same international price of p^*, exports have increased from x_0 to x_1. Equivalently, the export supply curve shifts downward, from X to X', by the amount of the subsidy s.[24]

---

[24] This downward shift of the export supply curve occurs because we are measuring the international price p^* on the vertical axis of panel (b), in both Figure 8.6 and Figure 8.7.

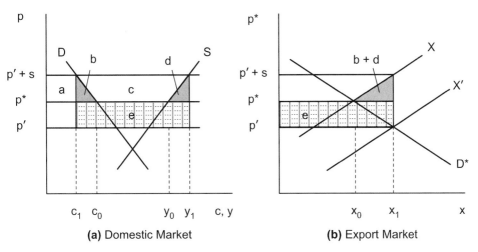

Figure 8.7   Large Country.

The welfare effect of the subsidy can be ready calculated in panel (a) as $-(a + b)$ consumer surplus loss $+(a + b + c)$ producer surplus gain $-(b + c + d)$ subsidy cost $= -(b + d)$, which is always negative. Area $b + d$ is the deadweight loss of the subsidy, and is also shown as the triangle under the export supply curve in panel (b). This area is analogous to the deadweight loss that we found for a tariff, in the last chapter. Therefore, the small country also loses due to an export subsidy.

Consider now the case of a large country, in Figure 8.7. In panel (b), we show again the rightward shift of the domestic export supply curve, from X to X'. Because this country is a large producer in world markets, it faces a downward-sloping demand curve D^* from the rest of the world. Therefore, the rightward shift of its export supply curve leads to a *fall* in the price of its exports, from p^* to p'. The exporting country experiences a decline in its terms of trade, which leads to a *further* welfare loss. In Figure 8.7, the deadweight loss of the export subsidy is still shown by the triangle $b + d$, while the terms of trade loss is shown by the rectangle e, so the welfare loss is the sum of these. So unlike the case of an import tariff, which improved the terms of trade gain and potentially raised welfare for a large country under perfect competition, we see that the export subsidy leads to an unambiguous welfare loss.

Many Goods

The above demonstration that export subsidies cannot be welfare improving implicitly assumed two goods—the export good in question and another good used to balance trade in the background (for example, the additively separable numeraire good introduced at the beginning of chapter 7). If there are other goods in the economy, then their prices are being held fixed (in terms of the numeraire). But what if there are other goods whose international prices *also change* with the export subsidy on the good in question. Is it possible for these other goods to have a terms of trade gain, which might overcome the terms of trade loss on the good being subsidized? If so, then the exporting country could gain from the subsidy.

Feenstra (1986) considers a three-good model where a subsidy on one export, which lowers its price, can nevertheless improve the overall terms of trade for a country and therefore be welfare improving. The condition to ensure this is that the subsidized good and the other export are sufficiently strong *complements*. In that case, the subsidy can lead to an increase in demand and price for the other export good that is enough to offset the terms of trade loss on the subsidized good. A simple example (not drawn from international trade) is the subsidy to travel, lodging, and food offered by many casinos as a way to attract customers: the casino recovers more than enough from gambling revenues to make this subsidy profitable.

The difficulty with the three-good example is that the results are very sensitive to the cross-elasticities in demand and production, about which it is difficult for researchers (let alone a government) to have accurate information. So is there a case where subsidies might be welfare improving even without relying on detailed elasticity information? It turns out that there is, and this due to Itoh and Kiyono (1987). These authors consider a Ricardian model with a continuum of goods, originally due to Dornbusch, Fischer, and Samuelson (1977). We have already used the Heckscher-Ohlin model with a continuum of goods in chapter 3, and the Ricardian version is simpler in that it uses only one factor—labor. Without presenting this model in detail, we will summarize the results found by Itoh and Kiyono.

The assumption of the Ricardian model is that countries differ in their technologies. Denote the continuum of goods by $z \in [0, 1]$, and let $a^*(z)$ denote the labor needed per unit of production abroad, while $a(z)$ is the labor needed per unit of production at home. We order these goods such that $a^*(z)/a(z)$ is *declining* in z, meaning that the home country has a comparative advantage in the goods of lowest index z. In equilibrium, the "borderline" good z' will have prices that are equal across countries, so that $wa(z') = w^* a^*(z')$, where w and w^* are wages at home and abroad. Then the home country will be producing and exporting goods in the range $[0, z')$, while the foreign country will be producing and exporting goods in the range $(z', 1]$. Notice that relative wages are determined in equilibrium by $w/w^* = a^*(z')/a(z')$.

Itoh and Kiyono first consider a home export subsidy of s to *all goods exported*. This has the effect of expanding the range of exports from $[0, z')$

to $[0, z_1)$, with $z_1 > z'$. The new borderline good satisfies $[wa(z_1) - s] = w^* a^*(z_1)$, where $wa(z_1)$ is the home price for that good and $[wa(z_1) - s]$ is the subsidized export price. Simplifying this equation, relative wages are

$$\frac{w}{w^*} - \left(\frac{s}{w^* a(z_1)} \right) = \frac{a^*(z_1)}{a(z_1)}. \tag{8.23}$$

As suggested by this equation, the direct effect of an export subsidy is to *raise* the relative home wage. There is also an indirect effect through the increase in z_1, which lowers $a^*(z_1)/a(z_1)$, but the net outcome is still an increase in w/w^* due to the subsidy $s > 0$.

However, with a subsidy granted to *all* home exports, the increase in relative wages does not lead to a welfare gain. The reason is that the revenue cost of the subsidy is too great: this cost would be a tax on labor, so that home labor earns $w - [s/a(z_1)]$ in its after-tax wage. The ratio of this after-tax wage to the wage of foreign workers is shown on the left side of (8.23). But since the right side of (8.23) is declining in z_1, then so is the relative after-tax wage on the left. So despite the fact that *gross* wages are increasing at home, the *net after-tax wage* falls relative to that abroad with the expansion of z_1, so the uniform export subsidy fails to raise home welfare.

Now consider instead a *targeted* export subsidy $s(z)$, which applies only to those goods in a range $[z_0, z_1]$, with $z_0 < z' < z_1$. Home workers still receive an increase in their relative wages w/w^*, as suggested by (8.23). But now the revenue cost of the subsidy can be lowered by suitable choice of z_0. All goods below this cutoff do not receive any export subsidy, but since relative home wages have been increased, they will sell in international markets at a higher relative price. Therefore, the increase in home wages corresponds to a *terms of trade increase* for those goods not receiving the subsidy. Indeed, Itoh and Kiyono demonstrate that by choosing z_0 and z_1 sufficiently close to z', the revenue cost of the subsidy is of the second order of smalls, whereas the terms of trade gain (which applies to all goods in the range $[0, z_0]$), is of the first order.[25] Therefore, the exporting country is better off.

The idea that a country might gain through *targeted* export subsidies is an intriguing one, which deserves more attention. Rodrik 1995b is among the few papers that takes targeted subsidies seriously, and he explores the ability of these policies to work in various countries.[26] That paper is recommended for further reading.

[25] The precise form of the export subsidy needed to raise welfare is described in Itoh and Kiyono 1987. Notice that goods below z' need to be subsidized since otherwise, with the increase in w, these goods would not longer be exported. Having such "gaps" in the range of exported goods needs to be avoided to raise welfare.

[26] See also World Bank 1993, which makes a strong distinction between export promotion programs (or "contests") that are run efficiently and those that are not.

Subsidies with Imperfect Competition

We next consider the effects of export subsidies under imperfect competition. In particular, suppose that a single home firm and a single foreign firm sell to a third market. The standard example here is sales of Boeing versus Airbus to a third market (such as China). We are interested in whether the home government can give its own firm a "strategic" advantage by subsidizing it. We shall require that the subsidy also be in the *national* interest, which means that profits for the exporter need to rise by more than the amount of the subsidy itself. We initially assume Cournot-Nash competition, as in Brander and Spencer (1985). Eaton and Grossman (1986) contrast the results from that case to Bertrand competition, as we shall also discuss.

Cournot Duopoly

We let x denote the sales of the home firm and x^* the sales of the foreign firm to the third market. We will treat x and x^* as differentiated products, so the home firm earns the price $p(x, x^*)$ and the foreign firm earns $p^*(x, x^*)$. It will be sufficient for our purposes to study the profit maximization of the home firm, as the foreign firm's problem is similar. Home profits from exporting are

$$\pi = p(x, x^*)x - C(x). \tag{8.24}$$

Maximizing this over the choice of x, the first-order condition is

$$\pi_x = p(x, x^*) + xp_x - C'(x) = 0, \tag{8.25}$$

and the second-order condition is $\pi_{xx} = 2p_x + xp_{xx} - C'' < 0$.

Using (8.25), we also solve for home exports x as a function of foreign sales x^*, written as the reaction curve $x = r(x^*)$. This reaction curve and the foreign counterpart $x^* = r^*(x)$ are graphed as RR and R*R* in Figure 8.8, and their intersection determines the Cournot equilibrium denoted by point C. The typical property of these reaction curves is that they are both downward sloping. For stability, the home reaction curve RR needs to cut the foreign reaction curve R*R* from above, as illustrated.[27] Notice that the iso-profit curves of π have higher profits in the downwards direction (i.e., for reduced x^*), and similarly the iso-profit curves π^* have higher foreign profits in the leftward direction (for reduced x), as illustrated.

---

[27] In problem 7.3, you are asked to derive these properties of the reaction curves.

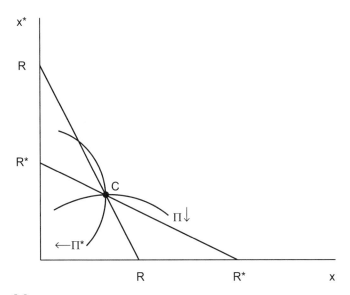

Figure 8.8

Now consider the impact of an export subsidy. Letting $p(x, x^*)$ denote the price paid by the buyer and s denote the *specific* subsidy, then $p(x, x^*) + s$ is the subsidized price received by the home firm. Home profits are, therefore,

$$\pi = [p(x, x^*) + s]x - C(x). \tag{8.26}$$

Maximizing this over the choice of x, the first-order condition is

$$\pi_x = p(x, x^*) + s + xp_x - C'(x) = 0, \tag{8.27}$$

where (8.27) defines a new reaction curve $x = r(x^*, s)$. To check how this reaction curve depends on the subsidy s, totally differentiate (8.27) to obtain

$$\frac{dx}{ds} = -\frac{1}{\pi_{xx}} > 0,$$

where this sign is obtained from the second-order condition for maximizing (8.26).

Thus, in Figure 8.9 the export subsidy unambiguously shifts the home reaction curve to the right, from RR to R′R′, so the equilibrium moves from point C to point D. Under the case we have shown with both reaction curves downward sloping, this will increase home exports x and reduce foreign exports x^*. It is readily confirmed that this will raise home profits, which is not surprising. Our interest is not just in the profits of the home firm, however, but in *social welfare*, defined as the profits earned by

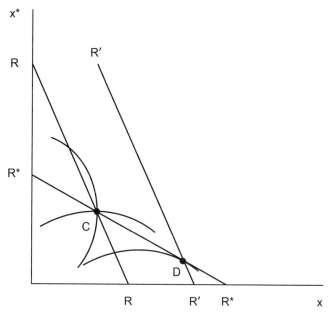

Figure 8.9

the home firm in the third market *minus* the revenue cost of the subsidy.[28] Since the subsidy cost is the amount sx, welfare becomes

$$W = [p(x, x^\star) + s]x - C(x) - sx = p(x, x^\star)x - C(x). \qquad (8.28)$$

Notice that the expression on the right side of (8.28) is identical to the *original* expression for home profits in (8.24). That is, by taking the subsidized profits in (8.26), and subtracting the amount of subsidy, we get back the initial profits. This means that the original iso-profit curves for the home firm, such as illustrated by π in Figure 8.8, now measure social welfare.

The difference between profits in (8.24) and social welfare in (8.28), however, is that they are evaluated at *different equilibrium quantities* $(x, x^\star)$. Whereas initial profits are evaluated at point C, the subsidy moves the equilibrium to point D. This clearly *increases* home welfare (since the iso-profit and welfare contours are increasing in the downward direction). Indeed, an *optimal* subsidy would be one for which the welfare contour is just tangent to the foreign reaction curve R*R*, as illustrated in Figure 8.9 at point D. We see that under Cournot-Nash competition, the export subsidy by the home government leads to a welfare improvement.

---

[28] Since the home and foreign firms are both operating in a third market, there is no impact on home consumers, so we do not need to take this into account in social welfare.

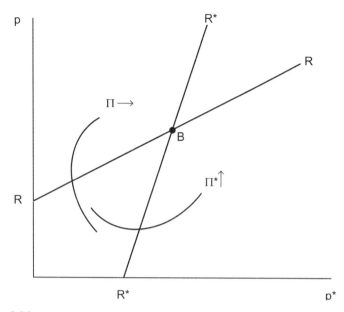

Figure 8.10

Bertrand Duopoly

We now contrast the results obtained above to a Bertrand duopoly, when the home and foreign firms are each choosing prices as the strategic variable, rather than quantities. Denote exports of the home firms to the third market by $x(p, p^*)$, where p is the price paid by the buyer. Letting s denote the *specific* subsidy, then $(p + s)$ is the subsidized price received by the home firm. Home profits are, therefore,

$$\pi = (p + s)x(p, p^*) - C[x(p, p^*)]. \qquad (8.29)$$

Maximizing this over the choice of p, the first-order condition is

$$\pi_p = x(p, p^*) + (p + s)x_p - C'(x)x_p = 0. \qquad (8.30)$$

Given the foreign price p^* and the subsidy, we can use (8.30) to solve for home export price p, obtaining the reaction curve $p = r(p^*, s)$. The analogous condition for the foreign exporter can be used to solve for foreign reaction curve $p^* = r^*(p)$. These are illustrated in Figure 8.10, with the typical properties that they are upward sloping and have a *dampened* response of each price to that of the competing good, so that

$$\frac{dp}{dp^*} \frac{p^*}{p} = r_{p^*}(p^*, s)\frac{p^*}{p} < 1, \quad \text{and} \quad \frac{dp^*}{dp} \frac{p}{p^*} = r_p^*(p)\frac{p}{p^*} < 1.^{29}$$

[29] In problem 7.6 you are asked to demonstrate these properties of the reaction curves.

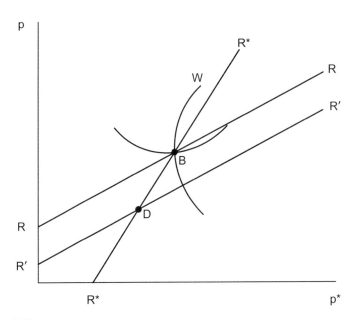

Figure 8.11

With a zero subsidy, the intersection of these determines the Bertrand equilibrium, at point B in Figure 8.10. The iso-profit curves of π have higher profits in the rightward direction (i.e., for higher p^*), and similarly the iso-profit curves π^* have higher foreign profits in the upward direction (for higher p), as illustrated.

Now consider how the application of an export subsidy shifts the home reaction curve. Totally differentiating (8.30), we obtain

$$\frac{dp}{ds} = -\frac{x_p}{\pi_{pp}} < 0, \tag{8.31}$$

where the sign of (8.31) is obtained because $x_p < 0$, and $\pi_{pp} < 0$ from the second-order condition for profit maximization. Thus, (8.31) shows that the export subsidy will unambiguously *lower* the price charged by the home firm for its exports (given the foreign price). In Figure 8.11, the equilibrium is moved from point B to a point like D.

To see how this affects home welfare, we again subtract the cost of the subsidy from (8.29) to obtain home welfare:

$$\begin{aligned} W &= (p + s)x(p, p^*) - C[x(p, p^*)] - sx(p, p^*) \\ &= px(p, p^*) - C[x(p, p^*)]. \end{aligned} \tag{8.32}$$

In (8.32), we once again obtain a measure of welfare that is identical to home profits in the absence of the export subsidy. This is shown by the iso-profit curve labeled π in Figure 8.10 and W in Figure 8.11, and increases in the rightward direction, that is, when the foreign price p^* increases. It is clear from Figure 8.11 that the export subsidy, by leading to a *fall* in prices, has *reduced* home welfare. The reason is that any increase in home profits—measured inclusive of the subsidy—is more than offset by the revenue cost of the subsidy, so that profits measured without the subsidy—which equals welfare—have declined.

In order for the home country to gain from an export policy, it must impose an export *tax* rather than a subsidy. This has the effect of moving the equilibrium above B, upwards along R^*R^* in Figure 8.11, and raising home welfare due to the increase in prices. These results are summarized with the theorem that follows.

Theorem (Brander and Spencer 1985; Eaton and Grossman 1986)

(a) Under Cournot duopoly, a subsidy to exports raises home welfare.
(b) Under Bertrand duopoly, a tax on exports raises home welfare.

Part (b), due to Eaton and Grossman (1986), shows that any "strategic" use of export subsidies is extremely sensitive to the form of competition. Since we do not expect the government to be able to distinguish the market conduct, it becomes impossible to implement these policies in a welfare-improving manner. Furthermore, even if the government knew that a market was operating under Bertrand competition, the home firm would generally oppose this policy, and in practice export taxes are rarely used.[30]

Eaton and Grossman have extended this theorem to discuss other forms of market conduct, which we do not cover. Regardless of the form of competition, however, there are a number of other reasons why export subsidies should not be expected to generate a welfare improvement. First, as we found with a tariff, the possible gains for the home country can be dissipated by free entry into the industry, so that profits are reduced to zero. This was demonstrated by Horstmann and Markusen (1986).

Second, we have assumed above that the home exporter takes the subsidy as exogenous; that is, the government sets the export subsidy in the first stage of the game, with the home and foreign firm competing in the second. But Carmichael (1987) argues that in the case of financing for export credits (such as provided by the U.S. Export-Import Bank to

---

[30] An interesting exception is the tax applied to U.S. exports of cotton in the Antebellum period, as discussed by Irwin (2002b).

purchasers of U.S.-produced aircraft), these subsidies should instead be viewed as endogenous: the government essentially guarantees a low interest rate to the buyers of aircraft in the second stage of the game, with firms optimizing over price in the first stage. In that case, Carmichael shows that even under Cournot competition the export subsidies no longer improve welfare. This result is similar in spirit to what we found in the previous chapter for antidumping duties, which fail to be welfare improving for the importing country when the foreign exporter treats them as endogenous.

Third, it may well be the case that exporters differ in their productivities, which are not observable to the government. Brainard and Martimort (1997) have analyzed this possibility in the context of Cournot competition between home and foreign exporters. With multiple home exporters, the home government needs to design a subsidy policy that induces them to truthfully reveal their productivities. It turns out that only the most efficient firms receive subsidies in this case, whereas the least efficient may very well be taxed.

Finally, even if the above concerns do not apply, the foreign country could very well respond by applying subsidies of its own. In that way, the two exporters end up in a "subsidy war," which lowers welfare for both of them but raises welfare for the importing country.[31] Of course, this concern also arises with tariffs, where a tariff applied by one country can invite retaliation by the foreign country and both countries can loose from this tariff war. This will be discussed in more detail in the next chapter. Interestingly, Janeba (1998) shows that when firms can choose their country of production, the incentive to use *nondiscriminatory* subsidies is greatly diminished, since these subsidies apply equally well to home firms and foreign firms located in the home market. In that case, Janeba finds that *zero subsidies* is the only equilibrium of the subsidy game between the countries, so that insisting on nondiscrimination is a simple device to assure this outcome.

Conversely, there are several reasons why export subsidies may be welfare improving regardless of the form of market conduct. Subsidies are often given to R&D rather than exports. Since R&D is a fixed cost that a firm must incur, these subsidies will influence the decision of a firm to enter the market or not. Dixit and Kyle (1985) investigate export subsidies in a model where these may deter entry by foreigners and encourage domestic entry, and find that they may be beneficial. Related to this issue is Maggi's (1996) investigation of subsidies to capacity rather than exports, in a model that is general enough to include both Bertrand and Cournot competition. He finds that these subsidies are weakly welfare improving; that is, they will raise or leave unchanged the welfare of the exporting country. Finally, export subsidies may be used in markets where learning is

---

[31] See problem 8.5.

important: either producers learning about costs, or consumers learning about product quality. Bagwell (1991) has analyzed the case of consumers learning about quality and finds a first-order gain due to export subsidies. The case of falling costs is important in the manufacture of semiconductors, for example, and also aircraft.[32] Then similar to the infant-industry argument for a tariff, subsidies may possibly be welfare improving.

Subsidies to Commercial Aircraft

A favorite industry to study the impact of export subsidies is aircraft. In large passenger aircraft, there have been just three competitors in recent decades: Boeing and McDonnell-Douglas in the United States and Airbus in Europe. The former two companies merged on August 1, 1997, so the industry effectively became a duopoly. Various types of subsidies have been used in both the United States and Europe to support their respective firms, so this is an ideal case to evaluate the theoretical results described above.

The idea that two countries can be in a "subsidy war" appears to apply in this industry. Recognizing this possibility, the United States and the Europe Community reached an agreement in 1992, which limited subsidies to 33% of development costs (see Tyson 1992; and Pavcnik 2002). In addition, the agreement prohibits production subsidies and limits the ability of government agencies to subsidize the interest rate on purchases of aircraft. Irwin and Pavcnik (2001) find that as a result of this accord, prices for commercial aircraft rose by something between 3.1% and 8.8%. They estimate that the reduction in subsidies granted is somewhat higher than this amount—between 7.5% and 12.5%.

There are recent claims that the terms of the 1992 agreement are being violated by a new aircraft under development by Airbus. As described by Irwin and Pavcnik (2001), commercial aircraft are comprised of two distinct product types: narrow-body aircraft with a single aisle, including the Boeing 737, 757 and Airbus A-320; and wide-body aircraft with two aisles, including the Boeing 747, 777, and Airbus A-300. Airbus has now announced plans for the production of another wide-body aircraft, the A-380, which will be even larger than the Boeing 747 and will compete directly with the 747 in long flights. The expenditures to develop the A-380 are estimated to be $12 billion, of which the governments of France, Germany, the Netherlands, Belgium, Spain, Finland, and the United Kingdom are expected to cover up to one-third. This subsidy has led to a trade dispute between the

---

[32] A simulation model of subsidies to aircraft is presented by Baldwin and Krugman (1988b), and the dynamics of production and sales in this industry are estimated by Benkard (2000a, 2000b).

United States and Europe over whether financing of the A-380 violates the 1992 agreement (described in Pavcnik 2002).

The goal of Irwin and Pavcnik (2001) is to estimate demand and mark-ups for wide-body aircraft, and then simulate the effect of A-380 entry on the market equilibrium. Airbus has stated that it needs to produce at least 250 planes to cover the development costs, but that it expects to sell 1,500 aircraft over the next 20 years. It had received initial orders for 60 planes (as of early 2001), but these purchasers appear to have received a discount of at least 10%, and perhaps as high as 35%, off the list price of $235 million per plane. Boeing, on the other hand, states that market de-mand for such a superjumbo will not exceed 700 aircraft over the next 20 years. We can expect the estimation of market demand and prices, and the simulation of A-380 entry, to inform us as to which projection (700 planes or 1,500 planes) is more accurate.

Demand for a differentiated product depends on the quality-adjusted prices, which we wrote earlier as $q_i = p_i/f(z_i)$. Suppose that we instead mea-sure quality-adjusted prices q_i by the *difference* between nominal prices p_i and quality $f(z_i)$. In addition, we assume that quality is a linear function of char-acteristics, so the quality-adjusted prices become $q_j = \alpha p_j - \beta' z_j - \xi_j$. In this notation, ξ_j reflects unmeasured characteristics of product j, which we treat as a random variable. Then the logit specification of demand is

$$s_i = \frac{e^{-q_i}}{\left[\sum_{j=1}^{N} e^{-q_j}\right]} = \frac{e^{\beta' z_i - \alpha p_i + \xi_i}}{\left[\sum_{j=1}^{N} e^{\beta' z_j - \alpha p_j + \xi_j}\right]}, \tag{8.33}$$

where s_i denotes the *market share* of product i, measured by quantity de-manded of product i relative to total quantity of all products $j = 1, \ldots, N$. As shown in Appendix B, the logit specification in (8.33) arises quite nat-urally from a discrete choice model and can also be viewed as the demand from a representative consumer using McFadden's aggregation theorem.

To estimate the parameters of (8.33), we take logs and difference with an "outside" good indexed by 0, to obtain

$$\ln s_i - \ln s_0 = \beta' z_i - \alpha p_i + \xi_i, \tag{8.34}$$

where the quality-adjusted price q_0 of the "outside" good is normalized to zero. Thus, in (8.34) we regress the difference in market shares on the prices and characteristics of product i, to estimate the parameters (α, β). The approach can be contrasted with the hedonic regression in (8.17), where we are regressing *prices* on characteristics, while in (8.34) we are regressing *market shares* on characteristics and price. In both cases, we interpret β as the consumer valuation of characteristics. We can think of (8.34) as an alterna-tive procedure to the hedonic regression, as proposed by Berry (1994).

Irwin and Pavcnik treat wide-body aircraft as differentiated into two market segments: those for medium-range and those for long-range trips. Denoting the products in each of these two groups by J_g, for $g = 1, 2$, it is shown by Berry (see Appendix B) that the quantity-share of demand for each type of aircraft is rewritten as

$$\ln s_i - \ln s_0 = \beta' z_i - \alpha p_i + \rho \ln s_{i|g} + \xi_i, \qquad i \in J_g, \qquad (8.35)$$

where s_i is the share of demand for wide-body aircraft i relative to all aircraft purchased annually; s_0 is share of demand for narrow-body aircraft (treated as the "outside" good); and $s_{i|g}$ is the share of wide-body aircraft i *within* the medium range or long-range group $g = 1, 2$. We expect that the parameter ρ is positive but less than unity, and Irwin and Pavcnik estimate ρ as 0.41 (standard error of 0.17) in their preferred specification.[33] This means that long-range wide-body aircraft are closer substitutes for each other than they are for medium-range aircraft. For example, the A-380 will compete more with the Boeing 747 than with the other medium-range aircraft sold by Airbus.

We can also use the demand equation (8.35) to obtain the optimal prices for multiproduct firms. Irwin and Pavcnik consider both Bertrand and Cournot competition, but we focus here on the former case. Suppose that the total demand for aircraft (wide-body plus narrow-body) is given by H units per year. The demand for each model is then $s_i H$. If the firm in question sells products $i = 1, \dots, M$, then its profit maximization problem is

$$\max_{p_i} \sum_{i=1}^{M} [p_i - g_i(z_i)] s_i H, \qquad (8.36)$$

where $g_i(z_i)$ denotes marginal costs. Maximizing this over the choice of prices p_i, we obtain the first-order conditions

$$s_i + \sum_{j=1}^{M} [p_j - g_j(z_j)] \frac{\partial s_j}{\partial p_i} = 0, \qquad i = 1, \dots, M. \qquad (8.37)$$

To simplify this expression, the derivatives of the market shares can be calculated from (8.35) and substituted into (8.37). In addition, we suppose that marginal costs are linear in characteristics, so $g_i(z_i) = \gamma' z_i + \omega_i$, where ω_i is a random error.

Irwin and Pavcnik (2001) estimate the demand parameters from (8.35) and substitute these into (8.37) in order to compute the markups. They

---

[33] When estimating (8.35) we need to use instruments to correct for the endogeneity of both $s_{i|g}$ and price on the right side, and the estimate of 0.41 comes when using the widest set of instruments.

find that these markups are high: current prices are about twice as high as marginal costs (under either Bertrand or Cournot competition), and even higher in past years. Having obtained estimates of demand and markups, they then simulate the effect of A-380 entry into the market. On the demand side, we know that this plane will be a close substitute for other long-range, wide-body aircraft such as the Boeing 747. But on the pricing side, having multiproduct firms means that Airbus will be *less* concerned than Boeing about this new product stealing demand away from its existing products. That is, Boeing will respond more aggressively than Airbus in lowering its own prices to prevent market share from falling (since Airbus is happy to have demand shifted towards its own products). These predictions are borne out in the simulations. Relative to their previous sales, the percentage decline in demand is smaller for Boeing than for Airbus, because Boeing responds more aggressively in cutting its prices. Nevertheless, including the new sales of A-380, the overall market share of Airbus increases.

How many of the new A-380s will Airbus sell? This depends, of course, on the price charged. Irwin and Pavcnik experiment with discounts from the list price of 0–30%. With the largest discount, they calculate that Airbus will sell 34 planes annually, or 680 over 20 years, yielding $110 billion in revenues. But annual sales of the A-380 are only one-half (one-quarter) as much when discounts of 20% (10%) are used instead, indicating that demand for the A-380 is highly elastic. High markups in this market are sustained because firms are selling multiple products, but at the full list price for the A-380, its demand is extremely low—only 4 or 5 planes annually, which would not cover development costs. Lack of detailed cost data means that we cannot estimate the profit-maximizing price for the A-380, but it is evident that high discounts are needed to achieve significant sales. Even with the 30% discount, however, demand falls well below the market projection of 1,500 planes made by Airbus. Rather, sales at that discount are closer to the 700 planes expected by Boeing, whose company representatives state that demand at that level will not allow the project to be profitable.

Conclusions

In the previous chapter, we identified three effects of a tariff on welfare: (*a*) a deadweight loss; (*b*) a terms of trade effect; (*c*) a reduction in the monopoly distortion if the output of home firms increase (without leading to inefficient entry). While we have not derived again the welfare criterion for an import quota, a similar decomposition would apply. However, any potential terms of trade gain becomes a loss if the importing country gives up the quota rents to the exporter, as under a VER. In that case, the only possible source of gain for the importing country would be under the third effect, if the import quota led to a significant increase in home output and offset a monopoly distortion. But we have found that the reverse case is more likely to hold: with either a home monopoly or Bertrand duopoly, the quota (say, at the free-trade level of imports) will lead to an increase in price and reduction in home quantity, so that the monopoly distortion is worsened rather than offset.

For export subsidies under perfect competition, the welfare criterion becomes: (*a*) a deadweight loss; (*b*) a terms of trade effect. Whereas the terms of trade will improve due to a tariff for a large country, it will instead *worsen* due to the export subsidy in a two-good model. We have noted, however, that with more goods there is the possibility that a subsidy on some goods will raise the terms of trade for others. The Ricardian model with a continuum of goods provides a good illustration and allows for welfare-improving export subsidies when they are targeted on a narrow range of goods. Determining whether this has occurred in any actual cases would be an interesting area for further research.

Under imperfect competition, the welfare criterion is simplified by considering sales to a third market. In that case the home firm earns profits from its export sales, and welfare is simply the difference between these and the revenue cost of the subsidy. This provides the clearest example of a potential role for "strategic" trade policy in shifting profits towards the home firm. As we have seen, however, subsidies may or may not be desirable: under Cournot competition export subsidies raise welfare, but under Bertrand competition they do not. Since it is very difficult to know the type of competition being used by firms, it becomes impossible for the government to implement this policy in a welfare-improving manner.

Empirically, the analyses of import quotas and export subsidies are linked because the industries involved are often producing discrete products, with multiproduct firms. This chapter has served as an introduction to the empirical techniques that can be used on such industries, including hedonic regressions and the estimation of demand and prices as in Berry 1994. The reader is referred to Appendix B for more details on discrete choice methods, which should be useful for many trade policy issues.

Problems

8.1 Suppose that the home and foreign firms are engaged in *Cournot* competition in the home market. Illustrate the free-trade equilibrium, and answer the following:

(a) Suppose that a VER is negotiated with the foreign firm, so that it agrees to *not sell more* than its free-trade quantity. What is the effect on the equilibrium?

(b) Suppose that the VER is negotiated at *below* the free-trade quantity. Show the effect on the equilibrium.

8.2 Suppose that the home firm and foreign firm are initially engaged in *Bertrand* competition in the home market, as discussed in the text. Suppose that the VER is negotiated at *below* the free-trade quantity. Show the effect on the equilibrium and on profits.

8.3 Building on problem 5.3 in chapter 5, consider the CES utility function written as in (8.2),

$$U = \sum_{i=1}^{N} a_i c_i^{\theta}, \quad \theta = (\sigma - 1)/\sigma,$$

where $a_i = f(z_i)^{\theta}$ is a transformation of the quality of each product, and can be treated as a parameter, $i = 1, \ldots, N$.

(a) Maximize this subject to the budget constraint, $\sum_{i=1}^{N} p_i c_i \leq I$, to obtain an expression for the demands c_i as a function of prices and income.
(b) Use these expressions to show that $\partial c_i / \partial p_j = \partial c_j / \partial p_i, i \neq j$.
(c) Also show that equation (8.9) holds, which we rewrite as

$$-\left(\sum_{j=1}^{M} \frac{\partial \ln c_i}{\partial \ln p_j}\right) = \sigma + (1 - \sigma)\left(\sum_{j=1}^{M} \frac{p_j c_i}{I}\right).$$

8.4 Consider the problem of maximizing profits subject to the VER constraint in (8.11). Using the same steps as in (8.6) to (8.9), show that the solution for prices is as in equation (8.15).

8.5 Consider a Cournot duopoly exporting to a third market, and suppose that *both* countries apply export subsidies. Illustrate where this "subsidy war" can end up; that is, illustrate the Nash equilibrium in subsidies for both governments.

Empirical Exercises

These exercises reproduce regression results from Feenstra 1988a. To complete the exercises, the files "car_7990.dta, truck_7990.dta" should be stored in c:\Empirical_Exercise\Chapter_8\. Then do the following:

8.1 Run the programs "pindex_c.do, pindex_t.do, unit_value.do" to reproduce the price indexes and unit-values for cars and trucks in Table 8.3. What formula is used for the price indexes, and how do these differ from the unit-values?

8.2 Run the program "car_reg.do" to reproduce column (1) in Table 8.4, and the program "truck_reg.do" to reproduce column (2). What weights are being used in the regression, and how does this affect the results?

8.3 Pooling car and truck data, run "system_7985.do" to reproduce columns (3) and (4) in Table 8.4 with the constraints specified in equation (8.22). How are these constraints built into the program for the non-linear regression?

8.4 Run the programs "unit_quality.do, qindex_c.do, qindex_t.do" to reproduce the quality indexes and unit-qualities for cars and trucks in Table 8.3. What formula is used for the quality of each model and the quality indexes, and how do these differ from the unit-qualities?

8.5 Pooling car and truck data, run "system_nocom.do" and "system_wcon.do" to reproduce columns (1)–(4) in Table 8.5, with constraints specified in equation (8.22).

Chapter 9

Political Economy of Trade Policy

IN THE PREVIOUS two chapters we have covered the basic analysis of trade policies, including models of imperfect competition. The idea that non-competitive markets give rise to opportunities for governments to gain from trade policies has been an important line of research. It has ultimately been concluded, however, that such opportunities for "strategic" use of trade policy are very limited. This raises the obvious question of why trade policies are used so often. One answer is that such policies are politically motivated: tariffs are granted in response to demands by special interest groups, such as industries and unions. The research issue is to understand how such demands are mediated through the political process. In this chapter we outline research on the political economy of protection, including the median voter model of Mayer (1984) and the "protection for sale" model of Grossman and Helpman (1994).

The "protection for sale" model has been extended in a number of directions. Mitra (1999) has shown how to introduce *endogenous* lobbies into that framework, as we shall discuss. Grossman and Helpman (1995a) further use this framework to analyze a tariff war between two countries, and the potential benefits from international agreements. Along the same lines, Bagwell and Staiger (1999, 2002) examine the economic rationale for the trade rules embodied in the General Agreement on Trade and Tariffs (GATT) and the World Trade Organization (WTO). These rules include GATT's principle of "reciprocity," whereby each country agrees to reduce its trade barriers in return for a reciprocal reduction by another. Bagwell and Staiger's framework is general enough to include both the median voter model and the "protection for sale" model, and we use it to show the outcome of a trade war, along with the benefits from reciprocal tariff reductions using GATT rules.

Another importance principle of GATT is the "most favored nation" (MFN) provision, which states that all member countries of GATT should be granted the same tariffs. This provision is violated when countries join into regional trade agreements, granting zero tariffs to countries *within* but not outside the agreement. Our third topic is to examine the incentives for countries to join regional trade agreements versus multilateral agreements. A key question here, raised by Bhagwati (1993; 2002, lecture 3), is whether joining a regional trade agreement *helps or hinders* the ultimate goal of multilateral free trade. Models indicating that regional agreements may hinder multilateral free trade include Krishna (1998) and McLaren (2002), and views on the other side include Baldwin (1995) and Ethier (1998). We will examine this issue using the median voter model, as in Levy 1997. In the basic version of this model a regional agreement cannot hinder a multilateral agreement, but in an extended version of the model (including product variety) this can occur.

We conclude the chapter with an application of political economy to a nondemocratic setting: the People's Republic of China. In this case the special interest groups do not take the form of well-funded lobbying groups as in the United States, but rather, include the large state-owned industries and the smaller but growing private industries, as well as foreign firms. The distribution of these firms is very uneven across provinces. China's recent entry into the WTO came only after regional concerns in China about the impact of import competition were overruled. We argue that the regional variation towards openness (as evidenced by the inflow of foreign firms), combined with the variation in location of state-owned firms, can be used to identify the political weights given to the various interest groups. We present the results of Branstetter and Feenstra (2002), who show how the Grossman-Helpman framework can be applied in this setting.

Median Voter Model

Used in many applications, the median voter model presumes that policies are established by majority vote. Provided that preferences are "single peaked" over the policy being voted upon (i.e., each person has a unique maximum), then it follows that the policy adopted will maximize the utility of the median voter. In the application to trade policy we assume that the policy is an import tariff or subsidy. The optimal tariff for the median voter will depend on the production structure in the economy, and for simplicity in this section we assume the two-by-two Heckscher-Ohlin (HO) model (Mayer 1984 also considers other structures). Then we will show that if the median voter owns a lower capital/labor ratio than overall for the economy, and imports are labor intensive, the economy will have a positive import tariff.

As in chapter 7, we will suppose that each individual has a quasi-linear utility function given by $c_0^h + U(c^h)$ where c_0^h is consumption of a numeraire export good, and c^h is the consumption of the import good for consumer $h = 1, \ldots, L$. (We use L rather than H to denote the number of consumers, since L also equals the number of workers.) Consumers all have the same increasing and strictly concave utility function U, so they have the same optimal consumption $c^h = d(p)$, $d'(p) < 0$, with remaining income spent on the numeraire good, $c_0^h = I^h - p'd(p)$. Then individual utility is

$$V(p, I^h) \equiv I^h - p'd(p) + U[d(p)]. \tag{9.1}$$

Both the export and the import goods are produced using labor and capital. The total endowments of labor and capital are L and K, respectively. The fixed world price of the import is denoted by p^*, and this good has a specific tariff of t, so the domestic price is $p = p^* + t$. We let $y(p)$ denote the supply of the import-competing good, with $y'(p) > 0$. Imports are then $m(p) = d(p)L - y(p)$, and tariff revenue collected is $T = tm(p)$, which is redistributed with a poll subsidy. We will suppose that individual h has one unit of labor and K^h units of capital, $h = 1, \ldots, L$, so that individual income is, $I^h = w + rK^h + (T/L)$. We can reexpress this as

$$I^h = \frac{1}{L}(wL + rK^h L + T) = \frac{1}{L}(wL + \rho^h rK + T), \tag{9.2}$$

where $\rho^h = K^h/(K/L)$ is the capital/labor ratio for the individual in question relative to the *overall* capital/labor ratio in the economy. Total GDP in the economy is $G = y_0(p) + py(p) = wL + rK$. It follows that we can rewrite individual income in (9.2) as

$$\begin{aligned}
I^h &= \frac{1}{L}[wL + rK + (\rho^h - 1)rK + T] \\
&= \frac{1}{L}[(\rho^h - 1)rK + y_0(p) + py(p) + T].
\end{aligned} \tag{9.2'}$$

Differentiating individual utility in (9.1) with respect to the tariff, we obtain

$$\begin{aligned}
\frac{dV^h}{dt} &= -d(p) + \frac{dI^h}{dt} \\
&= (\rho^h - 1)\frac{dr}{dp}\frac{K}{L} + \left[\frac{y(p)}{L} - d(p)\right] + \frac{1}{L}\frac{dT}{dp} \\
&= (\rho^h - 1)\frac{dr}{dp}\frac{K}{L} + \frac{t}{L}m'(p),
\end{aligned} \tag{9.3}$$

where the first line follows from Roy's Identity, the second line using (9.2') and the envelope theorem, and the third line using tariff revenue of $T = t[d(p)L - y(p)] = tm(p)$.

If the tariff is determined by majority vote, then the tariff prevailing will be that which maximizes the utility of the median voter. Denoting the median voter by m, with utility $V^m = V(p, I^m)$, this tariff will satisfy $dV^m/dt = 0$ and $d^2V^m/dt^2 < 0$. Setting (9.3) equal to zero, this tariff is

$$t^m = (1 - \rho^m)\frac{dr}{dp}\frac{K}{m'(p)}, \qquad (9.4)$$

where ρ^m is the capital/labor ratio for the *median* individual h relative to the overall capital/labor endowment for the economy. This ratio is less than one for all countries (Alesina and Rodrik 1994), so that $\rho^m < 1$. Then since $m'(p) < 0$, we see that the tariff t^m is *positive* when the import good is labor intensive, so that $dr/dp < 0$, but *negative* when the import good is capital intensive, so that $dr/dp > 0$. In other words, import tariffs should be used in capital-abundant industrialized countries, but import subsidies in labor-abundant developing countries.

In practice, import subsidies are rarely observed, despite this prediction from the median voter model. There are many reasons for this, some of which we will investigate later in this section. Setting aside this most obvious limitation of the median voter model, Dutt and Mitra (2002) ask whether there is some *other* prediction that might accord better with real-world evidence. In particular, suppose that we compare countries with varying degrees of inequality, which we measure by $(1 - \rho^m)$, that is, with lower values of the median voter's capital/labor endowment ρ^m, corresponding to higher inequality. Then differentiating the first-order condition $dV^m/dt = 0$, we obtain

$$\frac{d^2V^m}{dt^2}dt + \frac{d^2V^m}{d(1 - \rho^m)dt}d(1 - \rho^m) = 0,$$

so that from (9.3)

$$\frac{dt^m}{d(1 - \rho^m)} = \frac{dr}{dp}\frac{K}{L} \bigg/ \frac{d^2V^m}{dt^2}, \qquad (9.5)$$

where $d^2V^m/dt^2 < 0$ from the second-order condition.

It follows that for capital-abundant countries importing the labor-intensive good, so that $dr/dp < 0$, the median voter model predicts that *increased* inequality (a rise in $1 - \rho^m$) will lead to a *higher* tariff. Conversely, for labor-abundant countries importing the capital-intensive good, so that $dr/dp > 0$, the median voter model predicts that *increased* inequality (a rise in $1 - \rho^m$) will lead to a *reduced* tariff or increased subsidy (a fall in t^m). Stated less formally, we expect increased inequality to be associated with more restrictive trade policies in industrialized countries, but more open trade policies in developing countries.

Dutt and Mitra test this prediction by running the regression

$$TR^i = \alpha_0 + \alpha_1 INEQ^i + \alpha_2 INEQ^i(K/L)^i \qquad (9.6)$$
$$+ \alpha_3(K/L)^i + X^i\beta + \varepsilon_i,$$

where TR^i is an measure of trade restrictions in country i, INEQ^i is an index of income inequality in that country, $(K/L)^i$ is the capital/labor ratio in country i, and X^i is a matrix of other control variables. Taking the partial derivative of TR^i with respect to INEQ^i, we obtain

$$\frac{\partial \mathrm{TR}^i}{\partial \mathrm{INEQ}^i} = \alpha_1 + \alpha_2 (K/L)^i. \tag{9.6'}$$

The prediction from the median voter is that this derivative should be negative for low levels of the capital/labor ratio $(K/L)^i$, but positive for higher levels of the capital/labor ratio. This will occur if $\alpha_1 < 0$ and $\alpha_2 > 0$, with the turning point between the negative and positive derivatives occurring where $(9.6')$ equals zero, or at the capital/labor ratio $(K/L)^i = -\alpha_1/\alpha_2 > 0$.

In their estimates, Dutt and Mitra confirm these signs of α_1 and α_2 for several different measures of tariffs used for TR^i. The turning point $(K/L)^i = -\alpha_1/\alpha_2$ turns out to be quite close to the median capital/labor ratio in the sample (South Korea). For developing countries with lower capital/labor ratios, greater inequality leads to lower tariffs. Conversely, for industrialized countries with higher capital/labor ratios, greater inequality leads to higher tariffs. This provides striking support for the median voter framework in the context of the Heckscher-Ohlin model. In addition, Dutt and Mitra find that this relationship holds better in democracies than in dictatorships.

This confirmation of the median voter model seems at odds with its first prediction, that tariffs should be positive in advanced countries importing labor-intensive goods, but negative in developing economies importing capital-intensive goods. As we have mentioned, import subsidies are rarely observed. Fernandez and Rodrik (1991) provide one explanation for the "antitrade" bias of nearly all countries. Specifically, they argue that even if policies are determined by majority vote, when individuals do not know whether they will be included among the gainers or losers, there is a tendency for voters to prefer the status quo. This occurs even in a model where everyone is perfectly informed about the aggregate gains and losses in each industry, but cannot predict their individual returns. Therefore, there is a tendency to apply tariffs to offset import competition and preserve the status quo income distribution.[1] This can help to reconcile the positive tariffs observed in most countries with the median voter model, and the logic of Fernandez and Rodrik holds equally well in other models as well.

---

[1] The idea that trade policy is applied to preserve the status quo income distribution has also been proposed by Corden (1974), and is known as the *conservative social welfare function*; see also Deardorff 1987. In Fernandez and Rodrik 1991, this is the outcome of majority vote rather than a criterion imposed by the government.

Protection for Sale

The median voter model assumes that policies are determined by majority vote. This is an overly simplified description of representative democracies where the electorate votes for legislators, who then determine the policies. In such settings the policies chosen will be jointly influenced by votes, voice, and dollars from the campaign contribution of lobbying groups. The second model we consider, due to Grossman and Helpman (1994), proposes an elegant solution to the problem of how the government simultaneously considers the contributions of numerous lobbies, as well as consumer welfare, in determining trade policy.[2]

We assume that there are N goods plus the numeraire commodity, all of which are additively separable in utility. Consumer utility functions are $c_0^h + \Sigma_{i=1}^N u_i(c_i^h)$, where c_0^h is the numeraire export good, and c_i^h is the consumption of good $i = 1, \ldots, N$. Maximizing utility subject to the budget constraint gives the per capita consumption $d_i(p_i)$ of each good, $i = 1, \ldots, N$, with remaining income spent on the numeraire good, $c_0^h = I^h - p'd(p)$. We let $d(p) = [d_1(p_1), \ldots, d_N(p_N)]$ denote the vector of per capita consumptions, depending on prices $p = (p_1, \ldots, p_N)$. Then individual utility is similar to that in (9.1):

$$V(p, I^h) \equiv I^h - p'd(p) + \sum_{i=1}^N u_i[d_i(p_i)]. \tag{9.7}$$

Notice that the last two terms on the right of (9.7) give per capita consumer surplus, or $S(p) \equiv \Sigma_{i=1}^N u_i[d_i(p_i)] - p'd(p)$, so that consumer welfare can be written as

$$V^h(p, I^h) \equiv I^h + S(p), \tag{9.7'}$$

with $\partial S(p)/\partial p_i = -d_i(p_i)$, by Roy's Identity.

On the production side, each of the N industries has the production function $y_i = f_i(L_i, K_i)$, where capital K_i is *specific* to each sector. The numeraire commodity is produced with one unit of labor, so wages are fixed at unity. Given the product price p_i in each sector, the return to the specific factor in that sector is

$$\pi_i(p_i) = \max_{L_i}[p_i f_i(L_i, K_i) - L_i]. \tag{9.8}$$

---

[2] Earlier political economy models, such as Findlay and Wellisz (1982), simply assumed a functional relationship between lobbying contributions and tariffs. Hillman (1989) allowed for a government objective function with a general trade-off between the benefits to a special interest group and costs to consumers of tariff protection. The advantage of Grossman and Helpman 1994 is that these functional relationships are endogenously determined rather than assumed.

From (9.8) we can determine the optimal outputs $\pi_i'(p_i) = y_i(p_i)$ in each industry. The international prices of the goods are fixed at p_i^*, and each industry may receive a specific trade policy of t_i, $i = 1, \ldots, N$, where $t_i > (<) 0$ indicates a tariff (subsidy) in an import industry, and a subsidy (tariff) in an export industry. Imports of each good are then $m_i(p_i) = d_i(p_i)L - y_i(p_i)$ (which are negative for exports), and tariff revenue collected is $T(p) = \Sigma_{i=1}^N (p_i - p_i^*)m_i(p_i)$. We assume that this revenue is redistributed by a poll subsidy of (T/L) per person.

The specific factor in each industry i is owned by H_i members of the population, so that $H = \Sigma_{i=1}^N H_i$ is the total number of persons owning some capital. For simplicity, we suppose that every individual also owns one unit of labor. The total population is L, so there are an additional $(L - H) \geq 0$ persons who own one unit of labor but no capital. The owners of specific capital in each industry earn the return $\pi_i(p_i)$ from (9.8), and obtain their wages of unity plus consumer surplus, along with redistributed tariff revenue. Summing these various terms, the owners of specific capital in industry i earn

$$W_i(p) = \pi_i(p_i) + H_i[1 + S(p)] + (H_i/L)T(p), \quad i = 1, \ldots, N. \quad (9.9a)$$

The remaining $(L - H)$ persons obtain their wages plus consumer surplus and redistributed tariff revenue, so their welfare is

$$W_0(p) = (L - H)[1 + S(p)] + [(L - H)/L]T(p). \quad (9.9b)$$

Summing (9.9) over all workers and industries, we obtain total welfare:

$$W(p) = \sum_{i=0}^N W_i(p) = \sum_{i=1}^N \pi_i(p_i) + L[1 + S(p)] + T(p). \quad (9.10)$$

We suppose that a subset of the industries $j \in J_o$ is organized into lobbies, while the complementary set $j \in J_u$ is unorganized industries, with $J_o \cup J_u = \{1, \ldots, N\}$. The purpose of each lobby is to provide contributions to the government in return for influencing the tariff/subsidy schedule. Specifically, they announce a *campaign contribution* schedule $R_j(p)$ that they are willing to pay, depending on the vector of prices $p_i = p_i^* + t_i$ prevailing across the industries, $i = 1, \ldots, N$. The government values campaign contributions, but also weighs these against the consumer welfare of all individuals. Giving social welfare the weight of $\alpha > 0$, Grossman and Helpman assume that the government chooses tariffs and subsidies t_i to maximize

$$G(p) = \sum_{j \in J_o} R_j(p) + \alpha W(p). \quad (9.11)$$

The key question is how the lobbies in industries $j \in J_o$ determine their campaign contributions. The answer to this comes from the work of Bernheim and Whinston (1986). They argue that in the Nash equilibrium of the game we have described—with each lobby optimally choosing its contribution schedule $R_j(p)$ taking as given the schedules of the other groups, and knowing that the tariffs will be chosen to maximize (9.11)—then the lobbies can do no better than to select a contribution schedule of the form

$$R_j(p) = \max \{0, W_j(p) - B_j\}, \quad j \in J_o, \tag{9.12}$$

where B_j is a constant.[3] Bernheim and Whinston refer to this as a *truthful contribution schedule*, since it reflects the true welfare levels $W_j(p)$ obtained by the lobby for various tariffs. They argue that a *truthful Nash equilibrium*, where each lobby uses a schedule like (9.12), is included among the equilibria of the game.

Accepting this result of Bernheim and Whinston (1986), we can substitute (9.12) into (9.11) to obtain

$$G(p) = \sum_{j \in J_o} [(1 + \alpha)W_j(p) - B_j] + \sum_{j \notin J_o} \alpha W_j(p), \tag{9.11'}$$

where the summation over $j \notin J_o$ also includes the welfare W_0 of workers with no capital. Notice that this statement of the government's objective function indicates that it gives *differential weights* to the welfare of organized and unorganized industries: the organized lobbies have the weight $(1 + \alpha)$, whereas other industries plus workers have the weight α.

Choosing the tariffs t_i to maximize (9.11') is equivalent to choosing the domestic prices p_j, $j \in J_o$ to maximize it. Before computing the first-order condition, we can differentiate welfare for an organized industry, unorganized industry, and workers as

$$\frac{\partial W_j}{\partial p_j} = y_j - H_j d_j(p) + \left(\frac{H_j}{L}\right)$$
$$\times \left[m_j + (p_j - p_j^*)\frac{dm_j}{dp_j} \right], \quad \text{for } j \in J_o, \tag{9.13a}$$

$$\frac{\partial W_i}{\partial p_j} = - H_i d_j(p) + \left(\frac{H_i}{L}\right)$$
$$\times \left[m_j + (p_j - p_j^*)\frac{dm_j}{dp_j} \right], \quad \text{for } i \in J_u, \tag{9.13b}$$

---

[3] Notice that by using the truthful contribution schedules in (9.12), the welfare of each lobby *net* of the contributions becomes $W_j(p) - R_j(p) = \min\{W_j(p), B_j\}$, so B_j is an upper bound

$$\frac{\partial W_0}{\partial p_j} = -(L-H)d_j(p) + \left(\frac{L-H}{L}\right)\left[m_j + (p_j - p_j^*)\frac{dm_j}{dp_j}\right], \quad (9.13c)$$

where $m_j = d_j(p_j)L - y_j(p_j)$ is the imports of good j (which is negative for exports).

Then multiply (9.13a) by $(1 + \alpha)$, and (9.13b) and (9.13c) by α, and sum these over all organized and unorganized industries to obtain

$$\frac{\partial G}{\partial p_j} = (1+\alpha)y_j - \left(\sum_{i \in J_o} H_i\right)d_j(p) - \alpha L d_j(p)$$

$$+ (\lambda_o + \alpha)\left[m_j + (p_j - p_j^*)\frac{dm_j}{dp_j}\right], \quad j \in J_o \qquad (9.14)$$

where $\lambda_o \equiv \Sigma_{j \in J_o}(H_j/L)$ denotes the fraction of the population owning a specific factor in an organized industry, and this first-order condition holds for an *organized* industry j. For an industry that is *not organized* into a lobby, the term $(1 + \alpha)y_j$ that appears first on the right side of (9.13) would be replaced by αy_j, since the unorganized industry receives the weight α rather than $(1 + \alpha)$ in the government's objective function.

We can make use of the definition of imports, $m_j = d_j(p_j)L - y_j$, to simplify (9.13) as

$$\frac{dG}{dp_j} = y_j(1-\lambda_o) + (\alpha + \lambda_o)(p_j - p_j^*)\frac{dm_j}{dp_j}, \quad j \in J_o, \qquad (9.14')$$

while for an industry *without* a lobby, the term $y_j(1 - \lambda_o)$ on the right side is replaced by $-y_j\lambda_o$. Setting (9.14') and the modified condition for the unorganized industry equal to zero, we solve for the equilibrium tariffs $t_j = (p_j - p_i^*)$, $j = 1, \ldots, N$, as

$$\frac{t_j}{p_j} = -\left(\frac{\delta_j - \lambda_o}{\alpha + \lambda_o}\right)\left(\frac{y_j}{m_j}\right)\left(\frac{\partial m_j}{\partial p_j}\frac{p_j}{m_j}\right)^{-1}, \quad \text{where } \delta_j = \begin{cases} 1 & \text{for } j \in J_o \\ 0 & \text{otherwise} \end{cases}. \quad (9.15)$$

This simple equation linking the tariffs/subsidies to underlying determinants is the key prediction of the "protection for sale" model of Grossman and Helpman (1994). To interpret it, notice that the import elasticity appearing in (9.15) is negative, while δ_j is an indicator variable that equals unity for organized industries j, and zero otherwise. Recall that $\lambda_o \equiv \Sigma_{j \in J_o}(H_j/L)$ equals the fraction of the population owning a specific factor in an organized industry. Then by inspection, for $0 < \lambda_o < 1$ the tariffs in (9.15) are negative

---

on *net* welfare. Grossman and Helpman (1994, 843–47) discuss how B_j might be determined, as does Mitra (1999).

(i.e., import subsidies or export taxes) for unorganized industries, but are positive (i.e., import tariffs or export subsidies) for industries organized into a lobby. On the other hand, if either $\lambda_o = 0$ or $\lambda_o = 1$ (i.e., no one or everyone belongs to a lobby), then the tariffs in (9.15) are zero, so free trade is the political optimum.

The result that unorganized industries receive import subsidies or export taxes serves as a way to lower their domestic prices and therefore benefit consumers. The fact that these instruments are seldom observed in reality may reflect political opposition to them, or some other reason. We do not take this to be a refutation of the "protection for sale" model, any more than we took the fact that import subsidies are not observed in capital-scarce countries to be a refutation of the median voter model. Instead, to test the "protection for sale" model we look for other correlations implied by (9.15). Notice that the *magnitude* of the tariffs or subsidies depends on the ratio of production to imports (y_j/m_j), and also on the inverse of the import demand elasticity. Having higher domestic production relative to imports will lead to *higher* import tariffs or export subsidies for organized industries (since then $\delta_j - \lambda_o = 1 - \lambda_o > 0$), but *lower* import tariffs or export subsidies for unorganized industries (where $\delta_j - \lambda_o = -\lambda_o < 0$). These are the key predictions that will be tested.

Goldberg and Maggi (1999) denote the import demand elasticity (measured as a positive number) by e_j, and multiply (9.15) by this magnitude to obtain

$$e_j\left(\frac{t_j}{p_j}\right) = \beta_0 + \beta_1\left(\frac{y_j}{m_j}\right) + \beta_2\delta_j\left(\frac{y_j}{m_j}\right) + \varepsilon_j, \qquad (9.16)$$

where $\beta_1 = -[\lambda_o/(\alpha + \lambda_o)]$, $\beta_2 = 1/(\alpha + \lambda_o)$, and β_0 is a constant term.[4] Notice that $\beta_1 < 0$ indicates how the trade barriers vary with the output/import ratio in *any* industry, while $\beta_2 > 0$ reflects the *additional* impact of having the industry organized as a lobby. So a change in the output/import ratio in an unorganized industry affects the trade barrier by $\beta_1 < 0$, and in an organized industry affects the trade barrier by $(\beta_1 + \beta_2) > 0$.

We multiply through by the import demand elasticity because that variable is measured with error, which is therefore incorporated into the error term ε_j of (9.16). Data on e_j is taken from the compendium of import elasticities in Shiells, Stern, and Deardorff 1986. For the trade barriers (t_j/p_j), Goldberg and Maggi use *nontariff* barriers in the United States. The reason for using nontariff barriers rather than tariffs is that the latter

---

[4] Notice that a constant term in the tariff equation is not implied by the theory in (9.15), but it is generally a good idea to include it in empirical work. It turns out that β_0 is insignificantly different from zero in the estimates of Goldberg and Maggi (1999).

have been reduced by international agreements, so we might expect their level to be lower than that predicted by (9.16). Nontariff barriers are measured by the "coverage ratio" in each industry, that is, the fraction of disaggregate products in each industry covered by quotas or some other restriction on trade. The independent variables in (9.16) are the indicator variable δ_j for whether an industry is organized or not, and the output/import ratio. Goldberg and Maggi measure the former using a threshold of contributions by industries to the 1981–82 congressional elections in the United States, from Gawande 1995. The output/import ratio is treated as endogenous (since changes in trade barriers affect both output and imports), and estimation is performed using the instruments from Trefler (1993b). With this data, (9.16) is estimated over a cross-section of 107 U.S. industries.

In their results, Goldberg and Maggi find estimates of β_1 and β_2 of -0.0093 (0.0040) and 0.0106 (0.0053), respectively (with standard errors in parentheses). Both of these results coefficients have the expected sign, with $(\beta_1 + \beta_2) = 0.0013 > 0$ as predicted, though the latter estimate is not significantly different from zero. Recalling that $\beta_1 = -[\lambda_o/(\alpha + \lambda_o)]$, and $\beta_2 = 1/(\alpha + \lambda_o)$, we can use these estimates to recover $\alpha = 93$ and $\lambda_o = 0.88$. In alternative estimates, they obtain $\alpha = 53$ and $\lambda_o = 0.83$. Regardless of which we use, it is evident that the weight α on consumer welfare in the government's objective function is very high: between 50 and 100 times higher than the weight given to political contributions.

Gawande and Bandyopadhyay (2000) extend the Grossman-Helpman model to allow for trade in intermediate inputs. Final-goods industries that use the intermediate input suffer from a tariff on it, so the predicted tariffs in those final-goods industries are higher. In other words, controls are added to the right side of (9.16) to reflect the tariffs on intermediate inputs, but otherwise the estimating equation is similar, with $\beta_1 < 0$, $\beta_2 > 0$ and $(\beta_1 + \beta_2) > 0$ expected. Gawande and Bandyopadhyay use an expanded dataset of 242 U.S. industries, and again use nontariff barriers as the dependent variable. In their results, they estimate β_1 and β_2 of -0.000309 (0.00015) and 0.000315 (0.00016), respectively. Both of the coefficients have the expected sign, and again we find that $(\beta_1 + \beta_2) = 0.000006 > 0$, though this coefficient is not significant. Using these estimates, we recover the values of $\alpha = 3,175$ and $\lambda_o = 0.98$, so Gawande and Bandyopadhyay find even a higher weight on consumer welfare than do Goldberg and Maggi! In alternative estimates, they obtain $\alpha = 1,750$ and $\lambda_o = 0.95$, which is still a remarkably high weight on consumer welfare.

There have been a number of other empirical applications of the Grossman-Helpman model, including McCalman 2003, who applies it to Australia, Grether, de Melo, and Olarrega 2002, who apply it to Mexico, and Mitra, Thomakos, and Ulubasoglu 2002, who apply it to Turkey.[5] Rather than describe these applications, we shall explore other theoretical extensions of the "protection for sale" model.

Endogenous Lobbies

In the description of Grossman and Helpman's model above, we treated the existence of the lobbies as exogenous. This is a limitation, of course, and in reality we would expect lobbies to form when their potential returns are sufficiently high or costs of organizing are sufficiently low. By allowing for the endogenous formation of lobby group, following Mitra (1999), we will obtain some important additional insights from the "protection for sale" model.

Recall that $\lambda_o \equiv \Sigma_{j \in J_o} (H_j / L)$ denotes the fraction of the total population belonging to organized industries. This can be rewritten as $\lambda_o = (H/L) [\Sigma_{j \in J_o} (H_j / H)]$, and decomposed into two terms: (H/L) is the fraction of the population that owns some specific factor, and $[\Sigma_{j \in J_o} (H_j / H)]$ is the fraction of specific-factor owners who are orgaized. Let us impose some symmetry on the model, so that H_j is the same across all industries j, and also capital K_j and the production functions f_j are the same across all $j = 1, \ldots, N$. Then denoting the number of organized industries by $N_o \leq N$, it is immediate that $[\Sigma_{j \in J_o} (H_j / H)] = (N_o / N)$, which measures the fraction of industries that are organized. So we can rewrite the term λ_o as $\lambda_o = \lambda_k n_o$, where $\lambda_k \equiv (H/L)$ is the fraction of the population that owns some specific factor (i.e., capital), and $n_o \equiv (N_o / N) = [\Sigma_{j \in J_o} (H_j / H)]$ is the fraction of industries that are organized.

Substituting $\lambda_o = \lambda_k n_o$ into (9.16), the predicted trade policies are

$$\frac{t_j}{p_j} = -\left(\frac{\delta_i - \lambda_k n_o}{\alpha + \lambda_k n_o} \right) \left(\frac{y_j}{m_j} \right) \left(\frac{\partial m_j}{\partial p_j} \frac{p_j}{m_j} \right)^{-1},$$

$$\text{where } \delta_j = \begin{cases} 1 & \text{for } j \in J_o \\ 0 & \text{otherwise} \end{cases}. \tag{9.17}$$

In the Grossman-Helpman model, a *rise in either* λ_k *or* n_o *will lower* (t_j / p_j) across all industries in (9.17). That is, holding the import demand elasticity and output/import ratio constant, we have

$$\frac{d(t_j / p_j)}{d(\lambda_k n_o)} = \frac{(\alpha + \delta_j)}{(\alpha + \lambda_k n_o)^2} \left(\frac{y_j}{m_j} \right) \left(\frac{\partial m_j}{\partial p_j} \frac{p_j}{m_j} \right)^{-1} < 0, \tag{9.18}$$

---

[5] See also the survey by Gawande and Krishna (2003).

where the sign of (9.18) follows because the import demand elasticity is negative (or for exports, this supply elasticity is positive but (y_j/m_j) is negative). Continuing to hold this elasticity constant, if we also allow the output/import ratio to respond, then this would *reinforce* the negative sign on (9.18): the rise in either λ_k or n_o will lower (t_j/p_j) as in (9.18), which lowers the domestic prices $p_j = p_j^* + t_j$, and further lowers the output/import ratio (y_j/m_j).

Now let us work this thought experiment in reverse. A *decline* in λ_k corresponds to fewer people owning the stock of capital, which is a more unequal income distribution. This would *raise* (t_j/p_j) across all industries as in (9.18) and also raise all domestic prices, meaning that import tariffs and export subsidies rise in organized industries, while import subsidies and export taxes are reduced in unorganized import industries. It can be argued that this has a *greater* beneficial impact to the organized industries receiving protection than for the unorganized industries.[6] That would create an incentive for new groups to enter, so if n_o is treated as endogenous, then it would rise. But that would *offset* the initial decline in λ_k, since the increase in n_o would lower (t_j/p_j) in (9.17). So with the number of lobbies treated as endogenous, it is no longer clear whether a more unequal income distribution leads to more or less protection. That is the issue that Mitra (1999) aims to resolve.

To model the entry of groups, we impose a high degree of symmetry on the model. We already assumed K_i and H_i do not vary across industries, and further assume that demand and production functions are symmetric across products, as are international prices. Then the tariff/subsidies computed from (9.16) will be t_o/p_o for all organized industries, and t_u/p_u for all unorganized industries. These policies depend on the *product* of $n_o\lambda_k$ from (9.17), reflecting the fraction of organized industries (which will be endogenous), and the fraction of population that owns capital (which is exogenous). These policies fully determine the welfare $W_o(n_o\lambda_k)$ to capital owners in organized industries, and welfare $W_u(n_o\lambda_k)$ to capital owners in unorganized industries, as in (9.9a). The *gross benefits* to forming a lobby are then

$$\Delta W(n_o\lambda_k) \equiv W_o(n_o\lambda_k) - W_u(n_o\lambda_k), \qquad (9.19)$$

while the *net benefits* are obtained by subtracting the cost of political contributions:

$$\mathrm{NB}(n_o\lambda_k) \equiv \Delta W(n_o\lambda_k) - R_o(n_o\lambda_k). \qquad (9.20)$$

Following Mitra, some properties of these schedules can be derived. Given the symmetry we have assumed, the gross benefits in (9.19) are simply the

---

[6] See problems 9.1–9.3.

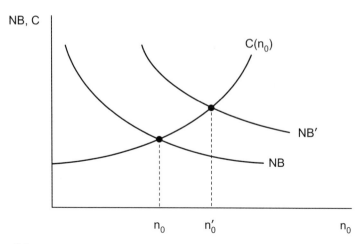

Figure 9.1

difference between the returns to the fixed factors in organized and unorganized industries: $\Delta W(n_o \lambda_k) = \pi(p_o) - \pi(p_u) > 0$. We argued above that as λ_k *declines*, leading to a rise in the tariff/subsidies as in (9.18), a greater benefit on the organized than unorganized industries is created, so that $\pi(p_o) - \pi(p_u)$ increases and gross benefits rise.[7] Thus, $\Delta W'(n_o \lambda_k) < 0$.

For net benefits, Mitra investigates the determinants of the truthful contribution schedules $R_o(n_o \lambda_k)$, including solving for the lower-bounds B_j to organized-industry welfare in (9.12). He is able to show that even when the impact of the number of lobbies n_o on contributions $R_o(n_o \lambda_k)$ is taken into account, it is still the case that net benefits rise if the number of lobbying groups falls. Thus, $\mathrm{NB}'(n_o \lambda_k) < 0$. The declining net benefits as a function of the number of organized industries is shown in Figures 9.1 and 9.2.

What about the costs of forming a lobby? In addition to the political contributions, there may be some significant costs of grass-roots organizing and communication between members so as to overcome the free-rider problem. Let us denote these costs (measured in terms of the numeraire good) by $C(n_o)$, where we assume that $C'(n_o) \geq 0$, so the cost of creating a new lobby is nondecreasing in the number of lobbies already there. This cost schedule is also illustrated in Figures 9.1 and 9.2. Then we suppose that lobbies form up to the point where net benefits just equal to the costs of creating a new lobby, which is illustrated by the lobbies n_o in both figures.

Now consider the effect of a fall in λ_k, which is a worsening of the income distribution. The impact effect from (9.17) (holding n_o constant) would be an increase in (t_j/p_j) and higher domestic prices for all industries. This creates

---

[7] See problems 9.1–9.3.

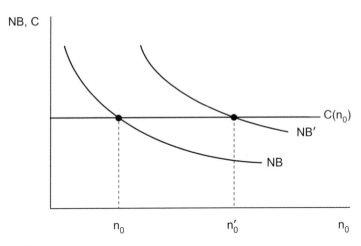

Figure 9.2

addition gains to organizing an industry, and in Figures 9.1 and 9.2, the net benefits schedule *rises* to NB′. Equivalently, net benefits remain the same if along with the decline in λ_k there is an equiproportional increase in n_o, so that the net benefit curves shifting *rightwards* by the amount $-d\lambda_k/\lambda_k$.

In Figure 9.1, where the cost of organizing lobbies is increasing, the induced increase in the number of lobbies from n_o to n_o' is clearly less than the rightward shift of the NB schedule. Therefore, $dn_o/n_o < -d\lambda_k/\lambda_k$, and it follows that $dn_o/n_o + d\lambda_k/\lambda_k < 0$, so that $n_o\lambda_k$ falls in equilibrium. This leads to an increase in the trade policies (t_j/p_j) from (9.17), so that organized industries receive higher import tariffs or export subsidies, and unorganized industries have reduced import subsidies or export taxes. Overall, there is a rise in domestic prices, and in this sense the net level of protection has increased due to the more concentrated income distribution and increased lobbying.

In Figure 9.2, by contrast, the cost of organizing lobbies is constant. In that case the increase in the number of lobbies from n_o to n_o' is just equal to the rightward shift of the NB schedule, so that $dn_o/n_o = -d\lambda_k/\lambda_k$ and $n_o\lambda_k$ is *unchanged* in equilibrium. Therefore the trade policies from (9.17) are also unchanged. We see that the overall impact of income inequality on protection is very sensitive to the structure of lobbying costs $C(n_o)$, which could reflect a wide range of legal and political features in a country. It would be difficult, then, to predict the effects of changes in income distribution on protection either within or across countries. This finding makes it all the more remarkable that in the median voter model, discussed earlier, Dutt and Mitra (2002) find a systematic (though nonmonotonic) relationship between trade barriers and inequality. Obtaining such time-series or cross-country empirical results from the "protection for sale" model would be more difficult. That model is ideally suited, however, to explaining *cross-industry* trade protection, as we have already discussed.

Two-Country Model

In the median voter model and the "protection for sale" model of Grossman and Helpman (1994), the governments treats the international price p^* as fixed. But what if instead the country is large, so that its tariffs affect the terms of trade? Obtaining a terms of trade gain creates an additional reason to use tariffs. In a two-country model, both countries would have this incentive, and we could conjecture that they would both end up with tariffs higher than those we solved for above. Bagwell and Staiger (1999, 2002) argue that this creates an important role for international institutions such as the GATT/WTO: to offset or eliminate the incentive to manipulate the terms of trade.

To formalize this idea, we return to the median voter or the "protection for sale" model. For simplicity, suppose that there are only two goods: the additively separable numeraire good that is exported from the home country, and a second good with demand $d(p)$ at home and supply $y(p)$. Home imports are then $m(p) = d(p) - y(p)$. Likewise, the foreign country has demand $d^*(p^*)$ for this good, and supply $y^*(p^*)$, depending on its own price p^*. Foreign exports are denoted by $x^*(p^*) = y^*(p^*) - d^*(p^*)$.

Home and foreign prices differ due to tariffs in both countries. Suppose that the home country applies an ad valorem tariff, and let τ equal *one plus the ad valorem tariff.* Then the home prices are $p = p^w \tau$, where p^w are the world prices. The foreign country applies an ad valorem tariff on its own imports, and let τ^* equal *one plus the foreign ad valorem tariff.* Since p^w is the world relative price of the home import and foreign *export*, then $1/p^w$ is the world relative price of the foreign *import*. Applying the tariff of τ^* means that the foreign price of its import good is τ^*/p^w, so the relative price of the foreign *export* is p^w/τ^*.

Using these prices, market clearing means that home imports equal foreign exports:

$$m(p^w \tau) = x^*(p^w/\tau^*) \implies p^w(\tau, \tau^*). \tag{9.21}$$

This equation determines the world equilibrium price $p^w(\tau, \tau^*)$, depending on the tariff in each country. Under the standard assumptions on the import demand and export supply curves, it is readily confirmed that

$$\frac{dp^w}{d\tau} < 0 < \frac{dp}{d\tau}, \quad \text{and} \quad \frac{dp^w}{d\tau^*} > 0 > \frac{dp^*}{d\tau^*}. \tag{9.22}$$

In other words, the home tariff *lowers* the world price of imports for the home country and raises the domestic price, while the foreign tariff *raises* the world price of its exports and lowers its local price of the export good.[8]

Let us now consider the government objective function in each country. In the median vote model the objective function was welfare of the median voter $V(p, I^m)$, where from (9.2′) income of the median voter was $I^m = [(\rho^m - 1)r(p)K + y_0(p) + py(p) + T]$.[9] Using the ad valorem tariffs defined above, tariff revenue in this expression is $T = (\tau - 1)p^w \times [d(p) - y(p)]$. Because domestic prices are $p = p^w\tau$, we can substitute this into tariff revenue and income and obtain an expression for income that depends on the world price and domestic tariff, $I^m(p^w, \tau)$. It follows that the objective of the home government is

$$G(p^w, \tau) = V[p^w\tau, I^m(p^w, \tau)]. \qquad (9.23)$$

Thus, the objective function of the home government can be written as a function of the world prices and the tariff. Bagwell and Staiger argue that this formulation of the objective function is general enough to encompass a number of models, including the median voter model and the "protection for sale" model of Grossman and Helpman.[10]

Furthermore, it is readily verified that the tariffs in the median voter model (equation 9.4) or in the "protection for sale" model (equation 9.15), satisfy the first-order condition

$$G_\tau(p^w, \tau) = 0. \qquad (9.24a)$$

That is, these tariffs are obtained by maximizing the government's objective while treating the world price p^w as *fixed*. For the foreign country there will be an analogous objective function $G^*(p^w, \tau^*)$, with first-order condition for the tariff

$$G_\tau^*(p^w, \tau^*) = 0. \qquad (9.24b)$$

Bagwell and Staiger refer to the tariffs satisfying (9.24) as *politically optimal*.

However, the tariffs satisfying (9.24) will generally *not be* chosen by a government that recognizes its ability to influence the terms of trade. Instead, the tariffs would be chosen in the home country to achieve

$$\frac{d}{d\tau}G[p^w(\tau, \tau^*), \tau] = G_p\frac{\partial p^w}{\partial \tau} + G_\tau = 0, \qquad (9.25a)$$

---

[8] You are asked to demonstrate (9.22) in problem 9.4.
[9] We now normalize the size of the population at $L = 1$ to simplify notation.
[10] Notice that G in (9.11) is a function of domestic prices p, but also depends on international prices p^* that we did not make explicit. Then $G(p, p^*)$ can be rewritten as $G(\tau p^*, p^*)$, so that G again depends on p^* and τ.

and in the foreign country,

$$\frac{d}{d\tau^*} G^* [p^w(\tau, \tau^*), \tau^*] = G_p^* \frac{\partial p^w}{\partial \tau^*} + G_{\tau^*}^* = 0. \qquad (9.25b)$$

Notice the obvious difference between the politically optimal tariffs in (9.24), and the first-order conditions (9.25) that incorporate the terms of trade effects. Bagwell and Staiger refer to the tariffs satisfying (9.25) as the *Nash equilibrium* tariffs, since they are the best response by each country given the tariff choice of the other.

The question then arises as to how the politically optimal tariffs (which ignore the terms of trade effects) compare with the Nash equilibrium tariffs (which incorporate these effects). To make this comparison, it is convenient to define the *reduced form* government objective functions as

$$\tilde{G}(\tau, \tau^*) \equiv G[p^w(\tau, \tau^*), \tau], \qquad (9.26a)$$

and in the foreign country,

$$\tilde{G}^*(\tau, \tau^*) \equiv G^*[p^w(\tau, \tau^*), \tau^*]. \qquad (9.26b)$$

These give the objectives as functions of the tariffs in the two countries. Notice that the Nash equilibrium in (9.25a) can be equivalently written as $\tilde{G}_\tau = 0$, which defines the best home response $\tau = r(\tau^*)$ to the foreign tariff. Similarly, the Nash equilibrium in (9.25b) can be written as, $\tilde{G}_{\tau^*}^* = 0$, which defines the best foreign response $\tau^* = r^*(\tau)$ to the home tariff.

The Nash equilibrium is defined by the intersection of these reaction curves $\tau = r(\tau^*)$ and $\tau^* = r^*(\tau)$. Assuming that this intersection is unique, it is illustrated by point N in Figure 9.3. Since this is the maximum of $\tilde{G}(\tau, \tau^*)$ subject to a given τ^*, the iso-curve of $\tilde{G}(\tau, \tau^*)$ has slope infinity at point N, and is increasing in the leftward direction, as illustrated. Similarly, the iso-curve of $\tilde{G}^*(\tau, \tau^*)$ has a slope of zero at point N, and is increasing in the downward direction, as illustrated. It is evident that there is a region *below and to the left* of point N, whose boundaries are defined by the iso-curves of $\tilde{G}(\tau, \tau^*)$ and $\tilde{G}^*(\tau, \tau^*)$, where *both countries are better off than at the Nash equilibrium*. Through this region, there lies the efficiency locus EE on which the iso-curves of $\tilde{G}(\tau, \tau^*)$ and $\tilde{G}^*(\tau, \tau^*)$ are tangent.

We have shown, therefore, that the Nash equilibrium does not lie on the efficiency frontier. This is the first half of the result given in the following theorem.

Theorem (Bagwell and Staiger 1999; Grossman and Helpman 1995a)

(a) The Nash equilibrium is not efficient.
(b) The political optimum is efficient.

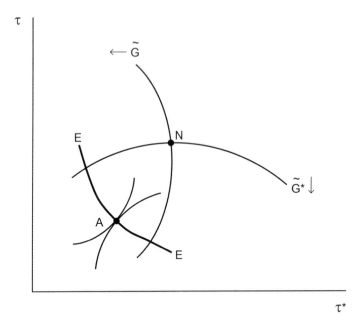

Figure 9.3

Grossman and Helpman (1995a) demonstrate part (a) by explicitly cal-culating the optimal tariffs for a *large* country in the "protection for sale" model. Rather than equation (9.15), which corresponds to the politically optimal tariffs $G_\tau(p^w,\tau) = 0$, they instead find that the tariffs are as in (9.15) *plus* the inverse elasticity of foreign export supply. Thus, the opti-mal tariffs are increased by exactly the same terms of trade effect that we discussed in chapter 7, and that is included in (9.25) by the terms $\tilde{G}_\tau$ and $\tilde{G}_{\tau^*}^*$.

To demonstrate part (b) of this theorem, let us calculate the condition for tangency of the iso-curves of $\tilde{G}(\tau, \tau^*)$ and $\tilde{G}^*(\tau, \tau^*)$. This is $\tilde{G}_\tau/\tilde{G}_{\tau^*} = \tilde{G}_\tau^*/\tilde{G}_{\tau^*}^*$. Using the definition of these reduced-form objective functions in (9.26), we can rewrite this tangency condition as

$$\frac{G_\tau + G_p \partial p^w/\partial\tau}{G_p \partial p^w/\partial\tau^*} = \frac{G_p^* \partial p^w/\partial\tau}{G_{\tau^*}^* + G_p^* \partial p^w/\partial\tau^*}. \tag{9.27}$$

Now substitute in the condition for the politically optimal tariffs, $G_\tau = G_{\tau^*}^* = 0$. Then (9.27) simply becomes $(\partial p^w/\partial\tau)/(\partial p^w/\partial\tau^*) = (\partial p^w/\partial\tau)/(\partial p^w/\partial\tau^*)$, which is obviously satisfied. Therefore, the political optimum lies on the efficiency locus, as illustrated by point A in Figure 9.3. It follows that the Nash equilibrium N is worse *for both countries* than the political optimum at point A.[11]

This raises the question of whether it is possible to improve on the Nash equilibrium by some simple rules agreed upon by both countries. Bagwell and Staiger (1999, 2002) argue that this creates an important role for the GATT, and in particular, justifies the GATT principles of reciprocity and nondiscrimination. As they describe (1999, 216–17): "the principle of reciprocity is a GATT norm under which one country agrees to reduce its level of protection in return for a reciprocal 'concession' from its trading partner. . . . The principle of nondiscrimination is a separate norm, under which a member government agrees that any tariff on a given product applied to the import of one trading partner applies equally to all other trading partners." We will examine the first of these principles.

How is reciprocity applied in practice? Bagwell and Staiger suggest the following definition in our two-country model: the tariffs τ and τ^* are reduced so that *import levels in both countries rise by the same amount.* Since these imports occur in different goods, they must be compared at some prices, so let us use the *initial* world prices p^{w0}. Then the tariff reductions are reciprocal if $p^{w0}\Delta m = \Delta m^*$, where m^* is foreign imports of the numeraire good. But from trade balance, the value of imports equals the value of exports abroad, so that $\Delta m^* = m^{*1} - m^{*0} = p^{w1}x^{*1} - p^{w0}x^{*0}$. But we also know that foreign exports equal home imports, so that $x^{*1} = m^1$ and $x^{*0} = m^0$. Therefore, Bagwell and Staiger's definition of reciprocity implies

$$\underbrace{p^{w0}\Delta m = p^{w0}m^1 - p^{w0}m^0}_{\Delta\text{Home imports}} = \underbrace{\Delta m^* = p^{w1}m^1 - p^{w0}m^0}_{\Delta\text{Foreign imports}}. \quad (9.28)$$

By inspection, this equality is satisfied if and only if world prices are constant, $p^{w1} = p^{w0}$. So the implication of reciprocity in the two-country model is that *mutual tariff reductions should leave the world price unchanged.*

Totally differentiating the world price $p^w(\tau, \tau^*)$, it is unchanged when

$$\frac{dp^w}{d\tau}d\tau + \frac{dp^w}{d\tau^*}d\tau^* = 0 \implies \frac{d\tau}{d\tau^*} = -\frac{dp^w}{d\tau^*} \bigg/ \frac{dp^w}{d\tau} > 0, \quad (9.29)$$

where the positive sign follows from the inequalities in (9.22). The locus of tariffs along which the world price $p^w(\tau, \tau^*)$ is held fixed at its Nash-equilibrium level is illustrated by PP in Figure 9.4. Since this line has a positive slope, and the iso-curves of $\tilde{G}(\tau, \tau^*)$ and $\tilde{G}^*(\tau, \tau^*)$ have slopes of

---

[11] We have not quite shown this last result, because it is possible that the countries are so asymmetric in size that the political optimum at point A lies on the efficiency locus EE, but *outside* the region bounded by the iso-curves of $\tilde{G}$ and $\tilde{G}^*$ in Figure 9.3. We assume that this asymmetric case does not apply.

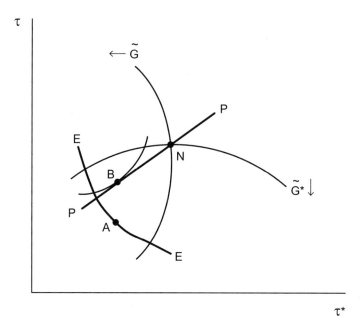

Figure 9.4

infinity and zero at point N, the PP locus clearly falls *inside* the region bounded by those iso-curve. Therefore, *reciprocal reductions in tariffs from the Nash equilibrium raise the government objective function for both countries.* This result provides strong justification for the GATT principle of reciprocity.

How far should the tariff reductions proceed? Bagwell and Staiger argue that if the two countries are symmetric in size, then the line PP will intersect the efficiency locus at precisely the political optimum at point A. That is, tariff reduction should proceed until both countries are applying tariffs as in the median voter or "protection for sale" model, and therefore avoiding the mutual losses associated with exploiting the terms of trade.

When countries are not symmetric in size, however, the situation is more complicated. As we move down the iso-price locus PP from point N in Figure 9.4, the government objective function of both countries initially rises. It might be the case, though, that the objective of one country is maximized on PP *before* we get to the efficiency locus EE. This is illustrated in Figure 9.4 by point B, where the government objective of the *home* country is maximized. At point B, both governments attain higher objectives than at the Nash equilibrium N, but further reciprocal reductions in tariffs would lower the objectives for the home country. So in this case, the political optimum at point A is not reached.

Bagwell and Staiger, as well as Grossman and Helpman (1995a), discuss various bargaining mechanisms that might enable the two countries to still agree on the political optimum at point A, or some other point on the efficiency locus. Bagwell and Staiger (1999, 2002) further discuss how other principles of GATT—including nondiscrimination—can be understood as being efficient. For further details the reader may refer to their work, which provides a quite general economic justification for GATT rules.[12]

Regional Trade Agreements

Another foundation of GATT is the MFN principle of nondiscrimination. Recall that this principle is embodied in Article I (see Table 6.1). This principle is violated, however, by Article XXIV, which allows for customs unions and free-trade areas in some circumstances. That raises the question of whether allowing for such regional trade agreements conflicts with the overall GATT goal of multilateral tariff reductions. Bhagwati (1993) has suggested that this question can be broken into two distinct issues: the "static impact effect" of regionalism, which is the impact of successive regional agreements (possibly leading towards global free trade) on world welfare; and the "dynamic time path," which is the issue of whether having the option of a regional trade agreement will impact countries' willingness to enter into a multilateral agreement. The first issue has been touched on at the end of chapter 6, drawing on the work of Krugman (1991a, 1991b) and Frankel (1997). We will examine here the second issue in the context of the median voter model, following Levy (1997).[13]

Levy proposes the following framework for thinking about sequential regional and multilateral agreements. In a multicountry world where the median voter in each country determines policy, suppose that a vote is taken initially on whether two countries should enter into bilateral free trade. For convenience, we treat the initial tariffs as prohibitive, so these countries are voting on whether to move from autarky to free trade between them, while retaining prohibitive tariffs with other countries. In the next period, a vote is then taken in each country as to whether to join into free trade with a larger group of countries, in a multilateral agreement. At this second stage, either country in the initial bilateral agreement has *veto power* over whether that agreement can be extended to incorporate new countries.

We shall assume that multilateral free trade brings benefits to both countries as compared to their autarky positions. That is, the median voters in both countries would approve a movement from autarky to multilateral free trade. The question is whether having bilateral free trade (with the assumed veto power of each country) acts as a "stepping stone" or a "stumbling block" towards multilateral free trade, to use the terminology of Bhagwati. To answer this, we need to consider four conceivable voting paths:

(1) The median voter in at least one country rejects the bilateral agreement, and then both countries agree to the multilateral agreement.
(2) The median voters in both countries agree to the bilateral agreement and then agree to the multilateral agreement.
(3) The median voters in both countries agree to the bilateral agreement and then both reject the multilateral agreement.
(4) The median voters in both countries agree to the bilateral agreement, but then one country vetoes the multilateral deal, whereas the other country would approve multilateral free trade.

Paths (1) and (2) are both possibilities, but in those cases the bilateral arrangement does not act as a hindrance to multilateral free trade. The multilateral deal is rejected in paths (3) and (4), so we need to examine whether these paths can actually occur. Case (4) can be *ruled out* by the assumption that the time spent in bilateral free trade is very short as compared to the time spent in multilateral free trade (if approved). This means that the median voter in the country that benefits from bilateral free trade, and then *also* benefits from multilateral trade, will anticipate that the *other* country will block the multilateral deal. Therefore, this median voter will refuse to approve the bilateral arrangement initially, correctly anticipating that multilateral free trade will still be achieved (since by assumption, this is better for both countries than autarky). By this argument, path (4) never occurs.

We are left, then, with only having to consider whether or not path (3) can occur: is it possible that the median voters in both countries are worse off going from bilateral to multilateral free trade, whereas they are better off going from autarky to bilateral or multilateral free trade? We will demonstrate that this is *impossible* with a HO production structure. After showing this, we discuss an extended model that incorporates monopolistic competition and product variety, under which path (3) can occur.

To demonstrate the impossibility of path (3) in the HO model, we use a simple but powerful graphical technique introduced by Levy. In Figure 9.5, a country's production possibility frontier (PPF) is illustrated, with the autarky equilibrium at point A. Treating all consumers as having identical homothetic tastes, there is an indifference curve tangent to the PPF at point A, with the autarky relative price of good 1 given by the slope of the line p^a. Also shown is a *smaller* PPF, which corresponds to just the labor and

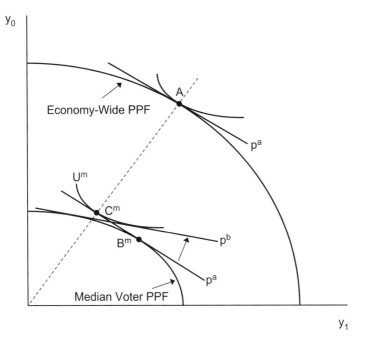

Figure 9.5

capital endowments owned by the median voter. Treating good 1 as labor intensive, and supposing that the median voter has a capital/labor ratio that is lower than that for the overall economy, this PPF is skewed towards good 1. Thus, at the autarky price ratio p^a, the median voter would have "individual production" at point B^m, and consumption at point C^m, with utility of U^m. It is evident that there are gains from the opportunity to trade with others in the economy, since consumption at point C^m is above the median voter's "individual PPF."

Now suppose that the economy enters into trade with another country (or group of countries). We assume that the countries are similar enough in their factor endowments for factor price equalization to occur, and let k^w denote the "world" capital/labor ratio in this integrated equilibrium (this would be the overall capital/labor ratio of the two countries with bilateral free trade, or all countries with multilateral free trade). With identical homothetic tastes across countries, the equilibrium relative price of good 1 can be written as a function $p(k^w)$, with $p'(k^w) > 0$ since good 1 is labor intensive.

If the economy shown in Figure 9.5 enters into trade with another country that has a *lower* capital/labor endowment than its own, this will *lower* the relative price of good 1, which then becomes the import good. A slight fall in p, from p^a in the direction of p^b, will clearly *lower* the welfare of the

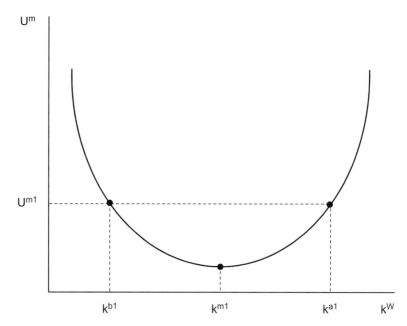

Figure 9.6

median voter. If this import price falls by a substantial amount, however, then the median voter can instead gain: at the price $p^b < p^a$ shown in Figure 9.5, the median voter has the *same* utility level U^m, so for $p < p^b$ the median voter will gain. Conversely, starting at the autarky equilibrium, if the economy enters into trade with another country that had a *higher* capital/labor endowment than its own, then the relative price of good 1 will rise as that good is exported, and for $p > p^a$ in Figure 9.5 the median voter again gains.

Summarizing these observations, in Figure 9.6 we graph the welfare of the median voter in country 1 against the capital/labor endowment k^w of the integrated world equilibrium. The endowment of the country is k^{a1}, so in autarky the relative price of good 1 is $p^{a1} = p(k^{a1})$, and the median voter obtains utility U^{m1}. If the country now trades in an integrated equilibrium with $p(k^w)$ *slightly lower* than p^{a1}, meaning that $k^w < k^{a1}$, we have argued above that the median voter is worse off. This is shown by utility declining in Figure 9.6 for k^w slightly below k^{a1}. But if the country trades in an integrated equilibrium with k^w *much lower* than k^{a1}, than we can obtain the price p^{b1} at which the median voter is back at their autarky utility level U^{m1}.

Let us denote the integrated capital/labor ratio at which the median voter achieves the same utility as in autarky by k^{b1}, with $p^{b1} = p(k^{b1})$. Then

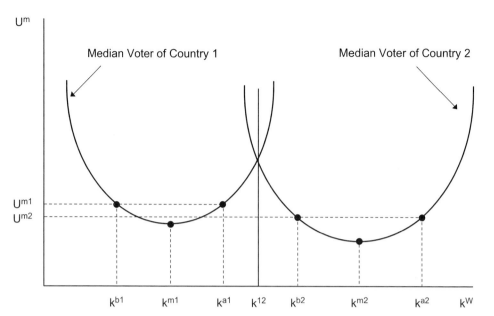

Figure 9.7

we see from Figure 9.6 that the median voter in country 1 will *reject free trade* with other countries when the integrated equilibrium has a capital/ labor endowment $k^w \in (k^{b1}, k^{a1})$, but otherwise will accept free trade for $k^w \notin (k^{b1}, k^{a1})$. Notice that the "rejection set" (k^{b1}, k^{a1}) is convex, which reflects the fact that utility of the median voter, $U^m(k^w)$, is a quasi-convex function of the capital/labor endowment in the integrated equilibrium.

Now consider the situation of countries 1 and 2 deciding whether to engage in bilateral free trade. In Figure 9.7 we graph the utilities of the median voter in each country. The "rejection sets" are (k^{b1}, k^{a1}) and (k^{b2}, k^{a2}), and in the case we have illustrated, country 2 is capital abundant, since its capital/labor endowment exceeds that of country 1, $k^{a1} < k^{a2}$. Then with bilateral free trade, the integrated world equilibrium has a capital/labor endowment denoted by $k^{12} = (K^1 + K^2)/(L^1 + L^2)$, and this lies in between the capital/labor endowments of the two countries, $k^{a1} \leq k^{12} \leq k^{a2}$. In order for the median voter *in both* countries to benefit from bilateral free trade, it must be the case that k^{12} lies *outside* both sets (k^{b1}, k^{a1}) and (k^{b2}, k^{a2}), as illustrated. Since we also have that $k^{a1} \leq k^{12} \leq k^{a2}$, it follows that bilateral free trade can benefit both countries only if the two "rejection sets" are *disjoint*, as illustrated.

Now let us ask whether countries 1 and 2, which are both better off from *bilateral* free trade, would be better or worse off from *multilateral* free trade. Let k^w denote the world capital/labor endowment in that integrated equilibrium. If $k^w = k^{12}$, then the two countries are obviously indifferent between bilateral and multilateral free trade (since the relative price is not affected). If k^w is slightly above k^{12}, then we can see from Figure 9.7 that country 1 would gain moving from bilateral to multilateral, but country 2 would lose. On the other hand, if k^w is much above k^{12}, so that $k^w > k^{a2}$ in Figure 9.7, then it is possible that both countries gain. Checking the other cases, if k^w is slightly below k^{12}, then country 2 would gain moving from bilateral to multilateral, but country 1 would lose; while if k^w is much below k^{12}, so that $k^w < k^{b1}$, then it is possible that both countries gain. In all cases, we see that *countries 1 and 2 cannot both lose in the move from bilateral to multilateral free trade.* Therefore, we have proved part (a) of the following theorem.

Theorem (Levy 1997)

(a) Under the two-by-two Heckscher-Ohlin production structure, if the median voters in both countries gain from bilateral free trade, then at least one country must gain from multilateral free trade.

(b) Allowing for product variety under monopolistic competition, it is possible that the median voters in both countries gain going from autarky to bilateral free trade, or from autarky to multilateral free trade, but lose going from bilateral to multilateral free trade.

Part (a) rules out path (3), and establishes that a bilateral free-trade agreement cannot act as a hindrance to a multilateral deal. The essential logic is that the two countries will accept the bilateral arrangement only if their "rejection sets" are *disjoint,* with their combined capital/labor endowment k^{12} lying in between these sets. This immediately rules out having the endowment k^w of a multilateral equilibrium contained in both sets. It is not difficult to see that this logic extends to an initial free-trade area involving any number of countries, who cannot subsequently all lose from multilateral free trade.

Having established this result for the two-by-two HO model, what about more general models? In part (b) of the theorem, we suppose that one sector produces a differentiated product under monopolistic competition, while another sector produces a labor-intensive homogeneous good. Furthermore, suppose that countries 1 and 2 are *identical.* There will still be gains from free trade between them, just as was demonstrated in Krugman's model at the beginning of chapter 5. So the median voters in countries 1 and 2 both prefer the free-trade area consisting of the country pair (1, 2).

Now suppose that there is country 3, with the same production structure as 1 and 2 but having a higher labor/capital endowment. Under multilateral free trade, it would produce more of the labor-intensive homogeneous good, and for convenience suppose that it is fully specialized in that good. Then the free-trade area consisting of (1, 2) obtains no further product variety gains from free trade with country 3, but there will still be a change in relative prices: since country 3 is labor abundant, free trade with it would lower the relative price of that good. This can quite possibly *lower* the welfare of the median voters in both country 1 and country 2. Therefore, it is entirely possible that the median voters in countries 1 and 2 *both lose* going from bilateral to multilateral free trade.

Finally, we need to check whether our initial assumption—that countries 1 and 2 are both better off with multilateral free trade than in autarky—is satisfied in this example. That is, we need to consider utility for the median voter in country 1 when it moves from autarky to free trade with countries (2, 3) combined. Country 1 then gains from increased product variety with the identical country 2, and possibly loses from the price change with labor-abundant country 3. Provided that the product variety gains *exceed* the losses for the median voter due to import competition, which is entirely possible, then country 1 gains overall from free trade with (2, 3). The same argument applies to country 2 when it moves from autarky to free trade with (1, 3). So despite the fact that multilateral free trade can bring gains as compared to *autarky*, we have found that it can bring losses as compared to *bilateral* free trade. In this situation, the bilateral agreement would prevent multilateral free trade from being pursued: it would indeed be a stumbling block rather than a stepping stone. This demonstrates part (b) of the theorem, and the general concern expressed by Bhagwati (1993; 2002, lecture 3) that regional trade agreements may inhibit the pursuit of multilateral free trade.[14]

Political Economy of Foreign Investment in China

All of the applications in the chapter so far have been to economies governed by direct democracy (with the median voter determining the optimal policy) or representative democracy (where voters elect representatives who then determine policies). Grossman and Helpman (2001) present a general formulation of democratic political systems where special interests exert an influence on policies. We conclude this chapter with an application of their framework to a nondemocratic system—the People's Republic of China. The motivation for this application is much the same as in Goldberg and Maggi 1999: to use the observed levels of some policy instrument or outcome to "reveal" the weights given by the government to various interest

---

[14] McLaren (2002) further argues that introducing *sector-specific sunk costs* can have a similar effect, under which a regional agreement can inhibit future multilateral deals.

groups. In the case of China, import tariffs have (until recently) been bound at relatively high and inflexible levels, so that that policy instrument cannot be used. Instead, we examine the policies towards foreign investment, as indicated by the entry of foreign firms into various provinces, to infer the weights in the government's objective function.

The model we use relies on the choice of policies to influence foreign investment. We shall not discuss the decisions of firms to enter foreign markets until the next chapter, but introduce here the idea that they may enter a market to "jump the tariff," that is, because they cannot export there due to tariff protection.[15] Grossman and Helpman (1996) have introduced foreign investment into their "protection for sale" model, and Branstetter and Feenstra (2002) make use of that model to analyze policies towards multinationals in China, as follows.

Consumers are assumed to have preferences over an additively separable numeraire good d_0, and a CES aggregate denoted by D:

$$U = d_0 + \left(\frac{\gamma}{\gamma - 1}\right) D^{(\gamma-1)/\gamma}, \quad \gamma > 0, \ \gamma \neq 1, \qquad (9.30a)$$

where the CES aggregate is

$$D = \left[N_h d_h^{(\sigma-1)/\sigma} + (N_f - M) d_f^{(\sigma-1)/\sigma} \right.$$
$$\left. + M d_m^{(\sigma-1)/\sigma} \right]^{\sigma/(\sigma-1)}, \quad \sigma > 1. \qquad (9.30b)$$

The values d_j denotes consumption of the differentiated varieties from sources: $j = h$ (home firms), of which there are N_h in number; $j = f$ (foreign imported products), of which there are $(N_f - M)$; and $j = m$ (multinationals in China) of which there are M. As usual, σ is the elasticity of substitution across individual varieties, while γ is the elasticity of demand for the aggregate good D, and we add the restriction that $\sigma > \gamma$.

Branstetter and Feenstra (2002) suppose that the domestic industry is owned by the government, as with state-owned firms in China. The profits earned by these firms receive extra weight in the government's objective function.[16] The presence of multinationals presents a potential threat to the state-owned enterprises through product market competition.[17]

---

[15] Bhagwati (1997) has taken this argument a step further and suggested that foreign firms may enter a market to "defuse" the threat of future protection, in what he calls "quid pro quo" foreign investment. See also Bhagwati et al. 1987; Dinopoulos 1989, 1992; and Wong 1989.

[16] As Naughton (1996) and other authors have noted, the Chinese government still relies on remittances from state-owned enterprises for about two-thirds of its revenue.

[17] Notice that foreign investment might also be complementary rather than competitive, because until recently in China the foreign firms were required to have local partners, which could benefit the state-owned enterprises. But a number of studies suggest that the Chinese

This creates a conflict between the entry of foreign firms and the profits of state-owned firms that must be resolved though government policy towards entry of the multinationals.

In designing the government policies, we allow the various *provinces* of China to exercise autonomous control over multinational entry. This is broadly consistent with the multiple layers of approval required for foreign investment in China. Only the largest projects (initially $30 million but later $50 million) require approval from the central government, whereas all projects require approval from the regional and provincial governments. In addition, we suppose that the separate provinces control trade between themselves through *internal* border barriers. The level of such barriers is the subject of current debate among experts on the Chinese economy. On the one hand, Young (2000) has argued that internal border barriers are rising, whereas Naughton (1999) disagrees. For reasons of modeling convenience, we take an extreme version of the view in Young and assume there is no trade between the provinces. This means that when a multinational enters one province, it is selling only to the local consumers. The utility function in (9.30) therefore applies to *each* province, which differs in the number of firms of each type found there.

We will suppose that labor is the only factor of production, and one unit of the numeraire is produced with one unit of labor, so wages are unity. We shall assume, however, that the multinational firms pay a *wage premium* of $(w - 1) > 0$. The wage premium is meant to proxy for a wide array of possible benefits that multinationals bring that are not captured in our model. Costs for the locally produced products are c_j, $j = h, m$. Costs for products produced abroad are c_f, but also face a specific tariff of t, so that marginal costs become $c_f + t$. Prices are a standard markup over these marginal costs, using the elasticity σ. We make the key assumption that $c_m < c_f + t$. This assumption ensures that the price charged by multinationals, p_m, is less than that for imports, p_f. It follows that as more multinationals enter (M increases) and these products are sold for $p_m < p_f$, the demand for products of the state-owned firms will decline due to substitution away from these products. This is how product market competition between the multinationals and domestic firms is captured in the model.

Each foreign firm faces the decision of whether to supply through imports, or through setting up a local plant that requires a fixed cost of $F > 0$. We suppose that the government also charges the multinational a profit tax of $\tau \geq 0$. This instrument is supposed to reflect the vast range of actual policies used in China to extract rents from multinationals, and not

---

government, both national and local, is acutely aware of this competition, and has taken steps to impede the ability of foreign firms to compete in the Chinese market (e.g., Li and Chen 1998; Rosen 1998).

just the corporate tax on multinationals.[18] By modeling these policies as a tax on profits, we are abstracting from the inefficiencies caused by actual policies.

The net profits earned locally are thus $(1 - \tau)\pi_m - F$, where $\pi_m = p_m d_m/\sigma$ is profits under the standard CES markup-pricing rule. Alternately, the multinational could just export to the home country, and earn $\pi_f = p_f d_f/\sigma$. Thus, entry will occur if and only if $(1 - \tau)\pi_m - F \geq \pi_f$. This condition is written as

$$(1 - \tau)\frac{p_m d_m}{\sigma} - F \geq \frac{p_f d_f}{\sigma}. \qquad (9.31)$$

Entry is influenced through the profits tax τ and the specific tariff t, so the number of multinational firms is written as a function $M(\tau, t)$. Multinationals react in the expected manner to changes in these policies: when (9.31) holds as an equality, then $dM/d\tau < 0$ and $dM/dt > 0$.

We now define the government's objective function over the various interest groups, beginning with consumer/worker utility U, which receives a weight of α. The profits of the home state–owned firms are $N_h \pi_h = N_h p_h d_h/\sigma$, which accrue to the regional and national government. We give revenue from state-owned firms a weight β in the objective function. Finally, the government extracts rents $M\tau\pi_m$ from the multinationals, and also collects tariff revenue of $(N_f - M)td_f$. These two sources of revenue are each given weights of unity. The objective function for each province is then defined by

$$G(M, \tau, t) \equiv \alpha U + \beta N_h \pi_h + M\tau\pi_m + (N_f - M)td_f, \qquad (9.32)$$

where the multinationals entering each province are endogenously determined from (9.31).

We suppose that the central and the provincial governments jointly determine the rents appropriated from the multinationals. The central government also chooses the tariff rate. Denoting provinces by the subscript i, we let $G_i[M_i(\tau_i, t), \tau_i, t]$ denote the objective function (9.32) for each. Then the profit tax and tariff are chosen to solve

$$\max_{\tau_j, t} \sum_i G_i[M_i(\tau_i, t), \tau_i, t]. \qquad (9.33)$$

---

[18] In fact, foreign firms are often taxed at zero or reduced rates for the first years of operation. Despite this, there are many ways that local and national agencies extract rents from the multinationals. For example, the fact that most multinationals have had to use local partners reflects an implicit tax on their profits, which are shared with the partner; similarly, the land-use fees that are commonly charged reduce the multinationals' profits, as do conditions of technology transfer and export requirements. Of course, bribes paid to allow multinationals to enter are another example of the profit tax. Wei (1998) argues that corruption in China, which includes the need for "questionable payments," acts as a significant deterrent to foreign direct investment.

We solve (9.33) over the choice of the profits tax rate τ_i, while a discussion of the solution for tariffs t is in Branstetter and Feenstra 2002. Differentiating (9.33), the first-order condition is that $\partial G_i / \partial M_i = - M_i \pi_{mi} / (\partial M_i / \partial \tau_i)$. This means that the gain from attracting one more multinational ($\partial G_i / \partial M_i$) is just balanced against the *fall* in the revenue $\tau_i M_i \pi_{mi}$ when the tax rate is lowered to attract another multinational. That is, the regions are acting as monopsonists in attracting foreign capital. This first-order condition for the choice of τ_i can be written as[19]

$$
\begin{aligned}
s_{mi} = & - \beta s_{hi} + \eta \left(\frac{w_i - 1}{w_i} \right) + \alpha(\sigma - 1) \left(\frac{w_i - 1}{w_i} \right)(s_{hi} + s_{fi}) \\
& - \sigma \left(\frac{t}{p_f} \right) s_{fi} + \left(\frac{M_i}{N_f - M_i} \right) s_{fi} + \varepsilon_i,
\end{aligned}
\tag{9.34}
$$

where $s_j, j = h, f, m$ denotes the *share of provincial consumption* purchased from home state–owned firms, imported products, or multinational products, respectively, and ε_i is a term involving unobserved profit levels that is treated as a random error.

The first term on the right side of (9.34) is the share of provincial consumption on state-owned firms, which enters with the coefficient $-\beta$. Thus, the weight on state-owned firms in the provincial objective function is simply obtained as the coefficient on their share in the regression (9.34). A high weight on the state-owned firms indicates that in provinces where these firms are more prevalent, the share of multinational firms will be correspondingly reduced. The next term on the right side of (9.34) is the wage premium paid by multinationals, which has the coefficient $\eta \equiv \alpha(\sigma - 1)(\gamma - 1)/(\sigma - \gamma)$, which is of ambiguous sign. Following this is the wage premium times the share of spending on state-owned firms plus imports. When the wage premium is higher, we expect that regions will be more willing to accept multinationals, and this is confirmed by having a positive coefficient $\alpha(\sigma - 1)$ on that variable.

The estimate of σ itself comes from the next term, which is the tariff rate times the share of spending on imports. This term reflects the loss in tariff revenue as multinationals enter, and the coefficient is $-\sigma$.[20] Thus, combining it with the former coefficient, we can recover an estimate of α. The final term reflects the number of multinationals times the share of imports. For simplicity we measure the number of multinationals M_i by their capital stock in each province, and treat the number of foreign firms wanting to export or invest in China, N_f, as constant over provinces and time and estimate it as a coefficient.

---

[19] This first-order condition is derived in Branstetter and Feenstra 2002.
[20] See our discussion of Brecher and Diaz-Alejandro 1977 in problem 11.1.

TABLE 9.1

Provincial Spending on Output of Multinational Enterprises as Dependent Variable

Independent Variable	Coefficient	OLS	TSLS	Weighted TSLS
		Estimation Method		
Provincial spending on state-owned production	$-\beta$	−0.41 (0.12)	−1.30 (0.40)	−1.66 (0.48)
Wage premium × (state-owned + imports)	$\alpha(\sigma-1)$	0.42 (0.23)	2.19 (0.87)	3.62 (1.16)
Tariff × imports	$-\sigma$	−0.15 (2.7)	−7.4 (3.3)	−15.9 (5.1)
Wage premium	$\dfrac{\alpha(\sigma-1)(\gamma-1)}{(\sigma-\gamma)}$	−118 (64)	−967 (435)	−3333 (1085)
FDI stock × imports	$1/N_f$	0.037 (0.022)	0.037 (0.017)	0.052 (0.013)
Provincial apparent consumption		0.11 (0.02)	0.15 (0.03)	0.15 (0.02)
R^2, N		0.85, 297	0.74, 280	0.76, 280

Note: The sample consists of 29 provinces (excluding Tibet) over 1984/95, using fixed effects for provinces and for time; only provinces with positive multinational output are included. All regressions except the first are estimated with TSLS. The weighted regressions use provincial GDP as a weight. White standard errors are reported in parentheses.

For estimation, a time subscript is added to most variables in (9.34). There is an obvious endogeneity problem in that the share of state-owned sales, on the right, will be correlated with the share of multinational sales (since all the shares sum to unity). To offset this, Branstetter and Feenstra estimate (9.34) in levels rather than shares (i.e., multiplying all variables by provincial apparent consumption) and also use instruments and weights.[21]

The results from estimating (9.34) using a panel of data for Chinese provinces over 1984–95, are shown in Table 9.1. Each of the three columns of results uses a different estimation technique, beginning with OLS, and

[21] The instruments are provincial electricity production (used as an instrument for expenditure on state-owned firms); indexes of urban, state, and overall wages (used as instruments for the wage premium); provincial GDP, population, average rural and urban income (used as instruments for apparent consumption); provincial processing imports (used as an instrument for ordinary imports); and various interactions between these terms. The weighted regressions use provincial GDP as a weight.

moving to weighted TSLS (standard errors are in parentheses). OLS estimates are largely uninformative, as we are unable to obtain reasonable estimates of σ. However, our estimates improve substantially when we move to two-stage least squares, and further weight the observations by provincial GDP. Each regression includes a full set of provincial and year fixed effects.

The estimate of the parameter β, the weight of state-owned enterprise output in the government's objective function, is taken from the regression coefficient on state-owned enterprise output, and ranges from 1.3 to 1.66 (ignoring the OLS estimate).[22] Estimates of α, the weight on consumer welfare, can be derived from the regression coefficients shown in the second and third rows of Table 9.1. For our preferred specification, which is the weighted TSLS estimate in the third regression, we obtain $\hat{\alpha} = 0.24$ as reported in Table 9.2. The difference between the state-owned and consumer weight is $\hat{\beta} - \hat{\alpha} = 1.42$, and the standard error of this difference is computed as 0.46. Thus, we find that the weight given to consumer welfare is *significantly lower* than that applied to the output of state-owned enterprises (at the 5% level), with their ratio being about *one-seventh* in our preferred estimates. Without using provincial GDP as weights, the TSLS estimate in the second regression gives $\hat{\alpha} = 0.34$, which is still *one-quarter* of the weight given to the state-owned enterprises. Turning to other parameters, we obtain high estimates of the elasticity of substitution σ (from 7 to 16), though these are somewhat imprecise.

A breakdown of the structural coefficients of interest is provided in Table 9.2 for later subsamples of the data, the 1988–95 period and the 1990–95 period. As we confine our view to the later subsamples, we lose observations and consequently precision in some of our estimates; sub periods smaller than 1990–95 do not yield many significant coefficients. In the later subperiods, the estimated magnitude of the weight on state-owned enterprises falls. This is consistent with the historical trend towards liberalization, of course. In the relatively liberal 1990–95 subperiod, for example, we find that the weight on state-owned enterprises is *unity*, which is still considerably higher than the weight on consumer welfare (though the difference between them is no longer significantly different from zero).

These estimates provide a stark contrast to the results of Goldberg and Maggi (1999) for the United States, where consumer welfare had a weight that was 50 to 100 times more than campaign contributions. For

---

[22] We note that the sign and magnitude of this estimate is contingent on including total provincial consumption as a control variable in the regression: controlling for total provincial spending, a decline in the spending on state-owned firms is associated with a rise in the spending on multinationals; but without this control variable, the sign of β is reversed. See the empirical exercise to reproduce Tables 9.1 and 9.2.

TABLE 9.2
Coefficient Estimates, by Time Period

| | | Coefficient | | |
Sample	N	α	β	σ
1984–1995	280	0.24 (0.07)	1.66 (0.48)	15.9 (5.1)
1988–1995	210	0.24 (0.13)	1.32 (0.50)	11.5 (6.7)
1990–1995	132	0.20 (0.15)	1.04 (0.49)	10.0 (7.6)

Note: Computed from the third regression reported in Table 9.1, but run over different samples. The estimation method is weighted TSLS. White standard errors are in parentheses.

China, we find that state-owned enterprises have a weight that is between four and seven times greater than that given to consumers. The evidence of a political premium on state-owned industries diminishes over time, but the point estimates still indicate these firms are favored. Branstetter and Feenstra (2002) further investigate the impact on provincial objective functions of the changes in tariff structure that China has promised under WTO accession. They find that these changes could potentially lower welfare in some provinces, due to the exit of multinationals. This provides some quantitative backing for skepticism that China, given the current political equilibrium, will actually follow through with the promised liberalization in all sectors and regions under its entry into the WTO.

Conclusions

In this chapter we have relied on two major models: the median voter model (first applied to trade policy by Mayer [1984]), and the "protection for sale" model of Grossman and Helpman (1994, 1995a, 1995b, 1996). There are many other models of the political economy of trade policy, and the reader is referred to Hillman 1989 and Rodrik 1995 for surveys. The median voter model relies on a voting mechanism under direct democracy, and despite this rather simplified framework, receives surprising empirical support from Dutt and Mitra (2002). In comparison, the "protection for sale" model allows for the government to be influenced by many industry lobbies. This has received strong empirical support for the United States from Goldberg and Maggi (1999) and Gawande and Bandyopadhyay (2000), along with numerous empirical applications to other countries, as surveyed by Gawande and Krishna (2003).

In their original formulations, the median voter and "protection for sale" models both treat international prices as fixed, so that tariffs shift income between interest groups, but cannot raise the welfare of all groups. In contrast, Bagwell and Staiger (1999, 2002) explicitly introduce a large-country model, under which tariffs can improve the terms of trade and raise a country's welfare. The government objective function used by them encompasses the median voter and "protection for sale" models, while Grossman and Helpman (1995a) also investigate terms of trade effects in the latter model. A country that uses an import tariff to improve its terms of trade does so at the expense of the other country (plus an added deadweight loss), so from the viewpoint of world efficiency, it would be better for countries to agree to avoid such actions. This creates an important role for the GATT, and the principle of *reciprocity* in tariff reductions provides a way to eliminate the incentive to manipulate the terms of trade. Notice that even under this principle, tariffs are still used in Bagwell and Staiger 1999, 2002 and Grossman and Helpman 1995a for political economy reasons.

We have also reviewed the role of regional trade agreements, and whether they help or hinder the movement towards multilateral free trade. Levy (1997) employs a median voter model to address this issue, while Grossman and Helpman (1995b) extend the "protection for sale" model in that direction. Empirically, it would be difficult to infer the impact of regional agreements on the pursuit of multilateral free trade, since the multilateral agreements of GATT are themselves so infrequent. But there are a number of related empirical questions that can be addressed. Krishna (2003) provides empirical evidence on the distance between countries and the potential welfare gains from regional agreements. He finds that close trading partners do not appear to have a "natural" advantage in created welfare-improving free-trade areas. Baier and Bergstrand (2002) and Magee (2002) introduce the endogeneity of free-trade agreements into a gravity equation, of the type discussed in chapter 5. These authors find that the impact of FTAs is significantly affected by treating these agreements as endogenous. The variables they include to explain free-trade areas also provide a test of the determinants of these regions, and these papers are recommended for further reading.

Problems

In the model of Mitra (1999), organized and unorganized industries are treated as symmetric, having the same world prices, capital stocks, and production and demand functions and differ only in their lobbying ability. Therefore, the return to the fixed factor in any industry can be written as $\pi(p_i)$ instead of $\pi_i(p_i)$, depending on the price but not on any other industry characteristic. Normalizing the world prices at unity, denote the price in organized industries by $p_o = 1 + t_o$, and in unorganized industries by $p_u = 1 + t_u$. The following questions derive additional results for that model.

9.1 Consider the return to the specific factor in sector i, from (9.8):

$$\pi(p_i) = \overset{\max}{\underset{L_i}{}}[p_i f(L_i, K) - L_i],$$

where we assume that $f_{LL} < 0$. By differentiating the first-order condition for this problem and using $\pi'(p_i) = y(p_i)$, show that profits are a convex function of the industry price.

9.2 Replace $\lambda_k n_o$ with λ_o in (9.17), and rewrite the optimal tariff $t_o > 0$ and subsidy $t_u < 0$ as

$$t_j = \left(\frac{\delta_j - \lambda_o}{\alpha + \lambda_o}\right) y(p_j) \left|\frac{\partial m}{\partial p_j}\right|^{-1},$$

where $\delta_o = 1$ and $\delta_o = 0$.

Output depends on the industry price, but for convenience, we treat the import derivative as fixed and equal across industries. Then compute $\dfrac{dt_o}{d\lambda_o}$ and $\dfrac{dt_u}{d\lambda_o}$, and show that $\left|\dfrac{dt_o}{d\lambda_o}\right| > \left|\dfrac{dt_u}{d\lambda_o}\right|$.

9.3 Continuing to denote $\lambda_k n_o$ by λ_o, consider the return to the specific factor in an organized rather than an unorganized industry, $\Delta W(\lambda_o) = \pi(p_o) - \pi(p_u)$. Using the results from problems 9.1 and 9.2, show that $\Delta W'(\lambda_o) = \pi'(p_o)(dt_o/d\lambda_o) - \pi'(p_u)(dt_u/d\lambda_o) < 0$.

9.4 The equilibrium prices $p^w(\tau, \tau^*)$ in (9.21) are defined by $m(p^w\tau) = x^*(p^w/\tau^*)$. Assuming that $m'(p^w\tau) < 0$ and $x^{*\prime}(p^w/\tau^*) > 0$, show that the inequalities in (9.22) hold.

Empirical Exercises

These exercises reproduce regression results in Branstetter and Feenstra 2002. To complete the exercises, the file "china_fdi.dta" should be stored in c:\Empirical_Exercise\Chapter_9\. Then do the following

9.1 Run the program "share_reg.do" to reproduce the regression results in Table 9.1. Notice that apparent consumption ("appcon3") is included as a control variable in these regressions. What happens if this variable is dropped?

9.2 Open the Excel file "standard_errors.xls" to see how the results in Table 9.2 are computed. What formula is used for α, and for its variance and standard error? Justify these formulas.

Hint: Consider the easier case of taking the difference between α and β. Then

$$\text{var}(\alpha - \beta) = E[(\alpha - \beta) - (\bar{\alpha} - \bar{\beta})]^2 = E f(\alpha, \beta),$$

where $f(\alpha, \beta)$ is the quadratic function indicated. To compute this expected value, we take a second-order Taylor series expansion:

$$
\begin{aligned}
f(\alpha, \beta) &\approx f(\bar{\alpha}, \bar{\beta}) + f_\alpha(\bar{\alpha}, \bar{\beta})(\alpha - \bar{\alpha}) + f_\beta(\bar{\alpha}, \bar{\beta})(\beta - \bar{\beta}) \\
&\quad + \tfrac{1}{2} f_{\alpha\alpha}(\bar{\alpha}, \bar{\beta})(\alpha - \bar{\alpha})^2 + \tfrac{1}{2} f_{\beta\beta}(\bar{\alpha}, \bar{\beta})(\beta - \bar{\beta})^2 \\
&\quad + f_{\alpha\beta}(\bar{\alpha}, \bar{\beta})(\alpha - \bar{\alpha})(\beta - \bar{\beta}).
\end{aligned}
$$

It follows that

$$Ef(\alpha, \beta) \approx \tfrac{1}{2} f_{\alpha\alpha}(\bar{\alpha}, \bar{\beta})\sigma_\alpha^2 + \tfrac{1}{2} f_{\beta\beta}(\bar{\alpha}, \bar{\beta})\sigma_\beta^2 + f_{\alpha\beta}(\bar{\alpha}, \bar{\beta})\,\text{cov}(\alpha, \beta).$$

So computing the derivatives of the quadratic function $f(\alpha, \beta)$, we obtain

$$\text{var}(\alpha - \beta) = E[(\alpha - \beta) - (\bar{\alpha} - \bar{\beta})]^2 \approx \sigma_\alpha^2 + \sigma_\beta^2 - 2\,\text{cov}(\alpha, \beta).$$

Now given the formula for α, use the same approach to justify its variance.

Chapter 10

Trade and Endogenous Growth

THE LINK BETWEEN trade and growth has long been a question of interest for both theory and policy. David Ricardo developed a dynamic model of corn and velvet production, with corn produced by land and labor and velvet produced with labor alone.[1] The need to pay labor from a "wage fund" established prior to production prevents all labor from being employed initially (i.e., there is a liquidity constraint on firms). Ricardo showed that in autarky the gradual expansion of the wage fund and growth of velvet production would lower its relative price, until a long-run equilibrium was reached. Opening trade, however, would allow the relative price of velvet to be maintained at world levels, thereby benefiting capitalists at the expense of landowners. This remarkable model demonstrates many of the issues that are of interest in modern discussions of trade and growth: the possibility that growth will be associated with continual changes in prices, and conversely, the impact of trade on prices and growth rates themselves.

In the first of these issues we will be primarily concerned with the effects of growth on the *terms of trade*, that is, the price of exports relative to imports. This brings us to the famous case of "immiserizing growth," due to Bhagwati (1958), growth that can actually lower a country's welfare due to a fall in the terms of trade. The idea that developing countries might be subject to a *decline* in their terms of trade, particularly for primary commodities, is associated with the Latin American economist Raul Prebisch (1950). While there is little evidence to support that hypothesis in general, it is still the case that declines in the terms of trade due to growth have been observed (Acemoglu and Ventura 2002; Debaere and Lee 2002).

In the second part of the chapter, we model the underlying determinants of growth through research and development. This class of models goes by the name '*endogenous growth*,' and their application to trade has been most thoroughly studied by Grossman and Helpman (1991). We will describe just one of the models presented by those authors, which is a dynamic version of the CES monopolistic competition model presented in

[1] See Findlay 1984, 187–91, who cites this model to Ricardo's *Essay on the Influence of a Low Price of Corn upon the Profits of Stock* (Ricardo 1951, 4:1–42).

chapter 5.[2] Even in this case, we will find that trade can have a fairly wide range of effects on product innovation within a country and therefore on growth. When there is free trade in *all goods*, including *free international flows of knowledge*, trade raises growth rates and brings gains to all countries; but this is not necessarily the case with free trade in only a subset of the goods without flows of knowledge. Empirically, then, the beneficial effect of trade on growth depends very strongly on whether there are international spillovers of knowledge, so we shall review the empirical evidence on that and other topics.

We begin with a discussion of how to measure productivity growth. This is quite easy in the case of perfect competition, but not under imperfect competition. In the latter case, it turns out that conventional measures of productivity growth are biased due to increasing returns to scale and the markup of price over marginal cost. Hall (1988) has proposed a method to correct for this problem and, at the same time, estimate the markups. In the context of trade reform it allows us to estimate the extent to which trade liberalization has led to a reduction in markups by firms facing import competition. This approach has been applied to Turkey by Levinsohn (1993) and to the Ivory Coast by Harrison (1994), as we shall discuss.

Measurement of Productivity

Growth in the output of a firm or industry can occur due to growth in inputs (labor, capital, and human capital), or due to an increase in output that is *not explained* by inputs: the latter is called productivity growth. Specifically, suppose that output y_i is produced using labor L_i and capital K_i, with the production function $y_i = A_i f(L_i, K_i)$, where A_i is a measure of Hicks-neutral technological progress. Totally differentiating this, we have $dy_i = dA_i f(L_i, K_i) + A_i f_{iL} dL_i + A_i f_{iK} dK_i$. Dividing this by $y_i = A_i f(L_i, K_i)$, and letting $\hat{z} = dz/z$ denote the percentage change in any variable, we see that

$$\hat{y}_i = \hat{A}_i + \left[\left(\frac{f_{iL} L_i}{f(L_i, K_i)} \right) \hat{L}_i + \left(\frac{f_{iK} K_i}{f(L_i, K_i)} \right) \hat{K}_i \right]. \qquad (10.1)$$

---

[2] This model was introduced by Judd (1985), Grossman and Helpman (1989, 1990), and Romer (1990), and also applied to trade by Rivera-Batiz and Romer (1991a, 1991b). The alternative to the CES model is the "quality ladders" model of product improvement, as described by Segerstrom, Anant, and Dinopoulos (1990), Grossman and Helpman (1991), and Taylor (1993). There are many other writings on endogenous growth and trade, including Taylor 1994 on the gains from trade and Dinopoulos and Segerstrom 1999a, 1999b on the dynamic effects of tariffs.

In general, then, output growth can be measured by productivity growth plus a weighted average of the growth in inputs, where the weights are the *elasticities of output with respect to each factor*. The difficulty is that these weights are not directly observable. With the added assumption of perfect competition, however, the marginal products equal $A_i f_{iL} = w/p_i$ and $A_i f_{iK} = r/p_i$, in which case the elasticities appearing in (10.1) are measured by $\theta_{iL} = wL_i/p_i y_i$ and $\theta_{iK} = rK_i/p_i y_i$, which are the *revenue shares* of labor and capital. Under the further assumption of constant returns to scale, these shares sum to unity, so that $\theta_{iK} = 1 - \theta_{iL}$. Then we see from (10.1) that technological progress $\hat{A}_i$ can be measured by the difference between the growth of output and a share-weighted average of the growth in inputs, which is the definition of total factor productivity (TFP) due to Solow (1957):[3]

$$\text{TFP}_i \equiv \hat{y}_i - [\theta_{iL}\hat{L}_i + (1 - \theta_{iL})\hat{K}_i]. \tag{10.1'}$$

Notice that this measure of productivity growth is indeed a "residual"—the portion of output growth that is not explained by inputs—or a "measure of our ignorance," in the memorable phrase of Abramovitz (1956).

Let us now weaken our assumptions and allow for imperfect competition and increasing returns to scale. To introduce increasing returns to scale, we assume that the production function is homogeneous of degree $\mu_i > 1$, so it follows that $\mu_i f(L_i, K_i) = (f_{iL}L_i + f_{iK}K_i)$.[4] Substituting this into (10.1), we obtain

$$
\begin{aligned}
\hat{y}_i &= \hat{A}_i + \mu_i\left[\left(\frac{f_{iL}L_i}{f_{iL}L_i + f_{iK}K_i}\right)\hat{L}_i + \left(\frac{f_{iK}K_i}{f_{iL}L_i + f_{iK}K_i}\right)\hat{K}_i\right] \\
&= \hat{A}_i + \mu_i\left[\left(\frac{f_{iL}L_i}{f_{iL}L_i + f_{iK}K_i}\right)\hat{L}_i + \left(1 - \frac{f_{iL}L_i}{f_{iL}L_i + f_{iK}K_i}\right)\hat{K}_i\right] \quad (10.2) \\
&= \hat{A}_i + \left(\frac{f_{iL}L_i}{f(L_i, K_i)}\right)(\hat{L}_i - \hat{K}_i) + \mu_i\hat{K}_i,
\end{aligned}
$$

where the last line follows from $\mu_i f(L_i, K_i) = (f_{iL}L_i + f_{iK}K_i)$ and simple arithmetic.

---

[3] In practice, total factor productivity in (10.1') would be measured using first differences rather than infinitesimal changes, as $\text{TFP}_i \equiv \Delta \ln y_i - [\theta_{iL}\Delta \ln L_i + (1-\theta_{iL})\Delta \ln K_i]$. We have already seen this definition of TFP in our discussion of chapter 4, as well as the dual definition, $\text{TFP}_i \equiv ([\theta_{iL}\Delta \ln w_i - \theta_{iK}\Delta \ln r_i) - \Delta \ln p_i$, where w_i is the wage, r_i is the rental on capital, and p_i is the price in industry i. Note that with the log change in input quantities or prices measured between two points in time, the factor cost shares θ_{ij} should be measured as the *average* between these two periods; this method is called the Törnqvist index of total factor productivity (see Appendix A).

[4] See problem 1.2.

With imperfect competition in the product market, the equilibrium condition for the hiring of labor is

$$p_i\left(1 - \frac{1}{\eta_i}\right)A_i f_{iL} = w, \tag{10.3}$$

where η_i is the (positive) elasticity of demand. It follows that the real wage equals $(w/p_i) = [(\eta_i - 1)/\eta_i]A_i f_{iL}$. The share of labor in total revenue is then

$$\theta_{iL} = \frac{wL_i}{p_i y_i} = \frac{(\eta_i - 1)A_i f_{iL} L_i}{\eta_i y_i} = \left(\frac{\eta_i - 1}{\eta_i}\right)\left(\frac{f_{iL} L_i}{f(L_i, K_i)}\right), \tag{10.4}$$

where the final equality follows from $y_i = A_i f(L_i, K_i)$. Thus, the labor share *understates* the elasticity of output with respect to labor, since $(\eta_i - 1)/\eta_i < 1$.

Substituting (10.4) into (10.2), we see that output growth is related to true productivity change by[5]

$$\hat{y}_i = \hat{A}_i + [\eta_i/(\eta_i - 1)]\theta_{iL}(\hat{L}_i - \hat{K}_i) + \mu_i \hat{K}_i. \tag{10.5}$$

Thus, we see that output growth is composed of true productivity change $\hat{A}_i$, plus the change in labor/capital growth times the coefficient $\eta_i/(\eta_i - 1)$, plus capital growth times the returns to scale parameters μ_i. The coefficient $\eta_i/(\eta_i - 1)$ equals the ratio of price to marginal cost, so any *changes* in this coefficient are interpreted as evidence of changes in the price-cost markup. Running (10.5) as a regression therefore allows us to measure the impact of trade liberalization on the markups charged, as well as estimate the returns to scale.

Harrison (1994) applies this technique to firm-level data for the Ivory Coast, which had an import liberalization beginning in 1985. The estimating equation is (10.5) but written with discrete rather than infinitesimal changes:

$$\begin{aligned} \Delta \ln y_{it} &= \Delta \ln A_{it} + \beta_t \theta_{iL}(\Delta \ln L_{it} - \Delta \ln K_{it}) + \mu \Delta \ln K_{it} \\ &= \alpha_i + \beta_t \theta_{iL}(\Delta \ln L_{it} - \Delta \ln K_{it}) + \mu \Delta \ln K_{it} + \varepsilon_{it}, \end{aligned} \tag{10.5'}$$

where in the second line we replace the true productivity change $\Delta \ln A_{it}$ by $\alpha_i + \varepsilon_{it}$, composed of a firm fixed-effect α_i and a random component ε_{it}.

---

[5] Alternatively, we can express (10.5) in first differences and deduct $[\theta_{iL}\Delta \ln L_i + (1 - \theta_{iL}) \Delta \ln K_i]$ from both sides, obtaining $\text{TFP}_i = \Delta \ln A_i + [1/(\eta_i - 1)]\theta_{iL}(\Delta \ln L_i - \Delta \ln K_i) + (\mu_i - 1) \Delta \ln K_i$, using the definition of TFP from note 3.

The estimated ratio of price to marginal cost, $\beta_t \equiv \eta_t/(\eta_t - 1)$, is treated as common across firms $i = 1, \ldots, N$ within each industry but is allowed to change in the pre- and postliberalization sample. Thus, by examining the change in β_t we can determine the effect of liberalization on markups.

Estimation is performed with both OLS and instrumental variables.[6] Initial estimates generally provide only insignificant changes in the estimated price-cost ratios. So rather than just letting the markups β_t change over time, Harrison instead interacts this variable with industry-level estimates of import penetration. Specifically, let $\beta_t = \beta_0 + \beta_1 M_t$, where M_t is the ratio of imports to consumption in each industry. Substituting this in (10.5′), we obtain an interaction term between M_t and $\theta_{iL}(\Delta\ln L_{it} - \Delta\ln K_{it})$, with the coefficient β_1. We expect that $\beta_1 < 0$, so that higher imports lead to lower markups. Harrison obtains an estimate of -0.25 for β_1 over the entire sample (standard error of 0.05). This indicates, for example, that an increase in import penetration from 0 to 50% would reduce the ratio of price to marginal cost by 12%. She also finds that reduced tariffs are associated with lower price-cost ratios, but that result is only significant at the 15% level. So the connection between import liberalization and reduced markups is weakly confirmed in her study.

Notice that in our derivation of (10.5) we *did not* assume that the rental on capital is observable, but only used the labor share. If instead the rental is observable, then the capital share is $\theta_{iK} = rK_i/p_iy_i = [(\eta_i - 1)/\eta_i] \times [f_{iK}K_i/f(L_i,K_i)]$, analogous to (10.4). Substituting these two equations into (10.1), we obtain an alternative relationship between output growth and true productivity change:[7]

$$\hat{y}_i = \hat{A}_i + \left(\frac{\eta_i}{\eta_i - 1}\right)(\theta_{iL}\hat{L}_i + \theta_{iK}\hat{K}_i). \tag{10.6}$$

Levinsohn (1993) applies equation (10.6), written using discrete changes, to firm-level data for Turkey, which embarked on an ambitious liberalization program in 1980. He replaces the true productivity change

---

[6] The error ε_{it} in (10.5′) is likely correlated with factor inputs on the right: a firm that experiences a boost to productivity will hire more inputs. Appropriate instruments should be correlated with factor usage by the firm, but not with productivity, and Harrison uses the nominal exchange rate, the price of energy, sectoral real wages, and the firm's reported debt. The endogeneity of inputs, and appropriate methods to correct for it, is also addressed by Hall (1988), Olley and Pakes (1996), and Levinsohn and Petrin (2001).

[7] Notice that (10.5) and (10.6) are identical if there are zero profits in the industry, so that price equals average cost. In that case, the ratio of average cost to marginal cost, which equals the returns to scale μ_i, also equals the ratio of price to marginal cost, which is $\eta_i/(\eta_i - 1)$. In addition, the labor and capital shares sum to unity, so that $\theta_{iK} = 1 - \theta_{iL}$.

$\Delta \ln A_{it}$ by $\alpha_t + \varepsilon_{it}$, composed of a year fixed-effect α_t that is common across firms and a random component ε_{it}. Once again, the estimated ratio of price to marginal cost, $\beta_t \equiv \eta_t/(\eta_t - 1)$, is treated as common across firms $i = 1, \ldots, N$ within each industry but is allowed to vary over time, as liberalization proceeds. In his results, Levinsohn finds a strong connection between the industries that experience liberalization and those where the estimated price-cost ratios are reduced: in three industries experiencing significant liberalization, the estimated ratios fell; whereas in two other industries experiencing increased protection, the ratios rose; and in the remaining five industries where the ratios where insignificantly different from unity (i.e., the industries are perfectly competitive), there was no clear pattern to the changes in the point estimates of β_t. So for both the Ivory Coast and Turkey, the evidence supports the hypothesis that import liberalization reduces markups.

Immiserizing Growth

We now turn to the link between growth and the terms of trade, and the case of "immiserizing growth" due to Bhagwati (1958). This case is illustrated in Figure 10.1, where good 1 is the exportable and good 2 is the importable. With the initial production possibility frontier (PPF), the economy produces at point B and consumes at point C. Due to growth the PPF shifts out. If the terms of trade were unchanged, then consumption would change to a point like C′ and the representative consumer would be better off. With a fall in the relative price of the export good, however, it is possible that consumption could instead be at point C″ with production at B″. This illustrates the borderline case where utility is unchanged due to growth, and with any further fall in the terms of trade, the representative consumer would be worse off.

   We are interest in solving for the conditions under which immiserizing growth can occur. To this end, it will be convenient to first solve for the conditions such that utility is *constant*, as illustrated in Figure 10.1. For simplicity we suppose that there are just two goods and choose the importable y_2 as the numeraire, so its price is unity. Let $G(p, \alpha) = py_1 + y_2$ denote the GDP function for the economy, where α is a scalar that represents a shift parameter for the PPF. For example, α can represent a factor endowment or technological progress in some industry. The total change in GDP is measured by

$$dG = \frac{\partial G}{\partial p} dp + \frac{\partial G}{\partial \alpha} d\alpha = y_1 dp + \left(p \frac{dy_1}{d\alpha} + \frac{dy_2}{d\alpha} \right) d\alpha. \qquad (10.7)$$

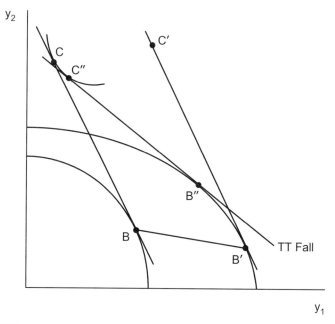

Figure 10.1

We presume that

$$\frac{\partial G}{\partial \alpha} = \left(p\frac{dy_1}{d\alpha} + \frac{dy_2}{d\alpha} \right) > 0 \text{ and } \frac{dy_1}{d\alpha} > 0,$$

meaning that growth at constant prices increases both GDP and production of the exportable.

As in chapter 7, we will allow for different consumers but suppose that the numeraire good is additively separable in consumption, so that consumer utilities can be summed. Total social welfare is then $W[p, G(p, \alpha)]$, which serves as an indirect utility function for the economy, where $\partial W/\partial p = -c_1 = -d_1(p)$ is the (negative of) consumption of good 1 and $\partial W/\partial G = 1$.[8] Then social welfare is constant due to growth if and only if

$$dW = \frac{\partial W}{\partial p}dp + \left(\frac{\partial G}{\partial p}dp + \frac{\partial G}{\partial \alpha}d\alpha \right) = (y_1 - c_1)dp + \frac{\partial G}{\partial \alpha}d\alpha = 0. \quad (10.8)$$

Thus, the drop in the export price that will just keep welfare constant is

$$dp = \frac{\partial G}{\partial \alpha}d\alpha/(c_1 - y_1). \quad (10.9)$$

[8] See problem 7.1 to derive the demand functions for an individual with quasi-linear utility.

Next, we solve for the equilibrium change in the relative price of exports and compare that to (10.9). Equilibrium in the export market means that $(y_1 - c_1) = m_1^*$, where m_1^* is import demand from the rest of the world. Totally differentiating this, we obtain

$$\frac{dy_1}{d\alpha}\,d\alpha + \left(\frac{\partial y_1}{\partial p} - \frac{\partial c_1}{\partial p}\right)dp = \frac{dm_1^*}{dp}\,dp.$$

Thus, the equilibrium change in the price of exports is

$$dp = \frac{\dfrac{dy_1}{d\alpha}\,d\alpha}{\left[\dfrac{dm_1^*}{dp} - \left(\dfrac{\partial y_1}{\partial p} - \dfrac{\partial c_1}{\partial p}\right)\right]}. \tag{10.10}$$

The denominator of (10.10) is negative, while the numerator is positive, so this expression indicates the drop in the export price due to growth. Welfare is constant if (10.9) = (10.10), and welfare falls if (10.10) < (10.9). This will occur if and only if

$$\frac{dy_1}{d\alpha}(y_1 - c_1)\bigg/\frac{\partial G}{\partial \alpha} > \left[\left(\frac{\partial y_1}{\partial p} - \frac{\partial c_1}{\partial p}\right) - \frac{dm_1^*}{dp}\right]. \tag{10.11}$$

Dividing this equation through by $(y_1 - c_1) = m_1^*$, and making use of $\dfrac{\partial G}{\partial \alpha} = \left(p\dfrac{dy_1}{d\alpha} + \dfrac{dy_2}{d\alpha}\right)$, we can express this necessary and sufficient condition

for immiserizing growth as

$$p\frac{dy_1}{d\alpha}\bigg/\left(p\frac{dy_1}{d\alpha} + \frac{dy_2}{d\alpha}\right) > \left[\left(\frac{\partial y_1}{\partial p} - \frac{\partial c_1}{\partial p}\right)\frac{p}{m_1^*} - \frac{dm_1^*}{dp}\frac{p}{m_1^*}\right]. \tag{10.12}$$

To interpret this expression, note that the first term on the right-hand side is the elasticity of export supply and is positive. For immiserizing growth to occur, it is therefore necessary that the term on the left-hand side *exceed*

the amount $-\left(\dfrac{dm_1^*}{dp}\dfrac{p}{m_1^*}\right)$, which is the elasticity of foreign demand for

imports. If this elasticity is less than unity, that is, foreign demand is inelastic, then immiserizing growth can occur even when the expression on the left side of (10.12) is also less than unity. However, if foreign demand for imports is elastic, then for (10.12) to be satisfied it must also be the case that the expression on the left side exceeds unity. By inspection, this occurs if and only if $dy_2/d\alpha < 0$, that is, when growth reduces the output of good 2 (at constant prices). Summarizing these results, we have the following theorem.

Theorem (Bhagwati 1958)

Immiserizing growth occurs if and only if (10.12) holds. Necessary conditions for this are that either (*a*) the foreign demand for imports is inelastic, or (*b*) growth reduces the output of the importable good (at constant prices).

Condition (a) is not surprising, since having inelastic demand for a product is the same condition that would permit farmers to be worse off after a bumper crop, as in the example given in introductory economics textbooks. What is more surprising is that immiserizing growth can occur even when foreign demand is *not* inelastic, but this requires that condition (b) hold, that is, that growth reduces the output of the importable good. We know from the Rybczynski theorem that this condition would hold in the two-by-two model if the factor used intensively in exports has grown. So this is one scenario in which immiserizing growth can occur. Are there others?

Findlay and Grubert (1959) answer this question in the affirmative. They considered Hicks-neutral technological progress in good 1. To demonstrate the effects of this, we work with the GDP function, defined as

$$G(pA_1, V) \equiv \max_{v_j \geq 0} pA_1 f_1(v_1) + f_2(v_2) \quad \text{subject to} \quad v_1 + v_2 = V. \quad (10.13)$$

That is, the parameter α that appeared in the earlier GDP function now equals A_1, which is the Hicks-neutral productivity parameter on good 1. Notice that pA_1 enters in a multiplicative form as an argument of the GDP function, since that is how it appears in the objective function.

We have demonstrated in chapter 1 that the derivative of the GDP function with respect to price equals the output of that good, or $\partial G/\partial p = y_1$. Letting $G_1(pA_1, V)$ denote the partial derivative of G with respect to its first argument, we therefore have

$$y_1 = \frac{\partial G}{\partial p} = \frac{\partial G}{\partial (pA_1)} \frac{d(pA_1)}{dp} = G_1(pA_1, V)A_1. \quad (10.14)$$

Totally differentiating this expression, we obtain $dy_1 = G_1 dA_1 +$

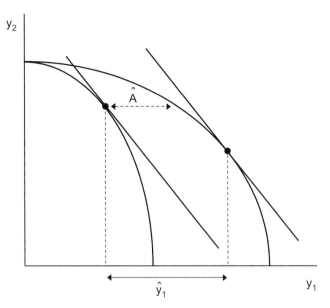

Figure 10.2

$A_1 G_{11} (p \, dA_1 + A_1 \, dp)$. Dividing through by $y_1 = G_1 A_1$, it follows that if *prices are constant*, then

$$\hat{y}_1 = \hat{A}_1 + \left(\frac{p A_1 G_{11}}{G_1} \right) \hat{A}_1 \geq \hat{A}_1, \tag{10.15}$$

where the inequality is obtained because the GDP function is convex in prices, so that $G_{11} \geq 0$. If we instead consider the cases where A_1 is constant and p changes, then it is readily shown that $(p A_1 G_{11}/G_1) = (\partial y_1/\partial p) \times (p/y_1) \geq 0$, which is the elasticity of supply in industry 1. When this inequality is strict, we obtain $\hat{y}_1 > \hat{A}_1$, so that the output of industry 1 increases by *more than* technological progress in the industry. The intuition for these results is that technological progress raises factor prices, so that industry 1 attracts resources from the rest of the economy.

This result is illustrated in Figure 10.2, where with *unchanged* inputs industry 1 would expand by $\hat{A}_1$ due to the technological progress, but after attracting resources from the rest of the economy, it expands by $\hat{y}_1 > \hat{A}_1$. Moreover, as illustrated in Figure 10.2, this will imply that *output in industry 2 must contract*, because it is losing factor inputs. Thus, there is a "Rybczynski-like" effect at work even when the source of growth is neutral technological progress in one industry, leading to a contraction of the other industry (at constant prices).[9] This type of growth therefore satisfies condition (b) of the above theorem, making immiserizing growth possible.

The result in (10.13) that the GDP function should have prices multiplied by the Hicks-neutral productivity parameter in each industry was already used in chapter 3 (see equation 3.24), where we reviewed the work of Harrigan (1997). He estimated a translog GDP function over the OECD countries while allowing for technology to differ across countries. Industry prices were treated as equal across countries (due to free trade), so it was *only* the technology parameters and factor endowments that appeared in the GDP function. The result in (10.15) that output expands by more than productivity in an industry then becomes a testable hypothesis: it will hold empirically provided that certain parameters of the translog GDP function satisfy appropriate conditions.[10] Thus, by estimating the GDP function we are able to test this result of Findlay and Grubert (1959). For example, Kee (2002) finds that the industry principally benefiting from productivity growth in Singapore is electronics, where TFP growth is 6.4% per year on average over 1970–99, whereas output growth is 15% per year. The difference between these is accounted for by labor and capital drawn into that sector, including foreign capital.

Endogenous Growth

Our discussion in the previous section did not model growth in any meaningful way, but simply treated it as a comparative statics increase in productivity or a factor endowment. Obviously, this is unsatisfactory. The celebrated model of Solow (1956) specified that capital accumulation should depend on investment, which equals to savings in the autarky one-sector economy, so that capital would gradually rise to its steady-state level. But that model still assumed that technological progress was *exogenous*, and a positive rate of technological progress or growth in the labor force was needed to obtain steady-state growth. The same assumptions were used in two-sector, open economy versions of this model, such as Smith (1977). Ultimately, interest in the profession has turned to models that instead allow for an *endogenous* rate of technological innovation, and we shall outline one of these models, taken from Grossman and Helpman (1990; 1991, chaps. 3, 8, and 9).

Many of the "endogenous growth" models build upon the monopolistic competition framework we introduced in chapter 5, but rather than thinking of differentiated final products, we instead consider *differenti-*

---

[9] In problem 10.1 you are asked to provide two other proofs of this result, using "Jones' algebra" and also graphically.
[10] See problem 10.2.

ated intermediate inputs. The idea is that an increase in the variety (N) of differentiated inputs will allow for an increase in output, much like an increase in variety of final goods allowed for higher consumer utility in chapter 5.[11] To make this precise, suppose that there is a single final good, with output y, produced with the CES production function

$$y = \left[\sum_{i=1}^{N} x_i^{(\sigma-1)/\sigma} \right]^{\sigma/(\sigma-1)}, \tag{10.16}$$

where x_i is the quantity of input variety $i = 1, \ldots, N$. As usual, we assume $\sigma > 1$, so that it is meaningful to think of changes in the number of inputs.[12]

If inputs are all priced equally in equilibrium, then their quantities are also equal, $x_i = x$, and so (10.16) can be rewritten as

$$y = N^{\sigma/(\sigma-1)} x = N^{1/(\sigma-1)} X, \tag{10.17}$$

with $X \equiv Nx$. We can think of X as the "aggregate" amount of the intermediate input, and holding this magnitude fixed, (10.17) shows that *increases in N raise output y* (since $\sigma > 1$). This amounts to a productivity gain in the final-good industry, due to the proliferation of differentiated intermediate inputs. Indeed, we could relabel $N^{1/(\sigma-1)}$ on the right side of (10.17) as A to obtain the simple production function $y = AX$, where technological progress A will depend on the number of new inputs.[13] By carefully modeling the dynamics of how N evolves due to the entry of new firms, we therefore have a story of endogenous technological progress, or endogenous growth.

Autarky Equilibrium

We begin by describing the autarky equilibrium. The price of the final good at each point in time is $P(t)$. If the consumer spends $E(t)$ on this good, then the quantity $y(t) = E(t)/P(t)$ will be purchased, and we assume that this provides instantaneous utility of $\ln y(t) = \ln E(t) - \ln P(t)$. The consumer's problem is then

---

[11] See problem 5.1. The use of differentiated inputs to generate economy-wide returns to scale is often attributed to Ethier (1979).
[12] If $\sigma < 1$, then output is zero whenever any input is zero. Thus, all inputs are essential to production, and we cannot think of introducing new inputs. In contrast, when $\sigma > 1$, output will increase by a finite amount when new inputs are introduced, as shown in (10.17).
[13] This is like the so-called '$y = AK$' production function used in some macroeconomic models.

$$\max_{E(\tau)} \int_t^\infty e^{-\rho(\tau-t)} [\ln E(\tau) - \ln P(\tau)] d\tau, \tag{10.18}$$

subject to the budget constraint

$$\int_t^\infty e^{-[R(\tau)-R(t)]} E(\tau) d\tau \leq \int_t^\infty e^{-[R(\tau)-R(t)]} w(\tau) L d\tau + B(t), \tag{10.19}$$

where $R(t)$ is the cumulative interest rate from time 0 to time t, so that $\dot{R}(t) \equiv dR/dt$ is the instantaneous interest rate. This budget constraint states that the discounted value of labor income $w(t)L$, plus initial assets $B(t)$, cannot exceed the discounted value of expenditure. The solution to this optimization problem is,[14]

$$\frac{\dot{E}}{E} = \dot{R} - \rho, \tag{10.20}$$

where we omit the time index on variables when doing so will not cause confusion.

Condition (10.20) states that when the nominal interest rate $\dot{R}$ exceeds the consumer's discount rate, then expenditure is rising. This is because with a high interest rate it is optimal to put a large amount of assets into savings initially, and gradually increase consumption thereafter. Generally, the nominal interest $\dot{R}(t)$ will depend on the normalization made on prices. Grossman and Helpman (1990, 1991) choose the normalization $E(t) \equiv 1$, which implies from (10.20) that $\dot{R}(t) \equiv \rho$, as we shall also use.

On the production side, the final good y is manufactured under perfect competition with the production function (10.17), where x_i is the quantity of each of N intermediate inputs (all these variables depend on t). These inputs are produced under monopolistic competition, and each unit of x_i requires one unit of labor, which is the only input. It follows that the price of each input is

$$p_i\left(1 - \frac{1}{\sigma}\right) = w, \quad \text{or} \quad p_i = w\left(\frac{\sigma}{\sigma-1}\right), \tag{10.21}$$

where w is the wage (which depends on t).

Input-producing firms have a fixed cost only when they begin production. The key question is how this fixed cost should be modeled. If we presume that the fixed cost is a fixed amount of labor α, as in the static monopolistic competition model, then there will be a limit to the number of products that can be profitably developed. In other words, growth of inputs $N(t)$ will cease at some point in time. The first dynamic monopo-

---

[14] As solved for in problem 10.3.

listic competition models had this feature (Judd 1985; Grossman and Helpman 1989), while the work of Romer (1990) and Grossman and Helpman (1990, 1991) avoided this outcome by presuming that fixed costs are *inversely proportional* to the number of products already developed, so that fixed labor costs are $\alpha/N(t)$. The idea is that the creation of products contributes to a "public stock of knowledge," which makes the invention of new products even easier. Notice that in a two-country model, this will allow for the potential spillover of public knowledge across borders, which will turn out to be very important.

With fixed labor costs of $\alpha/N(t)$, the nominal fixed costs are $\alpha w(t)/N(t)$. These are financed by consumers purchasing equity in the firms, which provides both dividends and capital gains. The instantaneous profits of the firms are

$$\pi_i = (p_i - w)x_i = \left(\frac{1}{\sigma - 1}\right)wx, \tag{10.22}$$

using (10.21) and symmetry of the equilibrium, so that $x_i = x$. The zero-profit conditions for the firms are that the present discounted value of instantaneous profits in (10.22) must equal the fixed costs $\alpha w(t)/N(t)$,

$$V(t) \equiv \int_t^\infty e^{-\rho(\tau - t)}\left(\frac{1}{\sigma - 1}\right)w(\tau)x(\tau)d\tau = \frac{\alpha w(t)}{N(t)}, \tag{10.23}$$

for all t.

Since (10.23) holds for all t, we can differentiate it with respect to t, obtaining

$$\dot{V} = -\left(\frac{1}{\sigma - 1}\right)w(t)x(t) + \rho\int_t^\infty e^{-\rho(\tau - t)}\left(\frac{1}{\sigma - 1}\right)w(\tau)x(\tau)d\tau$$
$$= \frac{\alpha\dot{w}}{N} - \frac{\alpha w\dot{N}}{N^2}. \tag{10.24}$$

To simplify (10.24), we can divide by the fixed costs $\alpha w/N$, obtaining

$$\underbrace{\left(\frac{1}{\sigma - 1}\right)\frac{Nx}{\alpha}}_{\substack{\pi/\text{Fixed cost} \\ \text{Dividends}}} + \underbrace{\left(\frac{\dot{w}}{w} - \frac{\dot{N}}{N}\right)}_{\substack{\dot{V}/V \\ \text{Capital gains}}} = \underbrace{\rho}_{\text{interest rate}}. \tag{10.25}$$

This is the key arbitrage condition of the endogenous growth model with expanding input variety, as derived by Grossman and Helpman (1990,

1991). The left-hand side of (10.25) is the sum of dividends plus capital gains, which should equal the discount rate on the right-hand side, which we interpret as the real interest rate.

With (10.25) in hand we can complete the model quite easily by using the full-employment condition for the economy. This can be written as

$$L = Nx + \left(\frac{\alpha}{N}\right)\dot{N}. \tag{10.26}$$

The left-hand side of (10.26) is the fixed endowment of labor, and the right-hand side equals the sum of labor used in production, $Nx = X$, and labor used in R&D, which is the fixed cost (α/N) times the growth of new products. Let us define the *growth rate* of inputs as $g \equiv \dot{N}/N$. Then we can rewrite (10.26) as $L = X + \alpha g$, or $X = L - \alpha g$. Substituting this into (10.25) we obtain

$$\left(\frac{1}{\sigma - 1}\right)\left(\frac{L - \alpha g}{\alpha}\right) + \left(\frac{\dot{w}}{w} - g\right) = \rho. \tag{10.27}$$

Now consider a steady-state solution with $\dot{w} = 0$. Substituting this into (10.27), we can readily solve for the autarky growth rate as

$$g^a = \left(\frac{1}{\sigma}\right)\left[\frac{L}{\alpha} - (\sigma - 1)\rho\right]. \tag{10.28}$$

Thus, the economy achieves steady-state growth even with a fixed labor supply, provided that $(L/\alpha) > (\sigma - 1)\rho$. Notice that with the growth rate fixed at g^a, the labor devoted to production is also fixed at $X = L - \alpha g^a$. Then from (10.17) we can solve for the growth rate of GDP as $\dot{y}/y = g^a/(\sigma - 1)$. So along with the continual growth of new products, there is also continual growth of GDP and utility.[15]

Trade Equilibrium with Knowledge Spillovers

Let us compare the autarky growth rate in (10.28) with that achieved under free trade between the two countries. Suppose that the foreign country has the same production function as at home and differs only in its labor endowment L^*. We will suppose that the final goods produced in

---

[15] While the economy achieves a continual growth of utility, it is not actually the case that welfare is maximized. That would require a choice of the growth rate different from g^a in (10.28). See problem 10.4.

the two countries are imperfect substitutes, with the instantaneous utility function in each country

$$U(y, y^*) = \ln\left[y^{(\eta-1)/\eta} + (y^*)^{(\eta-1)/\eta}\right]^{\eta/(\eta-1)}. \tag{10.29}$$

This is the log of a CES function with elasticity of substitution $\eta > 1$. We suppose that the final goods from home and abroad are freely traded, at the prices p_y and p_y^*, respectively.

Given expenditure E in the home country, it follows that the demand for the final goods of each country is[16]

$$y = (p_y/P)^{-\eta}(E/P), \quad \text{and} \quad y^* = (p_y^*/P)^{-\eta}(E/P), \tag{10.30}$$

where P refers to the overall price index of the final goods, defined as

$$P(p_y, p_y^*) = [p_y^{1-\eta} + (p_y^*)^{1-\eta}]^{1/(1-\eta)}. \tag{10.31}$$

Demand for the final goods from the foreign county is similar, and is obtained by just replacing home expenditure E by foreign expenditure E^* in (10.30).

Using (10.30), it is readily confirmed that utility in (10.29) equals $U(y, y^*) = \ln(E/P)$, or the log of real expenditures. We will suppose that the capital markets are fully integrated, so there is a single, cumulative world interest rate $R(t)$. Maximizing the presented discounted sum of home utility gives us the same objective function as in (10.18), so the first-order condition (10.20) still applies. If we again use the normalization $E(t) \equiv 1$, the real interest rate equals ρ, the discount rate in both countries.

With this setup, we want to contrast the effects of trade in two scenarios. In the first, we will suppose that in addition to free trade in the final goods and integrated capital markets, there is *also* free trade in the intermediate inputs and complete transfer of knowledge across countries. The latter assumption means that the fixed costs of creating a new product in either country are $\alpha/[N(t) + N^*(t)]$. Under this set of assumptions, the integrated world equilibrium with the two countries is simply a "blown up" version of either country in autarky. The effect of this increase in size is to *raise* the growth rate from that shown in (10.28) to

$$g^w = \left(\frac{1}{\sigma}\right)\left[\frac{(L + L^*)}{\alpha} - (\sigma - 1)\rho\right]. \tag{10.32}$$

The result that the growth rate increases in proportion to the size of the world economy is referred to as a '*scale effect*,' and is the dynamic analogue

[16] See equations (5.24) and (5.25), and also problem 5.2.

to the static gains from trade that we saw in Krugman's model in the beginning of chapter 5. This result has come under some criticism in the growth literature, not because of the result that trade increases growth, but rather, because of another result, that subsidies to R&D permanently raise the growth rate. Both of these propositions depend very strongly on our specification that fixed costs are *inversely proportional* to the number of products already developed. If this strict inverse proportionality does not hold—for example, if we specified fixed costs as α/N^{β}, with $0 < \beta < 1$— then new product development in the absence of population growth will eventually stop. Jones (1995a, 1995b) has referred to models of this type as "semi-endogenous" growth, and they imply that free trade or subsidies to R&D have only temporary effects on the growth rate. The empirical question, which class of models is most realistic, we shall discuss later.

Trade Equilibrium without Knowledge Spillovers

Let us now contrast the results from a fully integrated world economy to the case where there are *zero* spillovers of knowledge across borders, as in Grossman and Helpman 1991, chap. 8 and Feenstra 1996. This means that the fixed costs in each country are $\alpha/N(t)$ and $\alpha/N^*(t)$, respectively. Initially, we suppose that there is no trade in intermediate inputs, so that only trade in final goods and financial capital is permitted; later in the section, we will reintroduce free trade in intermediate inputs. We shall demonstrate that in the absence of knowledge spillovers across borders, free trade *will not* increase the growth rate for both countries, but rather, will slow down product development in the smaller country.

With the countries growing at different rates, we cannot simultaneously use the normalizations $E(t) \equiv 1$ and $E^*(t) \equiv 1$, so it is no longer the case that $\dot{R}(t) = \rho$. Accordingly, the profits of input-producing firms in (10.23) are discounted using the cumulative interest rate $R(t)$, and the arbitrage condition in each country is rewritten from (10.25) as

$$\left(\frac{1}{\sigma-1}\right)\frac{Nx}{\alpha} + \left(\frac{\dot{w}}{w} - \frac{\dot{N}}{N}\right) = \dot{R} \tag{10.33}$$

and

$$\left(\frac{1}{\sigma-1}\right)\frac{N^*x^*}{\alpha} + \left(\frac{\dot{w}^*}{w^*} - \frac{\dot{N}^*}{N^*}\right) = \dot{R}. \tag{10.34}$$

As before, we will use the notation $X \equiv Nx$ and $X^* \equiv N^*x^*$ to denote the amount of labor devoted to production of intermediate inputs in each country. In addition, let $g \equiv (\dot{N}/N)$ and $g^* \equiv (\dot{N}^*/N^*)$ denote the home and foreign growth rates of new inputs. The full-employment condition in each country implies that $X = L - \alpha g$ and $X^* = L^* - \alpha g^*$, and substituting these into (10.33) and (10.34), we can derive the growth rates:

$$
g = \left(\frac{L}{\alpha\sigma}\right) - \left(\frac{\sigma-1}{\sigma}\right)\left[\dot{R} - \left(\frac{\dot{w}}{w}\right)\right], \text{ and,}
$$

$$
g^* = \left(\frac{L^*}{\alpha\sigma}\right) - \left(\frac{\sigma-1}{\sigma}\right)\left[\dot{R} - \left(\frac{\dot{w}^*}{w^*}\right)\right]. \tag{10.35}
$$

These equations show that the growth rates are *inversely related* to the real interest rates $[\dot{R} - (\dot{w}/w)]$ and $[\dot{R} - (\dot{w}^*/w^*)]$: having a higher nominal interest rate $\dot{R}$ lowers the discounted value of profits and therefore expenditure on R&D; conversely, having a rising path of wages and prices leads to rising profits and a lower real interest rate, with higher R&D. Taking the difference between the two growth rates in (10.35), we obtain

$$
g - g^* = \left(\frac{L - L^*}{\alpha\sigma}\right) + \left(\frac{\sigma-1}{\sigma}\right)\left(\frac{\dot{w}}{w} - \frac{\dot{w}^*}{w^*}\right). \tag{10.36}
$$

Let us assume henceforth that the home country is larger, $L > L^*$. From (10.36) we see that this difference in size will tend to be associated with a faster growth rate at home, $g > g^*$. The growth rates are also affected, however, by the change in wages on the right-hand side. In the autarky equilibrium discussed above, we had focused on the steady-state solution with $\dot{w} = 0$. But now it is impossible to assume this for both countries: assuming $\dot{w} = \dot{w}^* = 0$ implies that $g > g^*$ from (10.36), and we will argue below that this implies rising relative wages for the home country, $\dot{w}/w > \dot{w}^*/w^*$, which is a contradiction. Thus, the assumption of a steady-state equilibrium is inconsistent with the dynamic equations for the two countries. Accordingly, we need to solve for the growth rates outside of the steady state.

We begin by solving for the change in wages, from the production function $y = N^{1/(\sigma-1)}X$ in (10.17), where X is the amount of intermediate inputs purchased at the price of $p_i = w\sigma/(\sigma-1)$. It follows that the marginal cost of producing the final good is $p_y = p_i/N^{1/(\sigma-1)} = w\sigma/[(\sigma-1)N^{1/(\sigma-1)}]$ at home, and $p_y^* = w^*\sigma/[(\sigma-1)(N^*)^{1/(\sigma-1)}]$ abroad. Differentiating these and taking the difference, we obtain

$$
\left(\frac{\dot{p}_y}{p_y}\right) - \left(\frac{\dot{p}_y^*}{p_y^*}\right) = \left(\frac{\dot{w}}{w} - \frac{\dot{w}^*}{w^*}\right) - \left(\frac{g - g^*}{\sigma-1}\right). \tag{10.37}
$$

This equation states that a higher growth rate at home tends to be associated with rising relative wages, but this also depends on the changes in the prices of the final goods in each country.

To determine these prices, we make use of the CES demands in (10.30), which imply that $(p_y/p_y^*) = (y/y^*)^{-1/\eta}$. Differentiating this equation using the production functions $y = N^{1/(\sigma-1)}X$ and $y^* = (N^*)^{1/(\sigma-1)}X^*$, we obtain

$$\left(\frac{\dot{p}_y}{p_y}\right) - \left(\frac{\dot{p}_y^*}{p_y^*}\right) = -\frac{1}{\eta}\left[\left(\frac{g - g^*}{\sigma - 1}\right) + \frac{\dot{X}}{X} - \frac{\dot{X}^*}{X^*}\right]. \qquad (10.38)$$

Then combining (10.36)–(10.38), we can derive the fundamental relation

$$g - g^* = \Delta\left(\frac{L - L^*}{\alpha\sigma}\right) - \Delta\left(\frac{\sigma - 1}{\eta\sigma}\right)\left(\frac{\dot{X}}{X} - \frac{\dot{X}^*}{X^*}\right), \qquad (10.39)$$

where

$$\Delta \equiv \left[1 - \frac{(\eta - 1)}{\eta\sigma}\right]^{-1} > 1. \qquad (10.40)$$

Equation (10.39) shows that the difference in the growth of new inputs across the countries depends on the difference in their size. There is also another term on the right-hand side of (10.39), depending on $\dot{X}$ and $\dot{X}^*$, but we can safely presume that this term approaches zero as $t \to \infty$. Notice that the difference in the *autarky* growth rates of the two countries is exactly $(L - L^*)/\alpha\sigma$, but in (10.39), the limiting growth rates of the countries will differ by this *times* the amount $\Delta > 1$. Therefore, in the absence of knowledge spillovers the effect of trade is to *magnify* the initial difference in the growth rates of the two countries.

We have not yet determined whether trade will increase the growth rate of the large country, or slow down the growth rate of the small country. Some additional calculations show that the first case is not possible: the growth rate of the large country must approach its autarky rate of g^a as $t \to \infty$.[17] Our results are then summarized by the following theorem.

Theorem (Feenstra 1996)

(a) $\lim_{t \to \infty} g = g^a$, which equals the autarky growth rate g^a of the large country.

---

[17] See problem 10.5.

(b) $\lim\limits_{t \to \infty} g^* = g^{a*} - (\Delta - 1)\left(\dfrac{L - L^*}{\alpha\sigma}\right)$, which is less than the autarky

growth rate g^{a*} of the small country, $g^{a*} = [(L^*/\alpha) - (\sigma - 1)\rho]/\sigma$.

(c) $\lim\limits_{t \to \infty}\left(\dfrac{\dot{w}}{w} - \dfrac{\dot{w}^*}{w^*}\right) > 0$, and $\lim\limits_{t \to \infty}\left(\dfrac{\dot{p}_y}{p_y} - \dfrac{\dot{p}_y^*}{p_y^*}\right) < 0$.

Parts (a) and (b) of this theorem have already been discussed above. The results in (c) follow from substituting the limiting growth rates into (10.37) and (10.38). Relative wages move in favor of the larger country, which reflects the rising productivity of that country due to the faster-growing number of intermediate inputs. But this same efficiency gain leads to a fall in the relative price of final goods. These different wage and price movements emphasize how difficult it is to make a general prediction of the terms of trade movement in this model: it depends on which goods/factors are used to measure the terms of trade.

The finding that the small country has its rate of product development slowed down does not necessarily translate into a welfare loss, though it might. That will depend on whether intermediate inputs are traded or not. Initially continue with our assumption that inputs are not traded. The welfare obtained by consumers in the small country will depend, of course, on the price index $P(p_y, p_y^*)$ for purchases of the final goods. Let us choose the foreign wage as the numeraire, $w^* \equiv 1$. Then since the number of intermediate inputs produced abroad is slowed down by trade, the price of its final good p_y^* is higher than in autarky. This will create a potential welfare loss. But the foreign consumers *also* have the final good from the home country available, which creates a potential welfare gain. Which of these effects dominates will depend on a comparison of elasticities: if $\eta > (\sigma + 1)$, then there is an overall welfare gain; but if $\eta \le (\sigma + 1)$, then there is a potential welfare loss.[18]

What about when the intermediate inputs are traded? Then the argument is quite different. Despite the fact that product development has been slowed in the small country, it can still purchase intermediate inputs from abroad. For t sufficiently large, it will definitely be the case that the efficiency gain from the additional imported inputs more than offsets the

---

[18] Specifically, Feenstra (1996, Proposition 2) finds that the price index under free trade exceeds that under autarky for t sufficiently high when $\eta \le (\sigma + 1)$, and a weak additional condition is satisfied. The finding that welfare in the smaller country can potentially fall is related to the fact that R&D is being undertaken at less than the socially optimal rate in autarky, as demonstrated in problem 10.4. Then trade in final goods but not in intermediate inputs worsens that distortion in that country. Markusen (1989) also discusses how trade in final goods, but not in intermediate inputs, can lead to a welfare loss even in a static model.

loss from the reduced number of local inputs, so that the price of the final good p_y^* is *lower* than in autarky. Thus, consumers in the small country benefit from a reduction in the price of their own final good as well as the imported final good, so there are welfare gains for both reasons.

It is worth emphasizing that our finding that trade can slow down the rate of product development occurs only when there are *zero* spillovers of knowledge. Provided that there are some positive spillovers, Grossman and Helpman (1991, chap. 9) and Rivera-Batiz and Romer (1991a, 1991b) argue that product innovation in both countries will increase. Indeed, this occurs even if knowledge spillovers are the *only* international flows, without any trade in final goods or inputs. So the assumption of zero international spillovers we have used above is an extreme case, but it serves to highlight how important these spillovers are to growth.

Empirical Evidence

Importance of Size

The first implication of the endogenous growth models is that "size matters" for growth. This follows directly from the equation for autarky growth rates in (10.28), where a higher labor stock (measured in units of effective R&D workers, or L/α) leads to a higher growth rate. This implication is analogous to what we found in Krugman's static model reviewed at the beginning of chapter 5: doubling a country's size would lead to efficiency gains through economies of scale, and additional consumer gains through increased variety. In the dynamic model outlined above, increasing a country's size leads to increased variety of intermediate inputs, which results in efficiency gains in producing the final good and also reduces the fixed costs $\alpha/N(t)$ of inventing new inputs. The latter reduction in fixed costs is what leads to a permanently higher growth rate due to larger country size.

How realistic is this result? Over very long time periods, it is perhaps reasonable to think that economies will grow in proportion to their size. Kremer (1993) considers the period from one million years ago to the present, and finds that the growth rate of population is proportional to its level. On the other hand, over shorter time spans, the implications of the "scale effect" in the endogenous growth model do not find support. Jones (1995a, 1995b) proposes a direct test of endogenous growth, whereby changes in policy should have permanent effects on the growth rate, and this hypothesis is decisively rejected on data for the United States and other advanced countries. As we discussed earlier, these negative results led Jones to propose the "semiendogenous" growth model, and there is now a class of growth models that operate *without* the scale effect.[19]

International Trade and Convergence

The second implication of the endogenous growth model was that, with international spillovers of knowledge, trade should increase growth rates. There is an active debate over whether this hypothesis holds empirically. Advocates of this view includes Dollar (1992), Sachs and Warner (1995), Edwards (1998), Ben-David (1993, 1998, 2001), and Frankel and Romer (1999). But their empirical results are all dismissed by Rodriguez and Rodrik (2000), and more specific criticisms on individual studies are made by Harrison (1996) and Slaughter (2001). In order to evaluate these arguments, it is useful to first relate them to another line of empirical research dealing with the *convergence* of countries to their steady-state growth rates.

The convergence literature is not motivated by the endogenous growth models at all, but rather, by the *exogenous* growth model such as Solow (1956) and extensions thereof. In those models, all countries converge to the same steady-state growth rate, but this pattern still allows for different levels of GDP per capita (depending on characteristics of the countries). So countries that are below their steady-state level of GDP per capita should grow faster, and conversely, countries that are above their steady-state GDP per capita should grow slower, so as to approach the steady state. This property follows directly from the diminishing marginal product of capital. There is both convergence in growth rates, and some degree of convergence in GDP per capita (though not necessarily to the same level across countries), and these two criteria tend to be used interchangably. The same is true for the studies dealing with trade, which examine either the impact on growth rates or on GDP per capita across countries.

In the initial work of Barro (1991) and Barro and Salai-i-Martin (1991, 1992) the convergence hypothesis found strong empirical support. It was also demonstrated by Mankiw, Romer, and Weil (1992), and led them to conclude that the original Solow model, suitably extended to allow for human capital, is "good enough" at explaining cross-country differences in growth rates: the endogenous growth models are apparently not needed! These findings, however, have been questioned in subsequent work that considers a broader range of countries. For example, Easterly and Levine (2000) emphasize a *divergence* in the absolute levels of income

---

[19] See Dinopoulos and Segerstrom 1999a and Dinopoulos and Syropoulos 2001 for applications to trade.

per capita across countries: the rich have grown richer, and some of the poorest countries have become even poorer.[20]

A similar approach to assessing the effects of trade is taken by the authors cited above. Sachs and Warner (1995) arrange their countries into two groups, one of which has an "open" trade regime and the other of which is judged to be "closed." Within the open group, they find evidence of convergence, with the poorer countries growing faster, but this is not true for those countries with closed trade regimes. By this argument, openness leads to convergence of incomes across countries. Ben-David (1993, 1998, 2001) groups countries based on their membership in regional trade agreements, or by the strength of their bilateral trade ties. He also finds significant evidence of income convergence *within* these groups, but not necessarily across the groups. Dollar and Kraay (2001a, 2001b) contrast the experience of a group of developing countries that have become more open (including China and India) with other developing countries. They argue that growth in the former group is explained by openness and has particularly benefited the poor. As noted above, all these studies are subject to empirical criticisms: among other difficulties, openness itself is fundamentally endogenous. Frankel and Romer (1999) deal with this endogeneity by first estimating a gravity equation, and then demonstrating that the *predicted* trade shares from this equation are indeed significant in explaining income per capita.

The finding that convergence occurs within groups, but not across groups, presents a challenge to the exogenous growth models. But this finding is in the spirit of the endogenous growth model without knowledge spillovers, discussed above, where the two countries converged to different growth rates. In a more general multicountry growth model that incorporates trade, Ventura (1997) also finds this result. In his model, capital *does not* have a diminishing marginal product due to Rybczynski effects: increases in capital raises the output of the capital-intensive good, and at fixed product prices, does not result in a reduced rental. Nevertheless, Ventura shows that in the global equilibrium, there is convergence to steady-state growth rates that differ across countries (as also demonstrated by Cuñat and Maffezzoli [2002]). The reason for convergence is that countries with expanding capital will have falling equilibrium prices for their capital-intensive goods, and therefore, a falling rental due to the Stolper-Samuelson theorem. So there is a general-equilibrium linkage between capital accumulation and the rental, even though there are no diminishing returns with fixed prices.

---

[20] Bernanke and Gürkaynak (2001) also question the conclusions of Mankiw, Romer, and Weil.

We might think of the model in Ventura (1997) as offering a third type of growth model, in which there are neither dimishing returns to capital as in the Solow model nor endogenous growth due to increased input variety, but growth *without* dimishing returns due to Rybczynski effects. Findlay (1996) argues that this framework may well be the most relevant one to analyze the growth experience of developing countries. These studies are recommended for further reading.

Spillovers of Knowledge

A third area of empirical investigation is international spillovers of knowledge. It is clear from our discussion that these are crucial: gains from trade are much more likely when knowledge flows across borders. Coe and Helpman (1995) test for the presence of such spillovers using data for the OECD countries.[21] Their hypothesis is that if international spillovers occur, the growth rates of countries should be correlated with both their *own* R&D expenditures and also the R&D expenditures of their trading partners. Thus, they construct measures of each country's R&D expenditures, and weight them using bilateral *import* shares to obtain an estimate of partner countries' R&D expenditures. They find that TFP growth rates at the country level are indeed correlated with own- and partner-country R&D expenditures, lending support to the idea that research and development carried out in one country "spills over" to its trading partners.

An econometric difficulty with the Coe and Helpman estimates is that the TFP growth rates and R&D expenditures are very likely to exhibit unit-roots in their time-series behavior. In that case, regressions of TFP on R&D could lead to estimates that are significantly different from zero using conventional *t*-tests, even though the relationship might be spurious. To investigate this, Keller (1998) reconstructs the weighted R&D expenditures of the trading partners used by Coe and Helpman, but using *random* rather than actual import weights. He shows that this measure still has a positive correlation with TFP, suggesting that the relationship has little to do with trade and may be spurious. The unit-roots problem can be corrected using recent panel co-integration techniques, as done by Funk (2001). He finds that there is no significant relationship between TFP growth and *import-weighted* R&D expenditures of partner countries. However, he does find a significant relationship between TFP and *export-weighted* R&D expenditures of partner countries, supporting the idea that exporters learn from their customers.

Keller (2002) has extended the results of Coe and Helpman using sectoral rather than aggregate country data. He again constructs a weighted

---

[21] Coe, Helpman, and Hoffmaister (1997) expand the sample to include developing countries.

average of R&D expenditures in other countries, but now uses the *distance* to each partner as the weight. Denoting the distance from country i to country j by d^{ij}, Keller weights the other countries' R&D expenditures by $e^{-\delta d^{ij}}$. The parameter δ measures how quickly the impact of other countries' R&D expenditures on TFP diminishes with distance. In fact, this parameter turns out to be positive and highly significant, implying that spillovers are quite highly localized. For the two closest countries in his sample, Germany and the Netherlands, one dollar of R&D expenditure in Germany has 31% of the impact on Dutch productivity that one dollar of R&D expenditure in the Netherlands has. The effects of foreign R&D are lower for all other countries; for example, the relative effect of American R&D on Canada is only 4% of the value of Canadian R&D on its own productivity. So Keller's results provide evidence of precisely estimated but small R&D spillovers across borders.

Spillovers of knowledge have also been assessed through the use of patent data. Many studies have applied this technique to firms within a country, and Branstetter (2001) has extended it to consider firms in both the United States and Japan. When firms apply for a patent in the United States, they must classify it in one or more product areas. We can treat each product area as a component of the vector $B_i = (b_{i1}, \ldots, b_{iK})$, where b_{ik} is the number of patents taken out by firm i in product area k. For two firms i and j, we can use the correlation between B_i and B_j as a measure of their *proximity* in technology space. Then we can construct a weighted average of the R&D expenditures of other firms, using the proximity with firm i as the weight. This gives us a measure of the *potential* spillovers from other firms. Branstetter constructs these measures separately for spillovers from U.S. firms and spillovers from Japanese firms.[22] Together with each firm's own R&D expenditures, these are regressed on a measure of each firm's performance (either number of patents taken out annually, or TFP growth), to determine the importance of the various spillovers.

In his results, Branstetter (2001, 75) finds that spillovers are primarily *intranational* in scope. Some regressions show that Japanese firms benefit from the weighted R&D activity of American companies, but this effect does not remain significant when the domestic spillovers are included in the regression. Conversely, there is no evidence that American firms benefit from the R&D activities of the Japanese. This raises the idea that knowledge spillovers may be *asymmetric*, and presumably flow from the most technologically advanced country outwards. In other work, Branstetter (2000) has explored whether Japanese firms that have foreign affiliates in the United States act as a "conduit" for knowledge flows, that

---

[22] Both measures are constructed using the patents that Japanese and American firms take out in the United States.

is, whether there is a greater spillover between these foreign affiliates and other American firms. It appears that this is indeed the case, so that foreign investment increases the flow of knowledge spillovers both to and from the investing Japanese firms.

Measuring Product Variety

All of the empirical applications we have discussed so far have been *indirect* tests of the endogenous growth model, relying on hypotheses arising from it but not actually measuring the variety of inputs. Our fourth and final empirical method will be to develop a *direct* test of endogenous growth, by constructing a measure of input variety that is "exact" for the CES production function, as in Feenstra 1994 and Feenstra and Markusen 1995. We show that this measure of product variety is correlated with productivity growth.

Let us begin with the CES production function in (10.16). The problem with using this function is that it is symmetric: at equal prices, every input would have the same demand. That assumption is made for convenience in our theoretical models, but is unacceptable empirically: we need to let demand be whatever the data indicates. So instead we will work with the nonsymmetric CES function

$$y_t = f(x_t, I_t) = \left[\sum_{i \in I_t} a_i x_{it}^{(\sigma-1)/\sigma} \right]^{\sigma/(\sigma-1)}, \sigma > 1, \qquad (10.41)$$

where $a_i > 0$ are parameters and I_t denotes the set of inputs available in period t, at the prices p_{it}. The CES unit-cost function dual to (10.41) is[23]

$$c(p_t, I_t) = \left[\sum_{i \in I_t} b_i p_{it}^{1-\sigma} \right]^{1/(1-\sigma)}, \sigma > 1, b_i \equiv a_i^{\sigma}. \qquad (10.42)$$

We are interested in determining how much unit-costs are reduced when the set of product varieties expands. To this end, let us first consider the case where $I_{t-1} = I_t = I$, so there is no change in the set of goods. Let us also assume that the observed input purchases x_{it} are cost minimizing for the prices and output, that is, $x_{it} = y_t(\partial c/\partial p_{it})$. In that case, the ratio of unit-costs can be measured by the price index due to Sato (1976) and Vartia (1976).[24]

---

[23] This is analogous to the CES price index in (5.25), and see also problem 8.3 to derive the CES demand system in the nonsymmetric case.
[24] The proof of this theorem and the next can be found in Feenstra 1994.

Theorem (Sato 1976; Vartia 1976)

If the set of inputs available is fixed at $I_{t-1} = I_t = I$ and inputs are cost minimizing, then

$$\frac{c(p_t, I)}{c(p_{t-1}, I)} = P_{SV}(p_{t-1}, p_t, x_{t-1}, x_t, I) \equiv \prod_{i \in I} \left(\frac{p_{it}}{p_{it-1}} \right)^{w_i(I)}, \quad (10.43)$$

where the weights $w_i(I)$ are constructed from the expenditure shares $s_{it}(I) \equiv p_{it} x_{it} / \sum_{i \in I} p_{it} x_{it}$ as

$$
\begin{aligned}
w_i(I) \equiv & \left(\frac{s_{it}(I) - s_{it-1}(I)}{\ln s_{it}(I) - \ln s_{it-1}(I)} \right) \Bigg/ \\
& \times \sum_{i \in I} \left(\frac{s_{it}(I) - s_{it-1}(I)}{\ln s_{it}(I) - \ln s_{it-1}(I)} \right).
\end{aligned}
\quad (10.44)
$$

To interpret this result, the numerator on the right-hand side of (10.44) is a logarithmic mean of the expenditure shares $s_{it}(I)$ and $s_{it-1}(I)$ and lies between these two values. The denominator ensures that the weights $w_i(I)$ sum to unity, so that the Sato-Vartia index P_{SV} defined on the right of (10.43) is simply a geometric mean of the price ratios (p_{it}/p_{it-1}). The theorem states that this index *exactly* equals the ratio of the CES unit-cost functions, provided that the observed input quantities used to construct the weight are cost minimizing.

Now consider the case where the set of inputs is changing over time, but some of the inputs are available in both periods, so that $I = I_{t-1} \cap I_t \neq \varnothing$. We again let $c(p, I)$ denote the unit-cost function defined over the inputs within the set I. Then the ratio $c(p_t, I)/c(p_{t-1}, I)$ is still measured by the Sato-Vartia index in the above theorem. Our interest is in the ratio $c(p_t, I_t)/c(p_{t-1}, I_{t-1})$, which can be measured as shown in the following theorem.

Theorem (Feenstra 1994)

Assume that $I = I_{t-1} \cap I_t \neq \varnothing$, and that the inputs are cost minimizing. Then for $\sigma > 1$,

$$\frac{c(p_t, I_t)}{c(p_{t-1}, I_{t-1})} = \left(\frac{\lambda_t(I)}{\lambda_{t-1}(I)} \right)^{1/(\sigma-1)} \prod_{i \in I} \left(\frac{p_{it}}{p_{it-1}} \right)^{w_i(I)} \quad (10.45)$$

where the weights $w_i(I)$ are constructed from the expenditure shares $s_{it}(I) \equiv p_{it} x_{it} / \sum_{i \in I} p_{it} x_{it}$ as in (10.44), and the values $\lambda_t(I)$ and $\lambda_{t-1}(I)$

are constructed as

$$\lambda_\tau(I) = \left(\frac{\sum_{i \in I} p_{i\tau} x_{i\tau}}{\sum_{i \in I_\tau} p_{i\tau} x_{i\tau}} \right) = 1 - \left(\frac{\sum_{i \in I_\tau, i \notin I} p_{i\tau} x_{i\tau}}{\sum_{i \in I_\tau} p_{i\tau} x_{i\tau}} \right), \quad \tau = t - 1, t. \quad (10.46)$$

To interpret this result, the product on the far right of (10.45) is simply the Sato-Vartia index, constructed over the set of inputs I that are common to both periods. This measures the ratio of unit-costs $c(p_t, I)/c(p_{t-1}, I)$, for the inputs available in both periods. The first ratio on the right-hand side of (10.45) shows how the Sato-Vartia index must be adjusted to account for the new inputs (in the set I_t but not I) or disappearing inputs (in the set I_{t-1} but not I). From (10.46), each of the terms $\lambda_\tau(I) \le 1$ can be interpreted as the *period τ expenditure on the inputs in the set I, relative to the period τ total expenditure*. Alternatively, this can be interpreted as *one minus the period τ expenditure on "new" inputs (not in the set I), relative to the period τ total expenditure*. When there is a greater number of new inputs in period t, this will tend to lower the value of $\lambda_t(I)$. Notice that the ratio $[\lambda_t(I)/\lambda_{t-1}(I)]$ on the right side of (10.45) is raised to the power $1/(\sigma - 1) > 0$, so that a lower value of $\lambda_t(I)$ due to new inputs will reduce the unit-cost ratio in (10.45) by more when the elasticity of substitution is lower.

To see the usefulness of this theorem, let us measure "dual" factor productivity as the log difference between the index of input prices and the ratio of unit-costs:

$$\text{TFP} \equiv \ln P_{SV}(p_{t-1}, p_t, x_{t-1}, x_t, I) - \ln[c(p_t, I_t)/c(p_{t-1}, I_{t-1})]. \quad (10.47)$$

Then using the above theorems, we immediately have

$$\text{TFP} = \frac{1}{(\sigma - 1)} \ln\left(\frac{\lambda_{t-1}(I)}{\lambda_t(I)} \right), \quad (10.48)$$

where the terms $\lambda_t(I)$ are defined in (10.46). Thus, the growth in new inputs, as reflected in a *falling* value of $\lambda_t(I)$, will lead to positive total factor productivity of the firm or industry using the inputs. This provides us with a direct test of the endogenous growth model with expanding input variety.

Feenstra et al. (1999) provide an application of this method to industry productivity growth in South Korea and Taiwan. The data used to measure product variety are the disaggregate *exports* from these countries to the United States. While is would be preferable to use national data on the *production of intermediate inputs* from these countries, this data is not available at a sufficiently disaggregate level. Despite the limitations of using *exports* to measure product variety, it has the incidental benefit of focusing on the link between trade and growth.

These authors analyze the relationship between changes in export variety and the growth in TFP across South Korea and Taiwan, in 16 sectors over 1975–91. The results lend support to the endogenous growth model. They find that changes in relative export variety (entered as either a lag or a lead) have a positive and significant effect on TFP in 9 of the 16 sectors. Seven of the sectors are classified as secondary industries, in that they rely on as well as produce differentiated manufactures, and therefore seem to fit the idea of endogenous growth. Among the primary industries, which rely more heavily on natural resources, the authors find mixed evidence: the correlation between export variety and productivity can be positive, negative, or insignificant. In addition, the authors also find evidence of a positive and significant correlation between *upstream* export variety and productivity in 6 sectors, 5 of which are secondary industries.

Funke and Ruhwedel (2001a, 2001b, 2002) have applied the same measure of product variety to analyze economic growth across the OECD and East Asian countries. Using panel datasets, they find that a country's export variety (relative to the United States) is a significant determinant of its GDP per capita and its export performance. Hummels and Klenow (2002) measure the product variety of exports for a broad sample of 110 countries in one year, and evaluate whether differences in the value of exports across countries are due to differences in product variety or due to differences in sales of goods that are commonly exported by countries. They find that differences in product variety are a principal explanation of cross-country export patterns, a finding confirmed by Schott (2001), who compares rich and poor countries. Notice that these measures of product variety, which are constructed from highly disaggregate trade data, are unlikely to suffer from the endogeneity problem that plagues aggregate trade flows (as addressed by Frankel and Romer 1999). Therefore, the construction of product variety indexes and their correlation with TFP offers a robust way to assess the importance of trade in economic growth.

Conclusions

This chapter began with a discussion of productivity growth for a firm or industry. The measure of total factor productivity (TFP) due to Solow (1957) is the growth of output minus a weighted average of the growth of inputs. The weights equal the elasticity of output with respect to the inputs. Under perfect competition and constant returns to scale, these weights are easily measured by the revenue shares of the inputs. Without these assumptions, however, the measurement of productivity growth becomes more difficult. Using the techniques of Hall (1988), we showed how "true" productivity growth can be identified, along with estimating the price-cost margins and returns to scale in an industry. This technique has been applied by Levinsohn (1993) and Harrison (1994) to measure the reduction in markups following liberalization in Turkey and the Ivory Coast, respectively.

Dropping the assumptions of perfect competition and constant returns to scale is also the starting point of the literature on endogenous growth. While there are several types of endogenous growth models, the one we considered in this chapter relied on expanding varieties of intermediate inputs. An essential assumption was that the fixed cost of inventing a new input is *inversely proportional* to the number of inputs already created. In the case where free trade in goods and inputs also brings international spillovers of knowledge, then trade leads to an increase in the growth rates of both countries (Grossman and Helpman 1990, 1991). But if there are no knowledge spillovers across borders, then free trade in goods has the effect of slowing down product development in the smaller country, which may also bring losses due to trade (Feenstra 1996). This leads to several important empirical questions: (*a*) Does free trade increase growth rates? (*b*) Are knowledge spillovers global or local? (*c*) Is there any direct evidence on the link between product variety and productivity? There is recent empirical work on all these questions, but still some unanswered questions.

In particular, it seems that the differences in per capita GDP across countries, which are as large as ever, must be due to *technology differences* across countries (Easterly and Levine 2000). This brings us right back to chapter 2, where we found that the HO model can account for trade patterns only if it is extended to incorporate such technology differences. What is the source of these? The endogenous growth model in this chapter has economy-wide increasing returns to scale, whereby larger countries create more inputs and are thereby more productive. It seems to me that we have not yet related this potential explanation for country productivity differences to the implied productivity differences arising from the HO model. Could it be the case that large countries (measured inclusive of proximity to neighbors) are the most productive due to their input variety, and that this productivity also accounts for their trade patterns? Addressing this question is one area for further research.

Problems

10.1   In the two-good, two-factor model with *constant* prices, suppose that good 1 experiences Hicks-neutral technological progress, that is, $y_1 = A_1 f_1(L_1, K_1)$, with A_1 rising. Also assume that good 1 is labor intensive.

Write down the zero-profit and full-employment conditions for the economy, and use the Jones' algebra to show the following:

(a) $\hat{w} > \hat{A}_1 > 0 > \hat{r}$.

(b) $\hat{y}_1 > \hat{A}_1 > 0 > \hat{y}_2$. Note that this is tricky because the factor prices are changing from part (a)

(c) If you have read the appendix to chapter 1, use the Lerner diagram to demonstrate part (a) graphically. Using this result, can you think of a graph that will also demonstrate part (b)?

10.2   Let us adopt a translog functional form for the GDP function in (10.12), extended to include many outputs:

$$\ln G = \alpha_0 + \sum_{i=1}^{N} \alpha_i \ln(A_i p_i) + \sum_{k=1}^{M} \beta_k \ln V_k + \frac{1}{2}\sum_{i=1}^{N}\sum_{j=1}^{N}\gamma_{ij}\ln(A_i p_i)\ln(A_j p_j)$$

$$+ \frac{1}{2}\sum_{k=1}^{M}\sum_{\ell=1}^{M}\delta_{k\ell}\ln V_k \ln V_\ell + \sum_{i=1}^{N}\sum_{k=1}^{M}\phi_{ik}\ln(A_i p_i)\ln V_k.$$

Differentiating this with respect to $\ln p_i$, we obtain the output share equations

$$s_i = \alpha_i + \sum_{j=1}^{N}\gamma_{ij}\ln(A_j p_j) + \sum_{k=1}^{M}\phi_{ik}\ln V_k, \quad i = 1,\ldots, N.$$

where $s_i = p_i y_i / G$ is the share of each output in GDP.

(a) Write the quantity of each output as $\ln y_i = \ln(s_i G/p_i)$. Differentiate this with respect to $\ln p_i$ and obtain an expression for the output elasticity $(\partial \ln y_i/\partial \ln p_i)$. What restriction on the translog parameters must hold for this elasticity to be positive?

(b) Write the quantity of each output as $\ln y_i = \ln(s_i G/p_i)$. Differentiate this with respect to $\ln A_i$ and obtain an expression for the "Rybczynski-like" elasticity $(\partial \ln y_i/\partial \ln A_i)$. If the restrictions in part (a) are satisfied, what can we say about the magnitude of this elasticity?

10.3   Consider the problem of maximizing (10.18) subject to (10.19), where for convenience we set $t = 0$. Write this as the Lagrangian

$$\int_0^\infty e^{-\rho\tau}[\ln E(\tau) - \ln P(\tau)]d\tau$$

$$+ \lambda\left\{\int_0^\infty e^{-R(\tau)}w(\tau)Ld\tau + B(t) - \int_0^\infty e^{-R(\tau)}E(\tau)d\tau\right\}$$

$$= \int_0^\infty \left\{e^{-\rho\tau}[\ln E(\tau) - \ln P(\tau)] + e^{-R(\tau)}\lambda[w(\tau)L - E(\tau)]\right\}d\tau$$

$$+ \lambda B(t),$$

where in the second line we bring the Lagrange multiplier inside the integral. The expression inside the integral must be maximized at every point in time. So differentiate this expression with respect to $E(\tau)$ and then τ to obtain the first-order condition (10.20).

10.4 Consider a central planner who chooses the time path of output to maximize utility. This problem can be written as

$$\max_{Y(\tau)} \int_t^\infty e^{-\rho(\tau-t)} \ln y(\tau) d\tau,$$

subject to

$$y = N^{\sigma/(\sigma-1)} x = N^{1/(\sigma-1)} X \quad \text{and} \quad L = X + \alpha(\dot{N}/N),$$

where $X \equiv Nx$ and the constraints are the production function (10.17) along with the full-employment condition (10.26). Let us restrict our attention to steady-state solutions where $N(\tau) = N(t)e^{g(\tau-t)}$. Substituting this equation along with the constraints into the objective function, differentiate it with respect to g to compute the socially optimal growth rate g^* of new products. Show that $g^* > g^a$, and interpret this result.

10.5 Let us solve for the limiting values of the growth rates in (10.35):

$$g = \left(\frac{L}{\alpha\sigma}\right) - \left(\frac{\sigma-1}{\sigma}\right)\left[\dot{R} - \left(\frac{\dot{w}}{w}\right)\right],$$

and

$$g^* = \left(\frac{L^*}{\alpha\sigma}\right) - \left(\frac{\sigma-1}{\sigma}\right)\left[\dot{R} - \left(\frac{\dot{w}^*}{w^*}\right)\right].$$

To do so, we use the share of world expenditure devoted to the products of the home country, which is $s = p_y y/(E + E^*)$, and the share devoted to products of the foreign country, which is $s^* = p_y^* y^*/(E + E^*)$, with $s + s^* = 1$. In the absence of trade in intermediate inputs, each final good is assembled entirely from inputs produced in the same country. The price of home inputs is $p_i = w\sigma/(\sigma - 1)$, so it follows that $p_y y = p_i X = w\sigma X/(\sigma - 1) = w\sigma(L - \alpha g)/(\sigma - 1)$, where in the last equality we make use of the home full-employment condition, $L = X + \alpha g$. Therefore, the expenditure share on home products can be written as $s = w\sigma(L - \alpha g)/[(E + E^*)(\sigma - 1)]$. Taking logs and differentiating, we obtain

$$\frac{\dot{s}}{s} = \frac{\dot{w}}{w} - \frac{\dot{g}}{(L - \alpha g)} - \left[\frac{\dot{E}}{E}\left(\frac{E}{E + E^*}\right) + \frac{\dot{E}^*}{E^*}\left(\frac{E^*}{E + E^*}\right)\right].$$

Using (10.20), the expression in brackets on the right-hand side equals $\dot{R} - \rho$. It follows that the home and foreign real interest rates are

$$\dot{R} - \frac{\dot{w}}{w} = \rho - \frac{\dot{s}}{s} - \frac{\dot{g}}{(L - \alpha g)}$$

and

$$\dot{R} - \frac{\dot{w}^*}{w^*} = \rho - \frac{\dot{s}^*}{s^*} - \frac{\dot{g}^*}{(L^* - \alpha g^*)}.$$

(a) The fact that the home country is developing more products than abroad means that $\lim_{t \to \infty} s = 1$. What does this imply about the limiting value of the home real interest rate? Therefore, what is the limiting value of the home growth rate?

(b) Since $\lim_{t \to \infty} s = 1$, then $\lim_{t \to \infty} s^* = 0$. What can we say about the limiting values of the foreign real interest rate, and the foreign growth rate?

Chapter 11

Multinationals and Organization of the Firm

DESPITE THE FACT that this book is about international trade, we have so far not introduced any role for *traders*. There has been little scope for firms, let alone economic organization more generally, to have any significant influence on trade patterns between countries. This contradicts the empirical fact that a good deal of trade occurs *internally* within firms located across countries. For the United States, for example, about one-third of exports and over 40% of imports consist of intrafirm trade between a U.S. or foreign firm and their affiliates (see Table 11.1). When a firm operates in several countries it is a *multinational enterprise*, and the investment made in the foreign country is referred to as *foreign direct investment* (FDI).[1] The first goal of this chapter is to introduce these features into our earlier trade models.

The classic treatment of a multinational is that it has some intangible asset (such as knowledge of a production process) that it can use to its advantage in a foreign market. It must decide whether to simply *export* there, or to *invest* in that market by building a plant and selling the product, or whether to engage in a *joint venture or other contractual arrangement* with a foreign firm to produce the good. We will initially focus on the first two decisions—whether to export to the foreign market or to build a plant and sell there. The third case—whether to engage in a joint venture with a foreign firm—will be discussed at the end of the chapter.

Notice that this classic statement of the FDI problem can equally well work in reverse, whereby the acquisition of a foreign firm can *bring with it* knowledge of value to the purchaser that could not be obtained by simply buying the products of that foreign firm. Blonigen (1997) argues that increased inflows of Japanese acquisition FDI into the United States after 1985 were motivated by the desire to acquire the knowledge assets of U.S. firms, combined with the low value of the dollar. Notice that by this argument, FDI flows depend on the level of exchange rates: when the

---

[1] We might define FDI as acquiring sufficient assets in a foreign firm to exercise some managerial control, though acquiring 10% or more of the assets of a foreign enterprise is the definition commonly used in practice.

TABLE 11.1
U.S. Imports and Exports through Multinational Corporations, 1992 ($ billions)

Total U.S. merchandise exports	448.2
Exports through U.S. multinationals	
U.S. parent to foreign affiliates	104.7
U.S. parent to other foreign firms	140.8
Other U.S. to foreign affiliates	15.6
Exports through foreign multinationals	
U.S. affiliate to foreign parent	48.8
Manufacturing,	11.6
Wholesale trade, of which	34.6
Motor vehicles & equipment	5.2
U.S. affiliate to other foreign firms	55.2
Total intramultinational exports	153.5
Percentage of total U.S. exports	34.2%
Total U.S. merchandise imports	532.7
Imports through U.S. multinationals	
Foreign affiliates to U.S. parent	92.6
Other foreign firms to U.S. parent	107.2
Foreign affiliates to other U.S.	16.6
Imports through foreign multinationals	
Foreign parent to U.S. affiliate	137.8
Manufacturing,	37.3
Wholesale trade, of which	89.2
Motor vehicles & equipment	28.7
Other foreign firms to U.S. affiliate	46.7
Total intramultinational imports	230.4
Percentage of total U.S. imports	43.3%

Source: Mataloni 1995, table 7, p. 48; U.S. Department of Commerce 1995, tables H-25, H-27, H-31, H-33; cited in Feenstra 1999.

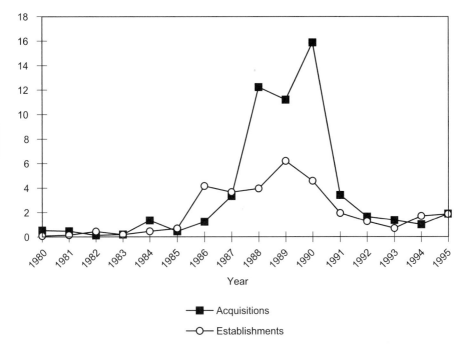

Figure 11.1   Japanese FDI into the United States.
Source: U.S. Department of Commerce, Bureau of Economic Analysis, *Foreign Direct Investment into the United States: U.S. Business Enterprises Acquired or Established by Foreign Investors 1980–91 and 1992–95* (Washington, D.C.), Tables 2, 5E, 6.1, 6.2, 6C, and 6D, diskette; cited in Feenstra (1999).

dollar depreciated after 1985, it became cheaper for foreign companies to purchase the intangible assets of U.S. firms.[2] There was, in fact, a surge in FDI into the United States during that period, particularly in the *acquisition* of U.S. companies. This is shown in Figure 11.1 for Japanese inflows of FDI, and Figure 11.2 for inflows from other countries.

We see that the decision to engage in FDI by a multinational therefore involves three interrelated aspects—*ownership* of an asset, *location* to produce, and whether to keep the asset *internal* to the firm—and these comprise the so-called OLI framework of multinational activity (Dunning 1977, 1981). In the following sections, we explore models giving insight into these various aspects. We begin with the simplest example where a firm considers shutting down its factory in one country and moving it to

---

[2] An alternative reason for an appreciation of foreign currencies to lead to increase FDI in the United States is through the wealth effect on foreign portfolios, as discussed by Froot and Stein (1991).

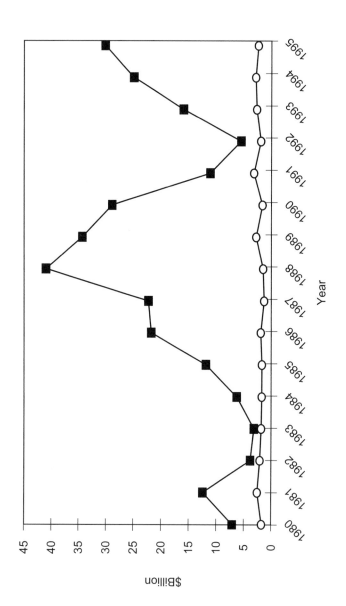

Figure 11.2   FDI into the United States from the United Kingdom, the Netherlands, Canada, Germany, and France.
Source: U.S. Department of Commerce, Bureau of Economic Analysis, *Foreign Direct Investment into the United States: U.S. Business Enterprises Acquired or Established by Foreign Investors 1980–91 and 1992–95* (Washington, D.C.), Tables 2, 5E, 6.1, 6.2, 6C, and 6D, diskette; cited in Feenstra (1999).

another, which can be modeled by a movement of physical capital across countries. While such a movement of capital does not necessarily occur with FDI (which may simply involve a change in ownership without any movement of physical capital), it is a useful place to begin our analysis.

After briefly reviewing capital inflows into a one-sector economy, we use the classic article by Mundell (1957) to investigate capital mobility in the two-sector Heckscher-Ohlin (HO) model. In that case we find that even small tariffs have a very large impact on the movement of capital from one country to the other. This phenomenon of "tariff-jumping" FDI is a typical occurrence in import-substitution regimes, but is not restricted to the developing countries: many industrialized countries have used tariffs or quotas to induce the entry of foreign firms. This policy has some economic rationale, since the entry of foreign firms in simple models leads to a welfare gain due to increased domestic wages. The link between foreign investment and wages is therefore an important topic for empirical research. In Mundell's analysis, domestic wages are not affected by the foreign investment (due to "factor price insensitivity" in the HO model), but it is still the case that the deadweight loss of the tariff is reduced due to the entry of foreign firms.

Multinationals need not lead to capital flows between countries, however, and may instead just involve the ownership and location of firms. We consider several models of that type, distinguishing *vertical* from *horizontal* multinationals. An example of the former case is a firm that has headquarters in one country but does production in another to obtain lower factor prices there (Helpman 1984c). The latter case occurs when a firm decides to duplicate production facilities and sell locally in two or more countries, due to tariffs or other barriers between them (Markusen 1984, 2002). We identify conditions under which a particular type of multinational is most likely to arise in equilibrium and, once again, find that trade policies can have a significant impact on multinational location.

Beyond trade that is internal to multinational firms, there is another large portion of trade that occurs *between* firms that have some special relationship. An example is when a firm outsources some of its production process to a lower-wage country. In chapter 4 we modeled this as the purchase of intermediate inputs, but in fact it often involves a longer-term relationship: the firm wanting to purchase the input is committing its money, and the selling firm is committing resources to production and development of the inputs. This relationship entails risk to both parties, and in many circumstances these risks cannot be offset by legal contracts. If the costs associated with these incomplete contracts are too great, then the firm wanting to purchase the inputs will instead vertically integrate into this activity, becoming a vertical multinational. Thus, a consideration of transactions costs under incomplete contracts allows us to model the *internalization* decision of a multinational firm. The recent work of Grossman and Helpman (2002a,

2002b, 2002c) and others puts this in a general equilibrium setting, and investigates the implications of internalization for trade.

Transactions costs are the first and foremost reason for firms to integrate, but there are others. For example, joint ventures between firms in different countries can bring with them knowledge of the supplier and distribution networks in each country, and any other intangible assets owned by either firm. Rauch and Trindade (2003) model this informational issue as a problem of "matching" firms across countries, where there is some inherent uncertainty in the ability to find a good partner. As we shall describe, the efficacy of achieving matches determines the extent to which markets are integrated, that is, the extent to which factor price equalization obtains. The study of the organization of firms and its implications for international trade is a very new area of research, and is an appropriate topic on which to conclude this book.

Capital Flows in a One-Sector Economy

We begin our analysis with the simplest case of a capital inflow into an economy producing just one good, as in MacDougall 1960. Suppose that the production function is given by $y = f(L, K)$, which is linearly homogeneous and concave. Normalizing the product price at unity, the rental on capital is $r = f_K(L, K)$, with $f_{KK} < 0$. Denote the domestic capital stock by K_0 and the foreign inflow of capital by K^*. The equilibrium rental in the absence of the foreign capital is shown by r_0 in Figure 11.3, and in the presence of the capital inflow by r_1. The foreign capital earns the amount $r_1 K^*$, which is taken out of the country. The increase in GDP due to the capital inflow is

$$\Delta y = \int_{K_0}^{K_0 + K^*} f_K dK = A + B. \tag{11.1}$$

Subtracting the payment to foreign capital, $r_1 K^* = B$, the net welfare gain to the home country is the area A. Thus, the inflow of foreign capital creates a welfare gain.

What is the source of this gain? It is evident from Figure 11.3 that as capital enters, it depresses the rental, so that the payments to foreign capital (B) are less than the total area under the demand curve ($A + B$). The other side of this is that the capital inflow *raises* the marginal product of labor and wages, $w = f_L(L, K)$. Indeed, the total increase in the wage bill equals the area $A + C$ in Figure 11.3.[3] Area C is the redistribution of income from capital to labor, whereas area A is the net welfare gain, and it accrues to labor.

---

[3] Because the production function is linearly homogeneous, $y_0 = w_0 L + r_0 K_0$, and $y_1 = w_1 L + r_1(K_0 + K^*)$. It follows that $\Delta y = (A + B) = (w_1 - w_0)L + (r_1 - r_0)K_0 + r_1 K^*$, and since

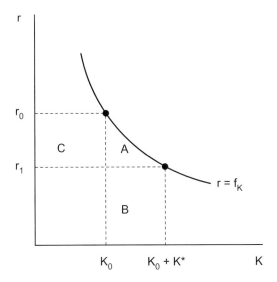

Figure 11.3

These simple observations have led to a good deal of empirical work as to whether industries experiencing an inflow of foreign capital pay higher wages. For the United States, Howenstein and Zeile (1994) and Doms and Jensen (1998) find that foreign plants pay higher wages than domestic plants. Blonigen and Tomlin (2001) further find that foreign plants typically grow faster than U.S. plants of similar size, and that they lead to a larger positive impact on local wages than does domestic investment. Combining U.S. data with information on Mexican and Venezuelan enterprises, Aitken, Harrison, and Lipsey (1996) also find a wage differential between domestic and foreign-owned enterprises, even after controlling for industry size and capital intensity.

Notice that these studies most often compare the wages paid by foreign and domestic plants, which is not exactly the same as the *general equilibrium* wage increase due to foreign investment predicted by Figure 11.3. For example, if foreign firms simply attract the highest-quality workers, wages would increase in comparison to domestic plants, but not necessarily welfare. This same problem of self-selection occurs in empirical studies of *technology transfer* between foreign and local firms (through joint ventures or other spillovers across firms). Evidence in support of technology transfer for Mexico is found by Blomstrom (1986), Blomstrom and Persson (1983),

---

$B = r_1 K^*$ and $C = (r_0 - r_1)K_0$, the wage bill changes by $(w_1 - w_0)L = (A + B) - (r_1 - r_0)K_0 - r_1 K^* = A + C$.

and Kokko (1994), and for Indonesia by Blomstrom and Sjoholm (1999). These studies correlate *industry* productivity with the presence of foreign firms. However, this leaves open the question of whether the higher productivity is due to the foreign plants themselves, or due to spillovers. This has been addressed using plant-level data by Haddad and Harrison (1993) for Morocco, and Aitken and Harrison (1999) for Venezuela. They find that the foreign plants indeed have higher productivity, but that there is a weak *negative* correlation between their presence and productivity of the *domestic* plants in the same industry. Thus, these findings cast some doubt on the hypothesis of positive technological spillovers between foreign and domestic firms; rather, foreign firms are just more productive.

Capital Flows in the Two-Sector Heckscher-Ohlin Model

We turn next to a famous example of capital flows in the two-sector HO model, due to Mundell (1957). Suppose there are two countries with identical technologies and homothetic tastes, initially engaged in free trade. With countries producing both goods and no factor intensity reversals, the rental on capital is uniquely determined by the goods prices, which we write as $r(p_1, p_2)$ for both countries. In Figure 11.4 the endowment of the two countries is shown at the point V^i, which we assume is inside the factor price equalization set so the rental on capital is the same across countries.[4] With free trade in goods, consumption of the two countries is proportional and occurs along the diagonal of Figure 11.4, such as the point AD^i (where D^i is the consumption vector of each country, and multiplying by the technology matrix A converts this to the factors embodied in consumption). In the case we have illustrated, country 1 is labor abundant, and the move from V^i to AD^i involves country 1 importing the capital-intensive good. Assume that good 1 is capital intensive, so that $\partial r(p_1, p_2)/\partial p_1 > 0$.

Now allow for capital mobility between the countries, and suppose that country 1 applies a specific import tariff of $t > 0$. This raises the domestic price of good 1 in that country, and since this good is capital intensive, by the Stolper-Samuelson theorem it increases the return to capital, $r(p_1 + t, p_2) > r(p_1, p_2)$. It follows that capital will flow from country 2 to country 1. In Figure 11.4, this shifts the effective endowment point vertically upwards from point V^i. The question is, where will this process end? The new equilibrium allowing for capital mobility requires that the return to capital be *equalized* across the countries. But with the tariff driving a wedge between the prices in the two countries, it is *impossible* for rentals to be equalized: $t > 0$ always implies that $r(p_1 + t, p_2) > r(p_1, p_2)$. Obviously, something in this equation must change to achieve a new long-run equilibrium!

[4] Refer to Figure 2.3 to review how this figure is constructed.

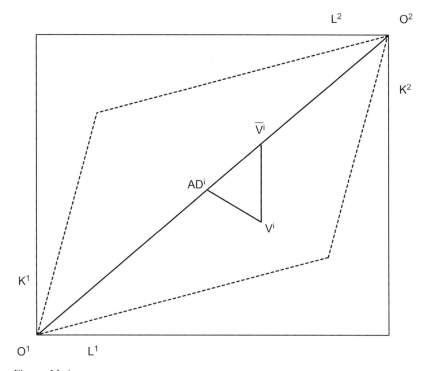

Figure 11.4

To see what changes, let us think about what happens as the endowments of the countries move upwards from point V^i. Capital is flowing towards country 1, which increases the output of industry 1 and reduces that of industry 2. Since good 1 is imported, the increased supply of that good *lowers* imports, and the reduced supply of good 2 also lowers exports. So as we move upwards from point V^i, trade between the countries is being reduced. This will continue until the endowments reach the diagonal, indicated by the point $\overline{V}^i$, at which point the capital/labor ratios in the two countries are identical. This means that there is no reason for trade: both economies are in autarky.

What about the rental on capital in each country? Since both countries are in autarky, with identical capital/labor ratios and identical homothetic tastes, this means that the equilibrium prices are the same across countries. It follows, therefore, that the equilibrium rental on capital is also the same across countries. The tariff that is being applied by country 1 is redundant: since there are no imports, the tariff no longer drives a wedge between the prices and rentals. So we conclude that the point $\overline{V}^i$ is the new equilibrium with capital mobility. Product prices and the rental on capital are unchanged from their original values before the tariff (since this is a property of a change in endowments within the FPE cone). Furthermore, the entire increase in the GDP of country 1 from point V^i to point $\overline{V}^i$ is repaid to the foreign capital located there.[5] If we deduct this amount from GDP, country 1 ends up back at its *original* consumption point AD^i, so its welfare is the same as before the tariff was applied!

This analysis by Mundell (1957) is important for several reasons: it shows that a tariff can lead to a large enough inflow of capital to eliminate trade; and it shows that the capital flow eliminates the deadweight loss due to the tariff. Both of these observations are realistic and can be illustrated by the VER applied to Japanese exports of automobiles into the United States, as discussed in chapter 8. While this trade policy took the form of a quota rather than a tariff, it still led a large inflow of Japanese auto firms into the United States—enough to make the VER redundant after 1987 (i.e., there were fewer imports from Japan than allowed by the VER). This means that its welfare cost was also reduced.[6]

This results of Mundell (1957) are sometimes summed up with the phrase "trade in factors is a substitute for trade in goods," since the capital inflow due to the tariff has the effect of eliminating trade. This hypothesis has been empirically tested. Blonigen (2001) investigates the extent to which FDI and imports are substitutes (with inflows of capital reducing imports) or complements (FDI leading to higher imports). He finds evidence for both hypotheses, as is also confirmed by Swenson (2003) for the United States and Goldberg and Klein (2000) using data from Latin America. The effect of U.S. antidumping duties on inward FDI is investigated by Blonigen (2002). He finds that this U.S. investment is a realistic option only for firms with prior multinational experience. While the raw data show a particularly high response rate for Japanese firms shifting their production to the United States, this is mainly explained by the fact that many of these firms are already multinationals.

Vertical and Horizontal Multinationals

We turn now from a discussion of capital flows to the modeling of multinational activity, where a firm chooses to operate plants in multiple countries. We distinguish the cases where the multinational chooses to operate its headquarters in one country and its production facilities in another—the

---

[5] To see this, measure GDP as the value of factor earnings. With unchanged product prices and factor prices, the new GDP at $\overline{V}^i$ is GDP $= wL^1 + rK^1 + rK^\star$, so deducting payment to foreign capital $rK^\star$, we obtain the original GDP of $wL^1 + rK^1$.

[6] Neary (1988) examines more systematically the welfare costs of tariffs and quotas under capital mobility.

so-called *vertical* multinational—from the case where it operates its head-quarters in one country but has production facilities in multiple countries—the *horizontal* multinational.

Vertical Multinationals

The vertical case was first analyzed by Helpman (1984c) in a two-factor framework with monopolistic competition. The incentive to operate headquarters in one country and production in another arises from factor price differences across the countries. As we shall see, however, the ability of a multinational to spread its facilities across several countries serves to ameliorate these factor price differences, and *enlarges* the region of factor price equalization.

Suppose that sector 1 produces a homogeneous good, while sector 2 produces a differentiated good with a CES utility function. A variety of the differentiated good requires α units of skilled labor H in its fixed costs (which we think of as "headquarters" services), and β units of unskilled labor L in its variable costs. Denoting the output of a differentiated variety by y_{2i}, the costs of production are $C_{2i}(w, q, y_i) = q\alpha + w\beta y_{2i}$, where q and w are the wages of skilled and unskilled labor, respectively. As dis-cussed in chapter 5, with a CES utility function there is a unique output $y_{2i} = \bar{y}$ at which profits are zero, where free entry also determines the number of varieties N_2 in sector 2. Then the demand for skilled labor for each variety produced is α, and the demand for unskilled labor is $\beta\bar{y}$.

Technologies are the same across countries, and we will focus on the "integrated world equilibrium" at which factor price equalization (FPE) is obtained. In sector 1, producing the homogeneous good, the require-ments of unskilled and skilled labor to produce *one unit* of output are denoted by a_{1L} and a_{1H}. In sector 2, the requirements to produce *one variety* of the differentiated product are $a_{2L} \equiv \beta\bar{y}$ and $a_{2H} \equiv \alpha$. Then we can let $A = \begin{bmatrix} a_{1L} & a_{2L} \\ a_{1H} & a_{2H} \end{bmatrix}$ denote the matrix of labor requirements in each industry, which applies in either country under FPE. Let $Y^j = (y_1^j, N_2^j)'$ denote the vector whose first component is the output of industry 1 in country j, and whose second component is the *number* of varieties of the differentiated product in sector 2 produced in country j. Then full em-ployment of resources in each country requires that $AY^j = V^j$, where V^j is the vector of endowments in country $j = 1, 2$.

Let us assume initially that the fixed costs of α and variable costs of $\beta\bar{y}$ for each differentated good have to be performed in the *same* country. Then the integrated world equilibrium can be illustrated in a fashion very much analogous to the two-factor HO model. In Figure 11.5, the FPE set is shown by the parallelogram $0^1Q0^2Q'0^1$. Starting at any endowment

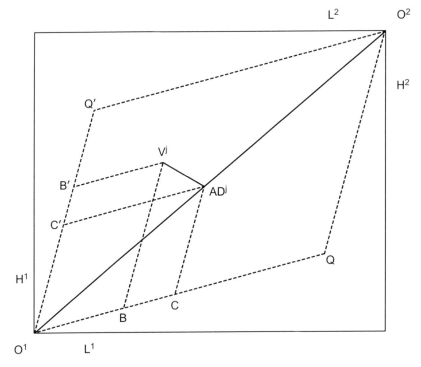

Figure 11.5

point such as V^j within this parallelogram, free trade in goods allows the economies to consume at points D^j that are proportional across countries, so that the factors embodied in consumption AD^j lie along the diagonal of the box.[7] The slope of the line between V^j and AD^j (in absolute value) is the equilibrium ratio of factor prices w/q.

Let us further assume that industry 1, producing the homogeneous product, is unskilled labor intensive, so that $a_{1L}/a_{1H} > a_{2L}/a_{2H} = \beta \bar{y}/\alpha$. Then from the endowment and consumption points we can readily compute the trade balance in each industry. Thus, in *production* country 1 uses the amount of labor 0^1B in industry 1 and $0^1B'$ in industry 2, which sum to the endowment point V^j. Similarly, in *consumption* country 1 uses the amount of labor 0^1C in industry 1 and $0^1C'$ in industry 2, which sum to the point AD^j. It follows that country 1 is an importer of good 1 ($OB < OC$), and a net exporter of the differentiated good ($OB' > OC'$).

---

[7] Note that the consumption in each country equals $D^j = [d_1^j, (N_2^1 + N_2^2)s^j]'$, where the first component is the quantity consumed in country j of the homogeneous good, and the second component is the *world* variety of the differentiated good times country j's share of world GDP.

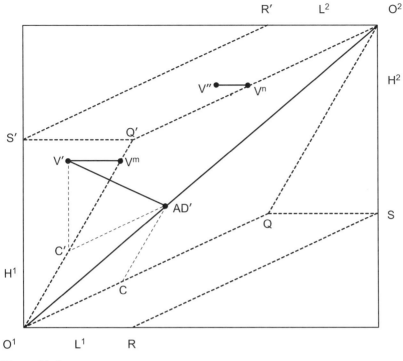

Figure 11.6

In addition, there is intraindustry trade in the differentiated goods sector.

Now let us change our assumptions and suppose that the fixed costs of α skilled labor and variable costs of $\beta\bar{y}$ unskilled labor for each differentiated good can be performed in *different* countries by a multinational firm. Then how does the ability to "fragment" the headquarters and production activities across countries affect the FPE set? A quick (and entirely correct) answer can be obtained by appealing to the FPE set with *multiple goods* developed by Dixit and Norman (1980), as discussed in chapter 3. Rank the activities beginning with the variable costs of producing the differentiated good, which uses only unskilled labor; followed by the production of the homogeneous product, which uses both factors; followed by the fixed costs of producing the differentiated good, which uses only skilled labor. This gives *three* rather than two factor requirements vectors, which are $(\beta\bar{y}, 0)$, (a_{1L}, a_{1H}), and $(0, \alpha)$. Multiplying each of these vectors by the total worldwide amount of each activity in the integrated equilibrium, and summing them, we will obtain the FPE set $0^1 R S 0^2 R' S' 0^1$ in Figure 11.6. This FPE region is clearly *larger* than the original parallelogram $0^1 Q 0^2 Q' 0^1$.

To understand how FPE is achieved in this expanded set, suppose that the factor endowments of the two countries are given by V' in Figure 11.6. This point lies *outside* the original FPE set, so that any firm in sector 1 would choose the country with lowest wage of skilled labor for headquarters, and the country with lowest wage of unskilled labor for production. Since country 1 is skilled labor abundant, we can presume that it would have the lower relative wage of skilled labor, and firms from either country would want to establish headquarters there. This will increase the demand for skilled labor in country 1, to the point where the entire endowment V' can be employed at the *same* factor prices as prevailing abroad. Intuitively, this is what allows FPE to hold in the expanded set.

Because there are three production activities and only two factors, there are actually many combinations of the activities across countries that are consistent with full employment and FPE. As in Helpman 1984c, we will focus on those combinations that lead to a minimum amount of trade. With factor endowments given by V' in Figure 11.6, country 1 could produce varieties of the differentiated good using resources shown by $0^1C'$, and then devote its remaining endowment of skilled labor, shown by $C'V'$, to headquarters services. These headquarters services would be combined with *unskilled* labor in country 2, of the amount $V'V^m$, in order to produce varieties of the differentiated product in that country. Additional resources in country 2, of the amount V^mQ', would also be devoted to produce varieties of the differentiated product, and the remaining resource of $Q'0^2$ would be used to produce the homogeneous product in sector 1. Factor price equalization is achieved through combining skilled labor for headquarters services in country 1 with unskilled labor for production in country 2.

What is the trade pattern implied by the multinational activity? For factor endowments in the region $0^1S'Q'$, as we have been discussing, the homogeneous good is produced only in country 2, so country 1 imports that good. But for the differentiated good, the trade pattern is not so clear. Indeed, in the case we have illustrated in Figure 11.6, it turns out that both countries have *balanced net trade* in the differentiated good. This can be seen by comparing the resources used in production and consumption. As discussed just above, country 1 uses the resources $0^1C'$ to produce varieties of the differentiated good. To determine its consumption, we can trace a line from its endowment point V' to its consumption of factors AD' (this line has the slope w/q). We then decompose the point AD' into the consumption of factors 0^1C in sector 1, and $0^1C'$ in sector 2. Notice that for the case we have illustrated, the *consumption* of factors $0^1C'$ in sector 2 is identical to those used in the *production* of differentiated varieties by country 1. It follows that trade is balanced in that sector, and the same will hold for country 2: they have balanced intra-industry trade in the differentiated good.[8]

How can country 1 be an importer of the homogeneous good, and yet have balanced net trade in the differentiated good? The answer is that this country receives *profits* from its multinationals engaged in production abroad, which would show up as investment income in the current account. Thus, its balance-of-trade deficit (due to importing the homogeneous good) is offset by receipts from its subsidiaries abroad, so that it has an overall current account balance. The *amount* of profits earned in country 2 will be proportional to the unskilled labor employed there by the multinationals, which is measured by $L^* \equiv V'V^m$. With $\beta\bar{y}$ units of unskilled labor needed per variety, the number of varieties produced by multinationals in country 2 is therefore $N^* = L^*/\beta\bar{y}$. The value of headquarters services provided by these multinationals through employing skilled labor in country 1 is then $\alpha N^* = \alpha L^*/\beta\bar{y}$.[9] This is an "invisible export" by country 1, which is used to pay for its imports of the homogeneous good.

As we move to other regions of the FPE set, the trade patterns change. For example, consider endowments within $0^2 R'S'Q'$, such as V''. Once again, multinationals with headquarters in country 1 will use some of the unskilled labor in country 2 so that FPE is achieved. In this case, the amount of unskilled labor employed in country 2 by multinationals is the distance $V''V^n$. We can think of the vector $0^1 V^n$ as the *employment* of resources by firms that have headquarters in country 1, as distinct from that country's *endowment* vector $0^1 V''$. In the absence of multinationals, the employment of resources must equal a country's endowment, but now they can differ. We can also construct the trade patterns in the region $0^2 R'S'Q'$. It turns out the country 1 can be either an importer or an exporter of the homogeneous product in this region, and also exports the differentiated product as well as headquarters services.[10]

Setting aside the details of the trade patterns, the most important message to take from Figure 11.6 is that vertical multinationals *enlarge* the FPE set. This is a deep insight from Helpman (1984c) and can be compared to our results in chapter 4, where we discussed trade in intermediate inputs and wages. We suggested there that the ability to fragment the production process, and purchase some unskilled-labor intermediate inputs from another country, could lead to an *increase* in the relative demand and

---

[8] It follows that for slightly different choices of the endowment point V', country 1 could be either a net exporter or a net importer of the differentiated good in the region $0^1 S'Q'$.

[9] Notice that the skilled labor of $\alpha N^* = \alpha L^*/\beta\bar{y}$ in country 1 is equivalently measured by the distance $C'V'$.

[10] Helpman (1984c) carefully solves for the trade pattern in this region, as well as showing how endowments affect the *volume* of trade in all regions of the FPE set.

wages of skilled labor in *both* countries. In comparison, we have argued above that such outsourcing by multinationals will lead to an enlargement of the FPE set, and therefore, a tendency for factor prices to equalize across countries. These two results are not necessarily inconsistent, but it is worth thinking about how the assumptions of Helpman (1984c) differ from those in chapter 4.

In the model of chapter 4 with a continuum of inputs, we showed that an increase in outsourcing would occur through the "borderline" activity being transferred from the home to the foreign country: that activity was *less* skill intensive than any other activity performed at home, but *more* skill intensive than any other activity performed abroad. Therefore, the relative demand for skilled labor rose in both countries, as did its relative wage. In contrast, in our discussion of Helpman's (1984c) model, we treated the production of the differentiated good as using only unskilled labor, with headquarters services using only skilled labor. The production activity is therefore *less* skill intensive than the homogeneous good produced in either country. The transfer of multinational production from country 1 to country 2 raises the relative demand for skilled labor in country 1, but lowers it in country 2. This will raise the relative wages of skilled labor in country 1, but lower them in country 2, thereby moving these relative wages towards *equality*, so that FPE is achieved.

We see that the assumptions on factor-intensities differ between chapter 4 and what we have used to describe Helpman's (1984c) model.[11] Obviously, other assumptions on factor intensities can be incorporated into Helpman's model, as well as alternative assumptions on fixed costs and trade barriers, as we shall explore in the next section.

Horizontal Multinationals

In Helpman's model, the multinational will never choose to operate production facilities in *both* countries, because with free trade, there is no benefit to doing so. But suppose that there are some trade barriers, such as the "iceberg" transport costs discussed in chapter 5. Suppose further that each plant has some specific fixed costs, which must be borne in the same country as production costs. Then we will say that *horizontal FDI* occurs if a firm chooses to operate production facilities in *multiple countries*, with each plant selling locally to that market. Horizontal FDI

---

[11] Helpman (1984c) actually uses more general assumption on factor intensities but, to illustrate the FPE regions, focuses on the case where the fixed costs use only skilled labor (which he calls a "general purpose" input H), and the variable costs use only unskilled labor. These are the same assumptions we have used above. In related theoretical work, Helpman (1985) allows for multinationals to produce multiple products.

requires that the gains from selling locally and thereby avoiding transport costs more than offset the plant-specific fixed costs. This case has been analyzed in a series of studies beginning with Markusen 1984 and culminating in Markusen 2002. These writings cover a whole range of vertical and horizontal multinationals, using unskilled and skilled labor in varying proportions. We will not attempt to summarize all these results, but shall develop one example of how horizontal multinationals can arise.

We suppose that a firm in country i is already producing for its home market and is deciding whether to export to country j or establish a production facility and sell there. This firm has already covered its fixed costs of headquarters services, as well as any plant-specific fixed costs in country i, and there is an additional fixed cost of establishing a plant abroad. We suppose there are "iceberg" transportation costs between the countries, so that $T^{ij} > 1$ units of the good must be exported from country i in order for one unit to arrive in j. We let p^i denote the f.o.b. price received by the firm in country i. Inclusive of the transportation costs, the c.i.f. price abroad is $p^{ij} = T^{ij} p^i$.

We borrow the demand structure from our treatment of monopolistic competition in chapter 5. With country j having a CES utility function over the differentiated product, its demand c^{ij} for a variety sent from country i is

$$c^{ij} = (p^{ij}/P^j)^{-\sigma}(Y^j/P^j), \qquad (11.2)$$

where Y^j is country j's GDP, and P^j refers to country j's overall price index, defined as

$$P^j = \left(\sum_{i=1}^{C} N^i (p^{ij})^{1-\sigma} \right)^{1/(1-\sigma)}, \qquad (11.3)$$

and where N^i is the number of products exported by each country $i = 1, \ldots, C$.

We treat labor as the only factor of production, and do not distinguish by skill type. The *exporting* firm in country i has the production function $L^i = \beta y^i$, where β is its marginal labor costs. Note that its plant-specific fixed costs are *already covered* by virtue of its home sales of this product. Revenue received from producing in country i and exporting to country j is $p^{ij}c^{ij} = p^i y^i$, where output is related to consumption by $y^i = c^{ij} T^{ij}$. The profits from exporting are then

$$p^i y^i - w^i \beta y^i = (p^i - w^i \beta) T^{ij} c^{ij}. \qquad (11.4)$$

Substituting for the CES demand from (11.2), and maximizing (11.4) over the choice of the price $p^{ij} = T^{ij} p^i$, we readily obtain the optimal price $p^i[1 - (1/\sigma)] = \beta w^i$. Substituting this back into (11.4), we obtain the maximized value of profits,

$$p^i y^i - w^i \beta y^i = \left(\frac{p^i y^i}{\sigma} \right) = \left(\frac{p^i T^{ij}}{\sigma} \right) \left(\frac{p^i T^{ij}}{P^j} \right)^{-\sigma} \left(\frac{Y^j}{P^j} \right)$$

$$= \frac{1}{\sigma} \left(\frac{p^i T^{ij}}{P^j} \right)^{1-\sigma} Y^j,$$

(11.5)

where the second equality follows using consumption from (11.2) with $y^i = c^{ij} T^{ij}$, and the third by simplification. From (11.5), we see that higher transport costs reduce profits from exporting, while higher GDP abroad increase profits.

Rather than exporting from country i, the multinational firm can instead establish a production facility in country j, and sell locally. In that case, it will face the production function $L^j = \alpha^j + \beta y^j$, including the plant-specific fixed costs paid abroad. For simplicity we treat marginal labor costs β as equal across countries, though the wages and fixed costs can differ. There are no transport costs when producing in country j and selling locally, so with the price p^j, the quantity sold is,

$$c^j = (p^j/P^j)^{-\sigma}(Y^j/P^j).$$

(11.2′)

Again, the optimal price is determined as $p^j[1 - (1/\sigma)] = \beta w^j$. Using this and (11.2′) to compute profits earned from the subsidiary in country j, we obtain

$$p^j y^j - w^j(\beta y^j + \alpha^j) = \frac{1}{\sigma} \left(\frac{p^j}{P^j} \right)^{1-\sigma} Y^j - w^i \alpha^j.$$

(11.5′)

Thus, in order for the multinational based in country i to wish to establish a second plant in country j, it must be the case that (11.5′) is at least as large as (11.5):

$$\frac{1}{\sigma} \left(\frac{p^j}{P^j} \right)^{1-\sigma} Y^j - w^j \alpha^j \geq \frac{1}{\sigma} \left(\frac{p^i T^{ij}}{P^j} \right)^{1-\sigma} Y^j.$$

(11.6)

Similarly, in order to be a horizontal multinational, it must be the case that it is *more profitable* to open a plant in country i than to simply export from a single plant in country j. The condition to ensure that is

$$\frac{1}{\sigma} \left(\frac{p^i}{P^i} \right)^{1-\sigma} Y^i - w^i \alpha^i \geq \frac{1}{\sigma} \left(\frac{p^j T^{ji}}{P^i} \right)^{1-\sigma} Y^i,$$

(11.6′)

where α^i is the plant fixed costs in country i. The left-hand side of (11.6′) is the profits from operating its plant in country i, while the right-hand side is the profits from exporting from country j to country i.

So in order to have a horizontal multinational operating plants in both countries, (11.6) and (11.6′) must both hold. These conditions can be re-expressed by moving the fixed costs to the right side, multiplying each equation by σ, and multiplying them together, in which case we obtain a *single necessary condition* to ensure that the multinational maintains plants in both countries:

$$
\left[1 - (T^{ij}T^{ji})^{1-\sigma}\right](Y^i Y^j)\left(\frac{p^i p^j}{P^i P^j}\right)^{1-\sigma}
$$

$$
\geq \sigma w^i \alpha^i Y^j \left(\frac{p^i T^{ij}}{P^j}\right)^{1-\sigma} + \sigma w^j \alpha^j Y^i \left(\frac{p^j T^{ji}}{P^i}\right)^{1-\sigma} \qquad (11.7)
$$

$$
+ \sigma^2 w^i \alpha^i w^j \alpha^j.
$$

This condition is more likely to hold in the regions of parameters given by the following theorem.

Theorem (Markusen and Venables 1998, 2000; Markusen 2002)

Horizontal multinationals will be more likely when (*a*) transport costs are higher; (*b*) plant-specific fixed costs are lower; (*c*) GDPs are higher or more similar across countries.

Conditions (a) and (b) of this theorem follow by inspection of condition (11.7).[12] Condition (c) requires some additional explanation. Notice that product of GDPs can be rewritten as:

$$
Y^i Y^j = (Y^i + Y^j)^2 s^i s^j = (Y^i + Y^j)^2 [1 - (s^i)^2 - (s^j)^2]/2, \quad (11.8)
$$

where $s^i = Y^i/(Y^i + Y^j)$ and $s^j = Y^j/(Y^i + Y^j)$ are country i's and country j's shares of GDP, with $(s^i + s^j) = 1$. It follows that $1 = (s^i + s^j)^2 = (s^i)^2 + (s^j)^2 + 2s^i s^j$, from which the last equality in (11.8) is obtained. In chapter 5, we referred to $[1 - (s^i)^2 - (s^j)^2]$ as a *size dispersion index* of the two countries, and it takes its *highest value* (of one-half) when the countries are the *same* size. Denoting this index by D^{ij}, we can divide (11.7) by $(Y^i + Y^j)$ and rewrite it as

---

[12] Notice that the left-hand side of (11.7) is increasing in the transport costs T^{ij} or T^{ji}, while the right-hand side is decreasing. In addition, the right-hand side is increasing in the fixed costs α^i or α^j.

$$\left[1 - (T^{ij}T^{ji})^{1-\sigma}\right](Y^i + Y^j)\left(\frac{D^{ij}}{2}\right)\left(\frac{p^i p^j}{P^i P^j}\right)^{1-\sigma}$$

$$\geq \sigma w^i \alpha^i s^j \left(\frac{p^i T^{ij}}{P^j}\right)^{1-\sigma} + \sigma w^j \alpha^j s^i \left(\frac{p^j T^{ji}}{P^i}\right)^{1-\sigma}$$

$$+ \frac{\sigma^2 w^i \alpha^i w^j \alpha^j}{(Y^i + Y^j)}.$$

$$(11.7')$$

We see that the left-hand side of $(11.7')$ is larger when the sum of GDPs $(Y^i + Y^j)$ is larger, and the right-hand side is smaller. In addition, the left is larger when the size dispersion index is higher, meaning that the countries are of similar size.[13] Under these conditions, $(11.7')$ is more likely to hold.

Markusen and Venables (1998) and Markusen (2002, chap. 5) demonstrate the above theorem in a model where firms produce a homogeneous good under Cournot-Nash competition, while Markusen and Venables (2000) and Markusen (2002, chap. 6) use monopolistic competition with a CES utility function. In both cases, the multinationals employ high- and low-skilled labor. So in addition to the similarity of GDP's that we obtain in condition (c), they also find that horizontal multinationals are more likely to hold when the *relative endowments* of high- and low-skilled workers are *similar*. Notice that this is the opposite of the result obtained from Helpman's (1984c) model: since vertical multinationals occur in the regions $0^1 S'Q'$ and $0^2 R'S'Q'$ of Figure 11.6, this requires that the relative endowments of skilled/unskilled workers are sufficiently *different*.

Estimating the Knowledge-Capital Model

The vertical and horizontal multinationals can be combined in a unified framework, which Markusen (2002, chaps. 7, 8) refers to as the "knowledge-capital" model. This term is used because the knowledge created at the headquarters is utilized at plants in multiple countries: it has the nature of a public good within the firm. This is the intangible asset that we identified in the introduction of the chapter as essential to any multinational firm. It is assumed that the ratio of skilled/unskilled labor used in headquarters services *exceeds* that used in plant production by multinationals, which in turn *exceeds* that used in production of the ho-

---

[13] Changes in the country shares will also affect the right-hand side of $(11.7')$, but only by a small amount if fixed costs, transport costs, and wages are similar across countries.

mogeneous competitive good. Then Markusen (2002, chap. 8) finds that increased investment by multinationals raises the relative wage of skilled/unskilled workers in the skill-abundant country, and possibly in the other country as well. The reason for this is that the skill-abundant country specializes more in headquarters services, while the other country specializes more in production by multinationals, which raise the relative demand for skilled labor in *both* countries. This outcome applies to either horizontal or vertical investment, and is very similar to what we obtained from outsourcing in chapter 4.[14]

The knowledge-capital model has been estimated by Carr, Markusen, and Maskus (2001), and hypothesis tests to distinguish the horizontal from the vertical model are performed by Markusen and Maskus (2001, 2002) as well as Blonigen, Davies, and Head (2003).[15] These studies differ somewhat in their precise specifications, and we will combine their various results in our discussion below.[16] The dependent variable used is the real sales of foreign affiliates of multinational firms, including both their local and export sales. For horizontal multinationals the local sales are most important, while for vertical multinational the export sales (back to the parent corporation) are most important.

The equation estimated by Carr, Markusen and Maskus (2001) is

Real Affiliate Sales

$$
\begin{aligned}
= {} & \beta_0 + \beta_1 (\mathrm{GDP}^i + \mathrm{GDP}^j) + \beta_2 (\mathrm{GDP}^i - \mathrm{GDP}^j)^2 \\
& + \beta_3 (\mathrm{Skill}^i - \mathrm{Skill}^j) + \beta_4 (\mathrm{GDP}^i - \mathrm{GDP}^j)(\mathrm{Skill}^i - \mathrm{Skill}^j) \\
& + \beta_5 (\alpha^j) + \beta_6 (\tau^j) + \beta_7 (\tau^j)(\mathrm{Skill}^i - \mathrm{Skill}^j)^2 \\
& + \beta_8 (\tau^i) + \beta_9 \mathrm{Distance}^{ij},
\end{aligned} \tag{11.9}
$$

where country *i* refers to the headquarters of a multinational and country *j* to the location of its a foreign affiliate. The first variable on the right side

---

[14] Notice that the skilled/unskilled labor used in plant product in the knowledge capital model lies *in between* the factor intensities of headquarters services and of the homogeneous competitive good. This is similar to factor intensity of the "borderline" activity that was transferred between countries in the outsourcing model of chapter 4, but differs from the assumption of Helpman (1984c).

[15] Brainard (1997) also estimates a horizontal versus multinationals model in which firms trade off the benefits from being close to customers against the benefits of concentrating production in one location.

[16] In the estimation of (11.9), Blonigen, Davies, and Head (2003) measure the skill difference and GDP difference as absolute values instead. They argue that the absolute values are closer to the specification in Markusen and Maskus 2002 and Markusen 2002, chap. 12, who allow for separate coefficients on the skill difference depending on its sign, along with separate coefficients on its interaction with the GDP difference.

of (11.9) is the sum of country GDPs, which we expect to be positively related to the presence of horizontal multinationals, and therefore real affiliate sales ($\beta_1 > 0$). Likewise, the second variable is the squared difference in real GDPs, which measures the size dispersion, and which we expect to be negatively related to horizontal multinationals ($\beta_2 < 0$). The variable α^j, reflecting host country investment costs, and τ^i and τ^j, reflecting trade costs, are included as controls.

What about for vertical multinationals? In the model of Helpman (1984c), neither the sum nor the difference of GDPs determines the magnitude of affiliate exports back to the parent country; rather, it is the relative factor endowments that determine the magnitude of these exports. For example, in Figure 11.6, the affiliate exports are proportional to the line segments $V' V^m$ and $V'' V^n$, which equal the amount of unskilled labor used for affiliate production. The position of the endowment points V' and V'' relative to the original FPE set is what determines these exports, not the country GDPs.

Thus, one test of the horizontal versus the vertical model is to compare the expected coefficients $\beta_1 > 0$ and $\beta_2 < 0$ for the horizontal case, with $\beta_1 = \beta_2 = 0$ for the vertical case. The estimation of (11.9) is performed with a dataset on inbound and outbound U.S. foreign direct investment, from 1986 to 1994. For each country pair, either i or j denotes the United States, with the other index being the location of either a U.S. affiliate or a foreign parent company with an affiliate in the United States. The hypotheses that $\beta_1 > 0$ and $\beta_2 < 0$ are strongly confirmed in the estimation, which supports the horizontal over the vertical multinational model.

The next two variables in (11.9) are related to the skill differences between the parent and host country, where Skill^i is measured by the share of the labor force in certain skilled occupations. In the horizontal model, it is expected that investment and affiliate sales are declining in the endowment differences of the countries, and this effect is more pronounced when the country GDPs also differ. Thus, the hypotheses $\beta_3 < 0$ and $\beta_4 < 0$ are obtained from the horizontal model. In contrast, with Helpman's model vertical investment is higher when the endowments of the countries differ more, so that $\beta_3 > 0$ is predicted. Markusen (2002, chap. 12) also finds in his simulations that countries that are both *small* and *skilled labor abundant* relative to their trading partners, such as the Netherlands, have the greatest concentration of headquarters for vertical multinationals. Thus, the interaction between relative country size and the skill endowment is positively related to vertical investment, so that $\beta_4 > 0$ also.

In the estimation of (11.9), the sign pattern $\beta_3 < 0$ and $\beta_4 < 0$ is strongly confirmed, so once again, the horizontal model is accepted and

TABLE 11.2
FDI Stock, 1980–95 ($ billions)

	1980	1985	1990	1995
Total inward stock	481.9	734.9	1716.9	2657.9
Developed economies	373.6	538.0	1373.3	1932.7
Developed share as % of total	77.5%	73.2%	80.1%	73.9%
U.S. inward stock	83.1	184.6	394.9	564.6
U.S. share of developed stock	22.2%	34.3%	28.8%	29.2%
Developing economies	108.3	196.8	341.7	693.3
Developing share as % of total	22.5%	26.8%	19.9%	26.1%
China inward stock	0.0	3.4	14.1	129.0
Chinese share of developing stock	0.0%	1.7%	4.1%	18.6%
Total outward stock	513.7	685.6	1684.1	2730.2
Developed economies	507.5	664.2	1614.6	2514.3
Developed share as % of total	98.8%	96.9%	95.9%	92.1%
U.S. outward stock	220.2	251.0	435.2	705.6
U.S. share of developed stock	43.4%	37.8%	27.0%	28.1%
Developing economies	6.2	21.2	69.4	214.5
Developing share as % of total	1.2%	3.1%	4.1%	7.9%
China inward flow	0.0	0.1	2.5	17.3
Chinese % of developing stock	0.0%	0.6%	3.6%	8.1%

Source: United Nations 1996, annex tables 3, 4; pp. 239–48; cited in Feenstra 1999.

the vertical model is rejected. This outcome is perhaps not surprising in view of the fact that the majority of foreign investments worldwide are between *industrial* countries, and not between developed and developing countries (Markusen 1995; Lipsey 1999, 2003). These investments would be more typical of horizontal rather than vertical linkages. This tendency can be seen from the data on the stocks and flows of global FDI over 1980–95, as shown in Tables 11.2 and 11.3.

Looking first at the inward *stock* of FDI in the upper half of Table 11.2, the proportion of FDI located in developing countries fluctuated between 19% and 26% over 1980–95, so the majority of FDI is in developed countries. There was a surge of investment into the developed countries during the second half of the 1980s, during which time the stock of investment in developed countries nearly tripled from $538 billion to $1,373 billion. At the same time, there was a considerable increase in foreign investment in the United States, which doubled from 1980 to 1985 and again from 1985 to 1990. Since 1990, the stock of investment located in the developing countries has grown more rapidly, which is in large part due to

TABLE 11.3
FDI Flow, 1983–1995 ($ billions)

	1983–88[a]	1989	1990	1991	1992	1993	1994	1995
Total inflow	91.6	200.6	203.8	157.8	168.1	207.9	225.7	314.9
Developed economies	71.8	171.7	169.8	114.0	114.0	129.3	132.8	203.2
Developed share as % of total	78.4%	85.7%	83.4%	73.8%	70.0%	64.8%	61.4%	68.4%
U.S. inflow	34.4	67.7	47.9	22.0	17.6	41.1	49.8	60.2
U.S. share of developed inflow	47.9%	39.4%	28.2%	19.3%	15.4%	31.8%	37.5%	29.7%
Developing economies	19.8	28.6	33.7	41.3	50.4	73.1	87.0	99.7
Developing share as % of total	21.6%	14.3%	16.6%	26.2%	30.0%	35.2%	38.6%	31.6%
China inflow	1.8	3.4	3.5	4.4	11.2	27.5	33.8	37.5
Chinese % of developing inflow	9.2%	11.8%	10.3%	10.6%	22.2%	37.6%	38.8%	37.6%
Total outflow	93.7	217.9	240.3	210.8	203.1	225.5	230.0	317.9
Developed economies	88.3	202.3	222.5	201.9	181.4	192.4	190.9	270.6
Developed share as % of total	94.2%	92.8%	92.6%	95.8%	89.4%	85.4%	83.2%	85.2%
U.S. outflow	14.2	25.7	27.2	33.5	39.0	69.0	45.6	95.5
U.S. share of developed outflow	16.1%	12.7%	12.2%	16.6%	21.5%	35.9%	23.9%	35.3%
Developing economies	5.4	15.6	17.8	8.9	21.6	33.0	38.6	47.0
Developing share as % of total	5.8%	7.2%	7.4%	4.2%	10.6%	14.6%	16.8%	14.8%
China outflow	0.5	0.8	0.8	0.9	4.0	4.4	2.0	3.5
Chinese % of developing outflow	8.5%	5.0%	4.7%	10.3%	18.5%	13.3%	5.2%	7.4%

Source: United Nations 1996, annex tables 1, 2; cited in Feenstra 1999.
[a] Annual average

increased FDI into China. This country accounts for 18.6% of the inward stock of developing countries in 1995, up from 4.1% just five years earlier. The vast majority of FDI entering developed and developing countries alike comes from the developed countries, as shown in the lower half of Table 11.2.

Similar to these stock figures, the majority of FDI *flows* shown in Table 11.3 are to developed countries, though China is also a large recipient. For example, in 1995 the United States received the most FDI, with an inflow of $60.2 billion, but China has the second-largest inflow of $37.5 billion. The surge in FDI flows during the second half of the 1980s both came from and was directed towards the developed countries: this flow reached $172 billion in 1989. This was followed by a fall in direct investment magnitudes from 1990 to 1991, with a recovery that was slow at first but increased to reach $203 billion in 1995. The inflow of investment into China grew most dramatically in 1990–92, and again in 1994–95.

From this very brief examination of the data, it is apparent that the majority of FDI flows is still between the industrial countries, but that an increasing fraction is being directed towards the developing countries, especially China. There are two major problems with using such data to test models of multinationals: first, the types of investments changed during the 1990s; and second, linkages between firms can come from contractual arrangements across countries that *need not* be reflected in multinational investments.

On the first problem, Hanson, Mataloni, and Slaughter (2001) use a more recent and detailed dataset to evaluate the types of investments made by U.S. multinationals. These data include detailed information on the various roles played by foreign affiliates: in importing inputs from their U.S. parents for further processing; in selling locally within the host countries; and in exporting from the host countries. The first of these roles illustrate vertical investment, while the second is horizontal investment, and the third could be either. These authors find that *both* types of investments are important in the data, with a growing share of vertical investments in some industries and regions. It is quite possible that pooling the data across industries and countries as in (11.9) will hide the underlying presence of both activities.

On the second problem, there is no way that data on multinationals will reflect the vast amount of outsourcing between unaffiliated firms. This is especially true of vertical relationships. Nike manufactures all of its running shoes in Asia, but does not own these plants; nevertheless, this is a vertical relationship very much in the spirit of Helpman's (1984c) model. So we should not expect data on multinationals alone to give the complete picture of horizontal and vertical relationships between firms. Estimating the determinants of these in a dataset that allows for both is therefore a challenge for future empirical research. But it is also a challenge for theoretical work: we would like to explain the division between activities that are kept *internal* to the multinational, and activities that external to the firm. This will be discussed in the remainder of the chapter.

Organization of the Firm

Both the vertical and the horizontal multinational models involved a firm deciding whether to open an additional plant in a foreign country, but neither of these models addressed the question of whether the foreign plant had to be *owned by* or *internalized within* the multinational or not. What would prevent the home firm from entering into a joint venture or some other contractual arrangement with a foreign firm rather than owning a foreign plant? In order to explain this, we need to add a richer structure to the models we have considered so far. Generally, Perry (1989, 187) identifies three reasons for firms to vertically integrate: technological externalities; transactions costs; and market imperfections, which can be due to the exercise of market power or imperfect information. We shall discuss each of these in turn.

Technological Externalities

Increasing returns to scale are one reason for firms to integrate: if two firms with given resources can produce more by combining, then there is a technological argument for doing so. Perry (1989, 187) uses the example of an integrated steel mill saving resources by not having to reheat its manufactured steel in order to make sheet metal. The model of horizontal multinationals we considered above had such a technological externality: the fixed cost of headquarters services only had to be paid in one country, whereas production could occur in multiple countries. It was assumed, however, that these headquarters services could only be transferred *within* a firm, thereby ruling out other contractual relationships between the firms. It would be preferable to derive the ownership structure endogenously in a framework where the firms might be integrated within a multinational, but might also engage in other contractual relationships, as considered next.

Transactions Costs

A general reason for the existence of firms provided by Ronald Coase (1937) is that there are costs involved with making transactions on the markets, and when these costs become too high, the activities are instead internalized within the firm. This idea was greatly elaborated by Oliver

Williamson (1975, 1985) and is associated with the twin concepts of "asset specificity" and the "holdup problem." To understand these concepts, suppose that firm A needs some new input. It could ask firm B to produce it, but that would be expensive for B to design and test. If firm B managed to successfully produce it and then sell it to A, what guarantee does firm B have that it will be paid enough to cover its costs of design, let alone its costs of production? If firms A and B could contract in the beginning to specify what the input would cost to develop and produce, that would resolve the problem, but it may be difficult to foresee in the beginning what these costs would be.

In the absence of complete contracts, firm B will be left with an input that may or may not be useful to buyers other than firm A: this is called *asset specificity*. We can presume that the better suited the input is to firm A's needs, the less valuable it is to alternative buyers. But in that case, firm B has very little bargaining power in refusing to sell the input to firm A: this is the "holdup problem." Because of the holdup problem, firm B might decide to produce an input that is not very well suited to firm A, but instead can be sold to other purchasers. So the incomplete contracts lead to an inefficient outcome. If this inefficiency is too great, firm A might decide to just design the input itself; that is, it will vertically integrate into the production of that good, and thereby become a bigger firm.

From this line of reasoning, we can see that the decision of a firm to integrate depends on the cost of making market transactions under incomplete contracts, and in particular, asset specificity and the holdup problem. These insights of Coase and Williamson have only recently been formalized into models of the firm; key references are Grossman and Hart 1986, Hart and Moore 1990, 1999, Holmstrom and Milgrom 1994, and Aghion and Tirole 1997. It is even more recent that these ideas have been incorporated into general equilibrium models of trade; references include McLaren 2000, Grossman and Helpman 2002a, 2002b, 2002c, Marin and Verdier 2001, Antràs 2003, and Puga and Trefler 2002. These studies are new enough that we do not attempt to summarize their contributions in this evolving area, but highly recommend them for further reading.

Market Power

Another reason for firms to integrate is to offset the exercise of market power. In the classic paper entitled "The Division of Labor Is Limited by the Extent of the Market," Stigler (1951) describes an example, a coal cartel at the end of the nineenth century, when steel companies kept acquiring mines to avoid paying the cartel's prices. That paper is primarily devoted to discussing a theorem of Adam Smith's, whose statement is used as the title, that firms will become less integrated (spinning off specialized activities) as the market grows. The example of backwards integration by the steel companies is used as an instance where vertical integration is caused by a failure of the competitive price system, rather than by the extent of the market. So firms may integrate to offset the exercise of market power by suppliers, and that activity can interact with the size of the market. Perry (1989) describes several models of that type within a single country. The closest application to multinationals comes from the studies of Hostmann and Markusen (1992) and Horn and Persson (2001), and further work in this area would be desirable.

Another case where the exercise of market power appears to be important is in the formation of *business groups* that are found in many countries: examples are the *keiretsu* in Japan and the *chaebol* in South Korea. The existence of these groups is often attributed to capital market imperfections, whereby the groups form to provide financing to their member firms. But Feenstra, Huang, and Hamilton (2003) argue that these groups, especially in Taiwan and Korea, can alternatively be described by the desire to sell inputs internally within a group at marginal cost, while charging optimally high markups for external sale of inputs.[17] By allowing business groups to optimally choose these markups, while also having free entry of business groups, means that there are *multiple equilibria* in the structure of business groups: an economy can have a small number of large business groups, charging high prices for inputs sold to other groups; or a larger number of smaller groups, charging lower prices for the sale of intermediate inputs. Therefore, historical conditions must be considered to determine which equilibrium occurs in a country, and Feenstra and Hamilton (2004) describe why South Korea ended up with large business groups, while Taiwan has smaller groups.

Imperfect Information

A final way to model the ownership decision is to introduce informational flows between the firms in the two countries, as done by Markusen (2002, chaps. 13–15) using several models of imperfect information. In one case (Horstmann and Markusen 1987), we suppose that the good produced by the multinational has a quality that is imperfectly observed by consumers, so that resources must be spent to maintain its quality reputation. If the multinational contracts with a foreign firm, the latter will have an incentive to shirk on this activity, so the parent company must transfer some rents to the foreign firm to avoid this shirking. If these rents become too costly, the multinational will just set up its own foreign affiliate instead. In

---

[17] Alternatively, Spencer and Qiu (2001) develop a transactions cost model of the *keiretsu* in Japan, which is empirically evaluated by Head, Ries, and Spencer (2002).

another version of this story (Ethier 1986; Ethier and Markusen 1996; Markusen 2001), the imperfect information comes in the form of the foreign plant manager learning the production technology, and then potentially leaving the firm. Again, the parent company must transfer rents to the manager to prevent this from occurring, and if these become too high, the multinational will prefer to establish its own foreign affiliate.

Both of these models rely on *moral hazard:* the foreign manager or firm is taking some action that cannot be directly observed by the multinational, and it becomes expensive to control this activity. A third model (Horstmann and Markusen 1996) uses *asymmetric information* about market conditions abroad, which are known to a foreign agent but not the multinational. In that case, if the multinational enters into a licensing agreement with the foreign agent, the multinational will have to transfer rents to elicit truthful reports of the foreign market conditions. If these rents are too high, the multinational will again establish its own foreign affiliate.

In a following section we will summarize another informational model due to Rauch and Trindade (2003), in which the integration of firms allows them to share information that each has about their own national markets.[18] For example, joint ventures between firms in different countries can bring with them knowledge of the supplier and distribution networks in each country, and any other intangible assets owned by either firm. But there is some inherent uncertainty in the ability to find a good partner. The efficacy of achieving matches determines the extent to which markets are integrated, that is, the extent to which factor price equalization obtains. This model is not solved using either a moral hazard or asymmetric information framework but, as we shall see, relies on the "matching" of firms across countries.

Matching of Firms across Countries

The starting point for Rauch and Trindade (2003) is similar to the one-sector model discussed at the beginning of the chapter, where capital combines with labor to produce a homogeneous good. We now suppose, however, that two producers must form a joint venture in order to successfully obtain output. These producers may both be in the same country (as in the autarky equilibrium) or may come from different countries (in the trade equilibrium with joint ventures). Let us initially focus on the autarky equilibrium.

The amount of output obtained by two producers depends on their complementarity with each other. For convenience, we will array the producers

---

[18] The work of Rauch and Trindade (2003) builds upon that in Casella and Rauch 2002 and Rauch and Casella 2003.

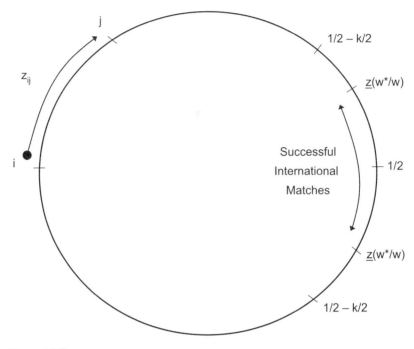

Figure 11.7

in each country around a circle of circumference unity, as illustrated in Figure 11.7. Let z_{ij} denote the shortest arc-distance between producers of type i and type j, which measures their complementarity. Notice that the maximum value of z_{ij} is $1/2$. Then we assume that the output obtained by a joint venture of these producers is $Y_{ij} = f(L_{ij}, z_{ij})$, where L_{ij} is the labor used. We do not include capital in this production function since the amount available from each producer is equal and fixed. We assume that $f(L_{ij}, z_{ij})$ is increasing and homogeneous of degree one in (L_{ij}, z_{ij}), so that producers farther away from each other obtain higher output.

If labor is available at the wage w, the profits obtained from this joint venture are

$$g(w, z_{ij}) \equiv \max_{L_{ij}} f(L_{ij}, z_{ij}) - wL_{ij}, \qquad (11.10)$$

where we have normalized the price of the output at unity. Under our assumption that $f(L_{ij}, z_{ij})$ is homogeneous of degree one in its arguments, then $g(w, z_{ij})$ will be homogeneous of degree one in z_{ij}: increasing the distance z_{ij} between producers will lead to an equiproportionate increase in labor hired, and in output and profits. It follows that we can write total profits earned as $g(w, z_{ij}) = z_{ij}\pi(w)$, where $\pi(w) \equiv g(w, 1)$. By the envelope theorem, the amount of labor hired by the joint venture is $L_{ij} = -z_{ij}\pi'(w) > 0$. Increasing the wage must reduce the labor hired, so that $dL_{ij}/dw = -z_{ij}\pi''(w) < 0$, which means that $\pi''(w) > 0$ so π is convex. For convenience in our discussion, we follow Rauch and Trindade in assuming that $\pi(w)$ has the iso-elastic form $\pi(w) = bw^{-\gamma}$, with $b, \gamma > 0$. This form will apply if the function $f(L_{ij}, z_{ij})$ is Cobb-Douglas.[19]

To solve for the autarky equilibrium, we need to match up producers in a single country. We assume that producers are uniformly distributed around the circle in Figure 11.7, and that at each point on the circle there is a unit-mass of producers: so the total distribution of them can be thought of as a "unit cylinder." The best matches are obtained when each producer has a joint venture with the one located on the opposite side of the circle, so that $z_{ij} = 1/2$. The profits earned from each of these matches are $z_{ij}\pi(w) = \pi(w)/2$. We assume that these are equally divided by the two participants, so each producer earns $\pi(w)/4$ in the autarky equilibrium. The equilibrium wage is determined by equating labor demand and supply. One-half of the producers are matching with the other half (on the opposite side of the circle), so the total number of matches is $1/2$. It follows that home autarky labor demand is

$$-z_{ij}\pi'(w^a)/2 = -\pi'(w^a)/4 = L, \qquad (11.11)$$

where the first equality is obtained because producers are matching with those on the opposite side of the circle ($z_{ij} = 1/2$), and the second equality sets labor demand equal to the endowment L to determine the autarky wage w^a.

Let us now introduce a foreign country, with the same technology but having a *higher* labor endowment $L^* > L$. Under autarky, the foreign wage satisfies $-\pi'(w^{a*})/4 = L^*$, and would therefore be lower than at home: $w^{a*} < w^a$ since $L^* > L$, using the convexity of π. In the trade equilibrium we allow joint ventures to form between producers *across* countries. We assume that in such a joint venture, the producers can employ labor in either country: given that foreign wages are lower, they will choose to locate there. This will tend to shift labor demand away from the labor-scarce home towards the labor-abundant foreign country, and therefore diminish the difference in their wages. How far will this process of wage equalization proceed? In the one-sector model used at the beginning of the chapter, *full* equalization of home and foreign wages would be achieved through capital mobility. That is, equalization of the rental rates across countries combined with identical technologies implies that wages are equalized, too.[20] The goal of the matching model is to see how this

[19] See problem 11.4.
[20] See problem 11.5.

result is modified when there are some frictions due to the information problems in finding a good partner.

To this end, suppose that producers can enter into a joint venture across countries. If these joint ventures prove to be unprofitable, then their "status quo" position is to enter into a joint venture domestically. Presuming that they still match with a domestic partner at the opposite side of the circle, then this would result in status quo payoffs of $\pi(w)/4$ and $\pi(w^*)/4$ for a producer in each country. Notice that these are evaluated at the equilibrium wages with international joint ventures, which will differ from the autarky wages. The international joint venture will yield profits of $z_{ij}\pi(w^*)$, where z_{ij} is the distance between the home and foreign producers and they employ labor in the foreign country. The two producers will divide the payoff $z_{ij}\pi(w^*)$ between themselves according to some rule, the details of which need not concern us.[21]

Given that the *total* payoff to a home and foreign producer who match domestically is $[\pi(w)/4 + \pi(w^*)/4]$, it is apparent that the international joint venture is equally profitable if it occurs between a home and foreign producer who are distance z apart, with

$$\underline{z}\,\pi(w^*) = [\pi(w)/4 + \pi(w^*)/4] \iff$$
$$\underline{z}(w^*/w) = (1/4)[1 + \pi(w)/\pi(w^*)]. \tag{11.12}$$

Under our assumption that $\pi(w)$ takes on the iso-elastic form $bw^{-\gamma}$, with $b, \gamma > 0$, we can write $\pi(w)/\pi(w^*) = (w^*/w)^\gamma$ as an increasing function of the relative foreign wage, and likewise for $\underline{z}(w^*/w)$. We will confirm below that foreign wages are less than those at home in the trade equilibrium with joint ventures, so that $\underline{z} < 1/2$. Recalling that the maximum distance between any two producers is $1/2$, then those international matches in the range $z_{ij} \in (\underline{z}, 1/2]$ will be strictly preferred to domestic matches.

Following Rauch and Trindade, let us add some structure to the international matches. We will assume that when a home producer i searches for a potential foreign partner j, the distance between them is randomly drawn from a uniform distribution defined over the interval $[1/2 - k/2, 1/2]$. Notice that when $k = 1$, this interval is $[0, 1/2]$, which means that partners are randomly distributed over the entire circle (recall again that the maximum distance in $1/2$). On the other hand, when $k = 0$, this interval becomes the point $1/2$, which is the best match possible. So the parameter $k \in [0, 1]$ indexes the extent of *uncertainty* in international joint ventures.

This structure of international matches is illustrated in Figure 11.7. For a domestic agent located at the point labeled i, the best match would be at

---

[21] Rauch and Trindade (2003) assume that the payoff $z_{ij}\pi(w^*)$ is divided according to the Nash bargaining solution.

the point labeled $1/2$ on the opposite side of the circle. The range of possible matches is in the interval $[1/2 - k/2, 1/2]$ on either side of the point $1/2$. On the other hand, the *successful* international matches must satisfy (11.12), which must be at least the distance $\underline{z}(w^*/w)$ away from the point i.[22]

We can now compute the probability P that an international match is successful. This is simply the length of the interval as $[\underline{z}(w^*/w), 1/2]$ as compared to $[1/2 - k/2, 1/2]$, or

$$P = \frac{(1/2) - \underline{z}(w^*/w)}{(1/2) - [(1/2) - (k/2)]} = \frac{1 - 2\underline{z}(w^*/w)}{k}. \tag{11.13}$$

Thus, the probability of a successful international match is higher when the ratio of wages w^*/w is lower (meaning that $\underline{z}$ is lower), or when the uncertainty k associated with international joint ventures is reduced.

To determine wages, we use labor market equilibrium in both countries. Home labor is demanded only by those domestic producers whose international matches were *not* successful, or a fraction $(1 - P)$ of home producers. The home demand for labor is therefore

$$-(1 - P)\, \pi'(w)/4 = L, \tag{11.14}$$

which can be compared to (11.11). Home labor demand has fallen from autarky due to producers employing labor abroad, so this results in a fall in the domestic wage, $w < w^a$.

Foreign labor demand has two components. The first is the demand from foreign producers whose international matches are not successful, and by analogy with (11.14), this is $-(1 - P)\pi(w^*)/4$. However, there is also labor demand from all the successful international matches. This is computed by taking the expected value of labor demand $-z_{ij}\pi'(w^*)$ over the successful matches in the range $z_{ij} \in [\underline{z}(w^*/w), 1/2]$. Therefore, the equilibrium condition in the foreign labor market is

$$-(1 - P)\, \pi'(w^*)/4 - \left(\frac{2}{k}\right)\int_{\underline{z}(w^*/w)}^{1/2} z_{ij}\pi'(w^*)dz_{ij} = L^*. \tag{11.15}$$

Notice that in the integral on the left of (11.15) we have multiplied by $(2/k)$, which is the density of the uniform distribution of international matches z_{ij} over its interval $[1/2 - k/2, 1/2]$, and converts that integral into an expected value.

---

[22] It can be confirmed that $\underline{z}(w^*/w)$ must lie within the interval $[1/2 - k/2, 1/2]$ in equilibrium. If this were not the case (i.e., if $\underline{z}(w^*/w) < 1/2 - k/2$), if then all home producers would enter into joint ventures with foreign producers, and the demand for home labor would be zero.

Then dividing (11.15) by (11.14), we obtain a single equation to determine the relative home wage:

$$(w/w^\star)^{\gamma+1}\left[1+\frac{8}{k(1-P)}\int_{\underline{z}(w^\star/w)}^{1/2} z_{ij}dz_{ij}\right] = L^\star/L, \qquad (11.16)$$

where we have simplified this expression using the iso-elastic form for $\pi(w)$, so that $\pi'(w^\star)/\pi'(w) = (w/w^\star)^{\gamma+1}$. Despite the complexity of (11.16), it is readily shown that the left-hand side is a strictly increasing function of $(w/w^\star)$, which starts at unity when $(w/w^\star) = 1$ and approaches infinity as $(w/w^\star) \to \infty$.[23] It follows that there is a unique solution for $(w/w^\star)$ from (11.16). This establishes the first part of the following theorem.

Theorem (Rauch and Trindade 2003)

(a) The trade equilibrium with international joint ventures exists and is unique.
(b) As $k \to 0$ so there is no uncertainty about international partners, then $(w/w^\star) \to 1$.
(c) $dw/dk > 0$ and $dw^\star/dk < 0$.
(d) $d\ln(w/w^\star)/d\ln(L^\star/L) < 1/(1+\gamma)$, is increasing in k, and $\lim_{k\to 0} d\ln(w/w^\star)/d\ln(L^\star/L) = 0$.

Part (b) of this theorem is obtained by inspection of the equilibrium condition (11.16). As $k \to 0$, the term multiplying the integral goes to infinity (meaning that $w/w^\star$ goes to zero), *unless* the lower limit of integration approaches $1/2$ so the integral goes to zero. The former case is easily ruled out as an equilibrium, so as $k \to 0$ we must have $\underline{z} \to 1/2$ in the lower limit of integration, which implies that the wages approach equality. Recall that this would be the outcome in the one-sector model used earlier in the chapter under perfect capital mobility. Therefore, the matching model approaches the outcome with perfect capital mobility as the uncertainty about international partners is eliminated. Part (c) of the theorem confirms that as international uncertainty increases, the equilibrium gets monotonically farther away from wage equalization: raising k increases domestic wages and lowers foreign wages, as fewer joint ventures are pursued.

In part (d), Rauch and Trindade investigate the sensitivity of relative wages to changes in the labor endowments. Notice that from (11.16), if

---

[23] Notice that $\underline{z}(w^\star/w)$ is decreasing in $(w/w^\star)$, which reduces the lower limit of integration so the value of the integral on the left-hand side of (11.16) is increasing in $(w/w^\star)$. Likewise, P in (11.13) is increasing in $(w/w^\star)$, and then so is $1/(1-P)$, which appears on the left-hand side of (11.16).

we hold z constant (so that P is also constant), then we readily obtain $d\ln(w/w^*)/d\ln(L^*/L) = 1/(1 + \gamma) > 0$. Relative wages are increasing in the relative labor endowment of the other country for fixed z, just as they are in autarky, because more labor abroad lowers foreign wages. In contrast, when wages are equalized across countries, then $d\ln(w/w^*)/d\ln(L^*/L) = 0$, as occurs in the one-sector model under perfect capital mobility used earlier in the chapter. We can interpret this as saying that perfect capital mobility leads to complete integration of the labor markets. Then part (d) states that the matching model leads to greater integration of the labor markets than in autarky, and monotonically approaches the case of perfect capital mobility as uncertainty k approaches zero.

There are many potential empirical and theoretical applications of this matching model. It is well known that wages respond to some degree to changes in local labor supplies (see Bernard and Jensen 2000), so that labor markets are not fully integrated across regions or countries. One explanation, according to this model, is the informational frictions involved in the movement of producers. This outcome is certainly not restricted to the one-sector, two-factor setting and would apply equally well to the two-sector HO model. The finding of "factor price insensitivity" discussed in the HO model (see chap. 1) relies on countries being able to freely export the goods that use intensively the factors that are growing in abundance. If there are informational frictions in the ability to match buyers and sellers in international trade, then factor price insensitivity would no longer hold: a growing labor force, for example, would necessitate increased exports of the labor-intensive goods, but if buyers are hard to find, then we would expect a terms of trade decline for those goods and therefore falling wages.[24]

The idea that selling goods on international market requires a "match" between buyers and sellers is explored empirically by Rauch and Trindade (2002). Earlier work by Gould (1994) for the United States and Head and Ries (1998) for Canada had confirmed the importance of immigrant networks in promoting trade with their home countries. Rauch and Trindade (2002) expand this to consider global bilateral trade, and show the importance of *Chinese ethnic networks* in enhancing trade. These networks are measured by the level or fraction of the population in a country that is of Chinese ethnic background, which is entered along with other typical regressors in a gravity equation.

Following earlier work by Rauch (1999), the trade flows in the gravity equation are distinguished depending on whether the products are homogeneous, with published prices; differentiated, with prices that are not available; or a middle category of "reference priced" products. It is found

---

[24] The same logic holds in any large-country model with labor migration. See problem 11.6.

that the variable measuring Chinese networks enters most significantly in the bilateral trade equations for *differentiated* goods. This supports the idea that the informational difficulty in assessing these goods is more severe than from homogeneous goods, and that having traders of the same ethnic background can overcome this difficulty to some extent.

Other empirical results that indicate the informational difficulties in international trade come from studies of the large traders in Hong Kong, such as Li and Fung (Slater and Amaha 1999). Their activities include matching firms or consumers who are the buyers of goods, with the most appropriate producers of the goods, located in China or elsewhere in Asia. The value of these informational activities to the buyers and sellers involved will depend on the type of good (homogeneous versus differentiated), uncertainty in prices and quality, market "thickness," and income levels of the buyers. Feenstra and Hanson (2001) find that these regressors are significant explanations of the markups charged on goods reexported through Hong Kong. This further indicates the importance of information in allowing for successful "matches" in international trade.

Conclusions

In this chapter we have reviewed a large literature on the role of foreign direct investment (FDI) and multinationals. The early contributions of Mundell (1957) and MacDougall (1960) dealt with capital flows between economies, though FDI can instead involve a change in ownership and location of firms, without capital flows. The later contributions of Helpman (1984c) and Markusen (1984) focused on the decision to establish vertical or horizontal foreign subsidiaries. The fact that the parent company had invested in headquarters services gave it an asset that could be transferred to the subsidiary. It was assumed by Helpman and Markusen that this asset was kept internal to the firm, but of course, that need not be the case: a great deal of international trade occurs between unaffiliated firms. This creates both an empirical and theoretical challenge of explaining cross-firm versus within-firm transactions.

At the theoretical level, transactions are kept internal to a firm when the cost of pursuing them between firms is too great. This is the starting point for the *transactions cost* explanation for the organization of the firm. This idea has been elaborated in the recent industrial organization models of Grossman and Hart (1986), Hart and Moore (1990, 1999), Holmstrom and Milgrom (1994) and Aghion and Tirole (1997) and has just begun to be incorporated into international trade models. This is a new and exciting topic, which may well replace increasing returns and imperfect competition (in the 1980s), endogenous growth (in the first half of the 1990s) and political economy (in the second half of the 1990s) as the next major research area in trade.

One objective of this research is to identify types of trading relationships that lie between the two extremes of market transactions and vertical integration, such as when firms engage in a joint venture or other ongoing relationship. We can refer to such trade as a "link" between the two firms, and the set of links between buyers and sellers is referred to as a "network."[25] As an extension of our study of multinationals, we are naturally led to a discussion of *networks* in international trade. These are relationships that represent more than market transactions, but less than full integration within a firm. There are many types of economic and social networks that can be considered (Rauch 2001; Rauch and Casella 2001), and we have discussed just one, arising from the "matching" of agents across international borders. Since firms will want to be linked with good partners abroad, we can expect that agents will find it profitable to undertake this matching activity. A model along these lines is developed by Rauch and Watson (2002), where individuals with expertise choose to become "international trade intermediaries." This also creates a role for governments to support such intermediation activities, through trade fairs, associations, and so on. Evidently, these ideas are bringing the *trader* back into international trade, where he or she should have been all along!

Problems

Our analysis of capital flows in the HO model compared the equilibrium before and after the tariff, with a complete flow of capital. It is of interest to ask what happens to the welfare of the country imposing the tariff *during the transition*. That is, as the capital inflow moves the countries from point V^i to $\overline{V}^i$ in Figure 11.4, how does the welfare of the capital-importing country change? This question is addressed by Brecher and Diaz-Alejandro (1977). To answer it, we can work in reverse and ask what happens if capital *leaves* the country starting at the point $\overline{V}^i$, with the tariff on the capital-intensive good applied by country 1.

The outflow of capital from the point $\overline{V}^i$ will reduce production of the capital-intensive good in country 1 and increase production of the labor-intensive good. Normally, this would lead to the capital-intensive good being imported. However, due to the tariff in that industry, there will be *some range* of capital outflow that *does not* lead to any imports; instead, country 1 remains in autarky but with a change in relative prices. This is illustrated in Figure 11.8 by the point E^i, lying on the line between V^i and $\overline{V}^i$, such that for the range of endowments between $\overline{V}^i$ and E^i, both

---

[25] This terminology follows Kranton and Minehart (2001).

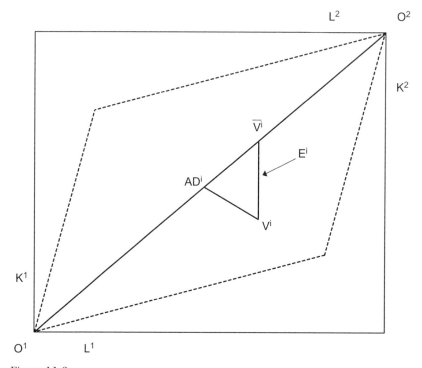

Figure 11.8

countries remain in autarky due to the tariff applied by country 1. Now answer problems 11.1–11.3.

11.1   As capital enters country 1, going from V^i to E^i, treat international prices as *fixed*. The welfare of a representative consumer in that country can be written as $V(p, I)$, where $p = p^* + t$ is the domestic relative price of imports and t is the tariff. As in earlier chapters, we assume that the exportable is additively separable in utility, so that consumption of the import good is $\partial V/\partial p = -d(p)$ and $\partial V/\partial I = 1$. Total national income equals GDP plus tariff revenue minus payments to foreign capital, so that $I = w(p)L + r(p)(K + K^*) + tm(p) - r(p)K^*$, where K^* is the foreign capital, $m(p) = d(p) - y(p, L, K + K^*)$ are imports, and $y(p, L, K + K^*)$ is production of the import good, which depends on the labor and capital endowments with the usual Rybczynski effects. Notice that national income simplifies to $I = w(p)L + r(p)K + t[d(p) - y(p, L, K + K^*)]$.

Then differentiate consumer utility with respect to the capital inflow K^*, and sign and interpret this result, assuming that the import good is capital intensive.

11.2 The results in problem 11.1 apply for inflows of foreign capital between points V^i and the point E^i. At E^i, country 1 is now in autarky. Suppose that capital *continues* to flow in:

  (a) What is the effect of the capital inflow on equilibrium prices for goods, and on the rental?
  (b) Thus, what is the effect of the capital inflow on consumer welfare in country 1? (Hint: illustrate the effect on the rental as in Figure 11.3).

11.3 Summarize your results from problems 11.1 and 11.2 by graphing the relationship between the capital inflow and welfare of the representative consumer in country 1. How does welfare at $\overline{V}^i$ compare to the free-trade welfare at V^i?

11.4 Suppose that $f(L_{ij}, z_{ij})$ takes on the Cobb-Douglas form $f(L_{ij}, z_{ij})$ $= L_{ij}^\alpha z_{ij}^{(1-\alpha)}$, $0 < \alpha < 1$. Then solve equation (11.10) and show that $\pi(w)$ $\equiv g(w, 1)$ can be written in the iso-elastic form $\pi(w) = bw^{-\gamma}$, with $b, \gamma > 0$.

11.5 In the one-sector model with perfect capital mobility, assume that the technologies are identical across countries and homogeneous of degree one.

  (a) If the rental rates are equalized across countries, what does this imply about the labor-capital ratios used in production?
  (b) Therefore, how do wages compare across countries?

11.6 Rather than capital flows, let us instead consider inflows of labor to a country through immigration. We will contrast the results of two models:

  (a) If there is only one sector in the economy, with fixed capital and fixed output price, then illustrate the effect of immigration on the home wages, and on welfare.
  (b) Suppose instead that we are in a Ricardian model, as discussed in chapter 1. Let labor flow from the foreign to the home country, and illustrate the impact on the welfare of workers at home (not including the new migrants). This Ricardian case is discussed in greater detail by Davis and Weinstein (2002b).

Appendix A

Price, Productivity, and Terms of Trade Indexes

At various points throughout this book we have relied on index numbers to measure prices or total factor productivity. There is a good deal of theory, dating back more than a hundred years, that we can rely on to guide us in the choice of index number formulas. Like econometrics, an understanding of index numbers can be very helpful in empirical research. Unlike econometrics, these methods are seldom taught. So in this appendix we present a self-contained treatment of index numbers, focusing on price indexes.[1]

We begin with some examples of price indexes. Let $p = (p_1, \ldots, p_N) > 0$ denote a vector of prices, and $q = (q_1, \ldots, q_N) \geq 0$ denote the corresponding vector of quantities. We let p^i and q^i denote these vectors in situation $i = 0, 1$. We can think of $i = 0, 1$ as measuring two time periods, or later in the appendix, as measuring two countries. A bilateral index number formula $P(p^0, p^1, q^0, q^1)$ uses just this information on prices and quantities to measure the "average" change in prices from situation 0 to 1. For example, the Laspeyres price index is

$$P_L(p^0, p^1, q^0, q^1) \equiv \frac{\sum_{i=1}^{N} q_i^0 p_i^1}{\sum_{i=1}^{N} q_i^0 p_i^0}. \tag{A.1}$$

Thus, the Laspeyres weights the prices in each period by the *quantities in the base period*.

Conversely, if we use the *current period quantities* to weight the prices, we obtain the Paasche price index:

$$P_P(p^0, p^1, q^0, q^1) \equiv \frac{\sum_{i=1}^{N} q_i^1 p_i^1}{\sum_{i=1}^{N} q_i^1 p_i^0}. \tag{A.2}$$

---

[1] This appendix draws extensively from Alterman, Diewert and Feenstra 1999, chap. 2.

We might expect the Paasche price index to give a *lower* value than the Laspeyres index when applied to a consumer choice problem, because by using current period quantities, the Paasche index incorporates consumer substitution *away* from goods with the highest price increase. We will show below that this is indeed the case. A third commonly used formula is Irving Fisher's (1922) ideal price index, P_F;

$$P_F(p^0, p^1, q^0, q^1) \equiv [P_L(p^0, p^1, q^0, q^1) \, P_P(p^0, p^1, q^0, q^1)]^{1/2}, \quad (A.3)$$

which is the geometric mean of the Laspeyres and Paasche indexes.

Another important formula is the Törnqvist (1936) price index P_T, defined as a geometric mean of the price ratios (p_i^1/p_i^0), using as weights the average of the expenditure shares $s_i^0 \equiv p_i^0 q_i^0 / \Sigma_{i=1}^N p_i^0 q_i^0$ and $s_i^1 \equiv p_i^1 q_i^1 / \Sigma_{i=1}^N p_i^1 q_i^1$ in the two periods:

$$P_T(p^0, p^1, q^0, q^1) \equiv \prod_{i=1}^N (p_i^1/p_i^0)^{(s_i^0 + s_i^1)/2}, \quad (A.4)$$

or in logs,

$$\ln P_T(p^0, p^1, q^0, q^1) = \sum_{i=1}^N (1/2)(s_i^0 + s_i^1) \ln(p_i^1/p_i^0). \quad (A.4')$$

How can we choose between these various formulas? The economic approach to index numbers is to ask how well each formula reflects the behavior of consumers or firms. On the consumer side, we would need to take into account that tastes may be nonhomothetic (see Diewert 1974, and Pollak 1989). We will focus here on the problem for firms, where we consider either an index of the *input prices* faced by a firm or the *output prices*. In either case, we will also want to develop an index of *productivity change* for the firm, and with an open economy, an index of the *terms of trade*.

Input Price Indexes

Let $p = (p_1, \ldots, p_N)$ denote a positive vector of input prices that producers face in period t, and let y denote an M dimensional vector of nonnegative outputs that the production sector might be asked to produce in period t. Then the *cost function* using period t technology is defined as

$$C^t(p, y) \equiv \min_q \{p'q : (q, y) \text{ belongs to } S^t\}, \quad (A.5)$$

where S^t denotes the period t technology set. Thus $C^t(p, y)$ is the minimum cost that the economy can achieve in period t, given that the vector of outputs y must be produced. Productivity improvements are reflected in an expansion of the technology set S^t, and this is why the cost function $C^t(p, y)$ is also indexed by the period $t = 0, 1$.

Generally, the goal of price and productivity indexes will be to measure changes in the value of costs C^t over time: costs increase as input prices rise, and decrease as productivity improves. The difficulty is that we do not observe the *separate* effect of each, but rather, just observe the total change in costs. We would like to decompose the total change in costs into components that can be attributed to input prices, productivity, and changes in output.

Toward this end, we can use the function C^t to define the economy's period t technology *theoretical input price index* P^t between any two periods, say period 0 and period 1, as follows:

$$P^t(p^0, p^1, y) = C^t(p^1, y)/C^t(p^0, y), \tag{A.6}$$

where p^t is the vector of output prices that the economy faces in period t, $t = 0, 1$, and y is a reference vector of outputs. We refer to this as a "theoretical" index because it *cannot* be computed from information on p^0, p^1, q^0, and q^1 alone, but also depends on the function C^t. Note that this theoretical index has the advantage that it is not influenced by technological change; rather, it is measured relative to a given period t technology. Our immediate goal is to see whether, for specific functional forms for the cost function in (A.5), there will correspond some observable price index formula (depending only on prices and quantities p^0, p^1, q^0, and q^1) that *will* equal (A.6), or at least provide upper and lower bounds to it.

We are interested in two special cases of the theoretical input price index (A.6): (*a*) $P^0(p^0, p^1, y^0)$, which uses the period 0 technology and the output vector y^0 that was actually used in period 0, and (*b*) $P^1(p^0, p^1, y^1)$, which uses the period 1 technology and the output vector y^1. Let q^0 and q^1 be the observed input quantities used in periods 0 and 1, respectively. We assume that these are *optimally chosen* to minimize costs in (A.5), so that

$$C^0(p^0, y^0) = p^{0\prime} q^0 \quad \text{and} \quad C^1(p^1, y^1) = p^{1\prime} q^1. \tag{A.7}$$

Under these cost-minimizing assumptions, we can adapt the arguments of Fisher and Shell (1972, 57–58) and Archibald (1977, 66) to show that the two theoretical indexes, $P^0(p^0, p^1, y^0)$ and $P^1(p^0, p^1, y^1)$ satisfy the following inequalities:

$$P^0(p^0, p^1, y^0) \equiv C^0(p^1, y^0)/C^0(p^0, y^0) \quad \text{using definition (A.6)}$$
$$= C^0(p^1, y^0)/p^{0\prime}q^0 \quad \text{using (A.7)}$$
$$\leq p^{1\prime}q^0/p^{0\prime}q^0 \quad \text{since } q^0 \text{ is feasible for the}$$
minimization problem

that defines $C^0(p^1, y^0)$ and

so $C^0(p^1, y^0) \leq p^{1\prime}q^0$

$$\equiv P_L(p^0, p^1, q^0, q^1),$$

where P_L is the Laspeyres price index. Similarly, we have

$$P^1(p^0, p^1, y^1) \equiv C^1(p^1, y^1)/C^1(p^0, y^1) \quad \text{using definition (A.6)}$$
$$= p^{1\prime}q^1/C^1(p^0, y^1) \quad \text{using (A.7)}$$
$$\geq p^{1\prime}q^1/p^{0\prime}q^1 \quad \text{since } q^1 \text{ is feasible for the}$$
minimization problem

that defines $C^1(p^0, y^1)$ and

so $C^1(p^0, y^1) \leq p^{0\prime}q^1$

$$\equiv P_P(p^0, p^1, q^0, q^1),$$

where P_P is the Paasche price index. So we find that the Laspeyres index of input prices P_L is an *upper bound* to the theoretical price index $P^0(p^0, p^1, y^0)$, and that the Paasche index of input prices P_P is a *lower bound* to the theoretical price index $P^1(p^0, p^1, y^1)$. To further explore these bounds, we separately discuss the cases of constant and changing technology.

Constant Technology

If technology is constant, then the Paasche and Laspeyres price indexes provide bounds to the "true" price index. That is, if technology is constant, the cost function can be written as $C(p, y)$, so the bounds above immediately imply that

$$P_P(p^0, p^1, q^0, q^1) \leq C(p^1, y^1)/C(p^0, y^1),$$

and

$$\text{(A.8)}$$

$$C(p^1, y^0)/C^0(p^0, y^0) \leq P_L(p^0, p^1, q^0, q^1).$$

These expressions can be further simplified by assuming that there is a single output, and that the technology has constant returns to scale, so that

$C(p, y) = y c(p)$, where $c(p)$ is the unit-cost function. Then the inequalities in (A.8) simplify to

$$P_P(p^0, p^1, q^0, q^1) \le c(p^1)/c(p^0) \le P_L(p^0, p^1, q^0, q^1). \qquad \text{(A.9)}$$

Thus, we see that the Paasche and Laspeyres price indexes provide lower and upper bounds to the ratio of unit-costs for the firm, which is the "true" price index. The same would apply to a consumer, where we would use the ratio of unit-expenditure functions in the two periods rather than the ratio of unit-cost. This confirms our assertion above that the Paasche price index is less than the Laspeyres price index for a consumer choice problem, provided that the quantities used are optimal for the consumer.

These observations lead us to ask whether it is possible to construct a price index that *exactly equals* the ratio of unit-costs, and that is the goal of the economic approach to index numbers. The strategy is to choose some specific functional form for the cost function, and then see whether there is a price index formula such that $P(p^0, p^1, q^0, q^1) = c(p^1)/c(p^0)$. For certain choices of the functional form for costs, it turns out that there is indeed an price index formula that will satisfy this equality. In this case, Diewert (1976) call the price index *exact*.

For example, suppose that we choose the quadratic production function $y = (q' A q)^{1/2}$, where $A = A'$ is a symmetric matrix of parameters. It is clear that this production function in homogeneous of degree one. Diewert (1976, 130) shows that this quadratic production function can approximate any linearly homogeneous function $f(q)$ to the second order around a point.[2] For this reason, Diewert calls the quadratic function $(q' A q)^{1/2}$ a "flexible" functional form. If A is invertible,[3] then it is not difficult to show that the cost function is $C(p, y) = y(p' B p)^{1/2}$, where $B = A^{-1}$, so the unit-cost function becomes $c(p) = (p' B p)^{1/2}$, which is again a "flexible" functional form.

Then corresponding to the quadratic production and unit-cost functions, we have the following theorem.

Theorem 1 (Diewert 1976)

If the production and unit-cost functions are quadratic and linearly homogeneous, and the observed quantities $q^t > 0$ are cost minimizing, then

$$\frac{c(p^1)}{c(p^1)} = P_F(p^0, p^1, q^0, q^1). \qquad \text{(A.10)}$$

---

[2] That is, the parameters A can be chosen such that $(q^{\star\prime} A q^\star)^{1/2} = f(q^\star)$, $A q^\star = f_q(q^\star)$, and $A = f_{qq}(q^\star)$, for any choice of a linearly homogeneous function $f(q)$.

[3] The solution for the unit-expenditure function when A is not invertible is discussed in Diewert 1976, 134.

The price index on the right of (A.10) is the Fisher ideal formula, defined by (A.3), which is therefore exact for the quadratic unit-cost function. Since the quadratic function is itself flexible, Diewert (1976) refers to the Fisher ideal price index as *superlative*. The remarkable feature of this theorem is that we achieve equality between the Fisher ideal index and the ratio of unit-cost function *for all values* of the parameters A and B. Intuitively, as these parameters change, so would the optimal choices q, so these choices are "revealing" what the underlying parameters must be. Using the data on the optimal choices q^t, combined with their prices p^t, we are able to measure the ratio of the unit-cost functions in (A.11) without knowing B. This shows the power of the economic approach to index numbers.

Changing Technology

With technology changing over time, the situation is more difficult. We are in the awkward position that the Paasche and Laspeyres indexes provide bounds to a theoretical price index $P^t(p^0, p^1, y)$ that itself depends on the period $t = 0, 1$. Fortunately, this issue can be resolved, and it is possible to define a theoretical price index that falls *between* the observable Paasche and Laspeyres price indexes. To do this, first we define a hypothetical cost function, $C(p, \alpha)$, that corresponds to the use of an α-weighted average of the technology sets S^0 and S^1 for periods 0 and 1 as the reference technology, and that uses an α-weighted average of the period 0 and period 1 net output vectors y^0 and y^1:

$$C(p, \alpha) \equiv \min_q \{p'q : (q, [1 - \alpha]y^0 + \alpha y^1) \text{ belongs to}$$
$$(1 - \alpha)S^0 + \alpha S^1\}. \tag{A.11}$$

We can now use this cost function to define the following family of theoretical price indexes:

$$P(p^0, p^1, \alpha) \equiv C(p^1, \alpha)/C(p^0, \alpha). \tag{A.12}$$

We can adapt the proof of Diewert (1983, 1060–61) to show that there exists an α such that the theoretical price index defined by (A.12) lies between the Paasche and Laspeyres output indexes, P_P and P_L.[4]

Theorem 2 (Diewert 1983)

There exists α between 0 and 1 such that

$$P_L \equiv p^{1\prime}q^0 / p^{0\prime}q^0 \le P(p^0, p^1, \alpha) \le p^{1\prime}q^1 / p^{0\prime}q^1 \equiv P_P$$
$$\text{or } P_P \le P(p^0, p^1, \alpha) \le P_L. \tag{A.13}$$

---

[4] The proofs for all theorems can be found in the sources cited.

If the Paasche and Laspeyres indexes are numerically close to each other, then (A.13) tells us that a "true" economic input price index is fairly well determined and we can find a reasonably close approximation to the "true" index by taking an average of P_L and P_P, such as Fisher's ideal price index P_F defined earlier by (A.3). This provides a justification for using the Fisher ideal formula even when the technology is changing.

Further results can be obtained by making more specific assumptions on the nature of technological change. In particular, suppose that the cost function takes on the *translog functional form* for $t = 0, 1$:[5]

$$\ln C^t(p, y) = \alpha_0^t + \sum_{i=1}^{N} \alpha_1^t \ln p_i + \sum_{k=1}^{M} \beta_k^t \ln y_k + \frac{1}{2} \sum_{i=1}^{N} \sum_{j=1}^{N} \gamma_{ij}^t \ln p_i \ln p_j$$

$$+ \frac{1}{2} \sum_{k=1}^{M} \sum_{\ell=1}^{M} \delta_{k\ell}^t \ln y_k \ln y_\ell + \sum_{i=1}^{N} \sum_{k=1}^{M} \phi_{ik}^t \ln p_i \ln y_k, \qquad (A.14)$$

where the parameters satisfy the restrictions $\gamma_{ij}^t = \gamma_{ji}^t$, and

$$\sum_{i=1}^{N} \alpha_i^t = 1 \quad \text{and} \quad \sum_{i=1}^{N} \gamma_{ij}^t = \sum_{i=1}^{N} \phi_{ik}^t = 0. \qquad (A.15)$$

These restrictions ensure that $C^t(p, y)$ is linearly homogeneous in the input price vector p (which is a property that any cost function must satisfy). Note that we are allowing the parameters that characterize the technology (the α's, β's, γ's, δ's, and ϕ's) to be completely different in each period, reflecting technological change.

Now let us add the restriction that the quadratic price parameters in (A.14) are *equal* across the two periods, that is, $\gamma_{ij}^0 = \gamma_{ij}^1$, though we still allow the other parameters to change over time. Then we can adapt the result in Caves, Christensen, and Diewert (1982, 1410) to show that the geometric mean of the theoretical price indexes in periods 0 and 1, $P^0(p^0, p^1, y^1)$ and $P^1(p^0, p^1, y^1)$, is equal to the Törnqvist price index P_T defined by (A.4).

Theorem 3 (Caves, Christensen, and Diewert 1982)

Assume that $\gamma_{ij}^0 = \gamma_{ij}^1$, and that the cost-minimizing input quantities q^t are strictly positive in both periods, $t = 0, 1$. Then

$$[P^0(p^0, p^1, y^0)P^1(p^0, p^1, y^1)]^{1/2} = P_T(p^0, p^1, q^0, q^1). \qquad (A.16)$$

The assumptions required for this result seem rather weak; in particular, there is no requirement that the technologies exhibit constant returns to scale in either period and our assumptions are consistent with technological

[5] This functional form was introduced and named by Christensen, Jorgenson, and Lau (1971). It was adapted to the expenditure or cost function context by Diewert (1974).

progress occurring between the two periods being compared. Because the index number formula P_T is *exactly* equal to the geometric mean of two theoretical price indexes, which correspond to the translog, and is itself a "flexible" functional form, this confirms that the Törnqvist index number formula is superlative.

To see the usefulness of this result, let us decompose the total change in costs between period 0 and period 1 in two alternative ways:

$$\frac{C^0(p^0,y^0)}{C^1(p^1,y^1)} = \frac{C^0(p^0,y^0)}{C^0(p^1,y^0)} \frac{C^0(p^1,y^0)}{C^0(p^1,y^1)} \frac{C^0(p^1,y^1)}{C^1(p^1,y^1)} \tag{A.17}$$

and

$$\frac{C^0(p^0,y^0)}{C^1(p^1,y^1)} = \frac{C^1(p^0,y^1)}{C^1(p^1,y^1)} \frac{C^1(p^0,y^0)}{C^1(p^0,y^1)} \frac{C^0(p^0,y^0)}{C^1(p^0,y^0)}. \tag{A.18}$$

In each of these decompositions, the first ratio on the right-hand side reflects the changing input prices; the second ratio reflects the changing output vector; and the third ratio reflects pure technological change. Let us define the measure of technological change, or *total factor productivity*, as a geometric mean of the final ratios in (A.17) and (A.18):

$$\text{TFP} \equiv \left[\frac{C^0(p^1,y^1)}{C^1(p^1,y^1)} \frac{C^0(p^0,y^0)}{C^1(p^0,y^0)} \right]^{1/2}. \tag{A.19}$$

This index reflects the fall in costs from period 0 to period 1 due to pure technological change, but as defined, it is not observable: neither the period 0 costs with period 1 prices and outputs, nor the period 1 costs with period 0 prices and outputs, are known. However, we can make use of theorem 3 to indirectly measure TFP. In particular, taking the geometric mean of (A.17) and (A.18), and using (A.19), we obtain

$$\frac{C^0(p^0,y^0)}{C^1(p^1,y^1)} = P_T(p^0,p^1,q^0,q^1)^{-1} \times \text{TFP}$$

$$\times \left[\frac{C^0(p^1,y^0)}{C^0(p^1,y^1)} \frac{C^1(p^0,y^0)}{C^1(p^0,y^1)} \right]^{1/2}. \tag{A.20}$$

Thus, the total change in costs from period 0 to period 1 is decomposed into the inverse of the Törnqvist input price index, total factor productivity, and the final term in (A.20), which reflects the change in outputs. We will see some techniques later in the appendix that allow us to measure the final term, but note here a particularly simply result.

If there is a single output, so that y^t is a scalar, and the cost function is linearly homogeneous in this output, then it can be written as $C^t(p, y) = yc^t(p)$ where $c^t(p)$ is the unit-cost function. In that case, the final bracketed term on the right-hand side of (A.20) is simply y^0/y^1. This ratio of outputs also appears on the left-hand side of (A.20), which equals (y^0/y^1) $[c^0(p^0)/c^1(p^1)]$, so it cancels from both sides. Then we can rearrange the terms in (A.20) to obtain total factor productivity as

$$\ln(\text{TFP}) = \ln P_T(p^0, p^1, q^0, q^1) - \ln[c^1(p^1)/c^0(p^0)]. \qquad (A.21)$$

If there is perfect competition in the industry, unit-costs equal price, so the ratio of unit-costs on the right of (A.21) is replaced by the ratio of output prices in the two periods. Then (A.21) becomes the *dual Törnqvist measure of total factor productivity* that we used in chapter 4, which is a weighted average of the change in input prices minus the change in output prices. The above results provide a rigorous justification for the use of this index (or its primal counterpart, the change in log output minus the log Törnqvist index of input quantities), which is widely thought to be the "best" measure of productivity change.

GDP Price Index

Our results above can be readily extended to the *GDP price index* for an economy. We suppose that the feasible set of outputs $q = (q_1, \ldots, q_N)$ and factor endowments $v = (v_1, \ldots, v_M) \geq 0$ during period t is a set S^t, a subset of $N + M$ dimensional space. We make the following conventions on outputs: if commodity i in the list of net outputs is an output in period t, then its corresponding quantity q_i^t is positive; however, if commodity i is an input in period t, then its corresponding quantity q_i^t is negative. The latter would include imported intermediate inputs, for example. Then the sum of price times quantity over all net outputs, $\Sigma_{i=1}^N p_i^t q_i^t$, equals net revenue or GDP for the economy.

Let $p = (p_1, \ldots, p_N)$ denote a positive vector of net output prices that producers face in period t. Then the *revenue or GDP function* using period t technology is defined as

$$G^t(p, v) \equiv \max_q \{p'q : (q, v) \text{ belongs to } S^t\}. \qquad (A.22)$$

Thus $G^t(p, v)$ is the maximum value of (net) output that the economy can produce, given that the vector of inputs v is available for use, using the period t technology.

The GDP function can be used to define the economy's period t technology *theoretical GDP price index* P^t between any two periods, say period 0 and period 1, as follows:

$$P^t(p^0, p^1, v) = G^t(p^1, v)/G^t(p^0, v), \tag{A.23}$$

where p^t is the vector of net output prices that the economy faces in period t, $t = 0, 1$, and v is a reference vector of factor endowments.

Note that there is a wide variety of price indexes of the form (A.23) depending on which (t, v) reference technology and input vector v that we choose. Again, we are interested in two special cases: (*a*) $P^0(p^0, p^1, v^0)$, which uses the period 0 technology and the input vector v^0 that was actually used in period 0, and (*b*) $P^1(p^0, p^1, v^1)$ which uses the period 1 technology and the input vector v^1. Let q^0 and q^1 be the observed net output vectors in periods 0 and 1 respectively. If there is competitive behaviour on the part of producers in periods 0 and 1, then observed GDP in periods 0 and 1 should be equal to $G^0(p^0, v^0)$ and $G^1(p^1, v^1)$ respectively; that is,

$$G^0(p^0, v^0) = p^{0\prime}q^0 \quad \text{and} \quad G^1(p^1, v^1) = p^{1\prime}q^1. \tag{A.24}$$

Then we can use these results of Fisher and Shell (1972, 57–58) and Archibald (1977, 66) to again develop a series of inequalities on the theoretical price indexes:

$$
\begin{aligned}
P^0(p^0, p^1, v^0) &\equiv G^0(p^1, v^0)/G^0(p^0, v^0) &&\text{using definition (A.23)}\\
&= G^0(p^1, v^0)/p^{0\prime}q^0 &&\text{using (A.24)}\\
&\geq p^{1\prime}q^0/p^{0\prime}q^0 &&\text{since } q^0 \text{ is feasible for the}\\
&&&\text{maximization problem}\\
&&&\text{that defines } G^0(p^1, v^0) \text{ and}\\
&&&\text{so } G^0(p^1, v^0) \geq p^{1\prime}q^0\\
&\equiv P_L(p^0, p^1, q^0, q^1),
\end{aligned}
$$

where P_L is the Laspeyres price index. Similarly, we have

$$
\begin{aligned}
P^1(p^0, p^1, v^1) &\equiv G^1(p^1, v^1)/G^1(p^0, v^1) &&\text{using definition (A.23)}\\
&= p^{1\prime}q^1/G^1(p^0, v^1) &&\text{using (A.24)}\\
&\leq p^{1\prime}q^1/p^{0\prime}q^1 &&\text{since } q^1 \text{ is feasible for the}\\
&&&\text{maximization problem}\\
&&&\text{that defines } G^1(p^0, v^1) \text{ and}\\
&&&\text{so } G^1(p^0, v^1) \geq p^{0\prime}q^1\\
&\equiv P_P(p^0, p^1, q^0, q^1),
\end{aligned}
$$

where P_P is the Paasche price index. Note that these inequalities are in the *opposite direction* compared to their counterparts for the input index, which reflects the fact that revenue is maximized in (A.22), whereas costs are minimized in (A.5).

As with the input index, it is possible to define a theoretical GDP price index that falls *between* the observable Paasche and Laspeyres price indexes. To do this, we first define a hypothetical GDP function, $G(p, \alpha)$, that corresponds to the use of an α-weighted average of the technology sets S^0 and S^1 for periods 0 and 1 as the reference technology, and that uses an α-weighted average of the period 0 and period 1 input vectors v^0 and v^1:

$$G(p, \alpha) \equiv \max_q \{ p'q : (q, [1-\alpha]v^0 + \alpha v^1) \text{ belongs to} \\ (1-\alpha)S^0 + \alpha S^1 \}. \tag{A.25}$$

Then we can define the following family (indexed by α) of theoretical GDP price indexes:

$$P(p^0, p^1, \alpha) = G(p^1, \alpha)/G(p^0, \alpha). \tag{A.26}$$

It turns out that for the theoretical index in (A.26), theorem 2 *continues to hold as stated*. That is, there exists α between 0 and 1 such that the theoretical GDP index in (A.26) lies between the observable Paasche and Laspeyres indexes. There is an important qualification to this result, however: as stated in (A.13), we do not know in general whether $P_L \geq P_P$ or $P_L \leq P_P$. For the input index, cost-minimizing behavior *with a constant technology* will cause the Laspeyres price index to exceed the Paasche price index, since the former uses base-period quantities that do not reflect the substitution by firms *away* from the inputs whose prices increase the most. Conversely, for the GDP price index, firms will substitute *towards* the goods with the greatest increase in price, and *with a constant technology* this will lead the Paasche price index to exceed the Laspeyres price index. In practice, however, even for GDP price indexes we typically find that the *Laspeyres price index exceeds the Paasche price index*. The same holds for quantity indexes: the Laspeyres quantity index typically exceeds the Paasche quantity index.[6] This empirical regularity is called the "Gerschenkron effect," after the work of Alexander Gerschenkron (1951).[7]

---

[6] Using the formulas (A.1) and (A.2), the Laspeyres and Paasche quantity indexes are defined as $Q_L(p^0, p^1, q^0, q^1) \equiv P_L(q^0, q^1, p^0, p^1)$ and $Q_P(p^0, p^1, q^0, q^1) \equiv P_P(q^0, q^1, p^0, p^1)$, that is, just reversing the role of prices and quantities in the price indexes. It is readily confirmed that $Q_L(p^0, p^1, q^0, q^1) P_P(p^0, p^1, q^0, q^1) = Q_P(p^0, p^1, q^0, q^1) P_L(p^0, p^1, q^0, q^1) = p^{1\prime}q^1/p^{0\prime}q^0$, which is the ratio of total spending on the goods in the two periods. Then having $P_L \geq P_P$ for the price indexes immediately implies $Q_L \geq Q_P$ for the quantity indexes as well.

[7] Recent examples of the Gerschenkron effect can be found in van Ark, Monnikhof, and Timmer 1999 for various OECD and transition economies, Dikhanov 1999 for the Soviet Union, and Alterman, Diewert, and Feenstra 1999 for the U.S. export price index.

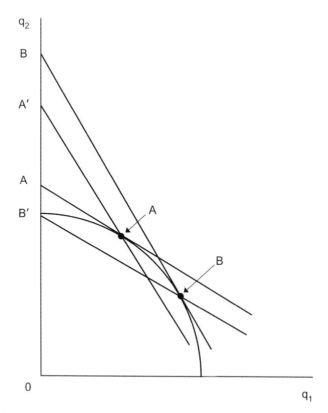

Figure A-1

The case where the Gerschenkron effect *does not* hold is illustrated in Figure A.1, where we hold technology constant along a given production possibility frontier (PPF). We choose good 2 as the numeraire and evaluate GDP by the intercepts on the vertical axis. The initial prices lead to outputs at point A, with GDP measured by 0A of good 2 along the vertical axis. At the new prices outputs occur at point B, with GDP measured by 0B of good 2. So the ratio 0B/0A is the theoretical GDP price index. The Laspeyres price index would evaluate the price change at the initial quantities, to obtain the ratio 0A'/0A < 0B/0A. On the other hand, the Paasche price index would evaluate the price change at the new quantities, to obtain 0B/0B' > 0B/0A > 0A'/0A, which exceeds that obtained from the Laspeyres price index. This confirms that the Paasche price index exceeds the Laspeyres index when technology does not change, due to output substitution by producers.

In Figure A.2, by contrast, we suppose that the PPF is shifting out due to technological change. At unchanged prices, GDP would increase from

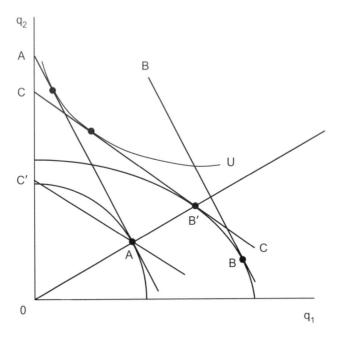

Figure A-2

point A to point B (i.e., GDP would increase from the intercept of AA and BB with the vertical axis). Suppose, however, that the relative price of good 1 falls due to its increased supply, so that the slope of the line CC shows the new prices. Production now occurs at point B′ rather than point B. We have drawn the case where the budget lines AA and CC are both tangent to an indifference curve U, indicating that the change in equilibrium prices is due to changing supply with constant utility.

In the case we have illustrated, the production points A and B′ lie on the same ray from the origin, so that the *relative outputs* of the two goods are unchanged. This means that the Laspeyres and Paasche price indexes, using the outputs at points A or B′, would be *identical*. In fact, evaluating the Laspeyres price index using the initial outputs at point A, we would obtain GDP of 0A along the vertical axis at the old prices and 0C′ at the new prices, so the price index is 0C′/0A < 1, indicating a substantial fall in the price of good 1. The Paasche price index, evaluated at the outputs at point B′, would give exactly the same result. If point B′ occurred along the PPF *slightly to the right* of the ray through the origin and A, however, then the higher supply of good 1, whose relative price has fallen, would cause the Paasche price index to be less than the Laspeyres price index. This would illustrate the Gerschenkron effect.

Finding that the Laspeyres GDP price index exceeds the Paasche is indirect evidence of changing technology (or factor endowments). The theoretical GDP price index $P(p^0, p^1, \alpha)$, defined in (A.26) holds technology and factor endowments constant, and is therefore a suitable measure of price change. Theorem 2 says that this theoretical index can be measured by an average of the Paasche and Laspeyres price indexes, which is one justification for using the Fisher ideal index for the output price index, as we also found for the input price index.

Further results can be obtained by using the translog form for the GDP function, where we allow its parameters to vary over time due to technological change:

$$
\begin{aligned}
\ln G^t(p, v) = \alpha_0^t &+ \sum_{i=1}^{N} \alpha_1^t \ln p_i + \sum_{k=1}^{M} \beta_k^t \ln v_k \\
&+ \frac{1}{2} \sum_{i=1}^{N} \sum_{j=1}^{N} \gamma_{ij}^t \ln p_i \ln p_j \\
&+ \frac{1}{2} \sum_{k=1}^{M} \sum_{\ell=1}^{M} \delta_{k\ell}^t \ln v_k \ln v_\ell \\
&+ \sum_{i=1}^{N} \sum_{k=1}^{M} \phi_{ik}^t \ln p_i \ln v_k.
\end{aligned}
\tag{A.27}
$$

In order to ensure that the translog GDP function is homogeneous of degree one in prices, we impose symmetry $\gamma_{ij}^t = \gamma_{ji}^t$ and the requirements

$$
\sum_{i=1}^{N} \alpha_1^t = 1 \quad \text{and} \quad \sum_{i=1}^{N} \gamma_{ij}^t = \sum_{i=1}^{N} \phi_{ik}^t = 0.
\tag{A.28}
$$

In addition, to ensure that the GDP function is homogeneous of degree one in endowments, we impose symmetry $\delta_{k\ell}^t = \delta_{\ell k}^t$ and the requirements

$$
\sum_{k=1}^{M} \beta_k^t = 1 \quad \text{and} \quad \sum_{k=1}^{M} \delta_{k\ell}^t = \sum_{k=1}^{M} \phi_{ik}^t = 0.
\tag{A.29}
$$

The next result is completely analogous to theorem 3 for the translog cost function, where again we require that the second-order parameters on prices γ_{ij}^t, remain constant. This result follows by adapting the arguments in Caves, Christensen, and Diewert (1982). It does not require the GDP function to be homogeneous of degree one in factor endowments, though we will make use of (A.29) later.

Theorem 4 (Caves, Christensen, and Diewert 1982)

Assuming that $\gamma_{ij}^0 = \gamma_{ij}^1$, and that the output quantities q^t are revenue maximizing at prices p^t, $t = 0, 1$, then

$$[P^0(p^0, p^1, v^0)P^1(p^0, p^1, v^1)]^{1/2} = P_T(p^0, p^1, q^0, q^1). \qquad (A.30)$$

Thus, a geometric mean of the theoretical GDP price indexes $P^0(p^0, p^1, v^0)$ and $P^1(p^0, p^1, v^1)$ equals the translog price index defined by (A.4). Unlike with theorem 3, we no longer need to assume that the quantities q^t are strictly positive: we are now letting $q_i^t > 0$ denote an output, and $q_i^t < 0$ denote an input, and a commodity can switch from one to the other across the two periods. This raises an important question of interpretation, however. Since $q_i^t < 0$ can reflect imported intermediate inputs,while $q_i^t > 0$ can reflect exported commodities, it appears that the output price index is mixing together terms of trade effects with other price movements. This is indeed the case, and in the next section we use the results of Diewert and Morrison (1986) and Kohli (1990b, 2001) to separately measure the terms of trade impact and productivity.

Terms of Trade and Productivity

Let us return to Figure A.2, where we illustrated a productivity improvement and a fall in the relative price of goods 1. We have already argued that the Paasche and Laspeyres output price indexes would be equal in the example illustrated and would indicate a very substantial decline in prices, of 0C′/0A < 1. Using good 2 as the numeraire, the resulting value of GDP (measured off the vertical axis) indicates a much smaller decline, from 0A to 0C, with the ratio 0C/0A. If we divide this change in GDP by the price index, we obtain a measure of the change in *real* GDP, which is just (0C/0A)/(0C′/0A) = 0C/0C′ > 1. Thus, we find that real GDP has risen, which is entirely appropriate since production has indeed increased from point A to point B′. Indeed, the ratio 0C/0C′ along the vertical axis is identical to the ratio 0B′/0A along the ray from the origin, which precisely measures the increase in outputs and real GDP. We conclude that our GDP price index, and the corresponding measure of real GDP, accurately reflects the outward shift in the PPF due to technological change or factor accumulation.

Now suppose we pose a different question, and ask what has happened to the cost of living for the representative consumer, with indifference curve shown by U in figure A.2. An exact cost of living index for the consumer would compare the initial expenditure 0A in Figure A.2 with the new expenditure 0C, both measured with good 2 as the numeraire and giving constant utility of U. Thus, an exact cost of living index would equal $0C/0A < 1$. Notice that this index is constructed using exactly the same *prices* as the GDP price index, but now using different *quantities* as weights: the cost of living index uses the quantities demanded, whereas the GDP price index uses the quantities supplied. For this reason we can expect the indexes to differ, and in our example, the cost of living index $0C/0A$ *exceeds* the GDP price index, which was $0C'/0A$. Indeed, the difference between the two indexes is entirely due to the *terms of trade change* for the economy. The fall in the relative price of good 1 is reflected *more* in the GDP price index than in the cost of living index, because this export good has production exceeding consumption.

The above argument suggests the following definition of the *terms of trade index*:

$$(\text{Terms of trade index}) \equiv (\text{GDP price index})/ \quad (\text{A.31})$$
$$(\text{Cost of living index}),$$

where all of these indexes are computed over the set of final goods sold in an economy. To further motivate this definition, consider the Törnqvist index in (A.4) or (A.4′). Let $P_T(p^0, p^1, q^0, q^1)$ denote the cost of living index, computed with prices p^t and quantities *consumed* q^t, $t = 0, 1$. In addition, let $P_T(p^0, p^1, y^0, y^1)$ denote the GDP price index, computed with prices p^t and quantities *produced* y^t, $t = 0, 1$. Net exports of final goods are simply $x^t = y^t - q^t$, and let us assume for simplicity that trade is balanced, so that $p^{t\prime}x^t = p^{t\prime}y^t - p^{t\prime}q^t = 0$. Then it follows immediately from (A.4′) that

$$\ln P_T(p^0, p^1, y^0, y^1) - \ln P_T(p^0, p^1, q^0, q^1)$$
$$= \sum_{i=1}^{N} \left(\frac{1}{2}\right)\left(\frac{p_i^0 x_i^0}{p^{0\prime}y^0} + \frac{p_i^1 x_i^1}{p^{1\prime}y^1}\right)\ln(p_i^1/p_i^0). \quad (\text{A.32})$$

The left-hand side of (A.32) is the difference between the log GDP price index and the log cost of living index, while the right-hand side is a price index constructed using as weights the average value of net exports relative to GDP in the two periods. These weights are negative for imports, so the right-hand side of (A.32) is indeed interpreted as a terms of trade index.

These results can be extended to the case where imports include intermediate inputs, as in Diewert and Morrison 1986. To achieve this extension, let us identify three groups of commodities: those for final domestic demand (quantity $q_{di}^t > 0$ and price $p_{di}^t > 0$, for $i = 1, \ldots, N_d$); those for export ($q_{xi}^t > 0$ and $p_{xi}^t > 0$, for $i = 1, \ldots, N_x$); and those imported as intermediate inputs ($q_{mi}^t < 0$ and $p_{mi}^t > 0$, for $i = 1, \ldots, N_m$). The quantity vector for all commodities is $q^t = (q_d^t, q_x^t, q_m^t)$, with prices $p^t = (p_d^t, p_x^t, p_m^t)$. Then the GDP function for the economy is still defined as in (A.22), where q^t is the revenue-maximizing choices by firms. We will suppose that GDP takes on the translog form as in (A.27)–(A.29).

For this GDP function, let us define the *theoretical productivity index*:

$$R(p,v) = G^1(p,v)/G^0(p,v). \qquad (A.33)$$

This theoretical index holds prices and factor endowments fixed and considers only the change in productivity between periods 0 and 1. We are interested in two special cases: (*a*) the Laspeyres productivity index, $R_L \equiv R(p^0, v^0) = G^1(p^0, v^0)/G^0(p^0, v^0)$, which uses prices and endowments from period 0; (*b*) the Paasche productivity index, $R_P \equiv R(p^1, v^1) = G^1(p^1, v^1)/G^1(p^1, v^1)$, which uses prices and endowments from period 1. Each of these is unobservable, but as in our earlier discussion of productivity in (A.19)–(A.21), we can measure their geometric mean.

Theorem 5 (Diewert and Morrison 1986)

Assuming that the GDP function takes on the translog form in (A.27)–(A.29), and the revenue-maximizing quantities q^t are nonzero, then

$$(R_L R_P)^{1/2} = \left(\frac{p^{1\prime}q^1}{p^{0\prime}q^0}\right) \Big/ [P_T(p^0, p^1, q^0, q^1)\, Q_T(w^0, w^1, v^0, v^1)]. \quad (A.34)$$

The first term on the right-hand side of (A.34) is the ratio of GDP in the two periods, or the growth in nominal GDP. This is deflated by the two other terms on the right side: the first is the Törnqvist price index of GDP using the formula in (A.4); and the second is a Törnqvist quantity index of *factor endowments*, defined by

$$\ln Q_T(w^0, w^1, v^0, v^1) \equiv \sum_{i=1}^{N} \left(\frac{1}{2}\right)\left(\frac{w_i^0 v_i^0}{w^{0\prime}v^0} + \frac{w_i^1 v_i^1}{w^{1\prime}v^1}\right)\ln(v_i^1/v_i^0). \qquad (A.35)$$

Thus, this is a factor share–weighted average of the growth in primary inputs for the economy. Notice that under our assumption in (A.29) that the GDP function is linearly homogeneous in v, $p^{t\prime}q^t = w^{t\prime}v^t$, so the shares in the Törnqvist price index and the Törnqvist quantity index are both measured relative to GDP. Theorem 5 generalizes our earlier derivation of TFP in (A.19)–(A.21), to allow now for multiple inputs and outputs.

Let us now take the Törnqvist price index of GDP that appears on the right side of (A.34) and decompose it into the portion dealing with domestic goods, exports, and imports:

$$
\ln P_T(p^0, p^1, q^0, q^1) = \sum_{i=1}^{N_d} \left(\frac{1}{2}\right) \left(\frac{p_{di}^0 q_{di}^0}{p^{0\prime} q^0} + \frac{p_{di}^1 q_{di}^1}{p^{1\prime} q^1} \right) \ln(p_{di}^1 / p_{di}^0)
$$

$$
+ \sum_{i=1}^{N_x} \left(\frac{1}{2}\right) \left(\frac{p_{xi}^0 q_{xi}^0}{p^{0\prime} q^0} + \frac{p_{xi}^1 q_{xi}^1}{p^{1\prime} q^1} \right) \ln(p_{xi}^1 / p_{xi}^0) \qquad \text{(A.36)}
$$

$$
+ \sum_{i=1}^{N_m} \left(\frac{1}{2}\right) \left(\frac{p_{mi}^0 q_{mi}^0}{p^{0\prime} q^0} + \frac{p_{mi}^1 q_{mi}^1}{p^{1\prime} q^1} \right) \ln(p_{mi}^1 / p_{mi}^0).
$$

We will refer to the first summation on the right-hand side of (A.36) as the cost of living index, because it uses the quantities and prices of final goods demanded by the consumer. The exponent of this first summation is denoted by the Törnqvist price index $P_T = (p_d^0, p_d^1, q_d^0, q_d^1)$, where the shares are computed relative to total GDP $p^{t\prime} q^t$. The second and third terms are the difference between the export and import price indexes, respectively (recall that $q_{mi}^t < 0$). Let us denote the exponent of these two summations by the Törnqvist index $P_T(p_{xm}^0, p_{xm}^1, q_{xm}^0, q_{xm}^1)$, where again, the shares are computed relative to total GDP $p^{t\prime} q^t$.

Then we can rewrite the result in (A.34) in the following form:

$$
\left(\frac{p^{1\prime} q^1}{p^{0\prime} q^0} \right) = (R_L R_P)^{1/2} P_T(p_d^0, p_d^1, q_d^0, q_d^1) P_T(p_{xm}^0, p_{xm}^1, q_{xm}^0, q_{xm}^1)
$$
$$
\times Q_T(w^0, w^1, v^0, v^1). \qquad \text{(A.37)}
$$

Thus, the ratio of nominal GDP is decomposed as a total factor productivity index, a cost of living price index, a terms of trade index, and a quantity index of endowment growth. Kohli (2004) argues that if we wish to deflate the growth in GDP to obtain a measure of welfare change for the representative consumer, then we should use the cost of living index rather than the GDP price index as a deflator. That is, a measure of *welfare change* would be

$$
\left(\frac{p^{1\prime} q^1}{p^{0\prime} q^0} \right) / P_T(p_d^0, p_d^1, q_d^0, q_d^1) = (R_L R_P)^{1/2} P_T(p_{xm}^0, p_{xm}^1, q_{xm}^0, q_{xm}^1)
$$
$$
\times Q_T(w^0, w^1, v^0, v^1). \qquad \text{(A.38)}
$$

This decomposition allows productivity growth, improvements in the terms of trade, and endowment growth in factors to all contribute positively to welfare. Notice that this measure of welfare is quite different from the normal method of calculating growth in real GDP, which is to deflate the ratio of nominal GDP by the GDP price index, obtaining

$$\left(\frac{p^{1\prime}q^1}{p^{0\prime}q^0}\right) \bigg/ P_T(p^0, p^1, q^0, q^1) = (R_L R_P)^{1/2} \, Q_T(w^0, w^1, v^0, v^1). \quad (A.39)$$

The log of (A.39) is reported as real GDP growth in national income statistics, but it *leaves out* changes in the terms of trade as a source of welfare gain. In (A.38), by contrast, we deflate nominal GDP by the price index computed for domestic goods only, that is, by the price index for domestic absorption, $C + I + G$. By applying this cost of living index to all components of GDP, $C + I + G + X - M$, including exports and imports, we obtain a measure of "real welfare" that is more appropriate to assess changes in the representative consumer. Kohli (1990b, 2004) shows that deflating nominal GDP by the cost of living index leads to a considerably higher growth in "real welfare" for some countries (such as Switzerland) than real GDP growth. This is explained by the terms of trade improvements for such countries in recent years.

Discrete Choice Models

Discrete choice models are commonly taught in econometrics, but the economic generality of these models is sometimes unclear. This is especially true when we consider models that incorporate not just demand but also the optimal prices charged by firms under imperfect competition. In that case, we want to derive demand and prices in a mutually consistent fashion, as will be discussed in this appendix.

We begin with an aggregation theorem due to McFadden (1978, 1981). He has shown that when individuals have random utility over discrete alternatives, the decisions they make can sometimes be aggregated up to a representative consumer. McFadden focuses on the case where individuals have utility functions that are linear in income, and where the goods over which a discrete choice is being made are purchased in the quantity 0 or 1. Under certain conditions, it is possible to generalize this to the case where utility is nonlinear in income, and where the discrete-choice good is purchased in continuous quantities. This is a principal result of Anderson, de Palma, and Thisse (1992, chaps. 2–5), who show, for example, that the representative consumer can have a CES utility function, as we also demonstrate below.

At the same time we present these aggregation results, we will discuss the empirical strategy to estimate discrete choice models due to Berry (1994). In this approach, we suppose that the individual-level data on consumer choices is not available. Rather, we just observe the market-level data on the quantity purchased of each product, as well as prices and characteristics. The goal is to infer the individual taste parameters from this market-level data on quantities and prices, as well as parameters of marginal cost, so that price-cost margins can be estimated.

Discrete Choice Model

Suppose there is a population of consumers h, and we normalize its size to unity. Each consumer must decide which of a discrete number of alternatives $j = 1, \ldots, N$ to purchase, and receives the following utility from consuming one unit of product j:

$$V_j^h = u_j + \varepsilon_j^h, \tag{B.1}$$

where u_j is the utility obtained from product j by *every* consumer, while ε_j^h is an additional part of utility obtained by consumer h. We will treat ε_j^h as a random variable with cumulative density function $F(\varepsilon)$, where each consumer obtains a different draw of $\varepsilon = (\varepsilon_1, \ldots, \varepsilon_N)$. Given this draw, the consumer chooses the product with highest utility. The probability that a consumer will choose product j is

$$
\begin{aligned}
P_j &= \text{Prob}[V_j \geq V_k, \text{ for all } k = 1, \ldots, N] \\
&= \text{Prob}[u_j + \varepsilon_j \geq u_k + \varepsilon_k, \text{ for all } k = 1, \ldots, N] \qquad (B.2) \\
&= \text{Prob}[\varepsilon_j - \varepsilon_k \geq u_k - u_j, \text{ for all } k = 1, \ldots, N].
\end{aligned}
$$

We can think of (B.2) as the probability that any consumer will choose alternative j, or equivalently, as the expected fraction of the population that chooses that alternative. The solution for these choice probabilities depends on the distribution function $F(\varepsilon)$, as well as on the specification of utility u_j. A simplified version of utility used by Berry (1994) is

$$
u_j = y + \beta' z_j - \alpha p_j + \xi_j, \quad \alpha > 0. \qquad (B.3)
$$

Thus, utility is linear in individual income y and decreasing in the price p_j, and also depends on the characteristics z_j of the product.[1] The term ξ_j is another random element in utility, but unlike ε_j^h, it *does not* vary across consumers. We could think of ξ_j as some unmeasured characteristics of product j, which are random across products but not consumers.

In general, computing the choice probabilities from (B.2) is computationally intensive since it requires integration over various subsets of the domain of $F(\varepsilon)$. However, McFadden has shown that for a class of distribution functions $F(\varepsilon)$ known as the *generalized extreme value*, the expected demands can be *equivalently* obtained by simple differentiation.

Theorem 1 (McFadden 1978, 80; 1981, 227)

Let H be a nonnegative function defined over R_+^N that satisfies the following properties:

  (i) H is homogeneous of degree one.
  (ii) $H \to \infty$ as any of its argument approaches infinity.
  (iii) The mixed partial derivatives of H with respect to k variables exist and are continuous, nonnegative if k is odd and nonpositive if k is even, $k = 1, \ldots, N$.

---

[1] This utility function is not homogeneous of degree zero in income y and price p_j. To obtain this property, we should measure y and p_j relative to a numeraire price p_0, so that utility becomes $u_j = y/p_0 - \alpha p_j/p_0 + \beta' z_j + \xi_j$, which is homogeneous of degree zero in (y, p_j, p_0).

Define the generalized extreme value distribution function,

$$F(\varepsilon_1, \ldots, \varepsilon_N) \equiv \exp[-H(e^{-\varepsilon_1}, e^{-\varepsilon_2}, \ldots, e^{-\varepsilon_N})]. \tag{B.4}$$

Then the expected value of consumer utility (up to a constant) is given by the aggregate utility function,

$$G(u_1, \ldots, u_N) \equiv \ln H(e^{u_1}, e^{u_2}, \ldots, e^{u_N}), \tag{B.5}$$

and the choice probabilities P_j in (B.2) can be obtained as

$$P_j = \partial G / \partial u_j. \tag{B.6}$$

To interpret this theorem, consider the linear utility function in (B.3). Substituting this into (B.5) and using the linear homogeneity of H, the aggregate utility function is

$$\tilde{G}(p_1, z_1, \ldots, p_N, z_N, y) = y + \ln H(e^{\beta' z_1 - \alpha p_1 + \xi_1}, \ldots, e^{\beta' z_N - \alpha p_N + \xi_N}). \tag{B.5'}$$

Notice that $\partial \tilde{G} / \partial y = 1$, and consider the case where $\alpha = 1$. Then price is inversely related to utility ($du_j = -dp_j$), so the choice probabilities in (B.6) can be computed as $P_j = \partial G / \partial u_j = -(\partial \tilde{G} / \partial p_j)/(\partial \tilde{G} / \partial y)$. Thus, the result that $P_j = \partial G / \partial u_j$ in (B.6) of the theorem can be interpreted as saying that Roy's Identity holds at the aggregate level.

The conditions on H in (i)–(iii) are technical properties needed to ensure that the $F(\varepsilon)$ defined in (B.4) is indeed a cumulative distribution function. There will be many choices of H satisfying these conditions, and for each, we obtain the aggregate utility function in (B.5), whose demands are identical to those aggregated from the individual choice problem in (B.1)–(B.2). Furthermore, this aggregate utility function can be used to make welfare statements about the individual consumers, since it reflects expected individual utility.

To see the usefulness of this result, we consider the well-known example where the random utility ε_j in (B.1) from consuming each product is independently distributed across products, with the extreme value distribution.

Example 1: Logit Demand System

Let us choose the function H as linear in its arguments:

$$H(e^{-\varepsilon_1}, e^{-\varepsilon_2}, \ldots, e^{-\varepsilon_N}) = \sum_{j=1}^{N} e^{-\varepsilon_j}. \tag{B.7}$$

Substituting (B.7) into (B.4), the distribution function is

$$F(\varepsilon_1, \ldots, \varepsilon_N) = \prod_{j=1}^{N} \exp(-e^{-\varepsilon_j}). \tag{B.8}$$

This cumulative distribution function is therefore the product of N iid "double-exponential" or extreme value distributions, which apply to the random utility terms in (B.1). Therefore, the random term in utility is distributed as iid extreme value.[2]

Computing the choice probabilities as in (B.6) using (B.7) and (B.3), we obtain

$$P_j = \frac{e^{u_j}}{\left[\sum_{k=1}^{N} e^{u_k}\right]} = \frac{e^{\beta' z_j - \alpha p_j + \xi_j}}{\left[\sum_{k=1}^{N} e^{\beta' z_k - \alpha p_k + \xi_k}\right]}, \tag{B.9}$$

which are the choice probabilities under the logit system.

Berry (1994) discusses how estimates of α and β can be obtained even if we do not have data on the purchases by each individual, but just observe the quantity share s_j of each product in demand, as well as their prices and characteristics. Then the probabilities in (B.9) would be measured by these quantity shares s_j. Suppose in addition there is some outside option $j = 0$, which gives utility normalized to zero, $u_0 = 0$. Then setting $s_j = P_j$, and taking logs of the ratio of (B.9) to s_0, we obtain

$$\ln s_j - \ln s_0 = \beta' z_j - \alpha p_j + \xi_j. \tag{B.10}$$

In addition, we follow Berry to solve for the optimal prices of the firm, where we assume for simplicity that each firm produces only one product. Denoting the marginal costs of producing good j by $g_j(z_j)$, and ignoring fixed costs, the profits from producing model j are

$$\pi_j = [p_j - g_j(z_j)] s_j. \tag{B.11}$$

Maximizing (B.11) over the choice of p_j, treating the prices of all other products as fixed, we obtain

$$p_j = g_j(z_j) - s_j / (\partial s_j / \partial p_j) = g_j(z_j) - (\partial \ln s_j / \partial p_j)^{-1}. \tag{B.12}$$

For the special case of the logit system (B.9) with $s_j = P_j$ denoting the quantity shares, we compute that $\partial \ln s_j / \partial p_j = -\alpha(1 - s_j)$. If we also specify marginal costs as $g_j(z_j) = \gamma' z_j + \omega_j$, where ω_j is a random error, then from (B.12) the optimal prices are

$$p_j = \gamma' z_j + \frac{1}{\alpha(1 - s_j)} + \omega_j, \tag{B.13}$$

[2] A discussion of the "double exponential" or extreme value distribution is provided by Anderson, de Palma, and Thisse (1992, 58–62).

which can be estimated jointly with (B.10). It is apparent, though, that the random error ξ_j influences the market shares in (B.10), and therefore from (B.13) will be correlated with prices p_j. Accordingly, the joint estimation of (B.10) and (B.13) should be done with instrumental variables.[3]

The problem with this simple logit example is that the demand elasticities obtained are implausible. From the market shares $s_j = P_j$ in (B.9) we readily see that s_j/s_k is independent of the price or characteristics of any third product i. This property is known as the '*independence of irrelevant alternatives*' in the discrete choice literature, and it implies that the cross-elasticity of demand between products j and k and the third product i must be equal. To improve on this limitation, we consider the nested logit system.

Example 2: Nested Logit Demand System

Now suppose that the consumers have a choice between two levels of the differentiated product. First, an individual decides whether to purchase a product in each of $g = 1, \ldots, G$ groups (for example, small cars and big cars), and second, the individual decides which of the products in that group to purchase. Suppose that the products available in each group g are denoted by the set $J_g \subset \{1, \ldots, N\}$, while J_0 denotes the outside option. Utility for consumer h is still given by (B.1), where the errors ε_j are distributed as extreme value but are *not* independent. Instead, we suppose that if consumer h has a high value of ε_j^h for some product $j \in J_g$, then that person will *also* tend to have high values of ε_k^h for all other products $k \in J_g$, so ε_j is positively correlated across products in each group. For example, an individual who has a preference for some small car also tends to like other small cars.

To achieve this correlation between the random errors in (B.1), McFadden (1981, 228) chooses the function H as

$$H(e^{-\varepsilon_1}, \ldots, e^{-\varepsilon_N}) = \sum_{g=0}^{G} \left[\sum_{j \in J_g} e^{-\varepsilon_j/(1-\rho_g)} \right]^{(1-\rho_g)}. \tag{B.14}$$

To satisfy property (iii) of theorem 1, we need to specify that $0 \leq \rho_g < 1$. Using this choice of H, we obtain a distribution function $F(\varepsilon)$ from (B.4),

$$F(\varepsilon_1, \ldots, \varepsilon_N) = \exp\left(\sum_{g=0}^{G} \left[\sum_{j \in J_g} -e^{-\varepsilon_j/(1-\rho_g)} \right]^{(1-\rho_g)} \right), \tag{B.15}$$

[3] Berry (1994, 249) suggests that appropriate instruments for prices in (B.10) are characteristics of other models z_k, as well as variables that affect the costs of producing product j.

where ρ_g roughly measures the correlation between random terms ε_j within a group.[4] Computing the choice probabilities as in (B.6) using (B.14), we obtain

$$P_j = \frac{e^{u_j/(1-\rho_g)}}{D_g} \frac{D_g^{(1-\rho_g)}}{\left[\sum_{g=0}^{G} D_g^{(1-\rho_g)}\right]}, \qquad \text{for } j \in J_g, \qquad \text{(B.16)}$$

where the term $D_g \equiv \sum_{k \in J_g} e^{u_k/(1-\rho_g)}$ appearing in (B.16) is called an *inclusive value*, since it summarizes the utility obtained from all products in the group g.

Berry (1994, 252) motivates this nested logit case somewhat differently. He rewrites the random errors ε_j^b as

$$\varepsilon_j^b = \zeta_g^b + (1-\rho_g)e_j^b, \qquad \text{for } j \in J_g, \qquad \text{(B.17)}$$

where the errors e_j^b are iid extreme value. The random variable ζ_g^b in (B.17) is *common* to all products within group g, and therefore induces a correlation between the random utilities for those products. Cardell (1997) shows that there exists a distribution for ζ_g^b (depending on ρ_g) such that when e_j^b are iid extreme value, then ε_j^b are *also* distributed extreme value but are *not* independent. Notice that as the parameter ρ_g approaches unity, ε_j^b are perfectly correlated within the group g (since they equal ζ_g^b), whereas when ρ_g approaches zero (in which case ζ_g^b also approaches zero) then ε_j^b become independent. Using the errors in (B.17) gives the same choice probabilities as shown in (B.16).

Using the nested logit choice probabilities in (B.16), we can rederive the estimating equations for market share and optimal prices, as does Berry (1994, 252–53). The first term on the right-hand side of (B.16) is the probability that an individual will choose product $j \in J_g$ *conditional on* having already chosen the group g. Let us denote this conditional probability by $s_{j|g}$. The second term on the right-hand side of (B.16) is the probability of choosing any product from group g, which we write as $\bar{s}_g$. So replacing P_j in (B.16) by the market shares s_j, we write this choice probability as $s_j = s_{j|g}\bar{s}_g$. In addition, we suppose that the outside good has has $u_0 = 0$ and inclusive value $D_0 = 1$, so that from (B.16), $s_0 = P_0 = [\sum_{g=0}^{G} D_g^{(1-\rho_g)}]^{-1}$. Taking logs of the ratio $s_j/s_0 = s_{j|g}\bar{s}_g/s_0$ and using the linear utility u_j in (B.3), we therefore have

$$\ln s_j - \ln s_0 = \frac{(\beta'z_j - \alpha p_j + \xi_j)}{(1-\rho_g)} - \rho_g \ln D_g. \qquad \text{(B.18)}$$

---

[4] Johnson and Kotz (1972, 256) report that the parameters $(1-\rho_g)$ equal $\sqrt{1-corr(\varepsilon_j, \varepsilon_k)}$, for $i, k \in J_g$ and $i \neq k$, so that $corr(\varepsilon_j, \varepsilon_k) > 0$ for $\rho_g > 0$.

To solve for the inclusive value D_g, recall that $\bar{s}_g$ equals the second term on the right of (B.16). Therefore, $\bar{s}_g / s_0 = D_g^{(1-\rho_g)}$ and so $\ln \bar{s}_g - \ln s_0 = (1-\rho_g)\ln D_g$. Using this in (B.18) and simplifying with $s_j = s_{j|g}\bar{s}_g$, we obtain

$$\ln s_j - \ln s_0 = \beta' z_j - \alpha p_j + \rho_g \ln s_{j|g} + \xi_j, \qquad j \in J_g. \qquad (B.19)$$

This gives us a regression to estimate the parameters (α, β), where the final term $\ln s_{j|g}$ measures the market share of product j within the group g, and is endogenous. Once again, we can use instrumental variables to estimate (B.19).[5]

In addition, we follow Berry (1994, 255) to solve for the optimal prices of the firm, assuming for simplicity that it produces only one product j. Profits are still given by (B.11), and the first-order condition by (B.12). For the nested logit system with $s_j = P_j$ in (B.16), the derivative of the log market shares is $\partial \ln s_j / \partial p_j = -\dfrac{\alpha}{(1-\rho_g)}[1 - \rho_g \bar{s}_{j|g} - (1-\rho_g)s_j]$.

With marginal costs as $g_j(z_j) = \gamma' z_j + \omega_j$, where ω_j is a random error, from (B.11) the optimal prices are

$$p_j = \gamma' z_j + \frac{(1-\rho_g)}{\alpha[1 - \rho_g \bar{s}_{j|g} - (1-\rho_g)s_j]} + \omega_j, \qquad (B.20)$$

which can be estimated simultaneously with (B.19) using instrumental variables. This pricing equation was generalized in chapter 8 to allow for multiproduct firms, as used by Irwin and Pavcnik (2001) in their study of export subsidies to commercial aircraft.

The nested logit allows for more general substitution between products than does the simple logit model (and does not suffer from "independence of irrelevant alternatives"). Goldberg (1995), for example, has used the nested logit in her study of automobile demand in the United States and the impact of the voluntary export restraint (VER) with Japan. Even more flexibility in the pattern of demand across autos can be achieved by introducing greater consumer heterogeneity, as done by Berry, Levinsohn, and Pakes (1995, 1999) in their work on autos and the VER with Japan. They suppose that the utilities in (B.3) instead appear as

$$u_j^h = \beta^{h'} z_j - \alpha p_j + \xi_j, \qquad \alpha > 0, \qquad (B.3')$$

where now the parameters β^h *depend* on the individual h, reflecting both demographic characteristics and income. Since individual income is included in β^h, without loss of generality we omit this variable from appearing explicitly in (B.3').

---

[5] Berry (1994, 254) suggests that appropriate instruments will include the characteristics of other products or firms in group g.

If we observed both individual characteristics and also their discrete choices, then it would be possible to estimate the other parameters appearing in (B.3′) using standard econometric programs for discrete choice. However, when we observe only the *market-level* demands and overall distribution of individual characteristics, then estimating the parameters of (B.3′) becomes much more difficult. To see this, let us suppose that the individual characteristics β^h are distributed as $\bar{\beta} + \eta^h$, with mean value $\bar{\beta}$ over the population and η^h a random variable that captures individual tastes for characteristics. Substituting this into (B.3′) and then into (B.1), we obtain utility,

$$V_j^h = \bar{\beta}'z_j - \alpha p_j + \xi_j + (\eta^{h'}z_j + \varepsilon_j^h), \tag{B.1′}$$

where now the random error includes the interaction term $\eta^{h'}z_j$ between individual tastes and product characteristics. The presence of this interaction term means that theorem 1 *cannot* be used: the cumulative distribution of the combined error $(\eta^{h'}z_j + \varepsilon_j^h)$ is more general than allowed for in theorem 1. It follows that there is no closed-form solution such as (B.6) for the choice probabilities.

Instead, the choice probabilities need to be calculated numerically from (B.2). That is, given the data (p_j, z_j) across products, we can simulate the distribution of $(\eta^{h'}z_j + \varepsilon_j^h)$. For each draw from this distribution, and for given parameters $(\alpha, \bar{\beta}, \xi_j)$, we can calculate utility V_j^h for each product. The choice probabilities P_j in (B.2) are computed as the proportion of draws for which product j gives the highest utility. Then the parameters $(\alpha, \bar{\beta}, \xi_j)$ are chosen so that these choice probabilities match the observed market shares s_j as closely as possible. Likewise, the predicted *change* in the market shares due to prices, $(\partial s_j / \partial p_j)$ in (B.12), would be calculated numerically by seeing how the choice probability P_j varies with prices p_j. This also depends on the parameters $(\alpha, \bar{\beta}, \xi_j)$, which are then chosen so that the pricing equations fit as closely as possible. Thus, the market share and pricing equations are simultaneously used to estimate the underlying taste and costs parameters, using simulated distributions of the random term in utility. This is the idea behind the work of Berry, Levinsohn, and Pakes (1995, 1999), which may be consulted for more details.[6]

It is also useful to compare the above approaches with a *third* approach to discrete choice models: rather than using a representative consumer, or individuals with random utility, we could instead use individuals that differ in terms of their *preferred* characteristics, in what is sometimes called the

---

[6] Estimating a discrete choice model by simulating the taste parameters is referred to as "mixed logit." A distance learning course on discrete choice methods including software to estimate mixed logit models is available from Kenneth Train at http://elsa.berkeley.edu/~train/distant.html.

"ideal variety" approach. Anderson, de Palma, and Thisse (1992) derive an equivalence between all three approaches. Bresnahan (1981) was the first to estimate a discrete choice model for autos in which consumers differ in their ideal varieties, and found that higher-priced models tended to have higher percentage markups. Feenstra and Levinsohn (1995) generalized the model of Bresnahan by allowing characteristics to differ multidimensionally, rather than along a line as in Bresnahan, and showed that the optimal prices of firms will vary with the distance to their neighbors.

Discrete Choice with Continuous Quantities

Setting aside the issue of consumer heterogeneity, there is another direction in which we can attempt to generalize theorem 1, while still allowing the aggregate utility function to exist so that demands can be computed using Roy's Identity. We again suppose that consumers are still choosing over products $j = 1, \ldots, N$, and now have the utility function

$$V_j^h = \ln y - \ln \phi(p_j, z_j) + \varepsilon_j^h, \quad j = 1, \ldots, N, \quad (B.21)$$

where p_j is the price of product j, z_j is a vector of characteristics, y is the consumers' income, and ε_j is a random term that reflects the additional utility received by consumer h from product j. Thus, income no longer enters utility in a linear fashion, and we will allow individuals to consume *continuous* quantities (not restricted to 0 or 1) of their preferred product j.

Each consumer still chooses their preferred product j with probability

$$P_j = \text{Prob}\,[V_j \geq V_k, \quad \text{for all } k = 1, \ldots, N]. \quad (B.22)$$

If product j is chosen, then the quantity consumed is determined from the indirect utility function in (B.21), using Roy's Identity:

$$c_j = -\frac{\partial V_j^h / \partial p_j}{\partial V_j^h / \partial y} = y(\partial \ln \phi / \partial p_j). \quad (B.23)$$

It follows that expected demand for each product is

$$X_j = c_j P_j. \quad (B.24)$$

This formulation of the consumer's problem is somewhat more general than that which we considered earlier, because now we are allowing the consumer to make a *continuous* choice of the quantity purchased. This falls into the category of so-called continuous/discrete models (see Train 1986, chap. 5). Our formulation of the problem is simplified, however, because there is no uncertainty over the *quantity* of purchases in (B.23);

the random term in utility affects only the choice of product in (B.22).[7] It turns out that in this setting, the aggregation results of McFadden (1978, 1981) apply equally well, and we can extend theorem 1 as theorem 2.[8]

Theorem 2

Let H be a nonnegative function defined over R_+^N that satisfies conditions (i)–(iii) of theorem 1. Define the cumulative distribution function F as in (B.3), and define an aggregate indirect utility function,

$$G(p_1, z_1, \ldots, p_N, z_N, y)$$
$$= \ln y + \ln H[\phi(p_1, z_1)^{-1}, \ldots, \phi(p_N, z_N)^{-1}] \qquad (B.25)$$

Then

   (a) Expected demand computed from (B.24) equals $-(\partial G/\partial p_j)/(\partial G/\partial y)$.
   (b) G equals the expected value of individual utility in (B.21) (up to a constant).

Thus, we can still compute demand using Roy's Identity as in part (a), and use the aggregate utility function to infer welfare as in part (b). Notice that expected utility can be rewritten in a more familiar form by taking the monotonic transformation $\tilde{G} = \exp(G)$, so that

$$\tilde{G}(p_1, z_1, \ldots, p_N, z_N, y) = yH[\phi(p_1, z_1)^{-1}, \ldots, \phi(p_N, z_N)^{-1}]. \quad (B.25')$$

This can be interpreted as an indirect utility function for the representative consumer.

To see the usefulness of this result, we consider again a random utility ε_j in (B.21) that is independently distributed across products, with the extreme value distribution, and derive a CES aggregate utility function.

Example 3: CES Demand System

Let us specify the individual utility functions as[9]

$$V_j^h = \ln y - \alpha \ln[p_j/f(z_j)] + \varepsilon_j^h, \qquad \alpha > 0, \qquad (B.26)$$

---

[7] In contrast, Dubin and McFadden (1984) consider an application where there is uncertainty in both the discrete choice of the product and the continuous amount to consume.
[8] The proof of theorem 2, based on the results of McFadden, is provided in Feenstra 1995, prop. 1.
[9] This utility function is not homogeneous of degree zero in income y and price p_j. To obtain this property, we should measure y and p_j relative to a numeraire price p_0, so that utility becomes $\ln(y/p_0) - \alpha \ln[(p_j/p_0)/f(z_j)]$, which is homogeneous of degree zero in (y, p_j, p_0).

where we are measuring prices relative to consumers' perceived "quality" of products $f(z_j)$. We will choose the function H as linear in its arguments, as in (B.7). It follows that the cumulative distribution function in (B.8) is the product of N iid extreme value distributions, so the errors in (B.26) are distributed as iid extreme value.

Then using (B.7), (B.25), and (B.26), we obtain the aggregate utility function as

$$G(p_1, z_1, \ldots, p_N, z_N, y) = y \sum_{j=1}^{N} [p_j / f(z_j)]^{-\alpha}, \tag{B.27}$$

so that expected aggregate demand is

$$-\frac{\partial G / \partial p_j}{\partial G / \partial y} = y \left(\frac{\alpha p_j^{-\alpha-1} / f(z_j)^{-\alpha}}{\sum_{k=1}^{N} [p_k / f(z_k)]^{-\alpha}} \right). \tag{B.28}$$

Thus, we obtain a CES indirect utility function in (B.27) for the aggregate consumer, with elasticity of substitution with $\sigma = 1 + \alpha$, and the associated CES demand in (B.28). This is an alternative demonstration of the result reached by Anderson, de Palma, and Thisse (1989; 1992, 85–90), that the CES utility function arrives from a discrete choice model with iid extreme value errors in random utility. Notice that this CES demand system is obtained with exactly the same assumptions on the random term in utility as the logit system (both used iid extreme value distributions), but differs from the logit system in allowing for *continuous* quantities demanded of the discrete good.

Example 4: Nested CES Demand System

As in our above discussion of the nested logit model, suppose that the consumers have a choice between two levels of the differentiated product. First, an individual decides whether to purchase a product in each of $g = 1, \ldots, G$ groups, and second, the individual decides which of the products in that group to purchase. Let the products available in each group g be denoted by the set $J_g \subset \{1, \ldots, N\}$, while J_0 denotes the outside option. Utility for consumer h is still given by (B.26), where the errors ε_j are distributed as extreme value but are *not* independent. We will specify the function H as in (B.14), with the cumulative density function F as in (B.15).

Then using (B.14), (B.25), and (B.26), we obtain the aggregate utility function

$$G(p_1, z_1, \ldots, p_N, z_N, y) = y \sum_{g=0}^{G} \left(\sum_{j \in J_g} [p_j / f(z_j)]^{-\alpha/(1-\rho_g)} \right)^{(1-\rho_g)}. \tag{B.29}$$

Applying Roy's Identity, we can readily obtain the expected demand for product j,

$$
X_j = -\frac{\partial G/\partial p_j}{\partial G/\partial y} = \left(\frac{\alpha y}{p_j}\right)\frac{[p_j/f(z_j)]^{-\alpha/(1-\rho_g)}}{D_g}
$$

$$
\times \frac{D_g^{(1-\rho_g)}}{\left[\sum_{g=1}^{G} D_g^{(1-\rho_g)}\right]}, \quad \text{for } j \in J_g, \tag{B.30}
$$

where the term $D_g \equiv \sum_{j\in J_g}[p_j/f(z_j)]^{-\alpha/(1-\rho_g)}$ in (B.30) is again the "inclusive value," analogous to (B.16). Notice that expected demand on the right-hand side of (B.30) is composed of three terms: the first term, $(\alpha y/p_j)$, is a conventional Cobb-Douglas demand function, reflecting the continuous demand for the product given the utility function in (B.26); the second term, $[p_j/f(z_j)]^{-\alpha/(1-\rho_i)}/D_g$, is the share of product j in the demand for group g; and the third term, $D_g^{(1-\rho_g)}/[\sum_{g=1}^{G} D_g^{(1-\rho_g)}]$, is the share of group g in the total demand for the product. The latter two terms both appear in the nested logit system (B.16), so the new feature of (B.30) is the continuous demand of $(\alpha y/p_j)$.

We can easily relate the parameters ρ_0 and ρ_i to the elasticity of substitution between products. Notice that for two products $i, j \in J_g$, we obtain relative demand from (B.30),

$$
\frac{X_i}{X_j} = \left(\frac{f(z_i)}{f(z_j)}\right)^{\alpha/(1-\rho_g)}\left(\frac{p_i}{p_j}\right)^{-[\alpha/(1-\rho_g)]-1}, \quad i, j \in J_g. \tag{B.31}
$$

Thus, the elasticity of substitution between two products in the same group is $1 + [\alpha/(1-\rho_g)] > 1$.

In addition, we can compute from (B.29) the ratio of expenditure on products from two different groups g and h:

$$
\frac{\sum_{i\in J_g} p_i X_i}{\sum_{j\in J_h} p_j X_j} = \frac{D_g^{(1-\rho_g)}}{D_h^{(1-\rho_h)}}, \quad i \in J_g \text{ and } j \in J_h. \tag{B.32}
$$

Let us define the price index for the products in group g as

$$
P_g \equiv \left[\sum_{j\in J_g}[p_j/f(z_j)]^{-\alpha(1-\rho_g)}\right]^{-(1-\rho_g)/\alpha} = D_g^{-(1-\rho_g)/\alpha}.
$$

Then we can rewrite the ratio of expenditures in (B.32) as

$$\frac{\left(\sum_{i \in J_g} p_i X_i\right)\Big/ P_g}{\left(\sum_{j \in J_h} p_j X_j\right)\Big/ P_h} = \left(\frac{P_g}{P_h}\right)^{-\alpha-1}, \quad i \in J_g, \text{ and } j \in J_h. \qquad (B.33)$$

The left side of (B.33) is ratio of expenditures on groups g and h, deflated by their price indexes, so it can be interpreted as a ratio of real expenditures. We see that this depends on the ratio of price indexes for the two groups, with the elasticity $1 + \alpha > 1$. Feenstra, Hanson and Lin (2002) have used a slightly more general version of this nested CES structure to estimate the gains from having Hong Kong traders act as intermediaries for firms outsourcing with China.

References

Abramovitz, Moses. 1956. "Resource and Output Trends in the U.S. since 1870." *American Economic Review: Papers and Proceedings* 46, no. 2:5–23.

Acemoglu, Daron, and Jaume Ventura. 2002. "The World Income Distribution." *Quarterly Journal of Economics* 117:659–94.

Acemoglu, Daron, Simon Johnson, and James A. Robinson. 2001. "The Colonial Origins of Comparative Development: An Empirical Investigation." *American Economic Review* 91:1369–1401.

Aghion, Phillipe, and Jean Tirole. 1997. "Formal and Real Authority in Organizations." *Journal of Political Economy* 105:1–29.

Aho, C. Michael, and Thomas O. Bayard. 1984. "Costs and Benefits of Trade Adjustment Assistance." In Robert E. Baldwin and Anne O. Krueger, eds., *The Structure and Evolution of Recent U.S. Trade Policy*. Chicago: University of Chicago Press and NBER.

Aitken, Brian, and Ann E. Harrison. 1999. "Do Domestic Firms Benefit from Foreign Investment? Evidence from Venezuela." *American Economic Review* 89:605–18.

Aitken, Brian, Ann E. Harrison, and Robert Lipsey. 1996. "Wages and Foreign Ownership: A Comparative Study of Mexico, Venezuela, and the United States." *Journal of International Economics* 40:345–71.

Akerlof, George, Andrew Rose, Janet Yellen, and Helga Hessenius. 1991. "East Germany in from the Cold: The Economic Aftermath of Currency Union." *Brookings Papers on Economic Activity* 1:1–87.

Alchian, Armen A., and William R. Allen. 1964. *University Economics*. Belmont, Calif.: Wadsworth.

Alesina, Alberto, and Dani Rodrik. 1994. "Distributive Politics and Economic Growth." *Quarterly Journal of Economics* 109:465–90.

Alterman, William F., W. Erwin Diewert, and Robert C. Feenstra. 1999. *International Trade Price Indexes and Seasonal Commodities*. Washington, D.C.: U.S. Department of Labor, Bureau of Labor Statistics.

Anderson, James A. 1979. "A Theoretical Foundation for the Gravity Equation." *American Economic Review* 69:106–16.

———. 1985. "The Relative Inefficiency of Quotas: The Cheese Case." *American Economic Review* 75:178–90.

———. 1988. *The Relative Inefficiency of Quotas*. Cambridge: MIT Press.

Anderson James A., and J. Peter Neary. 1996. "A New Approach to Evaluating Trade Policy." *Review of Economic Studies* 63:107–25.

Anderson, James A., and Eric van Wincoop. 2003. "Gravity with Gravitas: A Solution to the Border Puzzle." *American Economic Review* 93:170–92.

Anderson, Simon P., Andre de Palma, and Jacques-Francois Thisse. 1989. "Demand for Differentiated Products, Discrete Choice Models, and the Characteristics Approach." *Review of Economic Studies* 56:21–35.

———. 1992. *Discrete Choice Theory of Product Differentiation.* Cambridge: MIT Press.

Anderton, Bob, and Paul Brenton. 1999. "Outsourcing and Low-Skilled Workers in the UK." *Bulletin of Economic Research* 51:267–85.

Antràs, Pol. 2003. "Firms, Contracts, and Trade Structure." NBER Working Paper no. 9740.

Antweiler, Werner, and Daniel Trefler. 2002. "Increasing Returns and All That: A View from Trade." *American Economic Review* 92:93–119.

Archibald, Robert B. 1977. "On the Theory of Industrial Price Measurement: Output Price Indexes." *Annals of Economic and Social Measurement* 6:57–72.

Armington, Paul S. 1969. "A Theory of Demand for Products Distinguished by Place and Production." *IMF Staff Papers* 16:159–78.

Arndt, Sven W. 1998a. "Globalization and the Gains from Trade." In K. Jaeger and K.-J. Koch, eds., *Trade, Growth, and Economic Policy in Open Economies.* New York: Springer-Verlag.

———. 1998b, "Super-specialization and the Gains from Trade." *Contemporary Economic Policy* 16:480–85.

Arndt, Sven W., and Henryk Kierzkowski, eds. 2001. *Fragmentation: New Production and Trade Patterns in the World Economy.* Oxford: Oxford University Press.

Autor, David, Lawrence F. Katz, and Alan B. Krueger. 1998. "Computing Inequality: Have Computers Changed the Labor Market?" *Quarterly Journal of Economics* 113:1169–1213.

Aw, Bee Yan. 1983. "The Interpretation of Cross-Section Regression Tests of the Heckscher-Ohlin Theorem with Many Goods and Factors." *Journal of International Economics* 14:163–67.

Bagwell, Kyle. 1991. "Optimal Export Policy for a New-Product Monopoly." *American Economic Review* 81:1156–69.

Bagwell, Kyle, and Robert W. Staiger. 1999. "An Economic Theory of GATT." *American Economic Review* 89:215–48.

———. 2002. *The Economics of the World Trading System.* Cambridge: MIT Press.

Baier, Scott, and Jeffrey H. Bergstrand. 2001. "The Growth of World Trade: Tariffs, Transport Costs, and Income Similarity." *Journal of International Economics* 53:1–27.

———. 2002. "On the Endogeneity of International Trade Flows and Free Trade Agreements." University of Notre Dame, manuscript.

Baldwin, Richard E. 1995. "A Domino Theory of Regionalism." In Richard E. Baldwin, P. Haaparanta, and J. Kiander, eds., *Expending Membership in the European Union.* Cambridge: Cambridge University Press.

Baldwin, Richard E., and Paul R. Krugman. 1988a. "Market Access and International Competition: A Simulation Study of 16K Random Access Memories." In Robert C. Feenstra, ed., *Empirical Methods for International Trade.* Cambridge: MIT Press. Reprinted in Gene M. Grossman, ed., *Imperfect Competition and International Trade* (Cambridge: MIT Press, 1992).

———. 1988b. "Industrial Policy and International Competition in Wide-Bodied Aircraft." In Robert E. Baldwin, ed., *Trade Policy Issues and Empirical Analysis.* Chicago: University of Chicago and NBER.

Baldwin, Robert E. 1969. "The Case against Infant-Industry Protection." *Journal of Political Economy* 77:295–305.

———. 1971. "Determinants of the Commodity Structure of U.S. Trade." *American Economic Review* 61:126–46.

Baldwin, Robert E., and G. G. Cain. 2000. "Shifts in Relative U.S. Wages: The Role of Trade, Technology, and Factor Endowments." *Review of Economics and Statistics* 82:580–95.

Baldwin, Robert E. and R. S. Hilton. 1984. "A Technique for Indicating Comparative Costs and Predicting Changes in Trade Ratios." *Review of Economics and Statistics* 64:105–10.

Barro, Robert J. 1991. "Economic Growth in a Cross-Section of Countries." *Quarterly Journal of Economics* 106:407–43.

Barro, Robert J., and Xavier Salai-i-Martin. 1991. "Convergence across States and Regions." *Brookings Papers on Economic Activity* 1:107–58.

———. 1992. "Convergence." *Journal of Political Economy* 100:223–51.

Bartelsman, Eric J., and Wayne Gray. 1996. "The NBER Manufacturing Productivity Database." NBER Technical Working Paper no. 205.

Ben-David, Dan. 1993. "Trade Liberalization and Income Convergence." *Quarterly Journal of Economics* 108:653–79.

———. 1998. "Convergence Clubs and Subsistence Economies." *Journal of Development Economics* 55:155–71.

———. 2001. "Trade Liberalization and Income Convergence: A Comment." *Journal of International Economics* 55:229–34.

Benkard, C. Lanier. 2000a. "A Dynamic Analysis of the Market for Wide-Bodied Commercial Aircraft." NBER Working Paper no. 7710.

———. 2000b. "Learning and Forgetting: The Dynamics of Aircraft Production." *American Economic Review* 90:1034–54.

Bergin, Paul R., and Robert C. Feenstra. 2000. "Staggered Price Setting and Endogenous Persistence." *Journal of Monetary Economics* 45:657–80.

———. 2001. "Pricing to Market, Staggered Contracts, and Real Exchange Rate Persistence." *Journal of International Economics* 54:333–59.

Bergsten, C. Fred, Kimberly Ann Elliott, Jeffrey J. Schott, and Wendy E. Takacs. 1987. "Auction Quotas and United States Trade Policy." Institute for International Economics, Washington, D.C.

Bergstrand, Jeffrey H. 1985. "The Generalized Gravity Equation, Monopolistic Competition, and the Factor-Proportions Theory in International Trade." *Review of Economics and Statistics* 71:143–53.

———. 1989. "The Gravity Equation in International Trade: Some Microeconomic Foundations and Empirical Evidence." *Review of Economics and Statistics* 67:474–81.

Berman, Eli, John Bound, and Zvi Griliches. 1994. "Changes in the Demand for Skilled Labor within U.S. Manufacturing: Evidence from the Annual Survey of Manufactures." *Quarterly Journal of Economics* 104:367–98.

Berman, Eli, John Bound, and Stephen Machin. 1998. "Implications of Skill-Biased Technological Change: International Evidence." *Quarterly Journal of Economics* 113:1245–80.

Bernanke, Ben S., and Refet S. Gürkaynak. 2001. "Is Growth Exogenous? Taking Mankiw, Romer, and Weil Seriously." In Ben S. Bernanke and Kenneth Rogoff, eds., *NBER Macroeconomics Annual, 2001.* Cambridge: MIT Press.

Bernard, Andrew B., and J. Bradford Jensen. 1997. "Exporters, Skill Upgrading, and the Wage Gap." *Journal of International Economics* 42:3–32.

———. 2000. "Understanding Increasing *and* Decreasing Wage Inequality." In Robert C. Feenstra, ed., *The Impact of International Trade on Wages.* Chicago: University of Chicago Press and NBER.

Bernheim, B. Douglas, and Michael D. Whinston. 1986. "Menu Auctions, Resource Allocation, and Economic Influence." *Quarterly Journal of Economics* 101:1–31.

Bernhofen, Daniel M., and John C. Brown. 2001. "A Direct Test of the Theory of Comparative Advantage: The Case of Japan." Clark University, August, manuscript.

———. 2002. "Estimating the Comparative Advantage Gains from Trade." Clark University, June, manuscript.

Bernstein, Jeffrey R., and David E. Weinstein. 2002. "Do Endowments Predict the Location of Production? Evidence from National and International Data." *Journal of International Economics* 56:55–76.

Berry, Steven T. 1994. "Estimating Discrete-Choice Models of Product Differentiation." *Rand Journal of Economics* 25:242–46.

Berry, Steven T., James A. Levinsohn, and Ariel Pakes. 1995. "Automobile Prices in Market Equilibrium." *Econometrica* 63:841–90.

———. 1999. "Voluntary Export Restraints on Automobiles: Evaluating a Trade Policy." *American Economic Review* 89:400–30.

Bhagwati, Jagdish N. 1958. "Immiserizing Growth: A Geometrical Note." *Review of Economic Studies* 25:201–5.

———. 1965. "On the Equivalence of Tariffs and Quotas." In Robert E. Baldwin et al., *Trade Growth and the Balance of Payments: Essays in Honor of Gottfried Haberler.* Chicago: Rand-McNally.

———. 1972. "The Heckscher-Ohlin Theorem in the Multi-commodity Case." *Journal of Political Economy* 80:1052–55.

———. 1987. "Quid Pro Quo DFI and VIEs: A Political-Economy-Theoretic Analysis." *International Economic Journal* 1:1–14.

———. 1993. Regionalism and Multilateralism: An Overview." In Jaime De Melo and Arvind Panagariya, eds., *New Dimensions in Regional Integration.* Cambridge: Cambridge University Press.

———. 2002. *Free Trade Today.* Princeton: Princeton University Press.

Bhagwati, Jagdish N., Richard A. Brecher, Elias Dinopoulos, and T. N. Srinivasan. 1987. "Quid Pro Quo Foreign Investment and Welfare: A Political-Economy-Theoretic Model." *Journal of Development Economics* 27:127–38.

Bhagwati, Jagdish N., and Marvin H. Kosters, eds. 1994. *Trade and Wages: Leveling Wages Down?* Washington, D.C.: American Enterprise Institute.

Bhagwati, Jagdish N.. and T. N. Srinivasan. 1980. "Revenue Seeking: A Generalization of the Theory of Tariffs." *Journal of Political Economy* 88:1069–87.

Blomstrom, Magnus. 1986. "Foreign Investment and Productive Efficiency: The Case of Mexico." *Journal of Industrial Economics* 35:97–110.

Blomstrom, Magnus, and A. Kokko. 1998. Multinational Corporations and Spillovers." *Journal of Economic Surveys* 12:247–77.

Blomstrom, Magnus, and H. Persson. 1983. "Foreign Investment and Spillover Efficiency in an Underdeveloped Economy: Evidence from Mexican Manufacturing Industry." *World Development* 11:493–501.

Blomstrom, Magnus, and F. Sjoholm. 1999. "Technology Transfer and Spillovers: Does Local Participation with Multinationals Matter?" *European Economic Review* 43:915–23.

Blonigen, Bruce A. 1997. "Firm-Specific Assets and the Link between Exchange Rates and Foreign Direct Investment." *American Economic Review* 87:447–66.

———. 2001. "In Search of Substitution between Foreign Production and Exports." *Journal of International Economics* 53:81–104.

———. 2002. "Tariff Jumping Antidumping Duties." *Journal of International Economics* 57:31–50.

Blonigen, Bruce A., Ronald B. Davies, and Keith Head. 2003. "Estimating the Knowledge-Capital Model of the Multinational Enterprise: Comment," *American Economic Review* 93:980–94.

Blonigen, Bruce A., and Stephen E. Haynes. 2002. "Antidumping Investigations and the Pass-through of Antidumping Duties and Exchange Rates." *American Economic Review* 92:1044–61.

Blonigen, Bruce A., and KaSaundra Tomlin. 2001. "Size and Growth of Japanese Plants in the United States." *International Journal of Industrial Organization* 19:931–52.

Blum, Bernardo. 2003. "Decomposing the U.S. Income Inequality into Trade, Technological, and Factor Supply Components: Theory and Data." University of Toronto, manuscript.

Boorstein, Randi, and Robert C. Feenstra. 1991. "Quality Upgrading and Its Welfare Cost in U.S. Steel Imports, 1969–74." In Elhanan Helpman and Assaf Razin, eds. *International Trade and Trade Policy*. Cambridge: MIT Press.

Borjas, George J., Richard B. Freeman, and Lawrence F. Katz. 1997. "How Much Do Immigration and Trade Affect Labor Market Outcomes?" *Brookings Papers on Economic Activity* 1:1–90.

Bowen, Harry P., Edward E. Leamer, and Leo Sveikauskas. 1987. "Multicountry, Multifactor Tests of the Factor Abundance Theory." *American Economic Review* 77:791–809.

Bowen, Harry P., and Leo Sveikauskas. 1992. "Judging Factor Abundance." *Quarterly Journal of Economics* 107:599–620.

Brainard, S. Lael. 1997. "An Empirical Assessment of the Proximity-Concentration Trade-off between Multinational Sales and Trade." *American Economic Review* 87:520–44.

Brainard, S. Lael, and David Martimort. 1997. "Strategic Trade Policy with Incompletely Informed Policymakers." *Journal of International Economics* 42:33–65.

Brander, James A. 1981. "Intra-industry Trade in Identical Commodities." *Journal of International Economics* 11:1–14.

Brander, James A., and Paul R. Krugman. 1983. "A Reciprocal Dumping Model of International Trade." *Journal of International Economics* 15:313–23. Reprinted in Gene M. Grossman, ed., *Imperfect Competition and International Trade* (Cambridge: MIT Press, 1992).

Brander, James A., and Barbara Spencer. 1984a. "Trade Warfare: Tariffs and Cartels." *Journal of International Economics* 16:227–42.

———. 1984b, "Tariff Protection and Imperfect Competition." In Henryk Kierzkowski, ed., *Monopolistic Competition and International Trade.* Oxford: Oxford University Press. Reprinted in Gene M. Grossman, ed., *Imperfect Competition and International Trade.* (Cambridge: MIT Press,1992).

———. 1985. "Export Subsidies and International Market Share Rivalry." *Journal of International Economics* 16:83–100.

Branstetter, Lee. 2000. "Is Foreign Direct Investment a channel of Knowledge Spillovers? Evidence from Japan's FDI in the United States," NBER Working Paper no. 8015.

———. 2001. "Are Knowledge Spillovers International or Intranational in Scope? Microeconometric Evidence from Japan and the United States." *Journal of International Economics* 53:53–79.

Branstetter, Lee, and Robert C. Feenstra. 2002. "Trade and Foreign Direct Investment in China: A Political Economy Approach." *Journal of International Economics* 58:335–59.

Brecher, Richard A., and Ehsan U. Choudhri. 1982a. "The Leontief Paradox, Continued." *Journal of Political Economy* 90:820–23.

———. 1982b. "The Factor Content of International Trade without Factor Price Equalization." *Journal of International Economics* 12:276–83.

Brecher, Richard A, and Carlos Diaz-Alejandro. 1977. "Tariffs, Foreign Capital, and Immiserizing Growth." *Journal of International Economics* 7:317–22.

Bresnahan, Timothy F. 1981. "Departures from Marginal Cost Pricing in the American Automobile Industry." *Journal of Econometrics* 17:201–27.

Burgess, David F. 1974a. "A Cost Minimization Approach to Import Demand Equations." *Review of Economics and Statistics* 56:225–34.

———. 1974b. "Production Theory and the Derived Demand for Imports." *Journal of International Economics* 4:103–17.

———. 1976. "Tariffs and Income Distribution: Some Empirical Evidence for the United States." *Journal of Political Economy* 84:17–45.

Campa, Jose Manuel, and Linda S. Goldberg. 2002. "Exchange Rate Pass-through into Import Prices: A Macro or Micro Phenomenon?" NBER Working Paper no. 8934.

Cardell, N. Scott. 1997. "Variance Components Structures for the Extreme-Value and Logistic Distributions with Application to Models of Heterogeneity." *Econometric Theory* 13:185–213.

Carmichael, Calum M. 1987. "The Control of Export Credit Subsidies and Its Welfare Consequences." *Journal of International Economics* 23:1–19.

Carr, David L., James R. Markusen, and Keith E. Maskus. 2001. "Estimating the Knowledge-Capital Model of the Multinational Enterprise." *American Economic Review* 91:693–708.

Casella, Alessandra, and James E. Rauch. 2002. "Anonymous Market and Group Ties in International Trade." *Journal of International Economics* 58:19–48.

Caves, D. W., L. R. Christensen and W. E. Diewert. 1982. "The Economic Theory of Index Numbers and the Measurement of Input, Output, and Productivity." *Econometrica* 50:1393–414.

Chamberlin, Edward. 1936. *The Theory of Monopolistic Competition: A Re-orientation of the Theory of Value.* Cambridge: Harvard University Press.

Chang, Won, and L. Alan Winters. 2002. "How Regional Blocs Affect Excluded Countries: The Price Effects of MERCOSUR." *American Economic Review* 92:889–904.

Cheng, Leonard, and Henryk Kierzkowski, eds. 2001. *Globalization of Trade and Production in South-East Asia.* New York: Kluwer Academic Press.

Chipman, John S. 1987. "Compensation Principle." In John Eatwell, Murray Milgate, and Peter Newman, eds., *The New Palgrave: A Dictionary of Economics*, Vol. 1. London: Macmillan; and New York: Stockton.

Choi, Yong-Seok, and Pravin Krishna. 2004. "The Factor Content of Bilateral Trade: An Empirical Test." *Journal of Political Economy*, forthcoming.

Christensen, Laurits R., Dale W. Jorgenson, and Lawrence J. Lau. 1971. "Conjugate Duality and the Transcendental Logarithmic Production Function." *Econometrica* 39, no. 4:255–56.

Clark, Gregory, and Robert C. Feenstra. 2003. "Technology in the Great Divergence." In Michael D. Bordo, Alan M. Taylor, and Jeffrey G. Williamson, eds, *Globalization in Historical Perspective.* University of Chicago Press and NBER, 277–313.

Clausing, Kimberley A. 2001. "Trade Creation and Trade Diversion in the Canada-U.S. Free Trade Agreement." *Canadian Journal of Economics* 34:677–96.

Coase, Ronald. 1937. "The Nature of the Firm." *Economica* 4:386–405.

Coe, David T, and Elhanan Helpman. 1995. "International R&D Spillovers." *European Economic Review* 39:859–87.

Coe, David T., Elhanan Helpman, and Alexander W. Hoffmaister. 1997. "North-South R&D Spillovers." *Economic Journal* 107:134–49.

Collins, Susan M., ed. 1998. *Imports, Exports, and the American Worker.* Washington, D.C.: Brookings Institution Press.

Corden, W. Max. 1974. *Trade Policy and Economic Welfare.* Oxford: Clarendon Press.

———. 1984. "Normative Theory of International Trade." In Ronald W. Jones and Peter B. Kenen, eds., *Handbook of International Economics.* Vol. 1. Amsterdam North Holland.

Corden, W. Max, and J. Peter Neary. 1982. "Booming Sector and De-industrialization in a Small Open Economy." *Economic Journal* 82:825–48.

Cox, David, and Richard G. Harris. 1985. "Trade Liberalization and Industrial Organization: Some Estimates for Canada." *Journal of Political Economy* 93: 115–45.

———. 1986. "A Quantitative Assessment of the Economic Impact on Canada of Sectoral Free Trade with the United States." *Canadian Journal of Economics* 19:377–94.

Cragg, M., and M. Epelbaum. 1996. "Why Has Wage Dispersion Grown in Mexico? Is It the Incidence of Reforms or the Growing Demand for Skills?" *Journal of Development Economics* 51:99–116.

Cuñat, Alejandro, and Marco Maffezzoli. 2002. "Neoclassical Growth and Commodity Trade." London School of Economics and Università Bocconi, manuscript.

Das, Satya P., and Shabtai Donnenfeld. 1987. "Trade Policy and Its Impact on the Quality of Imports: A Welfare Analysis." *Journal of International Economics* 23:77–96.

———. 1989. "Oligopolistic Competition and International Trade: Quantity and Quality Restrictions." *Journal of International Economics* 27:299–318.

Dasgupta, P., and Joseph Stiglitz. 1988. "Learning-by-Doing, Market Structure, and Industrial and Trade Policies." *Oxford Economic Papers* 40:246–68.

Davidson, Carl, and Steven J. Matusz. 2002. "Trade Liberalization and Compensation." Michigan State University, manuscript.

Davis, Donald R. 1995. "Intra-industry Trade: A Heckscher-Ohlin-Ricardo Approach." 39:201–26.

———. 1998. "The Home Market, Trade, and Industrial Structure." *American Economic Review* 88:1264–76.

Davis, Donald R., and David E. Weinstein. 1996. "Does Economic Geography Matter for International Specialization?" NBER Working Paper no. 5706.

———. 1999. "Economic Geography and Regional Production Structure: An Empirical Investigation." *European Economic Review* 43:379–407.

———. 2001. "An Account of Global Factor Trade." *American Economic Review* 91:1423–53.

———. 2002a. "Bones, Bombs, and Break Points: The Geography of Economic Activity." *American Economic Review* 92:1269–89.

———. 2002b. "Technological Superiority and the Losses from Migration." NBER Working Paper no. 8971.

———. 2003. "The Factor Content of Trade." In E. Kwan Choi and James Harrigan, eds., *Handbook of International Trade*. Oxford: Blackwell.

Deardorff, Alan V. 1979. "Weak Links in the Chain of Comparative Advantage." *Journal of International Economics* 9:197–209.

———. 1984a. "Testing Trade Theories and Predicting Trade Flows." In Ronald Jones and Peter Kenen, eds., *Handbook of International Economics*, Vol. 1. Amsterdam: North Holland.

———. 1984b. "The General Validity of the Law of Comparative Advantage." *Journal of Political Economy* 88:941–57. Reprinted in Edward E. Leamer, ed., *International Economics* (New York: Worth 2001).

———. 1987. "Safeguards Policy and the Conservative Social Welfare Function." In Henryk Kierzkowski, ed., *Protection and Competition in International Trade: Essays in Honor of W. M. Corden*. Oxford: Blackwell.

———. 2000. "Factor Prices and the Factor Content of Trade Revisited: What's the Use?" *Journal of International Economics* 50:73–90.

Deardorff, Alan V., and Robert W. Staiger. 1989. "An Interpretation of the Factor Content of Trade." *Journal of International Economics* 24:93–108.

Debaere, Peter. 2002. "Testing 'New' Trade Theory with Testing for Gravity: Re-interpreting the Evidence." University of Texas at Austin, manuscript.

———. 2003. "Relative Factor Abundance and Trade." *Journal of Political Economy* 111:589–610.

Debaere, Peter, and Hongshik Lee. 2002. "The Real-Side Determinants of Countries' Terms of Trade: A Panel Data Analysis." University of Texas at Austin, manuscript.

Debaere, Peter, and Ufuk Demiroglu. 2003. "On the Similarity of Country Endowments." *Journal of International Economics* 59:101–36.

Dell'mour, R., P. Egger, K. Gugler, and M. Pfaffermayr. 2000. "Outsourcing of Austrian Manufacturing to Eastern European Countries: Effects on Productivity and the Labor Market." In Sven Arndt, H. Handler, and D. Salvatore, eds., *Fragmentation of the Value Added Chain*. Vienna: Austrian Ministry for Economic Affairs and Labour.

Dicken, Peter, Philip F. Kelley, Kris Olds, and Henry Wai-Chung Yeung. 2001. "Chains and Networks, Territories and Scales: Towards a Relational Framework for Analyzing the Global Economy." *Global Networks* 1:99–123.

Diewert, W. Erwin. 1974. "Applications of Duality Theory." In M. Intriligator and D. Kendrick, eds., *Frontiers of Quantitative Economics*, Vol. 2. Amsterdam: North-Holland.

Diewert, W. Erwin. 1976. "Exact and Superlative Index Numbers." *Journal of Econometrics* 4:115–46.

———. 1983. "The Theory of the Output Price Index and the Measurement of Real Output Change." In W. E. Diewert and C. Montmarquette, eds., *Price Level Measurement*. Ottawa: Statistics Canada.

Diewert, W. Erwin, and Catherine J. Morrison. 1986. "Adjusting Outputs and Productivity Indexes for Changes in the Terms of Trade." *Economic Journal* 96:659–79.

Diewert, W. Erwin, Arja H. Turunen-Red, and Alan D. Woodland. 1989. "Productivity and Pareto Improving Changes in Taxes and Tariffs." *Review of Economic Studies* 56:199–216.

Dikhanov, Yuri. 1999. "A Critique of CIA Estimates of Soviet Performance from the Gerschenkron Perspective." In Alan Heston and Robert E. Lipsey, eds., *International and Interarea Comparisons of Income, Output, and Prices*. Chicago: University of Chicago Press.

Dinopoulos, Elias. 1989. "Quid Pro Quo Foreign Investment." *Economics and Politics* 1:145–60.

———. 1992. "Quid Pro Quo Foreign Investment and VERs: A Nash Bargaining Approach." *Economics and Politics* 4:43–60.

Dinopoulos, Elias, and Mordechai E. Kreinin. 1988. "Effects on the U.S.-Japan Auto VER on European Prices and on U.S. Welfare." *Review of Economics and Statistics* 70:484–91.

Dinopoulos, Elias, and Paul Segerstrom. 1999a. "The Dynamic Effects of Contingent Tariffs." *Journal of International Economics* 47:191–222.

———. 1999b. "A Schumpeterian Model of Protection and Real Wages." *American Economic Review* 89:450–72.

Dinopoulos, Elias, and Constantinos Syropoulos. 2001. "Globalization and Scale-Invariant Growth." University of Florida and Florida International University, manuscript.

Dixit, Avinash K. 1986. "Gains from Trade without Lump Sum Compensation." *Journal of International Economics* 21:111–22.

Dixit, Avinash K., and A. S. Kyle. 1985. "The Use of Protection and Subsidies for Entry Promotion and Deterrence." *American Economic Review* 75:139–52.

Dixit, Avinash K., and Victor Norman. 1980. *Theory of International Trade*. Cambridge: Cambridge University Press.

Dixit, Avinash K., and Joseph E. Stiglitz. 1977. "Monopolistic Competition and Optimum Product Diversity." *American Economic Review* 67:297–308.

Dollar, David. 1992. "Outward-Oriented Developing Economies Really Do Grow More Rapidly: Evidence from 95 LDCs, 1976–1985." *Economic Development and Cultural Change* 40:523–44.

Dollar, David, Edward N. Wolff, and William Baumol. 1988. "The Factor Price Equalization Model and Industry Labor Productivity: An Empirical Test." In Robert C. Feenstra, ed., *Empirical Methods for International Trade*. Cambridge: MIT Press.

Dollar, David, and Aart Kraay. 2001a. "Trade, Growth, and Poverty." World Bank Working Paper no. 2615.

———. 2001b. "Growth Is Good for the Poor?" World Bank, manuscript.

Doms, Mark E. and J. Bradford Jensen. 1998. "Comparing Wages, Skills, and Productivity between Domestic and Foreign-Owned Manufacturing Establishments in the United States." In Robert E. Baldwin, Robert E. Lipsey, and J. David Richardson, eds., *Geography and Ownership as Bases for Accounting*. Chicago: University of Chicago Press and NBER.

Dornbusch, Rudiger, Stanley Fischer, and Paul A. Samuelson. 1977. "Comparative Advantage, Trade, and Payments in a Ricardian Model with a Continuum of Goods." *American Economic Review* 67:823–39.

———. 1980. "Heckscher-Ohlin Trade Theory with a Continuum of Goods." *Quarterly Journal of Economics* 95:203–24.

Dubin, Jeffrey A., and Daniel L. McFadden. 1984. "An Econometric Analysis of Residential Electric Appliance Holdings and Consumption." *Econometrica* 52:345–62.

Dunning, John H. 1977. "Trade, Location of Economic Activity and the MNE: A Search for an Eclectic Approach." In B. Ohlin, P. O. Hesselborn, and P. M. Wijkman, eds., *The International Allocation of Economic Activity*. London: Macmillan.

———. 1981. *International Production and the Multinational Enterprise*. London: George Allen and Unwin.

Dutt, Pushan and Devashish Mitra. 2002. "Endogenous Trade Policy through Majority Voting." *Journal of International Economics* 58:107–34.

Easterly, William and Ross Levine. 2000. "It's Not Factor Accumulation: Stylized Facts and Growth Models." World Bank and University of Minnesota, manuscript.

Eastman, H. C. and S. Stykolt. 1967. *The Tariff and Competition in Canada*. Toronto: Macmillan.

Eaton, Jonathan, and Gene M. Grossman. 1986. "Optimal Trade and Industrial Policy under Oligopoly." *Quarterly Journal of Economics* 101:383–406. Reprinted in Gene M. Grossman, ed., *Imperfect Competition and International Trade* (Cambridge: MIT Press, 1992).

Eaton, Jonathan and Samuel Kortum. 2002. "Technology, Geography, and Trade." *Econometrica* 70:1741–80.

Edwards, Sebastian. 1998. "Openess, Productivity, and Growth: What Do We Really Know?" *Economic Journal* 108:383–98.

Engel, Charles, and John H. Rogers. 1996. "How Wide Is the Border?" *American Economic Review* 86:1112–25. Reprinted in Edward E. Leamer, ed., *International Economics* (New York: Worth, 2001).

Estevadeordal, Antoni and Alan M. Taylor. 2002a. "A Century of Missing Trade?" *American Economic Review* 92:383–93.

———. 2002b. "Testing Trade Theory in Ohlin's Time." In Ronald Findlay, Lars Jonung, and Mats Lundahl, eds., *Bertil Ohlin: A Centennial Celebration, 1899–1999*. Cambridge: MIT Press.

Ethier, Wilfred J. 1974. "Some of the Theorems of International Trade with Many Good and Factors." *Journal of International Economics* 4:199–206.

———. 1979. "Internationally Decreasing Costs and World Trade." *Journal of International Economics* 9:1–24.

———. 1982a. "Decreasing Costs in International Trade and Frank Graham's Argument for Protection." *Econometrica* 50:1243–68.

———. 1982b. "Dumping." *Journal of Political Economy* 90:487–506.

———. 1984. "Higher Dimensional Issues in Trade Theory." In Ronald W. Jones and Peter B. Kenen, eds., *Handbook of International Economics*, Vol. 1. Amsterdam: North Holland. 131–84.

———. 1986. "The Multinational Firm." *Quarterly Journal of Economics* 101:805–33.

———. 1998. "Regionalism in a Multilateral World." *Journal of Political Economy* 106:1214–45.

Ethier, Wilfred, and James R. Markusen. 1996. "Multinational Firms, Technology Diffusion, and Trade." *Journal of International Economics* 41:1–28.

Evenett, Simon J., and Wolfgang Keller. 2002. "On Theories Explaining the Success of the Gravity Equation." *Journal of Political Economy* 110:281–316.

Facchini, Giovanni, and Gerald Willmann. 1999. "The Gains from Duty Free Zones." *Journal of International Economics* 49:403–12.

Feenstra, Robert C. 1984. "Voluntary Export Restraints in U.S. Autos, 1980–81: Quality, Employment, and Welfare Effects." In R. E. Baldwin and A. O. Krueger, eds., *The Structure and Evolution of Recent U.S. Trade Policy*. Chicago: University of Chicago Press and NBER.

———. 1985. "Automobile Prices and Protection: The U.S.-Japan Trade Restraint." *Journal of Policy Modeling* 7:49–68.

———. 1986. "Trade Policy with Several Goods and 'Market Linkages'." *Journal of International Economics* 20:249–67.

———. 1988a. "Quality Change under Trade Restraints in Japanese Autos." *Quarterly Journal of Economics* 103:131–46.

———. 1988b. "Gains from Trade in Differentiated Products: Japanese Compact Trucks." In Robert C. Feenstra, ed., *Empirical Methods for International Trade*. Cambridge: MIT Press.

———. 1989. Symmetric Pass-through of Tariffs and Exchange Rates under Imperfect Competition: An Empirical Test." *Journal of International Economics* 27:25–45.

———. 1992. "How Costly is Protectionism?" *Journal of Economic Perspectives* 6:159–78.

———. 1993. "Measuring the Welfare Effect of Quality Change: Theory and Application to Japanese Autos." NBER Working Paper no. 4401.

———. 1994. "New Product Varieties and the Measurement of International Prices." *American Economic Review* 84:157–77.

———. 1995. "Exact Hedonic Price Indexes." *Review of Economics and Statistics* 78:634–53.

———. 1996. "Trade and Uneven Growth." *Journal of Development Economics* 49:229–56.

———. 1998. "Integration and Disintegration in the Global Economy." *Journal of Economic Perspectives* 12:31–50.

———. 1999. "Facts and Fallacies about Foreign Direct Investment." In Martin Feldstein, ed., *International Capital Flows*. Chicago: University of Chicago Press and NBER.

———. 2002. "Border Effects and the Gravity Equation: Consistent Methods for Estimation." *Scottish Journal of Political Economy* 49:491–506.

———. 2003. "A Homothetic Utility Function for Monopolistic Competition Models, without Constant Price Elasticity." *Economic Letters* 78:79–86.

———. ed. 2000. *The Impact of International Trade on Wages*. Chicago: University of Chicago Press.

Feenstra, Robert C., and Gary G. Hamilton. 2004. *Emergent Economies, Divergent Paths: Economic Organization and International Trade in South Korea and Taiwan*. Cambridge: Cambridge University Press, forthcoming.

Feenstra, Robert C., Gary G. Hamilton, and Deng-Shing Huang. 2001. "The Organization of the Taiwanese and South Korean Economies: A Comparative Equilibrium Analysis." In Alessandra Casella and James E. Rauch, eds., *Networks and Markets*. New York: Russell Sage.

Feenstra, Robert C., and Gordon H. Hanson. 1996. "Foreign Investment, Outsourcing, and Relative Wages." In Robert C. Feenstra, Gene M. Grossman and Douglas A. Irwin, eds., *The Political Economy of Trade Policy: Papers in Honor of Jagdish Bhagwati*. Cambridge: MIT Press.

———. 1997. "Foreign Direct Investment and Relative Wages: Evidence from Mexico's Maquiladoras." *Journal of International Economics* 42:371–93.

———. 1999. "The Impact of Outsourcing and High-Technology Capital on Wages: Estimates for the U.S., 1979–1990." *Quarterly Journal of Economics* 114:907–40.

———. 2000. "Aggregation Bias in the Factor Content of Trade: Evidence from U.S. Manufacturing." *American Economic Review: Papers and Proceedings* 90, no. 2:155–60.

———. 2001. "Intermediaries in Entrepôt Trade: Hong Kong Re-exports of Chinese Goods." NBER Working Paper no. 8088.

———. 2003. "Global Production Sharing and Rising Inequality: A Survey of Trade and Wages." In E. Kwan Choi and James Harrigan, eds., *Handbook of International Trade*. Oxford: Blackwell.

Feenstra, Robert C., Gordon H. Hanson, and Songhua Lin. 2002. "The Value of Information in International Trade: Gains to Outsourcing through Hong Kong." NBER Working Paper no. 9328.

Feenstra, Robert C., Deng-Shing Huang, and Gary G. Hamilton. 2003. "A Market-Power Based Model of Business Groups." *Journal of Economic Behavior and Organization* 51:459–85.

Feenstra, Robert C., and James Levinsohn. 1995. "Estimating Markups and Market Conduct with Multidimensional Product Attributes." *Review of Economics Studies* 62:19–52.

Feenstra, Robert C., and Tracy R. Lewis. 1991a. "Distributing the Gains from Trade with Incomplete Information." *Economics and Politics* 3:21–39.

———. 1991b. "Negotiated Trade Restrictions with Private Political Pressure." *Quarterly Journal of Economics* 106:1287–1307.

———. 1994. "Trade Adjustment Assistance and Pareto Gains from Trade." *Journal of International Economics* 36:201–22.

Feenstra, Robert C., Dorsati Madani, Tzu-Han Yang, and Chi-Yuan Liang. 1999. "Testing Endogenous Growth in South Korea and Taiwan." *Journal of Development Economics* 60:317–41.

Feenstra, Robert C., and James R. Markusen. 1995. "Accounting for Growth with New Intermediate Inputs." *International Economic Review* 35:429–47.

Feenstra, Robert C., James R. Markusen, and Andrew K. Rose. 1998. "Understanding the Home Market Effect and the Gravity Equation: The Role of Differentiating Goods." NBER Working Paper no. 6804.

———. 2001. "Using the Gravity Equation to Differentiate among Alternative Theories of Trade." *Canadian Journal of Economics* 34:430–47.

Feenstra, Robert C., John McMillan, and Tracy R. Lewis. 1990. "Designing Policies to Open Trade." *Economics and Politics* 2:223–40.

Feenstra, Robert C., Tzu-Han Yang, and Gary Hamilton. 1999. "Business Groups and Product Variety in Trade: Evidence from South Korea, Taiwan, and Japan." *Journal of International Economics* 48:71–100.

Fernandez, Raquel, and Dani Rodrik. 1991. "Resistance to Reform: Status Quo Bias in the Presence of Individual-Specific Uncertainty." *American Economic Review* 81:1146–55.

Findlay, Ronald. 1984. "Growth and Development in Trade Models." In Ronald W. Jones and Peter B. Kenen, eds., *Handbook of International Economics*, Vol. 1. Amsterdam: North Holland.

———. 1996. "Modeling Global Interdependence: Centers, Peripheries, and Frontiers." *American Economic Review: Papers and Proceedings*, 86, no. 2:47–51.

Findlay, Ronald, and Harry Grubert. 1959. "Factor Intensities, Technological Progress, and the Terms of Trade." *Oxford Economic Papers* 1:111–21.

Findlay, Ronald, and Stanislaw Wellisz. 1982. "Endogenous Tariffs, the Political Economy of Trade Restrictions, and Welfare." In Jagdish N. Bhagwati, ed., *Import Competition and Response*. Chicago: University of Chicago Press and NBER.

Fisher, Franklin M., and Karl Shell. 1972. *The Economic Theory of Price Indexes*. New York: Academic Press.

Fisher, Irving. 1922. *The Making of Index Numbers*. Boston: Houghton Mifflin.

Francois, Joseph, and Tanguy van Ypersele. 2002. "On the Protection of Cultural Goods." *Journal of International Economics* 56:359–70.

Frankel, Jeffrey A. 1997. *Regional Trade Blocs in the World Economic System.* Washington, D.C.: Institute for International Economics.

Frankel, Jeffrey A., and David Romer. 1999. "Does Trade Cause Growth?" *American Economic Review* 89:379–99.

Freeman, Richard B. 1995. "Are Your Wages Set in Beijing?" *Journal of Economic Perspectives* 9:15–32.

Freeman, Richard B., and Lawrence Katz. 1994. "Rising Wage Inequality: The United States vs. Other Advanced Countries." In Richard Freeman, ed., *Working under Different Rules.* New York: Russell Sage Foundation.

Froot, Kenneth A., and Jeremy C. Stein. 1991. "Exchange Rates and Foreign Direct Investment: An Imperfect Capital Markets Approach." *Quarterly Journal of Economics* 106:1191–1217.

Fujita, Masahisa, Paul R. Krugman, and Anthony Venables. 1999. *The Spatial Economy.* Cambridge: MIT Press.

Funk, Mark. 2001. "Trade and International R&D Spillovers among OECD Countries." *Southern Economic Journal* 67:725–36.

Funke, Michael, and Ralf Ruhwedel. 2001a. "Product Variety and Economic Growth: Empirical Evidence from the OECD Countries." *IMF Staff Papers* 48:225–42.

———. 2001b. "Export Variety and Export Performance: Evidence from East Asia." *Journal of Asian Economics* 12:493–505.

———. 2002. "Export Variety and Export Performance: Empirical Evidence for the OECD Countries." *Weltwirtschaftliches Archiv* 138:97–114.

Gabaix, Xavier. 1999. "The Factor Content of Trade: A Rejection of the Heckscher-Ohlin-Leontief Hypothesis." Department of Economics, MIT, manuscript.

Gallaway, Michael P., Bruce A. Blonigen, and Joseph E. Flynn. 1999. "Welfare Costs of the US Antidumping and Countervailing Duty Laws." *Journal of International Economics* 49:211–44.

Gao, Ting. 2002. "Outsourcing and Wage Inequality in a Simple Economic Geography Model." University of Missouri, manuscript.

Gawande, Kishore. 1995. "Are U.S. Nontariff Barriers Retaliatory? An Application of Extreme Bounds Analysis in the Tobit Model." *Review of Economics and Statistics* 77:677–88.

Gawande, Kishore, and Usree Bandyopadhyay. 2000. "Is Protection for Sale? A Test of the Grossman-Helpman Theory of Endogenous Protection." *Review of Economics and Statistics* 82:139–52.

Gawande, Kishore, and Pravin Krishna. 2003. "The Political Economy of Trade Policy: Empirical Approaches." In E. Kwan Choi and James Harrigan, eds., *Handbook of International Trade.* Oxford: Blackwell.

Geishecker, Ingo. 2002. "Outsourcing and the Relative Demand for Low-Skilled Labour in German Manufacturing. New Evidence." German Institute for Economic Research, DIW-Berlin, Discussion Paper no. 313, November.

Gereffi, Gary, and Miguel Korzeniewicz, eds. 1994. *Commodity Chains and Global Capitalism.* Westport, Conn.: Praeger.

Gerschenkron, Alexander. 1951. *A Dollar Index of Soviet Machinery Output, 1927–28 to 1937.* Report R-197. Santa Monica: Rand Corporation.

Goldberg, Linda S., and Michael W. Klein. 2000. "International Trade and Factor

Mobility: An Empirical Investigation." In Guillermo Calvo, Rudiger Dornbusch, and Maurice Obstfeld, eds., *Festschrift in Honor of Robert Mundell.* Cambridge: MIT Press.

Goldberg, Pinelopi Koujianou. 1995. "Product Differentiation and Oligopoly in International Markets: The Case of the U.S. Automobile Industry." *Econometrica* 63:891–951.

Goldberg, Pinelopi Koujianou, and Michael M. Knetter. 1997. "Goods Prices and Exchange Rates: What Have We Learned?" *Journal of Economic Literature* 35:1244–72.

Goldberg, Pinelopi Koujianou, and Giovanni Maggi. 1999. "Protection for Sale: An Empirical Investigation." *American Economic Review* 89:1135–55.

Goolsbee, Austan. 2003. "Taxes and the Quality of Capital." *Journal of Public Economics*, forthcoming.

Görg, Holger, A. Hijzen, and R. C. Hine. 2001. "International Fragmentation and Relative Wages in the U.K." Leverhulme Centre for Research on Globalization and Economic Policy, University of Nottingham, Research Paper 2001/33.

Gould, David M. 1994. "Immigrant Links to the Home Country: Empirical Implications for U.S. Bilateral Trade Flows." *Review of Economics and Statistics* 76:302–16.

Graham, Frank. 1923. "Some Aspects of Protection Further Considered." *Quarterly Journal of Economics* 37:199–227.

Grether, Jean-Marie, Jaime de Melo, and Marcelo Olarrega. 2001. "Who Determines Mexican Trade Policy?" *Journal of Development Economics* 64:343–70.

Grinols, Earl L. 1981. "An Extension of the Kemp-Wan Theorem on the Formation of Customs Unions." *Journal of International Economics* 11:259–66.

———. 1984. "The Thorn in the Lion's Paw: Has Britain Paid Too Much for Common Market Membership?" *Journal of International Economics* 16:271–93.

———. 1991. "Increasing Returns and the Gains from Trade." *International Economics Review* 32:973–84.

Grinols, Earl L., and Kar-yiu Wong. 1991. "An Exact Measure of Welfare Change." *Canadian Journal of Economics* 24:429–49.

Grossman, Gene M., and Elhanan Helpman. 1989. "Product Development and International Trade." *Journal of Political Economy* 97:1261–83.

———. 1990. "Comparative Advantage and Long Run Growth." *American Economic Review* 80:796–815.

———. 1991. *Innovation and Growth in the Global Economy.* Cambridge: MIT Press.

———. 1994. "Protection for Sale." *American Economic Review* 84:833–850.

———. 1995a. "Trade Wars and Trade Talks." *Journal of Political Economy* 103:675–708.

———. 1995b. "The Politics of Free-Trade Agreements." *American Economic Review* 85:667–90.

———. 1996. "Foreign Investment with Endogenous Protection." In Robert C. Feenstra, Gene M. Grossman and Douglas A. Irwin, eds., *The Political Economy of Trade Policy: Papers in Honor of Jagdish Bhagwati.* Cambridge: MIT Press.

———. 2001. *Special Interest Politics.* Cambridge: MIT Press.

———. 2002a. "Integration versus Outsourcing in Industry Equilibrium." *Quarterly Journal of Economics* 117:85–120.

———. 2002b. "Outsourcing in a Global Economy." NBER Working Paper no. 8728.

———. 2002c. "Managerial Incentives and the International Organization of Production." NBER Working Paper no. 9403.

Grossman, Sanford J., and Oliver D. Hart. 1986. "Costs and Benefits of Ownership: A Theory of Vertical and Lateral Integration." *Journal of Political Economy* 94:691–719.

Haddad, Mona, and Ann E. Harrison. 1993. "Are There Positive Spillovers from Foreign Direct Investment? Evidence from Panel Data for Morocco." *Journal of Development Economics* 42:51–74.

Hall, Robert. 1988. "The Relation between Price and Marginal Cost in U.S. Industry." *Journal of Political Economy* 96:921–47.

Hamilton, Alexander. 1791. *Report on Manufactures.* Reprinted in U.S. Senate Documents, Vol. 22, no. 172. Washington, D.C.: U.S. Congress, 1913.

Hansen, Wendy, and Thomas J. Prusa. 1995. "The Road Most Taken: The Rise of Title VII Protection." *World Economy* 295–313.

Hanson, Gordon H. 1997. "Increasing Returns, Trade and the Regional Structure of Wages." *Economic Journal* 107:113–33.

———. 1998. "Market Potential, Increasing Returns, and Geographic Concentration." NBER Working Paper no. 6429.

Hanson, Gordon H. and Ann E. Harrison. 1999. "Trade, Technology, and Wage Inequality." *Industrial and Labor Relations Review* 52:271–88.

Hanson, Gordon H., Raymond J. Mataloni Jr., and Matthew J. Slaughter. 2001. "Expansion Strategies of U.S. Multinational Firms." In Dani Rodrik and Susan Collins, eds., *Brookings Trade Forum, 2001.* Washington. D.C.: Brookings Institution Press.

Harper, Michael J., Ernst R. Berndt, and David O. Wood. 1989. "Rates of Return and Capital Aggregation Using Alternative Rental Prices." In Dale W. Jorgenson and Ralph Landau, eds., *Technology and Capital Formation.* Cambridge: MIT Press.

Harrigan, James. 1995. "Factor Endowments and the International Location of Production: Econometric Evidence for the OECD, 1970–1985." *Journal of International Economics* 39:123–41.

———. 1996. "Openness to Trade in Manufactures in the OECD." *Journal of International Economics* 40:23–39.

———. 1997. "Technology, Factor Supplies, and International Specialization: Estimating the Neoclassical Model." *American Economic Review* 87:475–94.

———. 2000. "International Trade and American Wages in General Equilibrium, 1967–1995." In Robert C. Feenstra, ed., *The Impact of International Trade on Wages.* Chicago: University of Chicago Press.

———. 2003. "Specialization and the Volume of Production: Do the Data Obey the Laws?" In E. Kwan Choi and James Harrigan, eds., *Handbook of International Trade.* Oxford: Blackwell.

Harrigan, James, and Rita A. Balaban. 1999. "U.S. Wage Effects in General Equilibrium: The Effects of Prices, Technology, and Factor Supplies, 1963–1991." NBER Working Paper no. 6981.

Harrigan, James, and Egon Zakrajšek. 2000. "Factor Supplies and Specialization in the World Economy." NBER Working Paper no. 7848, and Federal Reserve Bank of New York Staff Report, no. 107, August.

Harris, Richard. 1984. "Applied General Equilibrium Analysis of Small Open Economies with Scale Economies and Imperfect Competition." *American Economic Review* 74:1016–32.

———. 1985. "Why Voluntary Export Restraints Are 'Voluntary'." *Canadian Journal of Economics* 18:799–809.

Harrison, Ann E. 1994. "Productivity, Imperfect Competition, and Trade Reform: Theory and Evidence." *Journal of International Economics* 36:53–73.

———. 1996. "Openness and Growth: A Time-Series, Cross-section Analysis for Developing Countries." *Journal of Development Economics* 48:419–47.

Hart, Oliver, and John Moore. 1990. "Property Rights and the Nature of the Firm." *Journal of Political Economy* 98:1119–58.

———. 1999. "Foundations of Incomplete Contracts." *Review of Economics Studies* 66:115–38.

Hartigan, James C. 1996. "Predatory Dumping." *Canadian Journal of Economics* 29:228–39.

Haskel, Jonathan E. and Matthew J. Slaughter. 2001. "Trade, Technology, and U.K. Wage Inequality." *Economic Journal* 110:1–27.

Head, Keith C. 1994. "Infant Industry Protection in the Steel Rail Industry." *Journal of International Economics* 37:141–66.

Head, Keith C., and John C. Ries. 1998. "Immigration and Trade Creation: Econometric Evidence from Canada." *Journal of International Economics* 31: 47–62.

———. 1999. "Rationalization Effects of Tariff Reductions." *Journal of International Economics* 47:295–320.

———. 2000. "Offshore Production and Skill Upgrading by Japanese Manufacturing Firms." *Journal of International Economics* 58:81–106.

———. 2002. "Increasing Returns versus National Product Differentiation as an Explanation for the Pattern of US-Canada Trade." *American Economic Review*, 91:858–76.

Head, Keith C., John Ries, and Barbara Spencer. 2002. "Vertical Networks and U.S. Auto Parts Exports: Is Japan Different?" University of British Columbia, manuscript.

Heckscher, Eli, and Bertil Ohlin. 1991. *Heckscher-Ohlin Trade Theory*. Ed. Harry Flam and M. June Flanders. Cambridge: MIT Press.

Helliwell, John F. 1998. *How Much Do National Borders Matter?* Washington, D.C.: Brookings Institution Press.

———. 2002. "Border Effects: Assessing Their Implications for Canadian Policy in a North-American Context." University of British Columbia, manuscript.

Helliwell, John F., and Genevieve Verdier. 2001. "Measuring Internal Trade Distances: A New Method Applied to Estimate Provincial Border Effects in Canada." *Canadian Journal of Economics* 34:1024–41.

Helpman, Elhanan. 1981. "International Trade in the Presence of Product Differentiation, Economics of Scale, and Monopolistic Competition: A Chamberlin-Heckscher-Ohlin Approach." *Journal of International Economics* 11:305–40.

———. 1984a. "The Factor Content of Foreign Trade." *Economic Journal* 94:84–94.

———. 1984b. "Increasing Returns, Imperfect Markets, and Trade Theory." In Ronald W. Jones and Peter B. Kenen, eds., *Handbook of International Economics,* Vol. 1. Amsterdam: North Holland.

———. 1984c. "A Simple Theory of International Trade with Multinational Corporations." *Journal of Political Economy* 92:451–71.

———. 1985, "Multinational Corporations and Trade Structure." *Review of Economic Studies* 102:443–57.

———. 1987. "Imperfect Competition and International Trade: Evidence from Fourteen Industrial Countries." *Journal of the Japanese and International Economies* 1:62–81.

———. 1990. "Monopolistic Competition in Trade Theory." International Finance Section, Princeton University, Special Papers in International Finance no. 16, June.

Helpman, Elhanan, and Paul R. Krugman. 1985. *Market Structure and Foreign Trade.* Cambridge: MIT Press.

———. 1989. *Trade Policy and Market Structure.* Cambridge: MIT Press.

Hillman, Arye L., 1989, *The Political Economy of Protection.* London: Harwood Academic.

Holmstrom, Bengt, and Paul Milgrom. 1994. "The Firm as an Incentive System." *American Economic Review* 84:972–91.

Horn, Henrik, and Lars Persson. 2001. "Equilibrium Ownership of an International Oligopoly." *Journal of International Economics* 53:307–33.

Hornig, Ellen, Richard N. Boisvert, and David Blandford. 1990. "Quota Rents and Subsidies: The case of U.S. Cheese Import Quotas." *European Review of Agricultural Economics* 17:421–34.

Horstmann, Ignatius J., and James R. Markusen. 1986. "Up the Average Cost Curve: Inefficient Entry and the New Protectionism." *Journal of International Economics* 20:225–47.

———. 1987. "Licensing versus Direct Investment: A Model of Internalization by the Multinational Enterprise." *Canadian Journal of Economics* 20:464–81.

———. 1992. "Endogenous Market Structures in International Trade." *Journal of International Economics* 32:109–29.

———. 1996. "Exploring New Markets: Direct Investment, Contractual Relationships, and the Multinational Enterprise." *International Economic Review* 37:1–20.

Howenstein, Ned G., and William J. Zeile. 1994. "Characteristics of Foreign Owned U.S. Establishments." *Survey of Current Business* 74:34–59.

Hsieh, Chang-Tai, and Keong T. Woo. 1999. "The Impact of Outsourcing to China on Hong Kong's Labor Market." Princeton University, manuscript.

Hummels, David. 1999. "Towards a Geography of Trade Costs." Purdue University, manuscript.

Hummels, David, Jun Ishii, and Kei-Mu Yi. 2001. "The Nature and Growth of Vertical Specialization in World Trade." *Journal of International Economics* 54:75–96.

Hummels, David, and Peter J. Klenow. 2002. "The Variety and Quality of a Nation's Trade." NBER Working Paper no. 8712.

Hummels, David, and James Levinsohn. 1995. "Monopolistic Competition and International Trade: Reinterpreting the Evidence." *Quarterly Journal of Economics* 110:799–836. Reprinted in Edward E. Leamer, ed., *International Economics* (New York: Worth, 2001).

Hummels, David, and Alexandre Skiba. 2002. "Shipping the Good Applies Out? An Empirical Confirmation of the Alchian-Allen Conjecture." NBER Working Paper no. 9023.

Hunter, Linda C., and James R. Markusen. 1988. "Per-Capita Income as a Determinant of Trade." In Robert C. Feenstra, ed., *Empirical Methods for International Trade*. Cambridge: MIT Press.

Irwin, Douglas A., 2001. "The Welfare Cost of Autarky: Evidence from the Jeffersonian Trade Embargo, 1807–1809." NBER Working Paper no. 8692.

———. 2002a. *Free Trade on Fire*. Princeton: Princeton University Press.

———. 2002b. "The Optimal Tax on Antebellum US Cotton Exports." *Journal of International Economics,* forthcoming.

Irwin, Douglas A., and Nina Pavcnik. 2001. "Airbus versus Boeing Revisited: International Competition in the Aircraft Market." NBER Working Paper no. 8648.

Itoh, Motoshige, and Kazuharu Kiyono. 1987. "Welfare-Enhancing Export Subsidies." *Journal of Political Economy* 95:115–37.

Janeba, Eckhard. 1998. "Tax Competition in Imperfectly Competitive Markets." *Journal of International Economics* 44:135–54.

Johnson, George, and Frank Stafford. 1999. "The Labor Market Implications of International Trade." in Orley Ashenfelter and David Card, eds., *Handbook of Labor Economics,* Vol. 3B. Amsterdam: Elsevier.

Johnson, Norman Lloyd, and Samuel Kotz. 1972. *Distributions in Statistics: Continuous Multivanjate Distributions.* New York: Wiley.

Jones, Charles I. 1995a. "Time Series Tests of Endogenous Growth Models." *Quarterly Journal of Economics* 110:495–526.

———. 1995b. "R&D-Based Models of Economic Growth." *Journal of Political Economy* 103:759–84.

Jones, Charles I., and Robert E. Hall. 1999. "Why Do Some Countries Produce So Much More Output per Worker Than Others?" *Quarterly Journal of Economics* 116:83–116.

Jones, Ronald W. 1956–57. "Factor Proportions and the Heckscher-Ohlin Theorem." *Review of Economic Studies* 24:1–10.

———. 1965. "The Structure of Simple General Equilibrium Models." *Journal of Political Economy* 73:557–72. Reprinted in Edward Leamer, ed., *International Economics* (New York: Worth, 2001).

———. 1971. "A Three-Factor Model in Theory, Trade, and History." In Jagdish Bhagwati et al., eds., *Trade, Balance of Payments, and Growth: Papers in International Economics in Honor of Charles P. Kindleberger*. Amsterdam: North-Holland.

Jones, Ronald W. 2000. *Globalization and the Theory of Input Trade*. Cambridge: MIT Press.

Jones, Ronald W., J. Peter Neary, and Francis P. Ruane. 1987. "International Capital Mobility and the Dutch Disease." In Henryk Keirzkowski, ed., *Protection and Competition in International Trade: Essays in Honour of W. M. Corden.* Oxford: Blackwell.

Jones, Ronald W., and Jose A. Scheinkman. 1977. "The Relevance of the Two-Sector Production Model in Trade Theory." *Journal of Political Economy* 85:909–35.

Ju, Jiandong, and Kala Krishna. 2000a. "Evaluating Trade Reform with Many Consumers." *Canadian Journal of Economics* 33:787–98.

———. 2000b. "Welfare and Market Access Effects of Piecemeal Tariff Reform." *Journal of International Economics* 51:305–16.

Judd, Kenneth. 1985. "On the Performance of Patents." *Econometrica* 53: 567–86.

Katz, Lawrence F., and David Autor. 1999. "Changes in the Wage Structure and Earnings Inequality." In Orley Ashenfelter and David Card, eds., *Handbook of Labor Economics*, Vol. 3A, Amsterdam: Elsevier.

Katz, Lawrence F., and Kevin M. Murphy. 1992. "Changes in Relative Wages, 1963–1987: Supply and Demand Factors." *Quarterly Journal of Economics* 107:35–78.

Kee, Hiau Looi. 2002. "Productivity versus Endowment: A Study of Singapore's Productivity Growth." World Bank, manuscript.

Keller, Wolfgang. 1998. "Are International R&D Spillovers Trade-Related? Analyzing Spillovers among Randomly Matched Trade Partners." *European Economic Review* 42:1469–81.

———. 2002. "Geographic Localization of International Technology Diffusion." *American Economic Review* 92:120–42.

Kemp, Murray C. 1962. "The Gain from International Trade." *Economic Journal* 72:803–19.

Kemp, Murray C., and Takashi Negishi. 1970. "Variable Returns to Scale, Commodity Taxes, Factor Market Distortions, and Implications for Trade Gains." *Swedish Journal of Economics* 72:1–11.

Kemp, Murray C., and Henry Wan Jr. 1976. "An Elementary Proposition concerning the Formation of Customs Unions." In Murray Kemp, *Three Topics in the Theory of International Trade: Distribution, Welfare, and Uncertainty.* Amsterdam: North Holland.

Kenney, Martin, and Richard Florida. 1994. "Japanese Maquiladoras: Production Organization and Global Commodity Chains." *World Development* 22:27–44.

Klenow, Peter, and Andrés Rodríguez-Clare. 1997. "Quantifying Variety Gains from Trade Liberalization." University of Chicago, manuscript.

Knetter, Michael M. 1989. "Price Discrimination by U.S. and German Exports." *American Economic Review* 79:198–210.

———. 1993. "International Comparisons of Pricing-to-Market Behavior." *American Economic Review* 83:473–86.

Kohli, Ulrich. 1981. "A Gross National Product Function and the Derived Demand for Imports and Supply of Exports." *Canadian Journal of Economics* 11:167–82.

———. 1981. "Nonjointness and Factor Intensity in U.S. Production." *International Economic Review* 22:3–18.

———. 1983. "Nonjoint Technologies." *Review of Economics Studies* 50:209–19.

———. 1990a. "Price and Quantity Elasticities in Foreign Trade." *Economic Letters* 33:277–81.

———. 1990b. "Growth Accounting in an Open Economy: Parametric and Nonparametric Estimates." *Journal of Economic and Social Measurement* 16:125–36.

———. 1991. *Technology, Duality, and Foreign Trade: The GNP Function Approach to Modeling Imports and Exports.* Ann Arbor: University of Michigan Press; and London: Harvester Wheatsheaf.

———. 1993a. "A Symmetric Normalized Quadratic GDP Function and the U.S. Demand for Imports and Supply of Exports." *International Economic Review* 34:243–55.

———. 1993b. "U.S. Technology and the Specific Factors Model." *Journal of International Economics* 34:115–36.

———. 2004. "Real GDP and Terms-of-Trade Changes." *Journal of International Economics*, forthcoming.

Kokko, Ari. 1994. "Technology, Market Characteristics, and Spillovers." *Journal of Development Economics* 43:279–93.

Kranton, Rachel E., and Deborah F. Minehart. 2001. "A Theory of Buyer-Seller Networks." *American Economic Review* 91:485–508.

Kremer, Michael. 1993. "Population Growth and Technological Change: One Million B.C. to 1990." *Quarterly Journal of Economics* 108:681–716.

Krishna, Kala. 1987. "Tariffs versus Quotas with Endogenous Quality." *Journal of International Economics* 23:97–113.

———. 1989. "Trade Restrictions as Facilitating Practices." *Journal of International Economics* 26:251–70. Reprinted in Gene M. Grossman, ed., *Imperfect Competition and International Trade* (Cambridge: MIT Press, 1992).

———. 1990. "Protection and the Product Line: Monopoly and Product Quality." *International Economic Review* 31:87–102.

Krishna, Kala. 2002. "Understanding Rules of Origin." Pennsylvania State University, manuscript.

Krishna, Kala, and Anne O. Krueger. 1995. "Implementing Free Trade Areas: Rules of Origin and Hidden Protection." In James Levinsohn, Alan Deardorff, and Robert Stern, eds., *New Directions in Trade Theory.* Ann Arbor: University of Michigan Press, 149–198.

Krishna, Pravin. 1998. "Regionalism and Multilateralism: A Political Economy Approach." *Quarterly Journal of Economics* 108:227–51.

———. 2003. "Are Regional Trading Partners 'Natural'?" *Journal of Political Economy* 111:202–26.

Krishna, Pravin, and Arvind Panagariya. 2002. "On Necessarily Welfare-Enhancing Free Trade Areas." *Journal of International Economics* 57:353–67.

Krueger, Alan B. 1997. "Labor Market Shifts and the Price Puzzle Revisited." NBER Working Paper no. 5924.

Krueger, Alan B., and Lawrence Summers. 1988. "Efficiency Wages and the Inter-industry Wage Structure." *Econometrica* 56:269–93.

Krueger, Anne O. 1974. "The Political Economy of the Rent-Seeking Society." *American Economic Review* 64:291–303.

Krugman, Paul R. 1979. "Increasing Returns, Monopolistic Competition, and International Trade." *Journal of International Economics* 9:469–79. Reprinted in Edward, E. Leamer, ed., *International Economics* (New York: Worth, 2001).

———. 1980. "Scale Economies, Product Differentiation, and the Pattern of Trade." *American Economic Review* 70:950–59. Reprinted as in Gene M. Grossman, ed., *Imperfect Competition and International Trade* (Cambridge: MIT Press, 1992).

———. 1981. "Intra-industry Specialization and the Gains from Trade." *Journal of Political Economy* 89:959–73.

———. 1984. "Import Protection as Export Promotion: International Competition in the Presence of Oligopoly and Economics of Scale." In Henryk Kierzkowski, ed., *Monopolistic Competition and International Trade*. Oxford: Oxford University Press. Reprinted in Gene M. Grossman, ed., *Imperfect Competition and International Trade* (Cambridge: MIT Press, 1992).

———. 1991a. "Is Bilateralism Bad?" In Elhanan Helpman and Assaf Razin, eds., *International Trade and Trade Policy*. Cambridge: MIT Press.

———. 1991b. "The Move towards Free Trade Zones." In *Policy Implications of Trade and Currency Zones*. Kansas City, Mo.: Federal Reserve Bank of Kansas City.

———. 1995. "Growing World Trade: Causes and Consequences." *Brooking Papers on Economic Activity* 1:327–62.

———. 2000. "Technology, Trade, and Factor Prices." *Journal of International Economics* 50:51–72.

Krugman, Paul R., and Anthony J. Venables. 1995. "Globalization and the Inequality of Nations." *Quarterly Journal of Economics* 110:857–80.

Kumar, Praveen. 2000. "Wage Inequality in the US: What Do Aggregate Prices and Factor Supplies Tell?" World Bank, manuscript.

Lancaster, Kelvin. 1975. "Socially Optimal Product Differentiation." *American Economic Review* 65:567–85.

———. 1979. *Variety, Equity, and Efficiency*. New York: Columbia University Press.

———. 1980. "Intra-industry Trade under Perfect Monopolistic Competition." *Journal of International Economics* 10:151–75.

Lawrence, Colins, and Pablo T. Spiller. 1983. "Product Diversity, Economics of Scale, and International Trade." *Quarterly Journal of Economics* 98:63–83.

Lawrence, Robert Z. 1994. "Trade, Multinationals, and Labor." NBER Working Paper no. 4836.

Lawrence, Robert Z., and Matthew Slaughter. 1993. "International Trade and American Wages in the 1980s: Giant Sucking Sound or Small Hiccup?" *Brookings Papers on Economic Activity: Microeconomics* 2:161–226. Reprinted in Edward E. Leamer, ed., *International Economics* (New York: Worth, 2001).

Leamer, Edward E. 1980. "The Leontief Paradox, Reconsidered." *Journal of Political Economy* 88:495–503. Reprinted in Edward E. Leamer, ed., *International Economics* (New York: Worth, 2001).

———. 1984. *Source of International Comparative Advantage: Theory and Evidence*. Cambridge: MIT Press.

———. 1987. "Paths of Development in the 3-Factor, N-Good General Equilibrium Model." *Journal of Political Economy* 95:961–99.

———. 1995. "The Heckscher-Ohlin Model in Theory and Practice." Princeton Studies in International Finance no. 77.

———. 1996. "The Effects of Trade in Services, Technology Transfer, and Delocalisation on Local and Global Income Inequality." *Asia-Pacific Economic Review* 2:44–60.

———. 1998. "In Search of Stolper-Samuelson Linkages between International Trade and Lower Wages." In Susan M. Collins, ed., *Imports, Exports, and the American Worker*. Washington, D.C.: Brookings Institution Press. Reprinted in Edward E. Leamer, ed., *International Economics* (New York: Worth, 2001).

———. 2000. "What's the Use of Factor Contents?" *Journal of International Economics* 50:17–50.

Leamer, Edward, E., and Harry P. Bowen. 1981. "Cross-section Tests of the Heckscher-Ohlin Theorem: Comment." *American Economic Review* 71: 1040–43. Reprinted in Edward E. Leamer, ed., *International Economics* (New York: Worth, 2001).

Leontief, Wassily W. 1953. "Domestic Production and Foreign Trade: The American Capital Position Re-examined." *Proceedings of the American Philosophical Society* 97:332–49. Reprinted in Richard Caves and Harry G. Johnson, eds., *Readings in International Economics* (Homewood, Ill.: Irwin, 1968).

Lerner, Abba P. 1952. "Factor Prices and International Trade." *Economica*, n.s. 19:1–15.

Levinsohn, James A. 1993. "Testing the Imports-as-Market-Discipline Hypothesis." *Journal of International Economics* 35:1–22.

———. 1997. "Carwars: Trying to Make Sense of U.S.-Japan Trade Frictions in the Automobile and Automobile Parts Markets." In Robert C. Feenstra, ed., *The Effects of U.S. Trade Protection and Promotion Policies*. Chicago: University of Chicago Press and NBER.

Levinsohn, James A., and Amil Petrin. 2001. "Estimating Production Functions Using Inputs to Control for Unobservables." University of Michigan and University of Chicago, manuscript.

Levy, Philip I. 1997. "A Political-Economic Analysis of Free-Trade Agreements." *American Economic Review* 87:506–19.

Li, David D., and Qi Chen. 1998. "Why Aren't Foreign Direct Investments Always Welcome?—a Political Economy Analysis." University of Michigan, manuscript.

Lipsey, Robert E. 1999. "The Role of FDI in International Capital Flows." In Martin Feldstein, ed., *International Capital Flows*. Chicago: University of Chicago Press.

———. 2003. "Foreign Direct Investment and the Operations of Multinational Firms: Concepts, History, and Data." In E. Kwan Choi and James Harrigan, eds., *Handbook of International Trade*. Oxford: Blackwell.

List, Friedrich. 1856. *National System of Political Economy*. Transl. G. A. Matile. Philadelphia: Lippincott.

Lopez de Silanes, Florencio, James R. Markusen, and Thomas F. Rutherford. 1994. "Complementarity and Increasing Returns in Intermediate Inputs." *Journal of Development Economics* 45:101–19.

MacDougall, G. D. A. 1960. "The Benefits and Costs of Private Investment from Abroad: A Theoretical Approach." *Economic Record*, special issue, March.

Magee, Christopher. 2002. "Endogenous Preferential Trade Agreements: An Empirical Analysis." Bucknell University, manuscript.

Maggi. Giovanni. 1996. "Strategic Trade Policies with Endogenous Mode of Competition." *American Economic Review* 86:237–58.

———. 1999. "The Role of Multilateral Institutions in International Trade Cooperation." *American Economic Review* 89:190–214.

Mankiw, N. Gregory, David Romer, and David N. Weil. 1992. "A Contribution to the Empirics of Economic Growth." *Quarterly Journal of Economics* 107:407–38.

Marin, Dalia, and Thierry Verdier. 2001. "Power Inside the Firm and the Market: A General Equilibrium Approach." University of Munich and DELTA, Paris, manuscript.

Marjit, Sugata, and R. Acharyya. 2003. *International Trade, Wage Inequality, and the Developing Economy: A General Equilibrium Approach.* Heidelberg: Physica Verlag.

Markusen, James R. 1981. Trade and the Gains from Trade with Imperfect Competition." *Journal of International Economics* 11:531–51. Reprinted in Gene M. Grossman, ed., *Imperfect Competition and International Trade* (Cambridge: MIT Press, 1992).

———. 1984. "Multinationals, Multi-plant Economies, and the Gains from Trade." *Journal of International Economics* 16:205–26.

———. 1989. "Trade in Producer Services and in Other Specialized, Intermediate Inputs." *American Economic Review* 79:85–95.

———. 1990. "De-rationalizing Tariffs with Specialized Intermediate Inputs and Differentiated Final Goods." *Journal of International Economics* 28:375–83.

———. 1995. "The Boundaries of Multinational Firms and International Trade." *Journal of Economic Perspectives* 9:169–89.

———. 2001. "Contracts, Intellectual Property Rights, and Multinational Investment in Developing Countries." *Journal of International Economics* 53:189–204.

———. 2002. *Multinational Firms and the Theory of International Trade.* Cambridge: MIT Press.

Markusen, James R., and Keith E. Maskus. 2001. "Multinational Firms: Reconciling Theory and Evidence." In Magnus Blomstrom and Linda S. Goldberg, eds., *Topics in Empirical Economics: A Festschrift in Honor of Robert E. Lipsey.* Chicago: University of Chicago and NBER.

———. 2002. "Discriminating among Theories of the Multinational Enterprise." *Review of International Economics* 10:694–707.

Markusen, James R., and Anthony J. Venables. 1998. "Multinational Firms and the New Trade Theory." *Journal of International Economics* 46:183–203.

———. 2000. "The Theory of Endowment, Intra-industry, and Multinational Trade." *Journal of International Economics* 52:209–35.

Martins, Joaquim Oliveira. 1992. "Export Behaviour with Differentiated Products: Exports of Korea, Taiwan, and Japan to the U.S. Domestic Market." In M. G. Dagenais and D. A. Muet, eds., *International Trade Modeling.* London: Chapman and Hall.

Mataloni, Raymond. 1995. "A Guide to BEA Statistics on U.S. Multinational Companies." *Survey of Current Business*, March, 38–55.

Mayer, Wolfgang. 1974. "Short and Long Run Equilibria for a Small Open Economy." *Journal of Political Economy* 82:955–67.

Mayer, Wolfgang. 1984. "Endogenous Tariff Formation." *American Economic Review* 74:970–85.

McCallum, John. 1995. "National Borders Matter." *American Economic Review* 85:615–23.

McCalman, Phillip. 2002. "Multilateral Trade Negotiations and the Most Favored Nation Clause." *Journal of International Economics* 57:151–76.

———. 2003. "Protection for Sale and Trade Liberalization: An Empirical Investigation," *Review of International Economics*, forthcoming.

McFadden, Daniel. 1978. "Modeling the Choice of Residential Location." In Anders Karlqvist, L. Lundqvist, F. Snickars, and J. Weibull, eds., *Spatial Interaction Theory and Planning Models*. Amsterdam: North-Holland.

———. 1981. "Econometric Models of Probabilistic Choice." In Charles F. Manski and Daniel McFadden, eds., *Structural Analysis of Discrete Data with Econometric Applications*. Cambridge: MIT Press.

McLaren, John. 2000. "'Globalization' and Vertical Structure." *American Economic Review* 90:1239–54.

———. 2002. "A Theory of Insidious Regionalism." *Quarterly Journal of Economics* 98:571–608.

Melitz, Marc. 2003. "The Impact of Trade on Intra-industry Reallocations and Aggregate Industry Productivity." *Econometrica*, forthcoming.

———. 2004. "When and How Should Infant Industries Be Protected?" *Journal of International Economics*, forthcoming.

Mill, John Stuart. 1909. *The Principles of Political Economy*. London: Longmans, Green.

Minhaus, Bagicha S. 1962. "The Homohypallagic Production Function, Factor-Intensity Reversals, and the Hecksher-Ohlin Theorem." *Journal of Political Economy* 70:138–56.

Mitra, Devashish. 1999. "Endogenous Lobby Formation and Endogenous Protection: A Long-Run Model of Trade Policy Determination." *American Economic Review* 89:1116–34.

Mitra, Devashish, Dimitrios Thomakos, and Mehmet Ulubasoglu. 2002. "'Protection for Sale' in a Developing Country: Democracy versus Dictatorship." *Review of Economics and Statistics* 84:497–508.

Mundell, Robert A. 1957. "International Trade and Factor Mobility." *American Economic Review* 47:321–35.

Mussa, Michael. 1974. "Tariffs and the Distribution of Income: The Importance of Factor Specificity, Substitutability, and Intensity in the Short and Long Run." *Journal of Political Economy* 82:1191–203.

———. 1979. "The Two-Sector Model in Terms of Its Dual." *Journal of International Economics* 9:513–26.

Naughton, Barry. 1996. "China's Emergence and Prospects as a Trading Nation," *Brookings Papers on Economic Activity* 2:273–343.

———. 1999. "How Much Can Regional Integration Do to Unify China's Markets?" University of California, San Diego, manuscript.

Neary, Peter. 1978. "Short-Run Capital Specificity and the Pure Theory of International Trade." *Economic Journal* 88:488–510. Reprinted in Edward Leamer, ed., *International Economics* (New York: Worth, 2001).

———. 1988. "Tariffs, Quotas, and Voluntary Export Restraints with and without Internationally Mobile Capital." *Canadian Journal of Economics* 21:714–35.

Nikaido, Hukukane. 1972. "Relative Shares and Factor Price Equalization." *Journal of International Economics* 2:257–63.

Obstfeld, Maurice, and Kenneth Rogoff. 2000. "The Six Major Puzzles in International Macroeconomics: Is There a Common Cause?" In Ben S. Bernanke and Kenneth Rogoff, eds., *NBER Macroeconomics Annual, 2000*. Cambridge: MIT Press.

Ohlin, Bertil. 1933. *Interregional and International Trade*. Cambridge: Harvard University Press.

Ohyama, M. 1972. "Trade and Welfare in General Equilibrium." *Keio Economic Studies* 9:37–73.

Olley, G. Steven, and Ariel Pakes. 1996. "The Dynamics of Productivity in the Telecommunications Equipment Industry." *Econometrica* 64:1263–97.

Overman, Henry, Stephen Redding, and Anthony J. Venables. 2003. "Trade and Geography: A Survey of Empirics." In E. Kwan Choi and James Harrigan, eds., *Handbook of International Trade*. Oxford: Blackwell.

Panagariya, Arvind. 2000. "Evaluating the Factor-Content Approach to Measuring the Effect of Trade on Wage Inequality." *Journal of International Economics* 50:91–116.

Pavcnik, Nina. 2002. "Trade Disputes in the Commercial Aircraft Industry." *World Economy* 25:733–51.

Perry, Martin K. 1989. "Vertical Integration: Determinants and Effects." In Richard Schmalansee and Robert Willig, eds., *Handbook of Industrial Organization*, Vol. 1. Amsterdam: North-Holland.

Phelps, Edmund S. 1997. *Rewarding Work*. Cambridge: Harvard University Press.

Pollak, Robert A. 1989. *The Theory of the Cost-of-Living Index*. Oxford: Oxford University Press.

Prebisch, Raul. 1950. *The Economic Development of Latin America and Its Principal Problems*. New York: United Nations.

Prusa, Thomas J. 1991. "The Selection of Anti-dumping Cases for Withdrawal." In Robert E. Baldwin, ed., *Empirical Studies of Commercial Policy*. Chicago: University of Chicago Press and NBER.

———. 1992. "Why Are So Many Antidumping Petitions Withdrawn?" *Journal of International Economics* 33:1–20.

———. 2001. "On the Spread and Impact of Anti-Dumping." *Canadian Journal of Economics* 34:591–611.

Puga, Diego, and Daniel Trefler. 2002. "Knowledge Creation and Control in Organizations," NBER Working Paper no. 9121.

Rauch, James E. 1999. "Networks versus Markets in International Trade." *Journal of International Economics* 48:7–37.

———. 2001. "Business and Social Networks in International Trade." *Journal of Economic Literature* 39:1177–203.

Rauch, James E., and Alessandra Casella. 2001. *Networks and Markets.* New York: Russell Sage.

———. 2003. "Overcoming Informational Barriers to International Resource Allocation: Prices and Ties." *Economic Journal* 113:21–42.

Rauch, James E., and Vitor Trindade. 2002. "Ethnic Chinese Networks in International Trade." *Review of Economics and Statistics* 84:116–30.

———. 2003. "Information, International Substitutability, and Globalization." *American Economic Review* 93:775–91.

Rauch, James E., and Joel Watson. 2002. "Entrepreneurship and International Trade." NBER Working Paper no. 8708.

Redding, Stephen. 2002. "Specialization Dynamics." *Journal of International Economics* 58:299–334.

Redding, Stephen, and Anthony J. Venables. 2000. "Economic Geography and International Inequality." Center for Economic Policy Research, Discussion Paper no. 2568.

Reid, Peter C. 1990. *Made Well in America: Lessons from Harley-Davidson on Being the Best.* New York: McGraw-Hill.

Ricardo, David. 1951. *The Works and Correspondence of David Ricardo.* Ed. P. Sfaffa. Cambridge: Cambridge University Press.

Richardson, J. David. 1982. "Trade Adjustment Assistance under the Trade Act of 1974: An Analytical Examination and Worker Survey." In Jagdish N. Bhagwati, ed., *Import Competition and Response.* Chicago: University of Chicago Press and NBER.

———. 1995. "Income Inequality and Trade: How to Think, What to Conclude." *Journal of Economic Perspectives* 9:33–56.

Ries, John. 1993. "Windfall Profits and Vertical Relationships: Who Gained in the Japanese Auto Industry from VERs?" *Journal of Industrial Economics* 41:259–76.

Rivera-Batiz, Luis A., and Paul Romer. 1991a. "Economic Integration and Economic Growth." *Quarterly Journal of Economics* 106:531–55.

———. 1991b. "International Trade with Endogenous Technological Change." *European Economic Review* 35:971–1004.

Robertson, Raymond. 2000. "Relative Prices and Wage Inequality: Evidence from Mexico." Macalester College, manuscript.

Robinson, Joan. 1933. *The Economics of Imperfect Competition.* London: Macmillan.

Rodriguez, Carlos A. 1979. "The Quality of Imports and the Differential Effects of Tariffs, Quotas, and Quality Controls as Protective Devices." *Canadian Journal of Economics* 12:439–49.

Rodriguez, Francisco, and Dani Rodrik. 2000. "Trade Policy and Economic Growth: A Skeptic's Guide to the Cross-National Evidence." In Ben S. Gernanke and Kenneth Rogoff, eds., *NBER Macroeconomics Annual, 2000.* Cambridge: MIT Press.

Rodrik, Dani. 1993. "Industrial Organization and Product Quality: Evidence from South Korean and Taiwanese Exports." In Paul Krugman and Alasdair Smith, eds., *Empirical Studies of Strategic Trade Policy.* Chicago: University of Chicago Press and NBER.

———. 1995a. "The Political Economy of Trade Policy." In Gene M. Grossman and Kenneth Rogoff, eds., *Handbook of International Economics*, Vol. 3. Amsterdam: Elsevier.

———. 1995b. "Taking Trade Policy Seriously: Export Subsidization as a Case Study in Policy Effectiveness." In Jim Levinsohn, Alan V. Deardorff, and Robert M. Stern, eds., *New Directions in Trade Theory*. Ann Arbor: University of Michigan Press.

———. 1997. *Has Globalization Gone Too Far?* Washington, D.C.: Institute for International Economics.

Romalis, John. 2001. "Factor Proportions and the Structure of Commodity Trade." University of Chicago, manuscript.

———. 2002. "NAFTA's and CUSFTA's Impact on North American Trade." University of Chicago, manuscript.

Romer, Paul. 1990. "Endogenous Technical Change." *Journal of Political Economy* 98:S71–S102.

———. 1994. "New Goods, Old Theory, and the Welfare Costs of Trade Restrictions." *Journal of Development Economics* 43:5–38.

Rose, Andrew K., and Eric van Wincoop. 2001. "National Money as a Barrier to International Trade: The Real Case for Currency Union." *American Economic Review* 91:386–90.

Rosen, Daniel. 1998. *Behind the Open Door: Foreign Firms in China*. Washington, D.C.: Institute for International Economics.

Rosen, Sherwin. 1974. "Hedonic Prices and Implicit Markets: Product Differentiation in Pure Competition." *Journal of Political Economy* 82:34–55.

Rybczynski, T. N. 1955. "Factor Endowments and Relative Commodity Prices." *Economica* 22:336–41.

Sachs, Jeffrey D. 2001. "Tropical Underdevelopment." NBER Working Paper no. 8119.

Sachs, Jeffrey D., and Howard J. Shatz. 1994. "Trade and Jobs in U.S. Manufacturing." *Brookings Papers on Economic Activity* 1:1–84.

———. 1998. "International Trade and Wage Inequality: Some New Results." In Susan M. Collins, ed., *Imports, Exports, and the American Worker*. Washington, D.C.: Brookings Institution Press.

Sachs, Jeffrey D., and Andrew Warner. 1995. "Economic Reform and the Precess of Global Integration." *Brooking Papers on Economic Activity* 1:1–118.

Samuelson, Paul A. 1949. "International Factor Price Equalization Once Again." *Economic Journal* 59:181–97. Reprinted in Edward E. Leamer, ed., *International Economics* (New York: Worth, 2001).

———. 1952. "The Transfer Problem and Transport Costs: The Terms of Trade When Impediments are Absent." *Economic Journals* 62:278–304.

———. 1953–54. "The Prices of Goods and Factors in General Equilibrium." *Review of Economic Studies* 21:1–20.

———. 1956. "Social Indifference Curves." *Quarterly Journal of Economics* 70:1–22.

———. 1962. "The Gains from International Trade Once Again." *Economic Journal* 72:820–29.

———. 2001. "The Ricardo-Sraffa Paradigm Comparing Gains from Trade in Inputs and Finished Products." *Journal of Economic Literature* 39:1204–14.

Sato, Kazuo, "The Ideal Log-Change Index Number." *Review of Economics and Statistics* 58:223–28.

Schiff, Maurice, and Won Chang. 2003. "Market Presence, Contestability, and the Terms of Trade Effects of Regional Integration." *Journal of International Economics* 60:161–76.

Schott, Peter K. 2001. "Do Rich and Poor Countries Specialize in a Different Mix of Goods? Evidence from Product-Level U.S. Trade Data." NBER Working Paper no. 8492.

———. 2003. "One Size Fits All? Heckscher-Ohlin Specialization in Global Production." *American Economic Review* 93:686–708.

Segerstrom, Paul, T. C. A. Anant, and Elias Dinopoulos. 1990. "A Schumpeterian Model of the Product Life Cycle." *American Economic Review* 80:1077–99.

Shiells, Clinton R., Robert M. Stern, and Alan V. Deardorff. 1986. "Estimates of the Elasticities of Substitution between Imports and Home Goods for the United States." *Weltwirtschaftliches Archiv* 122:497–519.

Slater, Joanna, and Eriko Amaha. 1999. "Masters of the Trade." *Far Eastern Economic Review:* July 22, 10–14.

Slaughter, Matthew J. 2000. "What Are the Results of Product-Price Studies and What Can We Learn from Their Differences?" In Robert C. Feenstra, ed., *The Effects of International Trade on Wages.* Chicago: University of Chicago Press.

———. 2001. "International Trade and Labor-Demand Elasticities." *Journal of International Economics* 54:27–56.

Smith, M. Alasdair. 1977. "Capital Accumulation in the Open Two-Sector Economy." *Economic Journal* 87:273–82.

Solow, Robert M. 1956. "A Contribution to the Theory of Economic Growth." *Quarterly Journal of Economics* 70:65–94.

———. "Technical Change and the Aggregate Production Function." *Review of Economics and Statistics* 39:312–20.

Spence, A. Michael. 1975. "Monopoly, Quality, and Regulation." *Bell Journal of Economics* 6:417–29.

———. 1976. "Product Selection, Fixed Costs, and Monopolistic Competition." *Review of Economic Studies* 43:217–35.

Spencer, Barbara J., and Larry D. Qiu. 2001. "Keiretsu and Relationship-Specific Investment: A Barrier to Trade?" *International Economic Review* 42:871–901.

Staiger, Robert. 1986. "Measurement of the Factor Content of Foreign Trade with Traded Intermediate Goods." *Journal of International Economics* 21:361–68.

Staiger, Robert W., and Frank A. Wolak. 1992. "The Effect of Domestic Antidumping Law in the Presence of Foreign Monopoly." *Journal of International Economics* 32:265–87.

———. 1994. "Measuring Industry-Specific Protection: Antidumping in the United States." *Brooking Papers on Economic Activity: Microeconomics* 1:51–118.

Stigler, George J. 1951. "The Division of Labor Is Limited by the Extent of the Market." *Journal of Political Economy* 54:185–93.

Stolper, Wolfgang F., and Paul A. Samuelson. 1941. "Protection and Real Wages." *Review of Economic Studies* 9:58–73.

Suomela, John W. 1993. *Free Trade versus Fair Trade: The Making of American Trade Policy in a Political Environment.* Turku, Finland: Institute for European Studies.

Swan, Peter L. 1970. "Durability of Consumption Goods." *American Economic Review* 60:884–94.

Swenson, Deborah. 2003. "Foreign Investment and the Mediation of Trade Flows." *Review of International Economics*, forthcoming.

Taylor, Christopher T. 2003. "The Economic Effects of Withdrawn Antidumping Investigations: Is There Evidence of Collusive Settlements?" *Journal of International Economics*, forthcoming.

Taylor, M. Scott. 1993. "'Quality Ladders' and Ricardian Trade." *Journal of International Economics* 34:225–43.

———. 1994. "'Once-off' and Continuing Gains from Trade." *Review of Economic Studies* 61:589–601.

Tinbergen, Jan. 1962. *Shaping the World Economy.* New York: Twentieth Century Fund.

Tombazos, Christis G. 1999. "The Role of Imports in Expanding the Demand Gap between Skilled and Unskilled Labor in the U.S." *Applied Economics* 31:509–16.

Törnqvist, L. 1936. "The Bank of Finland's Consumption Price Index." *Bank of Finland Monthly Bulletin* 10:1–8.

Train, Kenneth. 1986. *Qualitative Choice Analysis.* Cambridge: MIT Press.

Trefler, Daniel. 1993a. "International Factor Price Differences: Leontief Was Right!" *Journal of Political Economy* 101:961–87.

———. 1993b. "Trade Liberalization and the Theory of Endogenous Protection." *Journal of Political Economy* 101:138–60.

———. 1995. "The Case of Missing Trade and Other Mysteries." *American Economic Review* 85:1029–46. Reprinted in Edward E. Leamer, ed., *International Economics* (New York: Worth, 2001).

———. 1998. "The Structure of Factor Content Predictions." University of Toronto, manuscript.

———. 2001. "The Long and Short of the Canada-U.S. Free Trade Agreement." NBER Working Paper no. 8293.

Trefler, Daniel, and Susan Chun Zhu. 2000. "Beyond the Algebra of Explanation: HOV for the Technology Age." *American Economic Review* 90:145–49.

Turunen-Red, Arja H., and Alan D. Woodland. 1991. "Strict Pareto Improving Reforms of Tariffs." *Econometrica* 59:1127–52.

———. 2000. "Multilateral Policy Reforms and Quantity Restrictions on Trade." *Journal of International Economics* 52:153–68.

Tybout, James R., Jamie de Melo, and Vittorio Corbo. 1991. "The Effects of Trade Reform on Scale and Technical Efficiency:" New Evidence from Chile." *Journal of International Economics* 31:231–50.

Tybout, James R., and M. Daniel Westbrook. 1995. "Trade Liberalization and Dimensions of Efficiency Change in Mexican Manufacturing Industries." *Journal of International Economics.* 39:53–78.

Tyson, Laura D'Andrea. 1992. *Who's Bashing Whom: Trade Conflict in High Technology Industries.* Washington, D.C.: Institute for International Economics.

United Nations. 1996. *World Investment Report.* New York: United Nations.

U.S. Department of Commerce. Bureau of Economic Analysis. 1995. *Foreign Direct Investment in the United States: 1992 Benchmark Survey, Final Results.* Washington, D.C.

———. 1996. *Foreign Investment into the United States: U.S. Businesses Acquired or Established by Foreign Investors,* 1980–91 and 1992–95. Washington, D.C., diskette.

U.S. International Trade Commission (USITC). 1983. *Heavyweight Motorcycles, and Engines and Power Train Subassemblies Therefor.* Publication 1342. Washington, D.C.: USITC.

———. 1983–84. *Heavyweight Motorcycles: Quarterly Report on Selected Economic Indicators.* Washington, D.C.

van Ark, Bart, Erik Monnikhof, and Marcel Timmer. 1999. "Prices, Quantities, and Productivity in Industry: A Study of Transition Economies in a Comparative Perspective." In Alan Heston and Robert E. Lipsey, eds., *International and Interarea Comparisons of Income, Output, and Prices.* Chicago: University of Chicago Press.

Vanek, Jaroslav. 1968. "The Factor Proportions Theory: The N-Factor Case." *Kyklos* 21:749–54.

Vartia, Y.O. 1976. "Ideal Log-Change Index Numbers," *Scandinavian Journal of Statistics* 3:121–26.

Ventura, Jaume. 1997. "Growth and Interdependence." *Quarterly Journal of Economics* 107:57–84.

Viner, Jacob. 1950. *The Customs Union Issue.* New York: Carnegie Endowment for International Peace.

———. 1966. *Dumping: A Problem in International Trade.* New York: Augustus M. Kelley.

Wei, Shang-Jin. 1998. "Why Does China Attract So Little Foreign Investment?" Harvard University and NBER, manuscript.

Weinstein, David E. 1992. "Competition and Unilateral Dumping." *Journal of International Economics* 32:379–88.

Williamson, Oliver E. 1975. *Markets and Hierarchies: Analysis and Antitrust Implications.* New York: Free Press.

———. 1985. *The Economic Institutions of Capitalism.* New York: Free Press.

Wolf, Holger C. 1997. "Patterns of Intra- and Inter-state Trade." NBER Working Paper no. 5939.

———. 2000. "Intranational Bias in Trade." *Review of Economics and Statistics* 82:555–63.

Wong, Kar-yiu. 1989. "Optimal Threat of Trade Restriction and Quid Pro Quo Foreign Investment." *Economics and Politics* 1:277–300.

Wood, Adrian. 1995. "How Trade Hurt Unskilled Workers." *Journal of Economic Perspectives* 9:57–80.

Woodland, Alan D. 1977. "A Dual Approach to Equilibrium in the Production Sector in International Trade Theory." *Canadian Journal of Economics* 10:50–68.

———. 1982. *International Trade and Resource Allocation.* Amsterdam: North-Holland.

World Bank. 1993. *The East Asian Miracle: Economic Growth and Public Policy.* Oxford: Oxford University Press.

Xu, Bin. 2002. "Capital Abundance and Developing Country Production Patterns." University of Florida, manuscript.

Yeaple, Dennis. 2003. "A Simple Model of Firm Heterogeneity, International Trade, and Wages." University of Pennsylvania, manuscript.

Yeung, Henry Wai-chung. 2001. "Organizing Regional Production Networks in Southeast Asia: Implications for Production Fragmentation, Trade, and Rules of Origin." *Journal of Economic Geography* 1:299–321.

Yi, Kei-Mu. 2003. "Can Vertical Specialization Explain the Growth of World Trade?" *Journal of Political Economy* 111:52–102.

Yoffie, David B., and Benjamin Gomes-Casseres. 1994. *International Trade and Competition.* New York: McGraw Hill.

Young, Alwyn. 2000. "The Razor's Edge: Distortions and Incremental Reform in the People's Republic of China." *Quarterly Journal of Economics* 115:1091–1135.

Zhu, Susan Chun. 2001a. "Trade, Product Cycles, and Inequality within and between Countries." Michigan State University, manuscript.

———. 2001b. "Trade, Product Cycles, and Wage Inequality: An International Perspective." Michigan State University, manuscript.

Zhu, Susan Chun, and Daniel Trefler. 2001. "Ginis in General Equilibrium: Trade, Technology, and Southern Inequality." NBER Working Paper no. 8446.

Index